EDWARD W. MINIUM
San José State University

STATISTICAL REASONING IN PSYCHOLOGY AND EDUCATION

Second Edition

JOHN WILEY & SONS
New York • Chichester • Brisbane • Toronto • Singapore

The drawings in this book were designed and executed by John Balbalis with the assistance of the Wiley Illustration Department. The designer was Madelyn Lesure. Production was supervised by Janet Sessa.

Library of Congress Cataloging in Publication Data:

Minium, Edward W   1917–
    Statistical reasoning in psychology and education.

    Includes bibliographical references and index.
    1.   Psychometrics.   2.   Educational statistics.
I.   Title.
BF39.M56   1978   150′.1′82   77-19213
ISBN 0-471-60828-9

Printed in the United States of America

PREFACE

The goals in preparing the second edition of this book were those of refinement, modernization, and increased clarity and depth of understanding.

The introduction to inference is always an instructional challenge. The old tightly packed introductory chapter to this topic has been replaced by two chapters: the first presents the basics and the second deepens understanding. In response to the growing awareness of problems accompanying hypothesis testing and to the need for assessment of effect size, treatment of estimation has been expanded and placed in a separate chapter. The chapter on analysis of variance now includes an easy-to-understand approach to orthogonal contrasts and Scheffé comparisons. A new chapter presents selected nonparametric procedures.

The emphasis given to the interplay between substantive and statistical aspects of research has been increased. Some of the topics formerly included in the chapter on experimental design are now interwoven in earlier chapters with those topics with which they are closely associated.

Gone are coded score methods of calculation, some deviation score formulas, some alternative graphic methods, and some end-of-chapter proofs that seemed more to reflect author's pride than students' need. Computing procedures have been modified to take advantage of the available low-priced hand calculators. Some problems have been weeded out, and about 100 new ones added. In those involving computation, most use a few simple scores to help deemphasize computational drudgery. Answers to problems and exercises now appear in the text. There are more introductions and more summaries than before. Examples and illustrations have been reworked to increase clarity of how-to-do-it.

This edition has gained in flexibility. As with the first edition, it is possible to develop a topic in basic form and then to supplement it by appropriate selection according to the goals of instruction and available time. As before, a detailed analysis of these possibilities appears in the Instructor's Manual.

Many people helped in the development of this edition. I am grateful to instructors who used the first edition and who shared their insights and feelings in responding to a lengthy questionnaire. Their opinions mattered; I took their advice on many issues. I wish to thank the following for their advice during the development of this edition: Professors Gordon Bear of Ramapo College, Robert B. Clarke of San Jose State University, William A. Frederickson of Central State University, Oklahoma, George Mandler of the University of California, San Diego, Jana Mason of the University of Illinois, and Jeff Miller of the University of California, San Diego. Professor Bear's counsel went well beyond the normal obligation of a reviewer and the book is definitely the better for it. Professor Clarke again provided a most detailed and helpful analysis and evaluation. Besides recognizing his heroic work as a reviewer, I must say that his views on statistics and the teaching of it have had an important influence on my own and are therefore doubtless reflected in many ways in this book.

San José, California   EDWARD W. MINIUM
August 1977

PREFACE TO THE FIRST EDITION

Most of the students I teach are quite able to absorb the logic of statistics, but do not come to the subject well prepared in mathematics. This book is addressed first to them. It requires only an understanding of arithmetic and an elementary knowledge of equations, such as most acquire by the end of the ninth grade. To assist those who "once knew" but whose memory has now grown dim, there is an extended review of basic mathematical propositions in the Appendix. It is preceded by a pretest (with answers), and the questions are keyed to various sections of the review to facilitate further study. For those competent in ordinary algebra, mathematical notes are offered at the end of many chapters, but the text is designed to stand without them.

Although the book does not demand advanced mathematical competence, it is emphatically concerned with the student's conceptual growth. It develops statistical concepts, understanding of statistical logic, properties of statistical devices, assumptions underlying statistical tools, and considers what happens when theory meets reality. The development is accompanied by frequent summaries which stress these points.

Constant appeal is made to common experience and intuition. I have tried particularly to be clear on those points that tend to be stumbling blocks. For example, I have worked to obtain a treatment of statistical inference that is both accurate and understandable. At the same time, I have tried to avoid oversimplification. I have also tried to be clear on how-to-do-it aspects. If successful, instructors should have more time to devote to the difficult concepts.

Full treatment is given to descriptors. I believe that after inference is done, one must return to these measures to assess the meaning of the inquiry; they must be fully understood. Coded score methods of calculation are included. Those having access to calculators and computers may choose to omit them, but these methods often prove useful when one must work in terms of his own resources. Large sample procedures for inference about means receive the full treatment. Inference is hard enough to grasp without introducing the complicating characteristics of Student's distribution at the start; one step at a time.

Certain frequently neglected topics cried for treatment. Among them are: randomization as experimental control, determination of sample size required for inference about means, evaluation of the merits of the experiment versus the *in situ* study, the problem of regression in research, and the relative merits of hypothesis testing versus estimation. Topics such as these are introduced from time to time, but special consideration is given many of them in Chapter 19,* *Some Aspects of Experimental Design.*

In many texts, the statistics of measurement is given lesser attention than the statistics of experimental analysis. I felt that both interests ought to receive adequate recognition. Accordingly, derived scores and interpretive aspects of correlation and regression are given substantial treatment.

Problems and exercises appear at the end of each chapter. Some give practice in how-to-do-it, and others require the exercise of critical judgment. Since easy availability of answers often negates the requirement of thoughtful analysis, answers appear in the instructor's manual but not in the book.

This book should serve very well for a one-semester text, and many will find it appropriate for two. It has been developed in a way to facilitate the selection which will be necessary for a one-semester course. First, a graded approach is used in several areas. For example, the elements of hypothesis testing are introduced in Chapter 14;† Chapter 15‡ offers a detailed commentary on each of the steps. Similarly, there is a graded approach to correlation and regression: for each, the elements are presented in one chapter, and detailed interpretive analysis in another. The instructor of the one-semester course will often find it possible to develop a topic in basic form, and then, through appropriate selection, to supplement that development according to taste and time.

*Now Chapter 21.
†Now Chapter 15.
‡Now Chapter 16.

Second, topics which might be considered supplementary (e.g., the mean and standard deviation of a combined distribution) have been developed in a way such that their omission does not interrupt the continuity, and they are placed, wherever possible, at or near the end of the chapter.

To assist in making an appropriate selection, the Table of Contents lists section titles as well as chapter titles. In addition, a detailed analysis of the possibilities for selection is offered in a manual available to instructors.

These acknowledgments I make with pleasure. I am grateful to two former professors, Edwin E. Ghiselli and the late Edward C. Tolman, who taught me to say, "I don't know" when I don't, which is often, and that happiness in teaching comes from two sources: love of your subject and love of students.

The encouragement and understanding of my wife, Juanita, sustained me during the preparation of the manuscript. The enthusiastic and expert assistance of my former assistant, Mrs. Fonda Eyler, helped me finish it on time.

I am indebted to former students and present colleagues who read and criticised, and to those students who helped in some of the research.

I am indebted to Professor James B. Bartoo, of Pennsylvania State University, for his helpful comments. To Professor Robert B. Clarke, of San Jose State College, and to Professor William B. Michael of the University of Southern California. I owe a debt which can never be repaid. These gentlemen gave the manuscript the kind of detailed analysis that goes far beyond what a hopeful author has any right to expect. If the book appears to have merit, it may well be theirs, but if fault is found, it is mine.

Lastly, I am indebted to the several authors and publishers who granted permission to use tables and figures so necessary to this work. Among others, I am indebted to the Literary Executor of the late Sir Ronald A. Fisher, F.R.S., and to Oliver & Boyd Ltd, Edinburgh, for their permission to reprint Table V.A. from their book *Statistical Methods for Research Workers*.

San José, California   EDWARD W. MINIUM
April 1970

CONTENTS

To Students Who Want to Learn and Instructors Who Like to Teach

STATISTICAL REASONING IN PSYCHOLOGY AND EDUCATION

CHAPTER 1

1.1 DESCRIPTIVE STATISTICS

In a new school, a biology instructor contemplates the arrival of the first group of students. How much biological information will they already have? She wishes neither to bore them by underestimating their readiness, nor to lose them by assuming too much. Should she begin with a review of fundamentals? How extensive? In what areas? It would also be helpful to know if the students vary widely in background of biological knowledge. If so, the instructional method may need adjustment. Finally, she would like information about the students as individuals. Who needs special help during the initial weeks? Who is ready for special challenges?

Let us suppose that there is available a nationally developed test of biological knowledge subdivided into measures of botanical information and zoological information. She administers this test to her students at the first class meeting and

Introduction

finds the number of correct answers for each student. After reading the test to get some idea of the kind and difficulty of the questions, she could compare each student's score with what is reasonable to expect. This approach would be useful, since she is an experienced teacher, but it is possible to learn quite a bit more relative to her initial questions if she would "use statistics."

Let us assume that from the school research office, or from the test manual, she is able to learn how students in similar educational circumstances perform on this test. With this knowledge, she discovers, for example, that Bob Beaver's score in zoology is better than that of 90% of students who are in the same grade, but that only 15% of students get lower scores than Steve Sloth's.

Concerning the general level of knowledge of the students in this class, she finds that there are too many scores to keep in mind at once. A way is needed to simplify consideration of the group, so she finds the class average on each subtest and for the complete test. Then she compares these figures with the performance data of other similar students. This comparison shows that, as a group, these students are approximately at the expected level in botany and that their performance is superior in zoology. Pursuing the question of diversity within the class, she notes that the distances between the scores of the top student and those of the bottom student are not very great.

In each instance our instructor is making use of techniques that are part of the body of *descriptive statistics*. These tools help to describe the level and homogeneity of performance of her students and to compare their knowledge with that of known groups in a way that will help her go about teaching. This is an example of the primary function of descriptive statistics: to provide meaningful and convenient techniques for describing features of data that are of interest.

1.2 INFERENTIAL STATISTICS

What is the attitude of the voting public toward the elimination of capital punishment? Pollsters find it impossible to put this question to all members of this group. Instead, they study the responses of a portion of it, and from that knowledge they estimate the attitudes of the whole. The outcome, like any estimate, is subject to error. But, if the voters selected for study have been chosen according to statistical principles, it is possible to know what margin of error is involved.

A second branch of statistical practice, known as *inferential statistics,* provides the basis for answering questions of this kind. The object of these procedures is to draw an inference about conditions that exist in a larger set of observations from study of a part of that set. This branch of statistics is also known as *sampling statistics.*

Another application of inferential statistics is particularly suited to evaluation of the outcome of an experiment. Is it possible that a certain drug has an effect on speed of learning? Let us suppose that an investigator decides on the kind of subjects he wishes to study, selects at random two groups of 25 subjects each, and administers the drug to one of the groups. Both groups are given a learning task and are in all ways treated alike except for the drug. From the outcome of the study, he finds that the average learning score of the two groups differs by five points.

Now some difference between the groups would be expected even if they were treated alike, because of chance factors involved in the random selection of groups. The question faced by the experimenter is whether the observed difference is within the limits of expected variation. If certain preconditions have been met, statistical theory can provide the basis for an answer. If the experimenter finds that the obtained difference of five points is larger than can be accounted for by chance variation, he will infer that other factors must be at work. If examination of his experimental procedures reveals no reasonable cause for the difference other than the deliberate difference in experimental treatment, he may conclude that the drug is the responsible factor.

1.3 RELATIONSHIP AND PREDICTION

Experience tells us that there is some relationship between intelligence of parents and their offspring, and yet it is not perfect. We expect that the parents of the brightest child in the class are also bright but would not expect that they are necessarily the most intelligent of all parents of children in this group. Can we describe with greater exactness the extent of this relationship?

The personnel office of an industrial concern gives an aptitude test to its prospective clerical employees. Is there really any relationship between the score on this test and subsequent level of job proficiency? How much? If there is a relationship, what percent of applicants may be expected to succeed on the job if only those who score above a certain point on the test are accepted for employment? How does this compare with what would happen if the test were eliminated from the company's procedures?

These are examples of the type of question that probes the existence and extent of *relationship* between two (or more) factors and explores the possibility of *prediction* of standing in one factor from knowledge of standing in the other. This kind of analysis is so frequently of interest that a considerable body of statistical techniques has been developed to deal with it. Because of the importance and distinctiveness of these two questions, they have been separately identified here. Nevertheless, both are problems in description and inference, the two major categories of statistical endeavor.

1.4 KINDS OF STATISTICIANS

Those who work with statistics might be divided into four classes: (1) those who need to know statistics in order to appreciate reports of findings in their professional field, (2) those who must select and apply statistical treatment in the course of their own inquiry, (3) professional statisticians, and (4) mathematical statisticians. The main interest of those in the first two classes is in their own subject matter; statistics is an aid to them in organizing and making meaningful the evidence that bears on questions that have been raised. Among their ranks are the biologist, educator, psychologist, engineer, census taker, medical researcher, geologist, agriculturist, physicist, personnel officer, counselor, businessperson, and city manager; all these and many more regularly find that statistical procedures can be of assistance. We might think of them as amateur statisticians, and like amateurs in most areas, their statistical knowledge may range from novice to expert.

At the next level, we have the professional statistician. In earlier years, he or she may have been trained in a university mathematics department. A more recent graduate is probably a product of a department of statistics and has undergone extensive training in statistical theory and relevant mathematics. The practicing statistician acts as a "middleman" in the process of research, one who assists those with *substantive questions*† in finding and applying statistical models with which to

---

†A substantive question concerns the subject matter under study. For example: does reaction time depend on intensity of the stimulus? See Section 1.6 for further comment.

examine evidence relative to their inquiry. The professional statistician's advantage is that of expert knowledge of statistical theory and of its general applicability. However, lack of expertise in the field of application is a limitation.

The three types of persons thus far discussed all have in common a primary interest in applied statistics, although the latter two may indeed have interest in, and make contributions to, statistical theory. The primary interest of a mathematical statistician is in pure statistics and probability theory. Professional statisticians have been heard to complain wryly that mathematical statisticians think them too practical and that those whom they serve as consultants think them too theoretical. In fairness, it should be pointed out that the latter view is less likely to emerge when those seeking advice have had some elementary education in statistics.

1.5 FOR WHOM IS THIS BOOK INTENDED?

The reader has doubtless concluded correctly that this book is concerned with applied statistics and that it is directed to the prospective amateur. It is intended to be of particular assistance to those who will encounter studies that incorporate statistical treatment, or who need to understand the properties of tools (e.g. mental tests) where important characteristics are stated in statistical language.

This book is equally directed to those who will have occasion to apply statistical procedures in their own inquiries. Knowledge of this kind will help to translate an initial question into a plan of inquiry more likely to bear directly on the issue, to think critically about evidence, and to conduct a meaningful study more economical of time and effort than might otherwise result.

Those who will be in a position to call on the services of a professional statistician will find that some statistical education will help them to know when such expert services are needed, to formulate a problem in a way amenable to treatment and interpretation, and to communicate with this specialist.

1.6 THE ROLE OF APPLIED STATISTICS

From the discussion so far, we can see that applied statistics is a tool and neither a beginning nor an end by itself. An investigator, Dr. Elizabeth Walker, poses a problem. She may turn to statistical procedures to find a convenient and meaning-ful way to organize and view the data that she proposes to collect in her quest. *Statistical procedures provide only a statistical answer; they do not by themselves provide a substantive answer.* They will give her *one* view, a view characterized by certain properties. In choosing statistical techniques, she will have to decide which gives the view that is most illuminating, and she must keep in mind their limitations. To do this, she must know the properties of the technique. To interpret the data, statistical knowledge is necessary but not sufficient. Faced with the outcome of statistical analysis, she must then take into account the numerous factors peculiar to the conduct of her particular study before she can come to a substantive conclusion.

The use of statistical procedures is therefore always a middle step. The typical steps of an investigation are:

1 A *substantive question* is formulated and refined, and a plan is developed to obtain relevant evidence. A substantive question is a question of fact in a subject-matter area. Suppose one group of subjects learns a foreign language vocabulary by spending two hours a day for four days, while another learns by spending a half-hour a day for sixteen days. The total practice time is the same for both groups, but will the amount retained be equal? Some of the aspects of this step will include selection of the type of material to be learned, the kind of subjects to be studied, and the measure of retention to be used.

2 When appropriate, a statistical model is chosen to assist in organizing and analyzing the data to be collected. At this point, a *statistical question* may be developed, the answer to which may be expected to throw light on the substantive question. A statistical question differs from a substantive question in that it always concerns a *statistical* property of the data, such as the average of the set of measures. For example, in the problem above we may ask whether the average number of words retained differs so greatly under the two conditions of practice that chance variation cannot account for it. Often there are alternative statistical questions which are relevant to exploration of the substantive question. For instance, we might ask whether the *proportion* of subjects who retain three quarters or more of the words learned differs substantially under the two conditions of practice. Part of the study of statistics is to learn how to choose among alternative statistical approaches.

3 Upon applying the statistical procedure, one arrives at a *statistical conclusion*. For example, a possible outcome of the learning experiment is that the difference in average number of words retained under the two conditions is too great to be attributed to chance variation. Again, a statistical conclusion concerns a statistical property of the data: in this case, it is about averages.

4 Finally, a *substantive conclusion* is drawn. In the example above, the conclusion may be warranted that under the circumstances studied, retention is better when short practice periods are used. Although the substantive conclusion derives partly from the statistical conclusion, other

factors must be considered. If average performance under the two conditions is so different that chance variation among the groups cannot be considered the sole factor, it will not be clear that the difference in method of learning is the responsible factor unless the experiment has been so conducted as to rule out other factors. The investigator, therefore, must weigh both the statistical conclusion and the adequacy of the experimental design in arriving at a substantive conclusion.

When contemplating design of an investigation, the first and second steps ought to be considered together. It is often possible to include certain features in the plan of attack that will enable use of statistical techniques that are more relevant and economical than otherwise would be possible.

1.7 MORE ABOUT THE ROAD AHEAD

The preceding sections touch on some objectives for education in elementary statistics. For a clear view of the road ahead, a bit more needs to be said. One objective is to develop a better appreciation of the relation between questions that are asked and the role of a quantitative approach in answering them. Since statistical methods have a "point of view," it is necessary to understand their special characteristics in order to decide what analysis is appropriate to the problem.

Even when this seems satisfactorily settled, special characteristics of our data can affect alternative techniques in different ways. If properties of the techniques are understood, a basis exists for choosing from among them. Important assumptions often lie unseen behind a technique. We must know what they are and what happens when they are violated.

It is not enough to learn the properties of statistical techniques; we must also learn "how-to-do-it." This is essential not only for those who will themselves apply these procedures in their own work, but also for those who are simply attempting to become statistically literate. In addition to following the logic and comprehending the properties, a significant kind of understanding comes in the course of "making it work."

1.8 DIRTY WORDS ABOUT STATISTICS

A number of complaints are issued about statistics: it is dry, it is depersonalizing because it considers the mass and not the individual, and it is misleading. Disraeli said: "There are three kinds of lies: lies, damned lies, and statistics." Other complaints heard are that statistical methodology dictates the nature of investigations, and that it is too mathematical for anyone but an expert to understand. Since there is some truth in each of these charges, we shall examine them.

A statistical result is simply a statement about the condition of data. This is bound to be dry unless the person is interested in the question to which the data relate and understands the significance of those findings for the question. *It is the conclusion that may be drawn from the data rather than the state of the data that is of possible interest.* If an increase of 851 children is expected in the public schools of your city next fall, this information may not stir me greatly if your city is not mine. Even Sally Q. Citizen of your city may feel that she has been told more than she wants to know. Mentally translating the figure into "quite an increase," she thinks it would be wise to vote to approve the school bond issue in the coming election. However, the detailed nature of the number is of vital interest to the school superintendent because it tells how many new classrooms and teachers must be ready and how much adjustment will be needed in the budget.

It is true that a statistical statement is usually one that is made about a group rather than about an individual. Consideration of the individual is certainly possible, however. A batting average refers to the performance of a single person, and in the example at the opening of this chapter, our biology instructor used information about a group in order to get better knowledge about each individual. Her aim was the antithesis of depersonalization.

In study of groups there may be much that is significant for the individual. Consider a study in educational technique, in which elementary statistics is taught by "standard" methods and also by an experimental method. Suppose that, at the conclusion of the study, average performance is substantially higher for the experimental group, and that average level of student anxiety during the course is substantially lower for the same group. This outcome does not mean that *every* student will profit in these ways from the new technique; for some students the possibility exists that the new method is worse. However, *in the absence of further information,* this experiment says that the odds are in favor of students who have the opportunity to study under the new method. Thus, the "group" approach can often be turned to the *probable* advantage of an individual.

In a given state college, it may be that 80% of the total number of credit units of instruction were taught by instructors holding the doctorate, that 75% of the courses were taught by instructors holding the same qualification, and that 65% of instructors in the institution hold the doctorate. If a journalist's theme is the "rotten state of higher education," we can guess which figure is most likely to be mentioned. On the other hand, if an economy-minded representative of the taxpayers' association wishes to show that higher salaries are unnecessary to attract a fully qualified faculty, a different choice will be made. Unfortunately, if we are presented in a telling way with only one of these approaches, the possibility of others may never occur to us. We might remember the old saying: "figures never lie, but liars figure." Deception is not the only cause of trouble; many errors in thinking occur inadvertently. It is apparent that there can be value in knowing the properties of statistical procedures and in remembering to inquire about the circumstances of their particular use. Misuse of statistics is an important topic, but limitations of space prevent detailed treatment here. Fortunately, works exist that give attention to these matters.†

One complaint has been that statistical procedures dictate the nature of investigations. It is true that some investigations lean more toward that which is objective and easily measurable than they do toward that which is meaningful. Statistics is not the culprit, since it is only a tool. The problem, rather, lies in the attitude of investigators. It is well to remember that it is the *question* that is of significance, and we ought to be sure we are asking an important one.

Is it true that statistics is mathematical and that only experts can understand it? The realm of statistics extends considerably, well beyond the domain of this book. A number of propositions in elementary statistics owe their existence to sophisticated mathematical derivations. Nevertheless, it is quite possible to acquire a good working understanding of the statistical procedures and logic included in this book with a knowledge of common arithmetic and elementary principles of high school algebra. A few matters will have to be taken on faith. If we know what assumptions were made, and what happens when they are not satisfied, our position will be sound.

1.9 SOME TIPS ON STUDYING STATISTICS

Is statistics a hard subject? It is and it isn't. In general, learning how-to-do-it requires attention, care, and arithmetic accuracy, but it is not particularly difficult. Learning the "why" of things varies over a somewhat wider range of difficulty.

What about the expected reading rate for a book about statistics? Rate of reading and comprehension differ from person to person, and a four-page assignment in mathematics may require the same time as forty pages in history. Certainly one should not expect to read a statistics text like a novel, nor even like the usual history text. Some parts, like this chapter, will go faster, but others will require concentration and several readings. In short, don't feel stupid if you cannot race through a chapter and instead find that some "absorption time" is required. The logic of statistical inference, for example, is a new way of thinking for most people and requires getting used to. Its newness can create difficulties for those who are not willing to slow down.

Another point where students often anticipate difficulty concerns mathematics. This has been partially clarified in the previous section. Ordinary arithmetic and

†S. K. Campbell, *Flaws and Fallacies in Statistical Thinking*, Prentice-Hall, Inc., Englewood Cliffs, N.J., 1974; D. Huff, *How to Lie with Statistics*, W. W. Norton and Co., New York, 1954.

some familiarity with the nature of equations is needed. Being able to see "what goes on" in an equation is at least necessary to perception of the kinds of things that affect the statistic being calculated, and in what way. For students who feel at home in elementary algebra, algebraic notes are included at the end of several chapters. They are intended to provide a supplementary "handle" by which the significance of statistical techniques can be grasped. Appendix A is especially addressed to those who feel that their mathematics lies in the too distant past to assure a sense of security. It contains a review of elementary mathematics of special relevance for study of this book and discusses some other matters, such as interpolation and the use of tables, which will be needed but which may not have been encountered before. This appendix is preceded by a pretest, so the student may determine which elements, if any, could profitably stand review. Not all of these understandings are required at once, so there will be time to brush up in advance of need.

Questions and problems are included at the end of each chapter. Enough of these should be worked to feel comfortable. They have been designed to give practice in how-to-do-it, in the exercise of critical evaluation, in development of the link between real problems and methodological approach, and in comprehending statistical relationships. There is merit in giving some consideration to all questions and problems, even though fewer may be formally assigned.

If you feel that a concept is not clear, do not hesitate to consult other texts written at a similar level. A little time in the library will reveal which ones will be helpful, or your instructor can provide suggestions. Although special effort has been directed toward clarity, often different words on the same subject will add to one's insight.

A word should be said about the ladder-like nature of the course in elementary statistics. What is learned in earlier stages becomes the foundation for what follows. Consequently, it is most important that the student "keep up." If you have difficulty at some point, seek assistance from the library or from your instructor. Don't delay. Those who think matters may clear up if they wait may be right, but the risk is greater than in courses where the material is less interdependent. It can be like trying to climb a ladder with some rungs missing. Cramming, never very successful, is least so in statistics. Success in studying statistics depends on regular work, and if this is done, relatively little is needed in the way of review before examination time.

It will take special effort on your part to try constantly to "see the big picture," but the reward is high. First, this pays off in computation. Look at the result of your calculation. Does it make sense? Don't fail to be suspicious when you find the average to be 53 but most of the numbers are in the 60s and 70s. Remember Minium's First Law of Statistics: "The eyeball is the statistician's most powerful instrument." Second, a given concept is often applicable to various situations. Try to relate what you are currently studying to techniques you learned earlier. When this kind of effort is made you will find that statistics is less a collection of disparate techniques and more a sensible study—and easier to learn!

Finally, try always to relate the statistical tools to real problems. Imagine an inquiry of special interest to you, and consider which methods might be most suited to the hypothetical approach that you have designed in your mind. Statistics can be an exciting study, but only if you open your mind and reach out. It is a study with relevance to real problems.

PROBLEMS AND EXERCISES

Identify:

descriptive statistics   mathematical statistician
inferential statistics   substantive question
sampling statistics   statistical question
amateur statistician   statistical conclusion
professional statistician   substantive conclusion

1 An experimenter may "wear two hats": that of subject-matter expert and that of statistician. Is our experimenter wearing primarily the first hat, primarily the second, or both about equally when he or she: (*a*) Thinks up the problem. (*b*) Translates it into a statistical question. (*c*) Draws a conclusion that average performance of experimental and control groups is really different. (*d*) Decides that the imposed difference in treatment was responsible for the difference in average performance. (*e*) Relates this finding to those of previous studies.

2 In what sense is a conclusion about individuals in general meaningful for a particular individual? Not meaningful for a particular individual?

3 In Section 1.8, three different percentages were given concerning teachers, the holding of the doctorate, and courses offered. Explain how these discrepancies could exist.

4 Edgar Egghead was entranced by the capabilities of a particular statistical tool, and searched for a thesis problem that would allow him to use it. Is his enthusiasm misplaced? Explain.

CHAPTER 2

2.1 POPULATIONS AND SAMPLES

In statistical work, you will find much talk about *populations* and *samples*. As a first approach to these important concepts, we find that *population refers to a group of persons (or objects) about which the investigator wishes to draw conclusions, and that a sample consists of a part of that population.* If pollsters are trying to take the pulse of the nation prior to an election, their target population consists of those who will go to the polls and vote, whereas those whose opinions they actually obtain constitute a sample of that population.† In most research in social science, the investigator hopes that findings can be generalized to persons who are like those used in the study. Thus a sample is studied in the hope that it will lead to conclusions about the larger "target" population. Note too that inferential statistics (described in Section 1.2) has as its purpose the drawing of conclusions about a population from observations made on a sample. Sometimes, of course, the group

Preliminary
Concepts

at hand is the group that we want, and therefore is a population. If an instructor wants to know how the present class performed on the first midterm, the class members constitute the population and not a sample.

So far, we have used the word *population* to refer to a group of persons or objects. A somewhat different definition usually works better in statistics because it eliminates certain confusions. According to this definition, *population refers to the complete set of observations or measurements about which we would like to draw conclusions.* In this usage, the word refers not to people but rather to some observed characteristic. Thus in a study of learning, the population would consist of a set of learning scores of individuals, rather than the individuals themselves. We shall call a single observation or measurement an *element*. Thus if our interest is in the mathematics achievement of all currently enrolled pupils in Garfield Elementary School, the observation to be recorded is the achievement test score of each student, an element is the test score of a particular student, the scores of students in Mr. Jones' room is a sample, and the complete set of scores constitutes the population. Defining a population, as we now can see, is dependent on what

---

†There is another problem here: some of those polled will fail to vote.

the investigator wants to know and is therefore not a statistical problem, but a precondition to the use of statistics.

Under this second definition, it is possible for a population, statistically speaking, to exist even though we are talking about just one person. Suppose our interest is in determining reaction time for a particular person. The population would consist of the large number of possible reaction times which could be measured at various times for this person. Note how confusing this would be if we insisted on thinking of a population as people rather than observations.

2.2 RANDOM SAMPLES

There is nothing inherent in the definition of a sample that specifies how it is to be selected from a population. But that matters very much in statistics. At the heart of inferential statistics we shall find the notion of a *random sample,* a sample chosen in a very specific way. In fact, if a sample is selected at random, known principles of inference apply, and if it is not so chosen, they don't apply. The concept will be discussed with precision in chapters 13 and 14, as the study of inference is begun. At present we need an approximate understanding of its nature. For a sample to be random, it must have been selected in such a way that every element in the population had an equal opportunity of being included in the sample.

An example may be helpful. Suppose a deck of 52 cards is thoroughly shuffled, and 4 cards are drawn. The hand thus obtained may be considered to be a random sample of the population, because every card in the deck had an equal opportunity of inclusion in the hand, and every possible set of four cards had an equal opportunity of selection.

There are two properties of random samples that we need to know now. First, if several random samples are drawn from the same population, the elements of the sample will differ, and therefore the statistical characteristics will change from sample to sample. Thus if two polling organizations each draw a random sample of voters from the voting population, the elements of their samples will not be identical, and so their projections of the final vote will not be exactly the same. Similarly, in dealing the 52 playing cards from a standard deck to 4 players, we do not anticipate that each hand of cards will contain one ace, one king, etc., nor do we suppose that the number of cards from each suit (clubs, diamonds, hearts, spades) will of necessity be equally distributed in a given hand.

Second, the larger the sample, the less the variation of characteristics of the sample from random sample to random sample. This is of obvious importance in statistical inference, because it means that large samples will provide us with a more precise estimate of what is true about the population than we can expect from small samples.

2.3 THE SEVERAL MEANINGS OF "STATISTICS"

So far, the term *statistics* has been encountered in several contexts. It can mean *applied statistics,* the science of organizing, describing, and analyzing bodies of quantitative data. It can also mean *statistical theory.* In this sense it is best regarded as a branch of mathematics, owing much to the theory of probability.

In a third meaning, statistics refers to a *set of indices,* such as averages, which are the outcome of application of statistical procedures. The general public often uses the word in this sense, as reflected in the request, "Give me the statistics."

A fourth meaning, similar to the third, is of significance later in this book. In this sense, a statistic is an *index descriptive of a sample.* The same index, if descriptive of a population, is called a *parameter.* Thus, the average of a sample is a statistic; the average of the population is a parameter.

2.4 VARIABLES AND CONSTANTS

A *variable* is a characteristic that may take on different values. Typical examples are: intelligence test score, height, number of errors on a spelling test, position of a baseball team in the league standing, eye color, marital status, and sex. The concept of a variable does not imply that each observation must differ from all the others. All that is necessary is that the possibility of difference exists. Thus, if a school nurse interested in the height of seventh-grade students selects a sample of three for study and finds that they are all the same height, it is still proper to refer to height as a variable since the possibility of getting students of different height existed. On the other hand, her decision to study height only among the seventh-grade students means that grade level is a constant, rather than a variable, in this inquiry.

When, in terms of the definition of the study, it is not possible for a characteristic to have other than a single value, that characteristic is referred to as a *constant.* In a particular study, there are often several variables and constants to which consideration must be given. Suppose we are interested in religious attitude among students in a college. Of prime concern is the variable of religious attitude. However, other variables such as age, sex, and parental religious affiliation may have to be taken into account in interpreting our findings. At the same time, membership in the specific college and the time when the data were collected are constants. Different results might be obtained in another college, or at the same college had the study been made ten years earlier.

2.5 DISCRETE AND CONTINUOUS VARIABLES

If we ask how many were present at a meeting, we might learn that 73 persons attended, or 74, but no value between these two figures is possible. Variables having this kind of property are called *discrete variables*. Values of such variables are stepwise in nature. Other examples of such variables are the number of books in a library, number of rooms in a school, kinds of occupations, prices of magazines, and steps in a salary scale that changes only by 5% increments. A discrete variable is therefore one that can take only certain values, and none in between.

The second kind is known as a *continuous variable,* despite the assertion of a student that it is called an "indiscreet" variable. Consider the question of length. It is possible for an object to be 3 ft 1 in. or 3 ft 2 in. in length, or any conceivable amount in between. The characteristic of a continuous variable is that, within whatever limits its values may range, any value at all is possible. The discrete variable has gaps in its scale; the continuous variable has none. Examples of common variables that are reasonably conceived as continuous include weight, age, temperature, ability to perceive spatial relations, degree of approval of the current governmental administration, and musical talent.

The difference between the two types of variables has doubtless been noticed by everyone, although perhaps not completely analyzed. Although we accept as normal a statement that males of given age average 5.3 ft in height, we may find it a bit odd to be told that in the principality of Ruritania, 60-year-old males have had an average of 1.3 wives. The use of the average is, however, entirely appropriate in both instances. All that is required is to recognize what an average is, and that it does not necessarily characterize an individual.

Even though a variable is continuous in theory, the process of measurement always reduces it to a discrete one. Suppose we are measuring length and decide to record our observations to the nearest ten-thousandth of an inch. A particular observation will then be recorded as 1.3024 in. if the object appears to be closer in length to that figure than to 1.3023 or 1.3025. As a result, our *recorded* measurement will form a discrete scale in steps of one ten-thousandth of an inch.

2.6 ACCURACY IN A SET OF OBSERVATIONS

Numbers in a discrete series may be *exact numbers*. If we perform an experiment using 25 subjects, we may speak of 25 as an exact number, since there is *no* margin of error. Numbers lacking this kind of accuracy are known as *approximate numbers*. There are two ways in which we may be confronted with a set of approximate numbers. First, our method of collecting data may have degraded the potential accuracy in a set of discrete values.† This happens when we count the "house" at a theater by estimating how many seats are filled, or in reporting the national debt as \$182,000,000,000, rather than \$182,344,541,776.98. This may be appropriate when we are not interested in the detailed accuracy that could potentially be achieved.

Second, we have seen that recorded measures obtained from a scale that is essentially continuous constitute a discrete scale. However, such recorded values are approximate numbers. If we are measuring height to the nearest half inch, recorded height of 5 ft $4\frac{1}{2}$ in. means that the actual height lies somewhere within the range of 5 ft $4\frac{1}{4}$ in., and 5 ft $4\frac{3}{4}$ in. It should be clear that any measurement of a continuous variable must be treated as an approximate number.

In any event, it is up to the investigator to determine the degree of accuracy appropriate to his problem. A report of weight to the nearest pound will be adequate for determining your weight, but will not be satisfactory for buying candy, much less gold! Once the desired degree of accuracy is determined, it falls in the computational domain to adjust procedures so that in the process of numerical manipulation we do not arrive at an outcome that pretends to greater accuracy than is warranted, or that unnecessarily loses desired accuracy. Soon you will ask, "How many decimal places should I keep?" The answer is, "Whatever seems sensible." We now know some of the factors involved, but there is one more to consider: the effect of sampling variation.

Very often we are interested in studying the characteristics of a sample not merely for its own sake, but because of the implication that the sample findings may have for the population from which the sample was drawn. In this case, we must deal not only with accuracy in the data at hand, but with the fluctuation attributable to sampling. Of course, the characteristics that we obtain in a particular sample will not be exactly duplicated in a second sample. Although the observations taken might be exact numbers, they are subject to inaccuracy from the standpoint of our primary interest in the characteristics of the population.

In general, it is good to keep a little more accuracy in the course of a series of statistical computations than we think is the minimum to which we are entitled, since in a sequence of computations it is possible to compound inaccuracy. Once a statistical computation is completed, we should round back to a figure that seems sensible. Insofar as the factor of sampling variation is concerned, remember that an outcome based on a large sample has—other things being equal—greater stability than one based on a small sample.

---

† Here and elsewhere in this book, *degraded* refers to a reduction in accuracy; often purposeful, it is not necessarily a bad thing.

2.7 LEVELS OF MEASUREMENT

In measuring weight, we are accustomed to the idea that 40 pounds is twice as much as 20 pounds, and that the difference between 10 and 20 pounds is the same as that between 60 and 70 pounds. However, if we put baseball teams in order of their standing in the league, we should not think that the number two team is twice as bad as the number one team, nor would we expect that the difference in merit between the first and second team is necessarily the same as that between the second and third team. It is apparent that numbers have a different significance in the two situations. The difference in usage of numbers has been clarified by the identification of four major kinds of scales of measurement.

Some variables are qualitative in their nature rather than quantitative. For example, the two categories of sex are male and female. Eye color, types of cheese, and party of political affiliation are other examples of *qualitative,* or *categorical,* variables. The several categories of such a variable are said to constitute a *nominal scale.* The fundamental principle of the nominal scale is that of equivalence; all observations placed in the same category are considered to be equivalent. In the pure form of this scale, there is no question about one category having more of the quality concerned; all are simply different. Numbers may be used to identify the categories of a given scale, e.g. Cheese No. 1, Cheese No. 2, etc. Numbers used in this way are simply a substitute for names and serve only for purposes of identification. If one football player bears the number 10 on his back while another bears the number 20, there is no implication that one player is "more than" the other in some dimension, let alone that he has "twice as much" of something.

At the next level of complexity is the *ordinal scale.* In this type of measurement, numbers are used to indicate the order of magnitude of the observations. Thus a supervisor may be required to estimate the competence of seven workmen by arranging them in order of merit. The basic relation expressed in a series of numbers used in this way is that of "greater than." Among the persons ranked 1, 2, and 3, the first has a greater degree of merit than the man ranked second, and in turn, the second man has greater merit than the third. However, nothing is implied about the magnitude of difference in merit between adjacent steps on the scale. The difference in merit between the first and second workman may be small or large and is not necessarily the same as that between the second and the third workman. Further, nothing is implied about the absolute level of merit; all seven workers could be excellent, or they could be quite ordinary.

The next major level is the *interval scale.* This scale has all the properties of the ordinal scale, but with the further refinement that the distance between adjacent scores is meaningful. Examples of this type of scale are calendar years and degrees of temperature on the Fahrenheit or Centigrade scale. We can assume that as much time has elapsed between 1910 and 1920 as between 1940 and 1950. A given interval (e.g. 10 years) is considered to represent the same difference in the characteristic measured (e.g. time) irrespective of the location of that interval along the measurement scale.

When measurement is at this level, one may talk meaningfully about the ratio between intervals. For instance, one may say that twice as much time has elapsed between 1940 and 1960 as between 1900 and 1910. Nevertheless, it is not possible to speak meaningfully about a ratio between two measures. For example, it is not meaningful to assert that a temperature of 100° (Centigrade) is twice as hot as one of 50°, or that a rise from 90° to 99° is a 10% increase. The reason is that the zero point is arbitrarily determined, and does not imply an absence of heat. The point is illustrated in Figure 2.1. The first part of this illustration shows three temperatures in degrees Centigrade: 0°, 50°, and 100°. It is tempting to think of 100° as twice as great as 50°. However, the value of zero on this scale is simply an arbitrary reference point. The second part of the illustration shows the same three temperatures in degrees Kelvin. This scale uses the same unit for its intervals; e.g., 50 degrees of *change* in temperature is the same on both scales. However, the Kelvin scale has an absolute zero, indicative of an absence of heat. The values of 50° and 100° on the Centigrade scale are 323° and 373°, respectively, on the Kelvin scale. A little arithmetic shows that the rise of 50 degrees from 323° is an increase by a factor of 1.15, rather than by a factor of 2.

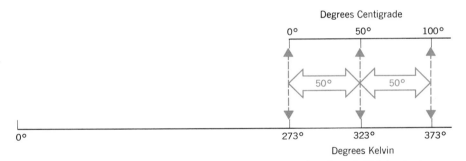

Figure 2.1 *Three Temperatures Represented on the Centigrade and Kelvin Scales.*

The *ratio scale* possesses all the properties of the interval scale and in addition has the property of an absolute zero. Temperature measured on the Kelvin scale, length, weight, and measures of elapsed time, such as age, years of experience, and reaction time are examples of measures of this type. Not only is the difference between 40 in. and 41 in. considered to be the same as the difference between 80 and 81 in., but it is also true that 80 in. is twice as long as 40 in.

Characteristics of the four measurement scales are summarized in Table 2.1.

Table 2.1 *Levels of Measurement and Their Characteristics*

Nominal scale:	Qualitative categories only. Observations sorted into categories by principle of equivalence. Scale categories differ from one another only in a qualitative sense. Example: eye color.
Ordinal scale:	Observations are ranked in order of magnitude. Numerical ranks express a "greater than" relationship, but with no implication about how much greater. Example: workmen sorted according to order of merit.
Interval scale:	Numerical value assigned indicates order of merit *and* meaningfully reflects relative distances between points along the scale. A given interval between measures has the same meaning at any point in the scale. Example: temperature in degrees Centigrade.
Ratio scale:	Scale has all properties of an interval scale, and in addition an absolute zero point. Ratio between measures becomes meaningful. Example: length.

2.8 LEVELS OF MEASUREMENT AND PROBLEMS OF STATISTICAL TREATMENT

An understanding of the major types of measurement scales provides a framework for understanding certain problems in the interpretation of data. In psychology and education, as well as in other behavioral sciences, most common measurements can *not* be demonstrated to have the full properties of interval or ratio scales. For example, a test of spelling, or any of the ordinary achievement tests (including examinations prepared for college classes) almost certainly do not have an absolute zero. A score of zero in spelling means that the person could not answer the simplest question, but easier questions probably exist. At the same time, it is not clear that such tests have the property of measurement according to equal intervals. This would certainly be doubtful in the case of the spelling test if the words varied in difficulty.

We should, therefore, be alert to the necessity of resisting several erroneous but tempting propositions, such as the assertion that a person with an IQ of 150 is twice as bright as one with an IQ of 75, or that the difference between 15 and 25 points on a spelling test necessarily represents the same increment in spelling ability as the difference between a score of 30 and 40 points on the same test. In psychological measurement, this problem may be particularly critical when a test does not have enough "top" or "bottom" to make adequate differentiation among the group measured. For example, imagine a test of ability that has a maximum possible score of 50 points and that is too easy for the group measured. Between two persons who score 50 points, the score for one may indicate maximum level of attainment, but the second person with the same score may be capable of a much higher level of performance: the measuring instrument is simply incapable of showing it.

"Scale problems" can sometimes cause headaches in interpretation of research outcomes. Consider, for example, the problem of evaluating a method of teaching spelling. We want to know whether the method is of differential effectiveness for high- and low-achieving students. We select two such groups, measure their spelling performance before and after exposure to the teaching method, and consider comparing the average gain made by one group with that made by the other. But, if the two groups do not start at the same level (and they most likely will not in this study), we are in a poor position to compare the gains unless it is possible to assume that a given gain at one point in the measurement scale represents the same increase in ability as an equal amount of gain in another part of the scale. In short, we must be able to assume an interval scale in order to be certain that we can make an entirely sensible interpretation of the comparison of gains. We are well advised to be alert to possible scale problems. Fortunately, the weight of the evidence suggests that in most situations, interpretability of statistical outcomes is not seriously incapacitated by uncertainty of the level of measurement achieved.

PROBLEMS AND EXERCISES

Identify

population	degraded data
sample	exact number
element	approximate number
parameter	sampling variation
statistics	levels of measurement
variable	nominal scale
constant	ordinal scale
qualitative variable	interval scale
discrete variable	ratio scale
continuous variable	

1 The example in Section 2.1 spoke of the population of intelligence test scores of all enrolled students in a particular school. If we were interested in the heights of these same students, should we speak of "the same population"? Explain.

2 In the same school, suppose we are interested in the number of chairs in each room. (*a*) What is the observation to be recorded? (*b*) What is an element? (*c*) What is the population?

3 If we are interested in ascertaining the existence of a TV set in the residences of Brownsville: (*a*) What is the observation to be recorded? (*b*) What is an element? (*c*) What is the population?

4 You are going on a diet with the intention of losing weight. You decide to weigh yourself now, before entering the diet, and one month from now. In order to refine your "study," what variables would you find it desirable to hold constant?

5 We wish to set up an experiment to test the relative effectiveness of morning hours and afternoon hours as a time for study. Identify several variables that it would be desirable to hold constant.

6 If the effect of the act of measurement is disregarded, which of the following variables are best regarded fundamentally as forming a discrete series, and which a continuous series? (*a*) temperature (*b*) time (*c*) sex (*d*) kinds of cigarettes (*e*) size of family (*f*) achievement score in mathematics (*g*) merit ratings of employees (*h*) score on an introversion–extraversion scale.

7 In a safety study, we might record the number of auto accidents incurred by each subject during a five-year period. This variable could be considered as discrete or, from another point of view, as continuous. Explain.

8 Is number of errors in a learning experiment an exact number or an approximate one? Explain.

9 The weights of nine children were recorded to the nearest pound, and their average weight was found to be 118.555 lb. What do you think about reporting the average as: (*a*) 118.555? (*b*) 118.6? (*c*) 120 (rounded to the nearest 10 lb)?

10 In one state, voters register as Republican, Democrat, or Independent. Can we consider this variable as one of the four "scales of measurement"? If so, which one?

11 Instructor, assistant professor, associate professor, and professor form what kind of scale?

12 Joe Casual, student, is asked whether he would rather have a grade of C for sure, or a 50-50 chance of getting a B or a D. He replies that he would prefer the certain C. It must be that for him the psychological distance between a B and a C is less than the distance between a C and a D. Therefore, the grades B, C, and D form a scale no higher in level of measurement than (which scale)?

13 If the student in the previous question had no preference, this would suggest that the three grades form for him a scale of what type?

14 Temperature in degrees Centigrade forms an interval scale. What kind of scale is formed by degrees Fahrenheit? Explain.

15 In an interval scale, is it proper to consider that an increase of 20 points is twice as much as an increase of 10 points? Explain.

16 Assume the following series of numbers form an interval scale: 0, 1, 2, 3, . . . , 19, 20. (*a*) Would it still be an interval scale if we added 10 points to each score? Explain. (*b*) Would it still be an interval scale if we multiplied each score by 10? Explain.

17 (*a*) If the numbers in Question 16 form a ratio scale, and 10 points is added to each, would we still have a ratio scale? Explain. (*b*) If we multiply each score by 10? Explain.

CHAPTER 3

3.1 THE NATURE OF A SCORE

Consider three possible adjacent scores on a social science achievement test: 51, 52, 53. It is reasonable to think that the score of 52 represents a level of knowledge *closer* to 52 than that indicated by a score of 51 or 53. Consequently, the score of 52 may be treated as extending from 51.5 to 52.5. This interpretation of a score is illustrated in Figure 3.1.

In general, the limits of a score are considered to extend from one-half of the smallest unit of measurement below the value of the score to one-half unit above.† If we were measuring to the nearest 10th of an inch, the range represented by a score of 2.3 in. is 2.3 ± .05 in., or from 2.25 to 2.35 in. If we were weighing coal to the nearest 10 pounds, a weight of 780 lb represents 780 ± 5 lb, or from 775 to 785 lb.

Some sets of scores may have negative values, as in a record of temperatures.

Frequency Distributions

Negative scores could also occur in use of a test scored by subtracting the number of wrong answers from the number of right answers. In measuring judgment of distance, it may be convenient to record the score in terms of error of over-estimation or underestimation, using positive and negative values to make this differentiation.

3.2 A QUESTION OF ORGANIZING DATA

Suppose that Héloïse Abelard, a college history instructor, has given a midterm examination, scored it, and returned the papers to her 50 students. Aside from the primary question about their grades, members of the class would like additional information. How do their scores compare with others in the class? What is the general level of performance of this class? One student asks, "Please tell us something about how the class did." In response, she writes the set of 50 scores on the blackboard. Since her gradebook is in alphabetical order, the result appears in

† Age is the only common exception; when a man says he is 52 he means his age is between 52.0 and 53.0.

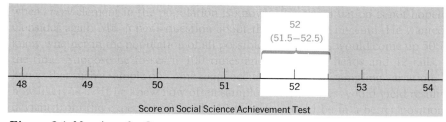

Figure 3.1 *Meaning of a Score.*

the form shown by Table 3.1. Before reading further, you are invited to imagine yourself in the place of a student whose score is 82, and to study this table.

You doubtless looked for some indication of the location of 82 among the mass and noted that there are a number of scores close to this figure, some higher and some lower. Perhaps you also saw that there are some scores in the 60s and some in the 90s, that they are few in number, and that no scores are lower or higher.

The simplest way to facilitate this kind of analysis is to put the scores in order. To do so, locate the highest and lowest score values. Then record all *possible* score values, including these two extremes, in descending order. Among the data of Table 3.1, the highest score is 96 and the lowest is 61. The recorded sequence is: 96, 95, 94, . . . , 61, as shown in Table 3.2. Now we return to the unordered collection of scores and, taking them in the order shown there, tally their occurrence against the new (ordered) list. The result is given in Table 3.2. Such a table, showing the scores and their frequency of occurrence, is called a *frequency distribution.*

Thus organized, many features of interest are easily perceived. We see that the score of 82 is a little above the middle of the distribution. Although scores range

Table 3.1 *Scores from Fifty Students on a History Class Midterm Examination*

84	82	72	70	72
80	62	96	86	68
68	87	89	85	82
87	85	84	88	89
86	86	78	70	81
70	86	88	79	69
79	61	68	75	77
90	86	78	89	81
67	91	82	73	77
80	78	76	86	83

Table 3.2 *Scores from Table 3.1, Organized in Order of Magnitude*

Score	Freq	Score	Freq	Score	Freq	Score	Freq
96	1	86	6	76	1	66	0
95	0	85	2	75	1	65	0
94	0	84	2	74	0	64	0
93	0	83	1	73	1	63	0
92	0	82	3	72	2	62	1
91	1	81	2	71	0	61	1
90	1	80	2	70	3		
89	3	79	2	69	1		
88	2	78	3	68	3		
87	2	77	2	67	1		

from 61 to 96, the bulk of the distribution lies between 67 and 91. There is one student whose competence stands above the rest, and two students who "aren't getting it." Eighty-two is not far from being quite a good performance in this class.

3.3 GROUPED SCORES

When scores range widely (as they do in the data we have been considering), reducing individual scores to a smaller number of groups makes it easier to display the data and to grasp their meaning. Table 3.3 shows two ways in which the scores

Table 3.3 *Scores from Table 3.1, Converted to Grouped Data Distributions*

A: Class interval width = 3		B: Class interval width = 5	
Scores	Freq	Scores	Freq
94–96	1	95–99	1
91–93	1	90–94	2
88–90	6	85–89	15
85–87	10	80–84	10
82–84	6	75–79	9
79–81	6	70–74	6
76–78	6	65–69	5
73–75	2	60–64	2
70–72	5		
67–69	5		
64–66	0		
61–63	2		

of Table 3.1 may be grouped into *class intervals*. When a graph is to be made from the distribution, grouping the scores helps present a more nearly regular appearance. Look ahead to Figure 4.8 in the next chapter and compare the three graphs shown there to see this effect.

There are, however, two matters that one should bear in mind when considering grouped scores:

1 When scores are grouped, some information is lost. For example, if we observe that there are five scores in an interval labeled 120–129, one can not say for sure whether they are all at one end of the interval, all at the other, or spread throughout in some way.

2 A set of *raw* scores (the term for a set of scores in their original form) does not result in a unique set of *grouped scores*. Table 3.3 shows, for example, two different sets of grouped scores that may be formed from the raw scores of Table 3.1.

3.4 CHARACTERISTICS OF CLASS INTERVALS

In converting raw scores to grouped data, there are several principles that should be kept in mind. As they are discussed, it will be helpful to refer to Table 3.3 from time to time.

1 *A set of class intervals should be mutually exclusive.* That is, intervals should be chosen so that one score cannot belong to more than one interval.

2 *All intervals should be of the same width.* Unequal intervals cause trouble when further statistical work is to be done.

3 *Intervals should be continuous throughout the distribution.* In part A of Table 3.3, there are no scores in the interval 64–66. To omit this interval and "close ranks" would create a misleading impression, and would make trouble when the distribution is used as a basis for further work.

4 *The interval containing the highest score value is placed at the top.* This convention saves the trouble of learning how to read each new table when we come to it.

5 For most work, *there should be not fewer than 10 class intervals, nor more than 20*. In Table 3.3, Distribution A meets this criterion; Distribution B does not. Fewer class intervals mean greater interval width, with consequent loss of accuracy. Many class intervals result in lesser convenience. When the number of cases is small or when graphic representation is to be the final product, a small number of intervals is often preferable. With a large number of cases (say, 150+), more intervals may work better.

Table 3.4 *Data of Table 3.3A, Showing Exact Limits and Tally*

Score limits	Exact limits	Tally	f
94–96	93.5–96.5	/	1
91–93	90.5–93.5	/	1
88–90	87.5–90.5	⬚ /	6
85–87	84.5–87.5	⬚ ⬚	10
82–84	81.5–84.5	⬚ /	6
79–81	78.5–81.5	⬚ /	6
76–78	75.5–78.5	⬚ /	6
73–75	72.5–75.5	/	2
70–72	69.5–72.5	⬚	5
67–69	66.5–69.5	⬚	5
64–66	63.5–66.5		0
61–63	60.5–63.5	/	2

6 It should be noted that in Table 3.3 the limits of each class interval are recorded in *score limits*. For example, the lowest class interval for Distribution A is 61–63. The intent is to include scores of 61, 62, and 63. However, following principles outlined in Section 3.1, the score of 61 extends from 60.5 to 61.5, and the score of 63 from 62.5 to 63.5. Consequently, the score limits of 61–63 include all scores that might have values between 60.5 and 63.5. When the limits are actually written this way, they are called *exact limits*. Intervals are typically written in terms of score limits because they are less cumbersome, but we must remember the exact limits implicit in such notation. Both types of limits are shown in Table 3.4. (The data are those of Distribution A of Table 3.3.)

3.5 CONSTRUCTING A GROUPED DATA FREQUENCY DISTRIBUTION

With these factors in mind, we are ready to translate a set of raw scores to a grouped data frequency distribution. We shall illustrate the procedure with the data of Table 3.1. The first step is to find the lowest score (61) and the highest score (96). The difference between these two figures is the *range* of scores. Therefore, the range is (96–61) = 35. Since there are to be from 10 to 20 class intervals, we must find an interval width satisfying this condition. Often this can be done by inspection. Alternatively, dividing the range by 10 gives the interval width necessary to cover all scores in 10 intervals. If 20 intervals were to be used, the width of the class interval would be exactly half this amount. Consequently, we may choose an interval width equal to any convenient whole number between these two values. For our data, one-tenth of the range is 3.5, and half of this number is 1.8. It is apparent that an interval width of 2 or 3 will be satisfactory for the present data. Suppose we decide to use an interval width of 3. In statistical work, interval width is symbolized by the letter i; for this problem, we have selected $i = 3$.

Next, we must determine the starting point of the bottom class interval. Since the lowest score is 61, the lowest interval (written in score limits) could be 59–61, 60–62, or 61–63. Often it is convenient to make the lower score limit a multiple of the class interval width. *This is especially true when interval width is 5 or 10 (or some multiple thereof).*

Next, refer to the collection of raw scores in whatever order they may be, and tally their occurrence, one by one, against the list of class intervals. Table 3.4 indicates the method of tally.† Then convert the tally to frequency (symbolized by f), as shown in the last column of Table 3.4. The total number of cases in the distribution is found by summing the several values of f and is symbolized by n if the distribution is considered as a sample, or by N if it is a population.

Note that when it comes to the selection of width of the class interval, a choice is usually available. The number of intervals desired is one factor in choosing, but convenience is sometimes another. Because of the nature of our number system, choosing a width of 5 or 10 or some multiple thereof (if these values are legitimately available) makes both the construction and interpretation of a distribution easier. The steps in constructing a frequency distribution are summarized below:

1 Find the value of the lowest score and the highest score.
2 Find the range by subtracting the lowest score from the highest.
3 Determine width of the class interval (i) needed to yield 10 to 20 class intervals.
4 Determine the point at which the lowest interval should begin.
5 Record the limits of all class intervals, placing the interval containing the highest score value at the top. Intervals should be continuous and of the same width.
6 Using the tally system, enter the raw scores in the appropriate class intervals.
7 Convert the tally count to frequency (f).

---

† The tally system shown in Table 3.4 (e.g. ▨ ▭) has all the advantages of the usual tally system (e.g. 卌 ///), and is less prone to error.

3.6 GROUPING ERROR

Once scores have been placed in class intervals, they lose their specific identity. For further work, we must often assume that the *midpoint* of the interval (the point halfway between the upper and lower limits) represents the scores therein, or that the scores are evenly divided throughout the interval. With poor luck, all scores might conceivably fall at one end of the interval. Of course, the more scores there are in the interval, the less the chance that this could happen. One factor related to potential inaccuracy is width of the class interval. Other things being equal, the narrower the class interval width, the less the potentiality for *grouping error*.

3.7 THE RELATIVE FREQUENCY DISTRIBUTION

We read that Catherine Candidate received 1375 votes for mayor in the last election. Is that a large number of votes? In a town where 1600 votes were cast, it is. In fact, it is 86% of the vote. In a city of 60,000 voters, the situation is different; it amounts to a little over 2%. For some purposes, an answer to the question "How many?" may give us what we want to know. For others the question "What proportion?" may be more relevant.

Table 3.5 *Relative Frequency Distributions*

Score limits	A: Group 1			B: Group 2		
	f	Prop. *f*	*% f*	*f*	Prop. *f*	*% f*
97–99				1	.01	1
94–96	1	.02	2	1	.01	1
91–93	1	.02	2	3	.04	4
88–90	6	.12	12	3	.04	4
85–87	10	.20	20	4	.05	5
82–84	6	.12	12	7	.09	9
79–81	6	.12	12	8	.10	10
76–78	6	.12	12	9	.11	11
73–75	2	.04	4	12	.15	15
70–72	5	.10	10	6	.08	8
67–69	5	.10	10	11	.14	14
64–66	0	.00	0	7	.09	9
61–63	2	.04	4	2	.02	2
58–60				3	.04	4
55–57				3	.04	4
	50	1.00	100%	80	1.01	101%

We can easily translate obtained frequencies for each class interval of a frequency distribution to *relative frequencies* by converting each to proportion or percent of the total number of cases. Part A of Table 3.5 shows the data of Part A of Table 3.3 expressed in this form. To obtain relative frequencies, we divide each frequency of a class interval by the total number of cases in the distribution (calculate f/n). This gives the proportion of cases in the interval, expressed as a decimal fraction, or parts relative to one. If percentage is preferable (parts relative to one hundred), this figure is multiplied by 100. Thus, the entry for the bottom class interval of Table 3.5 (Part A) is obtained by dividing the frequency of 2 by 50, which results in the decimal fraction .04, or 4%.† If you own a pocket calculator that permits the use of a "constant divisor," this feature will make the conversions particularly easy.

In final presentation of the results of calculation of relative frequencies, there is little point in retaining more than hundredths in resulting decimal fractions, or units in the percents unless the scores number several hundred.

Use of relative frequency is particularly helpful when comparing two or more frequency distributions in which the ns are unequal. Table 3.5 shows two distributions. In one $n = 50$, and in the other $n = 80$; comparison of the two sets of frequencies is not easy. Conversion to relative frequency puts both distributions on the same basis, and meaningful comparison is easier.

Caution is in order when the distribution is comprised of a small number of cases. It can be misleading to say that 50% of a community's auto mechanics are alcoholics when what is meant is that one of the two of them is.

3.8 THE CUMULATIVE FREQUENCY DISTRIBUTION

Henry earned a score of 52 in an arithmetic achievement test; how many of his class scored less well? How many scored better? Mary earned a score of 143 on a college entrance test. Among college applicants, what percent obtains lower scores? On the same test, what score is so low that only 10% of applicants do less well? What score divides the upper 25% of the distribution from the lower 75%? These are examples of questions that are more easily answered when the distribution is cast in *cumulative* form.

A cumulative frequency distribution shows how many cases lie below the upper exact limit of the particular class interval. To construct such a distribution, we begin with the usual frequency distribution, as illustrated in the first two columns of Table 3.6. Starting at the bottom, we record for each class interval the total frequency of cases falling below its upper limit. These figures are shown in the

---

† Consult Section A.6 in Appendix A if you think a refresher on fractions and proportions would be helpful.

Table 3.6 *Data from Table 3.3A Presented in Cumulative Form*

Exact limits	f	cum f	Prop. cum f	cum % f
93.5–96.5	1	50	1.00	100
90.5–93.5	1	49	.98	98
87.5–90.5	6	48	.96	96
84.5–87.5	10	42	.84	84
81.5–84.5	6	32	.64	64
78.5–81.5	6	26	.52	52
75.5–78.5	6	20	.40	40
72.5–75.5	2	14	.28	28
69.5–72.5	5	12	.24	24
66.5–69.5	5	7	.14	14
63.5–66.5	0	2	.04	4
60.5–63.5	2	2	.04	4
	$n = 50$			

third column, headed *cum f*. They are obtained by adding the frequency of the given class interval to the cumulative frequency recorded for the next lower class interval. As a check on computation, the cumulative frequency for the uppermost class interval should equal n.

If *relative frequency* is desired, the cumulative frequencies are converted by dividing each cumulative frequency by n. For example, in the interval 87.5–90.5, $cum\ f/n = 48/50 = .96$, the proportional cumulative frequency. These values are shown in the fourth column of Table 3.6. If desired, they may be converted to percent frequency by multiplying each by 100, as shown in the last column.

3.9 CENTILES AND CENTILE RANKS

The centile system is widely used in educational measurements to report the standing of an individual relative to the performance of a known group. It is based on the *cumulative percentage frequency distribution*. A *centile point* is a score point below which a specified percent of the scores in the distribution fall. It is often called a *centile*, or a *percentile*. The specified percent is the *centile rank* of the centile point. The two should not be confused: centile ranks may take values only between zero and 100, whereas a centile (point) may have any value that scores may have. It is perfectly possible to find that 576 is the value of a centile, for example. Suppose Mary earned a score of 143 on a college entrance test, and that this score is such that 75% of applicants score below it. Mary's centile is 143; her centile rank is 75.

We shall use the symbol C to represent a centile, and attach a subscript to indicate the centile rank. For Mary, we may write: $C_{75} = 143$. In Table 3.6, we find that C_{96} (the 96th centile point) is 90.5, the upper limit of the third-from-top class interval. Similarly, the same table shows that $C_{24} = 72.5$ and $C_{40} = 78.5$. In the next two sections, we shall learn how to compute centiles and centile ranks from cumulative frequency distributions. Evaluation of the merits of this method of reporting scores will be postponed until chapter 8, where comparison will be made with other systems.

3.10 COMPUTATION OF CENTILES FROM GROUPED DATA

In Table 3.7, the data of Table 3.5 (Part B) are presented in cumulative frequency form. This is the starting point for finding centiles. We shall suppose that our problem is to find the values of C_{25}, C_{50}, and C_{82}. What is C_{25}? It is the score point below which 25% of the cases fall. There are 80 cases, and since 25% of 80 is 20, C_{25} is the point below which 20 cases fall. Working up from the bottom of the distribution, we find that the 20th case will fall in the class interval 66.5–69.5 (we must be sure to think in terms of exact limits). At this point, it is not clear what score value should be assigned, since the point sought lies somewhere within the interval.

Table 3.7   *Cumulative Percentage Frequency Distribution and Centile Calculation*

Score limits	f	cum f	cum % f	Centile calculations
97–99	1	80	100.0	
94–96	1	79	98.8	
91–93	3	78	97.5	
88–90	3	75	93.8	$C_{82} = 81.5 + \left(\dfrac{4.6}{7} \times 3\right)$
85–87	4	72	90.0	$= 83.5$
82–84	7	68	85.0	
79–81	8	61	76.2	
76–78	9	53	66.2	
73–75	12	44	55.0	$C_{50} = 72.5 + \left(\dfrac{8}{12} \times 3\right)$
70–72	6	32	40.0	$= 74.5$
67–69	11	26	32.5	
64–66	7	15	18.8	
61–63	2	8	10.0	$C_{25} = 66.5 + \left(\dfrac{5}{11} \times 3\right)$
58–60	3	6	7.5	$= 67.9$
55–57	3	3	3.8	
	$n = 80$			

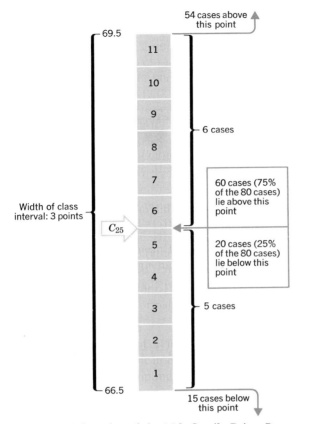

Figure 3.2 *Location of the 25th Centile Point: Data from Table 3.7.*

There are 11 scores in this interval, and to proceed, *we will make the assumption that they are evenly divided throughout the interval.*† The results of this assumption are pictured in Figure 3.2. From this point on, grasping the procedure will be made easier by close study of Figure 3.2. The value of the 25th centile point will be located at a point 20 scores (cases) up from the bottom of the distribution. Since there are 15 cases below the lower limit of the class interval concerned, we must come up five more to reach this position. This means that we are to come up five out of the 11 equal parts in the interval, or 5/11ths of the interval's width. The width of the interval is three score points, and the calculation is as follows: $(5/11) \times 3 = 1.4$ points. This quantity is therefore added to the lower exact limit of the interval.

$$C_{25} = 66.5 + 1.4 = 67.9$$

† This procedure is called *linear interpolation*. It is explained in Section A.10 of Appendix A.

A formula could be given for this calculation, but it is more important to follow the logic of the procedure. Once the logic is grasped, it is much easier to remember than any formula because it makes sense.

The steps in calculating a centile will be reviewed and summarized by determining C_{50}.

Problem: Find C_{50}.

1 First objective: find the class interval in which C_{50} falls.

    (a) C_{50} is the score point below which 50% of the cases fall.
    (b) 50% of $n = .50 \times 80 = 40$ scores.
    (c) The 40th score (from the bottom) falls in the class interval 72.5–75.5.

2 Determine the number of cases between the bottom of the distribution and the lower limit of the class interval containing the centile (in this case, 32).

3 Determine the additional number of cases required to make up the number of scores found in 1(c) (in this case, 8; $32 + 8 = 40$).

4 Assume the (12) scores in the class interval are evenly divided throughout the interval.

5 Find the additional distance into the interval needed to arrive at the score point (8/12ths of the interval width, or $(8/12) \times 3 = 2.0$).

6 Add this value to the lower limit of the class interval to obtain the centile:
$$C_{50} = 72.5 + 2.0 = 74.5$$

Elements of the calculation of C_{50} and C_{82} are shown in Table 3.7. To be certain that the procedure is grasped, you should verify that $C_5 = 58.5$ and that $C_{75} = 81.1$.

A good way to check calculation of centiles is to count *downward* in the distribution to the appropriate point. Checking the calculation of C_{25} by this method, one must come down 75% of the cases, or 60 scores. This is six cases below the upper limit of the class interval 66.5–69.5, and by the same reasoning applied above
$$C_{25} = 69.5 - (6/11 \times 3) = 67.9$$

A special situation arises when a centile point coincides with an empty class interval. In the data of Table 3.6, this occurs for C_4. By the definition of a centile point, C_4 could be said to be any score value between 63.5 and 66.5, inclusive. Preferred procedure is to split the difference; C_4 is therefore taken as the midpoint of this interval, 65.0.

3.11 COMPUTATION OF CENTILE RANK

Calculation of centile rank may be required rather than calculation of centiles. The assumption required is the same as for computation of a centile, and the general nature of the procedure is parallel in both instances. One illustration will suffice.

What is the centile rank of a score of 87? We must find the percent of cases that lie below 87.0. First, we find the number of them below this point. Consulting Table 3.7, we see that the score of 87.0 is located in the class interval 84.5–87.5. The interval width is three score points, and to reach 87.0 one must come up 2.5 of these points from the bottom of the interval (84.5 + 2.5 = 87.0). There are four cases in the interval, and we assume them to be evenly distributed. We must come up $(2.5/3) \times 4$, or 3.3 cases from the bottom of the interval. Since there are 68 scores below this lower limit, the point in question is $68 + 3.3 = 71.3$ cases up from the bottom of the distribution. Finally, $71.3/80 = .89$, or 89%. The score of 87 is therefore at a point below which 89% of the cases fall, and therefore its centile rank is 89. The calculation may be summarized as follows:

$$\left. \begin{array}{l} \text{Centile rank of} \\ \text{a score of 87} \end{array} \right\} = 100 \left[\frac{68 + \left(\frac{2.5}{3} \times 4 \right)}{80} \right] = 89$$

To be certain the procedure is understood, you should verify the following calculation of the centile rank of a score of 62:

$$\left. \begin{array}{l} \text{Centile rank of} \\ \text{a score of 62} \end{array} \right\} = 100 \left[\frac{6 + \left(\frac{1.5}{3} \times 2 \right)}{80} \right] = 9$$

For further practice, verify that the centile rank of a score of 72 is 39, and that the centile rank of a score of 91 is 94.

PROBLEMS AND EXERCISES

Identify:

raw scores	relative frequency
grouped scores	percentage frequency
i	cumulative frequency
f	distribution
n	cumulative percentage
N	frequency distribution
score limits	"less than" distribution
exact limits	centile
midpoint	centile rank
class interval	C_{75}
range	linear interpolation
grouping error	

1 Write the exact limits for the following scores: (*a*) A score of 52; measurement is to the nearest digit. (*b*) 17 years; measurement is to the last birthday. (*c*) 800 yd; measurement is to the nearest 100 yd. (*d*) 460 lb; measurement is to the nearest 10 lb. (*e*) .6 in.; measurement is to the nearest .1 in. (*f*) .47 sec; measurement is to the nearest .01 sec.

2 "The notion that there ought to be between 10 and 20 class intervals is fundamentally an arbitrary convention." Evaluate the foregoing statement.

3 List the possibly objectionable features in the following set of class intervals:

50 and up	20–25
44–49	14–19
38–43	8–13
26–31	0– 7

4 The lowest and highest scores are given below for different distributions. Assume grouping is to be done as a preliminary to further statistical calculation. For each, state (*a*) the range, (*b*) your choice of class interval width, (*c*) the score limits and the exact limits for the lowest class interval, and (*d*) the midpoint of that interval: (1) 36, 75; (2) 54, 117; (3) 27, 171; (4) −22, +21; (5) 1.13, 3.47; (6) 287, 821.

5 Suppose we are recording weight in pounds, and one class interval has these score limits: 10–19. What are its exact limits? Its midpoint? The lowest class interval is 0–9. What is the best way to view its exact limits? Its midpoint? Would you view the interval, 0–9, differently if it represented performance on a test scored by subtracting wrong answers from right ones? Explain.

6 When $i = 1$, how do we write the exact limits for these scores: 47, 48, 49? The score limits?

7 The following scores were obtained by university freshmen on an achievement test in history:

Data 3A

44	35	20	40	38	52	29	36	38	38
38	38	41	35	42	50	31	43	30	41
32	47	43	41	47	32	38	29	23	48
41	51	48	49	37	26	34	48	35	41
38	47	41	33	39	48	38	20	32	37
29	44	29	33	35	50	41	38	26	29
32	26	24	38	38	56	56	48	34	35
26	26	38	37	44	24	44	47	29	41

(*a*) Construct a frequency distribution using $i = 3$, and 20–22 as the score limits for the lowest class interval. (*b*) Construct another frequency distribution from the same scores, using $i = 3$, but using 18–20 as the first class interval. Is the midpoint of the interval 27–29 representative of the scores that should be so classified in Data 3A? (*c*) Compare the appearance of the two distributions. Are they generally similar in appearance? One place where they appear to differ is in class intervals covering scores of 45 to 52. What explains this?

8 Construct a frequency distribution from Data 3A using $i = 5$, with the lowest interval at 20–24. Compare the result with the distribution obtained in Problem 7, writing your impressions.

9 Convert the frequency distribution requested in Problem 7a into a percentage frequency distribution.

10 Convert the frequency distribution requested in Problem 7b into a percentage frequency distribution.

11 Comparing group 1 and 2 in Table 3.5, (a) which group has proportionately more scores of 88 and above? (b) 66 and below? (c) between 70 and 81?

12 In Table 3.6, in which class interval is the score below which (a) 90% of the cases fall? (b) 30 cases fall? (c) 50% of the cases fall? (d) 10 cases fall?

Data 3B

76	72	77	65	70	69	60	68	72	69
68	73	67	73	63	80	68	74	75	71
65	75	64	81	77	76	64	72	73	67
71	74	78	66	78	63	68	76	71	72
70	75	69	67	71	68	72	75	73	74

13 For Data 3B, (a) construct a frequency distribution suitable for further statistical calculation, (b) obtain the cumulative frequencies, (c) obtain the cumulative percentage frequencies.

14 From the cumulative distribution of Problem 13, find: (a) C_{10} (b) C_{25} (c) C_{60} (d) C_{95}.

15 Verify the centile calculations in Problem 14 by counting down from the top of the distribution and interpolating downward from the top of the interval.

16 From the cumulative distribution of Problem 13, find the centile rank of scores of (a) 79.5 (b) 64.5 (c) 70 (d) 75.

17 Is it possible for a centile to have a value such as 432? Explain.

Data 3C
Retention Scores for Subjects Who Learned
Under Different Conditions of Practice

Score	Method A	Method B
155–159		1
150–154	2	2
145–149	4	7
140–144	7	12
135–139	12	10
130–134	14	7
125–129	25	4
120–124	23	3
115–119	18	0
110–114	20	2
105–109	12	1
100–104	8	0
95– 99	3	1
90– 94	2	
	$n = 150$	$n = 50$

18 Present the distributions of Data 3C as (*a*) percentage frequency distributions, (*b*) cumulative frequency distributions, and (*c*) cumulative percentage distributions. Which method do you find makes comparison of the two easiest? Why?

19 From the cumulative distribution of the scores for Method A in Data 3C, find: (*a*) C_{20} (*b*) C_{60} (*c*) C_{75} (*d*) C_{95}.

20 Follow the procedure of Problem 15 to verify centile calculations made in Problem 19.

21 From the cumulative distribution of the scores for Method A in Data 3C, find the centile rank of (*a*) 139.5 (*b*) 126 (*c*) 100 (*d*) 97.

22 From the data for Method B in Data 3C, find: (*a*) C_8 (*b*) C_{22}.

23 Create a formula to express the process of finding a centile. Define the symbols you use.

24 In Table 3.5B, the percents add to 101 rather than 100. Why? In a table of ten class intervals, would it be possible for the total of the individual percents to be even farther from 100? Explain.

CHAPTER 4

4.1 INTRODUCTION

Should a frequency distribution be presented as a table or a graph? A graph is based entirely on the tabled data and therefore can tell no story that can not be learned by inspecting the table. However, graphic representation often makes it easier to see pertinent features of a set of data.

Graphic representation is one way of presenting all kinds of quantitative information, and there are many different kinds of graphs. Books are available that describe graphic procedures in variety and at length.† We shall limit consideration to the representation of frequency distributions. For this purpose, there are three main types of graphs: the *histogram* (and its variant, the *bar diagram*), the *frequency polygon*, and the *cumulative percentage frequency curve*. These graphs are illustrated in Figures 4.1, 4.2, 4.3, and 4.4, respectively.

Graphic Representation

4.2 THE HISTOGRAM

Table 4.1 presents a frequency distribution of intelligence test scores for a sample of 100 adults selected at random. These data are graphed in the form of a *histogram* in Figure 4.1. The graph consists in a series of rectangles, each of which represents the frequency of scores in one of the class intervals of the tabled distribution. The rectangle is erected so that its two vertical boundaries coincide with the exact limits of the particular interval, and its height is specified by the frequency of scores for that interval. Either frequencies or proportionate frequencies may be represented by a histogram.

There are some details of construction that apply to the histogram and to other graphs to be discussed in this chapter:

> **1** The graph has two axes: horizontal and vertical. The horizontal axis is often called the *abscissa*, or *X axis*, and the vertical axis the *ordinate*, or *Y axis*.

† One such is: H. Arkin and R. Colton, *Graphs: How to Make and Use Them*, 2nd ed., Harper and Brothers, New York, 1938.

Table 4.1 *Army General Classification Test Scores:*
100 Adults Selected at Random

Score limits	Exact limits	Midpoint	f
	159.5–169.5	*164.5*	
150–159	149.5–159.5	154.5	1
140–149	139.5–149.5	144.5	1
130–139	129.5–139.5	134.5	3
120–129	119.5–129.5	124.5	10
110–119	109.5–119.5	114.5	14
100–109	99.5–109.5	104.5	20
90–99	89.5–99.5	94.5	21
80–89	79.5–89.5	84.5	11
70–79	69.5–79.5	74.5	11
60–69	59.5–69.5	64.5	6
50–59	49.5–59.5	54.5	2
	39.5–49.5	*44.5*	
			$n = 100$

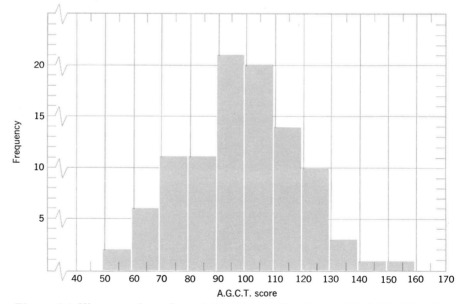

Figure 4.1 *Histogram: Army General Classification Test Scores; 100 Adults Selected at Random.*

2 It is customary to represent scores along the horizontal axis, and frequency (or some function of frequency) along the vertical axis.

3 According to mathematical practice, the intersection of the two axes represents the zero point on both scales. If it does not, the reader should be warned. In Figure 4.1, for example, a break is introduced in the horizontal axis to indicate that a portion of the scale has been omitted.

4 A small graph is hard to construct with accuracy and equally hard to read. If values are to be read from a graph, the larger the scale the better.

5 Convenient units should be chosen to identify position along the axes. Limits of class intervals or interval midpoints usually do not form the most convenient frame of reference for the horizontal axis. See Figures 4.1, 4.3, 4.4, and 4.5 for examples of convenient representation.

6 Whether the graph of a frequency distribution appears squat or slender depends on the choice of scale used to represent position along the two axes. Since it is desirable that similar distributions should appear similar when graphed, it is customary to choose a relative scale such that the height will be no less than .6 nor more than .8 of the width. Width and height are measured from the span of the graphed data rather than from the borders of the graph. In Figure 4.1, for example, the width extends from scores of 49.5 to 159.5. First, decide on a suitable scale for the horizontal axis (scores). Then determine the number of squares (on the graph paper) required for the width of the graph. Multiply this number by .6 and .8, respectively, to find how many squares are to be used for the graph's height. Some trial-and-error may be necessary to create a graph suitable in size and convenient in scale.

7 The graph of any frequency distribution should have a title, as well as labels on both axes. The title should be both succinct and informative. Ideally, a graph should not need accompanying explanation.

By now you will have noted that some procedures are basically arbitrary and governed by conventions. These conventions are useful because they result in representations that we learn to expect. Then we do not have to approach each situation as a problem-solving exercise before absorbing its meaning. We could read a book just as well if the page order were reversed, but it would be a nuisance to find out which way a book was printed every time we picked up a new volume.

4.3 THE BAR DIAGRAM

If the problem is to graph categorical data, the histogram is a possibility, but the *bar diagram* is still better. The bar diagram is very similar to the histogram, except that space is inserted between the rectangles, thus properly suggesting the essential

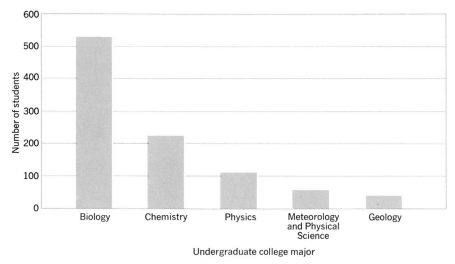

Figure 4.2 *Bar Diagram: Comparative Frequency of Academic Majors in a School of Science.*

discontinuity of the several categories. Figure 4.2 illustrates its use for nominal data. Since nominal categories have no necessary order, they may be arranged in order of magnitude of frequency, if desired. The bar diagram would also have merit in representing ordinal data or discrete data.

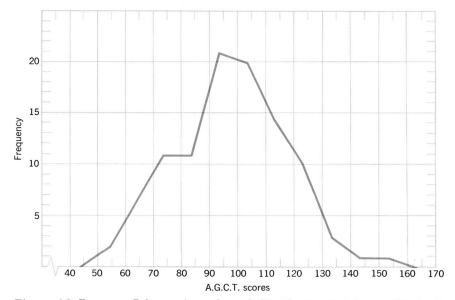

Figure 4.3 *Frequency Polygon: Army General Classification Test Scores: 100 Adults Selected at Random.*

4.4 THE FREQUENCY POLYGON

The same data plotted as a histogram in Figure 4.1 have been represented by a *frequency polygon* in Figure 4.3. In this type of graph, a point is plotted above the midpoint of each class interval at a height commensurate with the frequency of scores in that interval. These points are then connected with straight lines. If nothing further is done, the graph will not touch the horizontal axis. To rectify its otherwise peculiar appearance, we identify the two class intervals falling immediately outside those end class intervals containing scores. These are shown in italics in Table 4.1. The midpoints of these intervals are plotted at zero frequency, and these two points are connected to the graph. As with the histogram, either frequency or proportionate frequency may be represented in the frequency polygon.

4.5 THE CUMULATIVE PERCENTAGE CURVE

Both the *cumulative frequency distribution* and the *cumulative percentage frequency distribution* may be cast in graphic form. We illustrate only the latter, since the essentials are similar for both, and since the cumulative percentage curve is widely

Table 4.2 *Cumulative Percentage Frequency Distribution*

Score limits	f	cum f	cum % f
97–99	1	80	100.0
94–96	1	79	98.8
91–93	3	78	97.5
88–90	3	75	93.8
85–87	4	72	90.0
82–84	7	68	85.0
79–81	8	61	76.2
76–78	9	53	66.2
73–75	12	44	55.0
70–72	6	32	40.0
67–69	11	26	32.5
64–66	7	15	18.8
61–63	2	8	10.0
58–60	3	6	7.5
55–57	3	3	3.8
52–54		0	.0
	$n = 80$		

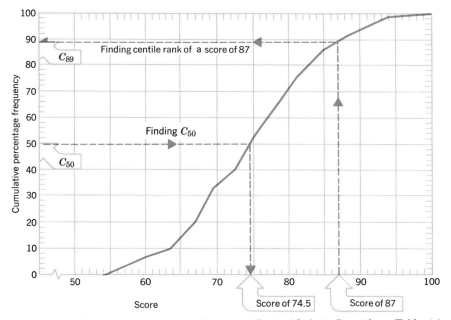

Figure 4.4 *Cumulative Percentage Frequency Curve (Ogive): Data from Table 4.2.*

applied in educational and psychological measurement. For convenience, the contents of Table 3.7 are again presented in Table 4.2; they are pictured in graphic form in Figure 4.4. You will recall that a particular cumulative percentage frequency indicates the percent of scores that lie below the upper limit of the associated class interval. Therefore, *in constructing cumulative percentage curves, the cumulative frequency is plotted at the upper exact limit of the class interval.* For example, the cumulative percentage frequency of 10 is aligned with the score of 63.5. Note that this procedure differs from that for the frequency polygon, where frequencies (uncumulated) were plotted at the midpoint of the interval.

Despite its rather different appearance, the conventions regarding construction discussed in Section 4.2 apply, including the rule relating height to width. The cumulative percentage curve has another name: the *ogive*. This name is significant; it implies an S-shaped figure, and the curve in Figure 4.4 has this characteristic. Graphs of cumulative frequency distributions will tend toward this form when there are more cases in the center of the corresponding uncumulated distribution than elsewhere. In Figure 4.5, Distribution B shows the uncumulated distribution for the same data presented in Figure 4.4 in cumulated form. You will find it instructive to compare them.

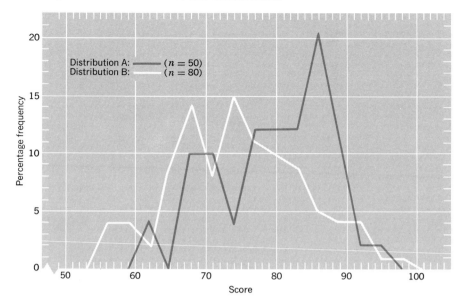

Figure 4.5 *Relative Frequency Polygons: Comparison of Two Groups: Data from Table 3.5.*

4.6 GRAPHIC SOLUTION FOR CENTILES AND CENTILE RANKS

The cumulative percentage curve may be used to determine the centile rank of a score or to find the centile corresponding to a particular centile rank. The dotted lines in Figure 4.4 illustrate this use. To find the centile rank of a score of 87, we locate it on the horizontal axis, and cast vertically upward until the curve is intersected. Then, reading horizontally to the vertical axis, we find the centile rank to be 89. The process may be reversed. If C_{50} is wanted, the graph shows it to be a score of 74.5; the second set of dotted lines illustrates this example.

Within limits of accuracy, graphic determination of centiles or centile ranks will yield the same result as that given by the computational procedures outlined in the previous chapter. Connecting the points on the cumulative curve with *straight* lines is the graphic equivalent of linear interpolation; both are the consequence of assuming that scores are evenly spread throughout the interval. The two points found by graphic solution above were found by direct computation in Sections 3.10 and 3.11. You may wish to refer to these sections for comparison.

4.7 COMPARISON OF DIFFERENT DISTRIBUTIONS

Comparison of two or more frequency distributions is often made easier by application of graphic methods. *When distributions are based on unequal numbers of cases, comparison is facilitated when relative frequencies are shown.* Figure 4.5 shows the comparison of the two sets of data taken from Table 3.5. Looking at Figure 4.5, it is easy to see that the bulk of the scores for Distribution A appear higher on the scale and that the range of performance is a little less than for Distribution B.

Comparison of cumulative functions is also possible. Again, relative frequency (proportional or percentage frequency) should be used when the number of scores differs in the distributions to be compared.

4.8 HISTOGRAM VERSUS FREQUENCY POLYGON

Representing frequencies by rectangular bars suggests that the scores are evenly distributed within each class interval and that the borders of the intervals are points of decided change. If a definite trend of increasing or decreasing frequency exists over a span of several consecutive class intervals, the frequency polygon will represent this trend more directly, since the direction of each straight line in the polygon is determined by frequencies in two adjacent class intervals, whereas the horizontal top of each rectangle in a histogram is responsive only to what occurs in one class interval. In general, because of this feature and because of the greater suggestion of continuity, the frequency polygon often seems better for displaying the distribution of a continuous variable. Study Figures 4.1 and 4.3 to get a feeling for the difference in mode of representation.

The frequency polygon is even more attractive when two or more distributions are to be compared, as in Figure 4.5. If the same comparison were attempted using two histograms, there would be considerable confusion created by overlapping rectangles. However, with categorical (nominal) data, the bar diagram may be used with some success for comparisons. Figure 4.6 illustrates this possibility.

Two points may be made in behalf of the histogram. First, the general public seems to find it a little easier to understand, and hence it may be a good choice for communicating with such a group. Second, the area in the bars of a histogram is directly representative of relative frequency. That is, *the area in any rectangle is the same fraction of the total area of the histogram as the frequency of that class interval is of the total number of cases in the distribution.* If 25% of scores lie below the upper limit of a particular class interval, then 25% of the area of the histogram will fall to the left of this point. This relationship is only approximately true in the frequency polygon.

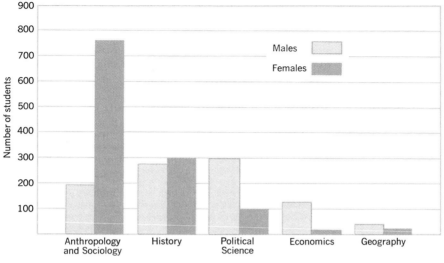

Figure 4.6 *Area of Concentration for Male and Female Students in a School of Social Science.*

4.9 THE UNDERLYING DISTRIBUTION AND SAMPLING VARIATION

Frequency distributions resulting from a very large number of scores often exhibit a pronounced regularity of shape. The particular shape may vary with circumstances; if you look ahead to Figure 4.11, you will find some typical forms. However, when a limited number of scores are taken from such a population, the fundamental pattern is subject to irregularity. This is a function of sampling variation, or "luck of the draw." In general, the fewer the cases, the greater the irregularity. Figure 4.7 shows three samples drawn from a normal distribution (which has a regular, bell-shaped appearance; see Figure 4.11 (F)). Note the greater regularity and closer resemblance to the parent distribution as sample size increases.

If the purpose of graphic representation is to see what regularity exists, we may want to consider alternatives that tend to suppress irregularity. Since more scores reduce irregularity resulting from chance fluctuation, use of fewer class intervals tends to favor a graph of smoother appearance. Figure 4.8 shows three representations of the same raw scores; they differ only in width of interval used in grouping. It may also be noted that the graph of the cumulative function presents a smoother picture than that of the noncumulated function of the same data, since the line connecting two points may be horizontal or rising, but never descending.

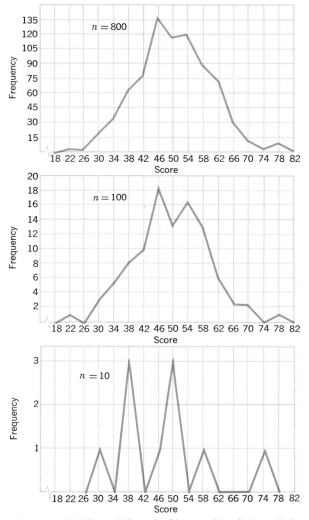

Figure 4.7 *Effect of Sample Size on Regularity of the Distribution (Samples Drawn from a Normal Distribution).*

Other methods of smoothing exist, such as the "running average," which bases the vertical position of a point not only on the frequency in the particular class interval, but also on the location of adjacent points. Such methods can easily be found elsewhere, but a warning is in order: smoothing is a "bootstrap" procedure. No clever amount of manipulation can make relatively few cases tell the story of a large number. Figure 4.8 stands as an object lesson on this point. The data pictured were obtained by drawing a random sample from a symmetrical distribu-

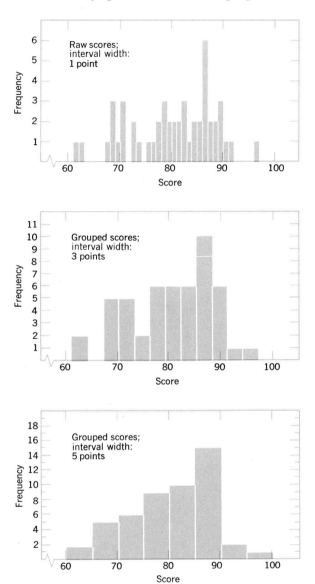

Figure 4.8 *Effect of Varying Width of Interval in Grouped Scores (Data from Table 3.2 and 3.3).*

tion like that shown in Figure 4.11 (F). Even the smoothing induced by widening class intervals does not, in this particular case, tend to make the child resemble its parent very closely; in fact, Figure 4.8 (C) tends to resemble the distribution pictured in Figure 4.11 (C).

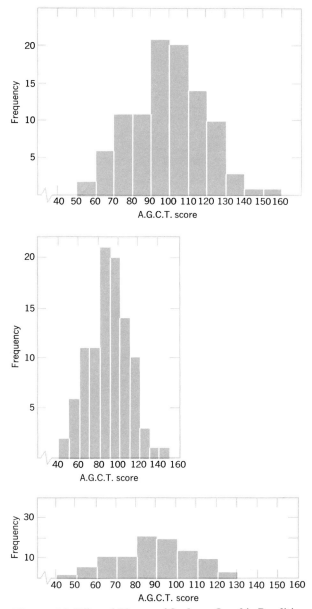

Figure 4.9 *Effect of Change of Scale on Graphic Rendition: Data from Table 4.1.*

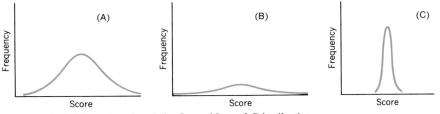

Figure 4.10 *Three Graphs of the Same Normal Distribution.*

4.10 THE MYTHICAL GRAPH

There is no such thing as *the* graph of a given set of data. First, the same set of raw scores may be grouped in different ways (see Figure 4.8). Such variation will be reflected in the graph of the distribution.

Even more important is the matter of relative scale. Frequencies and scores are like apples and cows; no principle specifies what is an "equivalent" number of each. Consequently, the decision on relative scale is fundamentally arbitrary, and the resulting graph can be squat or slender depending on the choice made. Figure 4.9 illustrates three different renditions of the data from Table 4.1. One of these complies with the convention that height of the figure should be between .6 and .8 of the width; the others do not.

Special attention is called to the so-called *normal curve,* a distribution omnipresent in statistical work. It is typically represented as shown at A in Figure 4.10. It is so often pictured this way that it is easy to think that it is *the* picture of the normal curve. However, B and C are also possible representations of the same distribution.

4.11 POSSIBLE SHAPES OF FREQUENCY DISTRIBUTIONS

Certain shapes of frequency distributions occur with some regularity in statistical work. Figure 4.11 illustrates the general nature of several of these. The *J-shaped distribution* is pictured at A. Curves of this type have resulted from plotting the speed with which automobiles went through an intersection where an arterial stop sign was present. B and C show *asymmetrical (skewed) distributions;* B might result from a test that is too difficult for the group taking it, and C from the opposite situation. D is an example of a *rectangular distribution* that, among other things, is the shape of the distribution of a set of ranks resulting from ordinal measurement. E shows a *bimodal distribution;* it could result from measuring strength of grip in a group consisting of both men and women. F shows the bell-shaped *normal*

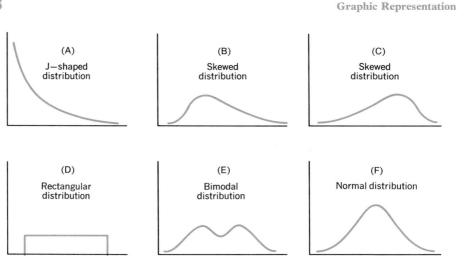

Figure 4.11 *Shapes of Some Distributions that Occur in Statistical Work.*

distribution that tends to characterize measurements of many different kinds and is of great importance in statistical inference. We shall encounter this distribution often, and the entirety of chapter 7 is devoted to its properties.

PROBLEMS AND EXERCISES

Identify:

bar diagram
histogram
frequency polygon
cumulative frequency curve
cumulative percentage
  frequency curve
proportionate frequencies
percentage frequencies
abscissa
ordinate
X axis
Y axis
zero point on a graph

relative scale of a graph
ogive
graphic equivalent of linear
  interpolation
sampling variation
smoothing of a graph
normal distribution
J-shaped distribution
asymmetrical distribution
rectangular distribution
bimodal distribution
skewness

1 It has been held that a statistically knowledgeable person would rather inspect a frequency distribution than a graph. What supports this position? What is an argument against it?

2 When should a graph be large? When would a small graph be acceptable?

3 (a) Construct a histogram from the data of Table 3.5 (B). (b) Construct a percentage frequency histogram from the same data.

4 Repeat the tasks of Problem 3, but use the data of Method A in Data 3C.

5 (a) Construct a frequency polygon from the data of Table 3.5 (B). (b) Construct a percentage frequency polygon from the same data.

6 Repeat the tasks of Problem 5, but use the data of Method A in Data 3C.

7 In a university, male psychology majors are distributed as follows: 24 freshmen, 61 sophomores, 109 juniors, 104 seniors, and 92 graduate students. Comparable figures for females (in the same order of classification) are: 74, 58, 99, 53, and 67. Construct a bar diagram suitable for displaying the comparative relation between the sexes. What conclusions appear significant from inspection of these data?

8 Read the graph in Figure 4.4, and find the value of (a) C_{10} (b) C_{25} (c) C_{40} (d) C_{75}. Compare your answer to C_{25} with the direct calculation shown in Table 3.7.

9 Read the graph in Figure 4.4, and find the centile rank of scores of (a) 60 (b) 75 (c) 80 (d) 92.

Data 4A

Reaction Time in Milliseconds
to Simple and Complex Stimuli

Time	RT: simple stimulus f	RT: complex stimulus f
300–319	1	3
280–299	1	6
260–279	2	10
240–259	4	18
220–239	3	25
200–219	6	35
180–199	11	28
160–179	12	16
140–159	8	7
120–139	2	2
	$n = 50$	$n = 150$

10 (a) Plot the percentage frequency polygons for the two sets of data in Data 4A. Put them both on the same graph. Compare the two distributions and record your conclusions. (b) Repeat for the two distributions of Data 3C.

11 For the distribution of reaction time scores to complex stimuli in Data 4A, do the following: (a) Tabulate the cumulative frequencies. (b) Convert the cumulative frequencies to cumulative percentage frequencies and tabulate them. (c) Plot the cumulative percentage frequency curve. (d) Find graphically C_{20} and C_{60}. Show with dotted lines how you found C_{20}. (e) Find graphically the centile rank of scores of 195 and 245. Show with dotted lines how you found the centile rank of the score of 195.

12 (*a*) Plot the ogives for the two sets of data in Data 4A on one graph. (*b*) Compare these graphs of the cumulative function with those of the noncumulative function of the same data which you plotted in Problem 10*a*.

13 Repeat parts (*a*) through (*d*) of Problem 11, but for the data of Method A in Data 3C. Find the centile rank of scores of 108 and 137.

14 Repeat Problem 12, but as applied to Data 3C. The noncumulative functions for comparison are those requested in Problem 10*b*.

15 Figure 4.5 shows the frequency polygons for the two distributions given in Table 3.5. (*a*) Construct cumulative percentage curves for these same distributions, plotting them on the same graph for comparison. (*b*) How does the fact that the level of performance is higher in Distribution A show up in these curves? (*c*) How does the greater spread of scores in Distribution B show up in these curves? (*d*) Study your cumulative curves in comparison with the noncumulated ones in Figure 4.5. Which type of representation appears smoother? (*e*) For what kind of question is each type of curve best adapted to provide information?

16 Would there be any difference in the shape of a cumulative frequency curve and a cumulative percentage frequency curve if both were constructed from the same basic frequency distribution and if height and width were the same for both types of graphs? Explain.

17 The cumulative curve tends toward an S-shape when the noncumulated distribution has more scores in the center than elsewhere. Draw an approximation to the cumulative curve that would result if the noncumulated distribution had a shape like that pictured in (*a*) Figure 4.11 (B), (*b*) Figure 4.11 (C), (*c*) Figure 4.11 (D), and (*d*) Figure 4.11 (E).

CHAPTER 5

5.1 INTRODUCTION

An investigator has constructed a test of manual dexterity and has before him the scores of a group of men and a group of women. He wants to know whether one group scored better than the other, and if so, to what extent. He could set the two distributions of scores side by side, but this will give him only an approximate answer. Instead, he finds the *average* score of each group and compares them.

Measures of this type are called *measures of central tendency*. Their purpose is to provide a single summary figure which describes the level (high or low) of a set of observations. There are three situations in which use of a measure of central tendency is helpful. First, we may wish to compare level of performance of a group with that of a standard reference group. A principal may want to compare the average reading test score of his 6th grade students with the state norm for such pupils. Second, such a measure may indicate a standard of performance not

Central Tendency

previously known. Suppose an investigator of airplane pilots' behavior finds that the average time required to observe a dangerous situation and complete the appropriate response is three seconds. Some redesign of safety equipment or procedures may be in order, since an aircraft can travel over half a mile in that time. Third, it may be desired to compare the level of performance under two (or more) conditions or of two or more existing groups. Is the ability to see at night better if diet is supplemented by extra quantities of vitamin A? Is the grade point average of freshman women higher or lower than that of freshman men?

There are numerous measures of central tendency. We will consider only those in common use: *mode, median,* and *arithmetic mean*. In this chapter we will take each in turn, define it, discuss computation, and then examine its properties. At the end of the chapter, a summary of the characteristics of each measure appears.

5.2 SOME STATISTICAL SYMBOLISM

Some additional symbolism is needed to provide a convenient language. The capital letter X is used as a collective term to specify the particular set of scores concerned. An individual score in the set may be identified by a subscript, such as X_1

(the first score), X_8 (the eighth score), etc. For example, consider the set of three scores: 31, 21, 41. We may identify them as follows: $X_1 = 31, X_2 = 21, X_3 = 41$. Note that the subscript serves only as an identification number and carries no connotation about the relative size of the scores. A set of scores in a sample may be represented like this:

$$X: \quad X_1, X_2, X_3, \cdots, X_n$$

In the example above:

$$X: \quad 31, 21, 41$$

If there are 42 scores in a set, the last score will of course be X_{42}. You remember that n stands for the number of scores in a sample and N for the number in a population. The last score in a sample can therefore be symbolized X_n; in a population it would be X_N.

When the scores in a set are to be summed, the capital Greek letter sigma, Σ, indicates that this operation is to be performed. It should be read "the sum of" (whatever follows). It is not called sigma because the lower-case sigma (σ) has a different meaning in statistics (as we shall see), and confusion could result. Use of this symbol is illustrated below.

$$\sum X = X_1 + X_2 + X_3 + \cdots + X_n$$

For the set of three scores in the example above,

$$\sum X = 31 + 21 + 41 = 93$$

When two groups of scores are involved, the letter Y is often used to symbolize the second set. In general, capital letters near the end of the alphabet (W, X, Y, for example) are used to symbolize variables. Be sure to use capital letters; lower-case letters are used in a different way (see Section 6.4). Constants are usually symbolized by letters from the front of the alphabet (A, B, C, and K are in common use). Constants may be represented either by capital letters or lower-case letters.

5.3 THE MODE

A common meaning of *mode* is "fashionable," and it has much the same implication in statistics. The mode is the score that occurs with the greatest frequency. In grouped data, it is taken as the midpoint of the class interval that contains the greatest number of scores. Its symbol is *Mo*.

5.4 THE MEDIAN

The median (symbol: *Mdn*) is the score point below which 50% of the scores fall. It is therefore another name for C_{50}, and for grouped data it is calculated by procedures given in Section 3.10. It may also be determined graphically from the ogive (cumulative percentage frequency distribution); see Section 4.6. When the median is found directly from a small number of raw scores, the refinement of interpolation is often omitted. Thus, for the following scores:

$$5, 7, 8, 8, 8, 8$$

the median is taken as 8 rather than the interpolated value of $7.5 + (\frac{1}{4} \times 1) = 7.75$. For raw scores, then, the median may be thought of as the middle score. When there is an even number of scores, there is no middle score, so the median is taken as the point halfway between the two scores that bracket the middle position. Note that this rule holds in the illustration above. Here are two more illustrations:

$$12, 14, 15, 16, 16, 22 \quad Mdn = 15.5$$
$$37, 41, 45, 46 \quad\quad Mdn = 43.0$$

5.5 THE ARITHMETIC MEAN

If we sum all of the scores in a set and divide by the number of them, we obtain the *arithmetic mean.* Many people call this measure the *average,* but we will avoid this term because it is sometimes used indiscriminately for any measure of central tendency. For brevity, the arithmetic mean is usually referred to as the *mean,* and we shall follow that practice.

The distinction between the mean of a sample and that of a population figures importantly in inferential statistics, so there are two symbols for the mean. The mean of a sample is represented by $\bar{X}$; read it as "X bar." The mean of a population is symbolized by μ (the Greek letter *mu,* pronounced "mew"). The fundamental formulas, and the ones that are directly applicable to calculation of the mean from raw scores, are as follows:

Raw Score Formulas

for the Mean

$$\mu = \frac{\sum X}{N} \quad \text{(mean of a population)} \quad\quad (5.1a)$$

$$\bar{X} = \frac{\sum X}{n} \quad \text{(mean of a sample)} \quad\quad (5.1b)$$

This distinction between sample and population is not crucial at a purely descriptive level, so to avoid unnecessary complication, symbolism appropriate to samples will be used whenever possible in these early chapters.

When the scores are grouped, we know only that scores in a given interval lie somewhere between the lower limit and the upper limit. To proceed, we assume that the *midpoint of the interval is the mean of the scores in that interval,* and we use it to represent the scores in the interval. This assumption will probably be exactly correct in only a few intervals. If we have used at least ten class intervals, the width of any one class interval will be small enough to limit the magnitude of the possible error.

Under this assumption, we calculate the mean ($\overline{X}$) for the data shown in Table 5.1. The summation (starting from the bottom) might begin:

$$42 + 42 + 47 + 47 + 47 + 52 + \cdots$$

But there is a better way. We can shorten the process by substituting multiplication for addition where appropriate. We multiply each midpoint (symbolized by X in the table) by the number of cases in the corresponding interval (f) and sum these products (fX) over all class intervals. For convenience, this process is expressed by a modification of Formula 5.1b:

Mean from Grouped Data $\qquad\qquad \overline{X} = \dfrac{\sum fX}{n}$ $\qquad\qquad\qquad$ (5.2)

where: $\sum fX = f_1 X_1 + f_2 X_2 + \cdots$, and the subscripts 1, 2, $\cdots$, identify the several class intervals.

Use of this formula is demonstrated in the example shown in Table 5.1. A calculator with a memory will be particularly effective for grouped data calculation, since the fX products can be stored and cumulated within the instrument.

Table 5.1 *Calculation of the Mean from Grouped Data*

Scores	X (midpoint)	f	fX	Calculation of the mean by Formula 5.2
90–94	92.0	2	184	
85–89	87.0	4	348	
80–84	82.0	9	738	
75–79	77.0	7	539	
70–74	72.0	10	720	$\overline{X} = \dfrac{\sum fX}{n}$
65–69	67.0	12	804	
60–64	62.0	9	558	
55–59	57.0	5	285	$= \dfrac{4557}{66} = 69.0$
50–54	52.0	3	156	
45–49	47.0	3	141	
40–44	42.0	2	84	
		$n = 66$	$\sum fX = 4557$	

5.6 EFFECT OF SCORE TRANSFORMATIONS

Consider the following set of scores: 4, 5, 9. Their mean is 6. If we add 10 points to each score, they become 14, 15, 19, and their mean is now 16, 10 points higher. *If some constant amount is added to each score in a distribution,* the entire distribution is shifted up by the amount of the constant, and *the mean will be increased by that same amount.* Similarly, *if a constant is subtracted from each score, the mean will be reduced by that amount.* Other measures of central tendency discussed in this chapter are affected in the same way.

This property may be put to good use in simplifying the process of finding the mean. Suppose there are 40 raw scores ranging in value from 503 to 535. If 500 is subtracted from each, the resultant values range from 3 to 35. The mean of these altered scores is easier to compute, and adding 500 points to the mean of this altered series recovers the mean of the original scores.

Scores may also be transformed by multiplying or dividing each score by a constant. If the scores 4, 5, and 9 are multiplied by 2, they become 8, 10, and 18; if multiplied by 10, they become 40, 50, and 90. Whereas the mean of the original set is 6, the mean of the second set is 12 (twice as large), and the mean of the third set is 60 (10 times as large). Evidently *multiplying each score by a constant also multiplies the mean by that amount.* Similarly, *dividing each score by a constant has the effect of dividing the mean by that amount.* If each score in the original set is divided by 10, the resultant scores are .4, .5, and .9, and their mean is .6, a value one-tenth of the original mean. The effect of multiplication or division by a constant holds true also for the mode and median.

Again, this property may be used to simplify calculation. If we have a series of scores such as:

$$3.42, \ 4.17, \ 5.56, \ \cdots$$

we may find it convenient to eliminate the decimal by multiplying each score by 100, find the mean of this set, and divide that value by 100 to obtain the mean of the original scores. Proof of the effect on the mean of these several transformations is given in Note 5.1 at the end of the chapter.

A score transformation is a process that changes a score to one on a different scale. The several transformations described above all fall under the heading of *linear transformations,* so called because a proportional, or straight-line, relationship is maintained between the original score values and their transformed equivalents. More about this matter in chapter 8 (Section 8.5).

5.7 PROPERTIES OF THE MEAN

The mean, unlike any of the other measures of central tendency, is responsive to the exact position of each score in the distribution. Inspection of the basic formula, $\Sigma X/n$, shows that if a score is increased or decreased by any amount, the value of the mean will reflect that change.†

The mean may be thought of as the balance point of the distribution, to use a mechanical analogy. If we imagine a see-saw consisting of a fulcrum (balance point), a board (the weight of which shall be neglected), and the scores of a distribution spread along the board, the mean corresponds to the position of the fulcrum when the system is in balance. Figure 5.1 pictures this analogy. As with the ordinary see-saw, if one score is shifted, the balance point will also change.

There is an algebraic way of stating that the mean is a balance point for the distribution: $\Sigma(X - \bar{X}) = 0$.‡ This says that if the scores are expressed in terms of the amount by which they deviate from their mean, and due account is taken of negative and positive deviations (scores below the mean deviate negatively from the mean), their sum is zero. To put it another way, the sum of the negative deviations exactly equals the sum of the positive deviations. Figure 5.1 shows that $\Sigma(X - \bar{X}) = 0$ for the data given. A general proof of this proposition is given in Note 5.2.

The mean *is more sensitive to the presence (or absence) of scores at the extremes of the distribution* than are the median and (ordinarily) the mode. Further discussion of this property of the mean will be forthcoming when properties of the median are examined.

When a measure of central tendency should reflect the total of the scores, the mean is the choice, since it is the only measure based on this quantity. If a coach wanted to

---

†Not quite true for grouped score calculation, of course.

‡$\Sigma(X - \bar{X})$ means: $(X_1 - \bar{X}) + (X_2 - \bar{X}) + \cdots + (X_n - \bar{X})$. For example, for the three scores 3, 4, 5, $\Sigma(X - \bar{X}) = (3 - 4) + (4 - 4) + (5 - 4) = 0$

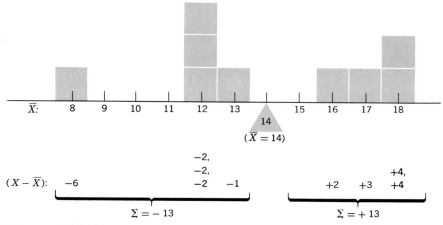

Figure 5.1 *The Mean as the Balance Point of the Distribution.*

know whether his four best quarter-mile runners have, as a group, improved their performance, the total time for the four is a good criterion, and hence the mean running time would probably best reflect his interest. Insurance companies express life expectancy as a mean value, because it is most closely related to total dollars of income and expenditure, a primary concern.

The mean is amenable to arithmetic and algebraic manipulation in a way that the other measures are not. In consequence, it fits in with other important statistical formulas and procedures. At the moment, it is enough to remark that the mean is often incorporated implicitly or explicitly in other statistical procedures. *When further statistical computation is to be done, the mean is likely to be the most useful of the measures of central tendency.*

A characteristic of great significance concerns sampling stability. Suppose that, from a large population of scores, samples were repeatedly drawn at random.† Means of such samples would have similar, but not identical, values. This would also be true for the medians of the same samples, and for their modes. However, for distributions encountered most frequently in statistical work, the means vary least among themselves. *Thus, under ordinary circumstances, the mean best resists the influence of sampling fluctuation.* This is obviously a very desirable property if we propose to engage in statistical inference (see Section 1.2).

5.8 PROPERTIES OF THE MEDIAN

The median is the point that divides the upper half of the scores from the lower half. In doing so, *the median responds to how many scores lie below (or above) it, but not to how far away the scores may be.* A little below the median or a lot: both count the same in determining its value.

Since the median is sensitive to the number of scores below it, but not to how far they are below, *the median is less sensitive than the mean to the presence of a few extreme scores.* Consider this simple distribution:

$$X: 5, 6, 7, 8, 24$$

The median is 7; the mean is 10. The value of the top score, 24, is quite different from that of the remainder of scores. It strongly affects the total, and hence the mean, but it is just another score above the median. If the score had been 9 rather than 24, the median would be the same.

Sometimes one encounters a distribution that is reasonably regular except for several quite deviant scores at one end. If it is feared that these scores will carry undue weight in determining the mean, a possible solution is to calculate the median. The median will respond to their presence, but no more than to others that lie on that side of its position. Similarly, *in distributions that are strongly asymmet-*

† See Section 2.2 for an introduction to the notion of a random sample.

rical (skewed; see Figure 4.11), the median may be the better choice if it is desired to represent the bulk of the scores and not give undue weight to the relatively few deviant ones. See Section 5.10 for further discussion of skewed distributions.

Of the measures of central tendency under consideration, *the median stands second to the mean in ability to resist the influence of sampling fluctuation* in ordinary circumstances. For large samples taken from a normal distribution, the median varies about one-quarter more from sample to sample than does the mean. For small samples, the median is relatively better, but still falls behind the mean.

The mean, as we learned in the last section, is frequently embodied in advanced statistical procedures. Not so the median. It has some use in inferential statistics, but much less than the mean.

Sometimes one encounters a distribution that is open-ended, such as the one shown below.

Scores	f
155–up	5
150–154	8
145–149	12
140–144	10
135–139	4
130–134	2

In this distribution the upper limit of the top class interval is not specified, and consequently the midpoint of the interval is unknown. *In open-ended distributions, the mean cannot be calculated, but calculation of the median remains possible.* Such distributions may therefore block the path to types of statistical analysis that would be very useful. The importance of thinking through the design of a study before gathering the data is apparent.

Finally, a word about ease of computation. Using grouped data, or raw scores when assisted by a calculator, the work involved in finding the mean and median is similar. However, from simple sets of ordered scores, the median is obtained with great ease by counting halfway up the distribution.

5.9 PROPERTIES OF THE MODE

The mode is easy to obtain, but it is not very stable. Further, when the data are grouped, the mode may be strongly affected by the width and location of class intervals. Another problem is that *there may be more than one mode for a particular set of scores.* In a rectangular distribution the ultimate is reached: every score shares the honor!

Sometimes the mode is just what we want. If a score is to be selected at random, the *modal score is the best bet if we must choose one "most likely" value.* It answers the question, "What is the *one* thing that happens the most frequently?" *It is the only measure that can be used for data that have the character of a nominal scale.* For example, no other measure of central tendency is appropriate for a distribution of eye color.

Some years ago, a national magazine made use of the mode in a way that capitalized ideally on its virtues. The magazine reported subscribers' ratings, ranging from "excellent" to "poor," of motion pictures that they had seen. The large number of pictures so rated was arranged alphabetically, coupled with the percentage frequency distribution of ratings. A hypothetical illustration is shown below:

	E	G	F	P
Purple Passion	0	10	40	**50**
Puzzle Me Not	5	25	**55**	15

. . . .

As shown in the illustration, the modal percentage frequency was printed in boldface type. One could quickly examine the "excellent" and "good" columns, find the pictures having a modal value in these classifications, and, if desired, study further the characteristics of the distribution for that film. The mode was quite adequately functional in speeding the prospective theatergoer's task of sorting his possibilities.

5.10 SYMMETRY AND OTHERWISE

In distributions that are perfectly symmetrical—i.e. in which the left half is a mirror image of the right half—mean, median, and (if the distribution is unimodal) mode will yield the same value. It is important to note that the widely occurring normal distribution falls in this category. Figure 5.2 shows what happens to mean, median, and mode in skewed distributions, as compared with the normal distribution. Equality of mean and median does not guarantee that the distribution *is* symmetrical, although it is not likely to depart very far from that condition. On the other hand, if the mean and median have different values, the distribution cannot be symmetrical. Furthermore, the more *skewed*, or lopsided, the distribution is, the greater the discrepancy between these two measures.

The distribution pictured at (A) in Figure 5.2 is said to be skewed to the left, or to be negatively skewed, and that at (B) is skewed to the right, or positively skewed. The nomenclature is easy to remember if you think of a closed fist with the thumb sticking out. If the fist represents the bulk of the scores and the thumb represents the tail of the distribution, the thumb points to the direction in which skewness is said to exist (see Figure 5.2).

In a smooth negatively skewed distribution (shown at A), the mode has the

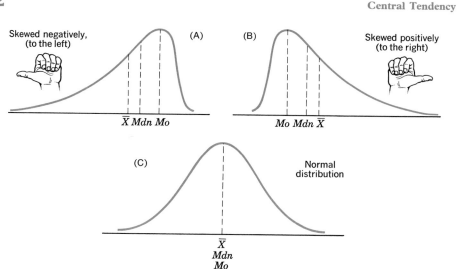

Figure 5.2 $\bar{X}$, *Mdn, and Mo in the Normal Distribution and in Skewed Distributions.*

highest score value, and the median falls at a point about two-thirds of the distance between that and the mean. The mean, as might be expected, has been specially affected by the fewer but relatively extreme scores in the tail, and thus has the lowest value. In a positively skewed distribution (B), exactly the opposite situation obtains.† As a consequence, the relative position of the median and the mean may be used to determine the direction of skewness in the absence of a look at the entire distribution. At a rough descriptive level, the magnitude of the discrepancy between the two measures will afford a clue to the degree of departure from a state of symmetry. More sophisticated measures of skewness exist, but we shall forego them in this elementary text.

Information about symmetry may also be obtained from examination of the comparative location of C_{25}, C_{50} (the median), the C_{75}. These three centile points

† Remember that it is the position of the score along the horizontal axis that indicates the value of these measures of central tendency, and not the height of the ordinate erected at these points. The height is simply an indicator of relative frequency of scores at the particular location.

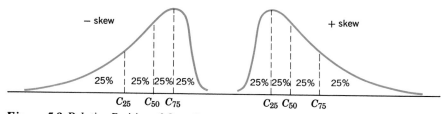

Figure 5.3 *Relative Position of* C_{25}, C_{50}, *and* C_{75} *in Negatively and Positively Skewed Distributions.*

divide the area (and hence the frequency of scores) of the distribution into four equal parts. In the negatively skewed distribution, the distance between C_{25} and C_{50} is greater than that between C_{50} and C_{75}. In the positively skewed distribution, the opposite is true. Figure 5.3 shows these characteristics. In manuals accompanying mental tests, for example, these figures are often available, and a quick inspection will tell us quite a bit about the distribution of performance of the group on which the test was standardized.

We may wish to calculate more than one measure of central tendency for a particular distribution simply because each measure conveys a different kind of information. With a distribution of family income for a particular year, it might be important to know that the income common to the greatest number of families was $9,500, that half of the families earned less than $11,500, and that the mean income was $12,500.

5.11 THE MEAN OF COMBINED SUBGROUPS

It sometimes occurs that means are known for several subgroups, and it is desired to find the mean of all of the scores when the subgroups are pooled. We could begin anew, sum all of the scores, and divide by the total number of cases. However, the sum of the scores can be expressed as the sum of the subgroup totals, and the sum of all the cases can be expressed as the sum of the cases in the several subgroups. Thus:

$$\bar{X}_c = \frac{\overset{\text{all}}{\underset{\text{cases}}{\sum}} X}{\underset{\text{cases}}{n_{\text{all}}}} = \frac{\sum X + \sum Y + \cdots}{n_X + n_Y + \cdots}$$

where: $\bar{X}_c$ is the mean of the combined distribution

X and Y are the scores from the first and second subgroups

n_X and n_Y are the number of scores in the first and second subgroups

Now since $\bar{X} = \Sigma X / n_X$, it follows that $\Sigma X = n_X \bar{X}$. Similarly, $\Sigma Y = n_Y \bar{Y}$. Substituting these equivalent expressions for ΣX and ΣY in the numerator of the formula above, we have:

Mean of Combined Subgroups

$$\bar{X}_c = \frac{n_X \bar{X} + n_Y \bar{Y} + \cdots}{n_X + n_Y + \cdots} \tag{5.3}$$

To illustrate, suppose two groups have been given the same test, and the mean of each group is known:

Given: $\bar{X} = 40$ $\bar{Y} = 30$
             $n_X = 50$ $n_Y = 25$

$$\bar{X}_c = \frac{n_X \bar{X} + n_Y \bar{Y}}{n_X + n_Y}$$

$$= \frac{(50)(40) + (25)(30)}{50 + 25} = 36.7$$

Note that the mean of the combined group is nearer to the mean of the first group (X) than to that of the second (Y). This makes sense, because there are more scores in the first group than in the second. If all subgroups are based on the same number of cases, Formula 5.3 is not needed; the unweighted mean of the subgroup means will give the correct value.

5.12 PROPERTIES OF THE MEASURES OF CENTRAL TENDENCY: SUMMARY

The *mean* is:

1 Responsive to the exact position of each score in the distribution.

2 The balance point of the distribution.

3 The point about which the sum of negative deviations equals that of positive deviations.

4 More sensitive to extreme scores than the median and the mode.

5 An indicator of skewness when used in conjunction with the median.

6 The measure that best reflects the total of the scores.

7 Widely used, implicitly or explicitly, in advanced statistical procedures.

8 Least sensitive to sampling fluctuation under ordinary circumstances.

The *median* is:

1 The point along the scale of scores that divides the upper half of the scores from the lower half.

2 Responsive to the number of scores above or below its value, but not to their exact location.

3 Less affected by extreme scores than the mean.

4 Sometimes a better choice than the mean for strongly skewed distributions.

5 Not as useful as the mean for purposes beyond the level of description.

6 Easier to calculate than the mean in a simple set of ordered scores.

7 Somewhat more subject to sampling fluctuation than the mean.

8 The only relatively stable measure that can be found for open-ended distributions.

The *mode* is:

1 Determined by the most frequently occurring score, or the class interval containing the largest number of cases.

2 More affected by choice of class interval than other measures.

3 Sometimes not a unique point in the distribution.

4 Subject to substantial sampling fluctuation.

5 Useful for rough or preliminary work.

6 Easy to obtain.

7 Of little use beyond the descriptive level.

8 The only measure suited to data of a nominal (categorical) character.

NOTES

In this chapter, we begin a series of mathematical notes. From now on, many chapters will contain such notes. They are not intended to provide a rigorous derivation of the statistical procedures considered, nor does their coverage of the material in the chapter pretend to be complete. They are offered as a means of providing additional insight into statistical relationships to the student who wants to know more about the subject. No knowledge of college mathematics is presumed, but a feeling of reasonable comfort in mathematical expression is helpful. *The student whose path of learning does not follow into these "woods" should understand that the text is designed to stand on its own without these notes:* they are part of an "enriched curriculum."

To use these notes, first turn to Appendix B to learn the few but necessary algebraic relationships that exist when the summation sign appears in an equation. What follows is predicated on the assumption that these principles are understood.

Note 5.1 The Mean of Transformed Scores (*Ref:* Section 5.6)
A. Let $\overline{X + C}$ be the mean of a distribution that has been altered by adding a constant, C, to each score. Then:

$$\overline{X + C} = \frac{\sum (X + C)}{n} = \frac{\sum X + nC}{n} = \frac{\sum X}{n} + C = \bar{X} + C$$

If C may take negative values, we have without further proof:

$$\overline{X - C} = \bar{X} - C$$

B. Let $\overline{CX}$ be the mean of a distribution that has been altered by multiplying each score by a constant. Then:

$$\overline{CX} = \frac{\sum CX}{n} = C\frac{\sum X}{n} = C\overline{X}$$

If C may take fractional values, we have without further proof:

$$\left(\overline{\frac{X}{C}}\right) = \frac{\overline{X}}{C}, \text{ or } \frac{1}{C}\overline{X}$$

Note 5.2 The Mean as a Balance Point (*Ref:* Section 5.7)
The algebraic way of saying that the mean is the balance point of the distribution is: $\Sigma(X - \overline{X}) = 0$. The proof is:

$$\sum(X - \overline{X}) = \sum X - n\overline{X}$$

$$= \sum X - n\frac{\sum X}{n}$$

$$= \sum X - \sum X$$

$$= 0$$

N.B.: $\overline{X}$ is a constant when summing over all values in the sample, so $\Sigma\overline{X} = n\overline{X}$

Note that no assumption has been made about the shape of the distribution.

PROBLEMS AND EXERCISES

Identify:

measures of central tendency	*Mdn*
mode	C_{50}
median	$\overline{X}$
arithmetic mean	μ
Y_7	positively skewed
Σ	negatively skewed
Mo	

1 Find the mean and median of these scores:
8, 12, 13, 20, 29

2 Find the mean and median of these scores:
14, 15, 19, 22, 23, 24

3 Find the mean and median of these scores:
27, 29, 33, 40

Data 5A		Data 5B	
scores	f	scores	f
60–64	4	60–65	4
55–59	7	54–59	9
50–54	6	48–53	7
45–49	3		

(The number of intervals is of course too small for these data. They are offered only in the interest of simplifying computation).

4 Find for Data 5A (*a*) the mode (*b*) the median (*c*) the mean.

5 Find for Data 5B (*a*) the mode (*b*) the median (*c*) the mean.

6 Data 5A and 5B were generated from the same set of raw scores. Why aren't the measures of central tendency the same in the two distributions?

7 Using the data from Table 3.3A, find (*a*) the mode, (*b*) the median, and (*c*) the mean (use Formula 5.2 to find the mean).

8 Using the data of Table 3.3B, find the mode, the median, and the mean (use Formula 5.2 to find the mean). Compare these values to the answers you found in Problem 7. The two distributions were generated from the same set of raw scores. Are the several measures of central tendency the same for distribution A and distribution B? Explain.

9 Find the median and the mode for Data 3C, Method A.

10 Find the median and the mode for Data 3C, Method B.

11 The mean of a group of scores is 21. What would the mean be if the scores were first altered by each of the following procedures: (*a*) 20 points are added to each score? (*b*) 5 points are subtracted from each score? (*c*) each score is multiplied by 2? (*d*) each score is divided by 3?

12 A counselor is interested in knowing whether the honor students, as a group, study more or fewer hours per day than the nonhonor students. What measure of central tendency would most likely reflect the counselor's interest? Explain.

13 A researcher finds that his collected data form a skewed distribution. He decides that he is interested in the bulk of the scores and does not want the few very deviant scores to alter extensively his measure of central tendency. Which measure will he use?

14 Which measure of central tendency would you use with the following distribution of scores? Explain.

Scores	f
32 up	3
29–31	5
26–28	6
23–25	2
20–22	3

15 A social science researcher finds that the mean of her distribution of measures is 120 and the median is 130. What can you say about the shape of the distribution?

16 If $C_{25} = 30$, $C_{50} = 65$, and $C_{75} = 90$, what can you say about the shape of the distribution?

17 For which distributions pictured in Figure 4.11 might the following be true? Explain. $C_{25} = 30$, $C_{50} = 40$, $C_{75} = 50$.

18 A personnel officer gave an aptitude test to three groups of job applicants. The group means were: $\bar{X}_1 = 52$, $\bar{X}_2 = 54$, and $\bar{X}_3 = 60$. The number of applicants in each group were: $n_1 = 10$, $n_2 = 20$, and $n_3 = 25$. What is the mean of all 55 applicants?

19 In finding the mean of combined subgroups, (*a*) Why must each subgroup mean be multiplied by the number of cases in the subgroup? (*b*) Under what condition is Formula 5.4 not necessary?

20 Some years ago, a newspaper editor claimed that more than half of American families earned a below-average income. Is there any sense in which this claim could be correct? Explain.

21 If the eventual purpose of the study involves statistical inference, which measure of central tendency is preferable (other things being equal)? Explain.

22 The National Association of Manufacturers claims that the "average" wage for workers in the steel industry is a figure higher than that stated by the steelworkers' union. Is it possible that both could be right? Explain.

23 (*Based on Notes*) By direct proof, show (*a*) that $\overline{X - C} = \bar{X} - C$, and (*b*) that $\overline{(X/C)} = \bar{X}/C$.

CHAPTER 6

6.1 INTRODUCTION

Measures of variability express quantitatively the extent to which the scores in a set scatter about or cluster together. Whereas a measure of central tendency is a summary description of the level of performance of a group, a measure of variability is a summary description of the spread of performance.

Information about variability is often at least as important as that about level. We would not be happy with a weight scale that gives our weight correctly *on the average,* but on any given occasion might read five pounds lighter or heavier than it should. A manufacturer is interested in the consistency of the quality of his product as well as the level of quality. The satisfaction of his customers who occasionally receive a far better product than they expected will not balance the ire of those who find that it falls apart before they can get good use out of it. A pollster must not only estimate the percentage of voters who favor a particular issue, but he must

Variability

know the amount of variation attributable to sampling fluctuation, the "margin of error" inherent in such estimates.

When measures of central tendency were first discussed (Section 5.1), it was observed that there were three situations in which such measures were helpful:

1 comparison with a known standard
2 establishment of a standard previously unknown, and
3 comparison of two or more sets of scores obtained under different conditions.

The same is true for measures of variability. Comparison with a known standard may be illustrated by returning to the school principal who was comparing the average reading test score of his 6th grade students with the state norms. If he finds that the competence of his students differs more widely than expected within the group, this will suggest the need for different approaches and materials for the further development of reading skills so as to suit the different levels of readiness that his students exhibit.

The second situation concerns the establishment of a standard. It is typical of mental tests that in their development there are no sound *a priori* grounds on which to conclude what the level and spread of performance should be. These characteristics depend heavily on such factors as the difficulty of the test items, the number of items, the time allotted for the test, and many other characteristics. Consequently, to develop a scale of measurement, it is necessary to give the test to a large number of persons to find out what performance will be. Measures of variability, as well as measures of central tendency, are needed to describe that performance.

The third situation is that of comparison of two groups. Consider an experiment designed to compare the effectiveness of two techniques of learning. Of course, we would want to know whether the mean amount learned was different. In addition, it would be important to know whether variability of performance was different under the two conditions. Even if the average amount learned was the same, it would be meaningful if it were found that the range of performance under one method was considerably greater than under the other method. The second picture in Figure 6.1 shows how the distributions might look if this situation existed.

Measures of variability are particularly important in statistical inference. In fact, measurement of variability is the keystone of this statistical structure. How much fluctuation will occur in random sampling? This question is fundamental to every problem in statistical inference; it is a question about variability.

We have said something about what measures of variability do; it is time to say what they do *not* do. A measure of variability does not specify how far a *particular* score diverges from the center of the group. It is a summary figure that describes the spread of the entire set of scores. A measure of variability does not provide information about the level of performance nor does it give a clue as to the shape of the distribution. Figure 6.1 shows that it is possible to have two distributions that

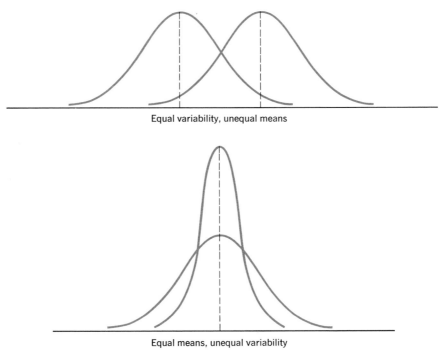

Equal variability, unequal means

Equal means, unequal variability

Figure 6.1 *Different Conditions of Central Tendency and Variability.*

have equal means but unequal variability, or that have equal variability but unequal means.

We shall consider four measures of variability: *range, semiinterquartile range, variance,* and *standard deviation.* Development will follow the same pattern used in the last chapter.

6.2 THE RANGE

We met the *range* earlier in constructing a frequency distribution. It is the difference between the highest and the lowest score. Like other measures of variability, the range is a *distance* and not, like measures of central tendency, a location. For example, all three of these simple distributions have the same range (20 score points):

$$3, 5, 5, 8, 13, 14, 18, 23$$
$$37, 42, 48, 53, 57$$
$$131, 140, 144, 147, 150, 151$$

In a frequency distribution, the range may be figured as the difference between the value of the lowest raw score that could be included in the bottom class interval and that of the highest raw score that could be included in the uppermost class interval.

All measures of variability *and* all measures of central tendency have one property in common: they are always expressed in a particular kind of measuring unit (e.g. feet, pounds, score points). As a consequence, it is not permissible to compare two distributions in terms of a measure of this type (e.g. the mean, or the range) unless it is certain that the same unit of measurement has been used in both. We would not be tempted to compare directly the means or ranges of two distributions when one set of measurements was in feet and the other in inches, but it is perhaps not so obvious that means (or ranges) of scores from two different mental tests may not be directly compared. The fact that both tests have the same title (e.g. "Verbal Aptitude," or "Spatial Visualization") does not make their scores comparable. The matter discussed in the fourth paragraph of Section 6.1 is pertinent to this understanding.

6.3 THE SEMIINTERQUARTILE RANGE

The *semiinterquartile range*,† symbolized by the letter Q, is defined as one-half the *distance* between the first and third quartile points, or,

Semiinterquartile Range $$\qquad\qquad Q = \frac{Q_3 - Q_1}{2} \qquad\qquad (6.1a)$$

† Also known as the *quartile deviation.*

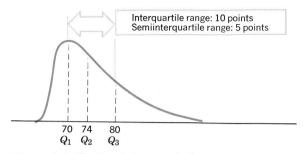

Figure 6.2 *The Semiinterquartile Range.*

The quartile points are the three score points which divide the distribution into four parts, each containing an equal number of cases. These points, symbolized by Q_1, Q_2, and Q_3, are therefore our old friends, C_{25}, C_{50}, and C_{75}, respectively. Formula 6.1a may therefore be rephrased in familiar terms:

$$Q = \frac{C_{75} - C_{25}}{2} \tag{6.1b}$$

Because computation of centile points has been covered in Section 3.10, it will not be repeated here.

One way of understanding Q is to realize that $2Q$ equals the range of the middle 50% of the scores. It may also be thought of as the mean distance between the median and the two outer quartile points. In Figure 6.2, we see an asymmetrical distribution. Q is one-half the 10-point distance between Q_1 and Q_3, or 5 points. But note that the distance between Q_1 and Q_2 is 4 points, the distance between Q_3 and Q_2 is 6 points, and that the mean of these two distances is 5 points, the value of Q.

6.4 DEVIATION SCORES

We have become acquainted with the concept of a raw score, but for the measures about to be introduced we need to know about another way of expressing a score: the *deviation score.*† *A deviation score expresses the location of a score by indicating how many score points it lies above or below the mean of the distribution.* The deviation score is symbolized by the lower-case letter x, to distinguish it from a raw score, which is symbolized by the upper-case letter X. In symbols, the deviation score may be defined:

$$x = (X - \bar{X})$$

---

†You met the deviation score in Section 5.7, but without the benefit of a formal introduction.

Consider the following raw scores (X) and their corresponding deviation scores (x):

X	$(X - \bar{X}) =$	x
1	$(1 - 4) =$	-3
5	$(5 - 4) =$	$+1$
7	$(7 - 4) =$	$+3$
3	$(3 - 4) =$	-1
$\Sigma X = 16$		$\Sigma x = 0$

$$\bar{X} = \frac{16}{4} = 4$$

When the mean ($\bar{X} = 4$) is subtracted from each of the raw scores, the resulting deviation scores state the position of the scores *relative to the mean*. For example, the raw score of 7 becomes $x = +3$, which says that this score is 3 points above the mean of 4. Similarly, the raw score of 3 becomes $x = -1$, indicating its location one point below the mean.

We now turn to two measures of variability of great importance. Both are based on the concept of the deviation score.†

6.5 DEVIATIONAL MEASURES: THE VARIANCE

One useful measure of variability is the *variance*. It can be defined as the mean of the squares of the deviation scores. σ^2 (the lower case Greek letter *sigma*) is the symbol for the variance of a population, and S^2 is the symbol for the variance of a sample. The defining formulas for the variance are as follows:

Variance of a Population
$$\sigma^2 = \frac{\sum(X - \mu)^2}{N} \quad \text{or} \quad \frac{\sum x^2}{N} \qquad (6.2a)$$

Variance of a Sample
$$S^2 = \frac{\sum(X - \bar{X})^2}{n} \quad \text{or} \quad \frac{\sum x^2}{n} \qquad (6.2b)‡$$

† It might appear that an attractive measure of variability could be obtained by calculating the mean of the distances between the scores and the mean of the distribution (deviation scores taken without regard to sign). In fact such a measure saw use in earlier years; it is called the *average deviation*. Despite its initial appeal, it has a mathematical intractability that severely limits its use. It is, for example, of absolutely no use in statistical inference.

‡ Although there is uniformity in defining the variance of a population, some statisticians prefer to define the variance of a sample as $\Sigma x^2/(n - 1)$. Since some other texts follow this usage, you should know about it. This difference in view derives from the problem of estimating the variance of a population when we have at hand only the data from a sample. Under these circumstances, dividing the sum of the squares of the deviation scores by $(n - 1)$ gives a better estimate than that offered by Formula 6.2b. We shall treat this problem of estimation as a separate issue (see Sections 15.4 and 16.10).

The variance is a most important measure that finds its greatest use in inferential statistics. At the descriptive level, it has a fatal flaw: its calculated value is expressed in terms of *squared* units of measurement. Consequently, it is little used in descriptive statistics, and therefore examination of its properties will not engage us at present. This defect, however, is easily remedied. By taking the square root of the variance, we return to a measure expressed in the original units of measurement. This solution yields the measure next to be discussed.

6.6 DEVIATIONAL MEASURES: THE STANDARD DEVIATION

The most important and widely used measure of variability is the *standard deviation*.† It is the square root of the variance, and therefore the defining formulas are:

$$\text{Standard Deviation of a Population} \qquad \sigma = \sqrt{\frac{\sum x^2}{N}} \qquad (6.3a)$$

$$\text{Standard Deviation of a Sample} \qquad S = \sqrt{\frac{\sum x^2}{n}} \qquad (6.3b)$$

† Another name for the standard deviation is *root mean square deviation*. It is seldom used now, but may be encountered in the older literature.

Table 6.1 *Calculation of the Standard Deviation: Deviation Score Method*

X	$(X - \bar{X})$	x	x^2	Steps
32	32–50.6	-18.6	345.96	1. Record each score
71	71–50.6	$+20.4$	416.16	2. Find $\bar{X}$
64	64–50.6	$+13.4$	179.56	3. Obtain x by sub-
50	50–50.6	$-.6$	.36	tracting $\bar{X}$ from each
48	48–50.6	-2.6	6.76	value of X
63	63–50.6	$+12.4$	153.76	4. Square each x
38	38–50.6	-12.6	158.76	5. Sum the values of x^2
41	41–50.6	-9.6	92.16	6. Enter Σx^2 and n in
47	47–50.6	-3.6	12.96	Formula 6.3b and
52	52–50.6	$+1.4$	1.96	simplify
$\Sigma X = 506$			$\Sigma x^2 = 1368.40$	

$$\bar{X} = \frac{506}{10} = 50.6 \qquad S = \sqrt{\frac{\sum x^2}{n}} = \sqrt{\frac{1368.40}{10}} = \sqrt{136.84} = 11.7$$

Calculation of the standard deviation by Formula 6.3b is illustrated in Table 6.1. You are invited to follow the procedure carefully, because it gives important insight into what the standard deviation is up to. However, from the standpoint of ease of calculation, this method leaves much to be desired. In general, the raw score method (described in Section 6.7) and the grouped data method (Section 6.8) will be better choices for practical computation.

What we have just learned about deviation score methods has wide applicability. In general, examining a deviation score formula is likely to be an excellent approach to understanding of a statistical device. But it is well to remember Minium's Second Law of Statistics: "For computation, if there is a choice between a deviation score method and some other method, choose the other method." †

6.7 CALCULATION OF THE STANDARD DEVIATION: RAW SCORE METHOD

In calculating the standard deviation by the deviation score formula, the main remediable nuisance is that of calculating Σx^2 directly from deviation scores. Without the bother of changing raw scores to deviation scores, this quantity can be found by the equation:‡

Raw Score Equivalent of Σx^2 $$\sum x^2 = \sum X^2 - \frac{\left(\sum X\right)^2}{n} \qquad (6.4)$$

Derivation of this formula is given in Note 6.1. The sum of the squares of the deviation scores may be calculated by Formula 6.4 and the resulting value substituted in Formula 6.3b. This method of calculation is illustrated for a set of ten scores in Table 6.2 (the data are from Table 6.1).

The following notes may be helpful:

1 Distinguish *carefully* between ΣX^2 and $(\Sigma X)^2$. To find the former, we square each score and then sum the squares. To find the latter, we sum the scores and then square the sum. The result is *not* the same.

2 Distinguish carefully between x and X, and thus between Σx^2 and ΣX^2.

3 The sum of the squares of the *deviation* scores, Σx^2, *must* be a positive number no matter what the raw score values are.

---

† In the next section, for example, we learn a method that avoids the necessity of subtracting the mean from each score before squaring and that substitutes the squaring of whole numbers for the squaring of deviation scores that incorporate decimal fractions.

‡ For the remainder of the chapter, only formulas appropriate to samples will be presented; modification appropriate to a population should be readily apparent.

Table 6.2 *Calculation of the Standard Deviation: Raw Score Method*

X	X^2	Steps (*for calculation by hand*)
32	1,024	1. Record each score
71	5,041	2. Record the square of each
64	4,096	score
50	2,500	3. Obtain ΣX, and ΣX^2, and n
48	2,304	4. Calculate Σx^2
63	3,969	5. Substitute numerical value
38	1,444	in formula for S
41	1,681	6. Complete calculation of S
47	2,209	
52	2,704	
$\Sigma X = 506$	$\Sigma X^2 = 26,972$	

Calculation of Σx^2:

$$\Sigma x^2 = \Sigma X^2 - \frac{\left(\Sigma X\right)^2}{n}$$

$$= 26972 - \frac{(506)^2}{10}$$

$$= 26972 - 25603.6$$

$$= 1368.4$$

Calculation of S:

$$S = \sqrt{\frac{\Sigma x^2}{n}}$$

$$= \sqrt{\frac{1368.4}{10}}$$

$$= \sqrt{136.84}$$

$$= 11.7$$

4 A small calculator is of great value in this calculation. If it has a memory system, the sum of squares can be cumulated internally, so there would be no need to write down the values of X^2.

5 Squares and square roots of numbers are given in Table A in Appendix F. Instructions for use of this table appear in Sections A.11 and A.12 of Appendix A. If you own a calculator without a square root key but with a floating decimal, there is an easy routine that will calculate square root. See Section A.13 of Appendix A.

6.8 SCORE TRANSFORMATIONS AND MEASURES OF VARIABILITY

In Section 5.6, we found that certain score transformations had a simple and predictable effect on measures of central tendency. What is the effect on measures of variability?

Consider the following set of scores: 12, 13, 15. The distance between the first and second score is one point, and between the second and third scores, two points. If we add 10 points to each score, they become 22, 23, and 25. The interscore distances, however, remain the same. If we had subtracted 5 points from each score, they would become 7, 8, and 10. Again, the interscore distances remain the same. Since measures of variability are indices of interscore distance, apparently these are not affected by either of these modifications. *Adding a constant to each score in the distribution, or subtracting a constant from each score, does not affect any of the measures of variability described in this chapter.*

This property can be quite useful. If we have 40 raw scores that range in value from 503 to 535, the method of calculation of the standard deviation described in the previous section would be somewhat cumbersome. If we subtract 500 from each score, the resultant values range from 3 to 35. The standard deviation of these altered scores is easier to compute, and the value obtained will be exactly the same as though the calculation had been performed on the original scores.

Scores may also be transformed by multiplying each score by a constant or by dividing each score by a constant. If scores of 12, 13, and 15 are multiplied by 2, they become 24, 26, and 30. In their original form, the interscore distances are one and two points, respectively. In their altered form, they are doubled, becoming two and four points. If the original scores are multiplied by 10, the scores become 120, 130, and 150, and the interscore distances are now 10 points and 20 points. Apparently, when each of a set of scores is multiplied by a constant, the interscore distances become multiplied by the same constant. If the original set of scores were altered by dividing each score by 10, the scores would be 1.2, 1.3, and 1.5. Interscore distances would now be .1 and .2, one-tenth of their original values. *When scores are multiplied or divided by a constant, the resultant measure of variability is also multiplied or divided by that same constant.* This also applies to all measures of variability discussed in this chapter except the variance.† Proof of the propositions concerning adding, subtracting, multiplying, and dividing by a constant is given in Note 6.2 at the end of the chapter.

These properties may also be used to simplify calculation of measures of variability. If we have a series of scores such as:

$$3.42, 4.17, 5.56, \ldots$$

it is convenient to eliminate the decimal by multiplying each score by 100, find the standard deviation, and divide that value by 100 to obtain the standard deviation of the original scores.

---

†Variance is expressed in terms of squared units of measurement. Consequently, if each score is multiplied or divided by a constant, C, the variance is multiplied or divided by C^2.

Table 6.3 *Calculation of the Standard Deviation: Grouped Score Method*

Scores	f	X	fX	fX^2 $(= fX \cdot X)$	Steps for hand calculation
70–74	2	72.0	144	10,368	1. Multiply each X by its
65–69	5	67.0	335	22,445	corresponding f to
60–64	9	62.0	558	34,596	obtain fX
55–59	8	57.0	456	25,992	2. Multiply each fX by X to
50–54	6	52.0	312	16,224	obtain fX^2.
	$n = 30$		$\Sigma fX = 1{,}805$	$\Sigma fX^2 = 109{,}625$	3. Sum the values to obtain ΣfX and ΣfX^2.
					4. Proceed as shown below.

Calculation of Σx^2:

$$\Sigma x^2 = \Sigma f X^2 - \frac{\left(\sum fX\right)^2}{n}$$

$$= 109625 - \frac{(1805)^2}{30}$$

$$= 109625 - 108600.8$$

$$= 1024.2$$

Calculation of S:

$$S = \sqrt{\frac{\sum x^2}{n}}$$

$$= \sqrt{\frac{1024.2}{30}}$$

$$= \sqrt{34.1}$$

$$= 5.8$$

Calculation of $\bar{X}$:

$$\bar{X} = \frac{\sum fX}{n}$$

$$= \frac{1805}{30}$$

$$= 60.2$$

6.9 CALCULATION OF THE STANDARD DEVIATION: GROUPED SCORES

When scores are grouped we assume that the midpoint of the interval represents the scores in the interval, just as we did in grouped score calculation of the mean (Section 5.5). The procedure is essentially the same as for the raw score method just described, except that we will shorten the process by substituting multiplication for addition wherever appropriate. A slightly modified form of the raw score formula for Σx^2 is needed:

Raw Score Equivalent of Σx^2 *for Grouped Data* $$\Sigma x^2 = \Sigma f X^2 - \frac{(\Sigma fX)^2}{n} \tag{6.5}$$

The method of calculation is illustrated in Table 6.3. Note that the mean is very easily obtained as a by-product of the procedure.

6.10 PROPERTIES OF THE STANDARD DEVIATION

The range and semiinterquartile range are measures that yield easily to intuitive grasp. It is ironic that the standard deviation is more important in statistical work than the others and less easy to understand. Rather than labor over the problem of grasping its nature intuitively, we will try to develop a picture of its functional properties.

The standard deviation, like the mean, is responsive to the exact position of every score in the distribution. If a score is shifted to a position more deviant from the mean, the standard deviation will be larger than before. If the shift is to a position closer to the mean, the magnitude of the standard deviation is reduced. Consequently, we may expect that the standard deviation is more sensitive to the exact condition of the distribution than measures that do not share this property (the range and semiinterquartile range do not).

The standard deviation is more sensitive than the semiinterquartile range to the presence or absence of scores that lie at the extremes of the distribution (the range is, of course, defined by the two outlying scores). Consider the following seven scores: 2, 5, 7, 8, 9, 11, 14. Table 6.4 shows S, Q, and the range for this set of scores. Now a new (and extreme) score is incorporated in the set: 2, 5, 7, 8, 9, 11, 14, 24. Table 6.4 shows the same measures of variability calculated after making this change. The figures showing the percent increase in magnitude of each measure of variability upon addition of the new score are the most important ones to study. Note that the standard deviation is affected more than the semiinterquartile range. The proportionate change would differ from distribution to distribution, but it is characteristic that the standard deviation is more profoundly affected by extreme scores than is Q. Because of this characteristic sensitivity, *the standard deviation may not be the best choice among measures of variability when the distribution contains a few very extreme scores or when the distribution is badly skewed.* For example, if we wished to compare the variability of two distributions where one of them contained several extreme scores and the other did not, the difference in extreme scores would tend to exert an influence on the magnitude of the standard deviation that was disproportionate to their relative number. Of course, if n is quite large and the extreme scores are very few in number, it will make little difference.

When the deviations are calculated from the mean, the sum of squares of these values is *smaller* than if they had been taken about any other point. Putting it another way,

$$\Sigma(X - A)^2 \text{ is a minimum when: } A = \bar{X}$$
(or when: $A = \mu_X$ in the case of a population)

Table 6.4 *Effect on Measures of Variability of Adding an Extreme Score to a Distribution*

	S	Q	Range
Original distribution ($n = 7$)	3.63	2.75	12.00
Distribution with extreme score added ($n = 8$)	6.29	3.25	22.00
Percent increase due to added score	73	18	83

Proof of this proposition appears in Note 6.3. This property may seem to be an oddity that only a mathematician could love. In fact it is an extremely important notion, one that reappears frequently in the further study of statistics.† For now, note that this gives us another way to define the mean: it is the point about which the sum of squares of the deviation scores is a minimum.

To illustrate the property, consider the scores 2, 3, 5, 10, which have a mean of 5. Calculate the sum of squares of deviation scores, taking the deviations from the mean. Then recalculate, this time taking the deviations from 4. Repeat again, taking the deviations from 6. What do you find?

One of the most important points favoring the standard deviation is its resistance to sampling fluctuation. In repeated random samples drawn from populations of the type most frequently encountered in statistical work, the numerical value of the standard deviation tends to jump about less than would that of other measures computed on the same samples. If our concern is in any way associated with inferring variation in a population from knowledge of variation in a sample, this property is clearly of worth.

When we come to study further methods of statistical analysis, the surpassing importance of the standard deviation will be better understood. *The standard deviation appears explicitly or lies embedded in many procedures of both descriptive statistics and inferential statistics.* Indeed, in inferential statistics, the range and semiinterquartile range are of very little use.

In many ways, the properties of the standard deviation are related to those of the mean. In usefulness for further statistical work, stability in the face of sampling fluctuation, responsiveness to location of each score, and sensitivity to extreme scores, the position of the standard deviation relative to other measures of variability has much in common with that of the mean among measures of central tendency.

6.11 PROPERTIES OF THE SEMIINTERQUARTILE RANGE

Like the average deviation, the semiinterquartile range has an approachable intuitive meaning. It is half the distance between C_{25} and C_{75}, or the mean distance between the median and C_{25} and C_{75}. To look at it another way, twice the semiinterquartile range is the distance that contains the central 50% of the scores.

The semiinterquartile range is closely related to the median, since both are defined in terms of centile points of the distribution. The median is responsive to the *number* of scores lying below it rather than to their exact position, and C_{25} and C_{75} are points defined in a similar way. We may therefore expect the median and the

† See, for example, Section 11.2.

semiinterquartile range to have properties in common. For example, C_{75} is sensitive only to the number of scores that lie above it. Consequently, all scores above C_{75} are of equal importance in determination of the semiinterquartile range, and a very extreme score counts no more and no less than a moderately extreme one in its determination. *The semiinterquartile range will therefore be less sensitive to the presence of a few very extreme scores than the standard deviation.* If a distribution is badly skewed or if it contains a few very extreme scores, the semiinterquartile range will respond to the presence of such scores, but will not give them undue weight.

If the distribution is open-ended (see Section 5.8), it is not possible to calculate the standard deviation or the range without additional (and probably hazardous) assumptions. *With open-ended distributions, the semiinterquartile range may be the only measure that it is reasonable to compute.* Unless more than a quarter of the scores lie in the indeterminate end category, the semiinterquartile range is computable in straightforward fashion.

Sampling stability of the semiinterquartile range is good, although not up to that of the standard deviation. Ease of computation is good if the scores are ordered or if they are grouped in class intervals. When either of these two conditions prevails, computation is likely to be faster than for the standard deviation.

The usefulness of the semiinterquartile range is essentially limited to the realm of descriptive statistics. It should be given particular consideration when its special properties can be put to good use and when the standard deviation would be adversely affected.

6.12 PROPERTIES OF THE RANGE

The range is a rough-and-ready measure of variability. In most situations, including those involving samples drawn from a normal distribution, the range *varies more with sampling fluctuation than other measures do.* Only the two outermost scores of a distribution affect its value; the remainder could lie anywhere between them. *It is thus not very sensitive to the total condition of the distribution.* In addition, *a single errant score is likely to have a more substantial effect on the range than on the standard deviation,* which we have seen is particularly sensitive to conditions at the extremes of a distribution. Like other measures, with the exception of the standard deviation, *it is of little use beyond the descriptive level.* In many types of distributions, including the important normal distribution, *the range is dependent on sample size, being greater when sample size is larger.* This is an important flaw when comparing two distributions that differ substantially in the number of cases on which they are based.

On the other hand, *the range is easier to compute than the others, and its meaning is direct. It is therefore ideal for preliminary work or in other circumstances where precision is not an important requirement.* Sometimes, of course, it provides precisely the information we need. We have seen it in this role in the course of transferring raw scores into grouped data.

6.13 MEASURES OF VARIABILITY AND THE NORMAL DISTRIBUTION

Since the measures of variability considered in this chapter are defined in different ways, we would expect them to yield different values if all were calculated for the same distribution. Their relative magnitudes cannot be exactly specified in terms of a generalization true for all distributions, because special characteristics of some distributions (e.g. the relative frequency of extreme scores) have a different effect on the different measures. The normal distribution, however, is so frequently useful that properties of these measures in that distribution ought to be given attention.

In the ideal normal distribution, the interval:

$$\mu \pm 1\sigma \quad \text{contains about 68\% of the scores}$$
$$\mu \pm 2\sigma \quad \text{contains about 95\% of the scores}$$
$$\mu \pm 3\sigma \quad \text{contains about 99.7\% of the scores}$$

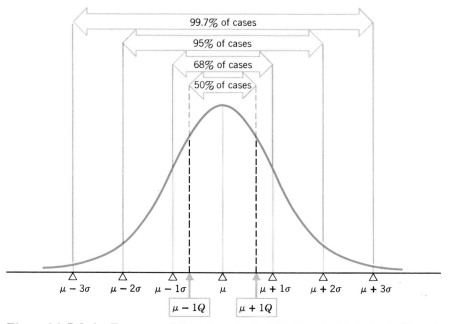

Figure 6.3 *Relative Frequency of Cases Contained within Certain Limits in the Normal Distribution.*

These relationships are pictured in Figure 6.3. Of course, in any sample drawn from a normal distribution there will be a certain degree of irregularity, and these statements will be only approximately true.

Figure 6.3 shows the interval $\mu \pm 1Q$, which contains 50% of the scores in the normal distribution. The illustration also shows that the numerical value of Q is smaller than that of σ. In the ideal normal distribution, $Q = .6745\sigma$.

Figure 6.3 also shows that the more extreme the score the greater the rarity of its occurrence in the normal distribution. Consequently, when a sample of limited size is drawn at random from a large number of scores that are normally distributed, very extreme scores may not be encountered. Roughly, the expected range of scores in a given sample approximates:

$$3S \text{ when } n = 10$$
$$4S \text{ when } n = 30$$
$$5S \text{ when } n = 100$$
$$6S \text{ when } n = 500$$

These relationships may be used as a rough check on the accuracy of computation of the standard deviation. Remember that they are only expectations, and that some departure due to sample variation is normal.

6.14 COMPARING MEANS OF TWO DISTRIBUTIONS

Suppose we found a difference of one point between the mean score for freshman males and freshman females. Is that a big difference? If the measure were College Entrance Examination Board (CEEB) test scores, the difference would be clearly negligible. If the scores were ratings on a five-point scale of satisfaction with the college experience, a difference of one point would be an amount of some importance, and if the scores were grade point averages, one point would be a very large difference. To sum up, the numerical size of the difference has little or no meaning without an adequate frame of reference by which to judge. That frame of reference can be provided by comparing the difference to the standard deviation of the variable. In the illustrations above, the standard deviation of CEEB scores is 100, and a typical standard deviation for a rating scale of the type mentioned would be .8, and, for grade point average, .4. If we now ask for each of the measures what the difference is when expressed as "number of standard deviations," the answer is $1/100 = .01$ standard deviation for CEEB test scores, $1/.8 = 1.25$ standard deviations for the rating scale, and $1/.4 = 2.5$ standard deviations for grade point average.

If we were to assume, for the moment, that the distributions were all normally distributed, these differences would be as shown in Figure 6.4.† Note the almost

---

†It is not likely that these three particular distributions will all be normally distributed.

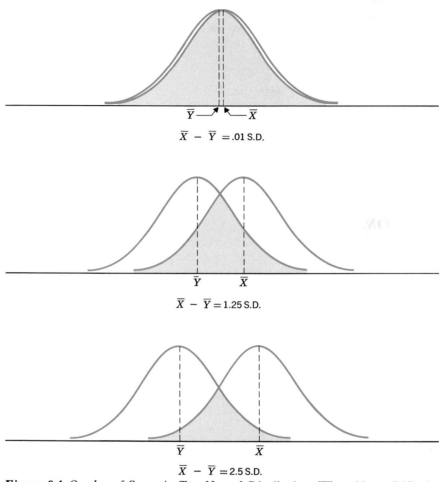

Figure 6.4 *Overlap of Scores in Two Normal Distributions Whose Means Differ by Varying Amounts.*

complete overlap of the two distributions in the first part of the illustration and the substantial separation that occurs in the second, and particularly in the third, situation.

In dealing with real variables, it is likely that the standard deviations of the two distributions to be compared will be similar but not identical. In such situations, it is reasonable to use the average of the two standard deviations for purposes of examining the magnitude of the difference between the two means. Just as a general guideline, we may think of a difference of .1 standard deviation as negligible, and one of .5 standard deviation of some importance.

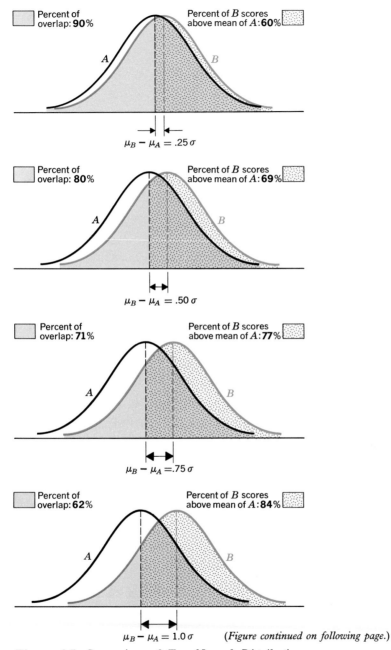

Figure 6.5 *Comparison of Two Normal Distributions Having Different Means.*

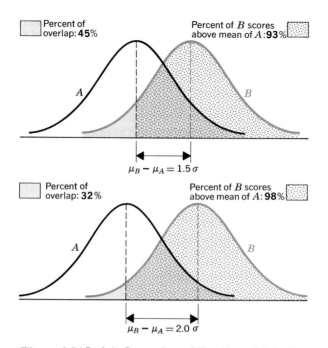

Figure 6.5 (*Con't.*) *Comparison of Two Normal Distributions Having Different Means.*

The problem of comparing means of two distributions occurs frequently, and it is very useful to get in the habit of thinking about the magnitude of that difference in terms of the number of standard deviations that it amounts to. To begin to develop a frame of reference, look at Figure 6.5. All of the normal distributions are alike with regard to variability, but their means differ by an amount ranging from .25 of a standard deviation to 2 standard deviations. One way of interpreting the pictures is to state the percent of scores in the higher distribution that exceed the mean of the lower distribution. Another is to state the amount of overlap of the two distributions; that is, the percent of scores in one group that could be matched by scores in the other group. Both of these ways of looking at the difference between the two distributions are shown in Figure 6.5.†

6.15 PROPERTIES OF THE MEASURES OF VARIABILITY: SUMMARY

The *variance* is:

1 The mean of the squares of the deviations of scores from their mean.

---

† The percentages shown characterize normal distributions and would not be exactly the same for distributions of other shapes.

2 A quantity expressed in squared score units.

3 Of little use at the level of descriptive statistics.

4 Important in statistical inference.

The *standard deviation* is:

1 The square root of the variance.

2 Defined in terms of deviations from the mean.

3 Responsive to the exact position of each score in the distribution.

4 Very good in its resistance to sampling variation.

5 Widely used, implicitly or explicitly, in advanced statistical procedures.

6 The most important measure at the descriptive level, and of great utility in inferential statistics.

7 More sensitive to extreme scores than the semiinterquartile range.

8 Smaller than if the same function were found, but with deviations taken about some point other than the mean.

The *semiinterquartile range* is:

1 The mean distance between the median and the first and third quartile points.

2 Related to the median in its constitution and properties.

3 Responsive to the number of scores lying above or below the outer quartile points, but not to their exact location.

4 Less sensitive to extreme scores than the standard deviation.

5 Particularly useful with open-ended distributions.

6 Of little use beyond the descriptive level.

7 Not as resistant to sampling fluctuation as the standard deviation, but substantially better than the range in most situations.

8 Easy to compute when scores are ordered or grouped.

The *range* is:

1 The distance spanned by the top and bottom scores of the distribution.

2 Unresponsive to the location of intermediate scores.

3 Dependent, in part, on sample size.

4 Generally poor in resistance to sampling fluctuation.

5 Of little use beyond the descriptive level.

6 Useful for rough or preliminary work.

7 Easy to obtain.

NOTES

Note 6.1 The Raw Score Equivalent of Σx^2 (*Ref:* Section 6.7)

$$\sum x^2 = \sum (X - \bar{X})^2$$
$$= \sum (X^2 - 2X\bar{X} + \bar{X}^2)$$
$$= \sum X^2 - 2\bar{X}\sum X + n\bar{X}^2$$
$$= \sum X^2 - 2\left(\frac{\sum X}{n}\right)\left(\sum X\right) + n\left(\frac{\sum X}{n}\right)^2$$
$$= \sum X^2 - 2\frac{\left(\sum X\right)^2}{n} + \frac{\left(\sum X\right)^2}{n}$$
$$= \sum X^2 - \frac{\left(\sum X\right)^2}{n}$$

Note 6.2 The Standard Deviation of Transformed Scores (*Ref:* Section 6.8).

A. Let $S_{(X+C)}$ be the standard deviation of a distribution that has been altered by adding a constant, C, to each score. Then:

$$S_{(X+C)}^2 = \frac{\sum [(X + C) - (\overline{X + C})]^2}{n}$$

From Note 5.1A, $(\overline{X + C}) = \bar{X} + C$, and

$$S_{(X+C)}^2 = \frac{\sum [X + C - \bar{X} - C]^2}{n}$$
$$= \frac{\sum [X - \bar{X}]^2}{n}$$
$$= S_X^2, \text{ and so } S_{(X+C)} = S_X$$

If C may take negative values, we have without further proof:

$$S_{(X-C)}^2 = S_X^2 \quad \text{and} \quad S_{(X-C)} = S_X$$

B. Let S_{CX} be the standard deviation of a distribution which has been altered by multiplying each score by a constant. Then:

$$S_{CX}^2 = \frac{\sum (CX - \overline{CX})^2}{n}$$

From Note 5.1B, $\overline{CX} = C\bar{X}$, and

$$S_{CX}^2 = \frac{\sum (CX - C\bar{X})^2}{n}$$
$$= C^2\frac{\sum (X - \bar{X})^2}{n}$$
$$= C^2 S_X^2, \text{ so } S_{CX} = CS_X$$

If C may take fractional values, we have without further proof:

$$S_{(X/C)}{}^2 = \frac{1}{C^2} S_X{}^2 \quad \text{and} \quad S_{(X/C)} = \frac{1}{C} S_X$$

Note 6.3 The Standard Deviation as a Minimum Value when Deviations Are Taken from the Mean (*Ref:* Section 6.10)

Let A be the point about which the deviation of each score is taken, and define it as a point which differs from the mean by an amount, d: $A = \bar{X} + d$. Then,

$$\sum (X - A)^2 = \sum [X - (\bar{X} + d)]^2$$
$$= \sum [(X - \bar{X}) - d]^2$$
$$= \sum [(X - \bar{X})^2 - 2d(X - \bar{X}) + d^2]$$
$$= \sum (X - \bar{X})^2 - 2d \sum (X - \bar{X}) + nd^2$$

From Note 5.2, $\Sigma(X - \bar{X}) = 0$, so

$$\sum (X - A)^2 = \sum (X - \bar{X})^2 + nd^2$$

Inspection of the right side of the above equation shows that $\Sigma(X - A)^2$ is smallest when $d = 0$. From the definition of d, this occurs when $A = \bar{X}$. Since $S = \sqrt{\Sigma(X - \bar{X})^2/n}$, it is apparent that S has a minimum value when deviations are taken from $\bar{X}$.

PROBLEMS AND EXERCISES

Identify:

measures of variability Q
range x
semiinterquartile range σ^2
average deviation S^2
variance σ
standard deviation S

1 Find (*a*) the range, and (*b*) the semiinterquartile range for the data of Table 4.1.

2 We want to compare the variability of the two sets of reaction time scores in Data 4A. (*a*) Find the range of both distributions. (*b*) Find the semiinterquartile range for both distributions. What can we say about relative variability under the two stimulus conditions?

3 Given these scores: X: 5, 8, 3, 5, 7; Y: 4, 2, 7, 4, 7. (*a*) What is the range of the X scores? The Y scores? (*b*) Find the standard deviation of the X scores by the deviation score method. Keep all work to 1 decimal. (*c*) Find S_X by the raw score method. Keep all work to one decimal. (*d*) Comment on the relative ease of calculation of the two methods.

4 Repeat parts (*b*), (*c*), and (*d*) of Problem 3, but as applied to the Y scores.

5 The standard deviation of a set of scores is 20. What would the standard deviation be if (*a*) 15 points were added to each score? (*b*) each score were divided by 5? (*c*) ten points were subtracted from each score and the resulting scores were divided by 2?

6 Calculate S for this set of scores: 2, 4, 6, 8. Use the raw score method.

7 Calculate $\bar{X}$ and S for each of the three simple sets of scores appearing in Section 6.2. Use raw score methods.

Data 6A		Data 6B		Data 6C	
Scores	f	Scores	f	Scores	f
33–35	5	65–69	3	50–59	8
30–32	7	60–64	5	40–49	14
27–29	11	55–59	7	30–39	11
24–26	7	50–54	5	20–29	7

(The number of intervals is of course too small for Data 6A, B, and C. They are offered only in the interest of simplifying computational practice.)

8 Calculate $\bar{X}$ and S for Data 6A.

9 Calculate $\bar{X}$ and S for Data 6B.

10 Calculate $\bar{X}$ and S for Data 6C.

11 Find the mean and standard deviation of the two sets of scores in Data 4A. What can we say about the differences between the two distributions?

12 Do the values obtained for the standard deviations in Problem 11 appear reasonable in view of the range of scores? Explain.

13 After the mean, median, range, Q, and S of a set of 40 scores had been computed, the researcher found that the highest score was slightly lower than originally recorded. Which of the measures would be affected by the change? Explain.

14 What are the advantages of the standard deviation over the other measures of variability?

15 An elementary statistics student decided to calculate the mean and standard deviation of a set of scores so that she could see if they followed the normal distribution. Comment.

16 What measure of variability do you suggest for the data of Problem 14, chapter 5? Explain.

17 A science teacher gives a standard test of knowledge of science to his class. The data for his students and for a national sample are as follows: Instructor's class: $\bar{X} = 90$, $S = 8$; National sample: $\bar{X} = 75$, $S = 14$. What is the meaning of these findings? What implication is suggested for teaching science to this class?

18 Compare the difference between mean performance of the X and Y groups in (*a*) Data 6D and (*b*) Data 6E. Do so by expressing the difference in terms of number of standard deviations. Do you suppose these differences would be considered substantial? Explain.

Data 6D		Data 6E	
$\bar{X} = 540$	$\bar{Y} = 555$	$\bar{X} = 2.43$	$\bar{Y} = 2.68$
$S_X = 100$	$S_Y = 100$	$S_X = .30$	$S_Y = .40$

CHAPTER 7

7.1 INTRODUCTION

In the development so far, there has been frequent reference to the *normal curve*. This stands as testimony to the pervasive significance of that function for statistical procedures. In the world of real variables, it is amazing how frequently distributions of measurements follow closely the handsome outlines of this bell–shaped curve. Examples are readily found in all disciplines–in physics, chemistry, geology, biology, and social science, as well as in psychological and educational measurement. We shall also find that the assumption of a normal distribution is an important requirement for many useful procedures in inferential statistics.

So the time has come to examine the normal curve more closely. We need to know what the normal curve is, what its properties are, the ways in which it is useful as a statistical model, and how to put it to work in answering questions. Some consideration of its history is in order because of its intrinsic interest and

The Normal Curve

because it throws some light on the character and widespread use of the normal curve as a model.

7.2 THE NATURE OF THE NORMAL CURVE

It is important to make a distinction between data that are normally distributed (or approximately so) and the normal curve itself. The normal curve is a mathematical abstraction having a particular defining equation (given in the Note at the end of this chapter). As a mathematical abstraction, it is not of necessity associated with (or determined by) any event or events in the real world. It is not, therefore, a "law of nature," contrary to the thought and terminology associated with it a century ago. Nevertheless, a specific normal curve may be useful in describing a given set of natural events under appropriate circumstances. In the same way, the equation of a circle is a mathematical abstraction and not a law of nature. We may find a boulder that has a circumference approximated by a circle having a particular equation, or observe that the circumference of the earth roughly conforms to the equation of another circle, or cut out a table top to agree with a third such equation. Nevertheless, the circular objects do not of necessity exist because of the mathematical abstraction called a circle. We shall return to this point in Section 7.4.

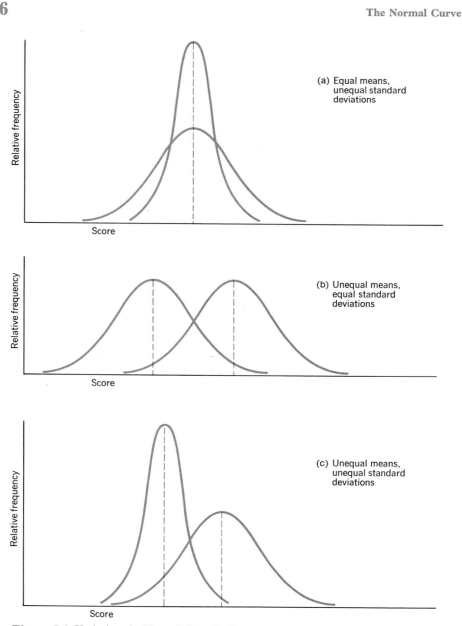

Figure 7.1 *Variations in Normal Distributions.*

Just as the equation of a circle describes a family of circles, some big and some small, so the equation of the normal curve describes a family of normal curves. The family of normal curves may differ with regard to their means, standard deviations, or area under the curve. In other respects, members of this family have the same characteristics. Figure 7.1 illustrates three possibilities: equal means and unequal standard deviations, unequal means and equal standard deviations, and unequal means and unequal standard deviations.†

All normal curves are *symmetrical;* that is, the left half of the normal curve is a mirror image of the right half. They are *unimodal,* with the mode at the center. Indeed, mean, median, and mode all have the same value. Starting at the center of the curve and working outward, the height of the curve descends gradually at first, then faster, and finally slower. A curious and important situation exists at the extremes of the curve. Although the curve descends promptly toward the horizontal axis, it never actually touches it, no matter how far out one goes. Such a curve is said to be *asymptotic* to the horizontal axis. One might think that if the curve never touches the X axis, a large proportion of the total area under the curve must lie in the extremes, but this is not so. For example, the area included within the range of $\mu \pm 3\sigma$ comprises approximately 99.7% of the total area under the curve, as we learned in Section 6.13.

The normal curve is *continuous.* This is of interest, because we remember that recorded values of observations always form a discrete series (see Section 2.5). It is our first indication that when the normal curve is used as a model for events of the "real world," it must be expected to be only approximate.

Finally, *for all members of the family of normal curves, the proportion of area under the curve relative to a particular location on the horizontal axis is the same when the location is stated on a comparable basis.* For example, approximately two-thirds (68%) of the area under a normal curve lies within the range of $\mu \pm 1\sigma$. Thus in a normal curve characterized by $\mu = 100$ and $\sigma = 20$, two-thirds of the area falls between the values of 80 and 120, and in a normal curve characterized by $\mu = 500$ and $\sigma = 100$, two-thirds of the area falls between the values of 400 and 600.

7.3 HISTORICAL ASPECTS OF THE NORMAL CURVE‡

The substantial beginnings of the development of statistical theory occurred in the middle of the 17th century. At that time, the first significant contributions were made to the principles associated with chance events, and hence to the theory of probability. To illustrate one such problem, suppose we toss eight coins and take as

---

†When it is appropriate to use the normal curve as a model for real events, it is most often the population of such events that is so modeled. Consequently, we shall use μ and σ in connection with the normal curve throughout this chapter, rather than $\overline{X}$ and S.

‡Those who wish to study further the historical development of statistical concepts will find the following reference of interest: H. M. Walker, *Studies in the History of Statistical Method,* The Williams & Wilkins Co., Baltimore, 1929.

our observation the number of heads. We shall suppose that each coin is as likely to come up heads as tails, and that the outcome of the toss of one of the eight coins in no way affects the outcome of the toss of another. Because of the operation of chance factors, we can not say precisely how many heads will appear on any one toss. But suppose we ask another question: if the act of tossing eight coins is repeated an extremely large number of times, what relative frequency of heads will occur? These early mathematicians developed a theory that provides the answer. The relative frequency distribution, derived from that theory, is shown in Figure 7.2. By inspection of the figure, we note that *on the average* there will be four heads and that the more divergent the number of heads and tails on any one toss (e.g. 7 heads and 1 tail), the lower the relative frequency of its occurrence.

We also see that if a normal curve were superimposed on the histogram in Figure 7.2, it would afford an approximate fit to the data. If 16 coins were tossed, rather than eight, there would be more bars in the histogram, and the normal curve would be an even better fit, as illustrated in Figure 7.3. It is apparent that the normal curve affords a good approximation to the relative frequency distribution generated by the operation of chance factors in a situation such as the one described. If the number of coins were increased indefinitely, the number of bars in the histogram would similarly increase and their outline, as represented in a histogram, would grow smoother and smoother.

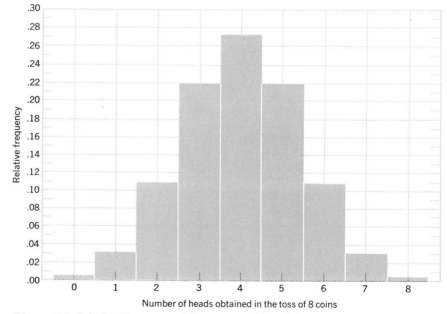

Figure 7.2 *Relative Frequency of Occurrence of Heads in Tossing 8 Coins.*

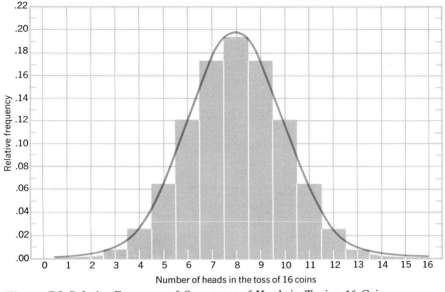

Figure 7.3 *Relative Frequency of Occurrence of Heads in Tossing 16 Coins.*

Indeed, in 1733 Abraham De Moivre discovered the formula for the normal curve as the limiting case characterizing an infinite number of such independent events. Because of this origin, the normal curve has frequently been connected with the notion that it occurs as a description of nature when a large number of factors are operating, each independent of the others and governed by chance.

Further significant development awaited the beginning of the 19th century. Indeed, it seems that Pierre-Simon (the Marquis de Laplace) and Carl Friedrich Gauss rediscovered the normal curve independently of De Moivre's work. Gauss's interest was associated with problems in astronomy; for example, determination of the orbit of a planet from a number of measurements (observations) that are subject to error. These problems led to the consideration of a theory of errors of observation with such strength that the normal curve came in that century to be known as the *"normal law of error"* (the name is now obsolete).†

Promotion of the applicability of the normal curve as a model for other situations is due primarily to Adolphe Quetelet, a Belgian, in the middle part of the 19th century. He was a teacher of mathematics and astronomy, originator of the basic methods of physical anthropometrics, and perhaps the founder of sociology. He believed that the normal curve could be extended to apply to problems in meteorology, anthropology, and human affairs. It was his opinion that "mental and moral traits," when measured, would conform to the "normal law." One of his concep-

†Vestiges of this terminology hang on. Note, in Chapter 13, the current term, *standard error.*

tions was *l'homme moyen*, or "average man." He compared the normal distribution to the notion that nature, in aiming at a mark (*l'homme moyen*), missed, and so produced a distribution of "error" in her effort.

In the latter part of the 19th century, Sir Francis Galton began the first serious study of individual differences, a domain very significant for psychology and education. He found that many mental and physical traits conformed reasonably to the normal curve and was greatly impressed by the applicability of the normal curve to natural phenomena. In 1889 he wrote:

> *I know of scarcely anything so apt to impress the imagination as the wonderful form of cosmic order expressed by the 'Law of Frequency of Error.' The law would have been personified by the Greeks and deified, if they had known of it. It reigns with serenity and in complete self-effacement amidst the wildest confusion. The huger the mob and the greater the apparent anarchy, the more perfect is its sway. It is the supreme law of Unreason. Whenever a large sample of chaotic elements are taken in hand and marshalled in the order of their magnitude, an unsuspected and most beautiful form of regularity proves to have been latent all along.*†

His enthusiasm is understandable and well worthy of our appreciation. His theory, however, must be tempered in light of current knowledge. A more balanced view will emerge in the next section.

7.4 THE NORMAL CURVE AS A MODEL FOR REAL VARIABLES

We now know that the normal curve is a rather good fit to an astonishingly large number of distributions of real data in a wide variety of sciences. The distribution has applications in physics, chemistry, microbiology, meteorology, engineering, and economics, to name but some. It appears to be a rather good fit to many (but not all) distributions of physical measurements made in biology and anthropology. For example, in reasonably homogeneous populations the distribution of stature follows the normal curve closely. As the mathematical astronomers found, it fits errors of observation in many circumstances. Again, it is often a good fit to the distribution of errors made in skill performance, such as shots aimed at a target, and it describes well the number of trials required by different subjects to learn a list of 25 words. Many measures of mental traits (e.g. scores earned on various aptitude tests, various achievement tests) tend to be normally distributed. In short, and specifically *with regard to psychological and educational data, the normal curve is in many instances a very good description of the distribution we shall get if we collect many observations and cast them into a frequency distribution.* The examples given

†F. Galton, *Natural Inheritance*, MacMillan and Co., London, 1889, p. 66.

only hint at the list of variables reasonably modeled by the normal curve. There is therefore every reason to understand Quetelet's and Galton's enthusiasm in uncovering so many variables that follow this distribution.

But is the normal curve a "Law of Nature," revealing some unifying principle that connects so many disciplines, perhaps even a principle that explains the generation of values consequently obtained? In a few cases it does seem to have an explanatory nature, as in determining the probability of obtaining a given number of heads in the coin-tossing illustration described in the previous section. But in most cases it must be accepted merely as a useful (and approximate) description of what will happen when observations are collected. Further, the hope of the 19th century that it might be a unifying principle of science seems no more justified than the view that the circle is a law of nature that unites the findings of the shape of a drop of oil in suspension, the pupil of the eye, and the wave made by dropping a pebble into still water.

In sum, the normal curve does not fulfill the earlier promise of a grand and unifying principle, one that explains the distributions of many real variables, but it does offer a convenient and reasonably accurate *description* of a great number of them. Even in that role, several words of caution are in order.

First, the normal curve as a model best describes an infinity of observations that are on a continuous scale of measurement. As we know, recorded observations are discrete rather than continuous, and, among concrete data, we do *not* have an infinity of observations. Real populations may be large, but they are not of infinite size. Although the normal curve closely approximates distributions of data of many kinds, it is a fair speculation that *no* real variable is *exactly* normally distributed. We conclude that this does not matter too much; it is the utility of the model that counts. We *are* reminded to examine the evidence and to decide whether the model is a close enough fit to warrant use.

Second, many variables are *not* normally distributed. Some variables that tend to show at least a degree of skewness are: human body weight, size of family income, reaction time, and frequency of accidents. Even variables that can exhibit a normal distribution in homogeneous populations may fail to do so under changed circumstances. The distribution of stature of a mixed group of men and women is bimodal, and a mental test that might yield a normal distribution of scores if appropriately constructed may produce distributions skewed to the left or right if the test is too easy or too hard for the group measured.

7.5 THE NORMAL CURVE AS A MODEL FOR SAMPLING DISTRIBUTIONS

The second way in which the normal curve functions as a model is for distributions of sample statistics, rather than for the raw observations. For instance, if one were to draw a very great number of random samples from a population and compute the mean of each sample, it would be found that the distribution of this large number of means tends to approximate the normal curve. In situations of this type, the fit of the normal curve is often very good indeed. This is a property of utmost importance in statistical inference, because the shape of such distributions must be known in order to provide information necessary to make the appropriate inference.

We shall find the normal curve in this role from time to time in the next few chapters, and then beginning with chapter 13 and throughout most of the remaining chapters it will be of central importance.

7.6 STANDARD SCORES (z SCORES) AND THE NORMAL CURVE

A question of the following type occurs frequently in statistical work: Given a normally distributed variable with a mean of 100 and a standard deviation of 20, what proportion of scores will fall above the score of 120? This question can be answered if we can find the area under the normal curve beyond the position of the score of 120, because *area under the curve is proportional to frequency of scores in the distribution*. By the methods given in the next section, we can determine that 16% of the area falls above the given point, and therefore we know that 16% of the scores fall above the same point. Look at Figure 7.4. We see that 16% of the area under the curve falls above a score of 120 (this was determined by the method explained in the next section). Since 16% of the area falls above a score of 120, we know that 16% of the cases in the distribution fall above that point. The relationship demonstrated here is a very important one, and we will make use of it again and again: *relative area under the curve equals relative frequency of cases in the distribution*.

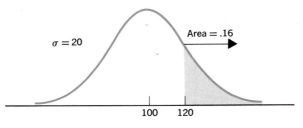

Figure 7.4 Proportion of Scores Exceeding a Score of 120 in a Normal Distribution Characterized by $\mu = 100$ and $\sigma = 20$.

Tables have been constructed that specify the area under the normal curve relative to particular locations along the horizontal axis. However, a way must be found to express location of a score in terms that are comparable for *all* normal curves. Raw scores will not do, since, for example, the score of 120 does not represent the same position in a normal distribution having a mean or standard deviation different from the values cited in the example above.

The solution is to convert the raw score to a *standard score*. A standard score, or *z score*, states the position of the score in relation to the mean of the distribution, using the standard deviation as the unit of measurement. In a distribution that has $\mu = 100$ and $\sigma = 20$, the score of 120 may be expressed as a z score of $+1$, indicating that the score is one standard deviation above the mean of the distribution. Similarly, a score of 85 is expressed as a z score of $-.75$, since it is three-quarters of a standard deviation below the mean. The z score may be stated in terms of a formula:

z Score in a Population $$z = \frac{X - \mu}{\sigma} \tag{7.1}$$

z Score in a Sample $$z = \frac{X - \bar{X}}{S} \tag{7.2}$$

The z score makes it possible to report scores from different normal distributions on a single, comparable basis. Consider a normal distribution that has $\mu = 50$ and $\sigma = 10$. In this distribution, a score of 60 lies one standard deviation above the mean; it may therefore be reexpressed as $z = +1.00$. This score, in its distribution, therefore falls at the same relative position as a score of 120 in a distribution that has $\mu = 100$ and $\sigma = 20$. Granted that both distributions follow the normal curve, we shall find that 16% of scores exceed the score of 60 in its distribution, just as 16% of scores exceed the score of 120 in its distribution. A single table of areas under the normal curve will therefore suffice for work with *all* normal distributions, irrespective of their means and standard deviations. All that is needed is to translate the relevant raw score to a z score in order to enter the table.

The idea of a z score is of great importance in statistical work, and it will appear again and again in this book. You will find it a great help to memorize Formula 7.2 and the following verbal definition of a z score: *a z score states by how many standard deviations the corresponding raw score lies above or below the mean of the distribution.*

There are three important properties of z scores:

1 *The mean of any set of z scores is always zero:* $\mu_z = 0$. This is apparent from the above definition, since the value of the mean is also the value of a score that is "no standard deviations away from the mean" and hence is represented by $z = 0$.

2 *The standard deviation of any set of z scores is always one:* $\sigma_z = 1$. Again, study of the definition of the z score reveals that it sets the standard deviation as the unit of measurement and therefore defines the standard deviation as unity. The z score of $+1$, for example, lies one standard deviation above the mean.

3 *A distribution of z scores has whatever shape is characteristic of the set of raw scores from which they were derived.*

Relative to the third point, one might be tempted to think that z scores are necessarily normally distributed because the notion of a z score has been introduced in connection with the normal curve, but this is not so. Reexpressing a raw score as a z score is one kind of linear transformation, and linear transformations of scores do not affect the shape of the distribution. We shall learn more about linear transformations in the next chapter.

7.7 FINDING AREAS WHEN THE SCORE IS KNOWN

This section and the next are concerned *only* with distributions that follow the normal curve; in other situations the outcomes presented would differ. Let us begin with the problem stated in the previous section: *Given a normally distributed variable with a mean of 100 and a standard deviation of 20, what proportion of scores will fall above a score point of 120?* The problem is illustrated in Figure 7.5.

The first step is to translate the score of 120 to a z score; its value is: $z = +1.00$. Table B (in Appendix F) is now of use. It gives the area under the normal curve that falls above or below a particular point when that point is expressed in standard score form. In this table, locate the value $z = 1.00$ in the first column and look across that row for the entry in the column marked "area beyond z." This entry is .1587, or if rounded, .16. The total area under the curve is defined as unity in this table, so the value, .16, may be interpreted as the proportion of the total area falling in the tail. As we noted in the last section, area under the curve is proportional to frequency of scores, so the question above is answered: .16 of the scores fall above the score point 120.

Suppose the problem had been to determine the proportion of scores lying below 80. Figure 7.5 also illustrates this problem. The z-score equivalent of 80 is -1.00. Negative z scores do not appear in the table. Because the normal curve is symmetrical, as many scores fall below a z of -1.00 as fall above a z of $+1.00$. The distinction between positive and negative values is therefore not needed. The column heading "area beyond z" takes care of both situations, and our answer is the same, .16.

Consider another type of problem: *assuming a mean of 100 and a standard deviation of 20, what proportion of scores falls within the score range of 90 to 120?*

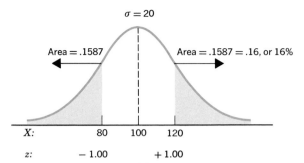

Figure 7.5 *Proportion of Scores Exceeding a Score of 120 and Falling Below a Score of 80 in a Normal Distribution Characterized by* $\mu = 100$ *and* $\sigma = 20$.

This problem is shown in Figure 7.6. Again, the first step is to obtain the z-score equivalents of these two scores. Using Formula 7.1, the values are found to be $z = -.50$ and $z = +1.00$, respectively. If we find the area under the curve between the z score of $-.50$ and the mean, and add this to the area between the mean and the z score of $+1.00$, we shall have the proportion of scores that fall within the given range. In Table B, the second column, "area between mean and z," gives the appropriate values:

area between $z = -.50$ and the mean: .1915
area between the mean and $z = +1.00$: <u>.3413</u>
total area: .5328

To two decimal places, the answer is .53, or 53%.

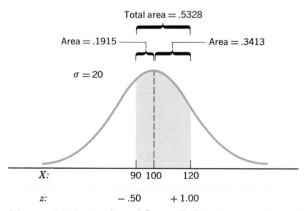

Figure 7.6 *Proportion of Scores Falling between 90 and 120 in a Normal Distribution Characterized by* $\mu = 100$ *and* $\sigma = 20$.

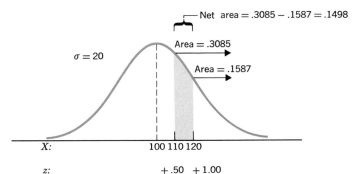

Figure 7.7 *Proportion of Scores Falling between 110 and 120 in a Normal Distribution Characterized by* $\mu = 100$ *and* $\sigma = 20$.

A third type of problem is illustrated by this question: *What proportion of scores falls between the values of 110 and 120?* We shall assume the same mean and standard deviation as before. One way to answer is to determine the proportion of scores falling above 110 and subtract from this value the proportion of scores falling above 120. The problem and its solution are illustrated in Figure 7.7. We begin, as usual, by converting the raw score values to z scores: $X = 110$ becomes $z = +.50$, and $X = 120$ becomes $z = +1.00$. Using Table B, the solution is:

$$
\begin{array}{lr}
\text{area above } z = +.50: & .3085 \\
\text{area above } z = +1.00: & -.1587 \\
\hline
\text{difference:} & .1498
\end{array}
$$

or, to two decimals, .15 of the scores.†

If the number of scores rather than the proportion of them is required, we have but to multiply the proportion by the total number of scores in the distribution. Thus, in the last problem, if there are 2000 scores in the distribution, $(.1498)(2000) = 299.6$, or 300 of them fall between the two points 110 and 120.

In solving problems of the sort described in this section, it is helpful to draw a picture of the kind used above.

7.8 FINDING SCORES WHEN THE AREA IS KNOWN

Consider the following problem: *Given a normal distribution, find the score that separates the upper 20% of scores from the lower 80%.* It is like some of the problems in the previous section, except that its form is inverted. There, the score was known

---

† In solving problems of this kind, beginners are sometimes tempted to subtract one z score from the other and find the area corresponding to that difference. A moment's thought shows that this will not work. *It is the difference between the two areas that is required.*

and the area required; here, the area is known and the score required. We *could* solve it by reading Table B "backward," locating the value in the column entitled "area beyond z" closest to .20 and then identifying the z score associated with it. However, Table C (in Appendix F) will facilitate this work. Consulting Table C, we look for the value of .20 in the column headed "the smaller area," and note that the z score associated with it is .8416. As before, the table does not distinguish between positive and negative z scores: we must supply that information. Noting that it is the *top* 20% that is to be distinguished from the remainder, it is clear that the value of the z score is positive: $z = +.8416$, or, to two decimals, $+.84$. Figure 7.8 presents this problem.

We can go no further in answering this question unless the mean and standard deviation of the distribution concerned are known. If, for example, the mean is 100 and the standard deviation is 20, we may proceed as follows. A z score of $+.84$ states that the score is 84/100 of a standard deviation above the mean. The value sought is therefore:

$$
\begin{array}{rl}
\text{mean} & = 100.0 \\
(+.84)(20) & = +16.8 \\
\hline
& 116.8
\end{array}
$$

If the question asked for the point separating the *lower* 20% of scores from the remainder, the z score would be $-.84$ and the raw score equivalent is:

$$
\begin{array}{rl}
\text{mean} & = 100.0 \\
(-.84)(20) & = -16.8 \\
\hline
& 83.2
\end{array}
$$

Another kind of question arises: *What are the limits within which the central 50% of scores fall?* Figure 7.9 illustrates this problem. If 50% of the cases fall between the two symmetrically located scores, 25% must fall above the upper limit and 25% below the lower limit. What is the score beyond which 25% of the cases fall? From Table C, it is found to be a z score of .6745. The scores are therefore located .6745

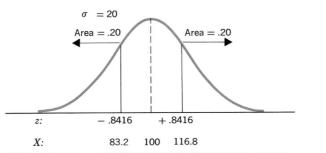

Figure 7.8 *The Score Dividing the Upper 20% of Observations (or the Lower 20%) from the Remainder in a Normal Distribution Characterized by* $\mu = 100$ *and* $\sigma = 20.$

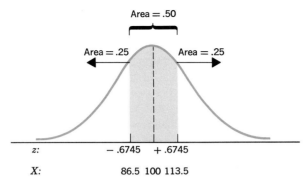

Figure 7.9 *The Limits That Include the Central 50% of Observations in a Normal Distribution Characterized by* μ = 100 *and* σ = 20.

of a standard deviation above and below the mean. If the mean is 100 and the standard deviation is 20, the limits are as follows:

Lower Limit	Upper Limit
$z = -.6745$	$z = +.6745$
mean = 100.0	mean = 100.0
$(-.6745)(20) =$ $-$ 13.5	$(+.6745)(20) =$ $+$ 13.5
raw score = 86.5	raw score = 113.5

In the illustrations above, the transitions from z score to raw score have been made in recognition of the meaning of a z score. The equivalent formula for making this transition may be obtained by solving Formula 7.1 for X:

Formula for Translating a
z Score to a Raw Score $X = \mu + z\sigma$†   (7.3)

Applying it to the solution of the upper limit in the problem above, we find:

$$X = 100 + (+.67)(20) = 113.5$$

the same value obtained previously.

NOTE

The Equation of the Normal Curve (*Ref:* Section 7.2)
  The equation of the normal curve is:

$$Y = \frac{N}{\sigma \sqrt{2\pi}} e^{-(X-\mu)^2/2\sigma^2}$$

†For samples, rather than populations, Formula 7.3 becomes: $X = \bar{X} + zS$.

As a model for a frequency distribution, it may be interpreted as follows:

$$Y = \text{frequency}$$
$$N = \text{number of cases}$$
$$X = \text{a raw score}$$
$$\mu = \text{mean of the set of scores}$$
$$\sigma = \text{standard deviation of the set of scores}$$
$$\left.\begin{array}{l} \pi = 3.1416 \\ e = 2.7183 \end{array}\right\} \text{mathematical constants}$$

The variables that determine what Y will be are: X, μ, σ, and N. Basically, the area under the curve is determined by N, the location of the center of the curve by μ, and the rapidity with which the curve approaches the abscissa by σ.

If one chooses to speak of a normal curve of unit area, in which the scores are standard scores, then: $N = 1$, $\mu = 0$, $\sigma = 1$, and the equation becomes:

$$Y = \frac{1}{\sqrt{2\pi}} e^{-(z^2/2)}$$

In this form, the value of z is the only variable that determines Y, the relative frequency. It is this function for which areas are tabled in Table B, in Appendix F.

Strictly speaking, Y in the normal curve is not interpretable as frequency; it is simply the height of the curve corresponding to a particular (point) value of X. Frequency *is* interpretable as the area under the normal curve that falls between two values of X (the frequency of scores within that range). The frequency of scores between limits of given width differs, depending on where such an interval is located on the abscissa. If the distance between the two values of X is decreased to a very small but finite quantity, the area between these limits becomes approximately proportional to the height of the curve at the midpoint of the limits. It is in this sense that we suggest that Y in the normal curve may be taken as an indication of frequency.

PROBLEMS AND EXERCISES

Identify:

normal curve	De Moivre
normally distributed	Laplace
data	Gauss
symmetrical distribution	Quetelet
unimodal distribution	Galton
asymptotic curve	normal law of error
continuous distribution	standard score
discrete distribution	z score

1 For normally distributed scores, what proportion of scores would fall: (*a*) above $z = +1.00$? (*b*) above $z = +2.00$? (*c*) above $z = +3.00$? (*d*) below $z = -2.00$? (*e*) below $z = -3.00$?

2 For normally distributed scores, what proportion of scores would fall: (*a*) above $z = -1.00$? (*b*) below $z = 0$? (*c*) below $z = +2.00$?

3 For normally distributed scores, what proportion of scores would fall: (*a*) between $z = +.25$ and $z = +1.25$? (*b*) between $z = -1.00$ and $z = -2.00$? (*c*) between $z = -1.00$ and $z = +1.00$? (*d*) between $z = -2.00$ and $z = +2.00$? (*e*) between $z = -3.00$ and $z = +3.00$?

4 If the distribution consists of 400 scores, what is the answer to each part of Problem 3 in terms of the number of scores involved?

5 For normally distributed scores, what proportion of scores would fall: (*a*) between $z = -1.25$ and $z = -.50$? (*b*) between $z = -.75$ and $z = +.25$? (*c*) outside the limits: $z = -.40$ and $z = -.20$? (*d*) outside the limits: $z = -1.00$ and $z = +2.00$?

6 If scores are normally distributed with a mean of 500 and a standard deviation of 100, what proportion of the scores fall: (*a*) above 550? (*b*) above 600? (*c*) below 420? (*d*) above 350? (*e*) between 550 and 750? (*f*) between 300 and 625? (*g*) between 625 and 725? (*h*) between 380 and 480?

7 In a normal distribution of 1000 aptitude test scores, with a mean of 60 and a standard deviation of 8, how many scores fall: (*a*) above 76? (*b*) below 80? (*c*) above 50? (*d*) below 46? (*e*) between 48 and 52? (*f*) between 58 and 70?

8 Among normally distributed scores, what z score (*a*) divides the upper 5% of scores from the remainder? (*b*) divides the upper 2.5% of scores from the remainder? (*c*) divides the upper 1% of scores from the remainder? (*d*) divides the upper .5% of scores from the remainder?

9 Among normally distributed scores, what are the z score limits that identify the central: (*a*) 99% of scores? (*b*) 95% of scores? (*c*) 50% of scores?

10 In a normal distribution of scores, what is (are) the z score(s): (*a*) above which 20% of the scores fall? (*b*) below which 65% of the scores fall? (*c*) above which 70% of the scores fall? (*d*) below which 6% of the scores fall? (*e*) between which the central 64% of the scores lie.

11 In a normal distribution of 200 scores, what is (are) the z score(s): (*a*) above which 20 scores fall? (*b*) below which 124 scores fall? (*c*) above which 156 scores fall? (*d*) below which 12 scores fall? (*e*) between which the central 100 scores lie?

12 In a normal distribution of employment screening test scores, with a mean of 25 and a standard deviation of 5, what is (are) the score(s): (*a*) above which 5% of the scores fall? (*b*) below which 52% of the scores fall? (*c*) above which 88% of the scores fall? (*d*) below which 10% of the scores fall? (*e*) between which the central 30% of the scores lie?

13 In a normal distribution of 500 intelligence test scores, with a mean of 100 and a standard deviation of 15, what is (are) the score(s): (*a*) above which 10 scores fall? (*b*) below which 175 scores fall? (*c*) above which 355 scores fall? (*d*) below which 32 scores fall? (*e*) between which the central 80% of scores lie?

CHAPTER 8

8.1 THE NEED FOR DERIVED SCORES

A student friend has been worried about his performance in a history examination. You see him for the first time in two weeks; the examination period is now over. "How did you do on the history examination?", you ask. "I got a score of 123," he replies. You consider his answer, not knowing whether to rejoice with him or to sympathize. "What was the class average?", you inquire. "One hundred and five," he responds. You are happy for him, but press the inquiry further: "What was the range?" "The low score was 80, and the high score was 125," he replies.

The example above illustrates the problem of meaning that is typical of scores obtained in psychological and educational measurement. The raw score, by itself, is really uninterpretable. A frame of reference is needed to decide whether a given score is indicative of a good performance or a poor one. In the example above,

Derived Scores

learning the value of the mean of the distribution contributed to understanding of his level of performance. Additional information was acquired by asking about the range; his answer indicated that his performance was very near to the best in the class. In this instance, the raw score, originally without meaning, became interpretable by relating it to a measure of central tendency and a measure of variability of a reference distribution.

The problem of making scores meaningful, in any dimension, is one of providing an adequate frame of reference. If we measure the length of an object in feet, the measurement obtained is meaningful, first because the length obtained is the same whether measured by your yardstick or mine, and second because we have some understanding of how long a foot is. In mental measurement, the problem is different. In measuring achievement in history, or intelligence, or mechanical aptitude, there is no standard raw score unit of measurement, nor should we expect one. On tests of these functions, the size and spread of scores that result depend on the number of test items, the number of points assigned to each test item, the difficulty of the items, and other factors. The problem is aggravated by two related matters. First, a test of intelligence, for example, is a *sample* of questions designed to tap this function. Another test of the same function will therefore constitute a somewhat different sample, with somewhat different outcome. Second, since we are not in perfect agreement as to what intelligence is, two test constructors may

123

sample domains which are not exactly alike. All of these factors mean that, unlike the measurement of distance, one "yardstick" of intellectual functioning is not necessarily the same as another.

With measures of this kind, meaningfulness is contributed by relating the position of individual scores to the distribution of scores obtained by a group whose characteristics are known.† We have already met two kinds of *derived scores* that serve this function: centile ranks and z scores.

The advantage of derived scores, then, is that they provide a standard frame of reference within which the meaning of a score can be better understood. Derived scores also make possible, under certain conditions, the comparison of scores from different measures. This property will be explained in Section 8.7.

There are two major kinds of derived scores: those that preserve the proportional relation of interscore distances in the distribution and those that do not. Linear transformations of the raw scores, including z scores, belong to the first category. Centile ranks and such scores as T scores and stanines belong to the second category. We shall consider each of these in turn.

8.2 STANDARD SCORES: THE z SCORE

The granddaddy of all standard scores is the z score. Its properties were given in the last chapter, but they are summarized here for review. A *z score states by how many standard deviations the corresponding raw score lies above or below the mean of the distribution*. This definition of the z score reveals that the standard deviation is set as the unit of measurement. In terms of a formula, z is calculated:

$$z = \frac{X - \bar{X}}{S}$$

The mean and standard deviation of a set of z scores are 0 and 1, respectively, no matter what the mean and standard deviation of the distribution of raw scores from which they were formed.‡ The fact that the mean and standard deviation always have the same values is the characteristic that earns the z score its other name: *standard score*.

Transforming raw scores to z scores changes the mean to 0 and the standard deviation to 1, but *it does not change the shape of the distribution*. By shape of the distribution, we really mean the proportional relation that exists among the

---

†A reference group of individuals with known characteristics is called a *norm group*, and the distribution of test scores obtained from such a group is known as the *test norms*.

‡See Section 7.6.

distances between the scores. For example, consider the following scores and their z score equivalents:

four scores from a distribution where $\bar{X} = 80$ and $S = 10$:   70   75   85   100

interscore differences among raw scores: 5   10   15

equivalent z scores: -1 $-\frac{1}{2}$ $+\frac{1}{2}$ $+2$

interscore differences among z scores: $\frac{1}{2}$ 1 $1\frac{1}{2}$

Note the relation between the interscore distances exhibited for the above raw scores and the z scores. The proportional magnitude of difference between successive raw scores, $5:10:15$, is exactly the same in z-score terms, $\frac{1}{2}:1:1\frac{1}{2}$.

Knowing the z score does not necessarily tell us exactly what proportion of scores fall above or below it in the distribution. *If* the original scores were normally distributed, precise information becomes available through the methods described in the last chapter. We know, for instance, that in a normal distribution approximately 98% of scores lie below the value of $z = +2$. Such percentages may be rather different when the z scores are generated from raw scores that are not normally distributed. Exactly what they would be depends on the specific shape of the distribution.

8.3 STANDARD SCORES: OTHER VARIETIES

There are minor inconveniences associated with the use of z scores. First, both negative and positive values will occur in any given distribution. Second, it is generally necessary to report the scores to one or two decimal places in order to achieve sufficient refinement in indicating location. Third, there can be a communication problem in dealing with a public unused to them. Imagine, if you will, a conference in which the teacher is attempting to explain to a mother that her son's performance in spelling, indicated by a score of zero, is for him really rather good.

To circumvent these difficulties, other varieties of standard scores have been devised. Each of them is like the z score in that it has a fixed mean and standard deviation; this is what is "standard" about them. The following are examples of those most commonly used:

Type	Mean	Std Dev	Example of Use
1	50	10	(Various)
2	100	20	Army General Classification Test, World War II
3	100	15	Wechsler Intelligence Scale IQs
4	500	100	Graduate Record Examinations (GRE)

The fundamental characteristic of all of these types of standard scores is that they, like the z score, locate the score by stating by how many standard deviations it lies above or below the mean of the distribution. For example, on the scale having a mean of 50 and a standard deviation of 10, a score of 40 is 10 points below the mean, and since the value of the standard deviation is 10 points, we know that this score is one standard deviation below the mean. On the remaining scales, scores of 80, 85, and 400, respectively, would inform us that each was one standard deviation below the mean. Despite the inconveniences attributed above to the z score, it does have the singular merit of giving its meaning directly. For example, the meaning of a score of 120 on a standard score scale where the mean is 100 and the standard deviation is 20 is that this score lies one standard deviation above the mean. However, that information is given *directly* by its z-score equivalent, $z = +1.00$.

Another important property of the standard scores described above is that they, like the z score, preserve the shape of the original distribution of raw scores. Figure 8.1 illustrates what happens when a set of raw scores having a mean of 66

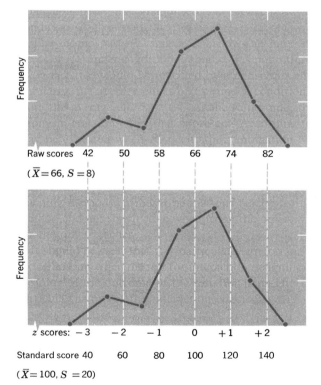

Figure 8.1 *Comparison of Shape of a Raw Score Distribution and a Standard Score Distribution.*

and a standard deviation of 8 is reexpressed as a set of standard scores with a mean of 100 and a standard deviation of 20.

Two final points should be noted. First, the term *standard score* is often used indiscriminately for z scores and for other types. It is easy to tell from context when the z score is meant, since its values hover close to zero. Second, standard scores with a mean of 50 and a standard deviation of 10 are sometimes called T scores. This is unfortunate, because that name was originally given to another kind of score, one described in Section 8.8. The T score described there also has a mean of 50 and a standard deviation of 10, but in addition the distribution of scores has been altered to conform to the normal curve. When the term T *score* is encountered, remember to find out which type of score is intended.

8.4 TRANSLATING RAW SCORES TO STANDARD SCORES

Suppose we have a score of 68, obtained from a distribution having a mean of 80 and a standard deviation of 8. What score is equivalent to this in a distribution where the mean is 100 and the standard deviation is 20? We need a *principle of equivalence* to solve this problem. Using the fundamental characteristic of all standard scores, we arrive at the following principle of equivalence: *Two scores will be considered equivalent if they are the same number of standard deviations above (or below) the mean in their respective distributions.* The score of 68 is 1.5 standard deviations below the mean (80) of its distribution. In the new distribution, an equivalent score will be 1.5 standard deviations below the mean of 100. Since the standard deviation is 20, this amounts to 30 points below 100, or 70.

The question, "How many standard deviations is this score away from the mean?", is answered directly by the z score. Consequently, the transformation procedure converts the score from the original distribution to a z score and, from the information thus made available, to an equivalent score in the new distribution. A second illustration utilizing this point of view appears below:

Problem: In a distribution with a mean of 71 and a standard deviation of 18, there exists a score of 85. What is the equivalent score in a distribution with a mean of 50 and a standard deviation of 10?

Procedure: 1. Translate the score in the original distribution to a z score:

$$z = \frac{X - \bar{X}}{S} = \frac{85 - 71}{18} = +.78$$

2. The score is therefore .78 of a standard deviation above its mean. Find 78/100 of the standard deviation of the new distribution, add that amount to the mean of the new distribution, and round the value as desired:

$$\text{mean} = \quad 50$$
$$(+.78)(10) = + \quad 7.8$$
$$\overline{ 57.8} \approx 58$$

This method we shall call the "principle" method. If more than a few scores are to be translated, the "formula" method, described below, is more efficient.

The principle of equivalence can be stated symbolically:

$$z_n = z_o$$

In this formula, the subscripts n and o serve to identify the new distribution and the original distribution, respectively. In effect, this formula says that scores in the two distributions will be equivalent when their z-score positions are the same in their respective distributions. The principle can be restated in raw score terms.

$$\frac{X_n - \bar{X}_n}{S_n} = \frac{X_o - \bar{X}_o}{S_o}$$

This formula is not in its most convenient form for use in translating scores from one distribution to another. When solved for X_n, it becomes Formula 8.1, and is easier to use in practice:

Formula for Translating Scores in One Distribution to Equivalent Scores in Another
$$X_n = \left(\frac{S_n}{S_o}\right)X_o + \bar{X}_n - \left(\frac{S_n}{S_o}\right)\bar{X}_o \qquad (8.1)$$

In translating scores by the formula, it is better to refrain from inserting any value of X_o until the means and standard deviations have been substituted and the equation simplified. The procedure is illustrated below with the data of the immediately previous example:

$$X_n = \left(\frac{10}{18}\right)X_o + 50 - \left(\frac{10}{18}\right)71$$
$$= .56X_o + 10.24$$

The set of new scores may now be obtained by substituting the several values for X_o. In our example, the score of 85 is converted as follows:

$$X_n = (.56)(85) + 10.24$$
$$= 57.8$$

This answer is the same as obtained by the earlier "principle" method.

If scores are already in z-score form, equivalent values in a different standard score system may be found by the following modification of Formula 7.3:

Formula for Translating z scores to Equivalent Scores in Another Distribution
$$X_n = \bar{X}_n + zS_n \qquad (8.2)$$

In the example illustrated above, the z-score equivalent of the score of 85 is $+.78$. Hence $X_n = 50 + (+.78)(10) = 57.8$.

8.5 STANDARD SCORES AS LINEAR TRANSFORMATIONS OF RAW SCORES

Any transformation of scores performed by adding, subtracting, multiplying, or dividing by constants results in what is known as a linear transformation. The name *linear transformation* is owed to the fact that the equation that describes the transformation is the equation of a straight line.

Consider the formula for finding a z score:

$$z = \frac{(X - \bar{X})}{S}.$$

In words, this equation says that to find z scores, first subtract the constant $\bar{X}$ from each raw score and then divide each of these transformed scores by another constant, S. The z score thus meets the requirements stated in the first sentence of this section and is therefore a linear transformation of the raw scores. It is not immediately apparent that Formula 8.1, the formula for translating raw scores to any standard score system, is also a linear transformation, but it is. The general form of an equation of a straight line is $Y = bX + a$, where a and b are constants; remember that in illustrating the use of Formula 8.1, it became:

$$X_n = .56X_o + 10.24.$$

It is plain that raw scores are first to be multiplied by a constant ($.56$), and then these values are to be further transformed by adding another constant (10.24) to each.

All of the standard scores considered so far—z scores and the others—are therefore linear transformations of the original raw scores and can be expressed by the equation of a straight line. In Section 5.6 and 6.8 the effect on the mean and standard deviation of adding or subtracting a constant to each score or multiplying or dividing each score by a constant was examined. We now recognize that these alterations also constitute a linear transformation of the scores.

The major property of a straight-line transformation of scores is that it preserves the proportionality of interscore distances and hence the "shape" of the distribution. This property was illustrated in Figure 8.1.

The fact that standard score transformations may be described by the equation of a straight line suggests the possibility of constructing a graph of the particular straight line and transforming the scores by reading the graph. An example of such a graph is given in Figure 8.2. The data are those used to illustrate the transformation equation in the previous section. A formal treatment of the linear function

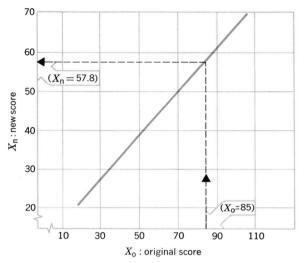

Figure 8.2 *Graph of the Transformation Equation*
$X_n = .56X_o + 10.24.$

is given in Section A.9 of Appendix A. It would be very good to review that material in connection with what has been presented above, and it also shows how to construct the graph of the transformation equation.

8.6 CENTILE SCORES

The basic characteristics of centile scores were presented in chapter 3 (beginning with Section 3.9). They are also derived scores, but their properties differ in some respects from those of standard scores. Like the standard scores described so far, the centile rank of a score describes its location relative to other scores in the distribution. It has an advantage in terms of directness of meaning, a property always to be desired. The idea that Johnny's centile rank of 75 in a science test means that he performs better than 75% of comparable students is easy to comprehend and relatively meaningful even to persons without statistical training. If ease of intelligibility were the only criterion, derived scores in the form of centile ranks would easily be the winner.

Unfortunately, there are certain disadvantages. Primarily, the problem is that *changes in raw scores are ordinarily not reflected by proportionate changes in centile rank.* When one centile rank is higher than another, the corresponding raw score of the one is higher than that of the other, but we do not know by how much. Indeed, changes in raw score are accompanied by proportionate changes in centile rank only when the distribution of scores is rectangular. Figure 8.3 illustrates this. For example, in the illustrated rectangular distribution, a change of ten points in centile

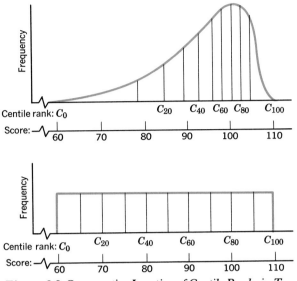

Figure 8.3 *Comparative Location of Centile Ranks in Two Distributions.*

rank reflects a change of five score points. In the other distribution, a change of ten points in centile rank reflects a change in score that may be larger or smaller than five points, depending on the location in the distribution.

In the normal distribution, the frequency of scores is greatest near the center of the distribution. The distance between two scores near the center is therefore represented by a relatively large difference in centile rank. On the other hand, as one approaches the extremes of the distribution, that same interscore distance is represented by a smaller and smaller difference in centile rank. This is illustrated in Figure 8.4. This figure shows, *in the normal distribution,* the relative scale for a wide variety of commonly used derived scores. It is worth close study, not only in connection with the matter currently under discussion, but in relation to the various types of derived scores discussed in other sections of this chapter. Some of the scores presented in this illustration will be introduced in later sections; e.g. *T* scores and stanines (Section 8.8).

To return to the problem of disproportionality of distances between centile ranks in the normal distribution, Figure 8.4 shows, for example, the actual score distance between two students who stand respectively at the fortieth and sixtieth centile rank. It is actually *smaller* than that between two students who stand respectively at the ninety-fifth and ninety-ninth centile rank. The standard scores discussed earlier do not suffer from this type of deficiency.

In summary, the centile scale is likely not to reflect proportionate raw score distances. When the basic raw score scale approaches the character of a normal

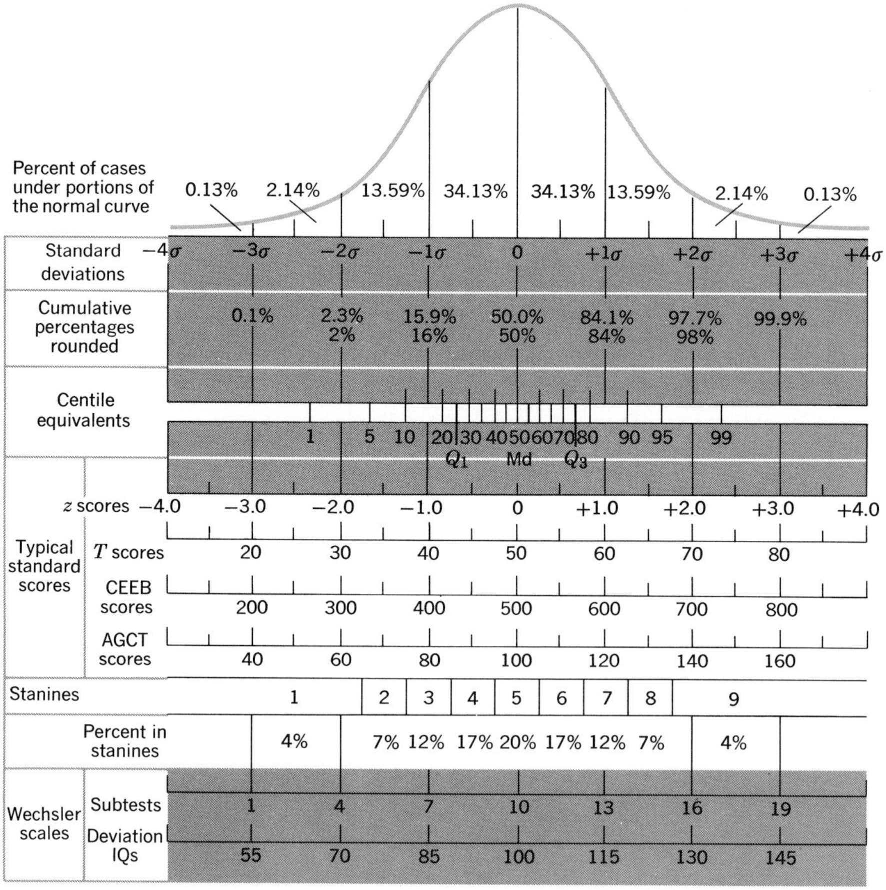

Figure 8.4 *Centiles and Standard Scores in a Normal Distribution (Adapted with Permission from Test Service Bulletin No. 48, The Psychological Corporation, New York).*

distribution, expression of scores in terms of centile ranks tends to leave the impression that there is a greater difference in performance between two individuals who fall near the center of the distribution than is actually warranted. On the other hand, individuals near the extremes tend to be inadequately differentiated. Note that $z = +2$ and $z = +4$ would be represented by C_{98} and C_{99}, respectively. If this system of derived scores is used, it is recommended that centile ranks beyond C_{99} be reported to at least one decimal.

A related problem arises when we wish to compare the performance of a particular group of individuals with that of another. For example, suppose a history teacher has scores for each member of the class on a standard test of achievement in history. The teacher wants to know how the average of the class compares with standards developed on a national sample. This can be done in straightforward fashion if the scores are in raw score or standard score form; the teacher can compute the mean for the class and observe where that value falls in the distribution for the reference group. If, however, students' scores are cast in terms of centile ranks, the mean of *these* values may lead to a different result. Consider, for example, the problem of finding the mean of a z score of zero and one of $+2.00$. The mean is a z of $+1.00$, and the centile rank of this score is 84 in a normal distribution. However, the centile rank of a z score of zero is 50, and of a z score of $+2.00$, 98, in a normal distribution. The mean of these two centile ranks is 74, a value differing from that of 84 obtained by the other procedure.

The difference obtained by the two procedures is dependent on the exact shape of the distribution. Generally, the better procedure is to pay attention to score values rather than to their ranks and therefore to calculate the mean (and standard deviation) of a set of scores *only* after translating centile ranks back into raw scores. Means of raw scores thus obtained may *then* be translated to centile rank if desired, and compared with data from the reference group. It should be noted that if interest is in the median rather than the mean of the distribution, there is no need to translate centile ranks to raw scores before finding this value, since the median of a set of centile ranks will be the same as the centile rank of the median score.

8.7 COMPARABILITY OF SCORES

Mary may earn a raw score of 37 in her mathematics examination and one of 82 in history. Suppose that in her mathematics class the score of 37 falls one-half of a standard deviation above class average ($z = +.5$) and that her history score of 82 is one-half of a standard deviation below class average ($z = -.5$). It appears that she is doing somewhat better in mathematics than in history. It also appears that standard scores permit comparison of performance even when the "measuring stick" is different. This may be correct, but there are some important qualifications.

If both courses were required of all freshmen, it is possible that the interpretation of Mary's performance stated above is correct. On the other hand, the picture is not so clear if the mathematics course is a remedial course required of freshmen who are deficient in that subject, but the history course is subject to enrollment only by honors students. *One element necessary for appropriate comparison is, therefore, that the reference groups used to generate the standard scores are comparable.* The prerequisite of comparable groups is just as important for comparison of centile ranks as it is for standard scores.

Even if the two norm groups are similar, standard scores will not be comparable unless the shapes of the distributions from which they arose are similar. The illustration in Figure 8.5 shows two distributions that are skewed in opposite directions. In the upper distribution, a score located at $z = +2$ is the top score in

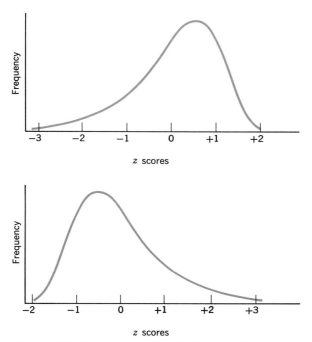

Figure 8.5 *Noncomparability of Standard Scores when Distributions Differ in Shape.*

the distribution. In the other, a score having the same z-score value is not the top score; some scores fall substantially beyond this point. Unless distributions from which standard scores are computed have the same shape, we shall find that equal standard scores may not have equal rank in their respective distributions. Thus, *standard scores should be used for comparing scores from two different distributions only if the two distributions have roughly the same shape.*

There is no satisfactory way in which the problem of noncomparable groups may be circumvented, but there is a solution to the problem of varying shape. One possibility is to use centile ranks. They are independent of the shape of the original distributions and thus may be used for comparison purposes even though the distributions differ in shape. Another solution is to convert scores to derived score distributions that have identical shapes as well as identical means and standard deviations. The next section describes transformations that do precisely this. In each case, scores are forced into a normal distribution in addition to being given standard values for the mean and standard deviation. Distributions treated in this fashion yield scores that are equal in rank as well as in score value. Some questions to consider before normalizing the distributions are discussed in the next section.

The limited meaning of the word "comparability" should be clearly recognized. It will not do to stretch it to include "equivalence," for example. The temptation to do so sometimes occurs when evaluating characteristics in what we perceive to be the "same" behavior domain. For example, it might be thought possible to estimate the Binet IQ of an individual from knowledge of his Army General Classification Test score, since both are tests of "intelligence." The cautions introduced in Section 8.1 should be remembered in such a situation. Those constructing the tests have sampled somewhat different aspects of the general domain, and therefore it would be inappropriate to presume that equivalent performance could be identified on the two instruments.

8.8 NORMALIZED STANDARD SCORES: *T* SCORES AND STANINES

The scores described in this section are like standard scores in that their means and standard deviations are specified, constant values. They differ, however, in that the process of transformation alters the shape of the original distribution of raw scores so that it follows the normal curve. Figure 8.6 shows, first, a skewed distribution of raw scores, and second, the normal distribution that results from transformations of this type.

The normalized standard score appearing most frequently in current work is probably the *T score*.† Transformation of raw scores to *T* scores produces a distribution with a mean of 50, a standard deviation of 10, *and* one that is normally distributed, irrespective of the shape of the original scores. Be sure to distinguish between *T* scores that are normalized and linearly transformed scores with the same mean and standard deviation, but which are *not* normalized. The scale of *T* scores in a normal distribution may be seen in Figure 8.4.

The *stanine* is another type of normalized standard score. The term *stanine* was devised by research workers in World War II. It is a contraction of "standard nine." Stanines have whole-number values ranging from 1 to 9. The mean is 5 and the standard deviation is 1.96, or approximately 2.0. Their fundamental advantage is that of simplicity: only a single digit is required to express its value. On the other hand, the stanine is a coarse unit of measurement, since the difference between successive stanine values is one-half of a standard deviation. Differentiation of performance is particularly poor at the extremes of the distribution. Figure 8.4 shows that stanines of 1 and 9 each cover a very broad range of performance. Methods of calculation for *T* scores and stanines appear in other books.‡

Why would one want to normalize the distribution? Some advanced statistical procedures may be based on the assumption that the data are normally distributed;

† Named after an early leader in educational measurement, E. L. Thorndike.

‡ One such is G. A. Ferguson, *Statistical Analysis in Psychology & Education,* 4th ed., McGraw-Hill, Inc., New York, 1976.

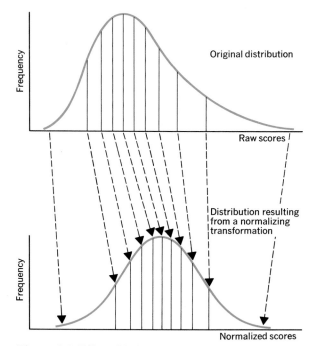

Figure 8.6 *Effect of Using a Normalized Standard Score Transformation.*

a normalizing transformation might be helpful here. If the departure from normality of the original scores is due only to an oddity in the construction of the measuring device, such as differences in difficulty of the test items, or the use of items too easy or too difficult for the group with which they are used, normalization may actually improve the nature of the scale of measurement. On the other hand, the use of the normal curve as a Procrustean bed to stretch and fit at will is arbitrary and artificial. Unless there is very good reason to force scores in the shape of a distribution different from that which they naturally exhibit, we will do better to use one of the standard score systems that preserve the original character of the raw scores.

The description of derived scores that appears so far in this chapter by no means exhausts the kinds of standard scores, whether of the linear function type or the normalized type. Those chosen for discussion include those most commonly used and serve to illustrate the general nature of the problem. Further consideration, systematically presented, can be found in other volumes. Particularly recommended is one by Lyman.†

†H. B. Lyman, *Test Scores and What They Mean,* 2nd ed., Prentice-Hall, Inc., Englewood Cliffs, N.J., 1971.

8.9 COMBINING MEASURES FROM DIFFERENT DISTRIBUTIONS

Suppose Professor Leonard Learned has given his class a quiz, a midterm, and a final examination, and now wishes to combine these numerical measures to obtain an index of performance for each student. If he wanted each to count equally he might think to add the three scores together, using the total as the indicator of each student's performance. But more than likely, he will want to give these measures different weight. Suppose he would like the final to count twice as much as the midterm, and the midterm twice as much as the quiz. If this is his thought, he may form the total by adding together the score on the quiz, two times the midterm score, and four times the score on the final.

In all likelihood, in neither situation will the procedure that he contemplates accomplish what he intends. The basic difficulty is that when several scores are summed, each one does *not* necessarily count equally in determining the total. It can be shown that *if the several scores are independent* (i.e. if the size of a person's score on one variable is in no way predictive of the size of that person's score on another variable), *then the contribution of each score to the total is proportional to the magnitude of the standard deviation of the distribution from which it came.* For example, if two tests have standard deviations of 15 and 10, respectively, and these two scores are summed, the contribution of the first test to the total is one-and-a-half times the contribution of the second, since the standard deviations are in the ratio of 1.5 to 1.

A simple example may be enlightening. Suppose two tests have the same mean, 50, but the scores on the first test spread from 30 to 70, while scores on the second spread from 40 to 60. If the two tests are to count equally in determining the total, a student whose scores are in the lowest position on the first test and in the highest position on the second test should receive the same total as a student whose scores are at the highest position on the first test and at the lowest position on the second test. We see that this is not the case. The first student's total is $30 + 60 = 90$, but the second student's total is $70 + 40 = 110$. The second student obtained the superior index because he had the good fortune to perform better on the test with the greater variability, whereas the opposite is true for the first student. This situation can be rectified by assuring that all of the test distributions from which scores are to be added to form the composite have the same standard deviation. One way to accomplish this is to translate scores from the several distributions to standard scores. The scores may *then* be summed (if equal weight is desired) or multiplied by the desired weights and summed.

One might wish that this were the end of the problem, but it is not. The careful reader will note that the above procedure was offered on the assumption that the several scores were independent. Most usually, this is not the case. For example, in the case of the instructor's two tests, it is likely that persons who score well on the first test will tend to do better than average on the second. If so, the two tests cannot be considered to be completely independent.

This is not a problem when only two measures are to be combined, but it is when there are more than two. With more than two measures, the procedure recommended above does not ensure that the weights assigned will result in the intended relative importance of the contribution of each to the whole. Nevertheless, it is better to follow the procedure outlined above than to allow the scores to be weighted by the amount of variability inherent in the distribution of each, since this is often a factor of irrelevant origin. Still more sophisticated alternatives exist, but they are beyond the scope of elementary statistics.

Two final points. First, the magnitude of the means of the several distributions have no bearing on the weight the scores carry; it is the relative size of the standard deviations that is important. Second, if one wished to talk about the mean of the combined scores rather than the total of them, the same principles apply, since for a given set of persons, the mean is found by dividing each person's score by a constant.

PROBLEMS AND EXERCISES

Identify:

norm group	equivalent score
test norms	principle of equivalence
derived scores	linear transformation
standard score	centile rank
mean and standard deviation	T score
of z scores	stanine

1 A student's grade on a very difficult English exam is 85. What can you say about the merits of the student's performance? Explain.

2 A distribution has a mean of 57.0 and a standard deviation of 12.0. Translate, by the "principle" method, the following scores to equivalent scores in a distribution having a mean of 100 and a standard deviation of 20: (a) $X = 63$ (b) $X = 72$ (c) $X = 48$ (d) $X = 30$.

3 A distribution has a mean of 108.0 and a standard deviation of 30.0. Translate, by the "principle" method, the following scores to equivalent scores in a distribution having a mean of 500 and a standard deviation of 100: (a) $X = 120$ (b) $X = 100$ (c) $X = 90$ (d) $X = 105$.

4 (a) Write the transformation equation required to solve Problem 2 by the "equation" method, and simplify it. (b) Use the equation to solve the several parts of Problem 2.

5 (a) Write the transformation equation required to solve Problem 3 by the "equation" method and simplify it. (b) Use the equation to solve the several parts of Problem 3.

6 $\bar{X} = 500$ and $S = 100$ for a set of normally distributed graduate entrance examination scores. What is the centile rank of a score of: (a) 450? (b) 700? (c) 550? (d) 625?

7 A high school principal wishes to compare the scores of his students on a standard achievement test with the scores of high school students in the adjacent district on the same test. Only the centile ranks of the students are available to him. What measure of central tendency would you suggest he use? Explain.

8 An instructor wants to compare her students' mathematics aptitude test score with their mathematics achievement score. The following are the means and medians for each of the two distributions: Math aptitude: $\bar{X} = 100$, $Mdn = 90$; Math achievement: $\bar{X} = 70$, $Mdn = 80$. How do you suggest that the comparison be made? Explain.

9 At the end of the school year, student A's science achievement score has changed from C_{50} to C_{70}, student B's score has changed from C_5 to C_{25}, and student C's score has changed from C_{65} to C_{85}. Assuming achievement test scores to be normally distributed, what can we say about the relative raw score gain of the three students?

10 Two students score as follows on Test X and Test Y:

	mean	std dev	Mary's score	Beth's score
Test X:	70	8	58	82
Test Y:	60	20	90	30

(a) Find Mary's mean raw score and Beth's mean raw score. (b) Translate the four scores into z scores. Find Mary's mean z score and Beth's mean z score. (c) Explain the discrepancy in outcome of (a) and (b).

11 A professor gave a midterm and a final examination to his students. The following data are available: midterm: $\bar{X} = 50$, $S = 9$; final: $\bar{X} = 65$, $S = 18$. He wants to base his course grade on the total of the two scores, but he feels that the final examination should count twice as much as the midterm. What is the simplest way to find a total for each student that will accomplish his aim?

12 One widely used way of attempting to give meaning to scores is to express the score as a percent of the total possible points. What fundamental limitation does this scheme have that the derived scores discussed in this chapter do not?

13 The mean of a set of z scores is always zero. Does this mean that half of a set of z scores will be negative and half positive? Explain.

14 If $\mu = 100$ and $\sigma = 20$, can there be negative scores? Explain.

CHAPTER 9

9.1 MEASUREMENT OF ASSOCIATION AND PREDICTION

What relation exists between stature and weight? Certainly taller persons tend to weigh more. On the other hand, we do not expect the tallest person to be the heaviest, the next tallest the next heaviest, and so on down to the shortest person. There is plainly a degree of association that exists between these two variables. Just how great is it?

We know that score earned on an academic aptitude test is related, to a degree, to the grade point average that the student will earn in college. A student who scores well on the aptitude test is therefore a better bet to do well in college than one who is not so talented. What grade point average shall we predict for a student who earns a particular score on the test? And what margin of error shall we attach to that

Correlation

prediction? If the relationship is not perfect, a particular prediction can only be considered to be a "good bet."

The first question concerns the degree of association between stature and weight and illustrates a problem in *correlation*. In this chapter and the next, we shall explore the problem of measuring the degree of association between two variables. The second question concerns the estimation of academic performance from knowledge of aptitude and illustrates a problem in *prediction*. In chapters 11 and 12, we shall explore the problem of prediction. The two problems are closely related. For example, we shall find that the closer the degree of association, the more accurately it is possible to predict standing in one variable from knowledge of standing in the other.

Determining degree of correlation and establishing rules of prediction are important in many areas of psychology and education. They are of particular importance in the study of individual differences. In this domain, two major problems are measuring traits in which individuals differ and determining the extent of relation between different kinds of characteristics. The notion of correlation is basic to the theory and practice of trait measurement. For example, many students will have encountered correlation in connection with the problem of test reliability (e.g. to what extent is initial performance on a test indicative of performance on the same test at a subsequent time?), and test validity (e.g. to what extent is score on a mechanical aptitude test related to on-the-job performance of machinists?). The second problem, that of interrelationship of individual differences, is illustrated by the two examples cited at the beginning of this section.

Other examples: Is there a relation between reading speed and reading comprehension? To what extent, if any, are physical factors, such as stature, related to mental characteristics, such as intelligence?

9.2 SOME HISTORICAL MATTERS

Fatherhood of the study of individual differences should without doubt be assigned to Sir Francis Galton, gentleman scholar of England during the latter part of the nineteenth century, man of astounding genius, and avid investigator of natural phenomena. In 1859, Galton's distinguished cousin, Charles Darwin, spelled out the theory of evolution and offered unimpeachable evidence in its behalf. This theory pointed to the importance of understanding the dimensions in which organisms differ and to the necessity for studying the role of heredity in transmission of these characteristics. These problems interested Galton. To study the inheritance of stature, for example, he put parent's height on one coordinate of a graph and offspring's height on the other coordinate, essentially in the manner illustrated in Table 9.1. In fact, the data are Galton's.[†] Distributions of this type are

[†] F. Galton, *Natural Inheritance,* MacMillan and Co., London and New York, 1889, p. 208.

Table 9.1 Bivariate Distribution of Midparent Height and Height of Adult Children (*All Female Heights Multiplied by 1.08*).

Height of adult children (in.)	Below 64	64–65	65–66	66–67	67–68	68–69	69–70	70–71	71–72	72–73	Above 73
Above 74							5	3	2	4	
73–74						3	4	3	2	2	3
72–73			1		4	4	11	4	9	7	1
71–72			2		11	18	20	7	4	2	
70–71			5	4	19	21	25	14	10	1	
69–70	1	2	7	13	38	48	33	18	5	2	
68–69	1		7	14	28	34	20	12	3	1	
67–68	2	5	11	17	38	31	27	3	4		
66–67	2	5	11	17	36	25	17	1	3		
65–66	1	1	7	2	15	16	4	1	1		
64–65	4	4	5	5	14	11	16				
63–64	2	4	9	3	5	7	1	1			
62–63		1		3	3						
Below 62	1	1	1			1		1			

called *bivariate distributions,* and their representation in the manner of Table 9.1, *scatter diagrams.* In this table, each cell entry is a frequency. For example, consider the entry in the cell at the intersection of the column headed 68–69 (midparent height), and the row 66–67 (height of children). It is 25. Of those parents whose midparent height was between 68 and 69 in., there were 25 children whose adult height was between 66 and 67 in. In diagrams of this kind, Galton perceived that a trend line could be fitted that would show the rate of increase in height of offspring as a function of increase in height of parent. He saw that a *straight line* was most often reasonably characteristic of the relationship observed, and that, other things being equal, the steepness of slope of the line was an indicator of the closeness of the relationship between the two variables. Some time later (1896), Karl Pearson, a scientist associated with Galton's laboratory, applied the mathematical basis now used to find the straight line of best fit and provided the fundamental formula for the correlation coefficient, an index of the strength of association. These procedures, as finally developed by Pearson, are the ones considered in this book.

Before leaving the subject of history, it is worth noting that Pearson was the outstanding contributor to the development of statistical techniques around the turn of the century. Many indispensable techniques are owed to him.

9.3 ASSOCIATION: A MATTER OF DEGREE

According to the development owed to Galton and Pearson, the degree of association shared by two variables is indicated by the coefficient of correlation; its symbol is r, although sometimes it is written with subscripts: r_{XY}. Again, we distinguish between the symbol for the population value of this coefficient and that for a sample drawn from the population. We shall let the Greek letter ρ *(rho)* stand for the population value and r for a sample value.† In this chapter the descriptive nature of the correlation coefficient is basic, and to avoid confusion the symbol r will be used consistently wherever possible. The principles and procedures for calculation described here apply equally to samples and to populations.

The coefficient is, in fact, a constant in the equation of Pearson's straight line of best fit, and it has properties convenient for expressing degree of relationship. When no relationship exists, its value is zero. When a perfect relationship exists, its value is one. An intermediate degree of relationship is represented by an intermediate value of r. The sign of the coefficient may be positive or negative. A positive value of r indicates that there is a tendency for high values of one variable (X) to be associated with high values of the other variable (Y), and low values of the one to be associated with low values of the other. The correlation between stature and

---

† The Greek letter ρ is often used to designate a variant of Pearson r; namely, Spearman's rank order correlation coefficient. When reading in other sources, be alert to possible variation in meaning assigned to this symbol. In the present volume we shall refer to Spearman's coefficient as r_s.

weight is an example of such a relationship. A negative value of r indicates that high values of X are associated with low values of Y, and vice versa. For example, we should expect IQ and number of errors made on a spelling test to be negatively correlated, i.e. the higher the IQ, the lower the number of errors. The sign of the coefficient indicates the direction of the association; it has nothing to do with its strength. For example, if the correlation between IQ and number of errors on the spelling test is $-.50$, the correlation between IQ and number of words correctly spelled would be $+.50$ (assuming that an "error" includes both misspelled words and words not attempted). For some variables, a high score is indicative of good performance, whereas for others a low score has the same meaning. The sign of the coefficient, therefore, will reflect the nature of the measure as well as the nature of the relationship. The scatter diagrams in Figure 9.1 illustrate various degrees of

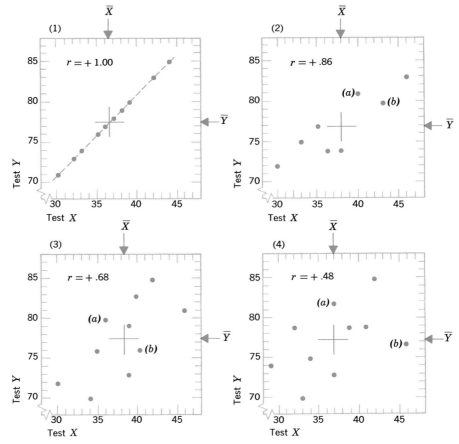

Figure 9.1 *Scatter Diagrams Illustrating Various Degrees of Correlation.*

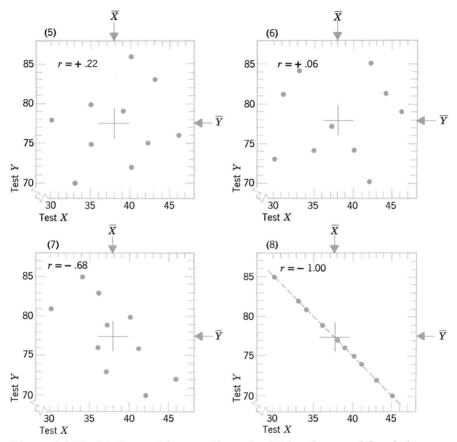

Figure 9.1 (*Con't.*) *Scatter Diagrams Illustrating Various Degrees of Correlation.*

correlation. In these illustrations, each dot represents a pair of scores, one for X and one for Y. In those diagrams characterized by a moderate positive correlation, note that although there is a general *tendency* for higher values in X to be associated with higher values of Y, it is easy to find specific instances of inversion. Such inversions may be seen by comparing points indicated at a and b in three of the diagrams. Note also that when $r = +1.00$ or -1.00, every point lies *exactly* on a straight line. This means that if we know the value of X, we can predict the value of Y without *any* error. It will not come as a surprise, therefore, to learn that in the "real world" of variables to be investigated, we do not encounter such perfect relationships except in trivial instances (e.g., the correlation will be -1.00 between the number of correct answers on a spelling test and the number of errors plus omissions).

9.4 A MEASURE OF CORRELATION

This section introduces formulas for computing the coefficient of correlation. As indicated above, the formulas are Pearson's and are intended for situations where two variables are involved and both are expressed in quantitative form. There are other related measures of correlation adapted to special situations, as we shall see in Section 9.10. In technical literature, the unqualified term *correlation coefficient* or the symbol *r* may usually be assumed to refer to the measure described in this chapter. This measure is also known as *Pearson r*, or *product-moment correlation*.

A problem in correlation begins with a set of paired scores. It could be height of parent and height of offspring, as with Galton's data; it could be performance on a mechanical aptitude test and trainee performance ratings of a group of apprentice sheet metal workers; it could be score on the first midterm and score on the final examination of a group of students; or many other things. But *the data always consist of scores paired in some meaningful way.*

We may consider the formula below (Formula 9.1) as the defining formula for the coefficient of correlation.

Correlation Coefficient;
Deviation Score Formula
$$r_{XY} = \frac{\sum xy}{n S_X S_Y} \tag{9.1}$$

where: $x = (X - \bar{X})$, $y = (Y - \bar{Y})$, $\sum xy$ is the sum of the products of the paired deviation scores, $n =$ number of *pairs* of scores, and S_X, S_Y are the standard deviations of the two distributions.

Note that the numerator consists of the sum of the products of pairs of scores (expressed in deviation score form). We meet two "old friends" in this equation. Implicit in the numerator is the mean ($x = X - \bar{X}$), and the standard deviation, S, appears explicitly in the denominator. We will calculate the value of a correlation coefficient using this formula, because it shows something about the factors that make the coefficient positive or negative and that result in a high or low value. However, the deviation score method of calculation is mainly of interest because it helps us to see what is going on. In practical computation, the raw score method, described in the next section, is much easier to work with (remember Minium's Second Law of Statistics?).

Table 9.2 illustrates computation of *r* by the deviation score formula. This table shows the midterm (X) and final examination (Y) test scores for each of ten students. First, the mean of each variable must be found. Then each raw score is translated to a deviation score (columns 3 and 4). To obtain the two standard deviations, we find the squares of the deviation scores (columns 5 and 6). For the numerator of the formula, the product of the pairs of deviation scores is obtained (column 7). For example, the *xy* value for student A is $+3.1$, obtained by multiplying his *x* score (-1.2) by his *y* score (-2.6). From the sums of the values in columns 5, 6, and 7, we obtain $\sum x^2$, $\sum y^2$, and $\sum xy$. The two standard deviations are then computed by the usual deviation score formula (see Section 6.6), and the correlation coefficient is found by substituting the appropriate values in Formula 9.1. Note that the order in which the pairs of scores appear makes no difference; the means, standard deviations, and sum of cross-products would remain the same. However, any shifting about requires that *both* members of a particular pair be moved at the same time. To do otherwise would affect the value of Σxy.

The data of Table 9.2 have been represented graphically in Figure 9.2. In this figure, each dot represents one of the ten pairs of scores. Beside each dot is a number indicating the product of the x value and the y value of the point expressed in deviation score form (the xy product). This diagram is divided into four quadrants by two lines, one located at the mean of X and one at the mean of Y. Points located to the right of the vertical line are therefore characterized by positive values of x and those to the left by negative values of x. Those points lying above the horizontal line are characterized by positive values of y and those below by negative values of y. For any point, the xy product may be positive or negative, depending on the sign of x and the sign of y. As shown in Figure 9.2, the xy products will be positive for points falling in quadrants I and III and will be negative for points falling in quadrants II and IV. On examination of the deviation

Table 9.2 *Calculation of r: Deviation Score Method*

Student	(1) First test X	(2) Second test Y	(3) x	(4) y	(5) x^2	(6) y^2	(7) xy
A	37	75	-1.2	-2.6	1.4	6.8	$+3.1$
B	41	78	$+2.8$	$+.4$	7.8	.2	$+1.1$
C	48	88	$+9.8$	$+10.4$	96.0	108.2	$+101.9$
D	32	80	-6.2	$+2.4$	38.4	5.8	-14.9
E	36	78	-2.2	$+.4$	4.8	.2	$-.9$
F	30	71	-8.2	-6.6	67.2	43.6	$+54.1$
G	40	75	$+1.8$	-2.6	3.2	6.8	-4.7
H	45	83	$+6.8$	$+5.4$	46.2	29.2	$+36.7$
I	39	74	$+.8$	-3.6	.6	13.0	-2.9
J	34	74	-4.2	-3.6	17.6	13.0	$+15.1$
$n=10$	$\Sigma X = 382$ $\bar{X} = 38.2$	$\Sigma Y = 776$ $\bar{Y} = 77.6$			$\Sigma x^2 =$ 283.2	$\Sigma y^2 =$ 226.8	$\Sigma xy =$ $+188.6$

$$S_x = \sqrt{\frac{\Sigma x^2}{n}} = \sqrt{\frac{283.2}{10}} = 5.3 \qquad r_{XY} = \frac{\Sigma xy}{nS_xS_Y} = \frac{+188.6}{(10)(5.3)(4.8)} = +.74$$

$$S_Y = \sqrt{\frac{\Sigma x^2}{n}} = \sqrt{\frac{226.8}{10}} = 4.8$$

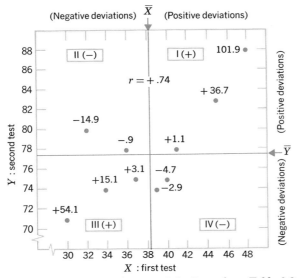

Figure 9.2 *Scatter Diagram of the Data from Table 9.2,*
Showing the xy Product of Each Pair of Scores.

score formula, $r = \Sigma xy/nS_X S_Y$, it is apparent that the sum of the products, Σxy,
determines whether the coefficient will be negative, zero, or positive. Moreover, if
other things are equal, the larger its magnitude the larger the magnitude of the
correlation coefficient. Note that the substantial positive correlation ($r = +.74$) is
owed to the relatively large positive contribution to Σxy made by those points lying
in quadrants I and III, while at the same time the negative contribution made by
those points lying in quadrants II and IV is small.

More generally, the correlation coefficient will be zero when the sum of the
negative xy products from quadrants II and IV equals the sum of the positive
products from quadrants I and III; the coefficient will be negative when the
contributions from quadrants II and IV exceed those from quadrants I and III; and
the coefficient will be positive when the reverse is true. The greater the predomi-
nance of the sum of products bearing one sign over those bearing the other, the
greater the magnitude of the coefficient. It is instructive to look at the several
scattergrams in Figure 9.1. The crosses at the center show the division into
quadrants I, II, III, and IV. In each diagram, compare the contribution of the
points in each quadrant with the calculated value of r.

9.5 COMPUTATION OF r: RAW SCORE METHOD

The deviation score formula for Pearson's r can easily be transformed to a useful
computing formula:

$$r = \frac{\sum xy}{nS_X S_Y} = \frac{\sum xy}{\cancel{n}\sqrt{\dfrac{\sum x^2}{\cancel{n}}}\sqrt{\dfrac{\sum y^2}{\cancel{n}}}} = \frac{\sum xy}{\sqrt{\left(\sum x^2\right)\left(\sum y^2\right)}}.$$ Thus:

Correlation Coefficient:
Computing Formula

$$r = \frac{\sum xy}{\sqrt{\left(\sum x^2\right)\left(\sum y^2\right)}} \qquad (9.2)$$

The two expressions in the denominator are the sum of squares of deviation scores for X and for Y. In Section 6.7 we learned how to compute such quantities using raw score equivalent formulas. They are repeated here for convenience:

$$\sum x^2 = \sum X^2 - \frac{\left(\sum X\right)^2}{n}, \qquad \sum y^2 = \sum Y^2 - \frac{\left(\sum Y\right)^2}{n}$$

What you see in the numerator of Formula 9.2 is known as the *sum of products of deviation scores*. This, like the sum of squares of deviation scores, may be found by raw score calculation:

Raw Score Equivalent
of Σxy

$$\sum xy = \sum XY - \frac{\left(\sum X\right)\left(\sum Y\right)}{n} \qquad (9.3)\dagger$$

In short, the two sums of squares and the sum of products are found by their raw score equivalent formulas and substituted in Formula 9.2 to find r. This method of calculation is illustrated in Table 9.3, using the data from Table 9.2 again. The sum of the raw scores, the sum of their squares, the sum of products of paired raw scores, and the number of paired scores are the building blocks from which everything else is generated. The squares and products of scores are, for the sake of completeness, shown in columns 3, 4, and 5 of the table. With an electronic calculator having a memory system it would not be necessary to record each of these values, since they can be stored internally by the instrument. The bottom part of the table shows the necessary steps (and their order) to complete the calculations.

9.6 SCORE TRANSFORMATIONS AND THE CORRELATION COEFFICIENT

In the chapters on central tendency and variability, we considered the effect of certain score transformations on the mean (Section 5.6) and standard deviation (Section 6.8). How will the correlation be affected if a constant is added to or

---

†Derivation of this formula is given in Note 9.1.

Table 9.3 Calculation of r: Raw Score Method

Student	(1) First test X	(2) Second test Y	(3) X²	(4) Y²	(5) XY
A	37	75	1369	5625	2775
B	41	78	1681	6084	3198
C	48	88	2304	7744	4224
D	32	80	1024	6400	2560
E	36	78	1296	6084	2808
F	30	71	900	5041	2130
G	40	75	1600	5625	3000
H	45	83	2025	6889	3735
I	39	74	1521	5476	2886
J	34	74	1156	5476	2516
$n = 10$	$\Sigma X = 382$	$\Sigma Y = 776$	$\Sigma X^2 =$ 14,876	$\Sigma Y^2 =$ 60,444	$\Sigma XY =$ 29,832

(1) $\displaystyle \sum x^2 = \sum X^2 - \frac{\left(\sum X\right)^2}{n} = 14876 - \frac{382^2}{10} = 283.6$

(2) $\displaystyle \sum y^2 = \sum Y^2 - \frac{\left(\sum Y\right)^2}{n} = 60444 - \frac{776^2}{10} = 226.4$

(3) $\displaystyle \sum xy = \sum XY - \frac{\left(\sum X\right)\left(\sum Y\right)}{n} = 29832 - \frac{(382)(776)}{10} = +188.8$

(4) $\displaystyle r_{XY} = \frac{\sum xy}{\sqrt{\left(\sum x^2\right)\left(\sum y^2\right)}} = \frac{+188.8}{\sqrt{(283.6)(226.4)}} = .75$

Usually we will also want both means and standard deviations:

(5) $\displaystyle \bar{X} = \frac{\sum X}{n} = \frac{382}{10} = 38.2 \qquad \bar{Y} = \frac{\sum Y}{n} = \frac{776}{10} = 77.6$

(6) $\displaystyle S_X = \sqrt{\frac{\sum x^2}{n}} = \sqrt{\frac{283.6}{10}} = 5.3 \qquad S_Y = \sqrt{\frac{\sum y^2}{n}} = \sqrt{\frac{226.4}{10}} = 4.8$

subtracted from each X score before obtaining the correlation between that variable and Y? And what is the effect of multiplying or dividing X by a constant? The answer, though not intuitively obvious, is most interesting: nothing happens. In each of the instances described above, the correlation between the altered variable and the remaining variable remains just as it was before the adjustment was made.

Proof of these propositions appears in Note 9.2 at the end of this chapter. In symbolic terms:

$$r_{(X+C)(Y)} = r_{XY} \quad r_{(X-C)(Y)} = r_{XY}$$
$$r_{(CX)(Y)} = r_{XY} \quad r_{(X/C)(Y)} = r_{XY}$$

It is also possible to transform X in one way (perhaps by adding a constant), and Y in another (say by multiplying by a constant), and the value of the coefficient remains unaltered.

These properties could be used to simplify the scores before calculating r. For example, if the X scores range from 506 to 548, 500 may be subtracted from each score and the resulting scores correlated with Y. The same answer will be obtained as if the alteration had not been made. Again, if scores are reported to one decimal point, we may multiply each by 10 (removing the decimal), and the subsequent correlation will be unaffected.

This property of invariance of r under various score transformations is also of considerable significance in understanding what a correlation coefficient means. Suppose we obtain the correlation between stature and weight as measured by inches and pounds, respectively. These propositions tell us that if the measurements were translated into centimeters and kilograms, the value of r would be unaffected.† Similarly, the correlation will remain the same whether the scores are expressed in raw score form, in deviation score form, or in z-score form. In fact, *as long as the translation of either (or both) variable(s) is a linear one (see Section 8.5), the correlation will be unaltered.* Again, consider the correlation between test and retest, as might be used to evaluate the consistency (reliability) of the measure. If practice results in some *constant* amount of improvement of performance on the occasion of the retest, this factor has, *per se*, no effect on the correlation between the two performances. What matters is whether those who had high scores on the first performance tend on the second testing to have scores that, *as compared with others on the second test*, are also high. To clarify this point, note that if scores on the first administration were augmented by adding 10 points to each score, and these values were correlated with the unaugmented scores, the correlation coefficient would be $+1.00$.

9.7 THE SCATTER DIAGRAM

Even though the correlation coefficient is calculated by the raw score method, it is often worthwhile to construct a scatter diagram to show visually the bivariate distribution formed by the pairs of scores. To do so, both X and Y are grouped in class intervals for ease of handling and visual inspection. The result will look like Table 9.1.

---

† A centimeter, for example, may be thought of as a "transformed inch." If measurements in inches are divided by .3937, the distances are expressed in centimeters.

The special advantage of this method is that one gets to see the way the data are related by studying the visual representation afforded by the scatter diagram. For the neophyte, this offers one of the very best ways to learn what is meant by a given magnitude of correlation. For the experienced data analyst, the scatter diagram provides a means of making an "eye check" on a number of factors that may influence the value of the coefficient or that should be taken into account in interpreting its meaning. This point will be better appreciated when we have studied these factors. For the present, note that inspection of a scatter diagram gives a rough check on the accuracy of computation of the correlation coefficient. If, for instance, the scatter plot looks like that in Figure 9.1, which corresponds to an r of $+.68$, but the computational outcome yields an r of $+.22$, we would be aware of the discrepancy and begin a recheck of our calculations. Using the raw score method, one would be unlikely to observe that something was wrong. When experienced workers are using the raw score method (or obtaining their results from a computer), they frequently find it helpful to construct a scatter diagram in order to study situations of particular interest, or to check values that appear unusual or dubious. For those who have access to a computer, it should be noted that the more sophisticated programs for computing correlation also make a provision for construction (by the computer) of the scatter plot.

9.8 CONSTRUCTING A SCATTER DIAGRAM

To construct a scatter diagram, we begin with a set of paired scores. Table 9.4 shows the faculty rating accorded to 40 psychology seniors, together with the scores for the same students on a comprehensive test of psychological knowledge. By the methods described in Section 3.5, class intervals are chosen in which to group the X scores. As usual, there should be 10 to 20 class intervals. When the number is between 10 and 15, the interests of accuracy are usually satisfactorily served, and convenience is maximized (in the illustration to follow, fewer intervals are used because of space limitations). The same kind of decision is then made about the scores in Y. It is not necessary to have exactly the same number of class intervals in X as in Y, nor is it necessary to use the same interval width in both variables. Indeed, if inches of rainfall were correlated with wheat yield in bushels, the range of the scores would be so different that it would be quite impossible to consider equating class interval width in X and Y.

The next step is to construct a grid in the manner exhibited in Figure 9.3. Graph paper with $\frac{1}{4}$ in. or 1 cm divisions is often convenient to use. First, the class intervals are recorded at the two margins of the graph. Remember to place the high score values of X to the right and the high values of Y toward the top.

The tally of the scores is done next. Referring to Table 9.4, we find that the first

Table 9.4 *Scores on an Achievement Test in Psychology (X), and Mean Faculty Rating of Potential as a Graduate Student (Y) (n = 40 Senior Psychology Students)*

Student	X	Y	Student	X	Y
1	106	2.3	21	107	3.8
2	101	2.4	22	124	4.8
3	129	5.0	23	126	4.8
4	128	4.1	24	133	4.0
5	113	2.6	25	132	4.9
6	116	2.9	26	116	3.3
7	117	4.0	27	112	2.8
8	138	4.0	28	103	3.0
9	131	4.2	29	103	3.2
10	132	3.8	30	128	4.6
11	111	3.1	31	135	4.2
12	96	4.0	32	103	2.1
13	100	3.7	33	101	2.7
14	100	1.9	34	105	3.2
15	102	3.3	35	119	4.2
16	114	3.3	36	122	3.4
17	122	4.3	37	112	2.6
18	118	4.5	38	120	3.7
19	102	3.0	39	132	3.2
20	106	2.5	40	109	1.7

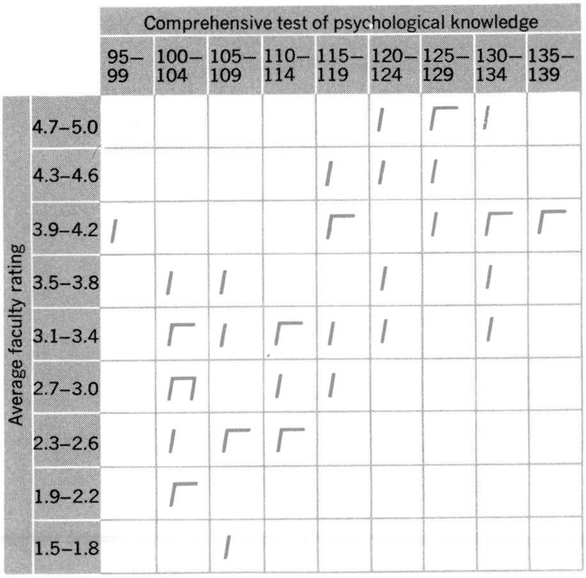

Figure 9.3 *Scatter Diagram: Initial State (Data from Table 9.4).*

student had a test score (X) of 106 and rating (Y) of 2.3. On the grid we locate the class interval in X in which the score of 106 will fall (105–109) and the class interval in Y in which the rating of 2.3 will fall (2.3–2.6). At the cell located at the intersection of this column and row, enter a lightly penciled tally mark. Do the same for each successive pair of scores until all pairs have been accounted for. The result will then look like Figure 9.3. The tally marks may then be erased and the equivalent Arabic numerals substituted if desired. It may be of interest to know that r as calculated from these data is $+.65$.

9.9 THE CORRELATION COEFFICIENT: SOME CAUTIONS AND A PREVIEW OF SOME ASPECTS OF ITS INTERPRETATION

One might think that interpretation of a given correlation coefficient would be a straightforward matter. Actually, this question is somewhat elusive. For the moment, we shall try to identify some of the more significant aspects pertinent to its understanding.

1   The degree of association is not ordinarily interpretable in direct proportion to the magnitude of the coefficient. For example, if we propose that "a correlation coefficient of $+.50$ means that there is 50% association between the two variables," a close analysis reveals that there are no objective referents by which this statement could be considered true; it turns out to be a nonsense statement. In general, a change of .10 point in the coefficient has greater consequence when applied to coefficients having high values than when applied to those having low values. For instance, accuracy of prediction is benefited more by an increase in the coefficient from .80 to .90 than by an increase from .20 to .30.

2   It is tempting to think that if two variables are substantially correlated, that one must be, at least in part, the *cause* of the other. This is not so. Mere association is insufficient to claim a causal relation between the two variables.

3   The strength of the association between two variables depends, among other things, on the nature of the measurement of the two variables as well as on the kind of subjects studied. It is not possible, then, to speak of *the* correlation between two variables without taking these factors into consideration.

4   You remember that Pearsonian correlation is based on the *straight* line of best fit to the bivariate distribution. Although a straight line is reasonably

considered to be the line of best fit in many situations, sometimes it is not. When it is not, the strength of association is likely to be underestimated by Pearson r.

5 The correlation coefficient is affected by the *range of talent* (variability) characterizing the measurements of the two variables. In general, the smaller the range of talent in X and/or Y, the lower the correlation coefficient, other things being equal. For example, in a given school the correlation between academic aptitude test score and grade point average may be $+.50$ for students in general. However, if the same correlation is determined using only those students who achieved a superior grade record, the correlation will be substantially lower.

6 Finally, the correlation coefficient, like other statistics, is subject to sampling variation. Depending on the characteristics of a particular sample, the obtained coefficient may be higher or lower than it would be in a different sample.

These and other factors will be discussed in some detail in the next chapter and in chapter 12.

9.10 OTHER WAYS OF MEASURING ASSOCIATION

Pearson's r is best suited when the two variables are both continuous and quantitative. There are a number of other measures of association adapted to special circumstances; many have been derived from the Pearsonian method. There is not space in this volume to develop them, but we shall identify major ones and say a few words about the situations for which they were designed. Several books describe them in greater detail and show how to calculate them.†

1 *Rank order correlation.* When scores are in the form of ranks (which for each variable will consist of successive whole numbers ranging from 1 to n), the rank order correlation coefficient may be used to determine the extent of correlation between two variables. This coefficient is derived from Pearsonian r, using certain simplifications that arise from the fact that the mean and standard deviation of a set of ranks can be derived just from knowing the number of ranks in the set and that the means and standard deviations of X and Y will be the same. This coefficient is sometimes known as *Spearman's rho*. Its calculation and use are demonstrated in chapter 24 (Section 24.3).

† One of these is: Q. McNemar, *Psychological Statistics*, 4th ed., John Wiley & Sons, Inc., New York, 1969.

2 *Biserial correlation; tetrachoric correlation.* The biserial correlation coefficient is suited for two variables where one is continuous and quantitative and the other *would* be, except that it has been expressed in only two categories. For example, biserial *r* is appropriate for determining the correlation between score on a mathematics test (continuous variable) and performance in a statistics class where each student's point total is designated simply as "above the median" or "below the median" (dichotomous variable). A special requirement is that the continuous distribution that appears in dichotomous garb would be, if the facts were known, normally distributed. Tetrachoric correlation is in order when both variables have the characteristics of the dichotomous variable described for biserial *r*. It would be appropriate above if performance on the mathematics test were also recorded as above or below the median. With tetrachoric correlation, normality is assumed for the underlying distributions of both dichotomous variables.

3 *Point biserial correlation; Phi coefficient* (ϕ). Point biserial correlation is like biserial correlation, except that the dichotomous variable is considered to be a discrete, "either-or" variable and not as one that has an underlying continuum. Qualitative variables meet this description; for example, male-female, Democrat-Republican, college-noncollege, prison record–no prison record. The phi coefficient is to point biserial correlation as tetrachoric *r* is to biserial *r*. It is appropriate when both variables are discretely dichotomous.

4 *Contingency coefficient.* This index of association is appropriate for two qualitative, unordered variables, each of which has more than two categories (if each has two categories, the phi coefficient is indicated). For example, it would be appropriate where *X* is father's eye color and *Y* is son's eye color and it is desired to measure the degree of hereditary resemblance.

5 *Correlation ratio:* η (*eta*). Pearson *r* properly represents the degree of association when a straight line is the line of best fit to the data. If a straight line is not the line of best fit, *r* will underestimate the degree of association. When the relation between the two variables is curvilinear, eta, known as the correlation ratio, is more appropriate. It has certain limitations that do not characterize Pearson *r*, so it should not be used for linearly related variables. Age and motor skill are two variables that are curvilinearly related. We would expect motor skill to be highest among the middle years and lower among the very young and the very old.

6 *Multiple correlation.* Suppose we want to predict performance of machinist trainees and find that scores on a test of spatial relations are related to this variable, as are scores on a mechanical aptitude test and a finger dexterity test. We do not have to choose only one predictor from among the three; the technique of multiple correlation makes it possible to combine the predictor variables and thus to make a better prediction than any one could do alone. In finding the coefficient of multiple correlation, we determine the weights to apply to each predictor variable so that the weighted total of these variables has the highest possible correlation with the variable we are attempting to predict. The coefficient of multiple correlation, symbolized by R, gives the Pearsonian correlation between the variable to be predicted and the best weighted composite of the several predictor variables. To calculate R, we must know the Pearsonian correlation between each variable and all the others.

7. *Partial correlation.* Partial correlation shows what the correlation between two variables would be if the influence of a third variable (or a third and a fourth variable, etc.) were removed. For example, the correlation between strength of grip and score on a mathematics test might be $+.75$ if our subjects range in age from 8 to 13. But the partial correlation between grip and math score with the influence of age removed drops to a value near zero.

NOTES

Note 9.1 The Raw Score Equivalent of Σxy (*Ref:* Section 9.5)

$$
\begin{aligned}
\sum xy &= \sum (X - \bar{X})(Y - \bar{Y}) \\
&= \sum (XY - \bar{X}Y - \bar{Y}X + \bar{X}\bar{Y}) \\
&= \sum XY - \bar{X}\sum Y - \bar{Y}\sum X + n\bar{X}\bar{Y} \\
&= \sum XY - \frac{\left(\sum X\right)\left(\sum Y\right)}{n} - \frac{\left(\sum Y\right)\left(\sum X\right)}{n} + \frac{n\left(\sum X\right)\left(\sum Y\right)}{(n)(n)} \\
&= \sum XY - \frac{\left(\sum X\right)\left(\sum Y\right)}{n}
\end{aligned}
$$

NOTE 9.2 Correlation between Transformed Scores (*Ref:* Section 9.6)

A. Let $r_{(X+C)Y}$ be the correlation between one variable (X) that has been altered by adding a constant (C) to each score, and another variable (Y).

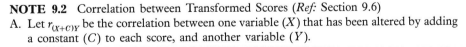

$$
r_{(X+C)Y} = \frac{\sum [(X + C) - \overline{X + C}]y}{n S_{(X+C)} S_Y}
$$

From Note 5.1A, $\overline{X + C} = \bar{X} + C$, and from Note 6.2A, $S_{(X+C)} = S_X$. Making these substitutions, we have:

$$r_{(X+C)Y} = \frac{\sum[(X + C) - (\bar{X} + C)]y}{nS_X S_Y}$$

$$= \frac{\sum[X - \bar{X}]y}{nS_X S_Y}$$

$$= \frac{\sum xy}{nS_X S_Y}$$

$$= r_{XY}$$

If C may take negative values, we have without further proof:

$$r_{(X-C)Y} = r_{XY}$$

B. Let $r_{(CX)Y}$ be the correlation between one variable (X) that has been altered by multiplying each score by a constant (C) and another variable (Y).

$$r_{(CX)Y} = \frac{\sum[CX - \overline{CX}]y}{nS_{CX} S_Y}$$

From Note 5.1B, $\overline{CX} = C\bar{X}$, and from Note 6.2B, $S_{CX} = CS_X$. Making these substitutions, we have:

$$r_{(CX)Y} = \frac{\sum[CX - C\bar{X}]y}{nCS_X S_Y}$$

$$= \frac{\cancel{C}\sum[X - \bar{X}]y}{n\cancel{C}S_X S_Y}$$

$$= \frac{\sum xy}{nS_X S_Y}$$

$$= r_{XY}$$

If C may take fractional values, we have without further proof:

$$r_{(X/C)Y} = r_{XY}$$

PROBLEMS AND EXERCISES

Identify:

correlation

correlation coefficient

prediction

negative value of r

product-moment correlation

quadrants I, II, III, IV

Galton $\qquad$ $\Sigma x^2, \Sigma y^2$
bivariate distribution $\qquad$ Σxy
scatter diagram $\qquad$ ρ, r
Pearson

1 Seven students made the following scores on two tests, X and Y:

Student:	A	B	C	D	E	F	G
Score on X:	3	9	7	8	4	7	5
Score on Y:	2	7	8	6	6	5	7

(a) Compute r to two decimals using the deviation score method. (b) Compute r to two decimals using the raw score method. (c) Did you get exactly the same answer in (a) and (b)? Explain. (d) Which method was easier? Why?

2 Five students made the following scores on two tests, X and Y:

Student:	H	I	J	K	L
Score on X:	9	4	5	3	5
Score on Y:	4	8	4	8	7

(a) Compute r, using the raw score method. (b) Compute $\bar{X}, \bar{Y}, S_X$, and S_Y, making the best use of quantities already found in computing r.

3 Four subjects obtained the following scores on two measures:

Subject:	M	N	O	P
Score on X:	7	6	5	8
Score on Y:	9	6	7	3

(a) Find r by the raw score method. (b) Find $\bar{X}, \bar{Y}, S_X, S_Y$.

4 Three subjects obtained these scores on two measures:

Subject:	Q	R	S
Score on X:	2	3	7
Score on Y:	5	4	11

(a) Find r by the raw score method. (b) Find $\bar{X}, \bar{Y}, S_X, S_Y$.

5 An r of $+.60$ was obtained between points earned on a spelling test and IQ for all current members of the sixth grade in a particular school. For each of the following, state whether the correlation would be affected, and if so, how. If it would be affected in an unpredictable manner, say so. Treat each question as independent of the others. (a) Score in spelling is changed to number of answers not correct rather than the number correct. (b) Each IQ is divided by 10. (c) Ten points are added to each spelling score. (d) Ten points are added to each spelling score *and* each IQ is divided by 10. (e) Spelling scores are converted to z scores. (f) Spelling scores are converted to z scores *and* IQ to standard scores with a mean of 50 and a standard deviation of 10. (g) r is calculated using only those paired scores for students whose IQ exceeds 100.

6 In Figure 9.1, one of the scatter diagrams is described by: $r = +.68$. The 10 pairs of scores are:

X:	30	34	35	36	39	39	40	40	42	46
Y:	72	70	76	80	73	79	76	83	85	81

(a) Verify, by the raw score method, that $r = +.68$. (b) Find $\bar{X}, \bar{Y}, S_X$, and S_Y.

Data 9A

In a statistics class, the instructor gave a test of elementary mathematics skills (X) on the first day. At the end of the course, he had available the score on the final examination (Y) for the same students. The data were as follows:

Student	X	Y	Student	X	Y	Student	X	Y	Student	X	Y
1	29	56	16	14	37	31	6	29	46	9	32
2	9	26	17	21	41	32	18	56	47	27	53
3	14	43	18	14	25	33	16	52	48	19	22
4	28	38	19	22	44	34	6	20	49	14	35
5	21	53	20	16	24	35	22	49	50	34	41
6	10	36	21	19	42	36	32	38	51	15	51
7	16	33	22	12	39	37	27	53	52	14	28
8	11	38	23	9	36	38	21	34	53	21	42
9	18	48	24	10	33	39	7	28	54	21	53
10	27	42	25	19	36	40	14	43	55	20	23
11	23	42	26	34	42	41	29	45	56	35	44
12	11	37	27	23	34	42	27	46	57	27	53
13	12	37	28	34	56	43	15	36	58	39	48
14	16	34	29	19	38	44	31	57	59	21	52
15	23	49	30	18	44	45	18	29	60	24	40

7 (*a*) Using a calculator, find r for the first 30 pairs of scores in Data 9A. (*b*) Calculate $\bar{X}$, $\bar{Y}$, S_X, S_Y.

8 (*a*) Using a calculator, find r for the 30 pairs of scores of subjects 31 through 60. (*b*) Calculate $\bar{X}$, $\bar{Y}$, S_X, S_Y.

9 Construct a scatter diagram for the first 45 pairs of scores in Data 9A, using 6–8 for the bottom class interval in X and 20–22 for the bottom interval in Y.

10 Construct a scatter diagram for the 45 pairs of scores for subjects 16 through 60 in Data 9A. Use the same class intervals as requested in Problem 9.

CHAPTER 10

10.1 CORRELATION AND CAUSATION

The meaning of the word *causation* has given wise men many hours of contemplation and debate. We cannot consider its subtleties here but shall take a commonsense approach, as in the statement that fly spray kills flies. In this sense, if variation in X is responsible for variation in Y, this must be reflected by evidence of some degree of association between X and Y, when the effect of interfering variables is appropriately controlled. However, the converse of this proposition is not true. The fact that X and Y vary together is a necessary, but not a sufficient condition for one to make a statement about causal relationship between the two variables. In short, evidence that two variables vary together is not necessarily evidence of causation. *If one is to speak of causation, it must be on grounds over and above those merely demonstrating association between the two variables.*

Factors Influencing the Correlation Coefficient

There is, for instance, a high correlation between length of left arm and length of right arm, but one is not the cause of the other. Again, if a sample of children ranging in age from 6 to 12 years is drawn and the correlation obtained between their scores on a test of reading comprehension and lengths of their big toes, a substantial positive correlation would be found. Of course, physical and mental maturity are parallel processes of growth, and the variation in state of growth affects the relationship. If the study were redone with children of *one particular age level*, the correlation coefficient would drop to a level close to zero. To speculate a bit, suppose that age has been held constant and that the correlation between length of big toe and reading comprehension is reliably found to be low and positive (but not zero). How could this occur? The following argument is speculative but possible and is offered for purposes of illustration. In a given cultural environment, it could be that differences in physique are due in part to the diet of the children, that their diet may be associated with the economic condition of the family, that the economic condition in turn is associated with intelligence of the parents, that intelligence of the parents is related to intelligence of their children, and hence with the reading comprehension scores that were obtained.

Figure 10.1 shows schematically four of the possibilities that may exist when the variables X and Y are correlated. First, it may be that the condition of Y is determined (in part, at least), by the condition of X. Second, the situation may be reversed, and Y is causing X to vary. Third, there may be a third factor that is influencing both X and Y, thus producing the observed association between the two. Fourth, the "third factor" may not be a unitary characteristic but in fact a complex of interrelated variables. This is certainly the case in the example given above concerning the association between reading comprehension and length of big toe. To invoke the concept of maturation makes it appear as though one were speaking of a single factor, but in fact it is a process of considerable complexity. To analyze the nature of the mechanism by which the particular physical traits and mental characteristics are associated through increase in age requires knowledge of substantial depth.

In correlational studies, the investigator must be particularly alert to the possible presence of extraneous variables (such as maturation in the example above) in order to exert an appropriate degree of control so that the interpretation of the obtained correlation coefficient may be as straightforward as possible.

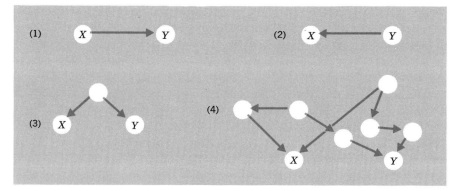

Figure 10.1 Diagrammatic Representation of Causal Relationships.

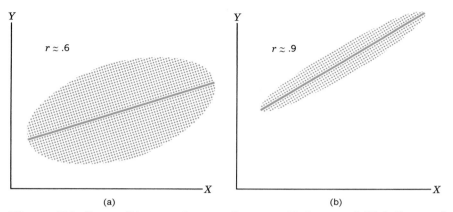

Figure 10.2 *Scatter Diagrams Corresponding to a Moderate and High Degree of Correlation.*

10.2 LINEARITY OF REGRESSION

Figure 10.2 shows a scatter diagram in which the correlation between X and Y is moderately low, and another in which the correlation is high. In each, the straight line of best fit has been included. In the diagram depicting the lower correlation, notice that the points scatter rather widely about the line. In the other picture, the points tend to hug the line quite closely. *In general, the more closely the scores hug the straight line of best fit, the higher the value of r.* A review of Figure 9.1 (in the previous chapter) offers further verification of this point. It shows scatter diagrams corresponding to correlation coefficients ranging in value from 0 to 1. In looking at those diagrams, one sees that if a straight line were fitted to each, the "hugging principle" described above would hold. When r is 0, the scores scatter as widely about the line as possible, and when r is 1, the scores hug the line as closely as possible (since they all fall exactly on the line). One meaning of this principle is that prediction of Y from knowledge of X can be made with greater accuracy when the correlation is high than when it is low. This consequence will be explored in detail in the next chapter. At the moment, our concern is with the relation between this principle and the notion of fitting a *straight* line to the bivariate distribution.

Pearson's solution to the problem of finding a measure of association (Sections 9.2 and 9.3) lay in fitting a straight line to the data; the correlation coefficient is a constant in the equation of this line. In a given set of data, a straight line may or may not reasonably describe the relationship between the two variables. When a straight line is appropriate, X and Y are said to be *linearly related*. More formally, the data are said to exhibit the property of *linearity of regression*. What happens

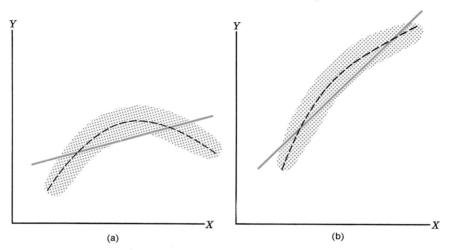

Figure 10.3 *Scatter Diagrams of Data That are Curvilinearly Related.*

when X and Y are not linearly related? Figure 10.3 illustrates two sets of data in which a curved line is apparently a better fit than a straight line. In the first picture, the curvature is pronounced, but a straight line has been fitted nonetheless. This therefore represents a situation in which Pearson r has been computed, but linearity of regression does not hold. How well do the scores hug the straight line? Obviously, not very well. As a result, when the correlation coefficient is calculated using the Pearsonian method, the obtained coefficient will reflect this fact and will have a low value. On the other hand, if the proper curved line had been fitted (illustrated by the dotted line), the scores would hug this line rather closely, reflecting a higher degree of association.

It can therefore be expected that *when the correlation is other than zero and the relationship is nonlinear, Pearson r will underestimate the degree of association.* Further, the greater the degree to which the data depart from a straight-line relationship, the more Pearson r will underestimate the strength of the association. In the second illustration of Figure 10.3, the relationship departs only slightly from a linear one, and the points hug the straight line better than in the first illustration. In this instance, Pearson r will underestimate the degree of association slightly rather than to a great extent.

Rather surprisingly, it has been found (as Galton earlier observed) that a great number of variables tend to exhibit a linear relationship, or one that is nearly so. Of course, this is why Pearsonian r is so useful in measuring association. Still, other types of relationship do occur, and their instance is not negligible. For example, score on a test of mental ability (or a measure of physical strength) would be curvilinearly related to age, if the span of age were taken, say, from 5 to 80 years. There are statistical tests that can be applied to determine whether the hypothesis of linearity is a reasonable one,† but the "eyeball test," made by inspecting the scatter diagram, is both a good and an easy way to learn whether a problem exists that should be examined with greater precision. Remember to allow for chance variation from a linear relationship.

10.3 HOMOSCEDASTICITY

In the last section, we found that if the scores scattered widely about the straight line of best fit, the value of r would be low, whereas if the scores hugged the line closely, r would be high. Look at Figure 10.4. In the first scatter diagram, no matter what value of X is chosen, the corresponding values of Y scatter to about the same extent. In the second diagram this is not so. Although Y does not vary much about the line when the value of X is low, it varies more when X has an intermediate value, and it varies greatly when X has a high value. Since r is a function of the degree to which the points hug the regression line, the value obtained for it has a meaning of general significance in the first diagram: it describes the closeness of association of X with Y *irrespective of the specific value of X (or Y)*.

In the second diagram, according to the "hugging criterion," there is a close association between X and Y for low values of X, a lesser degree of association when X has an intermediate value, and very little association when the values of X are high. It follows that if Pearsonian r is computed on the data in the second situation, it will reflect the "average" degree to which the scores hug the line and

† Q. McNemar, *Psychological Statistics,* 4th ed., John Wiley & Sons, Inc., New York, 1969.

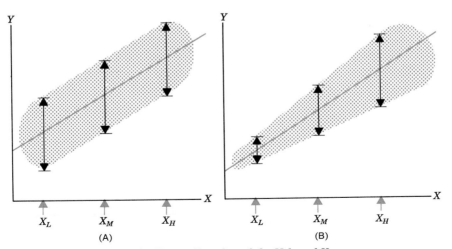

Figure 10.4 *Variability in Y as a Function of the Value of X.*

will characterize properly only the degree of relationship appropriate to interme-diate values of X and Y. The strength of association as measured by r will not, in these circumstances, have the general meaning that it does for the data of the first diagram. In the specific illustration (the second diagram), r will underestimate the extent of the relationship for low values of X and will over-estimate the relation-ship for high values.

When the amount of scatter is the same throughout, the bivariate distribution is said to exhibit the property of *homoscedasticity,* or, roughly translated from the classic tongue, *equal variability.* This property implies that if the data were sectioned into columns, the variability of Y would be the same from column to column, or if sectioned into rows, the variability of X would be the same from row to row. We can see that homoscedasticity characterizes the data shown in Part A of Figure 10.4 but not the data in Part B.

Obviously, the meaning to be attached to r will depend on whether the hypothe-sis of homoscedasticity is appropriate to the data. Tests of this property exist, but a simple way to make a preliminary check is to inspect the scatter diagram. One must allow, of course, for departure from perfect equality attributable to random sampling fluctuation. Fortunately, a reasonably homoscedastic relationship holds for many kinds of data. In Section 11.8 we shall learn how lack of homoscedasticity can affect the problem of prediction.

10.4 THE CORRELATION COEFFICIENT IN DISCONTINUOUS DISTRIBUTIONS

Suppose someone in the admissions office of a university wants to know the relation between entrance aptitude test score and freshman grade point average for last year's freshman class. At lunch with a friend from the student personnel office, he learns that a ready-made sample of personnel records awaits him; his friend is sending disqualification notices to those who failed during their first year and also sending notices of election to the Gold Star Society to those who qualified for that scholastic honor during their first year. His friend offers to pass on to him the records of these students when he is through, thus saving the effort of pulling rec-ords from the file. If the man from the admissions office accepts the offer, pools the two sets of personnel records, and computes the coefficient of correlation between test score and grade point average, his data might look like those pictured in Figure 10.5. Note that distributions that normally would be continuous have been rendered discontinuous because of the exclusion of students whose grade point average was at an intermediate level. A sample constituted in this manner will yield a correlation coefficient different from what would be obtained in drawing a sample

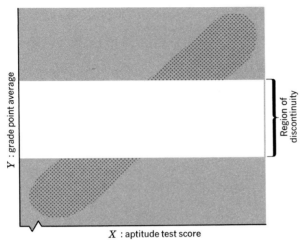

Figure 10.5 *Scatter Diagram for Discontinuous Data.*

so that all elements of the population had an opportunity to be selected. Usually, discontinuity results in a coefficient higher than otherwise.

This matter may be put in proper perspective by considering it from the point of view of adequacy of sampling. What population does the man from the admissions office want to study? Apparently, he intends to draw conclusions about the entire freshman class. Accordingly, he should draw a fair sample of such persons. The ready-made sample is a very special sample, composed only of students who made either outstandingly good or outstandingly bad records. It is appropriate only if one wants to draw conclusions about a population so constituted.

10.5 SHAPE OF THE DISTRIBUTIONS AND THE CORRELATION COEFFICIENT

If the correlation coefficient is to be calculated purely as a descriptive measure, nothing need be assumed about the shape of the distribution of X or Y. In particular, there is no requirement that the distributions be normal. However, two points must be mentioned concerning distribution shape. First, if one or both distributions are skewed, they may also be curvilinearly related. Therefore when the distributions are not symmetrical, it is particularly desirable to examine the data with an eye to the correctness of the linear hypothesis.

Second, obtaining the coefficient is often only the first step in analysis. When additional steps are undertaken, the assumption frequently must be made that X and Y are normally distributed. For example, this assumption is needed in making inferences about the population value of the coefficient (chapter 20) and in establishing limits of error in prediction (chapter 11).

10.6 RANDOM VARIATION AND THE CORRELATION COEFFICIENT

Sometimes we are interested only in describing how things are in the particular group of observations under study; in this case the correlation coefficient obtained with that group is exactly what we want to know. Most often, however, interest is in a population, but only a sample is available for study. The industrial psychologist is interested in how well job performance can be predicted from an aptitude test for employees-in-general of the type studied rather than for the specific workers with whom the correlation between these two variables was obtained. Another psychologist wants to know what relation exists between intensity of emotional feeling and pulse rate among people-in-general, and not solely among the 50 subjects he has studied.

In these circumstances, we want to make an inference about the state of affairs in the population from knowledge of the state of affairs in the sample. Like all statistics, the value of r varies from sample to sample, depending on the chance factors associated with selection of the particular sample. Suppose that for all eighth grade pupils in a large city, the correlation is $+.45$ between achievement test scores in history and mathematics. If by random selection we choose 35 of these students and obtain the correlation between these two measures, its value may be, say, $+.30$. Another sample selected in the same way may yield a value of $+.53$, and a third sample still a different value.

How to make appropriate inferences about conditions in the population from evidence obtained with a sample is a very important problem, but adequate consideration of it must be postponed until the principles and procedures of statistical inference are properly developed. This problem, with specific reference to correlation coefficients, is treated in chapter 20. Two general aspects of the question must be considered here.

The first point has already been made and is now summarized: when a coefficient has been obtained from a particular set of paired observations, it does not represent *the* correlation between the two variables; another sample will yield a somewhat different value. The second point concerns how big "somewhat" is. In general, large samples yield values of r that are similar from sample to sample, and thus the value obtained from a large sample will probably be close to the population value. For very small samples, r is quite unstable from sample to sample, and its value can not be depended upon to lie close to the population value. Table 10.1 illustrates this point. It shows, for selected sample sizes, the limits within which 80% of sample

Table 10.1 *Limits within Which 80% of Sample Values of r Will Fall when the True Correlation Is Zero*

Sample size	80% limits for r
5	−.69 to +.69
15	−.35 to +.35
25	−.26 to +.26
50	−.18 to +.18
100	−.13 to +.13
200	−.09 to +.09

coefficients will fall if the samples of that size are drawn at random from a population in which the true correlation is zero. Note, therefore, that 20% of such coefficients would actually fall *further* away from the "true" value than the points indicated by the limits. Note also that great variation characterizes the smaller sample sizes. Estimation of the degree of association from study of a sample is really not very satisfactory unless *n* is large enough to produce reasonably stable results.

10.7 THE CORRELATION COEFFICIENT AND THE CIRCUMSTANCES UNDER WHICH IT WAS OBTAINED

The influence of random sampling variation is but one reason why the obtained correlation coefficient is not *the* coefficient between the two variables under study. Consider the correlation between intelligence and achievement in a mathematics course. The extent of the relationship may depend on a variety of moderating circumstances. It may differ depending on the specific measures of "intelligence" and "achievement" that are used,† it may differ among fourth-grade pupils as compared with those in the eighth grade, it may differ among students from middle-class families as compared with those from economically deprived families or among children who are bilingual, and it may differ for students learning in an atmosphere of anxiety as compared with those operating in a more normal learning situation.

Suppose that, in a given industrial plant, score on a mechanical aptitude test correlates to the extent of +.45 with measures of job proficiency of assembly

---

† See Section 8.1.

workers. The test would be useful in selecting assembly workers. However, it is quite possible that the nature of the job will change substantially over a period of five years or so; worker characteristics required for success on the job may then be different. The mechanical aptitude test may then no longer satisfactorily predict job success, despite the fact that the job title is the same. It is all too easy to think that "the correlation between mechanical aptitude and job performance *is* +.45 for assembly workers in factory X." Obviously, what is needed is a periodic review to ascertain whether the fundamental situation has sufficiently changed so that a restudy is in order.

The degree of association between two variables depends (1) on the specific measure taken for each of the two variables, (2) on the kinds of subjects used for the investigation, and (3) on the particular circumstances under which the variables are operative. If any of these factors changes over time, the extent of the association may also change. Consequently, it is of utmost importance that a correlation coefficient be interpreted in the light of the particular conditions by which it was obtained. Any report of research, therefore, should include a careful description of the measures used and the circumstances under which the coefficients were obtained. Similarly, research results reported by others may or may not be directly applicable to the circumstances with which you are concerned. Such results should be taken only as a working hypothesis, subject to confirmation under the present circumstances.

10.8 OTHER FACTORS INFLUENCING THE CORRELATION COEFFICIENT

Two important factors that influence the magnitude of the correlation coefficient remain to be discussed: *range of talent* and *heterogeneity of samples*. Their influence can best be understood after the development of certain concepts. Since these concepts will be presented in chapter 11, consideration of these two factors is deferred until the beginning of chapter 12 (see Sections 12.1 and 12.2).

PROBLEMS AND EXERCISES

Identify:

linearity of regression   discontinuous distribution
homoscedasticity   "hugging principle"

1 In one transit company, the correlation between frequency of accidents and age of the bus drivers was $r = -.50$. It was recommended that the transit company try to hire older men for the job. Identify several factors that might suggest caution in adopting this recommendation.

2 Among a group of children selected at random from an elementary school, the correlation between strength of grip and score on an arithmetic achievement test was $r = +.65$. The study was repeated on a group of college seniors, and r was found to be $+.10$. Assuming both are representative findings, what is the likely explanation?

3 Given the following 20 pairs of scores:

Pair	X	Y	Pair	X	Y	Pair	X	Y
1	79	51	8	86	45	15	89	39
2	77	47	9	81	45	16	89	44
3	74	49	10	80	48	17	92	38
4	58	37	11	63	39	18	82	49
5	58	40	12	87	47	19	90	42
6	85	42	13	60	37	20	62	42
7	65	40	14	75	46			

(a) The bivariate distribution formed by these 20 pairs of scores exhibits two interesting features. Can you guess what they are from inspection of the above data? (b) On graph paper, plot the 20 points indicated by the pairs of scores. What two features appear? Would these be likely to affect the value of Pearson r? Explain.

4 Given the following 20 pairs of scores:

Pair	X	Y	Pair	X	Y	Pair	X	Y
1	64	45	8	85	71	15	62	45
2	63	43	9	83	62	16	71	47
3	66	50	10	56	38	17	59	39
4	66	44	11	62	42	18	70	57
5	63	47	12	60	42	19	77	67
6	73	50	13	79	52	20	89	56
7	60	41	14	58	41			

(a) The bivariate distribution formed by these 20 pairs of scores exhibits two interesting features. Can you guess what they are from inspection of the data above? (b) On graph paper, plot the 20 points indicated by the pairs of scores. What two features appear? Which one is more important for understanding the strength of the relationship? Explain.

5 A statistics instructor has a class of 30 students, half male and half female. Among the males, the correlation between aptitude score and achievement in statistics is found to be $r = +.50$; among the females, the correlation is $r = +.35$. One observer suggests that apparently the relationship is different among men than among women. Any objection?

6 The personnel director for Company A often has lunch with the personnel director for Company B. This noon, she mentions that they are having trouble selecting good

assembly workers. Her friend replies that they have had great luck with Aptitude Test X, and that the correlation, established on 400 of their assembly workers, is $+.60$ between test score and job performance. Have you any caution to offer Company A's director before she rushes out to adopt the test as a selective device?

7 In one company the correlation between units produced and score on a manual dexterity test is $+.60$. In a second company, the same two variables are essentially uncorrelated. Cite some factors that could account for this.

CHAPTER 11

11.1 THE PROBLEM OF PREDICTION

There is a substantial positive correlation between stature and weight. Therefore, if a man is tall, we expect that his weight will be above average. In general, if two variables are correlated, it is possible to predict, with better than chance accuracy, standing in one of them from knowledge of standing in the other. We know that when the correlation coefficient is zero, knowledge of X is of no help in predicting Y, and if the coefficient is ± 1, we can predict Y with perfect accuracy. Clearly, the degree of correlation is indicative of the predictive possibilities, yet knowing the value of the coefficient, by itself, does not tell us how to make the prediction.

Consider the bivariate distribution pictured in Figure 11.1. Suppose we wish to

Regression and Prediction

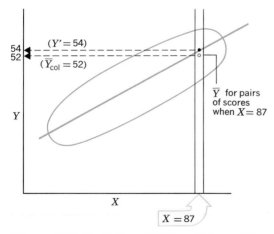

Figure 11.1 *Prediction of Y from Column Mean and from Line of Best Fit.*

predict the value of Y which might be expected if X is 87. Taking the simplest possible approach to prediction, we could erect a column at the location of that value of X and inquire as to the mean Y value of each of the points falling within the borders of the column. As shown in Figure 11.1, this would lead us to take $Y = 52$ as the predicted Y for those scoring 87 in X.

This method of prediction is satisfactory, but it has one handicap. This prediction is based *only* on the Y values of those scores falling in the particular column, a rather small number of cases. Other values of paired scores are ignored. As might be expected, predictions based on a small number of cases tend to be unstable, since another sample from the population of paired scores may yield different values in the particular column. If we follow this method, considerable instability attributable to random sampling fluctuation will be encountered.

How can the situation be improved? We note that for the data indicated, the hypothesis that X and Y are linearly related appears to be reasonable.† It is therefore possible to find the straight line of best fit to the Y values, a line determined by *all* of the scores in the bivariate distribution. Such a line is called a *regression line* and its equation a *regression equation*. *The prediction may then be made by noting the Y value of the point on the line that corresponds to the particular value of X.* Figure 11.1 shows that, following this procedure, the predicted value of Y (which we shall call Y') is 54 when X is 87. Prediction made in the simpler way (first described) would be better if one were concerned only with the present set of paired scores, i.e. if this set of points constituted the population of paired values. However, in this case "prediction" would have little meaning, since we would *know* the Y value for each X. When the data are only a sample of the larger population of interest (the usual situation), sampling fluctuation must be taken into account, and a prediction more resistant to this factor is obviously preferable. A prediction made by taking into account *all* the data is therefore a superior solution to the problem.

Two limitations still remain. First, the straight line fitted to the sample is probably not quite the same as the straight line that would be obtained if the population were available for study. Other things being equal, the larger the sample, the closer the approximation. Second, the adequacy of the procedure depends on the assumption that a straight line *is* a reasonable description of the interrelationship of X and Y. Fortunately, the linear hypothesis is often satisfactory; inspection of the scatter diagram is useful in checking possible exceptions. The present chapter will deal only with situations in which a linear relation between X and Y is a reasonable assumption.

† The hypothesis of linearity states that the line best describing the relationship between X and Y is a straight line. See Section 10.2.

11.2 THE CRITERION OF BEST FIT

It is all very well to speak of finding the straight line of best fit to the data, but how is one to know when the "best fit" has been achieved? Indeed, "best fit" could be defined in more than one (reasonable) way. Karl Pearson's solution to this problem was to apply the *least-squares criterion*. Let us consider the problem of predicting Y from X. Figure 11.2 shows a bivariate distribution in which the discrepancy between each actual value of Y and Y', its corresponding predicted value as determined by the regression line, is indicated by the symbol d. The least-squares criterion calls for the straight line to be laid down in such a manner that the sum of the squares of these discrepancies is as small as possible ($\Sigma d_y{}^2$ is a minimum value).

At first, the notion of minimizing the sum of the *squares* of the discrepancies seems to be an undue complication. Why not minimize the sum of the absolute magnitudes of the discrepancies rather than their squares? The answer has two parts: (1) it is very difficult to deal mathematically with the absolute discrepancies, whereas the treatment of squared discrepancies opens the way to mathematical developments that are of practical value in interpreting the regression equation, and (2) desirable statistical properties follow from using the least-squares criterion. One important property of the least-squares solution is that *the location of the regression lines and the value of the correlation coefficient will fluctuate less under the influence*

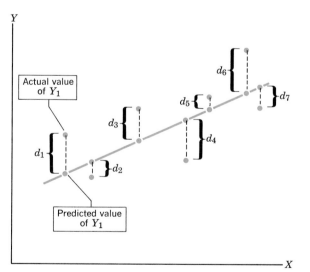

Figure 11.2 *Discrepancies between Y Values and the Line of Regression of Y on X.*

of random sampling than would occur if another criterion were used. In short, these values are more stably determined.

You may be thinking that this is not the first time that we have dealt with the sum of squared discrepancies, and that, indeed, one property of the mean is that the sum of the squares of the deviations of the scores from the mean is a minimum (Σx^2 is a minimum; see Section 6.10). Is there some connection between these facts and the current issues concerning correlation?

First, just as the regression line is a least-squares solution to the problem of the straight line of best fit, so the mean is a least-squares solution to the problem of finding a measure of central tendency. Both are chosen so as to minimize the sum of squares of discrepancies. It may be expected, therefore, that both will have analogous properties. Indeed, we note that resistance to the influence of sampling fluctuation characterizes them both.

Second, the regression line may actually be thought of as a kind of mean. One way to think of it is as a "running mean," a line that tells us the mean, or expected value of Y, for a particular value of X. In other words, $\overline{Y}$ is the mean of *all Y* values in the set, whereas Y' (Y predicted from the regression line) is an estimate of the mean of Y *given the condition that X has a particular value.*

Paradoxically, there is *another* straight line of best fit. If one wished to predict X from knowledge of Y, rather than the other way around, the least-squares criterion would be applied to minimize discrepancies in X [$\Sigma(X - X')^2$] rather than those in Y [$\Sigma(Y - Y')^2$]. Unless $r = \pm 1.00$, the two lines thus determined will not be

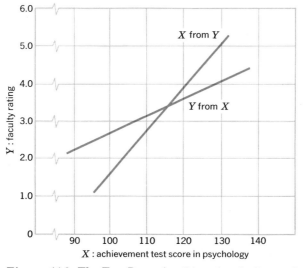

Figure 11.3 *The Two Regression Lines for the Data of Table 9.4.*

the same. Figure 11.3 shows the two regression lines for the data of Table 9.4 (chapter 9), where $r = +.65$.

In practical work in prediction, interest is in predicting in *one* direction, not both directions. Therefore, *it is always possible to define the variable to be predicted as Y and the variable used to make the prediction as X.* Consequently, it will suffice to discuss only the prediction of Y from X.

11.3 THE REGRESSION EQUATION: STANDARD SCORE FORM

The regression equation for predicting Y from X is, in standard score form:

Regression of Y on X:
Standard Score Formula
$$z'_Y = rz_X \qquad\qquad (11.1)$$

where:

z'_Y is the predicted standard score value of Y

r is the coefficient of correlation between X and Y

z_X is the standard score value of X from which z'_Y is predicted

Note the title of this equation; it is customary to speak of the regression of Y *on* X when we mean to say that the equation is appropriate for predicting Y from knowledge of X. This equation is seldom used in practical prediction, because the scores from which prediction is made are usually in raw score form. However, the equation is simple enough that studying it is instructive.

First, suppose the value from which prediction was made was the mean of X. Since the z-score equivalent of the mean is zero, the predicted standard score value of Y is

$$z'_Y = (r)(0) = 0,$$

or in other words, the mean of Y. We see that the prediction will be the same, irrespective of the value of r, so the regression line will always pass through the point defined by the mean of X and the mean of Y. This is illustrated in Part A of Figure 11.4.

Second, if $r = 0$, then the predicted standard score value of Y will always be zero. In raw score terms, *if the correlation is zero, the predicted value of Y is the mean of Y no matter what value of X is used to predict Y.* The implications are both interesting and logical. If knowing the value of X affords no advantage in predicting Y, what value of Y shall we predict? The mean of Y is not only an intuitively reasonable prediction, but it satisfies the least-squares criterion; the sum of the squares of errors of prediction will be minimized. Part B of Figure 11.4 shows the line of regression of Y on X when $r = 0$.

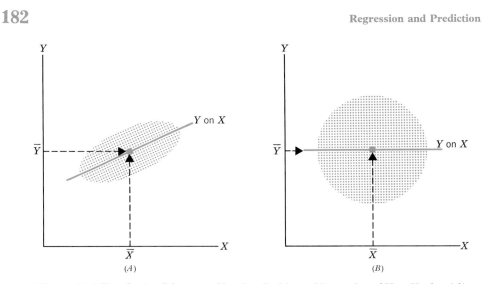

Figure 11.4 *Two Scatter Diagrams, Showing the Lines of Regression of Y on X when (A)* $r > 0$, *(B)* $r = 0$. *Note that Both Regression Lines Pass Through the Point* $X = \bar{X}$, $Y = \bar{Y}$.

Further study of the standard score form of the regression equation can reveal still more about interpretive aspects of association and prediction. This topic is taken up again in the next chapter (Sections 12.3 and 12.4).

11.4 THE REGRESSION EQUATION: RAW SCORE FORM

Although the standard score formula helps us to understand some of the characteristics of the straight line of best fit, most practical problems in prediction are couched in terms of raw scores rather than standard scores. The raw score formula for the regression of Y on X will therefore be more useful in this context. It can be developed from the defining standard score formula. First, replace z scores with their raw score equivalents:

$$\frac{Y' - \bar{Y}}{S_Y} = r\frac{X - \bar{X}}{S_X}$$

Then, if this equation is solved for Y', we have the raw score formula of the regression equation:

Regression of Y on X:
Raw Score Formula
$$Y' = \left(r\frac{S_Y}{S_X}\right)X - \left(r\frac{S_Y}{S_X}\right)\bar{X} + \bar{Y} \qquad (11.2)$$

where: Y' is the predicted raw score in Y
S_X and S_Y are the two standard deviations

$\bar{X}$ and $\bar{Y}$ are the two means

r is the correlation coefficient between X and Y.

The formula looks more complicated than it really is. To predict Y, we need to know the value of X from which the particular prediction is to be made, the two means, the two standard deviations, and the value of the correlation coefficient. Application of the formula for a problem in prediction is shown below. The data are from Table 9.4 and concern the interrelation between achievement score and faculty rating.

Given: Y: faculty rating; X: achievement test score

$$\begin{array}{ll} \bar{X} = 115.6 & \bar{Y} = 3.48 \\ S_X = 11.9 & S_Y = .85 \end{array} \quad r = +.65$$

Problem: John earns a test score of 130. What rating do we predict for him?

Solution: 1. Because rating is to be predicted from test score, assign Y as the symbol for rating and X for test score. Insert the means, standard deviations, and the correlation coefficient in the raw score equation and simplify it:

$$Y' = \left(r\frac{S_Y}{S_X}\right)X - \left(r\frac{S_Y}{S_X}\right)\bar{X} + \bar{Y}$$

$$= (.65)\left(\frac{.85}{11.9}\right)X - (.65)\left(\frac{.85}{11.9}\right)(115.6) + 3.48$$

$$= .0464X - 1.89$$

2. Insert the value of X from which the prediction is to be made, and find the predicted value of Y:

$$Y' = .0464X - 1.89$$
$$= (.0464)(130) - 1.89$$
$$= 4.14$$

Note that the particular value of X from which Y is to be predicted has not been inserted until the equation has first been simplified. This is particularly desirable if more than one prediction is to be made, as is usually the case. For example, if we now wish to predict Y when $X = 100$, it is possible to insert that value of X in the formula $Y' = .0456X - 1.82$, whereas if the equation were not first reduced to its simplest form, one would have to back up to an earlier point in the calculation before inserting the new value of X, and the ensuing series of calculations would be more of a nuisance.

Since the regression equation is a straight line, it is easy to make a graph of the equation and then to read the graph to make predictions from various values of X. Section A.9 in Appendix A explains how to graph a straight line. A graph of the regression equation illustrated above is shown in Figure 11.5, together with the prediction for John.

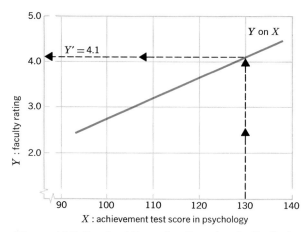

Figure 11.5 *Graph of Regression Equation for Predicting Faculty Rating (Y) from Achievement Test Score (X): Data from Section 11.4.*

11.5 ERROR OF PREDICTION: THE STANDARD ERROR OF ESTIMATE

The regression equation states what value of Y is expected (Y') when X has a particular value. Of course, Y' is not likely to be the *actual* value of Y that corresponds to the particular X. If a man is six feet tall, the appropriate regression equation may predict his weight to be 175 lb, but we do not expect a given six-footer to have exactly that weight. *The predicted value is only an estimate of mean value of weights of persons who are that height,* a "best estimate" of the person's weight. If the correlation is low, considerable variation of actual values about the predicted value may be expected. If the correlation is high, the actual values will cluster more closely about the predicted value. Figure 10.2 (in the last chapter) illustrates this. *Only when the correlation is unity will the actual values regularly and precisely equal the predicted values.*

What is needed is a way to measure the predictive error, the variability of the actual Y values about the predicted value (Y'). Such a measure would have desirable properties if it were cast in the form of a standard deviation (see Chapter 6). The *standard error of estimate*, S_{YX}, is exactly that kind of measure; its formula (with, for comparison, that of the standard deviation) is presented below.

Standard Deviation $$S_Y = \sqrt{\frac{\sum(Y - \bar{Y})^2}{n}}$$

Standard Error of
Estimate of Y on X
$$S_{YX} = \sqrt{\frac{\sum (Y - Y')^2}{n}} \qquad (11.3)$$

Figure 11.6 illustrates the discrepancies, $(Y - Y')$, on which Formula 11.3 is based. These are the same values we called "d_Y" in Section 11.2, and illustrated in Figure 11.2.

    The standard error of estimate is a kind of standard deviation: it is the standard deviation of the distribution of obtained Y scores about the predicted Y score. There is another way to look at this quantity. Suppose that for each value of X, we record the discrepancy between the actual value of Y and the value of Y predicted by the regression equation: $(Y - Y')$. This set of values may be thought of as the set of predictive errors. If the standard deviation of this set is then calculated, its value will be exactly S_{YX} (Note 11.2 at the chapter's end gives proof of this proposition). S_{YX} is therefore a measure of the magnitude of errors of prediction.

    When the correlation is perfect, every value of $(Y - Y')$ is zero, and therefore

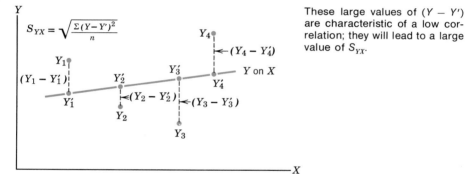

These large values of $(Y - Y')$ are characteristic of a low correlation; they will lead to a large value of S_{YX}.

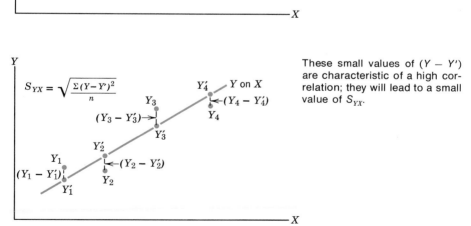

These small values of $(Y - Y')$ are characteristic of a high correlation; they will lead to a small value of S_{YX}.

Figure 11.6 *The Standard Error of Estimate (S_{YX}) as a Function of the Magnitude of the $(Y - Y')$ Discrepancies.*

S_{YX} is zero. In short, there is *no* error of prediction. When the correlation is zero, $Y' = \bar{Y}$ for all values of X. We may therefore substitute $\bar{Y}$ for Y' in Formula 11.3, and it becomes $\sqrt{\Sigma(Y - \bar{Y})^2/n}$, or S_Y. *The value of S_{YX} therefore ranges from zero when the correlation is perfect to S_Y when there is no correlation at all.* Table 11.1 shows the calculation of S_Y and S_{YX} for data taken from Table 9.2. The first two columns present the paired raw scores. Columns 3 and 4 contain the values needed for the calculation of S_Y. Column 5 presents the value of Y predicted by the regression equation from each value of X. Columns 6 and 7 contain the values needed for the calculation of S_{YX}. For these data, the correlation coefficient is $+.74$. As expected from the foregoing discussion, the value $S_{YX} = 3.2$ is less than that of $S_Y = 4.8$ but greater than zero.

Is S_{YX} really a standard deviation? Formula 11.3 looks very much like the formula for the standard deviation. In fact, the form of the equations for S_Y and S_{YX} are the same, except that Y' (rather than $\bar{Y}$) has been subtracted from each score in calculating S_{YX}. However, Y' is indeed a kind of mean (Section 11.2); it is the estimated mean of Y when X has a particular value. S_{YX} is therefore a genuine standard deviation.

If S_{YX} is really a standard deviation, it should have the properties of one. One such property is that the sum of the squares of the deviations of each score from the

Table 11.1 *Calculation of S_Y and S_{YX}: Data from Table 9.2*

(1) X	(2) Y	(3) $(Y - \bar{Y})$	(4) $(Y - \bar{Y})^2$	(5) Y'	(6) $(Y - Y')$	(7) $(Y - Y')^2$
37	75	-2.6	6.8	76.8	-1.8	3.2
41	78	$+.4$	.2	79.4	-1.4	2.0
48	88	$+10.4$	108.2	84.1	$+3.9$	15.2
32	80	$+2.4$	5.8	73.4	$+6.6$	43.6
36	78	$+.4$	.2	76.1	$+1.9$	3.6
30	71	-6.6	43.6	72.1	-1.1	1.2
40	75	-2.6	6.8	78.8	-3.8	14.4
45	83	$+5.4$	29.2	82.1	$+.9$	.8
39	74	-3.6	13.0	78.1	-4.1	16.8
34	74	-3.6	13.0	74.8	$-.8$	.6
Σ 382	776	0	227	776	0	101
Σ/n 38.2	77.6	0	22.7	77.6	0	10.1

$$S_Y = \sqrt{\frac{\sum(Y - \bar{Y})^2}{n}} \qquad S_{YX} = \sqrt{\frac{\sum(Y - Y')^2}{n}}$$

$$= \sqrt{22.7} \qquad\qquad = \sqrt{10.1}$$

$$= 4.8 \qquad\qquad\quad = 3.2$$

mean is a minimum (Section 6.10). Indeed, this is precisely the way in which the regression line is laid down. It is to be so located that the sum of the squares of the discrepancies between each value of Y and the corresponding value of Y' given by the regression line, $\Sigma(Y - Y')^2$, is minimized. A second property of the standard deviation is that the sum of the deviations of each score from the mean of the scores must be zero (Section 5.7). Consider the third and sixth columns in Table 11.1. The quantity $\Sigma(Y - Y')$ is zero, just as $\Sigma(Y - \bar{Y})$ is zero. Note 11.1 shows this property to be a general one, and not just an accident.

11.6 AN ALTERNATE (AND PREFERRED) FORMULA FOR S_{YX}

The formula given in the previous section for the standard error of estimate, $S_{YX} = \sqrt{\Sigma(Y - Y')^2/n}$, is in a form more convenient for studying the nature of the statistic than it is for actual work in prediction. For this purpose, it is better to use Formula 11.4.

Standard Error of Estimate of Y on X
$$S_{YX} = S_Y \sqrt{1 - r^2} \qquad (11.4)$$

It can be shown that Formula 11.4 is the exact algebraic equivalent of Formula 11.3. Note, for example, that if $r = 0$, $S_{YX} = S_Y$, and that if $r = \pm 1$, $S_{YX} = 0$. In the previous section, calculation of S_{YX} by Formula 11.3 was illustrated in Table 11.1. The value is the same if recalculated by Formula 11.4:
$$S_{YX} = 4.8 \sqrt{1 - (.74)^2} = 3.2.$$

11.7 ERROR IN ESTIMATING Y FROM X

From earlier study of the standard deviation, we learned certain useful facts that applied when confronted with a normal distribution. For example, in a normal distribution:

> 68% of scores fall within the limits: $\bar{X} \pm 1S$
> 95% of scores fall within the limits: $\bar{X} \pm 1.96S$
> 99% of scores fall within the limits: $\bar{X} \pm 2.58S$

These values can be easily verified by consulting Table C in Appendix F.

Since the standard error of estimate is a kind of standard deviation, the same kind of interpretation can be made if it is reasonable to assume that the obtained scores are normally distributed about the predicted scores, and that variability of Y about Y' is similar for all values of Y'. Thus,

68% of obtained Y values fall within the limits: $Y' \pm 1S_{YX}$
95% of obtained Y values fall within the limits: $Y' \pm 1.96S_{YX}$
99% of obtained Y values fall within the limits: $Y' \pm 2.58S_{YX}$

This type of interpretation is illustrated in Figure 11.7. One part of the picture shows schematically the limits within which 95% of obtained Y values would be expected to fall when predicting Y from a low value of X. The other shows the limits resulting from a prediction made from a higher value of X.

Specific application is best shown in a concrete example. The examples presented below illustrate the solution of two types of problems that may arise. It may be helpful to review Sections 7.6, 7.7, and 7.8, since the procedures described there are needed to solve the problems presented here.

Given: $\bar{X} = 80$ $\bar{Y} = 100$ $r = +.60$
            $S_X = 10$ $S_Y = 20$

Problems: 1. For those who score 90 in X, what proportion may be expected to score 120 or better in Y? 2. For those who score 90 in X, within what central limits

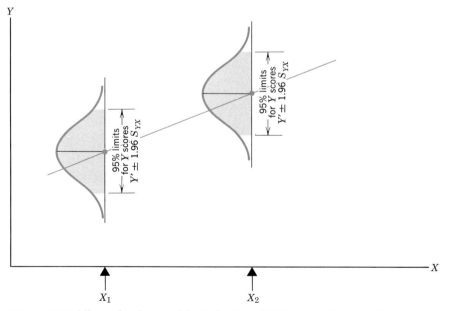

Figure 11.7 *Ninety-five Percent Limits for Actual Y Scores of Subjects Scoring at Particular Levels in X.*

may we expect 50% of their Y scores to fall? (These two problems are illustrated in Figure 11.8.)

Solutions: For both problems, the first step is to find the predicted value of Y.

$$Y' = \left(r\frac{S_Y}{S_X}\right)X - \left(r\frac{S_Y}{S_X}\right)\bar{X} + \bar{Y}$$
$$= (+.60)\left(\frac{20}{10}\right)X - (+.60)\left(\frac{20}{10}\right)(80) + 100$$
$$= 1.20X + 4.00$$

For $X = 90$, we have

$$Y' = (1.20)(90) + 4.00$$
$$= 112.00$$

Next, S_{YX} is calculated.

$$S_{YX} = S_Y\sqrt{1 - r^2}$$
$$= 20\sqrt{1 - (.60)^2}$$
$$= 16.00$$

Solution to Problem 1. As Figure 11.8 shows, the problem is to find, in the distribution of obtained Y scores for those who score 90 in X, the proportion of Y scores that exceed 120. We take the mean of this distribution to be 112 (the value of Y') and the standard deviation to be 16 (the value of S_{YX}). The problem now becomes one of the type described in Section 7.7. We must therefore translate the

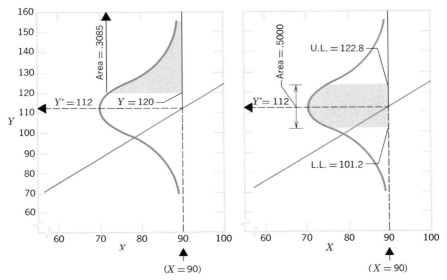

Figure 11.8 *Estimation of Predictive Error.*

score of 120 to z-score terms, and find the area that would lie above this point in a normal curve. Remembering that a z score is *(score − mean)/(standard deviation)*, we have:

$$z = \frac{Y_{obt} - Y'}{S_{YX}}$$
$$= \frac{120 - 112}{16}$$
$$= +.50$$

Consulting Table B in Appendix F, we find that .3085 of the cases will fall beyond a z of +.50 in a normal distribution (see Figure 11.8). This is the answer to the problem: For those who score 90 in X, 31 per cent may be expected to have Y scores of 120 or better.

Solution to Problem 2. The second problem is also concerned with the distribution of obtained Y scores for those who score 90 in X, a distribution in which the mean (Y') is 112, and the standard deviation (S_{YX}) is 16. Since we are after the boundaries that enclose the central 50% of cases, the points desired are therefore those in the normal curve beyond which .25 of the cases fall. Table C in Appendix F shows these points to be:

$$\text{Upper Limit: } z = +.6745$$
$$\text{Lower Limit: } z = -.6745$$

Translating these limits to raw score values,

$$Y = (z)(\text{standard deviation}) + (\text{mean})$$
$$\text{Upper Limit: } Y_{UL} = (+.6745)(16) + 112$$
$$= 122.8$$
$$\text{Lower Limit: } Y_{LL} = (-.6745)(16) + 112$$
$$= 101.2$$

Procedures of the kind illustrated above may be useful in various practical situations. For example, a university admissions officer may wish to predict the likelihood of academic success (as defined by achieving a given grade point average or better) for those who score at a given level on the institution's scholastic aptitude test. Using the procedures illustrated above, that official may find, say, that 65% of students who make the particular score on the aptitude test may be expected to earn a grade point average of 2.5 or better. Similarly, a personnel officer for an industrial organization might use this procedure to estimate the percentage of applicants who would succeed on the job when they score at a given level on a selection test. Information of this kind would also be useful in counseling.

11.8 CAUTIONS CONCERNING ESTIMATION OF PREDICTIVE ERROR

Correct application of the procedures described in the preceding section requires that several assumptions be satisfied. First, the regression equation was used to obtain the predicted value of Y; we must assume that a straight line *is* the line of best fit, or this predicted value may be too high or low. The first picture in Figure 11.9 shows that, with these curvilinearly related data, the straight line of best fit will make the right prediction for Y from X for only two values of X. For other values, Y' will underestimate or overestimate the correct value.

Second, S_{YX} is taken as the standard deviation of the distribution of obtained Y scores about Y', *irrespective of the value of X from which the prediction has been made.* It is therefore necessary to assume that variability is the same from column to column (the assumption of homoscedasticity; see Section 10.3). The formula, $S_{YX} = \sqrt{\Sigma(Y - Y')^2/n}$, shows that S_{YX} is a function of the *average* magnitude of the squared discrepancies between each Y value and Y'. If the data are like those pictured in the second part of Figure 11.9, S_{YX} will approximate the standard deviation of Y values when X is at an intermediate level but will overestimate error of prediction in Y when X is low, and will underestimate it when X is high.

Third, the procedures of the previous section depend on the assumption that the distribution of obtained Y scores (for a particular value of X) is normal. Remember that the obtained value of z was taken to the table of areas under the *normal* curve in order to find the proportion of cases expected to fall above or below the value of z.

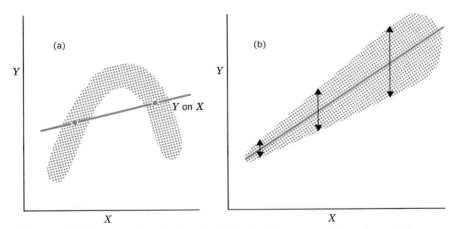

Figure 11.9 *Bivariate Distributions in Which the Properties of Linearity and Homoscedasticity Do Not Hold.*

The assumptions listed above must sound formidable. Fortunately, there are numerous occasions on which it is reasonable to assume that these conditions are sufficiently closely approximated that an estimate of predictive error made by the procedures of Section 11.7 is sensible. One hopes that it is not too much of a blow to add one more warning.

Procedures of Section 11.7 do not take into account the influence of random sampling variation. Since in any realistic prediction situation we are not dealing with the population of paired scores (why predict if you know?), but with a sample from that population, the "true" correlation coefficient, regression line, and standard error of estimate will probably differ somewhat from those characterizing the sample with which we are confronted. More sophisticated approaches that take this factor into account may be found in texts such as that by Hays.† We cannot pursue them here, because they require an understanding of statistical inference that has yet to be developed in this book. However, a certain kind of comfort can be offered: if the assumptions listed above hold for the *population* of paired values, and if sample size is reasonably large, the procedures here described will yield results close to those resulting from application of the more advanced procedures.

As might be expected, taking account of the additional variability attributable to sampling fluctuation will increase the width of the limits within which the actual values may be expected to be found. If sample size is 100, the more accurate procedures will yield limits for Problem 2 of the previous section that range from about 3% to 7% greater, depending on whether the value of X from which the prediction is made is centrally located or in the outer limits of the distribution. If sample size is greater than 100, the amount of error will be less. Suffice it to say that prediction and estimating error of prediction are best made when sample size is large enough to reduce the margin of error to a tolerable amount. One hundred cases is really rather small for this purpose.

NOTES

Note 11.1   Sum of the Deviations of Scores about Their Predicted Values (*Ref:* Section 11.5)

Substituting the raw score equivalent of Y' (from Formula 11.2) in the expression $\Sigma(Y - Y')$, we have:

$$\sum(Y - Y') = \sum\left[Y - \left(r\frac{S_Y}{S_Y}\right)X + \left(r\frac{S_Y}{S_X}\right)\bar{X} - \bar{Y}\right]$$

$$= \sum\left[(Y - \bar{Y}) - \left(r\frac{S_Y}{S_X}\right)(X - \bar{X})\right]$$

†W. L. Hays, *Statistics for the Social Sciences,* 2nd ed., Holt, Rinehart, and Winston, Inc., New York, 1973, chapter 15.

$$= \sum(Y - \bar{Y}) - r\frac{S_Y}{S_X}\sum(X - \bar{X})$$

Since $\Sigma(Y - \bar{Y}) = 0$ and $\Sigma(X - \bar{X}) = 0$ (See Note 5.2), $\Sigma(Y - Y') = 0$.

Note 11.2 S_{YX} as the Standard Deviation of the Errors of Prediction (*Ref:* Section 11.5)
Define $(Y - Y')$ as an error of prediction. Then:

$$S_{Y-Y'} = \sqrt{\frac{\sum[(Y - Y') - \overline{Y - Y'}]^2}{n}}$$

From Note 11.1, $\Sigma(Y - Y') = 0$, so $\overline{Y - Y'} = 0$, and

$$S_{Y-Y'} = \sqrt{\frac{\sum[Y - Y']^2}{n}}$$

$$= S_{YX} \text{ (Formula 11.3)}$$

PROBLEMS AND EXERCISES

Identify:

regression equation	error of prediction
least-squares criterion	hypothesis of linearity
regression of Y on X	homoscedasticity
regression of X on Y	z'_Y, Y'
standard error of estimate	S_{YX}

1 Under what two circumstances is prediction of Y from X better made from the linear regression equation than from the mean of the Y column corresponding to the particular value of X?

2 Identify two advantages of using the least-squares criterion of "best fit."

3 The following data are for freshman students at Spartan University:

Aptitude score: X Freshman grade point average (gpa): Y
$$\bar{X} = 560 \qquad\qquad \bar{Y} = 2.65$$
$$S_X = 75 \qquad\qquad S_Y = .35$$
$$r_{XY} = +.50$$

(*a*) Write the raw score regression equation for predicting Y from X and simplify it. (*b*) John and Will score 485 and 710, respectively, on the aptitude test. Predict the freshman gpa for each. (*c*) What assumption is necessary for this prediction to be valid? (*d*) What is the value of the standard error of estimate of Y on X? (*e*) For students whose aptitude score is the same as John's: 1. What proportion will be expected to obtain a gpa equal to the freshmen mean or better? 2. What proportion will be expected to obtain a gpa of 2.0 or below? 3. Within what central gpa limits will 95% of students with aptitude scores like John's be likely to be found? (*f*) For students whose aptitude score is the same as Will's: 1. What proportion will be expected to obtain a gpa equal to

2.5 or better? 2. What proportion will be expected to obtain a gpa of 3.0 or below? 3. Within what central gpa limits will 50% of students with aptitude scores like Will's be likely to be found? (g) What assumptions are necessary for the answers to 3(e) and 3(f) to be valid?

4 For the general data of Problem 3, write the regression equation of Y on X in z score form.

5 Given the following data: $\bar{X} = 50$, $S_X = 15$, $\bar{Y} = 100$, $S_Y = 20$, and $r_{XY} = +.70$, (a) Write the raw score regression equation for predicting Y on X and simplify it. (b) Mary and Alice score 60 and 30, respectively, in X. What Y score do we predict for each? (c) For persons whose X score is the same as Mary's: 1. What proportion will be expected to equal or exceed a score of 90 in Y? 2. What proportion will be expected to obtain a Y score of 100 or below? 3. Within what central limits will 99% of Y scores for such students be likely to be found? (d) For persons whose X score is the same as Alice's: 1. What proportion will be expected to equal or exceed a score of 90 in Y? 2. What proportion will be expected to obtain a Y score of 80 or below? 3. Within what central limits will 75% of Y scores of such students be likely to be found?

6 For the general data of problem 5, write the regression equation of Y on X in z score form.

7 Given the following data: $\bar{Y} = 50$, $S_Y = 10$, $\bar{X} = 150$, $S_X = 20$, $r = +.60$. For each of the following questions, use the standard score form of the regression equation to develop your answer, and try working the problems in your head: (a) Find z'_Y when $z_X = +2.00$. (b) Find Y' when $X = 190$. (c) Find Y' when $X = 170$. (d) Find Y' when $X = 130$. (e) Find Y' when $X = 110$. (f) Find Y' when $X = 150$.

8 If $r = 0$, then $Y' = \bar{Y}$, no matter what the value of X. What justification is there for such a prediction, aside from intuition?

9 If the regression equation of Y on X reads: $Y' = -.25X + 40$, (a) Could it be that the X and Y scores were expressed in z-score form? Explain. (b) Could it be that $r = 0$? Explain. (c) Is $r = -.25$? Explain.

CHAPTER 12

12.1 FACTORS INFLUENCING r: RANGE OF TALENT

The problem of range of talent is very important in understanding what a correlation coefficient means (or does not mean). First, let us lay a little groundwork.

According to Formula 11.4, $S_{YX} = S_Y \sqrt{1 - r^2}$. This equation can be solved for r:

Alternative Formula for r
$$r = \sqrt{1 - \frac{S_{YX}^2}{S_Y^2}}$$
(12.1)

This is not a practical formula for computing the correlation coefficient, but it is quite helpful in understanding the meaning of r. You will remember (Section 10.2) that it was contended that if the Y scores "hugged" the regression line closely, the correlation would be high, and if not, it would be low. We now have a

Interpretive Aspects of Correlation and Regression

more precise expression of this "hugging principle." Notice that *the magnitude of r is not solely a function of the size of S_{YX}*, the absolute measure of the variation of Y about the regression line, *but rather of the relative size of S_{YX} to S_Y.* If S_{YX} is zero, there is no error of prediction, and the correlation coefficient, according to Formula 12.1, is ± 1. On the other hand, if S_{YX} has the same value as S_Y, the

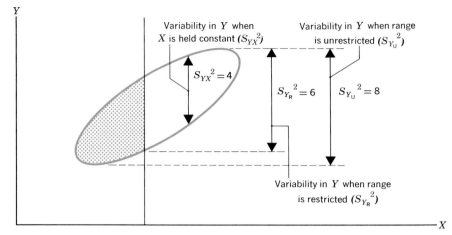

Figure 12.1 *Relation between S_{YX}^2 and S_Y^2 when Range of Talent Differs.*

correlation will be zero. It is of no consequence, therefore, to the determination of the degree of correlation, to state that the standard error of estimate "is small." What matters is whether it is small *in relation to S_Y*.

Figure 12.1 illustrates a bivariate distribution and shows the consequences of restriction of range. Imagine two situations: in the first, the range of X values is unrestricted and the bivariate distribution is represented by the entire oval in Figure 12.1; in the second, the scores to the left of the vertical line have been eliminated, and the bivariate distribution is represented only by that part of the oval that lies to the right of the vertical. It is clear that Y values would vary to a greater extent in the unrestricted situation. In line with this observation, let us suppose that $S_{Y_U}^2$, the variance of the Y scores in the unrestricted case, is 8, and $S_{Y_R}^2$, the variance of the Y scores in the restricted case, is 6.† Now chopping off the left side of the bivariate distribution shrinks the variability of Y, but if the assumption of homoscedasticity holds, S_{YX}^2, the variance of Y when X is held constant, *does not change*. We shall suppose that S_{YX}^2 is 4 for both the restricted and unrestricted situation. Let us calculate r by Formula 12.1 for both cases:

<table>
<tr><td align="center">Range of Talent
Unrestricted</td><td align="center">Range of Talent
Restricted</td></tr>
<tr><td align="center">$r = \sqrt{1 - \dfrac{S_{YX}^2}{S_{Y_U}^2}}$</td><td align="center">$r = \sqrt{1 - \dfrac{S_{YX}^2}{S_{Y_R}^2}}$</td></tr>
<tr><td align="center">$= \sqrt{1 - \dfrac{4}{8}}$</td><td align="center">$= \sqrt{1 - \dfrac{4}{6}}$</td></tr>
</table>

† Variance is the term used for the square of the standard deviation, S_Y^2 (see Section 6.5). It gets at the same basic characteristic as does the standard deviation—namely, variation in Y.

$$= \sqrt{\frac{1}{2}} \qquad\qquad = \sqrt{\frac{1}{3}}$$
$$= .71 \qquad\qquad = .58$$

To sum up, in moving from an unrestricted situation to a restricted one, S_Y^2 shrank, but S_{YX}^2 did not, so the ratio S_{YX}^2/S_Y^2 became larger and consequently r became smaller.

The immediate consequence of this knowledge is that the value of the correlation coefficient depends on the degree of variation characterizing the two variables as well as on the relationship present. It is common to find that the correlation coefficient between score on an academic aptitude test and academic achievement is highest among grade school children, lower among high school seniors, and still lower among college students. These differences may not so much indicate that something different is going on among the three groups as that the range of ability is greatest among the students in the lower grades and successively less as one progresses into the realms of higher education.

In a given situation, restriction of range may take place in X, in Y, or in both. The value of r will be smaller in those situations in which the range of either X or Y (or both) is less, other things being equal. This means that there is no such thing as *the* correlation between two variables, and that the value obtained must be interpreted in the light of the variability of the two variables in the circumstances in which it was obtained. *Other things being equal, the greater the restriction of range in X and/or Y, the lower the correlation coefficient.* When reporting a correlation coefficient, one should state the standard deviation of X and Y, so that others may judge whether the range of talent is similar to that with which they are concerned, or whether some allowance must be made.

It is possible to predict what the correlation will be in a situation characterized by a given degree of variability from knowledge of the correlation in a situation characterized by a different degree of variability. Guilford† offers a good discussion of this problem.

12.2 FACTORS INFLUENCING *r*: HETEROGENEITY OF SAMPLES

Section 10.7 cautioned that the correlation coefficient should be interpreted in terms of the circumstances under which it was obtained. Section 12.1 made one aspect of this warning explicit. Here is another.

Suppose Professor Haggerty, a natural science instructor, obtains the correlation

---

†J. P. Guilford, *Fundamental Statistics for Students of Psychology and Education*, 4th ed., McGraw-Hill Book Co., New York, 1965, pp. 341–345.

between academic aptitude test score and grade given in her course in natural science; let us say that it is $+.50$. She persuades Professor Eagan, a colleague of hers who also teaches the same course, to repeat the study in his class to verify the result. Professor Eagan does so and also finds the correlation to be $+.50$. In a moment of idle curiosity, Haggerty decides to pool the pairs of scores from the two classes and recalculate the correlation coefficient. She does so, and obtains a value of $+.30$! How could this be?

The answer lies in something well known to natural science students although perhaps inadequately appreciated by the instructors. The fact of the matter is that the first instructor is known as "Hard Nosed Haggerty," and the second as "Easy Aces Eagan." Professor Haggerty is a hard grader; once, 8 years ago, she had a student who she thought deserved an "A." Professor Eagan, on the other hand, thinks all students are wonderful, and rarely gives a grade below "C." Consequently, the scatter diagrams obtained from the two samples are like those shown in the first illustration of Figure 12.2. Note that the ability of the students appears to be about the same in the two classes (the X distributions), but the distributions of grades (the Y distributions) are not. The reason for the different correlation coefficient is that when the data are pooled, the scores no longer hug the regression line (which now must be a line lying amidst the two distributions) as closely as they do in either distribution considered by itself. In terms of our more recent knowledge, the ratio of S_{YX}^2 to S_Y^2 is smaller in either sample taken by itself than it is among the data when they are pooled.

In the particular case illustrated, the distributions differed, between samples, in the mean of Y but not in the mean of X. Other types of differences are quite possible. The second illustration in Figure 12.2 shows a situation in which a second sample differs in that *both* the mean of X and the mean of Y are higher than in the first sample. In this case, the fraction S_{YX}^2/S_Y^2 is *smaller* when the data are pooled

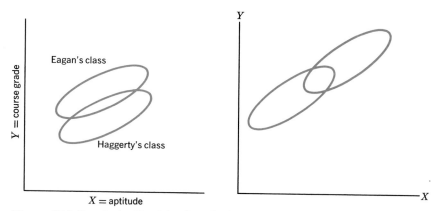

Figure 12.2 *Correlation Resulting from Pooling of Data from Heterogeneous Samples.*

than when each sample is considered separately, and the correlation will therefore be greater among the pooled data than among the separate samples.

12.3 INTERPRETATION OF *r*: THE REGRESSION EQUATION (I)

Earlier we observed that there was no simple way to interpret the meaning of the correlation coefficient; that, for example, it was not meaningful to say that a coefficient of +.50 indicates "50% association" between the two variables. In this section, we consider the first of several ways to interpret Pearson *r*. Others will appear in subsequent sections of this chapter.

The equation for any straight line can be put into the following form:

General Equation of a Straight Line
$$Y = bX + a \tag{12.2}$$

In this equation, *a* is a constant that identifies the point on the *Y* axis at which the line crosses it. It is known as the *Y intercept*. For the two lines in Figure 12.3, the equation of one is $Y = 3X - 4$ and the equation of the other is $Y = .25X + 2$.

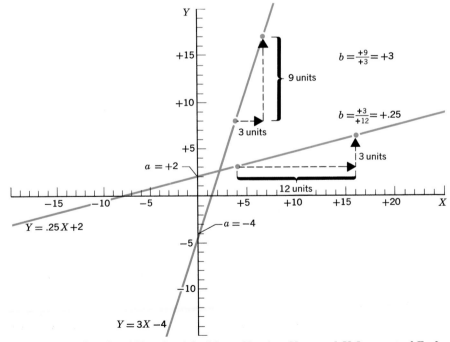

Figure 12.3 *Graphs of Two Straight Lines, Showing Slope and Y Intercept of Each.*

Note that in each case the value of a identifies the point on the Y axis at which the line crosses it.

The other constant in the equation is b; and it is called the *slope* of the line. It will be positive when the value of Y increases with increasing values of X, as is the case with the two lines pictured. It will be negative if the line slants the other way, i.e. when Y *decreases* as X increases. *The slope of the line specifies the amount of increase in Y that accompanies one unit of increase in X.* This can be appreciated by studying the lines pictured in Figure 12.3. Consider the line for which the equation is $Y = 3X - 4$. The dotted lines show that if X is increased by three units, Y increases by nine units. The ratio of the increase in Y (vertical distance) to the increase in X (horizontal distance) is the slope of the line. Thus, the slope is:

$$b = \frac{vertical\ change}{horizontal\ change} = \frac{+9}{+3} = +3.0$$

In the second equation, Y increases three units for every 12 units of increase in X, so the slope, b, is $3/12$, or $+.25$. Note that if Y *decreased* three units for every 12 units of increase in X, we would have a "negative increase" in the numerator of the fraction, and the resultant value of b would be $-.25$ rather than $+.25$.

Using this model, let us examine the several forms of the line of regression of Y on X.

General Equation of
a Straight Line
$$Y = \quad bX \quad + \quad a$$

Regression of Y on X:
Standard Score Formula
$$z'_Y = \quad \overset{b}{\hat{r}z_X} \quad + \quad \overset{(a=0)}{0}$$

Regression of Y on X:
Raw Score Formula
$$Y' = \overset{b}{\left(r\frac{S_Y}{S_X}\right)}X + \overset{a}{\left(-r\frac{S_Y}{S_X}\right)\bar{X} + \bar{Y}}$$

The value b is most interesting when the regression equation is cast in standard score form. In this case, the correlation coefficient *is* the slope of the regression line. *One interpretation of the correlation coefficient, therefore, is that it states the amount of increase in Y that accompanies unit increase in X when both measures are expressed in standard score units.* It indicates how much of a standard deviation Y will increase for an increase of one standard deviation in X.

When the regression equation for predicting Y from X is stated in raw score form, its slope, b, is $r(S_Y/S_X)$ rather than r. This expression is known as the *regression coefficient*. The regression coefficient may also be used to interpret the meaning of a given correlation. *It states the amount of increase in Y that accompanies unit increase in X when both measures are expressed in raw score terms.* In his early work in measuring association, Sir Francis Galton apparently thought that the slope of the line of best fit might be an indicator of the degree of association. From what we have learned in this section, it is clear that this would work if the two standard deviations were equal, since in that case $r(S_Y/S_X)$ reduces to r. Indeed, much of Galton's work on heredity involved just such variables. Think back, for example, to Table 9.1, which contains the data from his investigation of the relationship between parental height and adult height of offspring. But for many variables the two standard deviations will differ substantially.

12.4 INTERPRETATION OF *r*: THE REGRESSION EQUATION (II)

The regression equation provides a second way of interpreting r. Consider the standard score formula for the regression of Y on X: $z'_Y = rz_X$. Let us see what this equation says about the consequences of three possible values of r: 0, $+.50$, and $+1.00$. A graphic representation of the regression of Y on X is shown in Figure 12.4 for each of these situations together with the regression equation appropriate to each. As the figure shows, when the correlation is $+1$, the predicted standard score in Y is the same as the standard score in X from which the prediction is made. When the correlation is zero, the mean of Y ($z = 0$) is predicted, no matter what value X has. This is logical because information about X supplies no information that would improve upon a sheer guess as to the value of Y. The most interesting of the three situations is where r_{XY} has an intermediate value. Think, for example, of the correlation between intelligence of parents and offspring, which indeed has a value close to $+.50$. If parental intelligence is two standard deviations above the mean, the predicted intelligence of their offspring is one standard deviation above the mean. On the other hand, if the parents' intelligence is two standard deviations below the mean, the predicted intelligence of their offspring is only one standard deviation below the mean. To put it in other words, bright parents will tend to have children who are brighter than average, but not as bright as they, and dull parents will tend to have children who are dull, but not as dull as their parents. Remember that the predicted value is to be thought of as an *average* value; it is quite possible for bright parents to have a child brighter than they or one whose intelligence is below average.

This phenomenon is precisely what Sir Francis Galton observed in his studies of inheritance. He first referred to it as "reversion" and later as "regression." Today we refer to it as *regression on the mean*. You understand now why the straight line of best fit is called a regression line, and why the symbol r was chosen for the correlation coefficient.

The fact of regression on the mean is, of course, characteristic of *any* relationship in which the correlation is less than perfect. Consequently, we would expect that a very short person would tend to have short children, but children less short than he, and that the brightest student in the class would tend to earn a good grade, but not necessarily the best in the class.

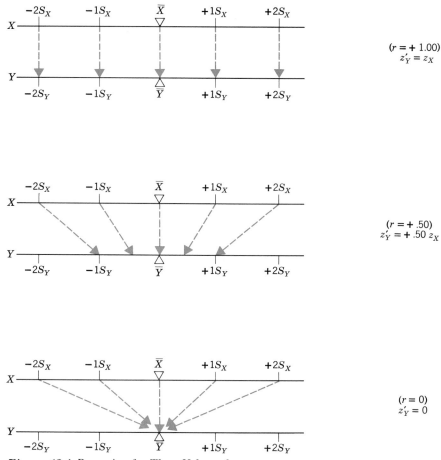

Figure 12.4 *Regression for Three Values of r.*

An interesting fact is that the more extreme the value from which prediction is made, the greater the amount of regression toward the mean. In the middle diagram of Figure 12.4, the amount of regression is one standard deviation when prediction is made from a value two standard deviations above the mean, whereas regression is half that amount when prediction is made from a value one standard deviation above the mean.

As the z-score form of the regression equation ($z'_Y = rz_X$) shows, the higher the value of r, the less the amount of regression. For $z_X = +1$, $z'_Y = +.9$ when $r = +.90$, $+.5$ when $r = +.50$, and $+.2$ when $r = +.20$.

12.5 REGRESSION PROBLEMS IN RESEARCH

The phenomenon of regression is frequently a factor in research design. For example, suppose it is hypothesized that special education at an early age can improve the level of intelligence of children who score low on such tests. A group of children are tested, and those with low IQ's are selected for the experimental training program. On completion of training, the children are retested, and the mean IQ is found to be higher than before. This is *not* adequate evidence that the training program improved the performance of the children on the intelligence test. The children were selected *because* they had low IQ's, and since the correlation between test scores on the two different occasions is less than perfect, we would, according to the regression equation, predict that their scores would be higher on retesting *even if no treatment intervened*. Therefore, it may be that the improvement in performance is simply another example of the phenomenon of regression on the mean. A better research design would be to select two groups of children of comparable initial level of intelligence, subject one group to the experimental treatment but not the other, retest them both, and compare these scores.

To sum up, when subjects are selected *because* of their extreme position (either high or low) on one variable, we expect their position on a correlated variable to be in the same direction, but less extreme. The two variables could be test and retest on the same measure, or they could be two different variables. For example, suppose students are selected for study because they are doing poorly in history. If we now inquire how they are doing in other courses, we expect to find that they are below average, but not as much below as they are in history. As we learned in the previous section, the amount of regression will depend on the size of the correlation between the two variables.

12.6 AN APPARENT PARADOX IN REGRESSION

If parents with extreme characteristics tend to have offspring with characteristics less extreme than themselves, how is it that, after a few generations, we do not find everybody at the center? Galton's attention was attracted to this apparent paradox. The answer is that *regression of predicted values toward the mean is accompanied by variation of obtained values about the predicted values, and the greater the degree of regression toward the mean, the greater the amount of variation*. The inward movement of regression is therefore accompanied by the expansive action of variability, which makes it possible for the more extreme values of Y to occur. Specifically, Y', the predicted value of Y, is only the predicted *mean* of Y for those

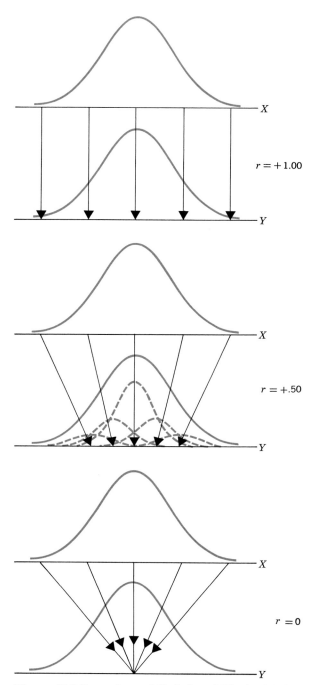

Figure 12.5 *Regression and Variation of Obtained Values about the Regressed Values.*

who obtain a particular score in X. The obtained Y values corresponding to that value of X will be distributed about Y' with a standard deviation equal to S_{YX}. The lower the value of the correlation coefficient, the greater the value of S_{YX}, so that the greater the degree of regression on the mean, the greater the variation of obtained Y values about their predicted values.

Figure 12.5 illustrates the situation. The top part of this figure shows that when $r = 1$, each obtained Y exactly equals its predicted value. If this were the correlation between height of fathers and their sons, we might presume that the distribution of height of sons would be the same as that of their fathers, unless factors *external* to the phenomenon of regression were operating. The middle part of Figure 12.5 illustrates an intermediate degree of correlation. There is partial regression, accompanied by a degree of variability of Y values about Y'. Again, unless external factors are involved, we see that the distribution of height of offspring would be the same as that of their parents. Finally, the third part of Figure 12.5 shows the situation when regression is complete ($r = 0$). Although the predicted value of Y is $\bar{Y}$ for every value of X, the variability of the obtained values of Y about their predicted value is S_Y (because $S_{YX} = S_Y$ when $r = 0$; see Section 11.6). Barring the influence of external factors, the same features (mean and standard deviation) of the parental distribution are recreated in that of the offspring.

12.7 INTERPRETATION OF r: k, THE COEFFICIENT OF ALIENATION

The measure of variability of scores about the regression line, or as we might call it, the measure of error of prediction, is given by the standard error of estimate, $S_{YX} = S_Y \sqrt{1 - r^2}$. The maximum possible error of prediction occurs when $r = 0$, in which case $S_{YX} = S_Y$. One interpretation of the correlation coefficient can therefore be made by comparing the magnitude of error in the present predictive circumstances with that which would obtain in the worst possible predictive circumstances, i.e., when $r = 0$. The ratio of S_{YX} to S_Y gives the proportion of the maximum possible predictive error that characterizes the present predictive circumstances. We have:

$$\frac{\begin{bmatrix} \textit{magnitude of predictive error} \\ \textit{characterizing our predictive} \\ \textit{situation} \end{bmatrix}}{\begin{bmatrix} \textit{magnitude of predictive error} \\ \textit{in the worst possible predic-} \\ \textit{tive situation } (r = 0) \end{bmatrix}} = \frac{S_{YX}}{S_Y} = \frac{S_Y \sqrt{1 - r^2}}{S_Y} = \sqrt{1 - r^2}$$

This quantity, $\sqrt{1 - r^2}$, is symbolized by the letter k, and it is called the *coefficient of alienation*:

Coefficient of Alienation $$k = \sqrt{1 - r^2} \qquad (12.3)$$

When the value of k is close to unity (its maximum value), the magnitude of predictive error is close to its maximum. On the other hand, when the value of k is close to zero, most of the possible error of prediction has been eliminated.

Table 12.1 presents values of k for selected values of r. In examining this table, a striking fact is that the magnitude of predictive error decreases very slowly as the correlation coefficient ascends from zero. For instance, note that when the correlation coefficient has reached .50, the standard error of estimate is 87% of the size that it would be if the correlation were zero. To put it the other way, the reduction in variability in predictive error amounts only to 13% for a coefficient of this

Table 12.1 *Values of Several Indicators of Utility of r for Different Levels of the Correlation Coefficient*

r_{XY}	k	r^2	A	B
1.00	.00	1.00	.50	1.00
.95	.31	.90	.40	.80
.90	.44	.81	.35	.71
.85	.53	.72	.32	.65
.80	.60	.64	.30	.59
.75	.66	.56	.27	.54
.70	.71	.49	.25	.49
.65	.76	.42	.23	.45
.60	.80	.36	.20	.41
.55	.84	.30	.19	.37
.50	.87	.25	.17	.33
.45	.89	.20	.15	.30
.40	.92	.16	.13	.26
.35	.94	.12	.11	.23
.30	.95	.09	.10	.19
.25	.97	.06	.08	.16
.20	.98	.04	.06	.13
.15	.99 −	.02	.05	.10
.10	.99 +	.01	.03	.06
.05	1.00 −	.00 +	.02	.03
.00	1.00	.00	.00	.00

k: coefficient of alienation (see Section 12.7)
r^2: coefficient of determination (see Section 12.8)
A: proportion of correct placements in excess of chance (see Section 12.9)
B: proportion of improvement in correct placement relative to the chance proportion of .50 (see Section 12.9)

magnitude. Note also that a change in r from .20 to .30 results in a reduction of .03 in the size of the coefficient of alienation, whereas a change in r from .80 to .90 results in a change of .16. This shows that a given change in the magnitude of a correlation coefficient has greater consequences when the correlation is high than when it is low.

12.8 INTERPRETATION OF r: r^2, THE COEFFICIENT OF DETERMINATION

When a number of scores are assembled, it is found that their values are not all the same. What is the source of this variation? If the question is applied to the Y scores in a bivariate distribution, the answer has two parts. First, some of the variation in Y is associated with changes in X. That is, assuming some degree of correlation between X and Y, Y takes different values depending on whether the associated value of X is high or low. However, if we settle on any single value of X, there is still some variability in Y (this second kind of variability is measured by S_{YX}). Total variation in Y may therefore be thought of as having two component parts: variation in Y that is associated with or attributable to changes in X, and variation in Y that is inherent in Y, and hence independent of changes in X.

It is possible to partition the total Y variation in such a way as to reflect the contribution of these two components. This partition must be done in terms of the *variance* of Y, which can be partitioned into additive components, rather than in terms of the standard deviation of Y, which cannot. We may begin by dividing the deviation of any Y score from its mean into two components:

$$(Y - \bar{Y}) = (Y - Y') + (Y' - \bar{Y})$$

Note that the equation is an algebraic identity, since on the right side of the equation the two values of Y' will cancel, if we wish, leaving the expression on the right the same as that on the left. Figure 12.6 illustrates the partition. We now have three deviation scores. Each measures variation of a particular kind:

$(Y - \bar{Y})$ This measures total variation among Y scores. When these deviations are squared, summed, and divided by their number, we have: $S_Y^2 = \Sigma(Y - \bar{Y})^2/n$, the variance of the Y scores defined in the usual manner.

$(Y - Y')$ This measures variation of obtained Y scores about the values predicted for them (Y'); it is variation in Y that remains when X is held constant. Therefore $(Y - Y')$ measures Y variation that is independent of changes in X. When these deviations are squared, summed, and divided by their number, we have: $S_{YX}^2 = \Sigma(Y - Y')^2/n$, the variance in Y that is *independent* of changes in X. This quantity is the square of the standard error of estimate (see Section 11.5 in chapter 11).

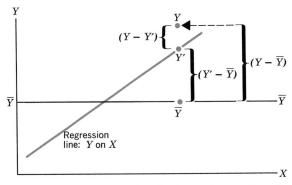

Figure 12.6 *Partition of a Deviation Score* $(Y - \bar{Y})$
into Component Deviations: $(Y - Y')$ *and* $(Y' - \bar{Y})$.

$(Y' - \bar{Y})$ This quantity, unlike the other two, is new to us. It measures variation of
the predicted Y values about the mean of Y and, as explained below,
measures variation in Y that is associated with changes in X. When these
deviations are squared, summed, and divided by their number, we have:
$S_{Y'}^2 = \Sigma(Y' - \bar{Y})^2/n$, the variance in Y that is associated with
changes in X.

A few more words about $S_{Y'}^2$ are in order. First, look at Figure 12.6 and find the
discrepancy $(Y' - \bar{Y})$ from which this variance is generated. What would happen
if $r = 0$? In this case the predicted value of Y is $\bar{Y}$, irrespective of the value of X
from which the prediction is made (see Section 11.3 in the last chapter). Then all
values of $(Y' - \bar{Y})$ would become $(\bar{Y} - \bar{Y}) = 0$, and $S_{Y'}^2$ becomes zero. In other
words, when $r = 0$, *none* of the Y variance is associated with changes in X. On the
other hand, if $r = 1.00$, each predicted value of Y is the actual value of Y. Then each
value of $(Y' - \bar{Y})$ would become $(Y - \bar{Y})$, and $S_{Y'}^2$ becomes S_Y^2. This would
mean that *all* the variation in Y is contributed by reason of the association with X.
We can express the relationships developed above in the following equation:

Partition of Y Variance
into Two Components

$$S_Y^2 \quad = \quad S_{YX}^2 \quad + \quad S_{Y'}^2 \qquad (12.4)$$

$$\begin{bmatrix} total\ Y \\ variance \end{bmatrix} = \begin{bmatrix} variance\ in\ Y \\ independent\ of \\ changes\ in\ X \end{bmatrix} + \begin{bmatrix} variance\ in\ Y \\ associated\ with \\ changes\ in\ X \end{bmatrix}$$

One interpretation of the correlation coefficient can be made in terms of the
proportion of the total Y variance that is associated with changes in X. This
proportion is given by:

$$\frac{\begin{bmatrix} variance\ in\ Y\ associated \\ with\ changes\ in\ X \end{bmatrix}}{[total\ variance\ in\ Y]} = \frac{S_{Y'}^2}{S_Y^2}$$

This expression can be simplified by appropriate substitution. Since

$$S_Y^2 = S_{YX}^2 + S_{Y'}^2$$

then

$$S_{Y'}^2 = S_Y^2 - S_{YX}^2$$

and

$$\frac{S_{Y'}^2}{S_Y^2} = \frac{S_Y^2 - S_{YX}^2}{S_Y^2}$$

$$= \frac{S_Y^2 - (S_Y\sqrt{1 - r^2})^2}{S_Y^2}$$

$$= \frac{S_Y^2 - S_Y^2(1 - r^2)}{S_Y^2}$$

$$= \frac{S_Y^2 - S_Y^2 + S_Y^2 r^2}{S_Y^2}$$

$$= r^2$$

So r^2 *gives the proportion of Y variance that is associated with changes in X.* r^2 is called the *coefficient of determination.* If $r = .50$, $r^2 = .25$. This means, for example, that 25% of Y variance is associated with changes in X (and 75% is not). Values of r^2 are given for selected values of r in Table 12.1. Note, once more, that the proportion of Y variance accounted for by variation in X increases more slowly than does the magnitude of the correlation coefficient. Not until $r = .71$ does $r^2 = .50$.

12.9 INTERPRETATION OF r: PROPORTION OF CORRECT PLACEMENTS

The interpretation of the meaning of r according to k or r^2 is certainly not very encouraging as to the value of r's of moderate magnitude. However, in practical problems of prediction, we are often interested in estimating, from knowledge of a person's score in X, the likelihood that he will "succeed" (i.e. score above a given point in Y). In these terms we can often do much better by using the predictor than by not doing so, even when the correlation is modest. Consequently, a somewhat more cheerful outlook may be had by considering the proportion of correct placements that occur when the regression equation is used to predict success. Assume a normal bivariate distribution, that success is defined as scoring above the median on the criterion variable (Y), and that those who are selected as potentially successful are those who score above the median on the predictor variable (X). If $r = 0$, 50% correct placement will be achieved by using score on the predictor for selection. Look at the first picture in Table 12.2. Successful predictions have been made for the 50 individuals who were predicted to succeed and did, plus the 50 who were predicted to fail and did, i.e. those individuals who fall in the first and third quadrants of the diagram. The proportion of successful placements is therefore 100 out of the 200 candidates, or 50%. Now look at the second picture in Table 12.2. In this case, the correlation coefficient is $+.50$, and the number of correct placements is $67 + 67 = 134$. The proportion of correct placements is therefore $134/200$, or .67. The proportion of correct placements in excess of chance proportion of such placements (.50) is .17. The proportion of improvement in correct placement relative to the proportion for chance placement (.50) is $.17/.50$, or .33.[†] Viewed this way, a correlation coefficient of .50 appears to have greater utility than some other interpretations suggest. The last two columns of Table 12.1 present, for selected values of r, the proportion of correct placements in excess of chance and the proportion of improvement in correct placements relative to the chance proportion of .50.[‡]

It should be remembered that the interpretation offered above is dependent on splitting the two variables at the median and on the assumption of a normal bivariate distribution. If these conditions are varied, a somewhat different result will follow. Some years ago, Taylor and Russell pointed out that effectiveness of prediction depended not only on the magnitude of the correlation coefficient, but also where the cut was made on the predictor variable.[††] Indeed, their work shows

[†] $.17/.50$ actually equals .34, but .33 is the right value; the discrepancy is due to rounding.

[‡] This interpretive approach, and the entries for columns A and B of Table 12.2, are owed to: W. B. Michael, "An Interpretation of the Coefficients of Predictive Validity and of Determination in Terms of the Proportions of Correct Inclusions or Exclusions in Cells of a Fourfold Table," *Educational and Psychological Measurement*, **26**, No. 2 (1966): 419-24.

[††] H. Taylor and J. Russell, "The Relationship of Validity Coefficients to the Practical Effectiveness of Tests in Selection: Discussion and Tables," *Journal of Applied Psychology*, **23**, (1939): 565-78.

Table 12.2 *Proportion of Successful Placements for Two Levels of r*

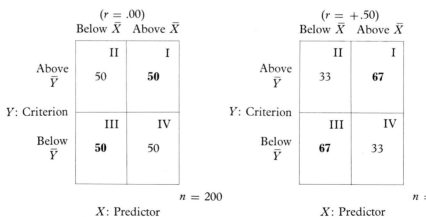

$n = 200$ $n = 200$

that a rather low coefficient may be quite useful in improving the quality of performance on the criterion when there are a large number of "applicants" but a small number to be selected. It also shows that a high correlation between predictor and criterion may be of little value if a large proportion of those who apply will be accepted. Their article is recommended for those who are concerned with this problem.

12.10 ASSOCIATION AND PREDICTION: SUMMARY

The fact that the correlation coefficient is zero when two variables are unrelated and unity when the relation is perfect suggests that the problem of assessing degree of association must be one of comforting simplicity. Alas, the last few chapters have revealed it to be much more complex than one might have supposed. We learned that Pearson's r is determined by the degree to which scores hug the straight line of best fit, and so the adequacy of this coefficient to describe the degree of association depends on the appropriateness of the hypothesis of linearity for the data at hand (Section 10.2). We also found that whether the coefficient can be given a general meaning or simply one "on the average" depends on whether or not the scores hug the line of best fit equally well throughout the data (Section 10.3). Furthermore, the value of the coefficient can be importantly affected by the circumstances under which it is obtained: continuity of the distributions (Section 10.4), range of talent (Section 12.1), and heterogeneity of samples (Section 12.2) are some of the factors that can affect it. Others include the kind of persons that constituted the sample, the particular measures taken for each of the two variables, and the specific circumstances under which these variables and persons operated (Section 10.7).

Although the correlation coefficient varies from zero to one, the degree of association is, as stated earlier, not ordinarily interpretable in direct proportion to its magnitude. Nevertheless, we have found several ways of saying what a given coefficient means. The slope of the straight line of best fit gives us one way: it specifies the amount of increase (or decrease) in one variable that accompanies one unit of increase in the other variable (Section 12.3). A second interpretation may be made through k, the coefficient of alienation (Section 12.7). This gives information about the reduction in magnitude of error of prediction accomplished by using the knowledge of the extent of association rather than by "just guessing." A third interpretation is given by examining r^2, the coefficient of determination. It states the proportion of variance of the one variable that is associated with change in the other. Study of the behavior of both k and r^2 shows that a change of given magnitude (.10, for example) in the correlation coefficient has greater consequence when applied to coefficients having a high value than those of low value. Finally, another way of interpreting correlation (and prediction) is in terms of the proportion of correct placements expected when the regression equation is used in practical problems of prediction (Section 12.9).

These several ways of interpreting correlation and prediction are quite diverse. It is clear not only that the problem of interpretation is not simple, but that there is also no one "best" way. The particular nature of the problem, theoretical or applied, and the context in which it is set must guide the investigator to an appropriate choice.

PROBLEMS AND EXERCISES

Identify:

range of talent   coefficient of alienation
homoscedasticity   coefficient of
heterogeneity of samples   determination
slope k
Y-intercept r^2
regression coefficient S_{YX}^2
$r(S_Y/S_X)$ $S_{Y'}^2$
regression on the mean

1   Solve the equation $S_{YX} = S_Y \sqrt{1 - r^2}$ for r, thus obtaining Formula 12.1.

2   Among a group of retarded 10-year-old children, it is found that the correlation between IQ and reading achievement is $+.25$. However, on a school-wide basis the correlation is $+.50$. Assuming these results to be typical, what explanation do you suggest?

3   To study the phenomenon of creativity, a number of outstandingly creative persons are assembled and tested. It is found that rating on creativity and IQ correlate to the extent of $r = +.20$ among this group. It is concluded that creativity is really quite different from intelligence. Any objections?

4   It is common to find that the correlation between airplane pilot aptitude test score and pilot proficiency is higher among aviation cadets than among experienced pilots. What could account for this?

5   One way to learn whether an aptitude test works is to test applicants for the particular job, hire them all, and subsequently correlate test score with a measure of job proficiency. Another way, usually more practical, is to test all currently employed workers of the particular type and obtain the same correlation. Is there any reason to think that the coefficient might be different when obtained in these two ways? Explain.

6   At certain stages in school, girls tend to be superior to boys in verbal skills. Suppose the correlation between spelling score and IQ is $+.50$ for a sample of girls and the same among a sample of boys. If the two sets of subjects were pooled and the coefficient computed on the total group, would you expect r to be about the same? Explain.

7 Suppose the correlation is $-.30$ between strength of grip and time in the 100-yard dash for a sample of men and the same among a sample of women. If the two samples are combined and r is recomputed, would it be about the same? Explain.

8 One regression equation reads: $Y' = 2X - 5$. (a) Could the scores be in standard score form? (b) Interpret r in terms of the slope of the regression equation.

9 Another regression equation reads: $Y' = -5X + 5$. (a) What can you say about r? (b) Interpret r in terms of the slope of the regression equation.

10 Another regression equation reads: $Y' = 3X$. Is that possible? Explain.

11 Another regression equation reads: $Y' = 12$. State all the things that we know from this about X, Y, and/or r.

12 If $r = -.50$, and Pete scores $\frac{1}{2}$ standard deviation below the mean in X, what (a) z score do we predict for him in Y? (b) score do we predict for him in Y if $\bar{Y} = 100$ and $S_Y = 20$? (c) score do we predict for him in Y if $\bar{Y} = 82$ and $S_Y = 16$?

13 It is proposed that those with an IQ below 70 be sterilized, in order to eliminate feebleminded children. Any objection, other than humanitarian?

14 Someone proposes a "hothouse" treatment for gifted children. Four-year-olds are tested, and those whose IQ appears to be above 140 are selected for special treatment. Before treatment, mean IQ of this group is 150. Let us suppose that the treatment has no effect on IQ. What mean IQ would you expect when the children are retested one year later? Explain.

15 In one company, it is found that frequency of accidents correlates about $+.40$ from one year period to the next. It institutes a safety course for the 10% least safe of workers last year. This year, the accident record of these men is distinctly better. Your comment?

16 Interpret the correlation coefficients .10, .30, .60, and .90 in terms of (a) the coefficient of alienation, (b) the coefficient of determination, (c) the proportion of correct placements when the split is at the median in X and Y.

17 By revising a test, we are able to increase the correlation between it and the criterion from .25 to .50. Interpret the gain made by revision according to (a) the coefficient of alienation, (b) the coefficient of determination, (c) the proportion of correct placements when the split is at the median in X and Y. (d) Do any of these interpretations suggest that the increase from .25 to .50 doubled the strength of the relationship?

18 When $r = \pm1.00$, what value would $\Sigma(Y - Y')^2/n$ have? Explain.

19 When $r = 0$, what value would $\Sigma(Y - Y')^2/n$ have? Explain.

20 Under what conditions will $S_Y = S_{Y'}$? Explain.

21 Under what conditions will $S_Y = S_{YX}$? Explain.

CHAPTER 13

13.1 INTRODUCTION: THE PLAN OF STUDY

For a person approaching statistics for the first time, statistical inference is loaded with new ideas, concepts, terminology, and for almost everybody, new ways of thinking. It is a heavy load for the learner. In recognition of this, the development will proceed along two tracks. The remainder of this chapter will pursue the most direct route, hewing as closely as possible to the main theme in the hope of avoiding intellectual indigestion. A number of concepts deserve more consideration than this "eye-on-the-ball" development can offer. These will be explored in the next chapter, which will serve as a more leisurely commentary that should promote a deeper understanding.

Absolutely basic to the development of statistical inference are the concepts of *population, sample,* and *random sample.* These were presented in Sections 2.1 and

The Basis of Statistical Inference

2.2 and should be reviewed before continuing with this chapter; what follows assumes that knowledge. The notion of a random sample is so vital that we shall be saying more about it both in this chapter and the next.

13.2 A PROBLEM IN INFERENCE: TESTING HYPOTHESES

A basic aim of statistical inference is to form a conclusion about a characteristic of a population from study of a sample taken from that population. In inference, the fundamental factor that must be taken into account is that sample outcomes vary. There are two types of inferential procedures: *hypothesis testing* and *estimation.* We will consider hypothesis testing in this section and estimation in the next.

Mr. Jones, wondering whether the coin he holds in his hand is a "fair" coin (i.e., is as likely to come up heads as tails), decides to put it to a test. He tosses the coin 100 times and observes the number of heads obtained in this series of trials.

Dr. Brown, director of institutional research at a large university, is aware of a nationwide survey of academic aptitude of college and university freshmen. She would like to know if the level of aptitude of the current freshman class at her institution is, as measured on the same test, the same as that obtained in the survey. In her institution, there are 5000 freshmen, too many to study conveniently. She therefore selects 250 students from among the 5000, finds their mean aptitude test score, and compares it with the mean of the nationwide group.

Dr. Smith, a psychologist, wants to know if reaction time is equally fast to red and green light. He chooses two groups of 50 subjects each and measures their reaction time when one group is exposed to the green stimulus and the other to the red. He then compares the mean reaction time of the two groups.

Jones, Brown, and Smith each have problems for which hypothesis testing procedures are appropriate. In each case we might first think of the problem in terms of a question, but the procedure for answering is easier if the question is translated into a hypothesis; that is, a statement to be subjected to test and, on the outcome of the test, to be retained or rejected. For example, Mr. Jones wants to know if the number of heads obtained in the sample of 100 tosses is in line with what could be expected if, in the population of all possible tosses, heads will occur half the time. For purposes of statistical examination, this question is rephrased as a hypothesis: *in the population of possible tosses, the proportion of heads is .50.* He then proceeds to compare the results for his sample of 100 tosses with the type of results that would be expected if the hypothesis were true. To be concrete about the matter, let us complete the example on intuitive terms. Suppose Mr. Jones obtained 54 heads in the 100 tosses. This is a reasonable result if the coin is fair, and therefore he has no reason to reject the hypothesis. On the other hand, suppose he obtained 95 heads in the 100 tosses. If the coin were fair, this outcome would be possible, but extremely unlikely. It is more reasonable to believe that the coin is not fair, and so he will reject the hypothesis.

Dr. Brown and Dr. Smith will also cast their questions in the form of hypotheses. Dr. Brown will hypothesize that the mean of the population of freshman test scores at her institution is equal to the mean characterizing the national group. Dr. Smith wants to draw conclusions about the reaction times of subjects in general like the ones he studied, not just about the 100 subjects in his experiment. He will therefore hypothesize that the mean of the *population* of responses to a red light is the same as the mean of the *population* of responses to a green light. To evaluate their hypotheses, both researchers will ask what type of sample results one would expect to obtain if the hypothesis were correct. If their sample outcome is not in accord with what they would expect, they will reject their hypotheses.

In each of the problems described, the data at hand are *not* those about which the investigators really wish to draw their conclusions. Mr. Jones wants to know about the proportion of heads and tails "in the long run," not just in the sequence of 100 tosses that he studied. Dr. Smith really wants to know about the speed of reaction to the two colors of light among people in general, not merely among the particular

100 people he studied. In short, they want to draw conclusions about the population represented by the sample they studied and not simply about the particular sample itself.

13.3 A PROBLEM IN INFERENCE: ESTIMATION

In hypothesis testing, we have a particular value in mind; we hypothesize that the value we have in mind characterizes the population of observations. The question is whether that value is reasonable in the light of the evidence from the sample. In estimation, on the other hand, no particular population value need be stated. Rather, the question is, what *is* the population value?

What proportion of the eligible voters favor, at this point in time, passing of the bond issue? What is the degree of correlation between knowledge of basic math and achievement in the first course in statistics? What is the difference in mean response time to red and green light? These are examples of problems in estimation. In each case it is impractical to study the characteristic of interest in the entire population. Instead, a sample is drawn, studied, and an inference made about the population characteristic.

It has been stated that the object of inference is to form a conclusion about the nature of a characteristic of a population. That characteristic may be a proportion, a mean, a median, a standard deviation, a correlation coefficient, or any other of a number of statistical parameters. Inference may also be concerned with the difference between populations with regard to a given parameter, as in Dr. Smith's interest in the possible difference in reaction time to light of two colors.

13.4 BASIC ISSUES IN INFERENCE

The fundamental fact of sampling is that the value of the characteristic we are studying will vary from sample to sample. Suppose Dr. Smith repeated his experiment several times. On each repetition he will obtain a different selection of subjects from the population he has chosen to study. *Even if there is no differential effect of color on reaction time,* the means of his two samples and the difference between them will not be exactly the same from repetition to repetition.

Now the task of statistical inference is to draw a conclusion about a characteristic of a population (or populations) from study of the characteristics of a *part* of that population. Because of the fact of sampling variation, it will not be possible to make such an inference and *know for certain that it is correct.*† Certainty comes only

---

† There are trivial exceptions.

when *every* element in the population is known. But the situation is not hopeless. Consider again Mr. Jones's question about the fairness of his coin. He wanted to know whether in the population of all possible tosses heads would come up 50% of the time. Suppose he tosses it 100 times and obtains 58 heads and 42 tails. He knows that such a sample outcome *could* occur as a result of sampling variation. But how likely is it? If he knew how often samples of 100 tosses would yield results as deviant from the expected 50 heads–50 tails, he would be in a better position to decide whether (a) the hypothesis could be true (because 58–42 is a sampling outcome that would readily occur if the hypothesis *were* true), or (b) the hypothesis is probably false (because 58–42 is so deviant that it would be unlikely to occur if the hypothesis were true).

The key to any problem in statistical inference is to discover what sample values will occur in repeated sampling, and with what relative frequency. A sample is drawn and the mean is computed. A second sample of the same size yields a mean of somewhat different value. A third, still another value. What kind of distribution will be formed by these means when sampling is repeated time after time? A distribution of this type is known as a *sampling distribution.* We must be able to describe it completely if we are to say what would happen when samples are drawn.

To learn what sample values will occur and with what relative frequency, there must be known rules that connect the "behavior" of samples to the population from which they are drawn. Such rules can be known only if a systematic method of drawing samples is adopted and used *consistently.* As it turns out, there is just one basic method of sampling that permits the rules to be known. This is to draw *probability samples*—samples for which the probability of inclusion in the sample of each element of the population is known. One kind of probability sample is the *random sample;* it is the kind considered in this book. If a random sample has been drawn, the necessary facts can be known about the distribution of the statistic under consideration, permitting inference of the type illustrated earlier.

13.5 PROBABILITY AND RANDOM SAMPLING: AN INTRODUCTION

To continue our development we need some understanding of *probability.* Several useful approaches are possible; we will consider one now, and another in the next chapter. What is the probability that when:

A coin is tossed, it will come up heads?
A score is selected blindly from a distribution, its value will exceed C_{75}?

In each case it is possible to think of a single trial (for example, a particular toss of a coin) and of a series of trials extending indefinitely.† In both instances rational considerations lead us to a particular expectation. In the first question, given a fair coin fairly tossed, we expect that in the long run heads will come up as often as tails. In the second situation three-quarters of the scores fall below C_{75} and one-quarter above. On any given trial the outcome may be one way or the other. But, if the number of trials is increased indefinitely, the relative number of outcomes that satisfy the condition specified in each question will approach one-half and one-quarter, respectively. We offer, therefore, the following definition of probability:

The probability of the occurrence of A on a single trial is the proportion of trials characterized by A in an infinite series of trials, when each trial is conducted in like manner.

According to this definition, the probability that the coin will come up heads is $\frac{1}{2}$, and the probability that when a score is drawn it will exceed C_{75} is $\frac{1}{4}$. Probability, then, can be ascribed a numerical value. The values it may take range from zero to one. The probability is *zero* that the coin will come up *neither* heads nor tails, and it is *one* that it will come up *either* heads or tails, to use a trivial example. Further consideration of probability will be found in Sections 14.2 and 14.3.

A random sample is a sample so drawn that each possible sample of that size has an equal probability of being selected.

Note that it is the method of selection, and not the particular sample outcome, that defines a random sample. If we were given a population and a sample from that population, it would be impossible to say whether the sample was random without knowing the method by which it was selected. Although characteristics of random samples *tend* to resemble those of the population, those of a particular random sample may not. If we deal 13 cards from a 52-card deck, each of the four suits (clubs, hearts, diamonds, spades) will usually be represented. Somewhat infrequently, a hand of 13 cards will contain cards from only three suits, and even less frequently, only two suits. It is possible that the hand might consist of cards from just one suit, but this is indeed a rare random sampling result: the probability is approximately .000000000006.

One important characteristic of a random sample is that every element in the population has an equal probability of inclusion in the sample. Suppose a sample of five scores is to be selected from a population of 50 scores. We write the value of each score on a ticket, place the 50 tickets in a can, shake the can thoroughly, and

---

† In selecting a score from the distribution, the outcome is noted but the score is returned to the distribution. Thus on each trial the set of scores from which selection is to be made remains identical, and the possible number of trials is indefinitely large.

make a blindfold selection of five tickets, withdrawing them one at a time.† The sample so selected is a random sample, and each ticket (and therefore each element) has an equal opportunity for inclusion in the sample. If done with care, the "tickets in a can" method results in a random sample. In most practical statistical work, better reliability and convenience can be guaranteed by using a table of random numbers.‡ This technique is described in Section 14.7. Further discussion of problems in drawing a random sample will be found in Section 14.4.

13.6 THE RANDOM SAMPLING DISTRIBUTION OF MEANS: AN INTRODUCTION

Although inference could be about one of a number of characteristics of a population (parameters), we shall focus on inference about means at first because of the basic utility of that measure in answering questions about data.

Suppose there is a very large population with mean, μ, equal to 100. We now draw from this population a random sample of 25 cases; its mean, $\bar{X}_1$, proves to be 97.4. We now replace the 25 cases in the population, "stir well," and select a second sample of 25 cases at random. Its mean, $\bar{X}_2$, is 101.8. This sampling procedure might be repeated indefinitely, and in each sample the mean is calculated and recorded. Figure 13.1 illustrates the situation.

If these sampling trials *were* continued indefinitely (for an infinity of trials), and if all sample means were then cast into a relative frequency distribution, we would have the answer to that key question posed in Section 13.4: "What sample values

---

†*Each* of the 50 scores is an element of the population. If, therefore, several scores have the same value, there must still be a ticket for each.

‡Computers can be programmed to generate random numbers and therefore also to select random samples.

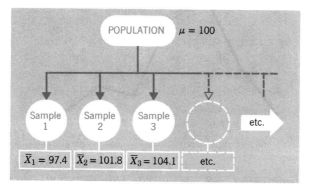

Figure 13.1 *Means of Successive Random Samples.*

will occur in repeated sampling, and with what relative frequency?"† The distribution of means thus generated is known as the *random sampling distribution* of means. Now it would be impossible to perform an experiment that would actually produce this distribution, because it calls for an infinity of sampling trials. However, mathematicians have been able to derive its characteristics and are thus able to tell us what would happen *if* an infinite series of trials were conducted. It is the fact that the samples are selected *at random* that makes it possible for them to do this.

13.7 CHARACTERISTICS OF THE RANDOM SAMPLING DISTRIBUTION OF MEANS

A distribution is completely defined by specifying its mean, standard deviation, and shape. First, the mean of any random sampling distribution of means is the same as the mean of the population of scores. To put it symbolically:

Mean of the Sampling Distribution of Means
$$\mu_{\bar{X}} = \mu \qquad (13.1)$$

Second, the standard deviation of the random sampling distribution of means is:

Standard Error of the Mean
$$\sigma_{\bar{X}} = \frac{\sigma}{\sqrt{n}} \qquad (13.2)$$

where σ is the standard deviation of the population and n is the size of the sample.‡ This formula is called the *standard error of the mean*. It calculates the standard deviation of the sampling distribution of means based on samples of a specified size. The term *standard error* is used in place of *standard deviation*. This term serves notice that theory leads us to its value, rather than actual calculation from the sample means in the distribution. Nevertheless, its value is the same as if that had been done, and therefore it *is* a standard deviation. The formula is worth study. It shows that (*a*) means vary less than scores do (when sample size is at least two), (*b*) means vary less where scores vary less, and (*c*) means vary less when sample size is greater.

Note that Greek letters were used to specify the mean and standard deviation of the sampling distribution ($\mu_{\bar{X}}$, $\sigma_{\bar{X}}$). They remind us that the sampling distribution constitutes a population of values, not a sample of them. This distribution represents *all possible* means of samples of a specified size and therefore constitutes the population of them—not just *some* of them.

---

† You remember that a relative frequency distribution is one in which proportional frequency or percent frequency is given, rather than raw frequency. See Section 3.7.

‡ Strictly speaking, this formula is not quite right if the population is finite in size and samples are drawn so that no element can appear in a sample more than once. In practice, this is not likely to be a problem in psychological and educational research. The issue will be fully treated in Section 14.5.

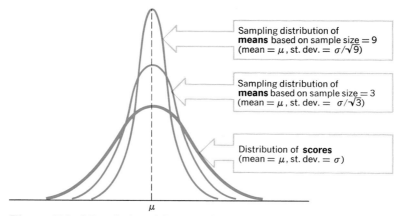

Figure 13.2 *A Population of Scores and Random Sampling Distributions of Means for n = 3 and n = 9.*

With regard to the shape of the distribution, *if the population of scores is normally distributed, the sampling distribution of means will also be normally distributed.* The random sampling distribution of means, demonstrating these three properties, is shown in comparison with the normally distributed population of scores in Figure 13.2. Note particularly how the sampling distribution changes with a change in sample size. This picture reminds us that there is not just one random sampling distribution corresponding to a given population, but a *family* of such distributions, one for each possible sample size.

Now all is well and good if the population is normally distributed. But what if it is not? Fortunately, a remarkable bit of statistical theory comes to the rescue: the *Central Limit Theorem.* This theorem informs us that the *random sampling distribution of means tends toward a normal distribution irrespective of the shape of the population of observations sampled and that the approximation to the normal distribution becomes increasingly close with increase in sample size.* With many populations, the distribution of scores is sufficiently similar to a normal distribution so that little assistance from the Central Limit Theorem is needed. But even when the population of scores differs substantially from a normal distribution, the sampling distribution of means may be treated as though it were normally distributed when sample size is reasonably large. How large is large? Depending on the problem, 25 to 100 cases might be quite large enough.

Figure 13.3 gives some idea of the tendency of the sampling distribution of means to become normalized as sample size rises. At A, two populations of scores are shown: one forming a rectangular distribution and one that is skewed. At B the sampling distributions appear for samples based on $n = 2$. Note that the shapes of these distributions differ from those of their parent populations of scores and that the difference is in the direction of normality. At C we find the sampling distributions for means of samples based on $n = 25$. In both cases the degree of resemblance to the normal distribution is remarkable, though the resemblance is closer for means of samples drawn from the rectangular distribution.

In any event, the usefulness of the Central Limit Theorem for inference about means can hardly be overestimated. It makes possible use of the normal curve as a statistical model for the sampling distribution of means in a wide variety of practical situations. If this were not so, many problems in inference would be very awkward to solve, to say the least.

In this section the random sampling distribution of means has been viewed as the result of an infinite series of sampling trials. An alternative view is also instructive; it is presented in Section 14.6.

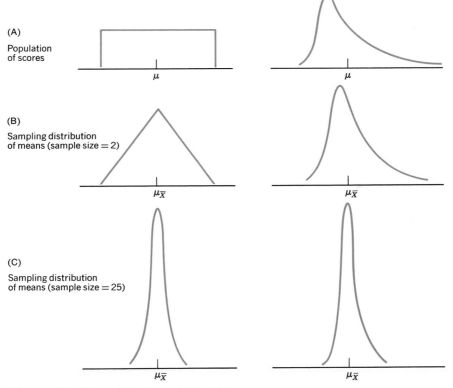

Figure 13.3 *Effect of the Central Limit Theorem.*

13.8 THE SAMPLING DISTRIBUTION AS PROBABILITY DISTRIBUTION

Any frequency distribution may be considered as a *probability distribution* when expressed in terms of proportional frequencies. Suppose an instructor has a statistics class of (Heaven forbid!) 200 students, and at the end he has assigned course grades as follows:

grade	f	p
A	30	.15
B	60	.30
C	80	.40
D	20	.10
F	10	.05
	$n = 200$	1.00

Considered as a frequency distribution, these data show that .15 of the students made an A grade. Viewed as a probability distribution, the same table tells us that if a student were selected at random, the probability is .15 that his course grade would be that of A. Similarly, if we ask the probability of drawing a student who earned a B or better, the answer is .15 + .30 = .45.

In just the same way, the random sampling distribution of means may be interpreted to tell what proportion of sample means would fall between certain limits, or alternatively, to give the probability of drawing such a mean in random sampling. Figure 13.4 illustrates this. It shows a sampling distribution of means that follows the normal curve and has a mean of 100 and standard deviation (standard error) of 5. The mean of 105 lies one standard deviation above the mean ($z = +1.00$). Applying the principles learned in earlier work with the normal curve (Section 7.7), it is possible to determine that .16 of the area under the normal curve falls beyond $z = +1.00$. Now since proportion of area under the curve corresponds to proportion of scores in the distribution, we can say that .16 of sample means will fall to the right of that same location. Alternatively, *we can say*

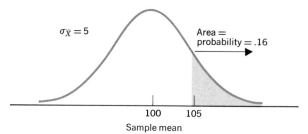

Figure 13.4 *Probability of Obtaining a Mean of 105 or Higher when* $\mu = 100$ *and* $\sigma_{\bar{X}} = 5$.

that in this sampling distribution, the probability of obtaining a sample mean of 105 or higher in random sampling is .16. We will be using these concepts in Section 13.10 and in further work.

13.9 THE FUNDAMENTALS OF INFERENCE AND THE RANDOM SAMPLING DISTRIBUTION OF MEANS: A REVIEW

Let us return, for review, to the issues stated at the beginning of this chapter. A basic aim of statistical inference is to draw conclusions about a characteristic of a population from study of a sample taken from that population. The value of the population characteristic is fixed, if unknown, but the value of that characteristic, as observed in the sample, will vary from sample to sample. The key to the problem of inference is to discover what sample values may be expected to occur in repeated sampling. More precisely, we must know the nature of the sampling distribution of that characteristic. To make this knowledge possible, a method of drawing samples must be specified and used consistently. Random sampling is the fundamental method that makes it possible to discover the properties of the sampling distribution. When sampling is random, it is possible to know the properties of the sampling distributions of many different statistics, e.g., the mean, standard deviation, proportion, etc.

In this chapter, we have developed the properties of the random sampling distribution of means. Its mean is μ, the mean of the population of observations, and its standard deviation is $\sigma/\sqrt{n}$, the standard error of the mean. If the population of observations is normally distributed, so will be the sampling distribution of means. If not, the normal distribution will still be a close, and therefore usable approximation, if sample size is not too small, due to the good offices of the Central Limit Theorem.

13.10 PUTTING THE SAMPLING DISTRIBUTION OF MEANS TO USE

From Chapter 7 we know that many useful questions can be answered when confronted with a normal distribution of known mean and standard deviation. Those procedures are applied in this section to answer four common types of questions that arise in inference. It is assumed that the methods of chapter 7 (see especially Sections 7.6, 7.7, and 7.8) are understood.

Given: A normally distributed population, with $\mu = 70$ and $\sigma = 20$. (Assume sample size is 25.)

Problem 1: What is the probability of obtaining a sample mean of 80 or higher?

Solution; Step 1. Calculate the standard deviation of the sampling distribution, i.e., the standard error of the mean.

$$\sigma_{\bar{X}} = \frac{\sigma}{\sqrt{n}} = \frac{20}{\sqrt{25}} = 4.00$$

Step 2. Restate the location of the sample mean of 80 as a z score. The general formula for a z score is: (*score − mean*)/(*standard deviation*). In a sampling distribution of means, the sample mean is the score, the mean of the population of scores is the mean, and the standard error of the mean is the standard deviation. Therefore,

$$z = \frac{80 - 70}{4} = +2.50$$

Step 3. Take the z score to the table of areas under the normal curve (Table B, in Appendix F), and determine the proportionate area beyond z. It is .0062. In random sampling, therefore, means of 80 or higher would occur with a relative frequency of .0062 for samples of size 25. The probability of obtaining such a mean in random sampling is therefore .0062. Figure 13.5 illustrates the problem.

Problem 2: What is the probability that the sample mean will differ from the population mean by 10 points or more? In Problem 1, the mean of 80 fell 10 points above the mean (70) of the sampling distribution. Since the normal curve is symmetrical, the same area lies below a mean of 60 (10 points below 70) as above one of 80 (10 points above 70). The z score will have the same magnitude; we must double the corresponding area to find the required probability. The probability of

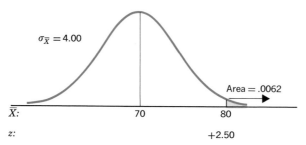

Figure 13.5 *Finding the Proportion of Sample Means Exceeding a Given Value.*

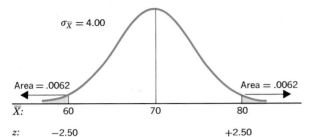

Figure 13.6 *Finding the Proportion of Sample Means that Differ from the Population Mean by More Than a Given Amount.*

obtaining a sample mean differing from the population mean by 10 points or more is therefore $(2)(.0062) = .0124$. The problem is illustrated in Figure 13.6.

Problem 3: What mean has such a high value that the probability is .05 of obtaining one as high or higher in random sampling?

Solution; Step 1. From Table C in Appendix F find the z score above which .05 of the area under the normal curve falls; it is $z = +1.6449$, or, to three decimals, $+1.645$.

Step 2. The value of z informs us that the desired value is 1.645 standard deviations above the mean of the distribution. Therefore (remembering that our concern is with the sampling distribution and that *its* standard deviation is $\sigma_{\bar{X}}$, not σ_X):

$$\bar{X} = \mu_{\bar{X}} + z\sigma_{\bar{X}}$$
$$= 70 + (+1.645)(4.00)$$
$$= 70 + 6.58$$
$$= 76.58$$

Five percent of sample means will have a value of at least 76.58; the probability is .05 of selecting such a mean. The problem is illustrated in Figure 13.7.

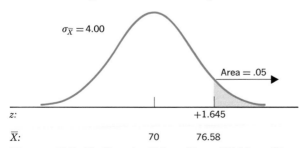

Figure 13.7 *Finding the Value Above Which a Given Proportion of Sample Means Will Fall.*

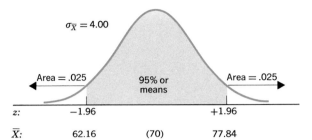

Figure 13.8 *Finding the Centrally Located Score Limits between Which a Given Proportion of Sample Means Will Fall.*

Problem 4: Within what limits would the central 95% of sample means fall? If .95 of the values are to fall in the center, the remaining .05 must be divided equally between the two tails of the distribution. Therefore, we must find the value of z beyond which .025 of the area is located. The method is the same as for Problem 3, and the solution is outlined below:

Lower Limit

$$z_{LL} = -1.96$$
$$\bar{X}_{LL} = \mu_{\bar{X}} + z_{LL}\sigma_{\bar{X}}$$
$$= 70 + (-1.96)(4.00)$$
$$= 70 - 7.84$$
$$= 62.16$$

Upper Limit

$$z_{UL} = +1.96$$
$$\bar{X}_{UL} = \mu_{\bar{X}} + z_{UL}\sigma_{\bar{X}}$$
$$= 70 + (+1.96)(4.00)$$
$$= 70 + 7.84$$
$$= 77.84$$

Ninety-five percent of sample means fall between 62.16 and 77.84. In random sampling, the probability is .95 of obtaining a mean within these limits and .05 of obtaining one beyond these limits. The problem is illustrated in Figure 13.8.

PROBLEMS AND EXERCISES

Identify:

hypothesis testing
estimation
population
sample
probability sample
random sample
random sampling distribution
    of means
standard error of the mean

Central Limit Theorem
probability
relative frequency
   distribution
three properties of a
   sampling distribution
$\mu_{\bar{X}}$
$\sigma_{\bar{X}}$

1 The principal notes that the mean reading test score of Miss Bates's class is 35.5 this year but was 37.5 last year. Any question before we recommend that he have a talk with her about "shaping up"?

2 An instructor gives a 100-item multiple choice examination. Each question has four alternatives. If the student knows nothing about the subject and selects answers by chance, (*a*) What is the probability for a given question that it will be answered correctly? (*b*) What is the expected number of correct answers for a given student (assume he attempts all questions)?

3 A die is cast. What is the probability of rolling (*a*) a five? (*b*) a one or a six? (*c*) a three or higher?

4 Consider the table in Section 13.8. What is the probability that a student selected at random will be one who passed the course?

5 Given: a normally distributed population, with $\mu = 150$, and $\sigma = 24$. If samples of size 36 are drawn at random, what is the probability of obtaining (*a*) a sample mean of 154 or higher? (*b*) a sample mean that differs from 150 by 6 points or more?

6 Given: A normally distributed population with $\mu = 120$ and $\sigma = 10$. If samples of size 25 are drawn at random, what is the probability of obtaining (*a*) a sample mean of 118.25 or lower? (*b*) a mean that differs from 120 by 2 points or more?

7 Given: A normally distributed population with $\mu = 150$ and $\sigma = 25$. If samples of size 100 are drawn at random, what is the probability of obtaining (*a*) a sample mean of 156 or higher? (*b*) a sample mean that differs from 150 by 7 points or more?

8 For the data of question 5, (*a*) What sample mean is so great that it would be exceeded but 1% of the time in random sampling? (*b*) Within what central limits would 99% of sample means fall?

9 For the data of question 6, (*a*) what sample value is so small that the probability of one smaller is .02? (*b*) within what central limits would 95% of sample means fall?

10 For the data of question 7, (*a*) what sample mean is so high that 10% of means would be higher? (*b*) within what central limits would 90% of sample means fall?

CHAPTER 14

14.1 INTRODUCTION

The last chapter presented the minimum essentials of the basis of statistical inference. It can stand by itself as the background necessary for chapter 15 and those chapters to follow. For the "short course" in statistics, then, it would be possible to skip the present chapter and proceed to the next.

The purpose of this chapter is to enlarge upon material introduced in the previous one, to develop qualifications that appear in application, and to give additional background that should deepen understanding of statistical inference, particularly as conducted in real-life settings. You will find, for example, further development of principles of probability, further exploration of the fundamental concept of the random sample and problems in obtaining one, a discussion of some of the "look-alike" relatives of true random sampling and their utility (or lack of it), and a presentation of an alternative approach to understanding the random

The Basis of Statistical Inference: Further Considerations

sampling distribution of means, an approach that because of its concrete nature should provide a good intuitive understanding of that vital concept.

14.2 ANOTHER WAY OF LOOKING AT PROBABILITY

In the previous chapter (Section 13.5) probability was defined in terms of relative frequency of occurrences in an indefinitely large series of sampling trials. Sometimes the possible outcomes of a sampling trial can be considered to be equally likely to occur. In a toss of a fair die, the values 1, 2, 3, 4, 5, and 6 are equally likely to occur. In selecting a score at random from a distribution, we are as likely to obtain a score above the median as below. This idea leads to a second way of looking at probability:

> *Given a population of possible outcomes, each of which is equally likely to occur, the probability of occurrence on a single trial of an outcome characterized by A is equal to the number of outcomes yielding A, divided by the total number of possible outcomes.*

In a deck of 52 cards, there are 13 spades. If a card is drawn at random, there are 52 equally likely ways in which a card may be drawn. Since there are 13 ways in which a spade may be drawn out of the 52 possible ways, the probability of drawing a spade is 13/52, or 1/4. Similarly, the probability of drawing an Ace is 4/52, the probability of drawing an Ace in a red suit is 2/52, and the probability of drawing a card (of any denomination) in a red suit is 1/2. In a distribution of 100 scores, there are 25 scores above C_{75} and 75 below. In drawing blindly, each score is equally likely to be selected. Therefore, there are 25 ways to select a score above C_{75}, out of the 100 ways in which a score can be selected. The probability of selecting a score above C_{75} is, then, 1/4.

A distinction can be made between *theoretical probability* and *empirical probability*. In the former case, rational grounds lead us to the probability value. In the latter, it is experience. Thus, we assume that if a fair coin is tossed fairly, the probability that it will come up heads is 1/2. An empirical probability value, on the other hand, is obtained by observation of the relative frequency of occurrence of an event over a finite series of trials, short or long. An empirical probability is but an estimate of the true value, and confidence is to be placed in it according to the number of observations on which it is based. For example, a survey of 1000 homes selected at random in a city may show that 85% have telephones. We therefore presume that a home selected at random has a probability of .85 of having a phone. With a sample from the entire city (the population) of this size, .85 is likely to be close, but not exactly equal to the correct probability.

Probability refers to uncertainty of outcome of an event. It is the outcome that is important, and not our knowledge of it. If we are *about* to toss a coin, the probability is one-half that it will come up heads. If the coin *has* been tossed, but the outcome not revealed, the probability of heads is no longer one-half; it is one or zero, but we do not know which.

14.3 TWO THEOREMS IN PROBABILITY

Let us look again at a problem introduced in the previous section. In a deck of 52 cards, what is the probability of drawing an Ace? We observed that there were four ways of drawing an Ace out of the 52 ways in which a card might be drawn. According to the principle of relative frequency among equally likely outcomes the probability of drawing an Ace is 4/52.

The same problem may be viewed another way. The probability of drawing an Ace of Spades is 1/52, and the same is true for the Ace of Hearts, the Ace of Diamonds, and the Ace of Clubs. The probability of drawing the Ace of Spades *or* the Ace of Hearts, *or* the Ace of Diamonds, *or* the Ace of Clubs is the sum of the individual probabilities, i.e., $1/52 + 1/52 + 1/52 + 1/52 = 4/52$. Similarly, the probability of obtaining a 5 *or* a 6 on a single toss of a die is $1/6 + 1/6 = 2/6$.

These examples illustrate the *addition theorem* of probability:

> *The probability of occurrence of any one of several particular outcomes is the sum of their individual probabilities, provided that they are mutually exclusive.*

Note that this proposition is valid only when the outcomes are *mutually exclusive;* that is, when the occurrence of one precludes the possibility of the occurrence of any of the others. In the examples above, the card drawn may be the Ace of Spades *or* the Ace of Hearts, but it can not be both. Similarly, a die may come up five *or* six, but we can not have it both ways. If you will look back to the table in Section 13.8 in the previous chapter, you will find a distribution of grades given to a class of 200 students. The question of the probability of earning a B or better can be approached through the addition theorem. Since grades of A and B are mutually exclusive outcomes, Pr (A or B) = Pr (A) + Pr (B) = .15 + .30 = .45.

Of the students at a given college, suppose that (1), 60% are men and 40% are women and (2), that 50% of the students are in the lower division, 40% in the upper division, and 10% in the graduate division. The addition theorem may be applied to state that in selecting a student at random, the probability that he will be either a lower division or an upper division student is .50 + .40 = .90. However, the same theorem may *not* be applied to obtain the probability that the student will be either a graduate student or a male; these are not mutually exclusive outcomes. A modification of the addition theorem appropriate when outcomes are not mutually exclusive is presented in Note 14.1.

Another useful theorem concerns joint events. Two coins are tossed. What is the probability that both will come up heads? Let us view the tossing of two coins as an experiment which is to be repeated indefinitely. In the long run, the first coin will come up heads half of the time. The second coin will come up heads in but half of those trials in which the first coin came heads. Therefore, the proportion of *all* trials in which both coins will come up heads is $(\frac{1}{2})(\frac{1}{2}) = \frac{1}{4}$. The probability of obtaining two heads on a single trial is therefore $\frac{1}{4}$.

This illustrates the *multiplication theorem* of probability:

> *The probability of several particular outcomes occurring jointly is the product of their separate probabilities, provided that the events that generate these outcomes are independent.*

Again, we have a qualification; the events must be independent. *Independence* of events means that the outcome of one event must have no influence on and in no way be related to the outcome of the other event (or events).† In the example cited, the way the first coin falls has no influence on the way the second coin will fall. The outcome of the toss of two coins is therefore the outcome of two independent events. Note that the rule, as stated, is extended to more than two independent events. If we ask the probability of obtaining three heads when three coins are tossed, it is $(\frac{1}{2})(\frac{1}{2})(\frac{1}{2}) = \frac{1}{8}$.

People being what they are, it is not unusual for them to act as though events are not independent when in fact they are. This failure occurs so often that it has been given a name: the Gambler's Fallacy. If we look over the shoulder of a person playing roulette, we may find him keeping track of the numbers that have come up, with the idea that he will bet on one that has not appeared recently, and so is "due." Such a system comes to naught. Assuming a fair wheel, fairly spun, there is no way in which the outcome of an earlier trial may affect the outcome of the present trial.

Many events are, of course, *not* independent. What is the probability of selecting a student who is above the median in English *and* above the median in spelling? If the one is true, the other is more likely to occur. The multiplication theorem does not apply. Indeed, any two events that are correlated (see chapter 9) are necessarily dependent, at least to some extent. A modification of the multiplication theorem appropriate to dependent events is presented in Note 14.4 (but read Notes 14.2 and 14.3 first for the necessary background).

Those just getting acquainted with probability sometimes become confused about mutually exclusive outcomes and independent events. Look carefully at the explanations that accompany their introduction; they do not mean the same thing. For example, the particular outcomes that may result from a *single* trial are always completely dependent if they are mutually exclusive: the occurrence of one predicts with certainty that the other(s) will *not* occur. The multiplication theorem applies only to situations where two or more "trials" are considered together, as in the tossing of two coins or the result of tossing one coin twice.

14.4 MORE ABOUT RANDOM SAMPLING

In the previous chapter, a random sample was defined as a sample so drawn that each possible sample of that size has an equal probability of selection. If a sample is drawn in this way, it is necessarily true that every element in the population has an equal chance of being selected. The reverse is *not* true; giving equal probability to the elements does not necessarily result in equal probability for samples. Consider

---

† Formal consideration of independence in a probability sense is given in Note 14.3. To understand this note, Note 14.2 must be read first.

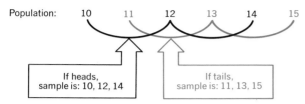

Figure 14.1 *The Two Possible Samples Resulting from a Systematic Sampling Scheme.*

the following *population* of scores: 10, 11, 12, 13, 14, and 15. Suppose our task is to draw a sample of three different scores at random. It might occur to us to toss a coin, and if it comes up heads we will take as our sample the first, third, and fifth scores. Otherwise our sample will be the second, fourth, and sixth scores. With this scheme just two samples are possible: 10, 12, 14, or 11, 13, 15. This is shown in Figure 14.1. Now what is the probability under this sampling method that 10 will appear in the sample? Clearly, 1/2. What about 14? Also 1/2 since it will be included if the coin comes up heads. But that is also true of 11 and of 13, and indeed of each and every element in this population. The sampling method therefore satisfies the equal probability requirement for elements. However, it does *not* satisfy the requirement that each sample of size 3 that could be formed shall have an equal opportunity of selection; only two samples are possible. The sample 10, 11, 12, for example, has no chance of selection. Will this make a difference in the random sampling distribution of means? It certainly can, and in this instance it does. In true random sampling the sample means will range from 11.0 (for a sample consisting of the three lowest scores) to 14.0. But in our case variability of means will be less because only the means 12.0 and 13.0 are possible.

In the real world of data, it is often difficult or costly (and sometimes impossible!) to draw a simple random sample from the population that the investigator would truly like to study. To do it the right way, we would have to identify every element of the population and then arrange to follow the implications of the definition of a random sample. Sometimes we are tempted to use a shortcut to reduce the amount of work. Three popular shortcuts are described below.

The first is to draw cases by what is usually known as a *systematic sampling method*. For example, one may decide to draw a sample of the students currently enrolled in school by selecting every tenth one in an alphabetical list. In many cases samples obtained by such a procedure probably closely approximate samples obtained through a random sampling. But did you notice that this is exactly the procedure described earlier in this section? If the names are in any order that proves to be related to the observation we are taking, or if there is a cyclical trend in the data that happens to coincide with the periodicity of selection of cases, we are in trouble. Think carefully before using this method, remembering Murphy's Law: "If anything can go wrong, it will."

A second substitute is to attempt to obtain a *representative sample,* one deliberately chosen to have characteristics that resemble the population as closely as possible. But if this is done with success, sample means will vary rather less than in random sampling. *Any* sample, however deviant from the expected, has *some* chance of occurring. How much less? *That's* the problem; we can no longer say. We are therefore in no position to specify the standard deviation of the sampling distribution, and accurate inferential conclusions are not possible.

The third method is to select what might be called a *casual sample.* The essence of this method is that the investigator attempts to act as a human randomizer. He tries to choose "at random" from the available subjects, and it will more likely fail than succeed. Suppose he wants to ascertain the public's view on the adequacy of compensation of women who work. But suppose also that he dearly prefers talking to pretty young women than to older women, and to women than to men. Would you trust the adequacy of his sampling procedure, however earnest he was? What about assigning rats from the new shipment to two conditions of an experiment? Our research assistant reaches into the shipping containers to select those animals to receive Treatment A. Do you think animated and lethargic rats will have an equal chance of being chosen? What about those that bite at his fingers versus those that do not? Freud said it long ago in *Psychopathology of Everyday Life,* but it is most clearly stated in Minium's Third Law of Statistics: "The human being is a rotten randomizer." When it is possible to enumerate the elements of the population, by far the best method is to refer to a table of random numbers in order to select the sample.† This method is described in Section 14.7. Further discussion of the difficulties in attempting to select a random sample will be found in Section 15.11.

14.5 TWO SAMPLING PLANS

Although there is only one way to define a random sample, there are two *sampling plans* that yield a random sample. If there are 50 tickets in a lottery and we draw one ticket, set it aside, draw another, and so on until five tickets have been selected, we are *sampling without replacement.* The characteristic of this method is that no element may appear more than once in a sample.

On the other hand, if a ticket is selected, its number noted, and the ticket returned before the next ticket is chosen, we are *sampling with replacement.* Under this plan it is possible to draw a sample in which the same element appears more than once.

Both of these plans satisfy the condition of random sampling, but certain sample outcomes possible when sampling with replacement are not possible under the

---

† Or to use a computer program that accomplishes the same result.

other method. This is illustrated in the following example. Suppose a population consists of three scores: 2, 4, 6, and samples of size two are drawn from this population. Table 14.1 shows the possible samples that could result when sampling is done with and without replacement. Note that when sampling without replacement, the samples are the same as when sampling with replacement, except for those in which the same element appears more than once. In the table, the sample in which 2 was obtained on the first draw and 4 on the second is treated as a different sample from that in which 4 was obtained on the first draw and 2 on the second. *Both* are possible samples, and account must be taken of each. This point will be clarified in the next section.

You remember that there are three characteristics of a sampling distribution that define it: mean, standard deviation, and shape. The first and last of these are unaffected by choice of sampling plan, but *the standard deviation of the sampling distribution is smaller when sampling without replacement:*

Standard Error of the Mean:
Sampling without replacement
$$\sigma_{\bar{X}} = \frac{\sigma}{\sqrt{n}} \sqrt{\frac{N - n}{N - 1}} \tag{14.1}$$

In this formula, N is the size of the population. Note that the formula would be the same as for sampling with replacement (Formula 13.2), except for the "correction factor" appearing at the far right: $\sqrt{(N - n)/(N - 1)}$. *The correction will not amount to much if the sample is small relative to the size of the population.* For example, if the sample is .05 of the population, $\sigma_{\bar{X}} = .975(\sigma/\sqrt{n})$, approximately. In any situation where the sample is a still smaller fraction of the population, the correction would be even less.

Table 14.1 *Possible Samples of Size 2 Drawn from a Population of Three Scores under Two Sampling Plans*

Population: 2, 4, 6			
Possible samples: sampling with replacement		*Possible samples: sampling without replacement*	
1st draw	*2nd draw*	*1st draw*	*2nd draw*
2	2		
2	4	2	4
2	6	2	6
4	2	4	2
4	4		
4	6	4	6
6	2	6	2
6	4	6	4
6	6		

Despite the fact that most sampling in behavioral science is done without replacement, we typically use the other formula for the standard error of the mean. No harm is done in the usual case, where the sample may be thought to be substantially smaller than 5% of the population.

14.6 THE RANDOM SAMPLING DISTRIBUTION OF MEANS: AN ALTERNATIVE APPROACH

In the previous chapter (Section 13.6) the random sampling distribution of means was conceived as the result of an infinite series of sampling trials. Another view is possible; it is one that makes possible a more concrete understanding of that distribution: *the random sampling distribution of means is the relative frequency distribution of means obtained from all possible samples of a given size that could be formed from a given population.* This definition holds whether sampling is done with or without replacement; the difference lies in the fact that a "possible sample" is not the same under the two sampling plans.

Note that if the population is of finite size, the number of possible samples will also be finite. This makes it possible to generate an entire sampling distribution and to explore its properties in a way not open to us when the distribution is defined as the outcome of a never-ending series of sampling trials. But to do this we will have to keep things simple.

Consider a population of four scores: 2, 4, 6, 8, from which samples of size two are to be selected. What are the possible samples? When sampling is done with replacement, there are four ways in which the first score may be chosen, and also four ways in which the second may be chosen. Consequently, there are $4 \times 4 = 16$ possible samples. These are shown at the left in Table 14.2.

What is the probability of drawing the sample (2, 2)? When each score is given an equal opportunity of selection, the probability that the first element will be 2 is $\frac{1}{4}$, and, when the score is replaced before selecting the second element, the probability that the second element will be 2 is also $\frac{1}{4}$. Selection of the second element is in no way dependent on the outcome of selection of the first element, and the two events are independent. The probability, therefore, of obtaining the sample (2, 2) is the product of the two probabilities: $(\frac{1}{4})(\frac{1}{4}) = \frac{1}{16}$, according to the multiplication rule for independent events (see Section 14.3). By similar reasoning, the probability of occurrence of any one of the other samples is also $\frac{1}{16}$. These probabilities are shown in the second column of Table 13.3. It is apparent that if samples are selected in this manner, each of the 16 possible samples is equally likely to occur, and the basic condition of random sampling is satisfied.

Our fundamental interest is in the means of these samples rather than in the samples themselves. The mean of each sample is given in the third column of

Table 14.2 *Possible Samples and Sample Means for Samples of Size Two (Sampling with Replacement).*

	Population: 2, 4, 6, 8	
Sample	Probability of occurrence	Mean
2, 2	1/16	2.0
2, 4	1/16	3.0
2, 6	1/16	4.0
2, 8	1/16	5.0
4, 2	1/16	3.0
4, 4	1/16	4.0
4, 6	1/16	5.0
4, 8	1/16	6.0
6, 2	1/16	4.0
6, 4	1/16	5.0
6, 6	1/16	6.0
6, 8	1/16	7.0
8, 2	1/16	5.0
8, 4	1/16	6.0
8, 6	1/16	7.0
8, 8	1/16	8.0

Table 14.2. Note that, although there are 16 different samples, each equally likely, this does *not* result in 16 different means, each equally likely. For example, there is only one sample (2, 2) that yields the mean of 2.0, but there are two samples for which the mean is 3.0: (2, 4), and (4, 2).† The probability of obtaining a sample with a mean of 2.0 is therefore $\frac{1}{16}$, whereas the probability of obtaining a sample with a mean of 3.0 is $\frac{1}{8}$, twice as great. This reminds us that *random sampling results in equal probability of occurrence of any possible sample, not in equal probability of occurrence of any possible sample mean.*

The 16 means may be cast in a relative frequency distribution, as shown in Table 14.3. This relative frequency distribution is, of course, the random sampling distribution of means for samples of size two drawn with replacement from the particular population of size 4.

This distribution is shown graphically in Figure 14.2. For comparative purposes two features have been added. First, the distribution of the population of scores appears in the same figure. Second, a normal curve has been fitted to the sampling distribution of means. What features appear in this sampling distribution?

---

† It is apparent that the sample (2,4) must be treated as distinct from the sample (4,2). Each is possible, and each yields a sample mean that must be accounted for.

Table 14.3 *Sampling Distribution of Means: Data from Table 14.2*

Sample means	Relative frequency
8.0	1/16
7.0	2/16
6.0	3/16
5.0	4/16
4.0	3/16
3.0	2/16
2.0	1/16

1 The mean of the sampling distribution of means is the same as the mean of the population of scores, that is, $\mu_{\bar{X}} = \mu_X = 5.0$.

2 The variability of the sampling distribution of means is *less* than the variability of the population of scores. The standard deviation of the population of scores is 2.236 ($\sigma_X = 2.236$), but the standard deviation of the distribution of means is 1.581 ($\sigma_{\bar{X}} = 1.581$).

3 The distribution of sample means tends to resemble the normal curve, although the population of scores is more like a rectangular distribution.

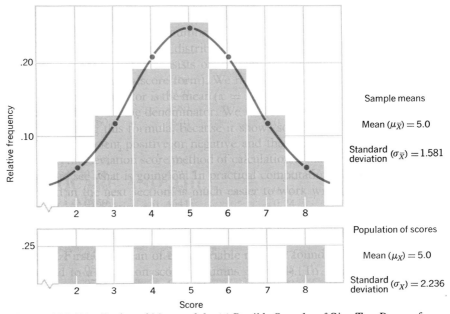

Figure 14.2 *Distribution of Means of the 16 Possible Samples of Size Two Drawn from a Population of Four Scores: Data from Table 13.4. Population: 2, 4, 6, 8.*

The standard deviation of the sampling distribution may be found by the formula for the standard error of the mean: $\sigma_{\bar{X}} = 2.236/\sqrt{2} = 1.581$. Because our sampling distribution consists of only 16 means, it is possible to verify that value by actually calculating the standard deviation of the set of 16 means; the answer is the same: 1.581.

What is really surprising is to see the power of the Central Limit Theorem in this limited situation. Look at the distribution of population scores, shown at the bottom of Figure 14.2. This is no normal distribution; if it had to be given a name, we might call it the Tooth Distribution of the Halloween Pumpkin. But look at what has happened to the random sampling distribution of means. This comes very close to the characteristics of a normal distribution. Compare the heights of the rectangles with the dots showing the elevation of the normal distribution at similar locations.

14.7 USING A TABLE OF RANDOM NUMBERS

How shall we select "at random"? Numerous experiments have demonstrated that human judgment can not be depended upon to perform this function, even when no apparent bias is present. The several variations of the "numbered tags in a box" scheme are at the very least awkward and under some circumstances unreliable. If each element of the population can be identified and assigned an identification number, a convenient and reliable procedure is to use a table of random numbers, such as Table I, in Appendix F. Such tables are usually constructed by computer, according to a program that ensures that each digit has an equal probability of occurrence.

A table of random numbers may be read as successive single digits, as successive two-digit numbers, as three-digit numbers, or otherwise. Thus, in Table I in the appendix, if we begin at the top left on the first page and read down, the random order of single digit numbers would be: 1, 9, 0, 7, 3, . . . If we wish to read two-digit numbers, they would be: 11, 96, 07, 71, 32, ...

Since the digits in the table are random, many schemes for selecting a set of random numbers are acceptable. For example, the desired numbers may be read vertically (in either direction) or horizontally (in either direction). To use them properly, some scheme must be adopted *in advance*. It should specify how the desired group of numbers (e.g., two-digit numbers) will be formed and how they will be read from the table (including how to proceed when the end of a column or row has been reached). In addition, it should specify how to enter the table. Well-shuffled slips of paper may be used to identify the page, column, and row that should mark the beginning.

To begin, each element of the population should be assigned an identification number. The order of the elements does not matter, since subsequent randomization will take care of that. Suppose that 30 scores are to be selected at random from a population of 700. Each element may be given a three-digit identification number, from 000 to 699, or 001 to 700, if preferred.† For the sake of simplicity, suppose that our scheme requires that we start at the upper left of the first page of the table and read down. The first random number is 113, and the first element to be included in the sample is therefore that bearing the identification number 113. The next random number is 969; it is skipped because it identifies no element of the population. The next number is 077, and identifies the second score to be included in the sample. We continue until 30 elements have been selected. If sampling is *with* replacement and the same element is selected twice, it must be included again. If sampling is *without* replacement, and an identification number appears a second time, it should be skipped.

NOTES

Note 14.1   Probability of Occurrence of A or B when A and B Are Not Mutually Exclusive (*Ref:* Section 14.3)

$$\mathrm{Pr}\,(A \text{ or } B) = \mathrm{Pr}\,(A) + \mathrm{Pr}\,(B) - \mathrm{Pr}\,(AB)$$

where: Pr (A) is the probability of A
Pr (B) is the probability of B
Pr (AB) is the probability of A
and B occurring together

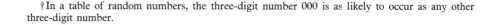

---

† In a table of random numbers, the three-digit number 000 is as likely to occur as any other three-digit number.

The outcome, (A *or* B), is satisfied if A occurs, if B occurs, or, when A and B are not mutually exclusive, if both A and B occur. Note the accompanying illustration, in which A and B are *not* mutually exclusive. If the number of outcomes characterized by A is added to the number characterized by B, their sum includes *twice* the number characterized by both A and B. To determine the number of outcomes characterized by A *or* B, this total must therefore be reduced by the number characterized by A *and* B, so that the latter quantity will be counted only once. Similarly, the probability of (A or B) ought to include but once the probability of (AB). When A and B *are* mutually exclusive, Pr (AB) = 0, and the formula for Pr (A or B) reduces to the addition theorem given in Section 14.3: Pr (A or B) = Pr (A) + Pr (B).

Note 14.2 Conditional Probability (*Ref:* Section 14.3)

Pr (A | B) is the symbolic representation for the probability of occurrence of A, *given that* B has occurred.† Probabilities of this type are called *conditional probabilities*. Consider the selection of a card, without replacement, from a 52 card deck. If we ask in advance as to the probability that the second card will be an Ace, it is $1/13$ (or $4/52$). But with additional knowledge, the probability changes. According to the above definition, Pr (2nd card is an Ace | 1st card is an Ace) = $3/51$, whereas Pr (2nd card is an Ace | 1st card is not an Ace) = $4/51$.

The notion of conditional probability is important in defining independence of events (see Note 14.3), in finding the probability of joint events (see Note 14.4), and in considering sampling without replacement (see Note 14.4). It is also relevant to an understanding of the likelihood of occurrence of error in testing hypotheses (see Section 16.7).

Note 14.3 Independence in a Probability Sense (*Ref:* Section 14.3).

(*N.B.* Note 14.2 provides proper background for this note.)

In Section 14.3, it was stated that independence of events means that the outcome of one event must in no way alter the probability of occurrence of the other. Symbolically, we may say that A and B are independent if Pr (A) = Pr (A | B). For example, in tossing coins, Pr (2nd coin comes heads) = Pr (2nd coin comes heads | 1st coin comes heads), and the two events are independent. However, in a given university, Pr (admission of an applicant) $\neq$ Pr (admission of an applicant | applicant's high school record is straight "A"); these two events are not independent.

The property of independence is pertinent in sampling *with* replacement (see Section 14.5). Consider a population of three scores: 2, 4, 6. What is the probability of selecting the sample (2, 6)?‡ The probability that the first element of the sample will be 2 is $1/3$. When that element has been replaced before selecting the second element, the probability that the second element will be 6 is also $1/3$; selection of the second element is independent of the outcome of selection of the first element. In terms of the definition of independence, Pr (second element is 6 | first element is 2) = Pr (second element is 6) = $1/3$. The probability, then, of selecting the sample (2, 6) follows the multiplication theorem for independent events (Section 14.3): Pr (2, 6) = $(1/3)(1/3) = 1/9$. See Note 14.4 for a comparable problem in sampling without replacement.

---

†The vertical bar is therefore to be read "given that," or perhaps "given the condition that."

‡The sample (2, 6) is considered to be one sample, and the sample (6, 2) another.

Note 14.4 Probability of Joint Occurrence of Dependent Events (*Ref:* Section 14.3)
(*N.B.* Notes 14.2 and 14.3 provide proper background for this note.)

When A and B are dependent events, probability of occurrence of both A *and* B is given by the product of the two probabilities: $\Pr(AB) = [\Pr(A|B)][\Pr(B)]$. This concept can be illustrated in application to sampling without replacement (see Section 14.5). Consider a population of three scores: 2, 4, 6. What is the probability of selecting the sample (2, 6)? The probability that the first element of the sample will be 2 is 1/3. Given that 2 has been selected (and removed from further selection), the probability that the second element will be 6 is 1/2. Since the outcome of selection of the first element affects the probability of occurrence of the second element, the two events are not independent. In terms of the definition of the probability of joint occurrence of dependent events, $\Pr(2, 6) = [\Pr$ (second element is 6 | first element is 2)][Pr (first element is 2)] $= (1/2)(1/3) = 1/6$. Compare this with the probability of occurrence of the same sample drawn with replacement (see Note 14.3).

According to Note 14.3, if $\Pr(A|B) = \Pr(A)$, A and B are independent. Therefore, when A and B are independent, the expression for probability of joint occurrence of A and B reduces to the multiplication theorem given in Section 14.3: $\Pr(AB) = [\Pr(A)][\Pr(B)]$.

PROBLEMS AND EXERCISES

Identify:

second "definition" of probability
theoretical probability
empirical probability
mutually exclusive outcomes
addition theorem of probability
independent events
multiplication theorem of probability
systematic sample
representative sample
casual sample
sampling with replacement
sampling without replacement
random sampling distribution of means, alternative definition
tables of random numbers
conditional probability (*from notes*)
independence in a probability sense (*from notes*)

1 Do you think weather predictions ("The chance of rain tomorrow is 3 in 10") are better considered as theoretical probabilities or empirical probabilities? Explain.

2 Two dice are tossed. (*a*) List the 36 ways the dice may fall (remember to distinguish between the outcome of die #1 and die #2). (*b*) Consider the sum of the points on the two dice; they may be from 2 to 12. With what relative frequency does each possible sum occur? (*c*) What is the probability of obtaining a 1 with the first die and a 3 with the second die? (*d*) What is the probability of obtaining a sum of points equal to 4? (*e*) What is the probability of obtaining a sum of points equal to 7 on one toss? (*f*) What is the probability of obtaining a sum of points greater than 7? Greater than 4? (*g*) What is the probability of obtaining a sum of points equal to 7 on two successive throws? Of 2 points on two successive throws?

3 Consider Table 14.3. In random sampling, what is the probability of obtaining a sample mean (*a*) of 3.0 or less? (*b*) of 4.0 or 5.0 or 6.0? (*c*) greater than 5.0?

4 From a deck of 52 cards, 2 cards are drawn *with* replacement (see Section 14.5). What is the probability that (*a*) Both cards will be the jack of diamonds? (*b*) Both cards will be jacks? (*c*) Both cards will be diamonds? (*d*) The first card will be an ace and the second a king? (*e*) One card will be an ace and the other a king?

5 You are a "person-in-the-street" interviewer for a radio station. Take as your population those who come near enough that you might buttonhole them for an interview. What biases do you think might prevent you from obtaining a truly random sample of interviewees? Stop when you have listed four.

6 By what percent would the standard error of the mean for sampling with replacement (For. 13.2) be reduced if sampling were *without* replacement and if (*a*) $N = 1,001$; $n = 50$? (*b*) $N = 1,001$; $n = 100$? (*c*) $N = 1,001$, $n = 500$?

7 Consider a population of five scores: 1, 2, 4, 7, 11. (*a*) Find the mean and standard deviation of this set of scores. (*b*) List the 25 possible samples of size 2 that may be composed from this population by sampling with replacement. (*c*) Calculate the mean of each of the 25 samples found in (*b*). (*d*) Cast the 25 means into a frequency distribution. (*e*) Find the mean and standard deviation of the distribution formed in (*d*). (*f*) Calculate the standard error of the mean of samples of size 2: $\sigma_{\bar{X}} = \sigma_{\text{pop}} / \sqrt{2}$. (*g*) Does $\mu_{\bar{X}} = \mu_X$? (*h*) Is $\sigma_{\bar{X}}$ as calculated in (*f*) the same as the standard deviation calculated in (*e*)? (*i*) The population of five scores does not form a symmetrical distribution. Does the distribution of means found in (*d*) appear to follow the normal curve? If not, does it seem closer to a normal distribution than the distribution formed by the population of five scores? What principle is involved?

8 Consider the X scores in Data 9A. Using the table of random numbers and the without-replacement sampling plan, select a sample of 20 scores from this set of 60 scores. Describe the steps in your procedure, including how you used the table of random numbers.

9 (*Based on Notes*) From a deck of 52 cards, 2 cards are drawn *without* replacement. What is the probability that (*a*) Both cards will be the jack of diamonds? (*b*) Both cards will be jacks? (*c*) Both cards will be diamonds? (*d*) The first card will be an ace, and the second a king?

10 (*Based on Notes*) Look ahead to Table 23.7. If a student were selected at random from among the 190, (*a*) What is the probability that the student will be male? (*b*) What is the probability that the student will aspire to the doctorate? (*c*) What is the probability that the student will aspire to the doctorate given the condition that he is male? (*d*) By inspection of Table 23.7, what is the probability that the student will be a male who aspires to the doctorate? Verify this by the theorem presented in Note 14.4, using the answers to earlier parts of this question. (*e*) If aspiring to a particular higher degree were independent of sex, what would be the expected probability that the student would be a male who aspires to the doctorate? (*f*) By inspection of Table 23.7, what is the probability that the student will be male *or* will aspire to the doctorate? Verify this by the theorem presented in Note 14.1.

CHAPTER 15

15.1 INTRODUCTION

In this chapter we shall learn how knowledge of the characteristics of the random sampling distribution of means can be used to test hypotheses about single means using the normal curve model. We shall study both the basic logic of the inferential process and the procedural steps in its accomplishment.

In these procedures theory requires the use of σ, the population standard deviation, but in practically all cases it will not be known and must be estimated from the sample at hand. Naturally, substituting an estimate for the real thing introduces some error, but the larger the sample the smaller the error. So, if sample size is large enough (say, $n \geq 40$), the error will be small enough that the normal curve model will be satisfactory. For this reason, the methods described in this chapter are sometimes known as "large sample procedures." Methods have been developed that take precise account of the error introduced, and that are preferable

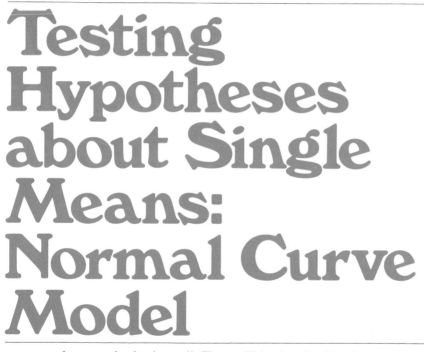

Testing Hypotheses about Single Means: Normal Curve Model

when sample size is small. They will be described in Chapter 19. There are other complications in applying the theoretical model to practical problems. These will receive attention in the last two sections of the present chapter.

As you study this chapter, you will probably find the question "Why?" frequently comes to mind. Indeed, a number of aspects of inferential procedure require further thought and explanation. Chapter 16 gives a commentary on the major questions that arise. The aspects of inference discussed there apply generally and are therefore not limited to problems concerning means.

Chapter 17 will describe how the normal curve model may be applied to problems of inference about two means. It is of particular importance because it forms the model for evaluating the outcome of an experiment in which two groups of subjects are treated differently and the question is whether the difference in treatment resulted in a difference in performance. Again, some parameters must ordinarily be estimated, so these procedures will be adequate only when sample size is large enough. The focus in the present chapter and in chapter 17 is on hypothesis testing. In chapter 18 we turn to interval estimation. In chapter 19 we discuss both types of inference when parameters must be estimated and sample size is small.

A number of factors must be considered in designing a study so that the risk of error in inference is known, the efficiency of the study is as high as possible, and the conclusions drawn at the outcome follow logically from the evidence. Problems of experimental design, such as those listed above, are discussed in chapter 21.

15.2 TESTING A HYPOTHESIS ABOUT A SINGLE MEAN

Dr. Frost, the research director of a large school district, reads in the test manual that the national norm for sixth-grade students on a particular test of achievement in mathematics is 85. He would like to know if the students in his district are performing at the same level. He selects at random 100 students from all the sixth-grade students in the district, and arranges to have the same test administered to them. The population of interest to him consists of the test scores of all currently enrolled sixth-grade students in the district. From study of the sample, he wants to draw an inference whether μ, the mean of *his* population is 85.

To answer this question, he will use the statistical model for testing hypotheses about single means. He will translate his question into a statistical hypothesis: that the mean of the population of sixth graders in his district is 85. This hypothesis will then be subjected to examination, and, at the end, accepted or rejected. To examine its validity, he will ask what sample means would occur if many samples of the same size were drawn at random from his population if the hypothesis that the population mean is 85 is true. The random sampling distribution of means appropriate to his problem provides this information. He will compare his sample mean with those that would result if the hypothesis were true. The relation between his sample mean and those of the random sampling distribution of means might look like that pictured at the left in Figure 15.1. If so, his mean is one that could reasonably occur if the hypothesis were true, and he will "accept" the hypothesis. If the relationship is like that pictured at the right, his mean is so deviant that it would

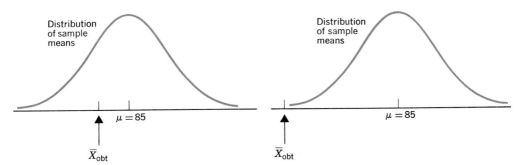

Figure 15.1 *Possible Locations of the Obtained Sample Mean Relative to the Distribution of Expected Sample Means when the Hypothesis Is True.*

be quite unusual to obtain such a value when the hypothesis is true. In this case, he will "reject" the hypothesis, believing it more likely that the mean of his population is not 85, as specified in the hypothesis.

15.3 GENERALITY OF THE PROCEDURE FOR HYPOTHESIS TESTING

The general logic and procedure for testing *all* statistical hypotheses, whether about means, frequencies, or other population characteristics, is essentially that described in the previous section:

1 A specific hypothesis is formulated about a parameter of the population (e.g. about the population mean).

2 A random sample is drawn from the population of observations, and the value of the sample statistic (e.g. the value of the sample mean) is obtained.

3 Characteristics of the random sampling distribution of the statistic under consideration are examined to learn what sample outcomes would occur (and with what relative frequency) if the hypothesis were true.

4 The hypothesis is accepted if the particular sample outcome is in line with the outcomes expected if the hypothesis were true; otherwise, it is rejected.†

---

† To "accept" the hypothesis has a special meaning. See Section 15.6.

15.4 ESTIMATING THE STANDARD ERROR OF THE MEAN WHEN σ IS UNKNOWN

To test hypotheses about means, it will be necessary to calculate the standard error of the mean:

$$\sigma_{\bar{X}} = \frac{\sigma}{\sqrt{n}}$$

Now this formula requires knowledge of σ, the standard deviation of the population, which in actual practice will be unknown and must be estimated from the sample. One would think that S, the sample standard deviation, would be the proper estimate, but it proves to be (on the average) a bit too small. This problem can be solved by calculating a new statistic, s, which provides a better estimate. Its formula is given in Equation 15.1:

Estimate of the Standard
Deviation of the Population $\qquad s = \sqrt{\dfrac{\sum x^2}{n-1}} \qquad\qquad (15.1)$

You will recall that the defining formula for S is $\sqrt{\sum x^2/n}$, so it is clear that s differs only in that the divisor is $n-1$ rather than n. We also see that the change in divisor makes s a bit larger than S. From now on, take care to distinguish between "big S" and "little s"; in print the symbols look much the same.

Substituting s for σ in the formula for the standard error of the mean yields the working formula for estimating the standard error of the mean:

Estimate of the Standard
Error of the Mean $\qquad\qquad s_{\bar{X}} = \dfrac{s}{\sqrt{n}} \qquad\qquad (15.2)$

Note that we have changed the symbol for the standard error of the mean to the lower-case s. *This serves as a reminder that the standard error of the mean is estimated.* Substituting s in making this estimate takes care of bias that would be introduced if S had been used, but different samples will still yield different estimates, and so the variable error introduced by substituting an estimate for the true value remains. As mentioned earlier, procedures described here do *not* make allowance for this error, so we must remember to use them only when samples are large enough.

'The procedure described above is the one that would ordinarily be followed when working a problem through from the beginning. However, suppose that S has already been calculated, or perhaps that S rather than s is desired for descriptive purposes. In either case, it will be convenient to use an alternative formula for estimating the standard error of the mean:

Estimate of the Standard Error
of the Mean; Alternate Formula $\qquad s_{\bar{X}} = \dfrac{S}{\sqrt{n-1}} \qquad\qquad (15.3)$

In this formula, adjustment for bias has been made in the denominator rather than in the numerator. Formula 15.3 produces results identical to those of Formula 15.2, so it may be used any time that S is available and s is not. Remember that $\sigma_{\bar{x}} = \sigma/\sqrt{n}$ is the *true* standard deviation of the sampling distribution of means; Formula 15.2 ($s_{\bar{x}} = s/\sqrt{n}$) and Formula 15.3 ($s_{\bar{x}} = S/\sqrt{n-1}$) are simply *equivalent* ways of estimating it.

It is curious that S should tend to underestimate σ. Closer study of this matter is definitely in order but will be postponed until the next chapter (see Section 16.10 and the Note at the end of chapter 16).

15.5 CAPTAIN BAKER'S PROBLEM: A TEST ABOUT μ

Suppose that the Army has declared that a new standard will be placed into effect as of next July 1: recruits should, after six weeks of basic training, earn on the average a score of 30 on something called the Army Wind and Muscle Test. The base commander wants to know whether his present physical conditioning program appears to be adequate to meet this standard. He turns the problem over to his research officer, Capt. Abel Baker, who will select a sample at random from among the large crop of soldiers just completing training and give them the new test. He does not really care about the mean of this particular sample, but he does want to know whether the mean of the population that has been sampled is 30. Therefore, he will hypothesize that the mean of the population *is* 30. If the mean of the recruit population differs from 30 in either direction, he would like to know it. Formally, his hypothesis will be expressed as follows:

$$H_0: \mu = 30$$
$$H_A \; \mu \neq 30$$

H_0 is called the *null hypothesis;* it is the hypothesis that he will subject to test and that he will decide to accept or reject. H_A is the *alternative hypothesis*. If the evidence is contrary to H_0 *and points with sufficient strength to the validity of* H_A, *he will reject* H_0; otherwise he will accept it.

Next, Capt. Baker selects the criterion by which he will decide to accept or reject the null hypothesis. If the sample mean is so different from what is expected when H_0 is true that its appearance would be unlikely, H_0 should be rejected. What degree of rarity of occurrence is so great that it seems better to reject the null hypothesis than to accept it? Common research practice is to reject H_0 if the sample mean is so deviant that its probability of occurrence in random sampling is .05 or less, or alternatively, .01 or less. Such a criterion is called the *level of significance* and is symbolized by the Greek letter α (alpha). Issues governing the choice of level of significance are discussed in Section 16.4. In the present illustration, we shall assume that Capt. Baker wishes to adopt the .05 level.

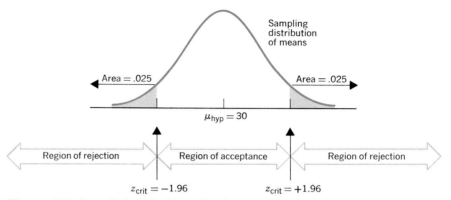

Figure 15.2 *Capt. Baker's Problem: The Random Sampling Distribution when* H_0 *is True.*

What sample means would occur if H_0 were true? If it were true, the random sampling distribution of means would center on μ_{hyp}, or 30, as shown in Figure 15.2. The figure also shows the region of rejection that follows from his decisions so far. He establishes a region of rejection in both tails of the distribution, so in case the evidence suggests either that μ is higher than 30 *or* that it is lower than 30, he will have some chance of rejecting the hypothesis that it is 30. According to the decision criterion adopted, H_0 should be rejected if the obtained sample mean is of the kind so deviant that its probability of occurrence, if the hypothesis were true, would be .05 or less. The critical magnitude of z is therefore that which separates the outer 5% of sample means from the remainder, as shown in Figure 15.2. From Table C in Appendix F, this value is found to be: $z = \pm 1.96$. The space between the two critical values of z (for Capt. Baker's problem, $z = -1.96$ and $z = +1.96$) is called the *region of acceptance,* because H_0 will be accepted if the obtained sample mean falls within these limits. Similarly, the space outside of these limits is called the *region of rejection.*

Before data can be collected one must decide what the size of the sample should be. If the sample is too small, sampling variation will be large and may mask a difference between μ_{hyp} and μ_{true} (i.e. the true value of μ) that it would be important to discover. In other words, the null hypothesis will not be rejected when it should be. Is it possible that a sample might be "too large"? Large samples increase precision by reducing sampling variation, but for a given study there is a limit to the precision needed. Once that has been determined, sample size can be specified. Using more cases can be considered as wasteful of time and effort. Section 21.11 shows how to determine optimum sample size for testing hypotheses about single means.

15.6 CAPTAIN BAKER'S PROBLEM: CONCLUSION

Having set up the conditions of the test, Capt. Baker now draws a random sample of 10 recruits. (This sample is far too small for the problem or for use of the normal curve model; we use it to make the demonstration simple.) The data for these men and the necessary calculations are shown in Table 15.1. The calculations begin by finding $\bar{X}$, s, and $s_{\bar{X}}$, shown in steps 1 through 6 in the table. Individual values of X^2 are recorded in the table but in actual calculation need not be written down if one uses a calculator that can cumulate internally.

What is the relative position of the obtained mean, $\bar{X} = 35.1$, among those expected if the hypothesis were true? To determine the mean's position it must be expressed as a z score. z has the form: $(score - mean)/(standard\ deviation)$. In the distribution of sample means, the sample mean is a score, the hypothesized

Table 15.1 *Calculations for Testing a Hypothesis about a Population Mean*

Subject	Score X	X^2	Calculations
A	43	1849	1. Find $\Sigma X = 351$
B	28	784	
C	24	576	2. Calculate $\bar{X} = \dfrac{\Sigma X}{n} = \dfrac{351}{10} = 35.1$
D	37	1369	
E	36	1296	3. Find $\sum X^2 = 12713$
F	31	961	
G	30	900	4. Calculate $\sum x^2 = \sum X^2 - \dfrac{\left(\sum X\right)^2}{n}$
H	39	1521	
I	44	1936	
J	39	1521	$= 12713 - \dfrac{351^2}{10}$
	$\Sigma X = 351$	$\Sigma X^2 = 12{,}713$	$= 392.9$

5. Calculate $s = \sqrt{\dfrac{\sum x^2}{n-1}} = \sqrt{\dfrac{392.9}{10-1}} = 6.61$

6. Calculate $s_{\bar{X}} = \dfrac{s}{\sqrt{n}} = \dfrac{6.61}{\sqrt{10}} = 2.09$

7. Calculate "z" $= \dfrac{\bar{X} - \mu_{hyp}}{s_{\bar{X}}} = \dfrac{35.1 - 30}{2.09} = +2.44$

8. Compare "z"$_{calc} = 2.44$ with $z_{crit} = 1.96$

9. Statistical conclusion: reject H_0

population mean is the mean, and the standard error of the mean is the standard deviation. Consequently, the location of the sample mean is expressed by:

$$z = \frac{\bar{X} - \mu_{\text{hyp}}}{\sigma_{\bar{X}}}$$

Now since σ is unknown, $\sigma_{\bar{X}}$ is also unknown, and the sample mean cannot be expressed as a true z. What we will do is to calculate it as an approximate z by substituting $s_{\bar{X}}$ for $\sigma_{\bar{X}}$:

Location of Sample Mean in the
Sampling Distribution of Means $\text{``}z\text{''} = \dfrac{\bar{X} - \mu_{\text{hyp}}}{s_{\bar{X}}}$ (15.4)
Expressed as an Approximate z

From now on z calculated by substituting such an estimate will be called an *approximate z* and symbolized "z".†

In the present problem, "z" is found to be $+2.44$, as shown in step 7. The location of "z" in the sampling distribution is shown in Figure 15.3. The value falls in the region of rejection, and so (step 8) Capt. Baker rejects H_0. In short, he concludes that it is *not* reasonable to believe that the mean of the population from which this sample came is 30. Under the circumstances, it seems reasonable to go a step further and say that the mean of his population is very likely greater than 30. The commander will doubtless be pleased and perhaps will fire off a note to the Pentagon suggesting that they come down and study *his* training methods.

If Capt. Baker had used $\alpha = .01$ as his decision criterion rather than $\alpha = .05$, the values of z which would separate the regions of rejection from the region of

† This reveals the heart of the problem in applying the normal curve model when σ must be estimated: we wind up comparing an approximate z with a true z in the sampling distribution (in the present example the true zs are the values of z_{crit}: ± 1.96). The smaller the sample the worse the approximation and the greater the error. The problem will be discussed more fully in chapter 19.

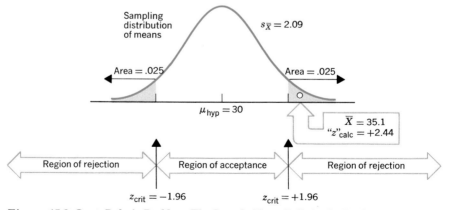

Figure 15.3 Capt. Baker's Problem: The Sample Mean Falls in the Region of Rejection.

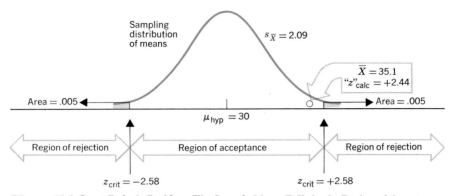

Figure 15.4 *Capt. Baker's Problem: The Sample Mean Falls in the Region of Acceptance.*

acceptance are: $z = \pm 2.58$. Figure 15.4 shows the sampling distribution of means, the location of these critical values of z, and the location of his sample mean. When this decision criterion is used, it is apparent that the sample mean falls in the region of acceptance, and therefore the decision would be to accept H_0. *The decision to "accept" H_0 does not mean that it is likely that H_0 is true, but only that it could be true.*† For example, if Capt. Baker had chosen to test the hypothesis that $\mu = 35$ at the .01 level of significance, his sample would have led him also to accept that hypothesis. His hypothesis, that $\mu = 35$, is but one of many possible hypotheses about which the decision to "accept H_0" would result, given Capt. Baker's sample mean of 35.1.

The critical values of z for a two-tailed test at $\alpha = .05$ ($z_{\text{crit}} = \pm 1.96$) and at $\alpha = .01$ ($z_{\text{crit}} = \pm 2.58$) are needed so commonly that it is well to commit them to memory.

15.7 DIRECTIONAL AND NONDIRECTIONAL ALTERNATIVE HYPOTHESES

In Capt. Baker's problem, H_A was stated: $\mu \neq 30$. Such an alternative hypothesis is said to be nondirectional. Use of a *nondirectional alternative* allows the investigator to reject the null hypothesis if the evidence points with sufficient strength to the possibility that μ greater than the value hypothesized, *or* to the possibility that it is less. Capt. Baker chose this form of the alternative hypothesis because the commander would want to know that his soldiers were superior if that were the fact *or* that they were substandard should that be true.

---

† For this reason, some statisticians prefer to say "fail to reject," or "retain," rather than "accept." For a fuller discussion of the meaning of the statistical decision, see Section 16.5.

Sometimes a *directional alternative* hypothesis is better suited to the problem at hand. If the base commander had been concerned only with the possibility that his soldiers might be substandard and that he would have to overhaul his training program, Capt. Baker might have adopted the following alternative hypothesis: $H_A: \mu < 30$. If he had done so, he would reject $H_0: \mu = 30$ only in the face of evidence that μ is *less* than 30. Consequently, he would place the entire region of rejection in the *left* tail of the sampling distribution rather than dividing it between the two tails. The illustration at the left in Figure 15.5 shows how the test would be conducted. If $\alpha = .05$, the critical value of z is -1.645. Capt. Baker's calculated value of "z" ($+2.44$) falls in the region of acceptance, and his decision must be to accept H_0. However, if he had adopted the alternative hypothesis $H_A: \mu > 30$, the region of rejection would be placed entirely in the *right* tail of the distribution. This is illustrated at the right in Figure 15.5. In this event, his sample mean falls in the region of rejection.

A directional alternative hypothesis is appropriate when it is *only* of interest to learn that the true value of μ differs from the hypothesized value *in a particular direction*. Look again at the situation described above in which Capt. Baker selected the alternative hypothesis $H_A: \mu < 30$, illustrated at the left in Figure 15.5. Accepting the null hypothesis, as he must do, is equivalent in substantive terms to saying "the evidence does not suggest that our recruits are substandard." If he chooses this approach, the procedure does not permit him to notice that the recruits are actually superior. This does not matter because he would choose this approach only if he were interested in learning whether his population was *below* the norm or not.

One must choose, therefore, between a directional alternative and a nondirec-

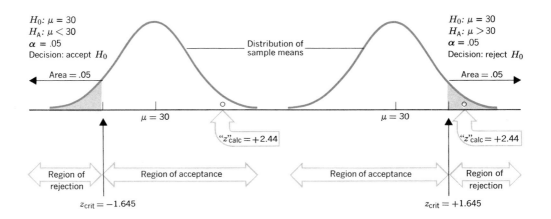

Figure 15.5 *Location of Regions of Acceptance and Rejection when H_A is Directional.*

tional one. The choice should be determined by the rationale that gave rise to the study, and should be made *before* the data are gathered. Further discussion of the issues involved in the choice appear in Section 16.3.

When a nondirectional alternative hypothesis is stated, the resulting test is referred to as a *two-tailed test*, because H_0 will be rejected if the obtained sample mean is located in an extreme position in *either* tail of the sampling distribution. Similarly, a directional alternative leads to a *one-tailed test*.

15.8 SUMMARY OF STEPS IN TESTING A HYPOTHESIS ABOUT A MEAN

1 Define the target population.

2 Specify the statistical hypothesis to be tested (H_0). It is determined according to the substantive question to be studied and stated in terms of a specific value of the population parameter, e.g. $H_0: \mu = 100$.

3 Specify the alternative hypothesis (H_A). A choice must be made between a directional and a nondirectional alternative, depending on the rationale of the substantive inquiry.

4 Specify the level of significance (α) to be used as the criterion for decision.

5 Decide on n and draw a random sample of that size from the specified population.

6 Calculate $\bar{X}$ and, if $\sigma_{\bar{X}}$ cannot be determined, calculate its estimate, $s_{\bar{X}}$†.

7 If $\sigma_{\bar{X}}$ can be determined, complete the test by the procedures of this chapter; they will be entirely appropriate. If $\sigma_{\bar{X}}$ is estimated by $s_{\bar{X}}$ *and $n \geq 40$*, proceed with the method indicated below or use the method of chapter 19. If $\sigma_{\bar{X}}$ is estimated by $s_{\bar{X}}$ and $n < 40$, use the method of chapter 19.

8 Calculate, in approximate z-score terms, the position of $\bar{X}$ in that sampling distribution of means that would result when sampling from a population in which H_0 is true.

9 Determine the z-score value or values that differentiate the region of rejection from the region of acceptance in the sampling distribution of means. Location is determined according to the specified level of significance and the directional or nondirectional nature of H_A.

10 Reject H_0 if $\bar{X}$ is located in the region of rejection; otherwise accept H_0.

†It will be extremely seldom in practice that σ (and hence $\sigma_{\bar{X}}$) will be known.

15.9 READING RESEARCH REPORTS IN BEHAVIORAL SCIENCE

When the outcome of a statistical test is reported in research literature, it is common to see statements such as "the difference was not significant," "none of the tests was statistically significant," and "the outcome was significant at the 5% level." What does it mean, for example, to say that "the outcome was significant at the 5% level"? In the more exact language that we have recently learned, this usually means that a null hypothesis and an alternative hypothesis were formulated, the decision criterion was $\alpha = .05$, and the evidence from the sample led to rejection of the hypothesis.† Similarly, the words "not significant" (sometimes abbreviated n.s.) imply that the hypothesis could not be rejected. When a report simply says "not significant" without stating the value of α, it is probably safe to assume that it was .05.

The use of the word *significant* in connection with statistical outcomes is unfortunate. In common English it implies "important," but in statistics it means only that the sample value was not within the limits of sampling variation expected under the null hypothesis. Whether the difference between what is hypothesized and what is true is large enough to be important is another matter (see Section 16.6).

When outcomes of statistical tests are reported in the manner described above, the researcher should make it clear whether the test was one-tailed or two-tailed. Unfortunately, this is not always made explicit, and it *does* matter. Recall that the critical values of z differ, depending on the choice of the alternative hypothesis.

Some researchers prefer to report the probability of obtaining a value so deviant (or more so) if the hypothesis were true. You may read, therefore, statements like these: "$p < .05$," "$p < .02$," "$p < .01$," or perhaps in cases where the sample outcome was not very deviant from what was hypothesized, "$p > .05$." Once again, look sharply to see if one-tailed or two-tailed probabilities are intended.

15.10 REVIEW OF ASSUMPTIONS IN INFERENCE ABOUT SINGLE MEANS

There are a number of conditions necessary for use of the normal curve model of statistical inference about single means to be *precisely* correct. Because these requirements have appeared in several chapters, they are listed below:

    1 A random sample has been drawn from the population.

    2 The sample has been drawn by the "with replacement" sampling plan.

---

† See Section 16.8 for another possible interpretation.

3 The sampling distribution of means follows the normal curve.

4 The standard deviation of the population of scores is known.

A truly random sample is often difficult to achieve in practice. Violation of this assumption may affect the mean and standard deviation of the sampling distribution in unpredictable ways. This problem is of sufficient importance that fuller discussion of it is reserved for the next section.

For the model of inference about single means described in this chapter to be strictly correct, it is assumed that sampling is with replacement (see Section 14.5). However, common practice is to sample without replacement. The consequent error in inference is quite small as long as sample size is a small fraction of population size (say, .05 or less). The effect of the error is to overestimate the standard error of the mean, which in turn tends to increase the probability of accepting H_0 when it should be rejected.

The third assumption is that the sampling distribution of means may be treated as a normal curve. As indicated in Section 13.7, this assumption is quite reasonably approximated in all but very small samples and when the scores in the population are reasonably close to a normal distribution. When the scores in the population are *not* normally distributed, the Central Limit Theorem comes to the rescue when sample size is reasonably large (Section 13.7). In this situation, assuming that the sampling distribution follows the normal curve results in minimal error.

The fourth assumption is that σ is known. In fact, we must almost always estimate it from the sample (see Section 15.1). If sample size is large, there is no substantial problem. As sample size decreases, the error thus introduced is intensified. With the procedures of this chapter, as sample size decreases there is an increasing probability of rejecting H_0 when it is in fact true. In general, when sample size drops below 40, an alternative approach that takes the error into account is required. A suitable method and further explanation of the issue involved are presented in chapter 19.

15.11 PROBLEMS IN SELECTING A RANDOM SAMPLE AND IN DRAWING CONCLUSIONS

The ideal way to conduct statistical inference is to define carefully the target population, identify each element of the population and assign it an identification number, and to draw a random sample by use of a table of random numbers. In behavioral science, only occasionally do real problems permit these specifications to be met. Let us look closely at Capt. Baker's problem. If the base commander really wants to define the target population as the *current crop* of recruits at *that base* who have *just finished,* then the ideal can easily be met. We need to keep in mind that, strictly speaking, *it is possible to generalize the inferential outcome only to a population from which the sample may be considered to be a random sample.*

But *does* he want to draw conclusions about the current crop of recruits? If pressed, he would probably say that he is really concerned whether his trainees will meet the standard after it goes into effect. He might agree that he would like to know about performance of recruits now, next July 1 (when the standard goes into effect), and for at least the next couple of years thereafter. If so, his target population consists of all of these soldiers. His sample cannot be considered a random sample from *this* population because not every element had an equal opportunity of inclusion in the sample. Does this matter? It certainly might; there are many factors that potentially affect the selection of recruits sent to that base.

Note also that the population consists of recruits at the particular base. A random sample of that group is not a random sample of recruits in general. Capt. Baker found these recruits to be superior, judged by the standard. But suppose the base commander is an enthusiast about athletics and uses his connections to channel sports figures into his recruit supply so that his base can have excellent teams in football, baseball, and other sports. There may be something more than just a good six-week training program to account for the superior showing made in this study.

Similarly, the theoretical scientist who is conducting a study of the behavior of "laboratory rats in general" cannot draw a truly random sample of this population but must study the behavior of those rats sent to him in the latest shipment from Superba Breeding Laboratories. As a consequence, the proper scientist realizes that he is dealing with a problem in limitation of generalization. To be sure, just as every son has a mother, every sample might be considered a random sample from *some* population. The question remains whether the referent population is appropriate to the substantive question posed. For instance, one problem that arises is that there are important differences among different strains of laboratory rats. You can see why it is so necessary in the scientific study of rats, people, or whatever to describe fully the characteristics of the sample studied and the circumstances under which it was drawn.

Another aspect of the problem often occurs with human subjects. If a scientist about to study a problem in learning, motivation, attitude change, perception,—or whatever—attempts to define the population about which he would really like to draw conclusions, he will usually be overwhelmed with the difficulties that would lie ahead. All elementary school children in the United States? All women? All members of a minority group? And if he could find them and identify them, how many could come to his laboratory, or for that matter, how many would be willing to participate under *any* conditions? He pushes these awful thoughts to the back of his mind and reaches for a convenient group of subjects to begin his exploration. This often turns out to be, for example, students currently enrolled in a general psychology class. He does not really wish to draw conclusions about a population of such students, but that is, at best, the population for which it is appropriate to generalize the outcome. In situations of this kind, it is common to refer to sampling from a *hypothetical population,* a polite term for a group that you didn't really want to study. This may be satisfactory for many pilot studies. Results found in such groups can be, if of interest, verified by restudy in a population of greater importance.

Many research reports sound as though a general conclusion had been reached, but since generalization can be made with total assurance only to the population sampled, a little probing may reveal that the conclusion applies to subjects of a particular sex, a particular age, a particular educational background, or a particular cultural and ethnic origin who happen to be attending a particular institution of higher education at that moment in time. Why do reports sound the way they do? One reason may be that the sampling problem is so overwhelming and so universal that there is a tendency to "forget" about it. A second reason may be that once the data are fed into the statistical testing hopper and the crank turned, out comes a statement that says "the hypothesis is probably false." This is a definite statement, derived "scientifically." So it must be true, right? What is often forgotten is that it applies only to the population sampled. If wider generalization is considered, it is incumbent on the researcher to repeat the study in the wider population or to make a reasonable showing that there is no relevant difference between the population sampled and the wider population about which it is desired to draw conclusions. The latter is a very difficult thing to do with confidence and requires the most profound knowledge on the part of the researcher. This is a far cry from the automaticity of turning the statistical crank. It should be clear that teaching a person statistics provides a tool but does not make him or her a researcher.

We now see that there are two very important and frustrating problems: the problem of sampling and the problem of generalization of results. And yet in many ways they are two aspects of the same thing. It is often very difficult if not impossible to get a true random sample of the population we would really like to study. If we do limit the population to what we can sample with reasonable adequacy, the outcome may, in a strict sense, be generalizable only to a trivial population.

What we have been discussing is closely related to a matter developed in chapter 1. In Section 1.6, the distinction was made between a statistical conclusion and a substantive one (one about the subject matter). The statistical conclusion says something about a parameter of the population, such as μ. But the substantive conclusion says something about the meaning of the study for psychology, or education, or some other discipline. The former can be done as an "automatic" process once statistics is learned. However, moving from the substantive question to an appropriate statistical question, and finally from a statistical conclusion to a substantive one, requires the highest qualities of knowledge and judgment on the part of the investigator.

PROBLEMS AND EXERCISES

Identify:

s, S, σ	one-tailed test
$s_{\bar{X}}, \sigma_{\bar{X}}$	two-tailed test
null hypothesis	H_0
alternative hypothesis	H_A
level of significance	α
region of acceptance	"z"
region of rejection	z_{crit}
directional hypothesis	not significant
nondirectional hypothesis	substantive conclusion

1 When would S and s be very similar? Very different? Explain.

2 If $\alpha = .10$, what would the values of z_{crit} be for a two-tailed test?

3 A sample consists of four scores: 3, 3, 5, 7. (*a*) Find Σx^2 by the raw score equivalent method described in Section 15.6. (*b*) Find s from Formula 15.1. (*c*) Find $s_{\bar{X}}$ from Formula 15.2. (*d*) Find S by the method shown in Table 6.2. (*e*) Find $s_{\bar{X}}$ from Formula 15.3. (*f*) Is your answer to (*c*) and (*e*) the same, within rounding error?

4 Given the following data: $\bar{X} = 63$, $s = 12$, $n = 100$, $H_0: \mu = 60$, $H_A: \mu \neq 60$. (*a*) Test the null hypothesis at the 5% significance level and state your conclusions. (*b*) Test the null hypothesis at the 1% significance level and state your conclusions. (*c*) What is the probability, in random sampling, of obtaining a mean of 63 or higher when samples of this size are drawn from a population in which $\mu = 60$? Of obtaining a sample mean which differs by three points or more (in either direction) from $\mu = 60$?

5 Repeat parts (*a*) and (*b*) of Problem 4, but assume that the alternative hypothesis reads $H_A: \mu > 60$.

6 Assume the same data as are given in Problem 4. Suppose that the alternative hypothesis reads $H_A: \mu < 60$. Test the null hypothesis at the 5% significance level and state your conclusions.

7 The eighth-grade national norm for a social science test is a score of 123. The research director of a school district wants to know how knowledge of pupils in his district compares with this standard. He selects a random sample of 81 students and finds that: $\bar{X} = 117$; $s = 36$. State the null hypothesis and alternative hypothesis best suited to the nature of his inquiry. Test the null hypothesis (*a*) at the 5% level of significance and state your conclusions; (*b*) at the 1% level of significance and state your conclusions. (*c*) What is the probability of obtaining, through random sampling, a sample mean so deviant (in either direction) from μ as his sample mean is?

8 Repeat Problem 7, but assume that $\bar{X} = 112$.

9 A sample consists of five scores: 6, 7, 7, 9, 10. (*a*) Test the hypothesis that $\mu = 9.6$ against a two-tailed alternative using $\alpha = .05$, and $\alpha = .01$. Use a picture to illustrate the problem. (*b*) What would the outcome be if: $H_A: \mu > 9.6$? If $H_A: \mu < 9.6$? Use $\alpha = .05, .01$ again. (*c*) Why is this problem appropriate only for demonstration?

10 A sample consists of these scores: 3, 5, 7, 8, 8. (*a*) Test the hypothesis that $\mu = 4$ against a two-tailed alternative, using $\alpha = .05$ and .01. Use a picture to illustrate the problem. (*b*) What would the outcome be if: $H_A: \mu > 4$? If $H_A: \mu < 4$? Use $\alpha = .05$ and .01 again.

11 If H_0 is rejected at the 5% significance level, can we be reasonably confident that H_0 is false? Explain.

12 If H_0 is accepted at the 5% significance level, can we be reasonably confident that H_0 is true? Explain.

13 A training director for a large company has been told that on completion of the training course, the average score of his trainees on the final evaluation should be 100. His only concern is whether he will have to begin remedial steps to ensure that the population of trainees is not below standard. A sample of 49 scores of recent trainees shows: $\bar{X} = 94$; $s_X = 21$. State the null hypothesis and alternative hypothesis best suited to the nature of his inquiry. Test the null hypothesis (*a*) at the 5% level of significance and state your conclusions; (*b*) at the 1% level of significance and state your conclusions. (*c*) What is the probability of obtaining, through random sampling, a sample mean so low or lower if μ is as stated in the null hypothesis?

14 A poll is designed to study habits of library usage among students at Spartan University. Various suggestions are made how to conduct the survey, as indicated below. What particular objection (or objections) might be made to each idea? (*a*) The survey is to be conducted just before midterms. (*b*) A booth is to be set up in front of the library, and those who pass by will be polled. (*c*) Freshman English is mandatory, so all students currently enrolled in those classes will be polled. (*d*) The Division of Humanities and Arts volunteers to poll all of its majors, so it is suggested that these students constitute the sample. (*e*) All students in 8:00 A.M. classes will be polled.

CHAPTER 16

16.1 INTRODUCTION

In the last chapter, we learned the basic steps that characterize inference about single means. Embedded in the process of testing a hypothesis are a number of issues that deserve further analysis. When should we conduct a one-tailed test? How does one decide on the value of α, the level of significance? Why is a "significant difference" not necessarily an important one? If "accepting" the null hypothesis doesn't mean that it is probably true, what *does* it mean? The present chapter affords a commentary on major aspects of hypothesis testing such as these. Although the last chapter concerned hypotheses about single means, and although the commentary offered here is oriented toward the same problem, the principles involved are quite general. As you study further problems in hypothesis testing, you may expect to find that the discussion presented here retains much of its relevance in those other contexts.

Further Considerations in Hypothesis Testing

16.2 STATEMENT OF THE HYPOTHESIS

There are two parts to the hypothesis: H_0, the hypothesis to be subjected to test, and H_A, the alternative hypothesis. H_0 is always a statement about the population parameter (or difference between two or more parameters if more than one population is involved). It is never a statement about the sample statistic. For example, if the hypothesis had been that the *sample* mean was 30, Capt. Baker would simply deny it because the sample mean is 35.1, and no inference is involved.

Second, the hypothesis to be tested, H_0, is expressed in terms of a point value, rather than a range. If the hypothesis is expressed as a point value, a single random sampling distribution of means applies, and the consequences of this particular distribution can be explored. If the hypothesis were expressed as a range, a multitude of sampling distributions would be relevant, each with a slightly different mean, and the problem of exploration becomes most awkward.

Third, the decision to accept or reject "the hypothesis" *always* has reference to H_0, and never to H_A. It is H_0 that is the subject of the test. The role of H_A is explained below.

Finally, H_0 is often referred to as the "null hypothesis." No special significance should be attached to this term; it is simply whatever hypothesis is to be subjected to test.

The alternative hypothesis describes the condition that, if the evidence of our sample is contrary to H_0 *and points toward it with sufficient strength,* leads us to reject H_0. We shall reject H_0, then, *only* when the evidence substantially favors H_A.

16.3 CHOICE OF H_A: ONE-TAILED AND TWO-TAILED TESTS

The alternative hypothesis may be directional or nondirectional, depending on the purpose of the study. When the alternative hypothesis is nondirectional, a two-tailed test results, and it is possible to detect a discrepancy between the true value and the hypothesized value of the parameter irrespective of the direction of the discrepancy. This capability is often desirable in examining research questions. For example, in most cases in which performance of a group is compared with a known standard, it would be of interest to discover that the group is superior *or* to discover that the group is substandard.

Sometimes a one-tailed test is more appropriate. Examples of situations in which a one-tailed test is indicated are:

1 A manufacturer wishes to test the length of life of light bulbs made by a new process. He wants to adopt the new process only if mean length of life is greater than 1500 hours.

2 The physical fitness of school children is tested. If mean performance is substandard, it will be necessary to institute a special physical training program.

3 The claim is made that when a particular hormone is ingested, more hair will grow.

4 A new teaching method is proposed; it is decided that the new method should be instituted if it can be demonstrated that learning accomplished under the new method is superior to that under the standard method.

In each of these situations, interest is in discovering whether there is a difference *in a particular direction* or not. For instance, in Example 2, the question is whether or not the children are substandard with regard to physical fitness. This may be tested by hypothesizing that the mean physical fitness score of the population of school children equals the standard value versus the alternative that it is less than this value. Note that if the children's physical fitness equals or exceeds the standard, no action is necessary. A special training program will be instituted *only* if their performance is substandard. Similarly, in the case of the Hairy Hormone Hypothesis, a finding of normal incidence of hair, or less hair than normal are equal in meaning: the research hypothesis is unsupported by the evidence. In this instance, one might test the hypothesis of normal hair, versus the alternative of more hair.

In general, *a directional alternative hypothesis is appropriate when there is no practical difference in meaning between finding that the hypothesis is true and finding that a difference exists in a direction* opposite *to that stated in the directional alternative hypothesis.* The reason for this advice is apparent in Figure 16.1. This figure illustrates the design for decision when testing $H_0: \mu = 100$ against the alternative hypothesis $H_A: \mu < 100$. As we see, the region of rejection is entirely at the left. A value of $\bar{X}$ which falls above 100 *cannot* lead to rejection of the null hypothesis, *no matter how deviant.* If this state of affairs is unacceptable, it means that a directional alternative is inappropriate and that a two-tailed test should be used.

The decision to use a one-tailed alternative must always flow from the logic of the substantive question, as illustrated above. The time to decide on the nature of the alternative hypothesis is therefore at the beginning of the study, before the data are collected. It will not do to observe the sample outcome and then set the region of rejection in the tail of the sampling distribution toward which the sample outcome tends. For example, if we adopt the 5% level of significance and follow this erroneous procedure systematically, we are really, in the long run, conducting two-tailed tests at the 10% significance level. Likewise, it is not satisfactory to set

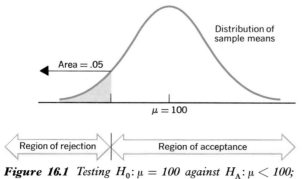

Figure 16.1 *Testing $H_0: \mu = 100$ against $H_A: \mu < 100$; $\alpha = .05$.*

our one-tailed trap in the direction in which we *think* the outcome might go, only to switch to a two-tailed test if the sample mean appears in the opposite direction. If tests are conducted in this manner, using $\alpha = .05$, they are equivalent to two-tailed tests at $\alpha = .075$, with an area of .05 in one tail, and .025 in the other—but with the larger area located by the prejudice of preconception. It is much better to decide in advance what kind of discrepancy is important to discover and to choose H_A accordingly.

16.4 THE CRITERION FOR ACCEPTANCE OR REJECTION OF H_0

The decision to accept or reject the null hypothesis is dependent on the criterion of rarity of occurrence adopted, commonly known as the *level of significance* (α). In recent years it has become common for research workers to evaluate the outcome of tests according to the .05 or .01 level of significance. In one sense these values are arbitrary, but in another they are not. It would be both possible and permissible to use values such as .02 or .04, for example. But consider the larger question: how shall we choose the level of significance? Should α be .05 or should it be .01, or perhaps some other value?

The problem becomes clearer when we realize that α is a statement of risk. Look at Figure 16.2, which shows how a two-tailed test would be conducted if α is set at .05. *When the hypothesis is true,* 5% of the sample means will nevertheless lead us to say that it is false. So when we decide to adopt $\alpha = .05$, we are really saying that we will accept a probability of .05 that the null hypothesis will be rejected when it is really true. Suppose we were to choose $\alpha = .25$. If the null hypothesis is true, 25% of sample means will fall in the region of rejection thus established, and one

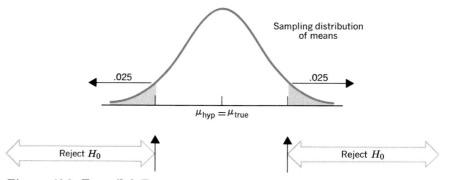

Figure 16.2 *Two-tailed Test at $\alpha = .05$; 5% of Sample Means Lead Incorrectly to Rejection of the Null Hypothesis when H_0 is True.*

test in four will lead to the erroneous conclusion that the hypothesis is false. The risk of committing this error seems uncomfortably high.

To reduce the risk, we may set α at a lower level. Suppose it is set very low, say .001. Now suppose a test is conducted and a mean obtained that is so deviant that its prior probability of occurrence under the null hypothesis is .002. According to the criterion adopted, we have insufficient evidence to reject the null hypothesis and therefore must accept it. In this case, we run a substantial risk of accepting the hypothesis when it is false. To turn to an intuitive example, suppose you are testing the honesty of a pair of dice belonging to the gentleman with the waxed mustache. In 20 out of 30 tosses, the dice come up seven. Are you willing to say, "Well, that *could* be chance; I have insufficient reason to reject the hypothesis of fair dice"?†

We now see that for general use, $\alpha = .05$ and $\alpha = .01$ make quite good sense. They tend to give reasonable assurance that the null hypothesis will not be rejected unless it really should be. At the same time, they are not so stringent as to raise unnecessarily the likelihood of accepting false hypotheses. How should one choose between $\alpha = .05$ and .01? Think about the practical consequences of rejecting the null hypothesis when it is true. In Capt. Baker's case, that would mean concluding that the population mean of recruits is better than standard or that they are worse than standard when they really meet the standard. If better, the commander will "point with pride" when the facts don't justify it; if worse, he will begin revising the training program when it is not necessary. What risk should be accepted for the two taken together? In general, one should translate the error into concrete terms and then decide what level of risk is tolerable.

Although the 5% and the 1% criteria are useful for general purposes, there are circumstances when selecting other values would make better sense. If it were important to be quite sure that the hypothesis was wrong before acting on that conclusion, we might wish to adopt an α even lower than .01. For example, if a change in educational procedure is implied by the rejection of the hypothesis, and if the change were costly (in time, effort, and/or money), we would want to be quite certain of our conclusions before making the change. Of course we would also want to know if the improvement expected by changing the procedure was large enough to be worth the trouble. But in a sense, the first question is whether there is any change at all. A lower value of α gives greater assurance that there is truly *some* difference.

On the other hand, if we were trying to uncover a possible difference with the idea of subjecting it to further confirmatory exploration, it might be desirable to set the value of α at .10 or perhaps .20. Such a situation might occur in preliminary stages of test construction, when it is more important to discover items of possible value than to be certain of eliminating the "duds."

---

† In this paragraph and in the preceding one, we meet the two types of errors that may occur in testing hypotheses: rejecting H_0 when it is true and accepting H_0 when it is false. These errors will be explored in Section 16.7.

Whatever the level of significance adopted, the decision should be made in advance. If, so to speak, we "peek" at the outcome of the sample data before arriving at this decision, there is a temptation to set the level of significance at a point that permits the conclusion to be in line with whatever preconception we may have. In any event, setting the level of significance should flow from the substantive logic of the study and not from the specific outcome obtained in the sample.

16.5 THE STATISTICAL DECISION

At the outcome of the test of a hypothesis, the decision is either to accept H_0 or to reject it. When testing the hypothesis that $\mu = 100$ versus the alternative that it is not, a decision to reject H_0 means that we do not believe the mean of the population to be 100. Moreover, the lower the probability of obtaining a sample mean of the kind that occurred when the hypothesis is true, the greater the confidence we have in the correctness of our decision to reject the hypothesis.

On the other hand, accepting the hypothesis does not mean that we believe the hypothesis to be true. Rather, *this decision merely reflects the fact that we do not have sufficient evidence to reject the hypothesis.* To put it another way, the decision to accept H_0 means simply that the hypothesis is a tenable one. Certain other hypotheses that might have been stated would also have been accepted if subjected to the same criterion. Consider the example above, where the hypothesis is: $\mu = 100$. If our sample mean is 101 and is related to the hypothesized sampling distribution as illustrated at the left in Figure 16.3, our decision will be to accept the hypothesis. But suppose the hypothesis had been: $\mu = 102$. If the same sample result had occurred, $\bar{X} = 101$, we would be led equally to accept the hypothesis that $\mu = 102$. This is shown at the right in Figure 16.3. In short, rejecting the hypothesis means that it does not seem reasonable to believe that it is true, but

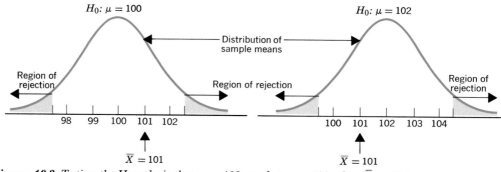

Figure 16.3 *Testing the Hypothesis that* $\mu = 100$, *or that* $\mu = 102$ *when* $\bar{X} = 101$.

accepting the hypothesis merely means that we believe that the hypothesis *could* be true. It does *not* mean that it must be true, *or even that it is probably true,* for there would be many other hypotheses that if tested with the same sample data would also be accepted.

16.6 A STATISTICALLY SIGNIFICANT DIFFERENCE VERSUS A PRACTICALLY IMPORTANT DIFFERENCE

To test the hypothesis that $\mu = 100$, we calculate "z" as

$$\text{``}z\text{''} = \frac{\bar{X} - \mu_{\text{hyp}}}{\frac{s}{\sqrt{n}}}$$

If "z" is large enough, the hypothesis will be rejected. Now the magnitude of "z" depends both on the quantity in the numerator *and* on the quantity in the denominator. Other things being equal, if sample size is very large, the denominator, $s/\sqrt{n}$, will be quite small. In this event, a relatively small discrepancy between $\bar{X}$ and μ_{hyp} may produce a value of "z" large enough to lead us to reject the hypothesis.† In cases of this kind, we may have a result that is "statistically significant" but in which the difference between μ_{true} and μ_{hyp} is so small as to be unimportant.

Recall Capt. Baker's problem. He asked if the mean physical fitness score of the population of recruits could be 30. To study this question, he drew a sample of 10 soldiers. Suppose someone in the Pentagon asked the same question about recruits in general and drew a random sample of 2500 trainees. Assuming the standard deviation of test scores to be the same as in Capt. Baker's case, the estimated standard error of the mean is $s_{\bar{X}} = 6.61/\sqrt{2500} = .13$. Adopting $\alpha = .05$ (as before), the Pentagon's researcher will reject the hypothesis that the mean is 30 if his calculated "z" is 1.96 or larger. This value will be reached when the sample mean differs from μ_{hyp} by only .26 of a score point. Although a value this discrepant is reasonably indicative that the mean of the population of trainees is not 30, it remains that a difference of this order is not worth bothering about.

We are reminded that the end product of statistical inference is a conclusion about descriptors, such as μ. Therefore, the simplest remedy is to return to them to evaluate the importance of a "significant" outcome. Look at how much difference

---

†The discrepancy between $\bar{X}$ and μ_{hyp} depends on random variation and, when the hypothesis is false, on the additional discrepancy between μ_{hyp} and μ_{true}. When samples are very large, the first component (due to random sampling) is small, and the second component, when present, is more "noticeable." A relatively small difference between μ_{hyp} and μ_{true} may therefore be detected in the test of significance with large samples. See Note at the end of chapter 17 for a related treatment.

exists between μ_{hyp} and the sample mean obtained. Is it of a size that matters? If the variable is one not familiar from previous experience, the actual number of points of discrepancy may not convey much meaning. In this case, divide the discrepancy by the standard deviation of the variable (s, not $s_{\bar{X}}$) to see how much of a standard deviation the difference amounts to. This procedure is also applicable to the problem of the difference between two means, described in the following chapter. See Section 6.14 for a related development. One caution: The procedure described above is most meaningful when fairly large samples have been employed. The larger the sample, the surer we can be that the important factor is the real difference that exists and not (to a large extent) sampling variation.

What about the statistical test when samples are quite small? In this case the standard error of the mean will be relatively large, and it will be difficult to discover that the null hypothesis is false, if indeed it is, unless the difference between μ_{true} and μ_{hyp} is quite large. This suggests that an important consideration in experimental design is the size of the sample that should be drawn. The question of optimum sample size for tests of hypotheses about means is explored in Section 21.11.

16.7 ERROR IN HYPOTHESIS TESTING

There are, so to speak, two "states of nature": either the hypothesis, H_0, is true, or it is false. Similarly, there are two possible decisions: to accept the hypothesis or to reject it. Taken in combination, there are four possibilities. They are diagrammed in Table 16.1. If the hypothesis is true and we accept it, or if it is false and we reject it, a correct decision has been made. Otherwise, we are in error. Note that there are two kinds of error. They are identified as Type I error and Type II error.

Table 16.1 *Two Types of Error in Hypothesis Testing*

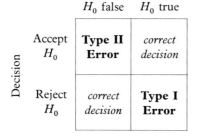

State of Nature

		H_0 false	H_0 true
	Accept H_0	**Type II Error**	*correct decision*
Decision	Reject H_0	*correct decision*	**Type I Error**

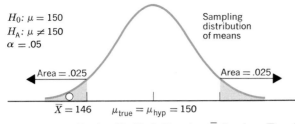

Figure 16.4 *Testing H_0:H_0 Is True but $\bar{X}$ Leads to Type I Error.*

A Type I error is committed when H_0 is rejected and in fact it is true. Consider the picture of the sampling distribution shown in Figure 16.4. It illustrates a situation that might arise in testing the hypothesis that $\mu = 150$ (against the alternative that it is not) when the 5% significance level has been adopted. Suppose the sample mean is 146, which, when the test has been conducted in the usual way, leads us to reject H_0. The logic in rejecting H_0 is that if the hypothesis were true, a sample mean this deviant would occur less than 5% of the time, and therefore it seems more reasonable to believe that this sample mean arose through random sampling from a population with a mean different from that specified in H_0. However, this sample mean *could* be one of those deviant values obtained through the vagaries of random sampling from a population where the hypothesis is true. By definition, the region of rejection identifies a degree of deviance such that, when the hypothesis is true, 5% of sample means will reach or exceed it. Therefore, when conducting tests according to this criterion, *and when the hypothesis is true,* 5% of sample means will lead us to an erroneous conclusion: rejection of the hypothesis.

In Section 16.4 we learned that the probability of committing this error is α. More formally:

$$\alpha = \text{Pr (Type I error)} = \text{Pr (rejecting } H_0 | H_0 \text{ is true)}†$$

Note that the probability of committing a Type I error exists *only* in situations where the hypothesis is true. If the hypothesis is false, it is impossible to commit this error.

A Type II error is committed when H_0 is accepted and in fact it is false. As in the previous example, suppose that the hypothesis is tested that $\mu = 150$, against the alternative that it is not. Again, the 5% level of significance is adopted. A sample is drawn, and its mean is found to be 152. Now it may be that, unknown to us, the mean of the population is really 154. This situation is pictured in Figure 16.5. In this figure, two sampling distributions are shown. The true distribution is shown with a dotted line and centers about 154, the true population mean. The other is

---

†The upright bar in the expression (rejecting $H_0 | H_0$ is true) is to be read: "given the condition that." Probabilities of this type are known as conditional probabilities; see Note 14.2.

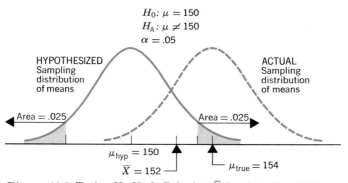

Figure 16.5 *Testing H_0:H_0 Is False but $\bar{X}$ Leads to Type II Error.*

the sampling distribution that would occur if H_0 were true; it centers on 150, the hypothesized mean. The sample mean actually belongs to the true sampling distribution. But, to test the hypothesis that $\mu = 150$, the mean is evaluated according to its position in the sampling distribution shown with a solid line. Relative to *that* distribution, it is not so deviant (from the mean of 150) as to call for rejection of H_0. The decision will therefore be to accept the hypothesis that $\mu = 150$. It is, of course, an erroneous decision; we have committed a Type II error. To put it another way, we have failed to claim that a real difference existed when in fact it did.

When considering a real-life problem it is useful to translate the abstract conception of a Type II error into practical consequences, just as we did in Section 16.4 when thinking about the meaning of α. Consider Capt. Baker's problem again. A Type II error would occur if he had accepted the hypothesis that the mean of the population of recruits was 30 (the standard), when in fact they were really above standard or below standard. How important would it be to avoid this error? Once that judgment is made, it can be taken into account in designing the study. We shall learn how to do that in chapter 21 (Section 21.11). It should be clear that thinking about such matters is properly a part of the planning stage, *before* the data are gathered.

The probability of committing a Type II error is given by:

$$\beta = \text{Pr (Type II error)} = \text{Pr (accepting } H_0 | H_0 \text{ is false)}$$

The Greek letter β (beta) is used to indicate this probability. Note that the probability of committing a Type II error exists *only* in situations where the hypothesis is false. If the hypothesis is true, it is impossible to commit this kind of error.

Several factors affect the probability of committing Type II errors. These are explored in chapter 21 (see Section 21.9).

16.8 α: DECISION CRITERION OR INDEX OF RARITY?

In Section 15.9 we learned that some researchers evaluate the outcome of the test of a hypothesis by showing the probability of obtaining a value as discrepant as the one obtained if the null hypothesis were true. For a given outcome they might report, say, that "$p < .03$." Now this probability statement is an expression of rarity of the sample outcome and nothing more. It *cannot* be interpreted as the value of α. By the definition of the previous section, α is the probability of rejecting H_0 when H_0 is true. It is, therefore, a decision criterion *established in advance* of conducting the test and determined by considering the risk the experimenter is willing to take of committing such an error when the sample is drawn. The p value, on the other hand, is not established in advance, and it is not a statement of risk; it simply describes the rarity of the sample outcome, whatever it might turn out to be. Those persons who employ *both* $\alpha = .05$ and .01 to evaluate the several tests they have conducted may be using these values in the sense of decision criteria *or* as a rough statement of rarity of sample outcome. You will usually have to look at the context to tell which is intended. One often suspects that the authors themselves have not thought through exactly what they intend.

16.9 MULTIPLE TESTS

Setting the level of significance at .05 means that the probability of wrongly rejecting the hypothesis when it is true ("finding something" when "nothing is there") is .05. That seems small enough for many purposes. But suppose that several tests are to be conducted using the same criterion. For each taken individually, the probability of a Type I error is .05, but taken as a group, the probability that at least one from among the several will prove to be a false positive is greater than .05 and continues rising as more tests are made. After all, the fact that α is set at .05 says that among 100 tests conducted on independent samples, five false positives are to be expected. To put it another way, 1 in 20 should be a Type I error and not a genuine "finding."

There appears to be a substantial tendency for humans to fail to take account of the increasing likelihood of encountering Type I errors as the number of tests conducted increases. It is therefore especially necessary to be aware of this potential for error in considering the results of our own research or that of others. For example, if we find two outcomes to be "significant at the .05 level" in a table showing 50 tests, it will not do to consider that these are gold that has been mined. Two in 50 is quite in line with the number of false positives to be expected.

16.10 THE PROBLEM OF BIAS IN ESTIMATING σ^2

The standard error of the mean is:

$$\sigma_{\bar{X}} = \frac{\sigma}{\sqrt{n}}$$

When σ is unknown, which is most often the case, it must be estimated from the sample. Intuition suggests substituting S, the sample standard deviation, as an estimate, but it tends to be a little too small (see Section 15.4).

The basic problem is that the sample variance, S^2, is a *biased estimator* of the population variance, σ^2. *When an estimator is* unbiased, *the mean of the estimates made from all possible samples equals the value of the parameter estimated.* For example, the sample mean is an unbiased estimator of the population mean, because the average of the means computed from all possible samples exactly equals μ. The same relationship does *not* hold between S^2, and σ^2: the mean value of S^2, calculated from all possible samples, is a little smaller than σ^2.

The formula for the sample variance (Formula 6.2*b*) is:

$$S^2 = \frac{\sum(X - \bar{X})^2}{n}$$

It has been shown that the tendency toward underestimation will be corrected if $\Sigma(X - \bar{X})^2$ is divided by $n - 1$, rather than by n. Formula 16.1 incorporates this correction.

Unbiased Estimate of the Population Variance $\qquad s^2 = \dfrac{\sum(X - \bar{X})^2}{n - 1}$ $\qquad\qquad$ (16.1)

The lower case letter, s^2, distinguishes this formula from that of S^2. Taking the square root of the formula, we have an estimate of the standard deviation of the population (Formula 15.1; see Section 15.4):

$$s = \sqrt{\frac{\sum(X - \bar{X})^2}{n - 1}}$$

Dividing by $n - 1$, rather than by n, will make little difference when n is large, but the smaller the sample, the greater the effect.

The characteristics described above may be demonstrated in one of the miniature populations described in chapter 14. Table 14.2 presented the 16 possible samples arising when samples of size two are drawn from a population of four observations. Calculation of the variance of the four scores by Formula 6.2*a* yields: $\sigma^2 = 5.0$. We may calculate s^2 using Formula 16.1 from each of the 16 possible samples. The 16 samples, together with the 16 variance estimates, are shown in the first two columns

Table 16.2 *Possible Samples, Together with Estimates of the Population Variance Computed from Each (Data from Table 14.2)*

Population: 2, 4, 6, 8 Population Variance: $\sigma^2 = 5.0$	
Sample	Estimate of population variance (s^2)
2, 2	0
2, 4	2
2, 6	8
2, 8	18
4, 2	2
4, 4	0
4, 6	2
4, 8	8
6, 2	8
6, 4	2
6, 6	0
6, 8	2
8, 2	18
8, 4	8
8, 6	2
8, 8	0
Mean value of s^2: 5.0	

of Table 16.2. We observe that the mean of these estimates is 5.0, which is also the true value of σ^2, the quantity estimated. This demonstrates that s^2 exhibits the qualities of an unbiased estimator of σ^2, since the average of all estimates equals the quantity estimated. Obviously, if the 16 estimates had been made by dividing by $n = 2$ rather than $n - 1 = 1$, the mean of *these* estimates would have been less than 5.0.

To return to the problem of estimating the standard error of the mean when σ is unknown, we may substitute s for σ in Formula 13.2. This yields Formula 15.2:

$$s_{\bar{X}} = \frac{s}{\sqrt{n}}$$

Although the correction introduced in estimating the standard error of the mean makes for a better estimate *on the average,* we should recognize that any particular sample will probably yield an estimate too large or too small. No explanation has been offered so far as to *why* S_X^2 tends to underestimate σ_X^2. The note appearing next explains this matter.

NOTE

Further Comments on Unbiased Estimates of σ^2 (*Ref:* Section 16.10)

The variance of a population of scores is given by Formula 6.2a: $\sum\limits^{N}(X - \mu)^2/N$, where N is the number of scores in the population. The best unbiased estimate of this quantity may be made by calculating: $\sigma_{X(\text{est})}^2 = \sum\limits^{n}(X - \mu)^2/n$. Note that the deviation of each score in the sample is taken from μ. Demonstration of the unbiasedness of this estimate may be had by calculating variance estimates according to this formula for each of the 16 samples shown in Table 16.2. It will be found that the mean of the 16 estimates is 5.0, precisely the value of σ^2.

When μ is unknown, it becomes necessary to take the deviation of each score from its own sample mean: $\sum\limits^{n}(X - \bar{X})^2$. Recall (Section 6.10) that the sum of the squares of deviation scores is a minimum when the deviations are taken from the mean of *that set of scores*, i.e., $\bar{X}$. But we should, if we could, compute $\sum\limits^{n}(X - \mu)^2$. Since $\bar{X}$ and μ will not ordinarily be identical, $\sum\limits^{n}(X - \bar{X})^2 < \sum\limits^{n}(X - \mu)^2$, and therefore $S^2 < \sigma_{X(\text{est})}^2$. To obtain an unbiased estimate of σ^2, $\sum\limits^{n}(X - \bar{X})^2$ must be divided by $n - 1$ rather than by n. This adjustment is incorporated in Formula 16.1: $s^2 = \sum\limits^{n}(X - \bar{X})^2/(n - 1)$.

It is tempting to think that S^2 tends to underestimate σ^2 because, when sampling from a normal distribution, very deviant scores are less likely to be present in any particular small sample than in a large one. Like most temptations, it should be resisted. Although the *number* of rare scores is expected to be less in small samples, their *proportional frequency* of occurrence is unaltered if sampling is random. Also, the shape of the population sampled is fundamentally irrelevant. Underestimation stems from use of $\bar{X}$, rather than μ, as the point about which deviations are taken.

One interesting point remains. Although s^2 is an unbiased estimator of σ^2, s still tends to underestimate σ, although s is an improved estimate. This does not cause important trouble in testing hypotheses about means. First, the degree of underestimation is quite small for samples in which $n > 10$. Second, when sample size is small, the procedures of chapter 19 are indicated. These procedures take *exact* account of the substitution of s for σ, and so no error is involved.

This result is due to the fact that the mean of the values of a variable tends to be less than the square root of the mean of the same squared values, a fact that follows from the nonlinear relation between numbers and their squares.

PROBLEMS AND EXERCISES

Identify:

reject H_0 Type I error
accept H_0 Type II error
α β

$z = 1.96, 2.58$ unbiased estimator

$z = 1.64, 2.33$ s^2

statistical significance S^2

practical significance μ_{hyp}, μ_{true}

1 A friend hands us a mysterious coin, saying that he thinks it is biased in favor of heads. We take as our null hypothesis that the coin is fair and as the alternative hypothesis that it is biased in favor of heads. On tossing the coin 100 times, we obtain 98 tails and 2 heads. If we make an intuitive significance test, what is our proper conclusion? Explain.

2 Why should the choice of a one- or two-tailed test be made before the data are gathered?

3 Why is it inadequate to choose a one-tailed test on the basis that we expect the outcome to be in that direction?

4 The meaning of "accepting H_0" is not exactly the opposite of "rejecting H_0." Explain.

5 Some investigators have praised the use of small samples in hypothesis testing, saying that such usage is better for the development of their science. (*a*) Explain the merit of this position. (*b*) Explain the limitations and/or defects of this position.

6 A man drew a sample of 400 cases, measured their IQs, and tested the hypothesis that $\mu_{IQ} = 100$. He obtained "z" $= +3.00$, which led him to reject the hypothesis. s was 15.0. (*a*) What was the standard error of the mean? (*b*) What was the mean of his sample? (*c*) The test yielded a statistically significant outcome. Does it appear to be an important one? Explain. (*d*) How much of a standard deviation did the discrepancy between $\bar{X}$ and μ_{hyp} amount to?

7 A man used $\alpha = .05$ for his test and accepted the hypothesis. Would it be correct to say he can be 95% sure that H_0 is true? Explain.

8 A woman used $\alpha = .05$ for her test and rejected the hypothesis. Would it be correct to say that she can be 95% confident that H_0 is false? Explain.

9 Eighteen different tests are tried out in an attempt to predict performance of airplane pilots. One of them, reaction time, yields a correlation of $+.45$. It is significantly different from zero at the 5% level and is the only test to meet that criterion. Your comment about the possible utility of this test?

10 Given: some hypotheses are true and some are false. A man rejects all hypotheses. (*a*) What is α? (*b*) What is β?

11 Given: some hypotheses are true and some are false. A man rolls a die. If it comes up 1 or 2 he accepts the hypothesis, otherwise he rejects it. (*a*) What is α? (*b*) What is β?

12 There are three urns. One urn contains two white balls, and the others each contain one white ball and one black ball. (*a*) Unable to see into the urns, we hypothesize that each urn contains at least one white ball. We will select one urn at random and accept the hypothesis if it contains at least one white ball; otherwise we reject it. What is α? (*b*) We hypothesize that each urn contains at least one black ball. Selecting an urn at random, we accept the hypothesis if it contains at least one black ball; otherwise we reject it. What is β?

13 A connoisseur of cigars claims that he can tell Puerto Rican cigars from Cuban cigars. We blindfold him and offer him two Cuban cigars and one Puerto Rican cigar. His task is to identify the Puerto Rican cigar. We hypothesize that the man is always right and establish the alternative hypothesis that he is right by chance. We give him one trial and accept H_0 if he correctly identifies the Puerto Rican cigar; otherwise we reject H_0. (*a*) What is α? (*b*) What is β?

14 (*Based on the Note*) In Table 16.2, we showed that the mean of the 16 variance estimates made by calculating $\sum^{2}(X - \bar{X})^2/1$ equaled $\sigma^2(5.0)$. For each of the 16 samples, calculate $\sum^{2}(X - \mu)^2/2$, and verify that the mean of these values also equals σ^2.

CHAPTER 17

In many fields of inquiry, including psychology and education, one of the most important ways of increasing knowledge is to ask whether it makes a difference when some characteristic is measured under two different conditions. Does supplementing the diet with extra quantities of vitamin A make a difference in ability to see under conditions of dim illumination? Is speed of reaction to a light stimulus the same as to a sound stimulus? Is ability to spell equal for male and female high school seniors? Is the error rate of typists the same when work is done in a noisy environment as in a quiet one?

Each of these questions is an example of a problem for which the test of the hypothesis of the equality of two means may be helpful in finding the answer. Consider the first question. Two sets of 50 subjects may be selected at random, and one fed a normal diet while the other receives the normal diet plus supplementary

Testing Hypotheses about Two Means: Normal Curve Model

vitamin A. After a suitable period under this regimen, each individual can be tested for visual acuity in conditions of dim illumination. A visual acuity "score" is thus obtained for each subject, and the mean score may be calculated for each group. We may imagine that the mean of the group receiving the vitamin A supplement is 47, and the mean of the other group is 43. However, it is not particularly instructive to compare the two sample means, *because we would expect two samples to yield different means even if the two groups had been treated alike.*

The important question is not about the samples, but about the populations from which the samples came. Is it possible that the mean of the population of visual acuity scores obtained under normal diet is the same as the mean of the population of observations obtained under normal diet plus supplementary vitamin A? The two *population* means should be the same if vitamin A had no effect. This question may be expressed as a statistical hypothesis to be subjected to test. If scores obtained under the vitamin A condition are designated by X and those under normal diet by Y, we have:

$$H_0: \mu_X - \mu_Y = 0$$
$$H_A: \mu_X - \mu_Y \neq 0$$

The test of the difference between two means always involves the question of the difference between measures of the *same* variable when taken under two conditions. For example, in the example above, X stands for vision scores of subjects treated one way, and Y stands for vision scores of subjects treated another way.

H_A may be directional or nondirectional. If interest were only in discovering whether vitamin A *improved* vision, $H_A: \mu_X - \mu_Y > 0$ would be the appropriate alternative. However, presumably we would want to know it if the effect were *either* to improve vision or to impair it. Consequently, a two-tailed test is in order.

From this point on, the procedure for testing the hypothesis follows the same basic principles outlined in chapter 15. First, the criterion for decision, α, must be chosen. Next, the characteristics of the pertinent sampling distribution are examined so that the present sample outcome can be compared with those outcomes expected when the hypothesis is true. In the sampling distribution, a region of rejection is established according to the nature of H_A and the value of α. In the present problem, if the difference between the two sample means is so great, in either direction, that it could not reasonably be accounted for by chance variation when the population means are the same, the hypothesis will be rejected. In short, the logic and general procedure for testing a hypothesis about the difference between two means are the same as for testing a hypothesis about a single mean.

17.2 THE RANDOM SAMPLING DISTRIBUTION OF THE DIFFERENCES BETWEEN TWO SAMPLE MEANS

The random sampling distribution of *single* means described the sample means that occur when sampling at random from a population having the mean specified in H_0. Here we are concerned with the *difference* between two means, and the pertinent reference distribution is the *random sampling distribution of differences between two sample means.* Just what *is* this distribution?

Suppose one sample is drawn at random from the population of X scores and another from the population of Y scores. The mean of each is computed, and the difference between these two means obtained and recorded. Let the samples be returned to their respective populations and a second pair of samples be selected in the same way. Again the two means are calculated and the difference between them noted and recorded. If this experiment is repeated indefinitely, the differences [values of $(\bar{X} - \bar{Y})$ thus generated] form the random sampling distribution of differences between two sample means.

The use to which the sampling distribution is put is, of course, to describe what differences would occur between $\bar{X}$ and $\bar{Y}$ when H_0 is true. In inquiry about the difference between two means, H_0, the hypothesis to be tested, is almost always that μ_X and μ_Y do not differ.† Now if pairs of samples are drawn at random from two populations, *and the means of the two populations are the same,* we will find that sometimes $\bar{X}$ is larger than $\bar{Y}$ [leading to a positive value for $(\bar{X} - \bar{Y})$] and sometimes it is the other way around [leading to a negative value for $(\bar{X} - \bar{Y})$]. It is easy to see that when all possible differences are considered, their mean will be zero. Hence, the mean of the sampling distribution of differences is zero when the difference between the two population means is zero. We will use $\mu_{\bar{X}-\bar{Y}}$ as the symbol for the mean of the sampling distribution of differences $(\bar{X} - \bar{Y})$. To summarize, then,

$$\mu_{\bar{X}-\bar{Y}} = 0$$

when $\mu_X - \mu_Y = 0$.

More generally, the mean of the sampling distribution of differences between two means is equal to the difference between the means of the two populations:

$$\mu_{\bar{X}-\bar{Y}} = \mu_X - \mu_Y$$

In Section 14.6, we found that another way of looking at the random sampling distribution of means is to consider it as the distribution of means of all possible samples. The same is true for the random sampling distribution of differences between $\bar{X}$ and $\bar{Y}$. If we specify sample size for X and Y, enumerate each possible sample that can be formed from the two populations, calculate the mean of each, couple in turn each sample mean of X with all of the possible sample means of Y, and obtain the difference between each resulting pair, we shall have the complete set of possible differences between pairs of sample means. The distribution of differences thus formed is equivalent to that formed by repeated sampling over an infinity of trials in that both lead to the same conclusions when interpreted as relative frequency, or probability distributions.‡

---

† H_0 *could* state that $\mu_X - \mu_Y = +5$, for example, and this hypothesis is capable of being tested. However, the nature of inquiry seldom leads to such a question.

‡ The sampling distributions described above are those that would be formed when the two random samples are selected *independently* from their respective populations. Sometimes samples are selected that do not meet this criterion. See Section 17.9 for further discussion.

17.3 AN ILLUSTRATION OF THE SAMPLING DISTRIBUTION OF DIFFERENCES BETWEEN MEANS

The set of differences between pairs of possible means is extremely large unless the populations are quite small. It is instructive to explore by actual enumeration the nature of the distribution of differences, but to do so, we shall have to confine our attention to miniature populations.

Suppose that the population of X scores consists of three scores: 3, 5, 7. Because the usual inquiry asks what would happen if the "treatment" had no effect, we shall also suppose that the population of Y scores consists of the same three scores: 3, 5, 7. If samples of two cases are drawn with replacement from either population, there are nine possible samples and therefore nine possible means that may occur. These are shown in Table 17.1. Note that we say that there are nine possible means, even though some of them have the same value. All must be taken into account.

To inquire what differences may occur between sample means in X and sample means in Y, we must consider that there are nine sample means in X, and that each may be coupled with any one of the nine sample means in Y. Thus, there are 81 possible pairings of means of X with means of Y. The possible sample means are shown on the margins of Table 17.2 and the 81 differences between pairs $(\bar{X} - \bar{Y})$ are shown in the body of the same table. *If samples are drawn independently and at random, each of the listed differences is equally likely to appear.* If we collect these differences in a frequency distribution, the result is as given in Table 17.3 and is graphically illustrated in Figure 17.1.

Table 17.1 *Possible Samples and Sample Means for Samples of Size Two (Sampling with Replacement)*

| Population of X scores: 3, 5, 7 | | $\mu_X = \mu_Y = 5$ | |
Population of Y scores: 3, 5, 7		$\sigma_X = \sigma_Y = 1.633$	
Sample from X population	$\bar{X}$	Sample from Y population	$\bar{Y}$
3, 3	3	3, 3	3
3, 5	4	3, 5	4
3, 7	5	3, 7	5
5, 3	4	5, 3	4
5, 5	5	5, 5	5
5, 7	6	5, 7	6
7, 3	5	7, 3	5
7, 5	6	7, 5	6
7, 7	7	7, 7	7

Table 17.2 *Differences between Pairs of Sample Means* $(\bar{X} - \bar{Y})$ *for All Possible Paired Samples of X and Y (Data from Table 17.1)*[a]

	$\bar{Y}$								
$\bar{X}$	3	4	4	5	5	5	6	6	7
7	4	3	3	2	2	2	1	1	0
6	3	2	2	1	1	1	0	0	−1
6	3	2	2	1	1	1	0	0	−1
5	2	1	1	0	0	0	−1	−1	−2
5	2	1	1	0	0	0	−1	−1	−2
5	2	1	1	0	0	0	−1	−1	−2
4	1	0	0	−1	−1	−1	−2	−2	−3
4	1	0	0	−1	−1	−1	−2	−2	−3
3	0	−1	−1	−2	−2	−2	−3	−3	−4

[a] The body of the table contains values of $(\bar{X} - \bar{Y})$.

Several features of the resulting frequency distribution are notable. First, the mean of the distribution is zero, the difference between μ_X and μ_Y. Second, the distribution is very reasonably approximated by the normal curve. In Figure 17.1, a normal curve has been fitted to the distribution, and it is apparent that the expected frequencies of the normal curve (shown by points on the curve) are close to the actual frequency of particular means (shown by the height of the bars in the histogram). If the sampling distribution of means for *X* and *Y* is approximately normal, the distribution of differences between pairs of means selected at random will also be approximately normal. In the present situation, the distribution of the population of scores in *X* and *Y* resembles a rectangular distribution more than it

Table 17.3 *Distribution of Differences between All Possible Pairs of Sample Means (Data from Table 17.2)*

$(\bar{X} - \bar{Y})$	f	
4	1	
3	4	
2	10	$\mu_{\bar{X}-\bar{Y}} = 0$
1	16	$\sigma_{\bar{X}-\bar{Y}} = 1.633$
0	19	
−1	16	
−2	10	
−3	4	
−4	1	
	$n = 81$	

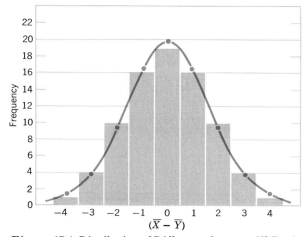

Figure 17.1 *Distribution of Differences between All Possible Pairs of Sample Means: Data from Table 17.3.*

does a normal distribution. Yet the distribution of differences between pairs of sample means resembles the normal curve. Thus the effect predicted for single means by the Central Limit Theorem (see Section 13.7) also has important bearing on the distribution of differences between sample means. The normal curve, therefore, remains as an important model for the sampling distribution of differences between means even when population distributions depart to some extent from normality.

17.4 PROPERTIES OF THE SAMPLING DISTRIBUTION OF DIFFERENCES BETWEEN MEANS

As we know, three characteristics completely define any distribution: mean, standard deviation, and shape. We now know that the mean of the random sampling distribution of differences between pairs of sample means, $\mu_{\bar{X}-\bar{Y}}$, is the same as the difference between the two population means, $\mu_X - \mu_Y$. We also know that the sampling distribution of differences will be normally distributed when the two populations are normally distributed, and that the sampling distribution tends toward normal even when the two populations are not normal. But what about its standard deviation? The answer depends on whether samples are independent or dependent.

Independent random samples exist when the selection of elements comprising the sample of Y scores is in no way influenced by the selection of elements comprising the sample of X scores, and vice versa. In ordinary random selection from two populations, this would be true. For example, the experiment concerning the influence of vitamin A, described at the opening of this chapter, falls in this category.

If the same subjects are used for both treatment conditions, or if the subjects for the two treatment conditions are matched in some way, the samples are dependent. We will consider first the procedure for independent samples.

The standard deviation of the sampling distribution of differences between two means is called the *standard error of the difference between two means,* and its symbol is $\sigma_{\bar{X}-\bar{Y}}$. If the sampling distribution is composed of differences between means of *independent* samples, its standard deviation is:

Standard Error of the Difference
between Two Independent Means
$$\sigma_{\bar{X}-\bar{Y}} = \sqrt{\sigma_{\bar{X}}^2 + \sigma_{\bar{Y}}^2} \qquad (17.1)$$

Like the formula for the standard error of the mean, it has been derived through theoretical considerations and on the assumption of random sampling with replacement.†

In the illustration of Section 17.3, the distribution of possible differences was constructed on the assumption of independence of sample means. According to Formula 16.1, its standard deviation should be

$$\sigma_{\bar{X}-\bar{Y}} = \sqrt{\left(\frac{1.633}{\sqrt{2}}\right)^2 + \left(\frac{1.633}{\sqrt{2}}\right)^2} = 1.633$$

Note that actual calculation of the standard deviation (see Table 17.3) yields the same value, 1.633.‡

Formula 17.1 requires the standard error of the mean of X and of Y and these, in turn, require that σ_X and σ_Y be known. As usual, in practice the two population standard deviations must be estimated from the samples (see Section 15.4). The formula for estimating $\sigma_{\bar{X}-\bar{Y}}$ is:

Estimate of $\sigma_{\bar{X}-\bar{Y}}$,
Independent Samples
$$s_{\bar{X}-\bar{Y}} = \sqrt{s_{\bar{X}}^2 + s_{\bar{Y}}^2} \qquad (17.2a)$$

For purposes of computation, this formula may be reexpressed:

$$s_{\bar{X}-\bar{Y}} = \sqrt{\frac{s_X^2}{n_X} + \frac{s_Y^2}{n_Y}}\text{††} \qquad (17.2b)$$

Estimating $\sigma_{\bar{X}-\bar{Y}}$ introduces a degree of error. If the size of *each* sample equals or exceeds 20, the error will be small enough that procedures described here will be

---

† See Section 14.5 for a discussion of the influence (ordinarily negligible) of sampling *without* replacement.

‡ It is a coincidence that in this problem $\sigma_X = \sigma_Y = \sigma_{\bar{X}-\bar{Y}}$.

†† If S is at hand (rather than s), one may calculate: $s_{\bar{X}-\bar{Y}} = \sqrt{S_X^2/(n_X - 1) + S_Y^2/(n_Y - 1)}$. See Section 15.4.

acceptable if not entirely correct. Methods that take precise account of the error are described in chapter 19.

17.5 TESTING THE HYPOTHESIS OF NO DIFFERENCE BETWEEN TWO INDEPENDENT MEANS: THE VITAMIN A EXPERIMENT

Does vitamin A make a difference in ability to see under conditions of dim illumination? We will test the hypothesis that:

$$H_0: \mu_X - \mu_Y = 0$$
$$H_A: \mu_X - \mu_Y \neq 0$$

using the 5% level of significance ($\alpha = .05$). Two samples of 10 cases each are selected at random from the target population. This number of cases is far too small for the procedures presented in this chapter but will be used for the sake of simplicity of exposition. Data for this problem and calculations are shown in Table 17.4. The calculations begin by finding the two means, the two estimates of the population standard deviations, and the standard error of the difference between means. These are shown in steps 1 through 3 in the table. Formula 17.2b requires s^2 for both variables, but we calculate s as well, because good practice requires reporting means and standard deviations as well as the outcome of the test (see Section 15.11).† s^2 is obtained from the next-to-last step in calculating s.

How deviant is our particular difference from the hypothesized difference of zero? To answer, the difference must be expressed in the form of a z score, where $z = (score - mean)/(standard\ deviation)$. In the sampling distribution of differences, our difference—$(\bar{X} - \bar{Y})$—is the score, the hypothesized difference is the mean, and $s_{\bar{X}-\bar{Y}}$ is the *estimated* standard deviation. As with problems involving single means (see Section 15.6), we have an approximate z rather than a true z, because an estimate of the standard deviation is substituted for the true value. The use of the symbol "z" will continue to remind us of this:

Location of $\bar{X} - \bar{Y}$ in the Sampling Distribution, Expressed as an Approximate z $"z" = \dfrac{(\bar{X} - \bar{Y}) - (\mu_X - \mu_Y)_{\text{hyp}}}{s_{\bar{X}-\bar{Y}}}$ (17.3)

In the present problem, "z" $= +1.32$, as calculated in step 4. Since the decision criterion is $\alpha = .05$ and the test is non-directional, the critical values of z are -1.96 and $+1.96$. The obtained difference is located within the region of accept-

---

† In preparing the research report, if it is desired to present S rather than s, it may be obtained from the calculated value of s thus: $S = s \sqrt{(n - 1)/n}$.

Table 17.4 *Calculations for Testing a Hypothesis about the Difference between Two Independent Means*

Supplementary Vitamin A: X	Normal Diet: Y	X^2	Y^2
38	37	1,444	1,369
41	34	1,681	1,156
42	45	1,764	2,025
47	40	2,209	1,600
42	43	1,764	1,849
45	40	2,025	1,600
48	42	2,304	1,764
31	22	961	484
38	28	1,444	784
30	31	900	961
$\Sigma X = 402$	$\Sigma Y = 362$	$\Sigma X^2 = 16{,}496$	$\Sigma Y^2 = 13{,}592$

(1) $\bar{X} = \dfrac{\sum X}{n_X} = \dfrac{402}{10} = 40.2 \qquad \bar{Y} = \dfrac{\sum Y}{n_Y} = \dfrac{362}{10} = 36.2$

(2a) $\sum x^2 = \sum X^2 - \dfrac{\left(\sum X\right)^2}{n_X} = 16\ 496 - \dfrac{402^2}{10} = 335.6$

$s_X = \sqrt{\dfrac{\sum x^2}{n_X - 1}} = \sqrt{\dfrac{335.6}{10 - 1}} = \sqrt{37.29} = 6.11$

(2b) $\sum y^2 = \sum Y^2 - \dfrac{\left(\sum Y\right)^2}{n_Y} = 13\ 592 - \dfrac{362^2}{10} = 487.6$

$s_Y = \sqrt{\dfrac{\sum y^2}{n_Y - 1}} = \sqrt{\dfrac{487.6}{10 - 1}} = \sqrt{54.18} = 7.36$

(3) $s_{\bar{X}-\bar{Y}} = \sqrt{\dfrac{s_X^2}{n_X} + \dfrac{s_Y^2}{n_Y}} = \sqrt{\dfrac{37.29}{10} + \dfrac{54.18}{10}} = \sqrt{9.15} = 3.02$

(4) $\text{``}z\text{''} = \dfrac{(\bar{X} - \bar{Y}) - (\mu_X - \mu_Y)_{\text{hyp}}}{s_{\bar{X}-\bar{Y}}} = \dfrac{(40.2 - 36.2) - 0}{3.02} = +1.32$

(5) Compare $\text{``}z\text{''}_{\text{calc}}$ with $(z_{\text{crit}} = \pm 1.96)$

(6) Statistical conclusion: accept H_0

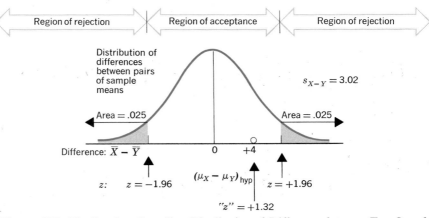

Figure 17.2 *The Random Sampling Distribution of Differences between Two Sample Means when H_0 is True.*

ance, so H_0 cannot be rejected. We conclude that the null hypothesis *could* be true. The outcome is illustrated in Figure 17.2.

17.6 THE CONDUCT OF A ONE-TAILED TEST

Suppose it had been important, in the problem of the previous section, only to discover whether supplementary feedings of vitamin A *improved* vision. In this case, a one-tailed test is in order. The null hypothesis and the alternative hypothesis would then be:

$$H_0: \mu_X - \mu_Y = 0$$
$$H_A: \mu_X - \mu_Y > 0$$

The region of rejection must, consequently, be placed entirely in the upper tail of the sampling distribution. Figure 17.3 illustrates the situation. The calculation of "z" is exactly the same as for a two-tailed test, and the obtained value remains: "z" $= +1.32$. In the normal distribution, $z = +1.645$ identifies the point above which 5% of the values will be found. The obtained z is not so deviant and therefore falls in the region of acceptance.

17.7 SAMPLE SIZE IN INFERENCE ABOUT TWO MEANS

When inference concerns two independent sample means, the samples may be of different size. However, if σ_X and σ_Y are equal, the *total* of the sample sizes

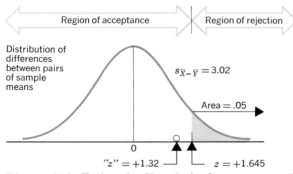

Figure 17.3 *Testing the Hypothesis that* $\mu_X - \mu_Y = 0$ *against the Alternative that* $\mu_X - \mu_Y > 0$; *Data from Section 17.5.*

$(n_X + n_Y)$ is used most efficiently when $n_X = n_Y$. This will result in a smaller value for $\sigma_{\bar{X}-\bar{Y}}$ than otherwise. For example, when one sample is twice as large as the other, $\sigma_{\bar{X}-\bar{Y}}$ is about 6% larger than if the same total sample size were distributed equally between the two samples.† The inflation of $\sigma_{\bar{X}-\bar{Y}}$ continues at an accelerated pace as the relative sample size becomes increasingly more discrepant. The advantage of a smaller $\sigma_{\bar{X}-\bar{Y}}$ is that, if there *is* a difference between μ_X and μ_Y, the probability of claiming it (rejecting H_0) is increased.

The discussion above relates to the *relative* size of the two samples. But what about the *absolute* magnitude of sample size? Other things being equal, large samples increase the probability of detecting a difference when a difference exists. The question of optimum sample size required for testing hypotheses about two means is given detailed consideration in Section 21.11.

17.8 RANDOMIZATION AS EXPERIMENTAL CONTROL

We have grown well acquainted with the role of random sampling in making it possible to know the characteristics of sampling distributions. When two or more groups are compared, randomization serves a second function not always fully appreciated: experimental control.

Consider a study of accuracy of perception. Two samples of subjects are drawn, one experimental condition is imposed upon one group, a second upon the other, and the perception score of each subject is recorded. If subjects are assigned by casual methods to one group or the other, there may well be factors associated with the assignment which are related to the performance being tested. If subjects first to

† This statement assumes that $\sigma_X^2 = \sigma_Y^2$.

volunteer are placed in one group, the two groups may differ in level of motivation, and so subsequently in performance. If subjects are inspected as they report for the experimental chore and assigned by whim, the experimenter may unconsciously tend to assign those without glasses to the condition where better performance is expected.

The primary experimental (as opposed to statistical) benefit of randomization lies in the chance (and therefore impartial) assignment of extraneous influence among the groups to be compared. Those who are likely to do well have just as much chance of being assigned to one treatment group as they have to another, and the same is true of those who are likely to do poorly. The beauty of randomization is that it affords this type of experimental control over extraneous influences whether or not they are known by the experimenter to exist. Now random assignment of subjects to treatment groups does not *guarantee* equality, any more than 50 heads are guaranteed every time we toss 100 coins. But randomization *tends* to produce equality, and that tendency increases in strength as sample size increases. In any event, if random assignment is practiced consistently, equality will result in the long run. Thus randomization ensures a lack of bias, whereas other methods may not.

One caution is in order. Inspection of the outcome of randomization sometimes tempts the experimenter to exchange a few subjects from group to group before proceeding with the treatment in order to obtain groups more nearly alike. Such a move leads to disaster. The standard error formulas are based on the assumption of randomization, and casual adjustment of this kind makes them inappropriate.

The specific advantage of experimental control, such as can be achieved through randomization (and other methods), is that the outcome of the study is more readily interpretable when adequate control is present. In a two-group comparison, we want to know if it is the difference in treatment that is responsible for a difference in outcome. If the two groups are balanced in all respects except the treatment imposed, conclusions are relatively straightforward. But if they differ in other respects, it will be harder to say (if not impossible) what is responsible for a difference if one is found. Randomization can be a great help in this regard, although it is not a cure-all. See Section 21.13 for discussion of its limitations.

Comparisons between two or more groups may be divided into two categories: those in which the investigator can assign to each subject the particular treatment condition that he wishes and those in which he cannot. The vitamin A study is an example of the first kind; the investigator can decide which subjects will receive the diet supplement and which will not. It is therefore possible for the investigator to choose to assign treatment condition at random to the subjects, thus achieving an important degree of control of extraneous variables.

Studies designed to inquire about possible differences between males and females in problem solving, or to explore effect of impact of a four-year college experience on values and attitudes, are examples of the second kind. In the problem-solving study, the "treatment" variable is difference in sex, a built-in characteristic of the individual and therefore not assignable by the investigator. Similarly, in the impact-of-college study, the "treatment" variable is four years of college vs. no college, a difference not within the power of the investigator to impose on his subjects according to his will. Consequently, the benefits of random assignment of treatment condition are not available, and interpretation of the outcome, should a difference be found, is much more difficult.

The problem considered here is one of the important problems that intervene in moving from substantive questions to statistical questions and from statistical answers to substantive conclusions. It is developed in greater depth in Sections 21.13 and 21.15.

17.9 COMPARING MEANS OF DEPENDENT SAMPLES

So far we have considered differences obtained from two independent random samples, where measurements in the two samples are unrelated to each other. Under proper conditions, it is also possible to conduct a study involving related measures.

In what circumstances would the sample means be dependent? Suppose the vitamin A experiment had been conducted by selecting a group of 50 subjects at random, feeding them a normal diet, testing their vision under dim illumination, *and then feeding them a normal diet plus supplementary vitamin A and retesting them.* In this case, we would have 50 pairs of observations, but each pair would be measured on the same subject. Presumably, a subject who was relatively good under one condition would tend to be relatively good on the other, aside from possible difference due to vitamin A.† Thus, with a given pair of observations, the value of Y is in part determined by (or related to) the particular value of X, and the samples cannot be said to be independent.

Samples may be dependent even when different subjects have been used. In an experiment with the same objective, it might occur to the experimenter that an extraneous source of variation is contributed by differences in basic visual acuity among individuals selected at random. He could eliminate this source of variation by pairing individuals matched on pretest performance in basic visual acuity. Thus the two members of the first pair of subjects may each have 20–40 vision, the members of the second pair 20–20 vision, etc. When paired in this way, the value of any particular Y score will be in part related to the value of its paired X score, and so the values of X and Y cannot be said to be completely independent.

---

† If the subjects differ in basic visual acuity, a man whose vision is 20–20 might be expected to perform better (relatively) under both conditions than one whose visual acuity was 20–40.

There are, then, two basic ways in which dependent samples may be generated: (1) the same subjects are used for both conditions of the study, and (2) different subjects are used, but they are matched on some variable related to performance on the variable being observed. When samples are dependent, the standard error of the difference between means must take account of the correlation induced by the existing relationship between the samples. It is:

Standard Error of the
Difference between $$\sigma_{\bar{X}-\bar{Y}} = \sqrt{\sigma_{\bar{X}}^2 + \sigma_{\bar{Y}}^2 - 2\rho_{XY}\sigma_{\bar{X}}\sigma_{\bar{Y}}}$$ (17.4)
Two Dependent Means

where: $\sigma_{\bar{X}}$ = standard error of the mean of X
  $\sigma_{\bar{Y}}$ = standard error of the mean of Y
  ρ_{XY} = correlation coefficient of the population
    of pairs of X and Y measures†

When the parameters are unknown, the formula that estimates $\sigma_{\bar{X}-\bar{Y}}$ is:

Estimate of $\sigma_{\bar{X}-\bar{Y}}$,
Dependent Samples $$s_{\bar{X}-\bar{Y}} = \sqrt{s_{\bar{X}}^2 + s_{\bar{Y}}^2 - 2rs_{\bar{X}}s_{\bar{Y}}}$$ (17.5)

Again, error will be introduced in substituting an estimate of $\sigma_{\bar{X}-\bar{Y}}$ for its true value. Evaluation of the approximate z (obtained by the procedures described in the next two sections) according to the characteristics of the normal curve will generally be acceptable, although not entirely accurate, when the number of *pairs* of scores = 40. When it is less, a method that takes account of the error is necessary. This method is described in chapter 19 (see especially Section 19.10).

17.10 TESTING THE HYPOTHESIS OF NO DIFFERENCE BETWEEN TWO DEPENDENT MEANS

Is reaction time different to a red light than to a green light? Suppose a group of subjects has been selected at random and given a preliminary test to determine the reaction time of each individual to a white-light stimulus. From among this group, pairs of subjects are formed such that the two members of any given pair are equal in speed of reaction to white light. Taking each pair in turn, one member is tested with a green light as the stimulus and the other with a red light. Which member of each pair receives which stimulus is determined at random. Reaction times are recorded in milliseconds. The two groups of subjects so selected constitute two dependent samples.

We shall test: H_0: $\mu_X - \mu_Y = 0$ (where X represents reaction time of those

† See Chapter 9 for the nature and computation of the correlation coefficient.

exposed to green light and Y reaction time of those exposed to red light) against: $H_A: \mu_X - \mu_Y \neq 0$, using the 5% significance level. The procedure for testing the hypothesis of no difference between the two treatment means is exactly the same as given in Section 17.5, except that allowance must be made for use of dependent rather than independent samples. This is done by using Formula 17.5 for the standard error of the difference rather than Formula 17.2. To illustrate the procedure, we shall suppose that ten pairs of subjects have been selected. This number of subjects is much too small for proper application of the procedures described in this chapter; the procedures of chapter 19 are appropriate.[†] We shall persist only for the sake of simplicity in demonstrating the necessary calculations.

The details of the test are shown in Table 17.5. This table contains the basic data, the calculations necessary for the test when raw score formulas are used, and the statistical decision.

The process of computation may be divided into two parts. First, find the basic quantities from which all calculations flow: $\Sigma X, \Sigma X^2, \Sigma Y, \Sigma Y^2, \Sigma XY$, and n. These are shown near the top of the table. Next, calculate the means, standard deviations, standard error of the means, correlation coefficient, standard error of the difference between means, and finally the approximate z. These are shown in steps 1 through 7. Steps 8 and 9 show the conclusion of the test.

17.11 AN ALTERNATIVE APPROACH TO THE PROBLEM OF TWO DEPENDENT MEANS

An alternative method is available for calculating z for the test of two dependent means. Depending on circumstances, it may save much computational labor. The outcome is identical with that of the method described in the previous section. That method dealt explicitly with the characteristics of the distribution of X and Y and required the correlation coefficient between the paired values of X and Y. *The present method focuses on the characteristics of the distribution of differences between the paired X and Y scores.*

Consider the hypothesis that $\mu_X - \mu_Y = 0$. If the hypothesis is true, then it is also true that the mean of the population of differences between paired values of X and Y is zero. If the difference between paired X and Y scores is designated by D, the initial hypothesis may be restated: $H_0: \mu_D = 0$. In the present method, we shall find $\bar{D}$, the mean of the sample set of difference scores, and inquire whether it differs significantly from the hypothesized mean of the population of difference scores, μ_D.[‡]

[†] The same example, properly evaluated by small sample procedures, is treated in Section 19.10.

[‡] Note that this transforms the test from a two-sample test to a one-sample test. Compare the test made here with that illustrated in Sections 15.5 and 15.6.

Table 17.5 *Test of the Hypothesis of the Difference of Two Dependent Means*

Pair	Reaction to green light stimulus X	Reaction to red light stimulus Y	X^2	Y^2	XY
1	28	25	784	625	700
2	26	27	676	729	702
3	33	28	1089	784	924
4	30	31	900	961	930
5	32	29	1024	841	928
6	30	30	900	900	900
7	31	32	961	1024	992
8	18	21	324	441	378
9	22	25	484	625	550
10	24	20	576	400	480
	$\Sigma X = 274$	$\Sigma Y = 268$	$\Sigma X^2 = 7718$	$\Sigma Y^2 = 7330$	$\Sigma XY = 7484$

$$(1) \quad \bar{X} = \frac{\Sigma X}{n} = \frac{274}{10} = 27.4 \qquad \bar{Y} = \frac{\Sigma Y}{n} = \frac{268}{10} = 26.8$$

$$(2a) \quad \sum x^2 = \sum X^2 - \frac{\left(\sum X\right)^2}{n} = 7718 - \frac{274^2}{10} = 210.4$$

$$(2b) \quad s_X = \sqrt{\frac{\sum x^2}{n-1}} = \sqrt{\frac{210.4}{10-1}} = 4.84$$

$$(3a) \quad \sum y^2 = \sum Y^2 - \frac{\left(\sum Y\right)^2}{n} = 7330 - \frac{268^2}{10} = 147.6$$

$$(3b) \quad s_Y = \sqrt{\frac{\sum y^2}{n-1}} = \sqrt{\frac{147.6}{10-1}} = 4.05$$

$$(4a) \quad \sum xy = \sum XY - \frac{\left(\sum X\right)\left(\sum Y\right)}{n} = 7484 - \frac{(274)(268)}{10} = +140.8$$

$$(4b) \quad r = \frac{\sum xy}{\sqrt{\left(\sum x^2\right)\left(\sum y^2\right)}} = \frac{+140.8}{\sqrt{(210.4)(147.6)}} = +.80$$

$$(5a) \quad s_{\bar{X}} = \frac{s_X}{\sqrt{n}} = \frac{4.84}{\sqrt{10}} = 1.53$$

Table 17.5 *Test of the Hypothesis of the Difference of Two Dependent Means (con't.)*

(5b) $s_{\bar{Y}} = \dfrac{s_Y}{\sqrt{n}} = \dfrac{4.05}{\sqrt{10}} = 1.28$

(6) $s_{\bar{X}-\bar{Y}} = \sqrt{s_{\bar{X}}^2 + s_{\bar{Y}}^2 - 2rs_{\bar{X}}s_{\bar{Y}}}$
$\qquad = \sqrt{1.53^2 + 1.28^2 - 2(+.80)(1.53)(1.28)} = .92$

(7) "z" $= \dfrac{(\bar{X} - \bar{Y}) - (\mu_X - \mu_Y)_{\text{hyp}}}{s_{\bar{X}-\bar{Y}}} = \dfrac{(27.4 - 26.8) - 0}{.92} = +.65$

(8) Compare "z"$_{\text{calc}}$ with $z_{\text{crit}} = \pm 1.96$

(9) Statistical conclusion: accept H_0

To conduct the test by the alternative method, the paired scores are recorded in tabular form, as shown in Table 17.6. Then each value of Y is subtracted from its paired value of X and the difference recorded in a new column, D. We must find the mean and (estimate of the) standard deviation of these difference scores ($\bar{D}$, and s_D).

To find the standard deviation, the square of each difference score is required. These values are shown in the column headed: D^2. Computation of $\bar{D}$ and s_D is shown in the table. Next, we find the standard error of the mean of the difference scores, $s_{\bar{D}} = s_D/\sqrt{n}$. "$z$" may then be calculated by Formula 17.6:

Table 17.6 *Test of the Hypothesis of the Difference between Two Dependent Means: Difference Score Method (Data from Table 17.5)*

Pair	X	Y	D	D^2	Calculations
1	28	25	3	9	$\bar{D} = \dfrac{\sum D}{n} = \dfrac{+6}{10} = +.6$
2	26	27	−1	1	
3	33	28	5	25	Let $d = (D - \bar{D})$, a deviation
4	30	31	−1	1	score in D. Then:
5	32	29	3	9	
6	30	30	0	0	$\left(\sum D\right)^2$
7	31	32	−1	1	$\sum d^2 = \sum D^2 - \dfrac{\left(\sum D\right)^2}{n}$
8	18	21	−3	9	
9	22	25	−3	9	$= 80 - \dfrac{(+6)^2}{10} = 76.4$
10	24	20	4	16	
			$\sum D = +6$	$\sum D^2 = 80$	And:

$s_{\bar{D}} = \dfrac{s_D}{\sqrt{n}} = \dfrac{2.91}{\sqrt{10}} = .92$

"z" $= \dfrac{\bar{D} - \mu_{D(\text{hyp})}}{s_{\bar{D}}} = \dfrac{+.6 - 0}{.92} = +.65$

$s_D = \sqrt{\dfrac{\sum d^2}{n - 1}} = \sqrt{\dfrac{76.4}{9}} = 2.91$

*Location of $\bar{D}$ in the
Sampling Distribution,
Expressed as a z Score*

$$\text{``}z\text{''} = \frac{\bar{D} - \mu_{D(\text{hyp})}}{s_{\bar{D}}} \qquad (17.6)$$

Note that the calculated value of "z" is exactly the same as obtained by the method of the previous section.

Although the simpler method, described in this section, reduces the computational burden substantially, it also yields less information. When we are done, we know the size of the difference between the two sample means ($\bar{D}$) and whether the difference was or was not significant according to the decision criterion adopted. In most research we will want to know (and will be obliged to report) the two means and the two standard deviations. If we are curious how much correlation was induced by pairing, we will also want to know r. But the short method yields none of this information. If these quantities are desired, we shall have to return to the data and compute them and so may find that the total amount of work is about the same as with the "longer" method described in the previous section.

17.12 SOME COMMENTS ON THE USE OF DEPENDENT SAMPLES

Section 17.8 developed the role of randomization from an experimental point of view. We saw that control could be obtained over the influence of extraneous variables when treatment condition could be randomly assigned to the subjects at hand, and that when random assignment cannot be followed, it is much more difficult to interpret the outcome. Those comments apply to studies using dependent samples as well as to those using independent samples. With matched subjects, the benefit of randomization as control can be achieved by assigning treatment condition randomly to the members of each pair, taking care to do so independently for each pair of subjects. The problem is more complicated when the same subjects are used for both treatment conditions. Here, random assignment would mean deciding randomly which treatment the subject will receive first and which will be given second. This will create some problems when the first treatment experience changes the subject in some way so that he performs differently under the second treatment. Practice effect and fatigue are two possible influences that might affect a subject's second performance.

As we learned earlier, in many important studies it is not possible to assign treatment condition at random. In these we may find that the matched samples design offers an advantage in that a potentially important but irrelevant influence may be controlled by matching subjects on that variable. Consider the study of sex differences in problem solving, mentioned earlier. Since standard tests of problem solving seem frequently to be constructed so that they depend to some extent on mathematical reasoning, and since it is probable that males and females receive differential reinforcement for doing well in mathematics, if we are after "genetic" sex differences, it would be reasonable to attempt control of this variable by matching males and females on mathematical competence. As a general stratagem this is doubtless a help, but it is not perfect: it is quite possible to "match out" too much or too little. These aspects of the logic of investigation are clearly of vital importance. They will be discussed in greater depth in Section 21.14.

From a statistical standpoint, there can be an advantage in electing to use paired observations rather than independent random samples, when a choice is available. Pairing observations makes possible elimination of an extraneous source of variation. For example, in the vitamin A study, variation between the two samples in basic visual acuity could be eliminated by pairing subjects in terms of this capability. The effect of doing so is to reduce the influence of random variation on the differences between means. The standard error measures this factor. Compare the standard error for dependent samples, $\sqrt{s_{\bar{X}}^2 + s_{\bar{Y}}^2 - 2rs_{\bar{X}}s_{\bar{Y}}}$, with the standard error for independent samples, $\sqrt{s_{\bar{X}}^2 + s_{\bar{Y}}^2}$; the former will be smaller, other things being equal. The effect of reducing the standard error of the difference by pairing is the same as reducing it by increasing sample size. The less the error (as measured by the standard error), the less likely it is to mask a true difference between the means of the two populations.† To put it more formally, a reduction in $\sigma_{\bar{X}-\bar{Y}}$ reduces the probability of committing a Type II error (see Section 16.7).

Note that the reduction of $\sigma_{\bar{X}-\bar{Y}}$ induced by pairing observations depends on the value of the correlation coefficient induced by pairing. In general, when pairing is on the basis of a variable importantly related to performance of the subjects, the correlation will be higher than otherwise, and the reduction in $\sigma_{\bar{X}-\bar{Y}}$ will consequently be greater. For example, matching subjects on the basis of visual acuity will probably be beneficial in the vitamin A study, and so will matching subjects to be used in an experiment on rate of learning on their intelligence test scores or, better, on pretest performance on a learning task similar to that used in the main experiment. When the correlation must be estimated from the sample, error is introduced to the extent that the sample coefficient differs from the population coefficient. For example, it might be that the correlation in the population is actually zero and yet the sample coefficient is, say, $+.20$. Consequently, we ought to be sure that the coefficient is substantial enough that the loss in efficiency through the introduction of error is more than recovered through the degree of dependency induced by pairing. In practice, this means that we do not match on a variable that "might help" but only on one that we are sure will have a reasonably strong influence.

---

† The Note at the end of this chapter compares the algebraic values of z when the hypothesis is true, and when it is not.

17.13 ASSUMPTIONS IN INFERENCE ABOUT TWO MEANS

The general assumptions required for inference about two means to be precisely correct according to the ideal model presented in this chapter are basically the same as for inference about single means. These were described in Section 15.10. For convenient reference here, the major points are summarized below in terms suited to inference about two means:

1 Each sample is drawn at random from its respective population.

2 The samples are drawn with replacement.

3 The sampling distribution of differences between pairs of sample means follows the normal curve.

4 The standard deviation of the population of each set of scores is known.

Section 15.10 offered a commentary on each of these points, and particularly crucial considerations were developed in Section 15.11. These comments are just as applicable here as there; it would be a good idea to reread them now. In addition, there are some considerations special to the problem of inference about two means.

For inference concerning *independent* means, the first assumption listed above must be further qualified by specifying that the two random samples be *independently* selected. For *dependent* means, the ideal model supposes that there exists a population of paired subjects matched on the basis of some characteristic (or characteristics) and that a sample is selected at random from this population. It also presupposes that ρ, the correlation between pairs of observations in the population, is known. In chapter 19 we develop a model that makes due allowance for the necessity to estimate ρ as well as σ_X and σ_Y.

The third point listed at the beginning of this section states that the sampling distribution of differences between pairs of sample means should follow the normal curve. When the distributions of both populations are normal and sampling is random, this condition will hold. As we saw in the case of the miniature sampling distribution constructed in Section 17.3, when these distributions are not normal, the Central Limit Theorem makes its influence felt, and the sampling distribution of differences tends toward normality. Since the procedures described in this chapter are appropriate for large samples, and since increased sample size tends to facilitate the benefits of the Central Limit Theorem, there is no need to worry about moderate degrees of departure from normality in the two populations.

NOTE

Comparison of z when the Hypothesis (H_0) Is True, and when It Is Not (*Ref:* Section 17.12)

To test H_0, z is calculated as follows:

$$z = \frac{(\bar{X} - \bar{Y}) - (\mu_X - \mu_Y)_{hyp}}{\sigma_{\bar{X}-\bar{Y}}}$$

When H_0 is *true*, z is in fact:

$$z = \frac{(\bar{X} - \bar{Y}) - (\mu_X - \mu_Y)_{true}}{\sigma_{\bar{X}-\bar{Y}}}$$

But when H_0 is *false*, the values of $(\bar{X} - \bar{Y})$ are distributed about $(\mu_X - \mu_Y)_{true}$ rather than about $(\mu_X - \mu_Y)_{hyp}$. In this case, z *as calculated to test H_0 is actually*:

$$z = \frac{[(\bar{X} - \bar{Y}) - (\mu_X - \mu_Y)_{true}] + [(\mu_X - \mu_Y)_{true} - (\mu_X - \mu_Y)_{hyp}]}{\sigma_{\bar{X}-\bar{Y}}}$$

Now the element at the left in the numerator tends to be proportionate to the denominator (the ratio of these two elements exceeds ± 1.96 only 5% of the time). Consequently, the larger the element at the right in the numerator, the more likely it will be that z is large (specifically, large enough to lead to rejection of H_0).

PROBLEMS AND EXERCISES

Identify:

sampling distribution of
  difference between means
independent samples
dependent samples
$\mu_{\bar{X}-\bar{Y}}$

control benefits
  of randomization
$\sigma_{\bar{X}-\bar{Y}}$
$s_{\bar{X}-\bar{Y}}$

1 Given: $\bar{X} = 165.0$, $s_X = 24.0$, $n_X = 36$, and $\bar{Y} = 175.0$, $s_Y = 21.0$, $n_Y = 49$; assume the samples are independent. (*a*) State formally the hypotheses necessary to conduct a nondirectional test of no difference between the two population means. (*b*) Calculate $s_{\bar{X}-\bar{Y}}$. (*c*) Calculate z. (*d*) Evaluate z according to $\alpha = .05$ and $.01$, and state your conclusions.

2 In Problem 1, suppose H_A was: H_A: $\mu_X - \mu_Y < 0$. Evaluate z according to $\alpha = .05$ and $\alpha = .01$, and state your conclusions.

3 In Problem 1, suppose H_A was: H_A: $\mu_X - \mu_Y > 0$. Evaluate z according to $\alpha = .05$ and $\alpha = .01$, and state your conclusions.

4 Repeat the steps of Problem 1 but as applied to these data: $\bar{X} = 97.0$, $s_X = 16.0$, $n_X = 64$; $\bar{Y} = 90.0$, $s_Y = 18.0$, $n_Y = 81$.

5 (In this problem, the samples are much too small for the procedures of this chapter to be appropriate; the problem is offered this way to eliminate lengthy computation.)

Given the following scores from two independent samples:

$$X: 6, 7, 8, 8, 11 \qquad Y: 3, 4, 4, 7, 7$$

(a) State formally the hypotheses necessary to conduct a nondirectional test of no difference between the two population means. (b) Calculate s_X and s_Y. (c) Complete the test at the .05 and .01 levels of significance, and state your conclusions.

6 Repeat the steps of Problem 5, but as applied to these data:

$$X: 2, 2, 5, 5, 6 \qquad Y: 8, 8, 8, 9, 12$$

7 We wish to compare mechanical aptitude scores of male high school seniors with female high school seniors. We draw a random sample of males and another of females to conduct the test. Should we consider these to be dependent samples because both groups are equated in the sense that they are high school seniors? Or are they independent samples? Explain.

8 Given the following data from two dependent samples: $\bar{X} = 88.0$, $s_X = 16.0$, $\bar{Y} = 85.0$, $s_Y = 12.0$, $n = 64$, $r = +.50$. (a) State formally the hypotheses necessary to conduct a nondirectional test of no difference between the two population means. (b) Calculate $s_{\bar{X}-\bar{Y}}$. (c) Complete the test at the .05 and .01 levels of significance, and state your conclusions.

9 (See parenthetical introduction to Problem 5.) Given the following pairs of scores from dependent samples:

$$\text{Pair: } 1\ 2\ 3\ 4\ 5$$
$$X: 4\ 4\ 6\ 5\ 9$$
$$Y: 5\ 2\ 3\ 1\ 6$$

(a) State formally the hypotheses necessary to conduct a nondirectional test of no difference between the two population means. (b) Calculate $\bar{X}$, $\bar{Y}$, S_X, S_Y. (c) Calculate r_{XY}. (d) Calculate $s_{\bar{X}-\bar{Y}}$. (e) Complete the test at the .05 and .01 levels of significance, and state your conclusions.

10 Using the data of Problem 9, test the hypothesis of no difference between population means by the difference method described in Section 17.11: (a) Calculate $\bar{D}$ and $s_{\bar{D}}$. (b) Calculate "z" and compare it with that obtained in Problem 9. (c) Evaluate "z" according to $\alpha = .05$ and .01, and state your conclusions.

11 Give two examples of studies other than those in the text in which (a) the investigator could assign treatment condition randomly to subjects, and (b) he cannot (or would not) assign treatment condition randomly.

12 Given: independent samples with $s_X = s_Y = 10$. (a) Calculate $s_{\bar{X}-\bar{Y}}$ from Formula 17.2b assuming $n_X = n_Y = 30$. (b) Recalculate $s_{\bar{X}-\bar{Y}}$ assuming $n_X = 15$ and $n_Y = 45$. (c) Compare the two values of $s_{\bar{X}-\bar{Y}}$. What principle does this outcome illustrate?

CHAPTER 18

18.1 INTRODUCTION

In testing a hypothesis about a single mean, we ask whether μ might have a particular value (Is $\mu = 100$?). In estimation no value is specified in advance; the question is, "What *is* the value of μ?" For some kinds of substantive problems, hypothesis testing is useless. Suppose someone wants to know what proportion of residences in Chicago contain color television sets; no specific hypothesis presents itself. On the other hand, estimation procedures are exactly suited to this problem. Although some problems are not amenable to hypothesis testing but can be approached through estimation, the reverse is not true. Any problem for which hypothesis testing might be useful can alternatively be approached through estimation. This fact is but a hint of the very considerable utility of estimation, a much underused procedure in behavioral science. This chapter will present the logic of estimation, develop the normal curve model for estimation of means and differ-

Estimation of μ and $\mu_X - \mu_Y$

ences between means, and discuss the relative merits of interval estimation and hypothesis testing. Procedures for means when samples are small appear in the next chapter; those for correlation coefficients are in chapter 20, those for proportions in chapter 23.

18.2 THE PROBLEM OF ESTIMATION

The problem of estimation may take two forms: *point estimation* and *interval estimation*. Sometimes it is required to state a single value as an estimate of the population value. Such estimates are called point estimates. What percentage of voters will vote for candidate X? What is the mean aptitude test score of applicants for admission to Spartan University? If it is impractical to find the proportion in the entire population (in the first example) or the mean of the population (in the second example), an estimate of the population characteristic may be made from a random sample.

Point estimates alone are made reluctantly, because they may be considerably in error. Interval estimates are more practical when conditions permit. In interval estimation, limits are set within which it appears reasonable that the population parameter lies. In the question about Candidate X, a point estimate might state that 49% of the population of voters favor him. If an interval estimate were made, the outcome might state that we are 95% confident that the portion of voters (in the population) who favor him is not less than 46% and not greater than 52%.

Of course, we may be wrong in supposing that the stated limits contain the population value. Other things being equal, if wide limits are set, the likelihood that the limits will include the population value is high, and if narrow limits are set, there is greater risk of being wrong.† Because the option exists of setting wider or narrower limits, any statement of limits must be accompanied by indication of the degree of confidence that the population parameter falls within the limits. The limits themselves are usually referred to as a *confidence interval* and the statement of degree of confidence as a *confidence coefficient*.

18.3 INTERVAL ESTIMATES OF μ

In a normal distribution, 95% of scores are no further away from the mean than 1.96 standard deviations. Similarly, if the sampling distribution of means is normally distributed, 95% of sample means are no further away from μ than $1.96\sigma_{\bar{X}}$. Now *if 95% of means are no further away from μ than $1.96\sigma_{\bar{X}}$, it is equally true that for 95% of sample means, μ is no further away than $1.96\sigma_{\bar{X}}$.* This fact makes it possible to construct an interval estimate of μ. Suppose for each sample mean the statement is made that μ lies somewhere within the range $\bar{X} \pm 1.96\sigma_{\bar{X}}$. For 95% of sample means, this statement would be correct, and for 5% it would not. In drawing samples at random the probability is therefore .95 that an interval estimate constructed according to the rule:

$$\bar{X} \pm 1.96\sigma_{\bar{X}}$$

will include μ within the interval.

Figure 18.1 illustrates application of this rule. Suppose we draw samples of size 100 from a population in which $\mu = 100$ and $\sigma = 20$. If a sample is drawn and its mean is 103, it would be claimed that μ lies somewhere within the interval $103 \pm (1.96)(2.00)$, or between 99.08 and 106.92. The interval so constructed is shown at (*b*) in Figure 18.1, and we see that the claim is correct. On the other hand, if $\bar{X}$ had been 95, it would have been one of the 5% of sample means that lie further from μ

---

†One might consider the point estimate as the ultimate in narrow limits, and the risk of being wrong is great indeed.

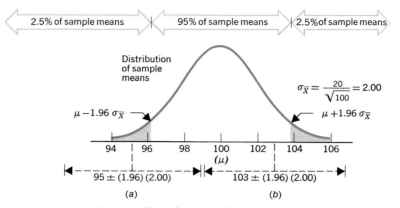

Figure 18.1 *Distribution of Sample Means Based on n = 100. Drawn from a Population Characterized by $\mu = 100$, $\sigma = 20$. (a) Interval Estimate of μ Constructed about $\bar{X} = 95$; Estimate Does Not Cover μ. (b) Interval Estimate of μ Constructed about $\bar{X} = 103$; Estimate Covers μ.*

than $1.96\sigma_{\bar{X}}$. Following the rule for constructing the interval, we would claim that μ lies within the interval $95 \pm (1.96)(2.00)$, or between 91.08 and 98.92. This interval is shown at (a); the claim is wrong.

We may wish to be even more sure that our estimate includes μ. Suppose that a probability of .99 is preferred to that of .95. Since 99% of sample means fall between $\mu \pm 2.58\sigma_{\bar{X}}$, an estimate may be made for which the probability is .99 that the interval will cover μ by the rule:

$$\bar{X} \pm 2.58\sigma_{\bar{X}}$$

Note that a wider interval will result than when a probability of .95 was used.

The two levels of probability, .95 and .99, are the ones commonly used in interval estimation. But it is possible to construct an interval estimate according to any desired level of probability. Suppose it is desired to find an interval such that the probability is .50 that μ is included within its limits. What is the value of z such that 50% of means are included within $\mu \pm z\sigma_{\bar{X}}$? From Table C in Appendix F, this value is found to be: $z = .6745$.† Consequently, the rule for constructing intervals such that the probability is .50 that the interval will contain μ is:

$$\bar{X} \pm .6745\sigma_{\bar{X}}$$

In general, intervals may be constructed according to a specified level of probability by the rule:

Rule for Constructing an Interval Estimate of μ $$\bar{X} \pm z_p\sigma_{\bar{X}} \qquad (18.1)$$

†Procedures for finding the value of z corresponding to a specified probability are described in Section 7.8.

where: $\overline{X}$ is the sample mean, obtained by random sampling

$\sigma_{\overline{X}}$ is the standard error of the mean

z_p is the magnitude of z for which the probability is p of obtaining a value so deviant or more so (in either direction)

The procedure so far described requires knowledge of $\sigma_{\overline{X}}$, which in turn requires that σ be known. As usual, most frequently $s_{\overline{X}}$ must be substituted as an estimate of $\sigma_{\overline{X}}$ (see Section 15.4). Accordingly, an approximate rule is:

Approximate Rule for Constructing an
Interval Estimate of μ $\qquad\qquad\qquad \overline{X} \pm z_p s_{\overline{X}} \qquad\qquad\qquad (18.2)$

When $n \geq 40$, little error will be introduced by substituting $s_{\overline{X}}$ for $\sigma_{\overline{X}}$. When sample size is smaller, procedures described in chapter 19 (Section 19.11) are in order.

The procedure for establishing confidence limits is illustrated below. Because σ is commonly unknown, the problems suppose that only a sample estimate is available. The sample problems, together with their solution, are presented in Table 18.1.

Table 18.1 *Construction of Confidence Intervals Concerning* μ *when* σ *Is Unknown and Sample Size Is Large*

Given:	$\overline{X} = 121.0$

$$s = 18.0^a \qquad \text{Therefore, } s_{\overline{X}} = \frac{s}{\sqrt{n}} = \frac{18.0}{\sqrt{144}} = 1.50$$

$$n = 144$$

Problem 1:   Estimate, at the 95% level of confidence, the location of μ.

Solution:
$$\overline{X} \pm (z_{.05})(s_{\overline{X}})$$
$$121.0 \pm (1.96)(1.50)$$
$$118.06 \text{ to } 123.94$$

$\begin{pmatrix}\text{Lower}\\\text{Limit}\end{pmatrix} \quad \begin{pmatrix}\text{Upper}\\\text{Limit}\end{pmatrix}$

Therefore, $C(118.06 \leq \mu \leq 123.94) = .95$

Problem 2:   Estimate, at the 99% level of confidence, the location of μ.

Solution:
$$\overline{X} \pm (z_{.01})(s_{\overline{X}})$$
$$121.0 \pm (2.58)(1.50)$$
$$117.13 \text{ to } 124.87$$

$\begin{pmatrix}\text{Lower}\\\text{Limit}\end{pmatrix} \quad \begin{pmatrix}\text{Upper}\\\text{Limit}\end{pmatrix}$

Therefore, $C(117.13 \leq \mu \leq 124.87) = .99$

---

^{a} Calculation of s is explained in Section 15.4.

When intervals are constructed according to the rule used in Problem 1, it is proper to say that the probability is .95 that an interval so constructed will include μ. *However, once the specific limits are established for a given set of data, the interval thus obtained either does or does not cover μ.* The probability is, at this stage, either 1.00 or 0 that the interval covers μ; we do not know which.† Consequently, it is usual to substitute the term *confidence* for probability in speaking of a specific interval. Thus, the outcome of Problem 1 is usually written as a *confidence interval:*

$$C(118.06 \leq \mu \leq 123.94) = .95$$

and the outcome of Problem 2:

$$C(117.13 \leq \mu \leq 124.87) = .99$$

The level of confidence is symbolized by C, the confidence coefficient. The first of these two statements may be translated as follows: we are 95% confident that μ falls between 118.06 and 123.94. But what does it mean to say that we are "95% confident"? We do not know whether the *particular* interval covers μ, but when intervals are constructed according to the rule, 95 of every 100 of them (on the average) will include μ. Remember that *it is the interval that varies from estimate to estimate, and not the value of μ. μ* is a fixed value, if unknown, and therefore does not vary.

For a given confidence coefficient, a small sample results in a wide confidence interval, and a large sample in a narrower one. How to choose sample size so that the resulting interval is of a desired width is discussed in Section 18.6.

18.4 AN INTERVAL ESTIMATE OF $\mu_X - \mu_Y$

Just as an interval estimate may be made of the value of μ, so also is it possible to estimate the true difference between μ_X and μ_Y. The logic of doing so and the general nature of the procedure are the same as for the case of the single mean. Figure 18.2 shows the random sampling distribution of differences between pairs of sample means when the true difference between μ_X and μ_Y is +5 points, and $\sigma_{\bar{X}-\bar{Y}} = 3.00$. Suppose for each sample difference, $(\bar{X} - \bar{Y})$, the claim was made that $\mu_X - \mu_Y$ lay somewhere within the range: $(\bar{X} - \bar{Y}) \pm 1.96\sigma_{\bar{X}-\bar{Y}}$. For example, if $(\bar{X} - \bar{Y}) = +1.00$, it would be claimed that $\mu_X - \mu_Y$ lay somewhere within the interval: $+1 \pm (1.96)(3.00)$ or between -4.88 and $+6.88$. This interval is shown in Figure 18.2. Note that the claim is correct.

If the difference between the two sample means is not further away from the difference between the two population means than $\pm 1.96\sigma_{\bar{X}-\bar{Y}}$, the claim will be correct. Otherwise, it will not. Since 95% of the obtained differences (under

† See Section 14.2.

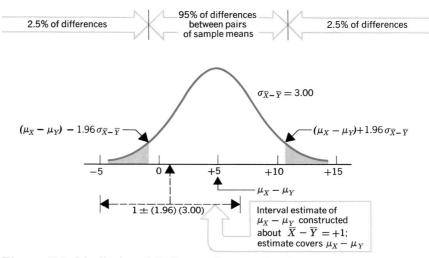

Figure 18.2 *Distribution of Differences between Two Sample Means, Drawn from Populations in Which* $\mu_X - \mu_Y = +5$ *and* $\sigma_{\bar{X}-\bar{Y}} = 3.00.$

random sampling) between the two sample means will be within this range, 95% of claims made by following this procedure will be correct. Accordingly, if a pair of samples are drawn at random, the probability is .95 that an interval estimate constructed by the procedure outlined above $[(\bar{X} - \bar{Y}) \pm 1.96\sigma_{\bar{X}-\bar{Y}}]$ will include the true value of $\mu_X - \mu_Y$. If the 99% confidence interval is required rather than the 95% interval just developed, substitute 2.58 for 1.96. Probabilities other than .95 and .99 may be selected if desired. See the previous section for the procedure.

In general, intervals may be constructed according to a specified level of probability by the rule of Formula 18.3:

Rule for Constructing an $$(\bar{X} - \bar{Y}) \pm z_p \sigma_{\bar{X}-\bar{Y}} \qquad (18.3)$$
Interval Estimate of $\mu_X - \mu_Y$

where: $(\bar{X} - \bar{Y})$ is the difference between the two sample means

$\sigma_{\bar{X}-\bar{Y}}$ is the standard error of the difference between two means

z_p is the magnitude of z for which, in the normal distribution, the probability is p of obtaining a value so deviant or more so (in either direction)

$p = 1 - C$, where C is the confidence coefficient

Once again, the procedure described above is dependent on knowledge of $\sigma_{\bar{X}}$ and $\sigma_{\bar{Y}}$ (and ρ, in the case of dependent samples), the values needed to obtain $\sigma_{\bar{X}-\bar{Y}}$. If only sample estimates are available (the usual case), $s_{\bar{X}-\bar{Y}}$ must be substituted for $\sigma_{\bar{X}-\bar{Y}}$. Accordingly, an approximate rule is:

Approximate Rule for Constructing $$(\bar{X} - \bar{Y}) \pm z_p s_{\bar{X}-\bar{Y}} \qquad (18.4)$$
an Interval Estimate of $\mu_X - \mu_Y$

When the size of each of the two samples equals or exceeds 20 for independent samples, or when the number of pairs of scores equals or exceeds 40 when samples are dependent, the error in such a substitution is usually tolerable. When sample size is smaller, the procedure described in Section 19.12 is in order.

The procedure for establishing confidence limits is illustrated in Table 18.2. Because the population values are commonly unknown, the problem supposes that only sample estimates are available.

The procedure described above applies to estimation of the difference between two population means for dependent samples as well as to independent samples. Of course, the formula for the standard error of the difference between two dependent means must be used. See Table 17.5 (Section 17.10) for an illustration of its calculation.

For a given confidence coefficient, a small sample results in a wide confidence interval and a large sample in a narrower one. How to choose sample size so that the resulting interval is of a desired width is discussed in Section 18.6.

Table 18.2 *Construction of a Confidence Interval Concerning $\mu_X - \mu_Y$ when σ_X and σ_Y Are Unknown, Samples Are Independent, and Sample Size Is Large*

Given: Independent random samples, where:

$$\bar{X} = 74.0 \quad \bar{Y} = 70.0$$
$$s_X = 14.0 \quad s_Y = 12.0$$
$$n_X = 49 \quad n_Y = 49$$

Problem: Estimate, at the 95% level of confidence, the value of $\mu_X - \mu_Y$.

Solution; Step 1: Calculate s_{X-Y} according to Formula 17.2b.

$$s_{\bar{X}-\bar{Y}} = \sqrt{s_{\bar{X}}^2 + s_{\bar{Y}}^2} = \sqrt{\frac{s_X^2}{n_X} + \frac{s_Y^2}{n_Y}}$$

$$= \sqrt{\frac{(14.0)^2}{49} + \frac{(12.0)^2}{49}}$$

$$= 2.63$$

Step 2: Calculate limits of the interval according to Formula 18.4.

$$(\bar{X} - \bar{Y}) \pm (z_{.05})(s_{\bar{X}-\bar{Y}})$$
$$(74.0 - 70.0) \pm (1.96)(2.63)$$
$$-1.15 \text{ to } +9.15$$
$$\begin{pmatrix} \text{Lower} \\ \text{Limit} \end{pmatrix} \quad \begin{pmatrix} \text{Upper} \\ \text{Limit} \end{pmatrix}$$

Therefore, $C[-1.15 \leq (\mu_X - \mu_Y) \leq +9.15] = .95$

18.5 EVALUATING AN INTERVAL ESTIMATE

In the first example in Table 18.1, the data were as follows: $\overline{X} = 121.0$, $s = 18.0$, and $n = 144$. The interval estimate of μ rounded to one decimal was: $C(118.1 \leq \mu \leq 123.9) = .95$. According to this estimate, μ is somewhere between 118.1 and 123.9. A statement of this kind is most meaningful when one is well enough acquainted with the variable to have reasonably good understanding of the meaning of different score values. For instance, in measuring height of males, we understand that 5′ 1″ would characterize an unusually short fellow, and that a person 6′ 4″ would be unusually tall. Psychologists and educators would understand reasonably well what a College Entrance Examination Board score of 400 or 750 meant. But many times we are not that familiar with the variable under study. In measuring change in electrical resistance of the skin under various kinds of emotional stimulation, the magnitude of our measure may depend on many factors, such as kind of measuring equipment used, the points on the skin between which resistance is measured, etc. In cases like this, an interval estimate expressed in terms of the variable measured may not be as meaningful as it might be.

One way to add meaning is to interpret the interval limits in terms of number of standard deviations of the variable rather than in terms of raw score points. The interval estimate cited at the opening of this section was constructed by calculating $121.0 \pm (1.96)(1.50)$, or 121.0 ± 2.9. In effect, then, the interval estimate as constructed states that μ is no further away from $\overline{X}$ than 2.9 raw score points. Let us reexpress that difference in terms of number of standard deviations of the variable. The estimated standard deviation is 18.0, so the difference becomes $2.9/18.0 = .16$. Thus reinterpreted, the interval estimate now states that μ is no further away from $\overline{X}$ than .16 of a standard deviation, which for most purposes would be considered fairly close.

One advantage of expressing the outcome of an interval estimate in this way is that it compensates for the fact that the importance of a given interscore distance depends on the size of the standard deviation of the variable. For example, a difference of .3 points is minuscule for GRE (Graduate Record Examinations) scores, which have a mean of 500 and a standard deviation of 100, but it is quite substantial if the subject is grade point average. By comparing the difference obtained to the standard deviation of the variable, interval estimates in both these dimensions would be placed on common ground.

To summarize the calculation described above for a single mean, we may find:

$$\boldsymbol{d}_1 = \frac{z_p s_{\overline{X}}}{s}$$

where $\boldsymbol{d}_1$ is the difference between $\overline{X}$ and the outer limits of the interval estimate expressed in number of standard deviations of the variable. This method will be most convenient if the ordinary interval estimate has been calculated first. If one prefers to go directly to this type of interpretation, it is a little faster to use an alternative formula:

$$d_1 = \frac{z_p}{\sqrt{n}}$$

The same approach can be applied to interval estimates of the difference between two means. Let us take the interval estimate, $C[-1.15 \leq (\mu_{\bar{X}} - \mu_{\bar{Y}}) \leq +9.15] = .95$, obtained in the example shown in Table 18.2. This interval estimate may be interpreted to say that the difference between the two population means is such that μ_X could be lower than μ_Y by as much as 1.15 score points, or that μ_X could be higher than μ_Y by as much as 9.15 points, or that the difference could be anywhere between these limits. To reexpress the difference in standard deviations, we need (an estimate of) the standard deviation of the variable. But we have *two* estimates: one for X and one for Y. If the two values of s are not widely different (the usual case) we may use their average.† For interval estimates involving the difference between two means, then, we may calculate:

$$d_2 = \frac{z_p s_{\bar{X} - \bar{Y}}}{s_{av}}$$

where d_2 is the difference between $(\bar{X} - \bar{Y})$ and the outer limits of the interval estimate, expressed in number of standard deviations of the variable, and s_{av} is the average of s_X and s_Y. Applying this formula to the present interval estimate, $d_2 = [(1.96)(2.63)]/[(14.0 + 12.0)/2] = .40$. This informs us that the true difference between the two means is within .40 standard deviation of the obtained difference.

If desired, the difference can be restated relative to a difference of zero rather than to the obtained difference between the two sample means. To do this, simply divide the upper and lower raw score limits of the confidence interval by s_{av}. In the present example, the lower limit becomes $-1.15/13 = -.09$, and the upper limit becomes $+9.15/13.0 = +.70$. This states that the difference between the two population means is such that μ_X could be lower than μ_Y by .09 standard deviation, or that μ_X could be higher than μ_Y by .70 standard deviation, or that the difference falls between these limits. When confidence limits are expressed this way, we need to keep in mind that the width of the limits must be considered in the light of the value of the confidence coefficient employed, just as we do when the limits are expressed in score points.

Section 6.14 (in chapter 6) contains development closely related to the present section. You may wish to look at it again.

---

† Taking the average will be reasonably satisfactory if n_X and n_Y are approximately the same size.

18.6 SAMPLE SIZE REQUIRED
FOR ESTIMATES
OF μ AND $\mu_X - \mu_Y$

Suppose it is desired to estimate μ so that it will not be further away from $\bar{X}$ than a given amount, with confidence coefficient equal to .95. If we can estimate σ, it is possible to estimate the size of the sample that will be required to produce this result. Required sample size is given by Formula 18.5:

Sample Size Required for an Interval
Estimate of Given Width of μ
$$n = \left[\frac{\sigma z_p}{w}\right]^2 \qquad (18.5)$$

where w is the maximum distance (in score points) desired between $\bar{X}$ and the limits of the estimate of μ. If σ is estimated to be 16 and it is desired to estimate μ with 95% confidence that it will not be further away from $\bar{X}$ than four points, the calculation will be:

$$n = \left[\frac{(16)(1.96)}{4}\right]^2 = 61$$

Note that the formula requires σ. Often an approximate estimate can be made from previous studies using the same variable. Even if the study is with a new variable, it may be possible to make some kind of guess. If it is important to be conservative, take more cases than Formula 18.5 suggests, using your guess.

When construction of the interval depends on estimating σ from the sample, and when an estimate of sample size has been made by the procedure described above, there are two points to remember. First, if the required sample size is small, the interval estimate should be made by the procedures described in chapter 19 (Section 19.11). Second, when the estimated sample size is small, it tends to be an underestimate. Consequently, when small sample procedures are in order, it is also desirable to use a sample larger by a few cases than that estimated by Formula 18.5.

It is also possible to estimate $\mu_X - \mu_Y$ with a given degree of confidence that it will not be further away from $(\bar{X} - \bar{Y})$ than a given amount. We discuss first the case for independent samples. The result will be satisfactory when samples are of (nearly) equal size, and when it is reasonable to believe that $\sigma_X = \sigma_Y$, or at least approximately so. The required size of *each* of the two samples may be found by calculating sample size according to Formula 18.5 *and multiplying that number by 2*. In this application of that formula, w is the maximum desired discrepancy (in score points) between $(\bar{X} - \bar{Y})$ and the limits of the estimate of $\mu_X - \mu_Y$. Again, in practical application it is usually possible to make at least an approximate estimate of σ.

Suppose it is desired to estimate $\mu_X - \mu_Y$ with 95% confidence that it will not be further away from $(\bar{X} - \bar{Y})$ than four score points and it can be estimated that $\sigma_X = \sigma_Y = 16$. What sample size will be required? The calculation is:

$$n = 2 \left[\frac{(16)(1.96)}{4} \right]^2 = 123$$

It is of interest to note that (within rounding error) *twice* as many cases are required for *each* sample to maintain the same distance, w, for the two-sample estimate as were required for the one-sample estimate illustrated in the previous section.

If the estimated sample size is small, the procedures of chapter 19 should be used (Section 19.12), and sample size should be larger than that indicated by the estimate by a few cases. The procedure described is for independent samples. If samples are dependent, the number of *pairs* of elements may be found by the same procedure, except that the resulting value of n should be multiplied by $(1 - \rho)$. Once again, ρ will have to be estimated.

Table 18.3 will give an idea of the degree of accuracy that may be achieved in interval estimation from samples of selected sizes. The entries represent w, expressed as a fraction of the standard deviation of the variable, for 95% confidence intervals. For example, the table says that if 100 cases are used in estimating μ, the 95% interval will be: $\bar{X} \pm .20s$. Values in the tables should be treated as approximations, particularly for the lowest three values of n.

Table 18.3 *Approximate Maximum Distance, (w), Measured in σ Units, Expected According to Selected Values of Sample Size Between (1) $\bar{X}$ and the Limits of the 95% Interval Estimate for Single Means and (2) $\bar{X} - \bar{Y}$ and the Limits of the 95% Interval Estimate for Two Independent Means[a]*

	Sample Size								
	10	15	25	50	75	100	200	500	1,000
Single Means: $\|\bar{X} - \mu\|/s$	.72	.55	.41	.28	.23	.20	.14	.09	.06
Difference between Two Independent Means: $\|(\bar{X} - \bar{Y}) - (\mu_X - \mu_Y)\|/s_{av}$	.94	.75	.57	.40	.32	.28	.20	.12	.09

[a] For two independent samples, n is the size of *each* of the two samples. It is assumed that $n_X = n_Y = n$, and that $\sigma_X = \sigma_Y$.

18.7 THE RELATION BETWEEN INTERVAL ESTIMATION AND HYPOTHESIS TESTING

Interval estimation and hypothesis testing are two sides of the same coin. For most population parameters or differences between two parameters, *the interval estimate contains all values of H_0 that would be accepted had they been tested using $\alpha = 1 - C$.* Consider a problem in which $\bar{X} - \bar{Y} = +12$ and $\sigma_{\bar{X}-\bar{Y}} = 5$. When the null hypothesis is tested, $z = +2.4$; the difference is significant at the .05 level. An interval estimate calculated from exactly the same data produces: $C[+2 \leqq (\mu_X - \mu_Y) \leqq +22] = .95.$† This interval says that the value of μ_X exceeds that of μ_Y by 2 to 22 points. Note that the interval does *not* include the possibility that the difference could be zero, the same message conveyed by the test of the hypothesis. In addition, the interval estimate informs us what the true difference *could* be. If the standard deviations of X and Y are about 15, the possible values appear to range rather widely.

Consider a second example: if an interval reads $C[-4 \leqq (\mu_X - \mu_Y) \leqq +10] = .95$, zero is among the possible values that the difference might take. Had the hypothesis of no difference been tested at $\alpha = .05$, it would have produced a z smaller than 1.96, and the hypothesis would have been accepted.

Here is a third interval: $C[+1 \leqq (\mu_X - \mu_Y) \leqq +4] = .95$. It shows that the true difference is not likely to be zero; instead, it shows that μ_X is probably higher than μ_Y by 1 to 4 points. If again the standard deviations of X and Y were about 15, we observe that although the difference is large enough that chance variation cannot account for it, it is nevertheless a small difference. Testing the null hypothesis with the same data produces $z = +3.3$. By itself, that indicates a difference quite unlikely to have arisen by chance, but it does not even hint at the fact that the true difference is quite small.

We are beginning to see that estimation may have some advantages over hypothesis testing in some instances. This is explored more systematically in the next section.

18.8 THE MERIT OF INTERVAL ESTIMATION

In the current research of the behavioral sciences, hypothesis testing is used much more often than is estimation. But close examination of the merits of the two suggests that in many studies interval estimation would have been superior. Let us

---

† For simplicity, $z_{.05} = 2$ has been substituted for $z_{.05} = 1.96$ in constructing interval estimates in this section.

see what can be said about the two approaches with particular regard for inference about means.

   1 The final quantitative output of an interval estimate is a statement about the parameter or parameters concerned. In hypothesis testing, the statement is about a derived score, such as z or t, or about a probability, p.

In either form of inference, the question is about the parameter(s). A confidence interval is a direct answer to the question, whereas hypothesis testing focuses on a derived variable. In hypothesis testing we have to be reminded to look at the values of the descriptors when inference is done; in estimation that view lies before our eyes.

   2 An interval estimate straightforwardly exhibits the influence of random sampling variation. The value of z, t, or p resulting from hypothesis testing is subject to *two* influences that cannot be disentangled without further study.

In interval estimation, the width of the interval forms a direct statement about the influence of sampling variation and the precision of our estimate. For example, estimation shows that the limits within which the population mean may lie are very wide when an estimate of its value is made from a small sample. In hypothesis testing, the magnitude of the derived variable depends on *two* factors: the difference between what was hypothesized and what is true, and the amount of sampling variation present. For example, a large value of z could occur in a study where the difference was small but the sample was large *or* where the difference was large and the sample was small. Unless we look at the descriptors and n, we shall not know which.

   3 Hypothesis testing is subject to an important confusion between a statistically significant difference and an important difference (Section 16.6). Essentially, this problem disappears with interval estimation.

Suppose $\bar{X} = 103$, $\sigma = 20$, and $n = 1,600$. If the hypothesis is tested that $\mu = 100$, a z of $+6$† will be obtained with a corresponding probability $< .000000001$. Impressive! However, an interval estimate of μ yields: $C(102 \leq \mu \leq 104) = .95$,† which brings us back to reality. Note that the interval estimate does not include the possibility that $\mu = 100$. Interval estimation works better here because it focuses on variation of the measure under consideration rather than on a derived variable, such as z or p.

   4 Interval estimation avoids the error of thinking that "accepting H_0" means that H_0 is true or probably true (Section 16.5).

---

† If we are allowed a little rounding error.

In interval estimation, no hypothesis is being tested, and therefore there is no occasion to "accept" or "reject." In the previous section we saw that interval estimation *could* be applied in most situations to inquire whether the population was characterized by a particular parameter value. If used in this way, the interval makes plain *all* of the values that might characterize the parameter, including, possibly, the value inquired about.

5 Since the null hypothesis is a *point* hypothesis, it is unreasonable to believe that it could be *exactly* true in any practical encounter. Interval estimation is therefore more realistic.

This point, though valid, is less important than it at first seems. Remember that hypothesis testing is a tool to aid the investigator. The investigator is not really concerned about declaring that a difference exists *unless that difference is large enough that he would want to know about it.* From a practical standpoint, then, he will not mind that the null hypothesis is accepted when a small difference exists. However, from the standpoint of a purist it does seem aesthetically unsatisfactory that many hypotheses will be accepted (or retained, if you prefer) when all hypotheses are false.

It should be mentioned that the merit of estimation is highest when the problem involves a single parameter or the difference between two parameters. In some forms of analysis, comparisons may be among more than two parameters taken as a group rather than pair by pair.† In this application, interval estimation loses much of its intuitive clarity, whereas hypothesis testing loses much less (relatively speaking).

The problems to which hypothesis testing has been applied may be divided into two categories. In the first, a decision must be made and a course of action followed. Once that action is taken, it is difficult or impossible to turn back. To cite an example in education, one decides to spend $75,000 on a learning laboratory or not to do so, depending on the estimate of benefit to be derived. Once the money is spent, it cannot be recalled. Problems of this type might be called "either-or" or "decision" problems. It is with this sort of problem that the strongest case can be made for considering hypothesis testing because of the dichotomous, "go-stop" character of the statistical conclusion. Even here, however, interval estimation can be considered as a workable alternative, because it will indicate what parameter values are possible, rather than reporting whether a particular value could be true or probably isn't.

In the second type of problem it is possible to come to a tentative conclusion and to use it as a "working hypothesis," mindful that further study may require revision of the conclusion. This is more characteristic of scientific studies initiated in the search for knowledge. Here the "go/no-go" character of decision making is less

---

†This occurs in the use of analysis of variance and chi square. See chapters 22 and 23.

applicable, and the advantages of interval estimation over hypothesis testing become particularly apparent.

In the past 15 years, psychologists and others have taken a much closer look at the logic, the merit, and the problems involved in hypothesis testing. A particularly thoughtful examination of some of the defects of this approach has been provided by Bakan.† Another source is a book edited by Morrison and Henkel.‡

PROBLEMS AND EXERCISES

Identify:

point estimation d_1
interval estimation d_2
confidence interval w
confidence coefficient C
logic of interval
     estimation

1 $\bar{X} = 63, s = 12, n = 100$. Construct an interval estimate of μ according to: (*a*) $C = .95$ (*b*) $C = .99$ (*c*) $C = .90$.

2 Repeat parts (*a*) and (*b*) of Problem 1, but with the condition that *n* is four times as large. Compare the size of the intervals obtained in the two problems. State your conclusion.

3 $\bar{X} = 117, s = 36, n = 81$. Construct an interval estimate of μ according to: (*a*) $C = .95$ (*b*) $C = .99$ (*c*) $C = .50$.

4 $\bar{X} = 165, s_X = 24, n_X = 36, \bar{Y} = 175, s_Y = 21, n_Y = 49$; assume samples are independent. Construct an interval estimate of $\mu_X - \mu_Y$ according to: (*a*) $C = .95$ (*b*) $C = .99$ (*c*) $C = .50$.

5 $\bar{X} = 97, s_X = 16, n_X = 64, \bar{Y} = 90, s_Y = 18, n_Y = 81$; assume samples are independent. Construct an interval estimate of $\mu_X - \mu_Y$ according to: (*a*) $C = .95$ (*b*) $C = .99$ (*c*) $C = .50$.

6 Two dependent samples yielded: $\bar{X} = 88, s_X = 16, n_X = 64, \bar{Y} = 85, s_Y = 12, n_Y = 64$, $r_{XY} = +.50$. Construct an interval estimate according to: (*a*) $C = .95$ (*b*) $C = .99$.

7 Using the data of Problem 1, interpret an interval estimate of μ in terms of d_1, using $C = .95$. Does it appear that the estimate has considerable precision or not? Explain.

8 Repeat Problem 7, but suppose *n* were 25.

9 $\bar{X} = 2.90, s = .30, n = 16$. (*a*) Construct an interval estimate of μ, using $C = .95$. (*b*) Your feeling about the precision of this estimate? (*c*) Calculate d_1. (*d*) Your feeling

† D. Bakan, "The Test of Significance in Psychological Research," *Psychological Bulletin* **66** (1966): 423–37.

‡ D. E. Morrison and R. E. Henkel (eds.) *The Significance Test Controversy*, Aldine Publishing Company, Chicago, 1970.

now about the precision of this estimate? (e) Comment on the appropriateness of applying the techniques of this chapter to this problem.

10 Using the data of Problem 4, interpret an interval estimate of $\mu_X - \mu_Y$ in terms of d_2, using $C = .95$. Does it appear that the estimate has considerable precision? Explain.

11 Construct the .95 confidence interval for the data of Problem 4, expressing the upper and lower limits in terms of the number of standard deviations relative to a difference of zero between μ_X and μ_Y.

12 Repeat Problem 10, but use the data of Problem 5.

13 A psychologist wishes to estimate mean reaction time such that he can be 95% confident that μ is not farther than 3 milliseconds (msec) away from his sample mean. He estimates that the standard deviation of reaction times is 15 msec. What size of sample should he draw?

14 Repeat Problem 13, but with the condition that the confidence coefficient should be .99.

15 With reference to Problem 13, our psychologist now wishes to change the nature of the reaction task and to compare mean reaction time on the original task with that on the altered task. He assumes that the standard deviation will be the same on both tasks and wants to estimate at the 95% level of confidence the difference between the two population means. He wants this difference to be within 5 msec of the difference between the sample means. (a) If he selects two random samples, what should be the size of each? (b) If he uses subjects matched on a pretest of reaction time and ρ is estimated to be $+.40$ between pairs of measurements, what should be the size of each sample?

16 Repeat Problem 15, but with the condition that the confidence coefficient should be .99.

17 $C(122 \leq \mu \leq 128) = .95$. (a) If $H_0: \mu = 127$ were tested at $\alpha = .05$ using a nondirectional alternative, what would the outcome be? (b) If $H_0: \mu = 118$ were tested at $\alpha = .05$, what would the outcome be? (c) Explain your answers to (a) and (b).

18 $C[-8 \leq (\mu_X - \mu_Y) \leq -2] = .95$. (a) What was $\bar{X} - \bar{Y}$? (b) If $H_0: \mu_X - \mu_Y = 0$ were tested at $\alpha = .05$ using a nondirectional alternative, what would the outcome be?

19 $C[-2 \leq (\mu_X - \mu_Y) \leq +12] = .95$. (a) What was $\bar{X} - \bar{Y}$? (b) If $H_0: \mu_X - \mu_Y = 0$ were tested at $\alpha = .05$ using a nondirectional alternative, what would the outcome be?

20 $\bar{X} = 83, s = 15, n = 625$. (a) Obtain z corresponding to a test that $\mu = 80$. (b) What, in "loose English," does that z tell us? (c) Construct the .95 interval estimate of μ. (d) What does that tell us? (e) Compare the information obtained by the two approaches.

CHAPTER 19

19.1 INTRODUCTION

In chapters 15, 17, and 18, models were developed for inference about single means and about the difference between two means. In those *ideal* models, the relevant standard errors are to be calculated from known population parameters. For example, in the ideal case the formula for the standard error of the mean is $\sigma_{\bar{X}} = \sigma / \sqrt{n}$, which requires knowledge of the standard deviation of the population of scores. If this could be known (and if other assumptions were met) a true z could be calculated and correctly evaluated on the normal curve. But almost never do we know the necessary parameters, and estimates obtained from the sample(s) must therefore be substituted ($s_{\bar{X}} = s / \sqrt{n}$, for example). This introduces a degree of error into the ideal procedure since we are now computing an approximate z (see Section 15.6). The error can be considered to occur in comparing the approximate

Inference about Means and the *t* Distribution

z at hand with the true z obtained from the normal curve that corresponds to the desired significance level.

Now the larger the sample the less the error. If samples are large enough and we persist in using the normal curve model, no great harm is done. The fact remains that error exists, and with smaller samples it may be substantial. In the present chapter we present another model, the t distribution, one that makes appropriate allowance for the use of estimated parameters.

The procedures described in this chapter are sometimes called "*small sample procedures,*" which might lead one to think that the basic issue is one of sample size. It should be clear that this is not so. The *fundamental* issue is whether the formulas for the standard errors are based on population parameters or on sample estimates of those parameters. If based on population parameters, the procedures of chapters

15, 17, and 18 are *exactly* correct *irrespective of sample size*. If based on *estimates* of population parameters, the procedures of this chapter are exactly correct.

19.2 INFERENCE ABOUT A SINGLE MEAN WHEN σ IS KNOWN AND WHEN IT IS NOT

Suppose the hypothesis that $\mu = 100$ is to be tested against the alternative that it is not, *and σ is known*. To do so, we calculate z:

$$z = \frac{\bar{X} - \mu}{\sigma_{\bar{X}}}$$

The value of z is then taken to the normal distribution for evaluation. For example, if the test is two tailed and $\alpha = .05$, the hypothesis will be rejected if the calculated value of z exceeds a magnitude of 1.96.

Is it right to treat z as a normally distributed variable? If the assumptions of Section 15.10 are satisfied, values of $\bar{X}$ will be normally distributed as we move from random sample to random sample, but the values of μ and $\sigma_{\bar{X}}$ will remain fixed. Consequently, values of z may be considered to be formed as follows:

$$z = \frac{(normally\ distributed\ variable) - (constant)}{(constant)}$$

where: $\bar{X}$ is the normally distributed variable
      μ is a constant
      $\sigma_{\bar{X}}$ is a constant

Subtracting a constant from each score in a normal distribution does not change the shape of the distribution, nor does dividing by a constant.† Consequently, z will be normally distributed when $\bar{X}$ is normally distributed, and the normal distribution is therefore the correct distribution to which to refer z for evaluation.

Consider the same problem, but this time *assume σ is not known* and must be estimated from the sample. To evaluate the position of the sample mean, we calculate the statistic:

t Required for Testing Hypotheses $t = \dfrac{\bar{X} - \mu}{s_{\bar{X}}}$ (19.1)
About Single Means

The expression on the right of the equals sign is *exactly what we termed an approximate z*, "*z*", in chapter 15. We now give it the name by which is universally known: *t*.

---

†The mean and standard deviation are affected by these operations, but the relative distances between scores (i.e. the "shape" of the distribution) remain unaltered. See Section 8.5.

This statistic differs from the z of the previous section in that *the denominator of the expression is a variable.* As we move from random sample to random sample, not only will values of $\bar{X}$ vary, but *each sample will yield a different estimate* ($s_{\bar{X}}$) *of* $\sigma_{\bar{X}}$.† The resulting statistic may be considered to be formed as follows:

$$t = \frac{(\textit{normally distributed variable}) - (\textit{constant})}{(\textit{variable})}$$

Because of the presence of the variable in the denominator, this statistic does *not* follow, with exactitude, the normal distribution. Just what distribution does it follow? Shortly after the turn of the century, William S. Gosset, writing under the name of "Student," solved this problem and presented the proper distribution for it. Since that time, the statistic has been called "t," and its distribution has been referred to as "Student's distribution," or "*Student's distribution of t*"; we shall so refer to it.

Before turning to Student's distribution, one comment seems in order. Beginners sometimes think that it is the sampling distribution of means that becomes nonnormal when $\sigma_{\bar{X}}$ must be estimated from the sample. This is not so. If the assumptions of Section 15.10 are met, $\bar{X}$ will be normally distributed *regardless of sample size.* However, *the position of $\bar{X}$ is not evaluated directly; rather, it is the value of the statistic* $t = (\bar{X} - \mu)/s_{\bar{X}}$. *Although $\bar{X}$ is normally distributed, the resulting value of t is not,* for the reason cited above. Indeed, $\bar{X}$ *must* be normally distributed for Student's distribution to be exactly applicable.

19.3 CHARACTERISTICS OF STUDENT'S DISTRIBUTION OF t

What may we expect of Student's distribution of t? When samples are large, the values of $s_{\bar{X}}$ will be close to that of $\sigma_{\bar{X}}$, and t will be much like z. Its distribution is, consequently, very nearly normal. The recommendations of chapters 15, 17, and 18 that we could treat t as normally distributed z were based on this fact. On the other hand, when sample size is small, the values of $s_{\bar{X}}$ will vary substantially about $\sigma_{\bar{X}}$. The distribution of t will then depart significantly from that of normally distributed z.

It is becoming clear that *Student's distribution of t is not a single distribution but rather a family of distributions.* The exact shape of a particular member of that family depends on sample size, or, more accurately, on the number of *degrees of freedom* (*df*), a quantity closely related to sample size.‡ When the number of degrees of freedom is infinite (*df* $= \infty$), the distribution of Student's t is exactly the

---

† It can be shown that the sampling distribution of $s_{\bar{X}}$ tends to be positively skewed.

‡ For example, $df = n - 1$ for problems of inference about single means. The concept of degrees of freedom will receive more explicit treatment in the next section.

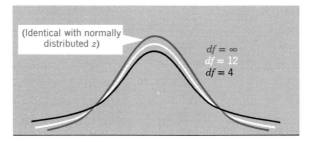

Figure 19.1 *The Distribution of Student's t for Three Levels of Degrees of Freedom.*

same as that of normally distributed z. As the number of degrees of freedom decreases, the characteristics of the t distribution begin to depart from those of normally distributed z. Figure 19.1 illustrates this point. It shows the normalized z distribution, and, in contrast, Student's distribution of t for $df = 12$ and $df = 4$.

When the number of degrees of freedom is less than infinite, the theoretical distribution of t and the normal distribution of z are alike in some ways, and different in others. They are alike in that both distributions:

1 have a mean of zero

2 are symmetrical

3 are unimodal

The two distributions differ in that the distribution of t:

1 is more *leptokurtic* than the normal distribution (a leptokurtic curve has a greater concentration of area in the center *and* in the tails than does a normal curve).

2 has a larger standard deviation (remember that $\sigma_z = 1$)

3 depends on the number of degrees of freedom

The different characteristics of Student's t have an important consequence in statistical inference. For example, if we test a hypothesis at $\alpha = .05$, the critical value of z is ± 1.96 for a two-tailed test. The tails of the t distribution descend less rapidly to the horizontal axis than do those of the normal distribution, and so in the t distribution it will be necessary to go to a *more extreme location* to find the point beyond which .025 of the area (in one tail) falls. This can be verified by studying Figure 19.1.

How much larger t must be than z to correspond to the same rarity of occurrence depends on sample size (or, more accurately, on the number of degrees of freedom). Table 19.1 illustrates this. It shows, for selected values of df, the critical magnitude

Table 19.1 *Magnitude of t for Which, in Student's Distribution, the Probability Is .05 of Obtaining a Value at Least as Deviant (in Either Direction)*

df:	5	10	25	50	100	500	∞
$t_{.05}$:	2.571	2.228	2.060	2.008	1.984	1.965	1.960

of t corresponding to a two-tailed test conducted according to the decision criterion: $\alpha = .05$. Note that:

1 For an infinite number of degrees of freedom, the critical magnitude of t is the same as the critical magnitude of z: 1.96.

2 The smaller the number of degrees of freedom, the larger the critical magnitude of t.

3 The behavior of t is extremely similar to that of z until the number of degrees of freedom drops below 100.

4 As the number of degrees of freedom decreases, the change in Student's distribution of t, slight at first, progresses at an increasingly rapid rate.

19.4 DEGREES OF FREEDOM AND STUDENT'S DISTRIBUTION

Basically, the term "degrees of freedom" refers to the freedom of observations to vary. In general, the number of degrees of freedom corresponds to the number of observations that are completely free to vary. One might at first suppose that this would be the same as the number of scores in the sample (or samples), but often conditions exist that impose restrictions so that the number of degrees of freedom is smaller. The concept of degrees of freedom is illustrated below in connection with the calculation of s.

Suppose a sample consists of three scores: X_1, X_2, X_3. If s is calculated by the deviation score formula, $s = \sqrt{\Sigma(X - \bar{X})^2/(n - 1)}$, the value of s will be determined by the values of the three deviation scores: $(X_1 - \bar{X})$, $(X_2 - \bar{X})$, and $(X_3 - \bar{X})$. Now only two (any two) of those are "free to vary." We could, if we wish, arbitrarily assign $(X_1 - \bar{X})$ the value $+3$, and $(X_2 - \bar{X})$ the value -7. But as soon as two of the three have been given numerical values, the third is no longer free to vary. Do you remember from chapter 5 that the *sum of the deviations taken about the mean is always zero?*† In other words, $\Sigma(X - \bar{X}) = 0$. So as soon as the first two deviations are fixed, the third must have a value such that the three deviations sum to zero. In the numerical example, $(X_3 - \bar{X})$ must be $+4$.

---

† See Section 5.7 and the proof in Note 5.2.

For a variance estimate made from a single sample, there will be *n* deviations. All but one of them will be "free to vary," but the last will be fixed by the constraint that $\Sigma(X - \bar{X}) = 0$. The number of degrees of freedom in a problem involving the calculation of *s* is therefore $n - 1$. For other kinds of problems *df* may be different; this will be considered as we turn to each type of problem.

19.5 USING STUDENT'S DISTRIBUTION OF *t*

The theoretical distribution of *t* appears in Table D in Appendix F. In using this table, it is important to remember that the area under a given distribution of *t* is taken to be 1.00, just as in the normal curve tables. The table makes no distinction between negative and positive values of *t*, since the area falling above a given positive value of *t* is the same as the area falling below the same negative value. This is illustrated in Figure 19.2.

Each row of the table specifies, according to the particular number of degrees of freedom, the value of *t* beyond which lies the area (in the tail of the curve) indicated at the top of the table. Characteristic use of the table may be best shown by some examples. Consider the following problem.

Problem: When $df = 20$, what value of *t* is so high that the probability in random sampling of obtaining one as high or higher is .05?

Solution: Consult Table D and identify the row corresponding to $df = 20$. Then find the column corresponding to *area in one tail* = .05. At the intersection of this row and column, read the entry of $t = 1.725$. Since, in effect, we are looking for the 95th centile point of the *t* distribution, its value is positive: $t = +1.725$. This is illustrated in Figure 19.2.

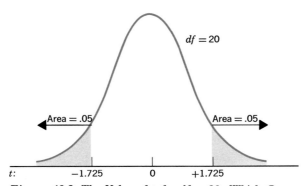

df = 20

Area = .05   Area = .05

t: −1.725   0   +1.725

Figure 19.2 *The Value of t for df = 20, Which Corresponds to Area in Each Tail of Student's Distribution = .05.*

If we had been testing the hypothesis that $\mu = 100$ against the directional alternative that $\mu > 100$, and were using the decision criterion, $\alpha = .05$, this would be the critical value of *t* when $df = 20$. Note that, according to the normal curve, the critical value of *z* would be: $z = +1.645$, a lesser value.

A second example explores another problem typically useful in inference.

Problem: When $df = 20$ and a two-tailed test is conducted at $\alpha = .05$, what values of *t* differentiate the region of rejection from the region of acceptance?

Solution: We must identify the values of *t* such that the central 95% of obtained *t*'s will be included within these limits. These are (1) the value of *t* below which 2.5% of *t*'s will be located, and (2) the value of *t* above which 2.5% of *t*'s will be located. The requisite magnitude of *t* may be read according to the heading *area in one tail* = .025. For $df = 20$, the value is: $t = \pm2.086$. The problem is illustrated in Figure 19.3.

It should be clear that the distribution of *t* may be interpreted as a probability distribution, just as may be done with the normal distribution. For example, when $df = 20$, and when sampling is random, the probability of obtaining a value of *t* exceeding the limits ±2.086 is .05.

In some cases we obtain a *t* and want to say what the probability is in random sampling of obtaining one so deviant in the given direction, or perhaps so deviant in either direction. Suppose $t_{\text{calc}} = 2.20$, based on $n = 25$. In this case $df = 24$, and from Table D we note that a *t* of $+2.064$ or greater would occur with probability equal to .025, and one of $+2.492$ or greater with a probability of .01. t_{calc} falls between these values, so to describe its rarity we could say: $\Pr(t \geq +2.20) < .025$. If the question is about a *t* of this magnitude *irrespective of*

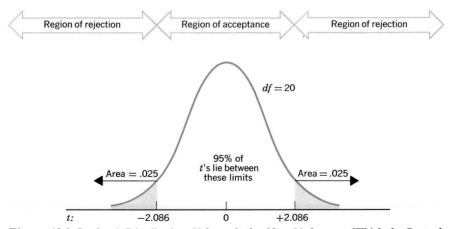

Figure 19.3 *Student's Distribution: Values of t for df = 20, between Which the Central 95% of t's Will Fall.*

direction, the probability becomes .05 rather than .025. In research reports that prefer to cite probabilities (see Section 15.9), it is customary to state t_{calc} and the associated probability (e.g. $p > .05, p < .025$, etc.). Watch to see whether a one- or two-tailed probability is intended.

19.6 APPLICATION OF THE DISTRIBUTION OF *t* TO PROBLEMS OF INFERENCE ABOUT MEANS

Student's distribution is applicable to the problems of testing hypotheses about single means, testing hypotheses about two means (both the dependent and the independent case), interval estimation of μ, and interval estimation of $\mu_X - \mu_Y$. In short, it is pertinent for all of the problems described in chapters 15, 17, and 18 in circumstances where the relevant standard error must be estimated from the sample.

The following sections of this chapter show how Student's distribution applies to these problems. The exposition is based on the assumption that the logic and procedures of chapters 15–18 are understood. A review of pertinent parts of those chapters may be desirable as collateral to study of the remainder of this chapter.

A distinction must be made between values of *t* calculated from sets of data, and the theoretical distribution of *t* as given in the appendix. Just as calculated values of *z* follow the normal distribution only under certain conditions, so calculated values of *t* follow Student's distribution of *t* only when certain assumptions are met. The necessary conditions are exactly the same as for the normal curve model, except that it is not required that the population standard deviations be known, and, in the case of two dependent means, it is not required that the population correlation coefficient be known. One further consideration occurs in the case of the difference between means of two *independent* samples, as we shall see in Section 19.8.

19.7 TESTING A HYPOTHESIS ABOUT A SINGLE MEAN

Suppose the claim has been made that the height of adult males is different from what it used to be, and that we wish to test this hypothesis. From a nationwide survey made 20 years ago, it is learned that the mean height of 21 year old males was, at that time, 69.5 inches.† To study the question, 25 males of the same age are selected at random, and measurements of height obtained. The research question is

---

† The data of this example, like others in this book, are hypothetical.

then translated into a statistical hypothesis, to be tested at $\alpha = .05$:

$$H_0: \mu = 69.5$$
$$H_A: \mu \neq 69.5 \qquad \alpha = .05$$

The mean of the 25 measurements proves to be 70.4, and because the population standard deviation is not available, it is estimated from the sample according to Formula 15.1. It proves to be 3.15. Next, the standard error of the mean is estimated according to Formula 15.2:

$$s_{\bar{X}} = \frac{s}{\sqrt{n}} = \frac{3.15}{\sqrt{25}} = .63$$

To test the hypothesis, we calculate t:

$$t = \frac{\bar{X} - \mu}{s_{\bar{X}}} = \frac{70.4 - 69.5}{.63} = +1.43$$

The estimate of the standard error of the mean, $s_{\bar{X}}$, was based on 25 observations, so $df = n - 1 = 24$. With a two-tailed test at $\alpha = .05$, the critical value of t is one that will in each tail of the distribution divide the outer 2.5% of the area from the remainder. From Table D in Appendix F, we learn that for $df = 24$, $t = \pm 2.064$ is the critical value. Figure 19.4 shows the critical value of t, the region of rejection thereby established, and the location of the calculated value of t. Since the sample mean of 70.4 is not sufficiently discrepant to lead to a t of 2.064 or larger, our decision will be to accept H_0.

In the example worked above, it was assumed that s had already been calculated. When the problem is begun with only the raw scores, see Section 15.6 for the method of calculation.

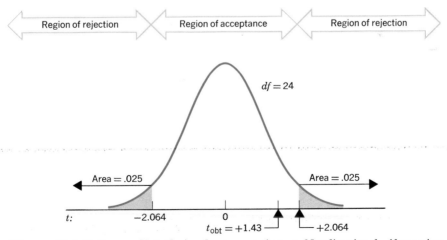

Figure 19.4 *Testing a Hypothesis about μ against a Nondirectional Alternative:* $\alpha = .05$.

19.8 TESTING A HYPOTHESIS ABOUT THE DIFFERENCE BETWEEN TWO INDEPENDENT MEANS

To test the difference between two independent means, we calculated:

$$\text{``}z\text{''} = \frac{(\bar{X} - \bar{Y}) - (\mu_X - \mu_Y)_{\text{hyp}}}{s_{\bar{X}-\bar{Y}}}$$

where:

$$s_{\bar{X}-\bar{Y}} = \sqrt{s_{\bar{X}}^2 + s_{\bar{Y}}^2}$$

When sample size is relatively large, "z" is very nearly normally distributed. As sample size decreases, its distribution departs from the normal, but, unfortunately, *neither is it distributed exactly as Student's t.*[†]

An eminent British statistician, the late Sir Ronald A. Fisher, showed that a slightly different approach results in a statistic that *is* distributed as Student's t. The change that Fisher introduced was, in effect, to assume that $\sigma_X^2 = \sigma_Y^2$. This is often called the *assumption of homogeneity of variance.* To understand the consequences of this assumption, it will be helpful to rewrite the formula for $\sigma_{\bar{X}-\bar{Y}}$. According to Formula 13.2, σ_X^2/n_X may be substituted for $\sigma_{\bar{X}}^2$ and σ_Y^2/n_Y for $\sigma_{\bar{Y}}^2$. The result is shown below:

$$\sigma_{\bar{X}-\bar{Y}} = \sqrt{\frac{\sigma_X^2}{n_X} + \frac{\sigma_Y^2}{n_Y}}$$

This formula clearly allows for the possibility that σ_X^2 might be different from σ_Y^2 and so does our working formula (Formula 17.2b), used when estimates of the two variances must be made from the samples:

$$s_{\bar{X}-\bar{Y}} = \sqrt{\frac{s_X^2}{n_X} + \frac{s_Y^2}{n_Y}}$$

If σ_X^2 and σ_Y^2 may differ, then it is quite correct for each sample to estimate its corresponding population value. Under the assumption of homogeneity of variance, however, both s_X^2 and s_Y^2 are estimates of the *same* population variance. If this is so, then rather than make two separate estimates, each based on a small sample, it is preferable to combine the information from both samples and make a single *pooled estimate* of *the* population variance. In general, the "best estimate" of a population variance is made as follows:

$$\sigma_{\text{est}}^2 = \frac{\textit{sum of squares of deviation scores}}{\textit{degrees of freedom}} [‡]$$

[†] Except in the special case when $n_X = n_Y$.

[‡] This is exactly what we do when we calculate $s^2 = \Sigma x^2/(n - 1)$.

A pooled estimate, made from the two samples, can be made by pooling the sums of squares of deviation scores from each sample and dividing by the total number of degrees of freedom associated with the pooled sum of squares. Thus, s_p^2 is:

Estimate of σ^2 Made by Pooling Information from Two Samples

$$s_p^2 = \frac{\sum x^2 + \sum y^2}{(n_X - 1) + (n_Y - 1)} \qquad (19.2)$$

This quantity may be substituted for s_X^2 and for s_Y^2 in the formula for $s_{\bar{X}-\bar{Y}}$.

$$s_{\bar{X}-\bar{Y}} = \sqrt{\frac{s_p^2}{n_X} + \frac{s_p^2}{n_Y}}$$

Factoring out s_p^2, the formula may be rewritten:

$$s_{\bar{X}-\bar{Y}} = \sqrt{s_p^2 \left(\frac{1}{n_X} + \frac{1}{n_Y} \right)}$$

If the expression for s_p^2 given by Formula 19.2 is substituted in this formula, we have:

Estimate of Standard Error of the Difference between Two Independent Means when $\sigma_X^2 = \sigma_Y^2$

$$s_{\bar{X}-\bar{Y}} = \sqrt{\frac{\sum x^2 + \sum y^2}{(n_X - 1) + (n_Y - 1)} \left(\frac{1}{n_X} + \frac{1}{n_Y} \right)} \qquad (19.3)$$

When the two n's are equal, $s_{\bar{X}-\bar{Y}}$ can be calculated by a simpler formula than that shown immediately above. It is:

Estimate of Standard Error of the Difference between Two Independent Means when $\sigma_X^2 = \sigma_Y^2$ and when $n_X = n_Y = n$

$$s_{\bar{X}-\bar{Y}} = \sqrt{\frac{\sum x^2 + \sum y^2}{n(n - 1)}} \qquad (19.4)$$

When t is calculated according to the following formula, *and $s_{\bar{X}-\bar{Y}}$ is calculated according to Formula 19.3 or 19.4,* t will be distributed according to Student's distribution:

t for Testing Hypotheses about the Difference between Two Means

$$t = \frac{(\bar{X} - \bar{Y}) - (\mu_X - \mu_Y)_{\text{hyp}}}{s_{\bar{X}-\bar{Y}}} \qquad (19.5)$$

An important question that arises in designing a two-group study concerns sample size. With too few cases, there may be a high risk of failing to find a difference that it would be important to discover (if it were present). On the other hand, too many cases will be wasteful. Chapter 21 (Section 21.11) describes how to choose sample size.

Table 19.2 *Small Sample Test of the Difference between Two Independent Means*

Estimates made in unbiased environment		Estimates made in biased environment	
X	X²	Y	Y²
38	1444	47	2209
35	1225	45	2025
37	1369	42	1764
40	1600	45	2025
45	2025	47	2209
34	1156	40	1600
40	1600	43	1849
36	1296	45	2025
43	1849	40	1600
41	1681	48	2304
$\Sigma X = 389$	$\Sigma X^2 = 15245$	$\Sigma Y = 442$	$\Sigma Y^2 = 19610$

(1) $\quad \bar{X} = \dfrac{389}{10} = 38.9 \qquad\qquad \bar{Y} = \dfrac{442}{10} = 44.2$

(2a) $\displaystyle \sum x^2 = \sum X^2 - \frac{\left(\sum X\right)^2}{n} = 15245 - \frac{(389)^2}{10} = 113$

(2b) $\displaystyle \sum y^2 = \sum Y^2 - \frac{\left(\sum Y\right)^2}{n} = 19610 - \frac{(442)^2}{10} = 74$

(3a) $\quad s_X = \sqrt{\dfrac{\sum x^2}{n_X - 1}} = \sqrt{\dfrac{113}{10 - 1}} = 3.54$

(3b) $\quad s_Y = \sqrt{\dfrac{\sum y^2}{n_Y - 1}} = \sqrt{\dfrac{74}{10 - 1}} = 2.87$

(4) $\quad t = \dfrac{(\bar{X} - \bar{Y}) - (\mu_X - \mu_Y)_{\text{hyp}}}{\sqrt{\dfrac{\sum x^2 + \sum y^2}{(n_X - 1) + (n_Y - 1)}\left(\dfrac{1}{n_X} + \dfrac{1}{n_Y}\right)}}$

$\qquad = \dfrac{(38.9 - 44.2) - 0}{\sqrt{\dfrac{113 + 74}{(10 - 1) + (10 - 1)}\left(\dfrac{1}{10} + \dfrac{1}{10}\right)}}$

$\qquad = -3.68$

(5) $\quad df = (n_X - 1) + (n_Y - 1) = (10 - 1) + (10 - 1) = 18$

(6) $\quad t_{\text{crit}} = \pm 2.878 \qquad$ **Decision:** Reject H_0

19.9 TESTING HYPOTHESES ABOUT TWO INDEPENDENT MEANS: AN EXAMPLE

A psychologist is interested in the effect of social pressure. He selects two groups of subjects at random. Each subject is asked to estimate by eye the length of a stick. In one group, the subject is placed in the presence of four other persons who, unknown to him, have been instructed to give estimates that are too large. Each of these persons gives his estimate orally to the experimenter before the subject is asked for his estimate. In the other group, the same procedure is employed, except that the four persons present (in addition to the subject) are instructed to make honest estimates. Estimates (in inches) made by each subject are given in Table 19.2.

The hypothesis to be tested is:

$$H_0 : \mu_X - \mu_Y = 0$$
$$H_A : \mu_X - \mu_Y \neq 0$$

We shall assume that the researcher has selected $\alpha = .01$ as the decision criterion. As usual, the first step is to find n_X, ΣX, ΣX^2, n_Y, ΣY, and ΣY^2. In the present illustration we have assumed 10 scores under each condition, but the numbers need not be equal. Next, we calculate the two means and the two sums of squares of deviation scores (steps 1 and 2).† While the two estimated standard

---

† If it should be that s_X and s_Y are already available, the sums of squares of deviation scores may be found by: $\Sigma x^2 = (n_X - 1)s_X^2$, and $\Sigma y^2 = (n_Y - 1)s_Y^2$. Similarly, if S_X and S_Y are known, $\Sigma x^2 = n_X S_X^2$, and $\Sigma y^2 = n_Y S_Y^2$.

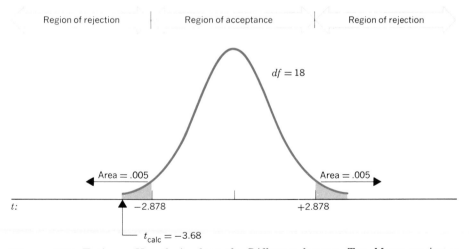

Figure 19.5 *Testing a Hypothesis about the Difference between Two Means against a Nondirectional Alternative: $\alpha = .01$.*

deviations are not required for the subsequent calculations, good practice requires reporting them as well as the outcome of the test; the necessary calculations are shown in step 3. If S should be preferred to s, it can be obtained by using the divisor n in this step, rather than $n - 1$, as shown. Step 4 shows the calculation of t, and steps 5 and 6 show the determination of the degrees of freedom according to a two-tailed test using $\alpha = .01$, the critical value of t obtained from Table D in Appendix F, and the statistical conclusion. The outcome of the test is shown in Figure 19.5. Formula 19.4 could have been used to practical advantage in calculating $s_{\bar{X}-\bar{Y}}$ in this example (since $n_X = n_Y$), but it seemed best to demonstrate the more general procedure, one that is appropriate when $n_X \neq n_Y$ as well as when both are the same.

19.10 TESTING A HYPOTHESIS ABOUT TWO DEPENDENT MEANS

The calculation of t for a test of the difference between two dependent means is *identical* with the calculation of "z" for the test according to the normal curve model. Therefore we calculate:

$$t = \frac{(\bar{X} - \bar{Y}) - (\mu_X - \mu_Y)_{\text{hyp}}}{\sqrt{s_{\bar{X}}^2 + s_{\bar{Y}}^2 - 2rs_{\bar{X}}s_{\bar{Y}}}}$$

The calculations were illustrated in Table 17.5 in Section 17.10 and therefore will not be repeated here. An alternative method (the difference method) was described in Section 17.11. Sometimes computationally advantageous, it yields the same value of "z" (and hence t) as the first method. The steps of its computation are shown in Table 17.6 in that section.

Once t has been obtained, it should be evaluated with

$$df = n - 1$$

where n is the number of *pairs* of scores.

In the illustrations cited in chapter 17, there were 10 pairs of scores, so there are $10 - 1$, or 9 degrees of freedom. The test was two-tailed and conducted according to the 5% significance level, so $t_{\text{crit}} = \pm 2.262$. t_{calc} was $+.65$ (the value given there as "z"); it falls within the critical limits, so H_0 must be accepted.

Note that $df = (n - 1)$ is but half of the $(n_X - 1) + (n_Y - 1)$ degrees of freedom that would obtain if the same study were conducted using independent samples. Why fewer degrees of freedom for dependent samples?

When samples are independent, the score recorded for the first subject in the first group and for the first subject in the second group are completely unrelated. But, when subjects are matched (or when the same subjects are used under both treatment conditions), this is not so. If a subject does very well as compared with others under one condition, his matched counterpart will tend to do well as compared with others under the other condition, if matching has been on a relevant variable. For example, suppose the study compares two methods of learning, and pairs of subjects have been formed on the basis of level of learning aptitude. We may expect that a pair of apt subjects will tend to perform relatively well, each in his own group. In short, performance of one "member" of the pair is *not* independent of that of the other "member." Thus, *when the score of one member of the pair is specified, that of the other is not completely "free to vary."* Consequently, only one degree of freedom can be ascribed to each *pair* of scores. Since there are *n* pairs of scores, there will be $n - 1$ degrees of freedom.

We close with two comments. First, unlike the test of the difference between two independent means, the assumption of homogeneity of variance is *not* required for the test between two dependent means. Second, choosing sample size is an important design problem. Section 21.11 shows how to go about it.

19.11 INTERVAL ESTIMATES OF μ

The logic of the confidence interval was presented in Section 18.3 as was also the construction of an interval estimate and the method of its evaluation according to the normal curve model. The development presented here shows the change in procedure necessary to make allowance for the error introduced by estimating the population standard deviation from the sample. The basic understandings were thoroughly covered there, and some familiarity with them is assumed.

The manner of constructing an interval estimate is identical with that described in Section 18.3, except that the appropriate value of *t* is substituted for *z*. To be specific, the upper and lower limits may be found according to the desired confidence coefficient (C) by calculating:

Rule for Constructing an Interval Estimate of μ $$\bar{X} \pm t_p s_{\bar{X}} \tag{19.6}$$

where: $\bar{X}$ is the sample mean

$s_{\bar{X}}$ is the estimate of the standard error of the mean

t_p is the magnitude of t for which the probability is p of obtaining a value so deviant or more so (in either direction)

p is $1 - C$

t_p must be identified according to $df = n - 1$, the number of degrees of freedom associated with s.

As an example, suppose it is desired to estimate the location of μ according to the 95% level of confidence when the sample data are:

$$\bar{X} = 85.0, \quad s = 15.0, \quad n = 25$$

We first calculate the estimated standard error of the mean.†

$$s_{\bar{X}} = \frac{s}{\sqrt{n}} = \frac{15.0}{\sqrt{25}} = 3.00$$

The number of degrees of freedom associated with s is $n - 1$, or 24 for the present problem. From Table D in Appendix F, the value of t—so great that the probability is .05 of equalling or exceeding its magnitude—is:

$$t_p = 2.064$$

The limits are, therefore:

$$\bar{X} \pm t_{.05}s_{\bar{X}}$$

$$\text{LL} = 85.0 - (2.064)(3.00) \qquad \text{UL} = 85.0 + (2.064)(3.00)$$
$$= 78.81 \qquad\qquad\qquad\qquad\quad = 91.19$$

Stated formally:

$$C(78.81 \leq \mu \leq 91.19) = .95$$

It is important to remember that μ, although unknown, is fixed. It is the *interval*, as constructed from sample data, that is the random variable, not μ. Figure 19.6 shows some of the intervals that might result if samples were selected at random and intervals constructed about the sample means by the procedures described above. We may expect that 95% of such estimates will include μ within their range when t_p is selected to agree with $C = .95$.

In Figure 19.6, note that as we move from sample 1 to sample 10, the *location* of the intervals differs according to the differences among the sample means. But note that the *width* of the intervals also differs. This is because interval width depends in

†Calculation of s and $s_{\bar{X}}$ are illustrated in Table 15.1, chapter 15.

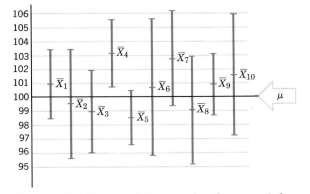

Figure 19.6 *Interval Estimates of μ Constructed from Means of Several Random Samples: σ Unknown.*

part on the varying estimates of the population standard deviation obtained from the several samples.

19.12 INTERVAL ESTIMATES OF $\mu_X - \mu_Y$

The rules for applying the normal curve model of estimation to the difference between two means were presented earlier. See especially Section 18.4 for a description of the procedure. The procedures now presented make allowance for the error introduced by estimating population parameters from the samples. The present procedures are exactly the same as those described earlier, except for (1) the substitution of t for z and the consequent use of Student's distribution rather than tables of normally distributed z, and (2) the use of a different standard error formula for the difference between means of *independent* samples (see Section 19.8 for the rationale). On the assumption that the developments mentioned are familiar, one example should suffice to clarify the procedure.

Suppose it is desired to estimate $\mu_X - \mu_Y$, the difference between two population means, according to the 99% level of confidence. We shall assume that the two samples are independent, and that the following information is available:

$$\begin{array}{ll} \bar{X} = 87.0 & \bar{Y} = 92.0 \\ s_X = 10.0 & s_Y = 12.0 \\ n_X = 13 & n_Y = 15 \end{array}$$

The upper and lower limits of the confidence interval may be found according to the desired confidence coefficient (C) by calculating:

Rule for Constructing an Interval Estimate of $\mu_X - \mu_Y$ $$(\bar{X} - \bar{Y}) \pm t_p s_{\bar{X} - \bar{Y}} \qquad (19.7)$$

where: $(\bar{X} - \bar{Y})$ is the difference between the two sample means

$s_{\bar{X} - \bar{Y}}$ is the estimate of the standard error of the difference between two means

t_p is the magnitude of t for which the probability is p of obtaining a value so deviant or more so (in either direction)

p is $1 - C$

For independent samples, $df = (n_X - 1) + (n_Y - 1)$, and t_p must be determined accordingly. In the present problem, $df = 26$, and the critical value of t is:

$$t_{.01} = 2.779$$

The standard error of the difference between the means is given by Formula 19.3:†

---

†Formula 19.4 may be substituted if $n_X = n_Y$.

$$s_{\bar{X}-\bar{Y}} = \sqrt{\frac{\sum x^2 + \sum y^2}{(n_X - 1) + (n_Y - 1)}\left(\frac{1}{n_X} + \frac{1}{n_Y}\right)}$$

This quantity is found by methods described in Section 19.9 and Table 19.2. Following those methods, we find that $s_{\bar{X}-\bar{Y}} = 4.21$.

The 99% confidence interval is therefore constructed as follows:

$$(\bar{X} - \bar{Y}) \pm t_{.01}s_{\bar{X}-\bar{Y}}$$

LL $= (87.0 - 92.0) - (2.779)(4.21)$ UL $= (87.0 - 92.0) + (2.779)(4.21)$
$\quad = -5 - 11.70$ $\quad = -5 + 11.70$
$\quad = -16.70$ $\quad = +6.70$

Formally, this is expressed:

$$C(-16.70 \leqq (\mu_X - \mu_Y) \leqq +6.70) = .99$$

This example illustrated procedures appropriate to *independent* samples. When samples are *dependent,* the procedure is the same except for calculation of $s_{\bar{X}-\bar{Y}}$. For dependent samples, it is:

$$s_{\bar{X}-\bar{Y}} = \sqrt{s_{\bar{X}}^2 + s_{\bar{Y}}^2 - 2r_{XY}s_{\bar{X}}s_{\bar{Y}}}$$

The method of its calculation is described in Section 17.10 (see especially Table 17.5). When samples are dependent, $df = n - 1$, where n is the number of *pairs* of scores (see Section 19.10). The value of t_p should be identified accordingly.

19.13 FURTHER COMMENTS ON INTERVAL ESTIMATION

When interval estimation is used with truly small samples, it becomes immediately apparent that the limits within which the parameter is expected to fall are wide. For example, in estimating $\mu_X - \mu_Y$ from two independent samples of 9 cases each, the 95% confidence interval will have a spread equal to *twice* the estimated standard deviation of the variable. Discouraging, but realistic. The same problem of lack of precision of course exists for those who use hypothesis testing with samples of this size, but unless the user knows how to look for it, it is not brought home so forcefully as when interval estimates are constructed. This should remind us of some of the attractive features of interval estimation relative to hypothesis testing. You may wish to review Section 18.8 for a closer look at these advantages.

It also reminds us that application of statistical techniques is no remedy for inherent design defects. Decide in the planning stage how much accuracy will be required, and then for interval estimation use the methods of Section 18.6 to determine how many cases will be required to produce that degree of precision.

Although interval estimation can quite properly be performed when parameters are estimated and samples are small, the alternative method of exploring the meaning of an interval estimate using the statistic *d* as described in Section 18.5 is subject to certain problems when sample size is small. It is best, therefore, to reserve its use for larger samples.

19.14 ASSUMPTIONS ASSOCIATED WITH INFERENCE ABOUT MEANS

The basic statistical conditions (such as random sampling) required to obtain wholly accurate output from the techniques described in this chapter are fundamentally the same as those previously described for the normal curve model. Look, therefore, to their enumeration and the detailed discussion to be found in Sections 15.10, 15.11, and 17.13. Nevertheless, there are two exceptions.

Under the earlier normal curve model, the *ideal* condition required that certain population parameters be known: σ, in the case of inference about a single mean; σ_X and σ_Y in the case of two independent means; σ_X, σ_Y, and ρ in the case of two dependent means. Use of the *t* statistic and evaluation of the outcome in terms of Student's distribution of *t* does away with these assumptions. This distribution makes allowance for estimation of these parameters from the sample(s).

The second exception applies only to inference about the difference between two *independent* means. In order for the *t* distribution to be exactly applicable, homogeneity of variance is assumed. At first, this assumption sounds formidable. In practical application, there is help from several quarters.

First, experience suggests that the assumption of homogeneity of variance appears to be reasonably satisfied in many cases. It is relatively rare that a striking difference in variance occurs. Second, violation of the assumption makes less disturbance when samples are large than when they are small. As a rule of thumb, it might be hazarded that moderate departure from homogeneity of variance will have little effect when each sample consists of 20 or more observations.

Finally, the problem created by heterogeneity of variance is minimized when the two samples are chosen to be of equal size. There are other benefits from using equal sample size; see Section 17.7. If sample size is small and it is suspected that the assumption of homogeneity of variance may not be satisfied, it is possible to test the significance of the difference between the two variance estimates (s_X^2 and s_Y^2). However, tests of homogeneity of variance are not very satisfactory in small sample situations. To combat the influence of nonhomogeneity of variance, *the best bet is to select samples of equal (or approximately equal) size, and the larger the better.*

Another point deserves special mention. A requirement, as you will remember, is that the sampling distribution of means, or of differences between two means, follows the normal distribution.† Strictly speaking, the sampling distribution will be normal only when the distribution of the population of scores is also normal. However, according to the Central Limit Theorem, the sampling distribution of means tends toward normality even when the population of scores is not normally distributed (see Section 13.7). *The strength of this tendency toward normality is pronounced when samples are large but less so when samples are small.*

Now *only* the Central Limit Theorem offers aid for potential nonnormality of the sampling distribution. The procedures here described have no remedial effect; they make no allowance for nonnormality in the population of scores. *Since the effect of the Central Limit Theorem is weakest when samples are small, it is particularly important to inquire as to the shape of the population (or populations) of scores when working with small samples.*

Fortunately, the normalizing effect of the Central Limit Theorem is rather pronounced unless sample size is quite small indeed. For example, a moderate degree of skewness in the population can probably be tolerated if sample size is, say, 20 or more. Indeed, empirical investigations have shown that the t test gives remarkably good results when applied in situations characterized by nonnormality, and, in the case of independent means, characterized by nonhomogeneity of variance.‡

When serious question still exists about the propriety of conducting tests about means because of nonnormality of the parent population, certain of the so-called "nonparametric" statistical tests may be considered. These techniques are, in some circumstances, less responsive to the totality of information conveyed by the data, but they are free of assumptions about the specific shape of the distribution of the population of scores. Some of these techniques are described in chapter 24. See Section 24.4 for the Mann-Whitney Test, an alternative to the test between two *independent* means. Section 24.6 describes the Sign Test and Section 24.7 describes Wilcoxon's Signed Ranks Test; both are alternatives to the test between two *dependent* means.

PROBLEMS AND EXERCISES

Identify:

Student	Fisher
Student's distribution	homogeneity of variance

† Remember that it is the distribution of t which is leptokurtic, *not* the sampling distribution of means, or of differences between means (see Section 19.2).

‡ See, for example: C. A. Boneau, "The Effects of Violations of Assumptions Underlying the t Test," *Psychological Bulletin* **57** (1960):49–64.

leptokurtic distribution s_p^2
degrees of freedom $t, t_p, t_{calc}, t_{crit}$

1 For a sample of three scores, the quantity $\Sigma(X - \bar{X})^2$ has associated with it 2 degrees of freedom. For the same sample, the quantity $\Sigma(X - \mu)^2$ is characterized by 3 degrees of freedom. Explain.

2 From Table D in Appendix F, identify the value of t that, for 15 degrees of freedom, (a) is so high that only 1% of t's would be higher, (b) is so low that only 10% of t's would be lower.

3 From Table D, identify the centrally located limits, for 8 degrees of freedom, that would include (a) 50% of t's, (b) 90% of t's, (c) 95% of t's, (d) 99% of t's.

4 From Table D, and for 25 degrees of freedom, what proportion of t's would be (a) less than $t = -1.316$? (b) less than $t = +1.316$? (c) between $t = -2.060$ and $t = +2.060$? (d) between $t = -1.708$ and $t = +2.060$?

5 From Table D, and for 20 degrees of freedom, what is the probability in random sampling of obtaining (a) $t \geq +2.6$ (b) $t \geq +1.8$ (c) $t \leq -1.9$ (d) $t = \pm 1.4$ or of greater magnitude (e) $t = \pm 2.2$ or of greater magnitude?

6 We adopt $\alpha = .05$ and test the hypothesis that $\mu = 50$ according to the small sample approach. What conclusion should we draw if (a) $n = 10$, $t_{calc} = +2.10$ and $H_A: \mu \neq 50$? (b) $n = 20$, $t_{calc} = +2.10$ and $H_A: \mu \neq 50$? (c) $n = 10$, $t_{calc} = +2.10$ and $H_A: \mu > 50$? Show the critical value of t for each problem.

7 Given the following data: $\bar{X} = 50.0$, $s = 12.0$, $n = 16$. Test, using $\alpha = .05$, (a) $H_0: \mu = 44.0$ versus $H_A: \mu \neq 44.0$ (b) $H_0: \mu = 55.0$ versus $H_A: \mu < 55.0$. Show the critical value of t for each problem.

8 Given the following scores: 2, 4, 4, 7, 8. (a) Calculate s by the raw score formula (see Section 15.6). (b) Calculate t required to test $H_0: \mu = 8.0$ versus $H_A: \mu \neq 8.0$. (c) Evaluate t for $\alpha = .05$ and state your conclusions. (d) Evaluate t for $\alpha = .01$ and state your conclusions.

9 Do Problem 10 of chapter 15 by the method of the present chapter.

10 Given the following data from two independent samples: $\bar{X} = 82.0$, $\Sigma x^2 = 120.0$, $n_X = 11$; $\bar{Y} = 88.0$, $\Sigma y^2 = 220.0$, $n_Y = 21$; (a) Calculate $s_{\bar{X}-\bar{Y}}$ according to Formula 19.3. (b) Test the hypothesis of no difference between the two population means against a nondirectional alternative using $\alpha = .05$.

11 Do Problem 5 of Chapter 17 by the method of the present chapter.

12 Do Problem 6 of Chapter 17 by the method of the present chapter.

13 Given the following data from two dependent samples: $\bar{X} = 40.0$, $s_X = 8.0$, $\bar{Y} = 36.0$, $s_Y = 12.0$, $n = 16$, $r = +.60$. (a) State formally the hypotheses necessary to conduct a nondirectional test of no difference between the two population means. (b) Calculate $s_{\bar{X}-\bar{Y}}$. (c) Complete the test at the .05 and .01 levels of significance, and state your conclusions.

14 For the data of Problem 7, construct an interval estimate of μ according to: (a) $C = .95$ (b) $C = .99$ (c) $C = .50$.

15 Do what is required in Problem 14, but use the data of Problem 8.

16 For the data of Problem 10, construct an interval estimate of $\mu_X - \mu_Y$ according to: (*a*) $C = .95$ (*b*) $C = .99$.

17 Do what is required in Problem 16, but use the data of Problem 5 in Chapter 17.

18 For the data of Problem 13, construct an interval estimate of $\mu_X - \mu_Y$ according to: (*a*) $C = .95$ (*b*) $C = .99$.

CHAPTER 20

20.1 INTRODUCTION

The Pearsonian correlation coefficient (see chapter 9), like other statistics, varies from sample to sample under the influence of random sampling variation. In most practical situations, we have knowledge only of the sample coefficient, but we want to know the state of affairs in the population. The two basic techniques of statistical inference, hypothesis testing and estimation, are therefore frequently pertinent to inquiries concerning degree of relationship as expressed by Pearson r.

In this chapter, we will consider procedures for inference about single coefficients and about the difference between two coefficients. An understanding of the basics of inference, such as may be found in chapters 13–18, is assumed. In addition, some of the procedures require knowledge of the distribution of Student's t (chapter 19).

Inference about Pearson Correlation Coefficients

20.2 THE RANDOM SAMPLING DISTRIBUTION OF r

Consider a population of pairs of scores (X and Y) that form a bivariate distribution. The Pearsonian correlation coefficient, calculated from the complete set of paired scores, is ρ_{XY}. When the coefficient is calculated from a sample, it is r_{XY}. If we draw a sample of given size at random from the population, calculate r, return the sample to the population, and repeat this operation indefinitely, the multitude of sample r's will form the *random sampling distribution of r* for samples of the particular size. The mean of this sampling distribution is approximately ρ, and the standard deviation is $\sigma_r = (1 - \rho^2)/\sqrt{n - 1}$. As we might expect (and can see from this formula), *the values of r will vary less from sample to sample when sample size is large.* Something that might not be anticipated is also apparent on study of

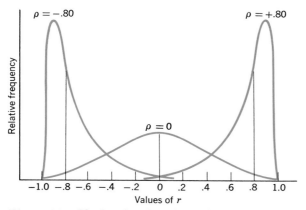

Figure 20.1 *The Random Sampling Distribution of r for Three Values of ρ: n = 8.*

the formula: *The values of r will vary less from sample to sample when the true correlation, ρ, is high than when it is low.*

If the sample values of *r* formed a normal distribution, we could proceed to solve problems of inference by methods already familiar (see chapter 15). *Unfortunately, the sampling distribution of r is not normally distributed.* When $\rho = 0$, the sampling distribution of *r* is symmetrical and nearly normal. But, when ρ has a value other than zero, the sampling distribution is skewed. In fact, the larger the value of ρ (either positively or negatively), the greater the skewness. Figure 20.1 shows the sampling distribution for $\rho = -.8$, 0, and $+.8$ when $n = 8$. It is not difficult to understand why the distribution is skewed when the value of *r* is high. When $\rho = +.8$, for example, fluctuations of random sampling might yield a sample coefficient as much as .2 point higher ($r = +1.0$), but it could be substantially lower than .2 point below $r = +.8$. Indeed, the lower absolute limit is -1.0.

The degree of skewness of the sampling distribution of *r* is also a function of sample size. When $\rho \neq 0$, the smaller the size of the sample, the greater the skewness of the sampling distribution.

Because the distribution of sample *r*'s is not normal, alternative solutions must be sought to provide a practical frame for inference. For some problems, the *t* distribution affords an appropriate model. For others, transformation of *r* to a variable which *is* (approximately) normally distributed offers the best solution.

20.3 TESTING THE HYPOTHESIS THAT $\rho = 0$

Without doubt, the most frequent question of inference about problems of association is whether there is any relationship at all between two variables. For example, if we are developing a test with the hope of predicting success in the job of insurance salesman, the primary question is whether the test has *any* relationship to a measure of job success. If, among a sample of salesmen, $r = +.30$ between test performance and job performance rating, it may still be that the true correlation (ρ) is zero, and that this value of r has occurred simply as a matter of random sampling variation. To answer this question, we test the hypothesis that $\rho = 0$ against the alternative that it is not.

The late Sir Ronald A. Fisher showed that when $\rho = 0$, the expression given in Formula 20.1 is distributed as Student's t with $n - 2$ degrees of freedom:

t Required for Testing the
Hypothesis That $\rho = 0$
$$t = \frac{r}{\sqrt{(1 - r^2)/(n - 2)}} \tag{20.1}$$

where: r is the *sample* coefficient and n is the number of *pairs* of scores in the sample.

To test the hypothesis that $\rho = 0$, we calculate t according to Formula 20.1 and evaluate it, according to the significance level adopted and $(n - 2)$ degrees of freedom, with reference to the values of t found in Table D, in Appendix F.†

This method is quite general. It can be used for a variety of levels of significance, and for one- or two-tailed tests. However, if tests are to be conducted at the usual 5% or 1% significance levels, Table E in Appendix F removes the chore of computing t. This table gives the critical values of r required to reach significance under these circumstances. To use this table, enter it with the appropriate value of df, and read the critical value of r according to the desired significance level. If r_{calc} exceeds the tabled value, the hypothesis of no correlation is rejected; otherwise it is not. For the example, if a two-tailed test is to be conducted at $\alpha = .05$, and if $r_{calc} = .30$ based on $n = 25$, first determine the degrees of freedom:

$$df = n - 2 = 25 - 2 = 23$$

Then enter Table E and look down the left column until this number of degrees of freedom is located. Then look across to find the entry in the column for a two-tailed test at $\alpha = .05$. This is the critical value of r:

$$r_{crit} = .396$$

Since our obtained value falls short of it, the hypothesis of no correlation cannot be rejected. Figure 20.2 illustrates this situation.

In terms of the *research* question posed, the finding of a significant r is only a preliminary. The next question is whether the correlation is large enough to be of practical or theoretical use. With large samples, an *un*usefully small r may prove to be "statistically significant." Although the approach described above is very frequently used, constructing interval estimates of the true value of the correlation coefficient offers a number of advantages. For one thing, with very large samples,

---

†Section 19.5 is particularly pertinent for those who wish to review use of the t distribution.

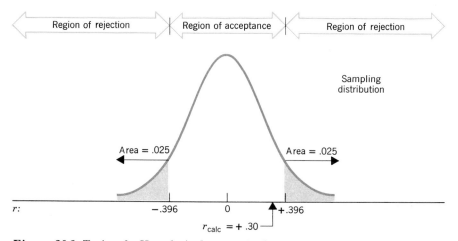

Figure 20.2 *Testing the Hypothesis that $\rho = 0$ when $r = +.30$ and $df = 23$.*

the interval estimate might inform us that ρ is somewhere between $+.05$ and $+.10$ (which tells us that the correlation is not zero, but it is so low as to be useless), rather than informing us that we have a "highly significant" coefficient (which would tend to make us think we had something worth while). The estimation procedure is described in Section 20.5. See also Section 16.6 for an earlier discussion of the difference between a significant difference and an important one, and Section 18.8 for consideration of the merits of interval estimation as an alternative to hypothesis testing.

20.4 FISHER'S z' TRANSFORMATION

Although the technique described in the previous section serves to test the hypothesis that $\rho = 0$, it cannot be used for other types of problems. Another approach is required, and, once more, it is the result of work by R. A. Fisher.

The fundamental problem is that the sampling distribution of r departs from the normal when $\rho \neq 0$. Moreover, the degree of skewness varies with the magnitude of ρ. Fisher derived a logarithmic function of r, which we shall call z' (z prime), that exhibits certain desirable properties:

1 The sampling distribution of z' is approximately normal irrespective of the value of ρ.

2 The standard error of z', unlike the standard error of r, is essentially independent of the value of ρ.

Because of these properties, we can, for several problems of inference about correlation coefficients, translate r to z' and conduct inference in terms of these converted values. The familiar properties of the normal curve can then be used in conducting the evaluation, and the outcome is the same as though inference were conducted directly in terms of r.

The formula for z' is:

Formula for Translating
r to Fisher's z'
$$z' = \tfrac{1}{2}[\log_e (1 + r) - \log_e (1 - r)] \qquad (20.2)$$

Note that the value of z' depends *wholly* on the value of r. The z' translation is therefore simply a mathematical reformulation that changes the scale of r. Note, also, that *Fisher's z' is not a z score, nor is it related in any way.* The similarity in symbolism is unfortunate; another symbol would be better. Fisher originally called his statistic z, which is completely unacceptable because of the wide use of that symbol for a standard score. Usage has perpetuated Fisher's symbolism, at least as closely as possible without creating utter confusion. We will shortly be using the symbols z and z' in close proximity; watch for the difference.

The improvement in scale can be most readily shown pictorially. Figure 20.3 shows the sampling distribution of z' that corresponds to $\rho = -.8$, $\rho = 0$, and $\rho = +.8$ when $n = 8$. Compare these distributions with those of r for the same values of ρ (Figure 20.1). Note that the sampling distribution of z' is essentially similar in shape and variability under these three conditions, whereas the sampling distribution of r is not.

It would be awkward to work through the formula for z' to translate an r to z', or vice versa. Fortunately, Table F, in Appendix F, makes the conversion easy. In this table, if r is positive, read the value of z' as positive, and if negative, read z' as negative.

It is rewarding to give this table a few moments of study, because it reveals what is accomplished by Fisher's translation. Note that when r is zero, z' is also zero, and

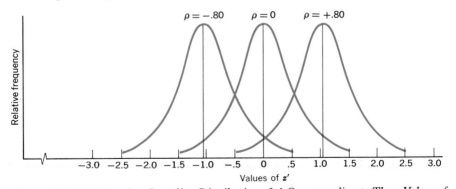

Figure 20.3 *The Random Sampling Distribution of z' Corresponding to Three Values of* ρ: $n = 8$.

that the two values are essentially equivalent up to, say, $r = .25$. As r progresses from zero to one, a discrepancy between r and z' begins to appear, z' being larger than its parent, r. The discrepancy increases more rapidly the higher the value of r. What is accomplished is that the scale of r (ranging from -1.00 through 0 to $+1.00$) is being stretched, very little at the center but increasingly more so at the extremes. Note that the original scale of r becomes, in terms of z', a scale ranging from approximately -3 to $+3$ (or even farther, if it is allowed that r might exceed $\pm.995$).

In the suggested uses of the z' transformation that follow, keep in mind that reasonable results will obtain unless sample size (n) is very small or ρ is very high. Actually, we have no justification for finding Pearsonian r among very small samples (see Section 20.8), nor do we ordinarily encounter correlation coefficients much above .9. Thus, the limitations are more academic than practical.

20.5 ESTIMATING ρ

Rather than testing the hypothesis that ρ is some specific value, it may be desirable to ask within what limits the population coefficient may be found. Accordingly, an interval estimate may be constructed corresponding to a selected level of confidence. The basic logic of formation of confidence intervals was developed in Section 18.3. The discussion here assumes that knowledge.

Because the sampling distribution of r is nonnormal (see Section 20.2), we make use of Fisher's normalizing z' transformation. A confidence interval may be constructed by translating the sample r to z', and following the rule:

Rule for Constructing an
Interval Estimate of ρ $$z' \pm z_p \sigma_{z'} \qquad\qquad (20.3)$$

where: z' is the value of z' corresponding to the sample r
$\quad\quad$ z_p is the magnitude of z for which the probability is p of obtaining a value so deviant or more so (in either direction)
$\quad\quad$ p is $(1 - C)$, where C is the confidence coefficient
$\quad\quad$ $\sigma_{z'}$ is the standard error of Fisher's z'

The formula for the standard error of z' is:

Standard Error of z' $$\sigma_{z'} = \frac{1}{\sqrt{n - 3}} \qquad\qquad (20.4)$$

Application of the above rule will result in a lower limit and an upper limit, both expressed in terms of z'. These must then be converted to r's by means of Table F in Appendix F.

The procedure is illustrated with the same data used in Section 20.3. The sample

r is $+.30$, based on 25 pairs of observations. What are the limits in which we can be 95% confident that they include ρ, the population value of the correlation coefficient? From Table F, we find that $z' = +.31$ corresponds to $r = +.30$. $\sigma_{z'} = 1/\sqrt{25 - 3} = .21$, and in a normal distribution, $z = \pm 1.96$ is the value so deviant that it would be exceeded but .05 of the time. According to the rule given in Formula 20.3, the limits of the 95% confidence interval are:

$$+.31 \pm (1.96)(.21)$$
$$\underset{\left(\substack{\text{Lower} \\ \text{Limit}}\right)}{-.10} \quad \text{to} \quad \underset{\left(\substack{\text{Upper} \\ \text{Limit}}\right)}{+.72}$$

Using Table F, these values of z' are translated back to values of r, and the limits are:

$$r_{\text{LL}} = -.10 \qquad r_{\text{UL}} = +.62$$

Formally, the confidence interval is expressed:

$$C(-.10 \leqq \rho \leqq +.62) = .95$$

Note that these limits are not equidistant from $r = +.30$. The upper limit is closer to $r = +.30$, as might be expected (see Section 20.2).

20.6 TESTING THE HYPOTHESIS OF NO DIFFERENCE BETWEEN ρ_1 AND ρ_2: INDEPENDENT SAMPLES

In the course of studying factors involved in academic success at Spartan University, an investigator wonders whether aptitude test score is related to freshman grade point average to the same degree for male and female students. Drawing a sample of 100 male students, he finds the correlation between these two variables to be: $r_1 = +.50$, and for a sample of 100 female students, the correlation between the same two variables is: $r_2 = +.35$.

We are faced with the problem that the two sampling distributions of r, corresponding to ρ_1 and ρ_2, are unknown and probably skewed. Hence, the sampling distribution of differences between pairs of coefficients will tend to be nonnormal. Fisher's z' transformation provides the avenue for solution, normalizing the sampling distribution. We shall therefore convert r to z', and conduct the test in terms of z'.

We first state the hypothesis and the desired significance level:

$$\begin{array}{ll} H_0: & \rho_1 - \rho_2 = 0 \\ H_A: & \rho_1 - \rho_2 \neq 0 \end{array} \qquad \alpha = .01$$

From Table F in Appendix F, we find the z' equivalents of r_1 ($z' = +.55$) and r_2 ($z' = +.37$). Then z (*not* z') is calculated according to Formula 20.5:

z Required to Test the Hypothesis
That $\rho_1 = \rho_2$ when Samples
Are Independent

$$z = \frac{(z_1' - z_2') - 0}{\sigma_{z_1' - z_2'}}$$ (20.5)

To use this formula, the equation for the standard error of the difference between two values of z', $\sigma_{z_1' - z_2'}$, is required. It is given by Formula 20.6:

Standard Error of the Difference
between Two Independent z''s

$$\sigma_{z_1' - z_2'} = \sqrt{\frac{1}{n_1 - 3} + \frac{1}{n_2 - 3}}$$ (20.6)

To conclude the test, we have:

$$\sigma_{z_1' - z_2'} = \sqrt{\frac{1}{100 - 3} + \frac{1}{100 - 3}} = .14$$

and,

$$z = \frac{(.55 - .37) - 0}{.14} = +1.29$$

Treating the obtained value of z ($+1.29$) as a normal deviate, we find that it falls short of the critical value of z ($z = \pm 2.58$) required to declare significance at the 1% level. The grounds are insufficient to reject the hypothesis; H_0 is accepted.

The procedure described above is suited *only* to situations involving two independent random samples. It is not appropriate, for example, when the two correlation coefficients have been obtained on the same set of subjects or when subjects have been matched.

20.7 TESTING THE HYPOTHESIS OF NO DIFFERENCE BETWEEN ρ_1 AND ρ_2: DEPENDENT SAMPLES

Is academic aptitude test score related to grade point average to the same degree for freshmen as for seniors? If the correlation between these variables is found among a sample of freshmen, and, 3 years later, among the *same* subjects when they are seniors, we have a problem involving dependent, rather than independent, samples. Again, suppose we have two predictors of job success and want to know whether the two are equally related to the criterion. If the two correlations (between predictor and criterion) have been obtained on the *same* sample of subjects, the samples are dependent. The method of the previous section is inappropriate to either of the above circumstances. For dependent samples, two cases may be distinguished. Case I is illustrated by the first example above, involving a correlation obtained at Time 1 and another obtained at Time 2. In Case I, *four* sets of measurements have been obtained, leading to two correlation coefficients. That is, aptitude score and grade point average obtained as freshmen yielded the first coefficient, and these variables, remeasured when the subjects were seniors, yielded the second. This comparison could be symbolized: r_{12} v. r_{34}.

Curiously, there is no entirely satisfactory test of the difference between two correlation coefficients obtained in such circumstances. Attempts have been made to solve this problem. Some proposals are of incompletely evaluated validity, and others are satisfactory but involve rather restrictive assumptions which may not be met in practical work. More detailed consideration of this problem may be found in a text by Johnson and Jackson.[†]

The second case, Case II, is illustrated by the second example above. In Case II, *three* sets of measurements have been obtained, leading to two correlation coefficients. In the example above, there is a set of measures for each of the two predictors, but there is just one set of scores on the criterion variable. This comparison could be symbolized: r_{13} v. r_{23}. This problem *does* have a solution, but because it is somewhat special we will omit its development here and make reference to other sources such as Johnson and Jackson, cited above.

20.8 CONCLUDING COMMENTS

From earlier chapters, you may recall that no assumption about the shape of the bivariate distribution is required when the correlation coefficient is used purely as a descriptive index. However, *all of the procedures for inference about coefficients described in this chapter are based on the assumption that the population of pairs of scores forms a normal bivariate distribution*. This implies that X is normally distributed, Y is normally distributed, and that the relation between X and Y is linear. If we are not dealing with a normal bivariate population, then these procedures for inference must be considered to yield approximate results.

Studies designed to ascertain the degree of association between two variables should be planned with an eye to adequacy of sample size. In many circumstances, the correlation coefficient can not be stably determined from small samples. In evidence of this, Table E in the appendix is worth study. This table may be interpreted to state the range that would include 95% (or 99%) of sample coefficients when the true correlation is zero. Note, for instance, that when n is 10 ($df = 8$), and $\rho = 0$, the 95% limits for r are $\pm.63$, and the 99% limits, $\pm.77$. Suppose, unknown to us, $\rho = +.60$, and our sample r happened to have exactly the same value. Nevertheless, if we were testing the hypothesis that $\rho = 0$, we would find no cause to reject it. Even when $df = 30$, the 95% limits are $\pm.35$, and the 99% limits are $\pm.45$. It should be obvious that a good-sized sample is needed to determine the extent of relationship with any degree of accuracy.

[†] P. O. Johnson and R. W. B. Jackson, *Modern Statistical Methods*, Rand McNally & Co., Chicago, 1959, pp. 353–356.

It is true that if ρ is nonzero, random sampling variation of r will be less. The otherwise relatively useless formula for the standard error of a correlation coefficient, $\sigma_r = (1 - \rho^2)/\sqrt{n - 1}$, helps to show this. Note that, according to this formula, if ρ were near ± 1.00, sampling variability in r would indeed be quite small. *In general, it would be good practice to make interval estimates of ρ much more often than is commonly done in research.* Such intervals call attention more directly to the inherent amount of sampling variation. It seems likely that research workers are often tempted to think that the population value of the coefficient is closer to the sample r at hand than inspection of the actual interval estimate would warrant.

Another benefit of interval estimation was described in Section 20.3. If samples are very large, a relatively small coefficient may lead to the conclusion that there is a real relationship between the two variables when the hypothesis of no correlation is tested. Though real, it may be so small as to be useless. Interval estimation avoids this trap.

PROBLEMS AND EXERCISES

Identify:

sampling distribution of r Fisher's z' transformation

σ_r $\sigma_{z'_1 - z'_2}$

1 Given: H_0: $\rho = 0$, H_A: $\rho \neq 0$, $r = +.35$, $n = 24$. Test the null hypothesis at $\alpha = .10$, .05, and .01.

2 Using Table E, in the appendix, test the hypothesis that $\rho = 0$ when: (a) $r = +.40$, $n = 28$, H_A: $\rho \neq 0$, $\alpha = .05$ (b) $r = -.55$, $n = 18$, H_A: $\rho \neq 0$, $\alpha = .01$ (c) $r = -.40$, $n = 22$, H_A: $\rho < 0$, $\alpha = .05$ (d) $r = +.45$, $n = 25$, H_A: $\rho < 0$, $\alpha = .05$. Show the critical value of r for each problem.

3 Would an r of $+.10$ be significantly different from zero if it were based on 1000 cases? Explain.

4 Professor Smith wants to know whether academic aptitude test score is related to freshman grade point average to the same extent for male college students as it is for female students. He obtains the following data from samples obtained at his institution: Males: $r = +.45$, $n = 103$; Females: $r = +.30$, $n = 103$. (a) State the null hypothesis and the alternative hypothesis appropriate to his question. (b) Test the hypothesis using $\alpha = .05$ and .01, and state your conclusions.

5 Given: $r = .65$, $n = 103$. Construct an interval estimate of ρ according to: (a) $C = .95$ (b) $C = .99$ (c) $C = .90$.

6 Repeat Problem 5, but assume these data: $r = .45$, $n = 19$.

7 In a particular study, it is reported that $r = +.75$ between predictor and criterion. Reading on, we find that this value was obtained on a sample of six cases. Comment.

8 In another study, it is reported that $r = +.12$ between predictor and criterion. This correlation is based on 500 cases. Is it significantly different from zero? Your comment?

CHAPTER 21

21.1 INTRODUCTION

The researcher is faced with two kinds of problems, as we learned early in this book: statistical problems and substantive (subject-matter) problems. On numerous occasions we have looked into both and into the interaction between them. In any exposition of statistics, primary emphasis must be accorded to properties of statistical devices. Nevertheless, it is important to clarify the relationships between experimental logic and statistical logic, and between substantive concerns and statistical properties.

In the course of inquiry, the investigator must perform such acts as to define the target population, select the alternative hypothesis, choose the level of significance, and determine the size of the sample. These decisions cannot be made in a vacuum; they must be made in consideration of the goals of the study. A number of areas of interaction between goals of the study and decisions about

Some Aspects
of
Experimental
Design

statistical procedures need further attention. The aim of this chapter is to give better treatment to certain of them.

21.2 TYPE I ERROR AND TYPE II ERROR

In Section 16.7, we learned that two types of error may occur in testing hypotheses: Type I error and Type II error. The probability of committing each is defined as follows:

Type I Error $\qquad \alpha = \Pr(\text{rejecting } H_0 \mid H_0 \text{ is true})$

Type II Error $\qquad \beta = \Pr(\text{accepting } H_0 \mid H_0 \text{ is false})$

In arranging the test of a hypothesis, the probability of committing a Type I error is relatively "visible," because the investigator must select the value of α he wishes to use. Issues to be faced in choice of α are discussed in Section 16.4.

The choice of α cannot be made in a vacuum. Since α specifies the risk of rejecting the null hypothesis when it is true, ask what that would mean in concrete terms in the setting of the study. Are you testing the null hypothesis to find if a new learning method is superior to a standard method? If so, α is the risk of finding the new method to be superior when it really isn't. Put in these practical terms, it is easier (but not necessarily easy!) to decide what level of risk can be assumed.

Although the investigator must choose a value for α, no such deliberate action is required for β, the risk of accepting the null hypothesis when it is false. Often the acceptable size of β is faced only indirectly, as in the question, "Is my sample large enough?" But this risk too can be faced directly and fixed by the investigator. Again, put the consequences of a Type II error in terms of practical consequences in order to consider its risk. In the illustration above, a Type II error would be committed if the investigator failed to find a difference between the two methods when in fact the new method was superior. What would the "cost" be of continuing to use the less effective method?

Once the level of acceptable risk is decided, one can consider certain aspects of experimental design with an eye to arranging them to achieve the specified level of protection. The next several sections examine factors affecting β. We will consider which of these might profitably be manipulated by the experimenter to obtain the desired protection, and in Section 21.11 we will show how to use the most important of the means available—selection of sample size—to achieve this end.

21.3 THE POWER OF A TEST

In statistical work one sees the expression, "the power of the test." A Type II error is committed when a false null hypothesis is accepted. The opposite occurs when a false null hypothesis is rejected. In the example of the previous section, rejecting a false null hypothesis would occur if as a result of the test we claimed that the new learning method was superior when in fact it really *was* superior. Since the probability of the former is β, the probability of the latter is $(1 - \beta)$:

$$(1 - \beta) = \Pr(\text{rejecting } H_0 \mid H_0 \text{ is false})$$

In other words, $(1 - \beta)$ is the probability of claiming a significant difference when a true difference really exists. The probability of doing so, $(1 - \beta)$, is called the *power of the test*. Among several ways of conducting a test, the most powerful one is that offering the greatest probability of rejecting H_0 when it should be rejected.

In the sections that follow we will examine factors that affect β. Since β and power are complementary, it must be remembered that any condition that decreases β increases the power of the test, and vice versa.

21.4 FACTORS AFFECTING TYPE II ERROR: DISCREPANCY BETWEEN THE TRUE MEAN AND THE HYPOTHESIZED MEAN

Suppose we conduct a two-tailed test of the hypothesis that μ has a particular value. If the hypothesis is true, the sampling distribution will center on μ_{hyp}, as shown by the distribution drawn in dotted outline at the top of Figure 21.1. This is the distribution from which the region of acceptance is determined, as shown in the same picture. Now if the hypothesis is false, the true sampling distribution of means will center on μ_{true}, rather than on μ_{hyp}.† This distribution is shown in solid outline. These are the means we shall actually get in random sampling when the hypothesis is false. We now recall that a Type II error is committed when a false hypothesis is accepted. What will lead to acceptance of the (false) hypothesis in the situation pictured? Clearly, getting a sample mean that falls within the limits of the region of acceptance. Since our sample means will actually be drawn from the true distribution, those means in the shaded area are the ones that will erroneously lead us to accept the null hypothesis. β, the probability of accepting a false hypothesis,

† In practice we would not know the value of μ_{true}. Here and in the next few sections we assume possible values for it for purposes of discussion.

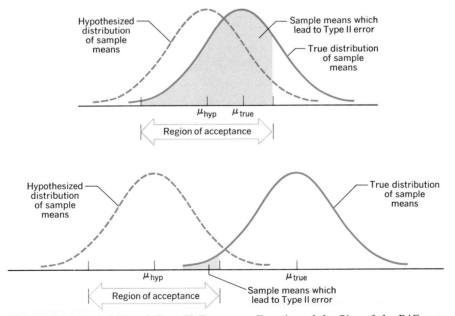

Figure 21.1 *Probability of Type II Error as a Function of the Size of the Difference between* μ_{hyp} *and* μ_{true}.

is therefore the probability of obtaining such a mean in random sampling; judging by eye in the picture, it appears that probability is about .8 (Section 21.10 will show how to calculate β).

In this section and in those that immediately follow, study of the influences that affect β will, for the sake of simplicity, be illustrated in the test of a single mean. The idea applies to tests of other hypotheses. For example, a similar analysis can be made for a test of the difference between two means.

The probability of a Type II error is related to the discrepancy between the hypothesized mean and the true mean. If the two are very close, the sample means obtained from the true sampling distribution will overlap the region of acceptance to a large extent. Consequently, many sample values will lead to the false acceptance of H_0. The diagram at the top in Figure 21.1 illustrates this situation; we estimated that about 80% of sample means will lead to the false acceptance of the hypothesis that $\mu = \mu_{hyp}$.

In the illustration at the bottom in Figure 21.1, the true mean and the hypothesized mean are substantially different. Here, few samples have means that will lead to the acceptance of H_0. *In general, the greater the discrepancy between μ_{true} and μ_{hyp}, the less the probability of falsely accepting the hypothesis.*

21.5 FACTORS AFFECTING TYPE II ERROR: SAMPLE SIZE

The probability of committing a Type II error is related to sample size. Consider the test of the hypothesis that $\mu = \mu_{hyp}$ when sample size is 100. The standard error of the mean will be $\sigma_{\bar{X}} = \sigma/\sqrt{100} = \frac{1}{10}\sigma$. If sample size were 400, the standard error of the mean would be $\sigma_{\bar{X}} = \sigma/\sqrt{400} = \frac{1}{20}\sigma$, only half as large. Figure 21.2 shows how the sampling distributions might appear when all factors are the same except for sample size. In general, the larger the size of the samples, the smaller the standard deviation ($\sigma_{\bar{X}}$) of the sampling distribution of $\bar{X}$. Com-

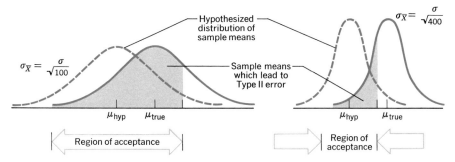

Figure 21.2 *Probability of Type II Error as a Function of Sample Size.*

parison of the two situations illustrated shows that when sample size is larger, there is less overlap between the two distributions. Consequently, the risk is less of drawing a sample that leads to (false) acceptance of the hypothesis. *Other things being equal, the larger the size of the sample, the lower the probability of committing a Type II error.*

The regulation of sample size offers the simplest avenue of controlling risk of a Type II error. In Section 21.11, we will consider how to take account of β in selecting sample size for tests of hypotheses about means.

21.6 FACTORS AFFECTING TYPE II ERROR: (1) VARIABILITY OF THE MEASURE; (2) DEPENDENT SAMPLES

The previous section showed that increase in sample size reduced the risk of Type II error by reason of its action in reducing the standard error of the mean. Since the standard error of the mean is $\sigma/\sqrt{n}$, another way to make it smaller is to reduce the size of σ. At first glance, one might think that this is beyond the control of the investigator. Actually, this opportunity is often open, but advance planning is necessary.

The standard deviation of the set of measures reflects variation attributable to the factors we wish to study, but it also reflects variation attributable to extraneous and irrelevant sources. Any source of extraneous variation tends to increase σ over what it would be otherwise, so an effective effort to eliminate such sources will tend to decrease σ and thus reduce β. For example, measures in behavioral science (e.g. tests, ratings) suffer from inconsistency to some degree.† Some are really rather poor in this regard. Improving the reliability of the measuring instrument will have the effect of reducing σ, other things being equal.

In comparing means of two groups, the dependent sample design makes it possible to reduce the standard error of the difference by controlling the influence of extraneous variables. The effect is accomplished by pairing observations rather than by reducing σ_X or σ_Y, but the effect on β is the same. Comparison of the formula for the standard error of the difference between two correlated means, $\sigma_{\bar{X}-\bar{Y}} = \sqrt{\sigma_{\bar{X}}^2 + \sigma_{\bar{Y}}^2 - 2\rho\sigma_{\bar{X}}\sigma_{\bar{Y}}}$, with that of the difference between two independent means, $\sigma_{\bar{X}-\bar{Y}} = \sqrt{\sigma_{\bar{X}}^2 + \sigma_{\bar{Y}}^2}$, shows the statistical improvement that can be accomplished by this method. Some aspects of this advantage of the dependent samples design were considered in Section 17.12. Further consideration of the design will appear later in the present chapter.

---

†Inconsistency means "rubber in the yardstick," or, in its technical sense, unreliability of measurement.

21.7 FACTORS AFFECTING TYPE II ERROR: CHOICE OF LEVEL OF SIGNIFICANCE (α)

β is also related to the choice of α. In Figure 21.3, the illustration at the top shows the probability of accepting H_0 when it is false, and when $\alpha = .05$. The illustration at the bottom shows the identical situation, except that $\alpha = .01$. In both diagrams, the sample means represented by the shaded area in the distributions shown in solid outline are those that fall in the region of acceptance. The proportionate frequency of such means is greater when $\alpha = .01$ than when it is .05. There is, therefore, a greater chance of obtaining a sample mean that will lead to the false acceptance of H_0 when α is smaller. *In general, reducing the risk of a Type I error increases the risk of committing a Type II error.*

Recognition of the relationship between α and β is reflected in the change in research practice from that of 40 years ago. In the "old days," it was common to require that "z" $\geq \pm 3$ before declaring the hypothesis to be rejected. This "z" is so discrepant that it would occur less than three times in one thousand in a normal distribution. In current practice, it is common to reject the hypothesis when the

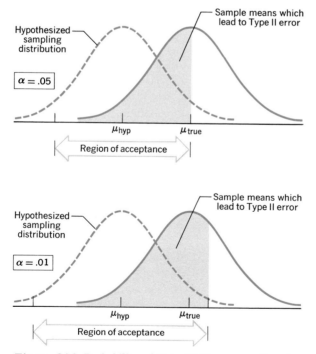

Figure 21.3 *Probability of Type II Error as a Function of α.*

discrepancy is so great that it would occur 5% of the time or less ($z_{crit} = \pm 1.96$), or 1% of the time or less ($z_{crit} = \pm 2.58$). The modern view is more satisfactory; it takes better account of the necessity of keeping Type II error under control, and still maintains an adequate watch over Type I error. Sometimes the older view is thought to be more "conservative," but it is now understood that conservatism in setting α is paid for by being a spendthrift with regard to β. See Section 16.4 for an earlier discussion of this point.

The primary consideration in selecting α should be, of course, the logic of the experiment, as discussed in Section 16.4. But unthinking conservatism in minimizing α will have an *unnecessarily* adverse influence on β.

21.8 FACTORS AFFECTING TYPE II ERROR: ONE-TAILED VERSUS TWO-TAILED TESTS

The risk of Type II error is affected by the choice of the alternative hypothesis. In conducting a one-tailed test of the hypothesis $H_0: \mu = \mu_{hyp}$ against the alternative $H_A: \mu > \mu_{hyp}$, H_0 is considered to be false (and therefore to be rejected) if and only if $\mu_{true} > \mu_{hyp}$. Figure 21.4 shows the test of H_0 when α is .05 and $\mu_{true} > \mu_{hyp}$. The two sets of diagrams represent identical test conditions except for the nature of

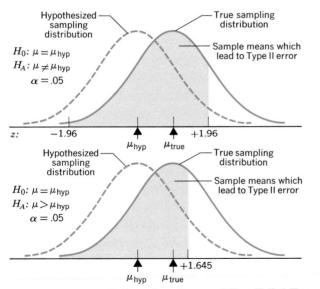

Figure 21.4 *Type II Error in a One- and Two-Tailed Test when $\alpha = .05$.*

the alternative hypothesis. When H_A is nondirectional, $z_{crit} = \pm 1.96$, and when H_A is directional, $z_{crit} = +1.645$. Compare the proportion of sample means leading to (false) acceptance of H_0 (the shaded area in the two figures). It is less for the one-tailed test. *Other things being equal, the probability of committing a Type II error is less for a one-tailed test than for a two-tailed test.*

The fact that a one-tailed test is more powerful (i.e. carries lower risk of Type II error) has sometimes been advanced in support of the proposition that one-tailed tests ought to be used more often. The position taken in this volume is that the choice of the alternative hypothesis ought to derive from the logic of the investigation. If that logic points to use of a one-tailed alternative, then the increase in power comes with it as an extra, or bonus benefit. See Section 16.3 for issues to be considered in making the choice.

21.9 SUMMARY OF FACTORS AFFECTING TYPE II ERROR

We found six factors that affect β, the probability of accepting H_0 when it is false:

1 The discrepancy between what is hypothesized and what is true: *the larger the discrepancy, the lower β*. The magnitude of this discrepancy is simply a fact of life; the experimenter has no control over it.

2 Sample size: *the larger sample size, the lower β*. This is the most important of all factors in controlling Type II error. The experimenter can choose the size he wants without having an adverse effect on other important considerations, and it is relatively easy to manipulate.

3 The standard deviation of the variable: *the smaller σ, the lower β*. The standard deviation can be reduced somewhat by improving the reliability of the measure, although usually the return is small for the effort expended.

4 Relation between samples (more than one mean): *dependent samples can lower β*. Choosing the dependent-samples design may have better potential for reducing β when comparing two (or more) means. In general, the higher the correlation induced by pairing, the stronger the effect on β. However, there are several problems with this design that do not characterize the independent-samples design. See Section 17.12 and, later in this chapter, Section 21.14.

5 The level of significance: *the larger the value of α, the lower β*. Although it would be possible to alter the choice of α in order to gain a desired value for β, it is a poor idea. α ought to be decided on its own merits and other means (see points 2 and 3 above) used to control β. The inverse relationship between α and β does remind us, however, of the danger of choosing an unnecessarily small value for α.

6 The choice of H_A: β is smaller for a one-tailed test that for a two-tailed test. Again, H_A is under control of the experimenter, but its choice ought to flow from the logic of the study, not from the desire to control β.

21.10 CALCULATING THE PROBABILITY OF COMMITTING A TYPE II ERROR

In this section we will learn how to calculate β. Now β can be calculated only when the true value of μ can be specified. Although this value is unknown, the ability to calculate β according to different possible values of μ_{true} allows us to see the consequences of testing hypotheses under various circumstances and thus to plan the test accordingly. The ability to perform these calculations provides the means of constructing tables or graphs from which one can determine the sample size required to keep β at a level of our own choosing. In the following section we will find tables of this kind and will learn how to use them.

Suppose the following hypothesis is to be subjected to examination:

$$H_0: \quad \mu_X = 80$$
$$H_A: \quad \mu_X \neq 80 \qquad \alpha = .05$$

If sample size is 25, and it is known that $\sigma = 20$, then $\sigma_{\bar{X}} = \sigma/\sqrt{n} = 4.00$. To test the hypothesis, we inquire as to the sampling distribution of means that occurs when

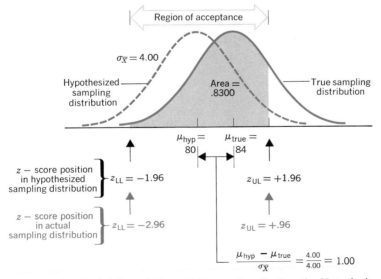

Figure 21.5 Probability of Type II Error when Testing the Hypothesis that $\mu = \mu_{hyp}$.

the hypothesis is true. This sampling distribution is shown in dotted outline in Figure 21.5. If, relative to this distribution, a sample mean is obtained that falls within the limits $z = \pm 1.96$, H_0 will be accepted.

Let us suppose that the hypothesis is false and further suppose that $\mu_{\text{true}} = 84$. In random sampling, the values of $\bar{X}$ actually obtained will follow the true sampling distribution, shown in solid outline in Figure 21.5. If the obtained sample mean is one of those shown in the shaded portion of this distribution, the decision will be to accept H_0: a Type II error will be committed. What is the probability of committing this error? It will be the probability of getting one of the means that falls in the shaded region of the true sampling distribution.

To find the area in the shaded portion of the curve, its boundaries must be expressed in z-score terms. We already know what the boundaries are in z-score terms *relative to the hypothesized population mean*: $z_{\text{LL}} = -1.96$ and $z_{\text{UL}} = +1.96$. But we must know what those z-score positions are in the true distribution. Note the magnitude, taken without regard for direction, of the difference between μ_{hyp} and μ_{true}; it is $|\mu_{\text{hyp}} - \mu_{\text{true}}| = 4.00$. Convert it to z-score units by dividing by $\sigma_{\bar{X}}$:

$$\frac{|\mu_{\text{hyp}} - \mu_{\text{true}}|}{\sigma_{\bar{X}}} = \frac{4.00}{4.00} = 1.00$$

We see that the lower boundary, which was 1.96 z-score units below μ_{hyp}, is $(1.96 + 1.00)$ units below μ_{true}. *Relative to the true distribution,* then, $z_{\text{LL}} = -2.96$. The upper boundary, 1.96 z-score units above μ_{hyp}, is $(1.96 - 1.00)$ units above μ_{true}. Its location, *relative to the true distribution,* is therefore $z_{\text{UL}} = +.96$. Finding the area between these boundaries may now be accomplished by the methods of Section 7.7, on the assumption of normality of the sampling distribution. The area between z_{LL} and the mean is .4985 and the area between the mean and z_{UL} is .3315, according to the table of areas under the normal curve. The sum of these two areas is .8300, the probability of obtaining a sample mean falling within the two boundaries, and is, therefore, β. The final phases of this solution are shown in Figure 21.6.

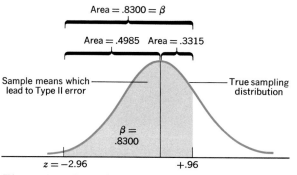

Figure 21.6 *Probability of Type II Error.*

In the calculations shown above, it was assumed that σ was known. When it must be estimated from the sample, the normal curve is only an approximate model, growing worse as sample size is reduced. Other models are available for these circumstances, but they cannot be considered here.

21.11 ESTIMATING SAMPLE SIZE FOR TESTS OF HYPOTHESES ABOUT MEANS

In testing hypotheses about means, convenience suggests the desirability of a small sample, but accuracy suggests a large one. Means of small samples vary widely from the mean of the population and so β, the probability of accepting a false hypothesis, is larger for small samples. But how large a sample is really needed? There is no point in taking a sample of 500 cases if 100 will do.

To answer this question, we must first decide what magnitude of discrepancy between the hypothesized value and the true value of the parameter is so great that, if one of this size or larger existed, we would want to be reasonably certain of discovering it. To put it another way, certain discrepancies are sufficiently small that if the hypothesis were (falsely) accepted, the error is one that we would be willing to overlook. For example, suppose a school principal tests the hypothesis that $\mu_{IQ} = 100$ for her population of school children. If she accepts that hypothesis when the mean IQ of the population is really 102, she might feel that the error was of no practical consequence. On the other hand, she would probably be quite unwilling to accept that hypothesis if the mean of the population were really 110.

Now it is fair to say that very likely *all* statistical hypotheses are false. The hypothesis is stated as a point value, and it is most unlikely, for example, that any real population has a mean IQ of *exactly* 100. *The value of hypothesis testing is that it can be used to reveal discrepancies that are large enough so that we care about them.* (See Section 16.6 for another discussion of "important" discrepancies.)

The decision as to just how big a discrepancy between the parameter's hypothesized value and its true value is important is fundamentally a substantive question and not a statistical one. It can be made only by a person who knows the meaning of a given discrepancy in the context of the question that gave rise to the study. If we can specify:

1 the magnitude of the *smallest* discrepancy that, if it exists, we wish to be reasonably sure of discovering and

2 the risk (β) we are willing to take of overlooking a discrepancy of that magnitude,

then the path lies open to determine the size of sample (or samples) that will be necessary.

For general use, it will be convenient to express the magnitude of this discrepancy in terms of the number of standard deviations of the measure under consideration. We shall refer to such a measure as d. For tests of hypotheses about single means:

$$d = \frac{\mu_{true} - \mu_{hyp}}{\sigma}$$

For tests of hypotheses about the difference between two means, *and on the assumption that* $\sigma_X = \sigma_Y = \sigma$:

$$d = \frac{(\mu_X - \mu_Y)_{true} - (\mu_X - \mu_Y)_{hyp}}{\sigma}$$

In each case, note that d expresses the discrepancy relative to the standard deviation of the set of measures, not to the standard error.

If $d = .5$, this means that the discrepancy between the true value and that hypothesized is one-half of a standard deviation of the variable measured. For example, for a common individual test of intelligence, mean IQ is 100, and the standard deviation is 16. If one were to decide that a discrepancy between μ_{true} and μ_{hyp} as large as eight IQ points should not be overlooked, then for this problem, $d = .5$. Table 21.1 presents information suited to one-tailed or two-tailed tests of hypotheses about single means for the two common levels of α, three levels of β, and several magnitudes of d. When these values are specified for the problem at hand, the table may be entered to find the required sample size.

Table 21.1 *Approximate Sample Size Required for Testing a Hypothesis about a Single Mean*

d	$\beta = .05$		$\beta = .10$		$\beta = .20$	
	$\alpha = .05$	$\alpha = .01$	$\alpha = .05$	$\alpha = .01$	$\alpha = .05$	$\alpha = .01$
			Two-Tailed Test			
1.50	8	12	7	10	6	9
1.00	15	22	13	19	10	15
.75	25	36	21	31	16	25
.50	55	74	43	64	34	51
.25	208	285	168	238	126	187
			One-Tailed Test			
1.50	7	10	6	9	5	7
1.00	13	19	10	16	8	13
.75	22	31	17	26	13	21
.50	46	65	36	54	27	42
.25	173	252	137	208	99	161

As an example of its use, suppose we have used the intelligence test described above and hypothesize that the mean IQ is 100. We have further decided on a two-tailed test and that if the true mean is as high as 108 or as low as 92, we wish to be quite certain of uncovering that discrepancy. Since the difference of eight IQ points is half of the standard deviation, $d = .5$. To guard against rejecting the hypothesis when it is true, we adopt $\alpha = .05$, and in order to be equally careful about accepting the hypothesis when it is false, we adopt $\beta = .05$. Entering the table with these values of α, β, and d, we find that 55 cases are required.

If the problem is that of testing the difference between two means, Table 21.2 is applicable. *Each* of the two samples must be of the size indicated. Entries in this table are based on the assumption that $\sigma_X = \sigma_Y$, that $n_X = n_Y$, and that the samples are independent. To find approximate sample size for a test between two dependent samples, find sample size from the table, multiply by $(1 - \rho)$, and increase this value by a few cases to compensate for the loss of degrees of freedom when ρ must be estimated from r.

For both tables, entries are derived on the assumption that populations of scores are normally distributed. Reasonable departure from this assumption will not seriously invalidate usage (see Sections 15.10 and 17.13). Both tables are appropriate when parameters such as σ must be estimated.†

† In both tables, values for $d = .25$ derive from the properties of the normal curve, others from the properties of noncentral t.

Table 21.2 *Approximate Sample Size Required for Testing a Hypothesis about the Difference between Two* Independent *Means*[a]

	$\beta = .05$		$\beta = .10$		$\beta = .20$	
d	$\alpha = .05$	$\alpha = .01$	$\alpha = .05$	$\alpha = .01$	$\alpha = .05$	$\alpha = .01$
			Two-Tailed Test			
1.50	14	20	12	17	9	14
1.00	28	40	23	34	18	27
.75	48	69	40	58	31	46
.50	106	150	87	125	66	100
.25	416	570	336	476	251	374
			One-Tailed Test			
1.50	11	17	9	15	7	12
1.00	23	34	19	29	14	23
.75	40	59	32	50	23	38
.50	90	130	71	108	51	85
.25	346	505	274	417	198	321

[a] The tabled values indicate required size for *each* of the two samples. It is assumed that $\sigma_X = \sigma_Y$ and that $n_X = n_Y$. For dependent samples, see text.

Frequently, studies are performed by setting the level of significance and then deciding intuitively on sample size. The tables above make possible a more rational approach to this problem. Using the tables, one decides on the maximum acceptable risk of committing a Type II error and then selects sample size accordingly. One practical defect in this approach is that σ must be known to determine accurately the value of d. Often a reasonable estimate can be made from results of other studies using the same variable, or from a pilot study. Or, in many instances it may be appropriate to "think in terms of σ units" directly, in which case the problem is avoided (see Section 6.14).

Tables 21.1 and 21.2 have been explained as useful in designing a study. They can also be used in the evaluation of adequacy of studies already reported. Obtain from the study information about α and sample size, and then select whatever value of β seems appropriate (perhaps .10). The tables may now be read to learn what value of d corresponds to these parameters. This will tell you what size of difference had a good chance of being discovered if it had existed. Suppose that a two-tailed test of the difference between two independent means had been conducted at the 5% level of significance and that each mean had been based on 40 cases. We turn to Table 21.2 and look at the top half of it, the part concerned with two-tailed tests. Looking in the column corresponding to $\beta = .10$ and $\alpha = .05$, we find that 40 cases per group corresponds to $d = .75$. Under the conditions of the test, a difference between μ_X and μ_Y of three-quarters of a standard deviation had a probability of $1 - \beta$, or .90, of being detected.

Extensive tables developed by Cohen permit much more fine-grained analysis than can be presented here.† They also provide similar analysis for other statistical indices, such as tests about correlation coefficients, proportions, and the like.

21.12 SOME IMPLICATIONS OF TABLE 21.1 AND TABLE 21.2

Close examination of the tables presented in the previous section points up a number of issues in experimental design. Some have been previously discussed in this chapter. To illustrate, reference is made to Table 21.1, in conjunction with the test of a single mean.

1 If it is satisfactory to discover a discrepancy only when it is large, fewer cases are required. In the first example of the previous section (single mean, two-tailed test, $\alpha = .05$, $\beta = .05$, $d = .5$), if it is required to reject the hypothesis only when the discrepancy is as great as 16 IQ points

† J. Cohen, *Statistical Power Analysis for the Behavioral Sciences*, rev. ed., Academic Press, New York, 1977.

($d = 1.00$), a sample of 15 cases would be adequate rather than one of 55 cases.

2 If it is important to discover a discrepancy as small as one-quarter of a standard deviation of the variable measured, sample size must be large. For the same circumstances as above, 208 cases are required.

3 If it is acceptable to increase the risk of a Type II error, smaller sample size is needed. If $\beta = .10$ is adequate (rather than $\beta = .05$) for the problem cited earlier, sample size of 43, rather than 55, will do the job.

4 If α is set at .01 rather than .05, a larger sample will be required to maintain the same protection level for β. For the problem cited, changing α from .05 to .01 means that 74 cases will be required, rather than 55.

5 If a one-tailed test is appropriate, a smaller sample will be required to maintain the same level of protection for β. In the same problem, if $H_A: \mu < 100$, rather than $H_A: \mu \neq 100$, a sample of 46 cases, rather than 55, will be required.

6 If the problem involves the difference between two means rather than a hypothesis about a single mean, approximately *twice* as many cases will be required in *each* of the two samples to achieve the same level of protection against committing a Type II error. Compare values in the two tables for equal values of α, β, and d.

21.13 THE EXPERIMENT VERSUS THE *IN SITU* STUDY

In the classic model of the experiment, all variables are controlled except the one subject to inquiry. The variable to be studied is then manipulated, and the effect on the variable under observation is then examined. For example, one may vary the form of motivation and observe its effect on speed of learning or length of retention. In an experiment, the variable subject to manipulation is called the *independent variable,* and that under observation is called the *dependent variable.*

The two primary characteristics of the experiment are (1) manipulation of the independent variable, and (2) control of extraneous factors. In the example above, the experimenter selects the kind of motivation and arranges conditions of the test so that if motivation does make a difference, its effect will not be clouded by group differences in kinds of subjects, learning task employed, circumstances of learning (other than motivation), etc.

In the basic two-group experiment, control may be achieved in a number of ways. One fundamental technique is to hold the condition of a possible interfering factor constant for every subject in the study. For example, the learning task should be the same for every subject in the learning study, irrespective of motivational treatment. In the study of the effect of vitamin A supplement on night vision that we have discussed from time to time, the fact that different subjects have different visual acuity *could* be controlled by accepting only subjects who have 20-20 vision. Note that there is an important price to be paid for seeking control in this manner: strictly speaking, conclusions from the learning study apply only to material of the specific type learned, and those from the vitamin A study would apply only to persons of 20-20 vision. In general, the tighter the control developed by holding many conditions constant, the more limited the generalization of the outcome.

Other means of control are possible. For example, the matched-groups design (see Section 17.12) equates subjects in the two groups on some characteristic, rather than holding the characteristic constant for all subjects. Randomization provides another most important source of control. It was considered in some detail in Section 17.8, and it would be worth rereading now. Random assignment of treatment condition achieves control over differences that subjects may bring to the study without limiting generalization in the way that would be done by holding these variables constant. Thus in the vitamin A study if subjects are assigned at random to the treatment condition, control is achieved over differences in visual acuity without limiting the full range of acuity normally present in the target population.

Although random assignment of treatment condition to subjects is a powerful experimental tool in controlling extraneous factors, it is no cure-all. It can take care of potentially interfering subject variables such as differences in learning aptitude, visual acuity, sex, ethnic background, educational background, age, reaction time, motivation, etc. But it cannot control certain other types of extraneous influence. Consider an experiment designed to evaluate the effectiveness of educational counseling of students who exhibit achievement deficiencies. Suppose 200 such students are identified, and they are divided at random into two groups, one of which receives counseling and the other does not. At the end of the semester, the mean grade point average of the two groups is compared. If the counseled group shows the better performance, it will not be clear whether that is owed to the specific counseling given, to the friendly interest of the counselor, or to the students' response to the fact that the college noticed what they were doing—or to some combination of these factors. Conducting the study as an experiment with random assignment of treatment conditions can be a great help in interpreting the meaning of the outcome of the statistical test, but it does *not* mean that the answer to the substantive question posed in the beginning is automatically provided by the statistical conclusion.

The significance of *adequate* control can not be overstressed. Only through such control is it possible to move from a statistical conclusion to a substantive conclusion without ambiguity. Statements of causal relationship, in the sense of asserting that certain antecedents lead to certain consequences, can be made with confidence only in such circumstances.

Many independent variables of potential interest are not subject to manipulation by the experimenter. Some are unmanipulable because we are unwilling to do so. For example, the effect of varying brain damage among human subjects must be studied by examining individuals to whom damage has occurred through injury or disease. Other variables are unmanipulable because they are inherent characteristics of the organism. Among such variables are stature, level of intelligence, ethnic group of origin, sex, and age. To study the effect of differences in such a variable, it may be possible to identify subpopulations possessing the desired differences. For example, to study the effect of differences in IQ on a particular learning task, the correlation between IQ and task performance may be obtained or subpopulations described as high IQ, medium IQ, and low IQ may be identified, sampled, and their mean performance on the learning task compared.

Studies in which the element of manipulation of the independent variable is absent cannot be called experiments. There is no universal name for this type of investigation; we may refer to them as *in situ* studies, in reference to the fact that the characteristic must be taken as we find it in the intact individual.† The important difference between experiment and *in situ* study is that in the latter, a significant degree of control is lost. This loss of control makes it more difficult to interpret the outcome of such studies. For example, suppose we learn that 50% of female chemistry majors marry, whereas 90% of female home economics majors do so. It is completely unjustified to conclude that marital practice is owed to differential educational experience. What about factors of personality, interest, and intellect which led these women to these educational paths? Had it been possible to assign women at random to the two majors, interpretation of the outcome of the study would be clearer.

When individuals are selected according to differences that they possess in the variable we wish to investigate, such as difference in college major in the example just cited, they inevitably bring with them associated differences in other dimensions. If differences in these extraneous dimensions are related to the dependent variable, we may well find that the different "treatment" groups are significantly different with regard to the dependent variable, but the origins of these differences may be so entangled that it is extremely difficult or even hopeless to sort them out. In short, it is most difficult to develop statements of causal relationship in studies of this type.

This is not to say that *in situ* studies are worthless. Some of the most important empirical questions are not approachable in any other way, and there are many instances in which such studies have made important contributions to knowledge. Advancement of knowledge through *in situ* studies often calls upon the highest degree of substantive knowledge and the most skillful devising of investigatorial tactics.

† *In situ* is pronounced: in sy-too, where "sy" rhymes with "try."

21.14 HAZARDS OF THE DEPENDENT SAMPLES DESIGN

Comparison between means of dependent samples was introduced in chapter 17. Because of its frequent use in psychology and education, and because a number of hazards are involved in its application, it deserves more detailed consideration. Some of the advantages and disadvantages of this design were considered in Sections 17.12. The present development assumes that background; review may be desirable.

Application and interpretation of the matched pairs design is straightforward when used as an adjunct to the experiment; a single population is sampled, matched pairs of subjects are formed, and the treatment conditions are randomly assigned to the two members of each pair. If matching has been on a variable strongly related to the observation being recorded (the dependent variable), the standard error of the difference between the two means will be smaller, and the power of the test will be increased (see Section 21.6).

Trouble begins when the design of the study departs from these conditions. Three problem situations may be identified.

1 Pairs of observations are formed by repeated observations on the *same* subjects. Assignment of treatment condition is random with regard to the two trials for a given subject.

When repeated measurements are made on the same subjects, it is possible that exposure to the treatment condition assigned *first* may change the subject in some way that will affect his performance on the treatment condition assigned *second*. An influence of this sort is called an *order effect*. Practice, fatigue, and change in set or attitude are examples of such influences. When an order effect is present *and* it can be assumed that the influence of one treatment upon the other is the same as that of the other upon the one, the outcome of the experiment may be interpretable, if treatment condition has been assigned at random with regard to order of treatment. However, the disturbing order effect will introduce an additional source of variation in each set of scores, according to the magnitude of its influence. This tends to increase the standard error and consequently to decrease the power of the test. The purpose of choosing the dependent-data design is ordinarily to *reduce* extraneous error, but the effect may be quite opposite. If the influence of one treatment upon the other is *not* the same as that of the other upon the one, *bias will be introduced* as well as unwanted variation. The outcome then becomes difficult or impossible to interpret. For example, if the two treatment conditions are mild and heavy shock, a subject receiving heavy shock first may have a different outlook toward the second trial than one who receives mild shock first.

2 Pairs of observations are formed by repeated observations on the *same* subjects. Assignment of treatment condition to the two trials for a given subject is nonrandom. (This design is typical of "growth" studies of the same subjects.)

If the design utilizes repeated observations on the same subjects but assignment of the treatment condition is not random with regard to order, we are in even graver difficulty. Any order effect will bias the comparison. In many investigations, it is not possible to avoid this problem. For example, it occurs in studies where the object is to determine what change has taken place in subjects over a period of time. Is a particular type of psychotherapy effective? The subjects' condition may be evaluated before and after therapy, and the results compared. "Before" and "after" can not be randomly assigned to a subject. The results of comparison are, of course, ambiguous. If there is improvement, is it the result of therapy, the person's belief that he is *supposed* to feel better, the mere fact that someone paid attention to him, or simply a natural recovery that would have taken place without therapy? To be meaningful, the study must include a comparison group, chosen in the same way and treated alike except for the therapy to be evaluated.

Studies of this type may also be subject to another source of bias: the *regression effect*. If subjects are selected *because* of their extreme scores on some measure, we expect remeasurement on the same variable to yield scores closer to the mean. Discussion of this effect and an illustration of it will be found in Section 12.5, but read section 12.4 first for the necessary background.

   3 The two groups consist of *different* subjects matched on an extraneous but related variable. Assignment of treatment condition to members of a matched pair is nonrandom.

These conditions are likely to arise when studying the effect of a nonmanipulable variable in intact groups. For example, one may wish to compare attitude test score of men and women who have been matched for level of education, or to compare personality characteristics of delinquent and nondelinquent children matched on parents' socioeconomic level. Such investigations fall in the category of *in situ* studies, described in the last section. They are open to all of the difficulties described there. There are several additional hazards:

   1 Matching may reduce, and therefore obscure, the influence of other important variables associated with the variable on which matching took place.

   2 When the two intact populations differ widely on the matching variable, it may be possible to form matched pairs only from among those in one group who have low scores on the matching variable and those in the other group who have (among members of that group) relatively high scores on the matching variable. Under these conditions, any conclusion reached will be generalizable only to peculiarly constituted subgroups of

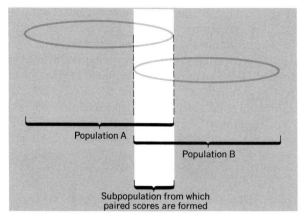

Figure 21.7 *Restriction of Generalization Resulting from Matching in Discrepant Populations.*

the two target populations. The restriction of generalization is diagrammed in Figure 21.7.

3 When subjects are selected for pairing because of their extreme scores on the matching variable, a regression effect may be expected. This is likely to occur in studying two intact populations that differ widely on the matching variable. Suppose we wish to compare the effect of educational counseling on mentally retarded students with that on students of normal intelligence, and decide to match subjects on achievement test score. To form matched pairs, students from the mentally retarded population will be selected *because* they have (relatively) high achievement test scores, and students from the normal population *because* they have (relatively) low achievement test scores. Since they were selected because of their extreme scores, a regression effect may be expected. If their achievement were remeasured, we would expect lower scores in the mentally deficient group and higher scores in the normal group. To the extent that this mismatch affects the outcome of counseling, bias has been introduced.

This section has touched upon some, but not all, of the problems in dependent analysis. A most comprehensive and valuable analysis of this problem may be found in the work of Campbell and Stanley.† Their treatment not only covers analysis of dependent samples, but considers systematically many problems of experimental design and is highly recommended to those who wish to explore this important matter. Two other useful works are those by Kerlinger and by Van

---

†D. T. Campbell and J. C. Stanley, "Experimental and Quasi-experimental Designs for Research on Teaching," in: N. L. Gage, ed., *Handbook of Research on Teaching,* Rand McNally & Co., Chicago, 1963.

Dalen.† Although the approach of all of these authors is oriented primarily to problems of design of educational research, their message is just as important for those engaged in psychological research.

21.15 THE STEPS OF AN INVESTIGATION

An outline of the role of applied statistics was developed early in this book (Section 1.6). There we considered the difference between a substantive question (Is reaction time the same for red and green light stimuli?) and a statistical one (Does $\mu_{red} = \mu_{green}$?), and the difference between a statistical conclusion and a substantive one. We also saw how statistical procedures were an intermediate part of an investigation. Now that we have learned so much more about the nature of statistical procedures, it is time to return to that overall picture and examine it at a more sophisticated level than was possible earlier.

Figure 21.8 shows the typical steps in the development of an inquiry in behavioral science. The rectangular boxes at the left show the progression in general terms, from the general body of knowledge back to the general body of knowledge again at the end. To the right of each of these boxes and connected to them by a straight line are brief statements that could represent this phase in a particular study of learning and retention.

Between the rectangular boxes appears a description representative of the kinds of actions that must be taken and questions that must be answered to provide the specifics required by the first of the boxes and to progress to the second of the boxes. These are listed by numbers: ① through ⑤. Notice the word "representative"; it is not possible to list all considerations that must be taken into account. Many of the statements or questions identified here involve not just a single step, but the interaction between factors characterizing one step and those pertaining to another. In some cases statements or questions have been underlined. These identify considerations that particularly demonstrate the interplay of statistical and substantive concerns.

Next, note that between the rectangular boxes appears a reminder that some form of judgment is required at each step. Statistical calculations, once one has learned how to do them, follow a "formula" that can be laid out in a simple sequence of cookbook instructions. But at its very best, that gets us from the statistical question to the statistical conclusion. In all other steps in the progression (and to some extent in the one just mentioned), judgment based on knowledge of

---

† F. N. Kerlinger, *Foundations of Behavioral Research*, Holt, Rinehart and Winston, Inc., New York, 1973, Part 6. D. B. Van Dalen, *Understanding Educational Research*, 3rd ed., McGraw-Hill Co., New York, 1973.

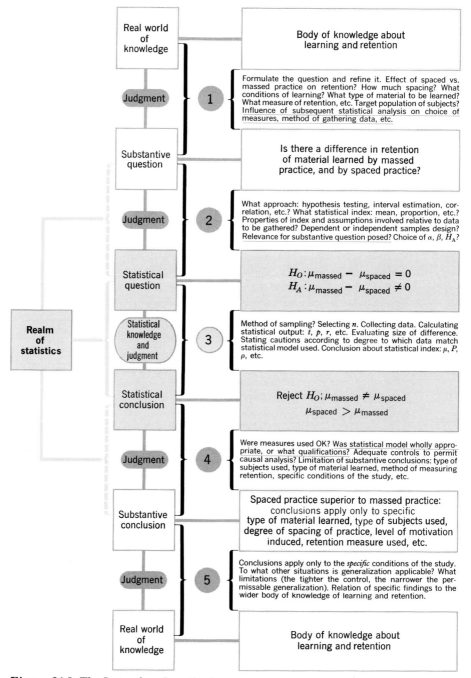

Figure 21.8 *The Steps of an Investigation.*

the substantive discipline and the logic of inquiry enter in most importantly. This reminds us that statistical procedures do not carry automatic authority but serve as merely one step in the chain.

Finally, note that the realm of statistics is indicated at the extreme left of the figure. Its central domain begins with the formulation of the statistical question and continues through the production of the statistical conclusion. Nevertheless, statistical considerations are important to take into account in moving from the substantive question to the statistical question, and again in moving from the statistical conclusion to the substantive one.

Much more deserves to be said about the steps of inquiry in behavioral science. The references cited in the previous section are particularly recommended for those who wish to study this matter more deeply. In closing, however, there are two important matters that must be mentioned here.

The first concerns attribution of causality. In the statistical conclusion of a study, we may be informed that mean performance is different for the two groups studied. But in moving to the substantive conclusion, we want to know *why* that difference occurred. The fact that a difference has occurred does not inform us as to the reason for it. It will not be clear that the difference in experimental conditions imposed upon the two groups is responsible for the difference *unless adequate controls exist*. The discussion in Section 21.13 and that concerning causation in Section 10.1 are particularly pertinent here.

Second, a few words about generalization. As indicated at ⑤ in Figure 21.8, the substantive conclusions apply, strictly speaking, only to the *particular* circumstances characterizing the study. See ① in that figure for examples of such specification. The problem in generalizing to other types of subjects, kinds of material learned, and conditions of learning is a serious one, because (again strictly speaking) it is necessary to demonstrate that the difference between the characteristics of the situation in which the study was conducted and those of the situation to which we wish to generalize would make no difference—a tall order indeed. Here is where great experience with the variables concerned can be most important in suggesting what can be safely ventured and what cannot.

The general (and ideal) model for the two-group comparison developed in this book is founded on the concept of drawing two random samples from a fully defined population and treating one group one way and the other another. In practice we are seldom so blessed but instead take a convenient group in hand and divide these subjects at random into two treatment groups. The first procedure is properly designated *random sampling,* and the recognized term for the second is *randomization.*† Now *both* techniques serve the purpose of experimental control, as described in Sections 17.8 and 21.13. But the result of random sampling may properly be generalized to the defined target population, whereas the outcome of a study using randomization applies *only* to the kind of subjects represented in the

---

†We confess that these terms have been used loosely up to now.

study. If these were subjects chosen for reasons of convenience and availability, they will not represent a truly relevant population but rather constitute a *hypothetical population* (see Section 15.11). In that case, the possibilities for wider generalization may be quite limited.

PROBLEMS AND EXERCISES

Identify:

Type I error	order effect
Type II error	regression effect
power of the test	d
independent variable	$1 - \beta$
dependent variable	random sampling
experiment	randomization
in situ study	

1 Give an example illustrating the difference between a substantive hypothesis and a statistical hypothesis.

Data 21A

$$H_0: \mu = 80.0 \qquad \sigma = 20.0$$
$$H_A: \mu \neq 80.0 \qquad n = 100$$

2 With regard to Data 21A, (a) If $\alpha = .05$ and $\mu_{true} = 81.0$, what is β? (b) If $\alpha = .05$ and $\mu_{true} = 82.0$, what is β?

3 With regard to Data 21A, (a) If $\alpha = .05$ and $\mu_{true} = 83.0$, what is β? (b) If $\alpha = .01$ and $\mu_{true} = 83.0$, what is β?

4 With regard to Data 21A, (a) If $\alpha = .05$ and $\mu_{true} = 82.0$, what is β? (b) If $\alpha = .05$, $\mu_{true} = 82.0$, but $\sigma = 10.0$, what is β?

5 With regard to Data 21A, (a) If $\alpha = .05$ and $\mu_{true} = 84.0$, what is β? (b) If $\alpha = .05$, $\mu_{true} = 84.0$, but $H_A: \mu > 80.0$, what is β?

6 A school research director notes that the norm for an eighth-grade reading test is 80.0. He would like to know whether his eighth-grade students may be considered to perform at this level, or whether they differ. He feels that the risk of making a Type I error should be .05, and that a risk of .10 of making a Type II error would be acceptable. From the data of the norm group, he estimates that the standard deviation of reading test scores is 12.0, and he feels that if the mean of his students is 6 points (or more) away from the norm, it would be important to know it. (a) State the hypothesis and the alternative hypothesis appropriate to his interest. (b) What sample size should he select to test this hypothesis?

7 In reference to Problem 6, what should sample size be if the research director felt that: (a) The risk of a Type II error should be .05? (b) It was important to know it if the mean of his students was 3 points (or more) away from the norm? (c) He would take

action only if his students were significantly below the norm. (Consider the three parts of this question to be independent.)

8 A psychologist wonders whether midsemester warning notices improve performance. She decides to select a sample of delinquent students and, at random, to send such notices to half of them and no notice to the other half. Experience suggests that among such delinquent students, $\sigma_{gpa} = .30$. She decides to adopt $\alpha = .05$, and $\beta = .05$. If the difference between warned and unwarned students is as great as .075 grade point, she would want to know it. (a) State the hypothesis and the alternative hypothesis appropriate to her interest. (b) What should the size of each sample be to test this hypothesis?

9 In reference to Problem 8, what should sample size be if the psychologist felt that: (a) She should choose $\alpha = .01$ and $\beta = .20$? (b) It was important to know it if the difference between the means was .15 point (or more)? (c) It was only desired to discover if the warning system were different from the nonwarning system, rather than superior to it? (Consider the three parts of this question to be independent.)

10 A community center for psychotherapy is so busy that it must turn away many applicants. It decides to evaluate its therapy program and divides applicants at random into two groups: those accepted for therapy and those who are not. At the end of 10 weeks all members of both groups are evaluated, and the "mental health" of the two groups is compared. (a) Name several variables that would be controlled by random assignment to the two groups. (b) Name several variables that would *not* be controlled.

11 Explain why using the paired samples design and reducing unreliability of the measuring instrument have the same effect on β. What *is* the effect?

12 In a nondirectional test of the difference between two independent groups of 20 cases each and using $\alpha = .05$, no significant difference was found. How big a difference (approximately) would there have had to be for it to have a probability of .8 to be discovered by this test?

CHAPTER 22

In chapters 17 and 19 we learned how to test the hypothesis of no difference between two means. This procedure is of great importance because it provides a statistical model for evaluating the outcome of the two-group investigation, the most basic weapon in the researcher's arsenal. For example, in the simplest form of the classic experiment, two groups are treated differently and examined with regard to the variable under observation to discover if the difference in treatment had an effect.

What if we wish to know about the relative effect of three or more different "treatments"? Does color of a light stimulus make a difference in speed of reaction time? We should want to use more than two colors in examining this question. Is there a difference in effectiveness among three methods of conducting psycho-

Elementary Analysis of Variance

therapy? Among five different genetic strains of rats available for laboratory use, is there a difference in speed of learning?

In each of these examples, the *t* test of the difference between two means could be pressed into service, making comparisons among each possible combination of two means. This method is inadequate in several ways. Consider the example involving five strains of rats. First, there must be ten tests of difference if each strain is to be compared with each of the others. Second, in any one comparison, use is made only of the information provided by the two groups compared; the remaining groups contain information that could make the tests stronger. Third, with so many tests, there is an increased likelihood of declaring that a difference exists among one or more of the comparisons when in fact there is no difference. Fourth, when the ten tests are completed, there are only ten bits of information but not a single, direct answer as to whether, taken as a whole, there is evidence of difference in performance among the five kinds of animals.

To provide a better answer in the face of these problems, we turn to *analysis of variance,* originally developed by the late Sir Ronald A. Fisher. Analysis of variance is a powerful aid to the investigator. It enables him to design studies more efficiently, to generalize more broadly, and to take account of the complexities of interacting factors. Analysis of variance is actually a class of techniques, designed to aid in hypothesis testing; entire volumes have been written about the subject. In this chapter, we shall develop its details only in its two simplest forms. The first is appropriate to the problems posed earlier in this section; it is variously called *simple analysis of variance, one-way analysis of variance,* or the *completely randomized design.* We shall consider it in the next few sections. The second is a form of the *factorial design,* and may be called *two-way analysis of variance.* Its consideration is begun in Section 22.11.

To follow the discussion of this chapter, certain background is needed. Particularly important is a basic understanding of sampling distributions (chapters 13 and 14) and hypothesis testing (chapters 15 and 16). Specific topics of pertinence, which you may wish to review, include:

1 the concept of variance (Section 6.5)

2 calculation of $\Sigma(X - \bar{X})^2$ (Section 6.7)

3 s^2 as an estimate of σ^2 (Section 16.10)

4 degrees of freedom in a variance estimate (Sections 19.4 and 19.8)

5 independent samples (Section 17.4)

6 t test of the difference between two means (Section 19.8)

7 homogeneity of variance (Sections 19.8 and 19.14)

8 Type II error (Section 16.7).

22.2 ONE-WAY ANALYSIS OF VARIANCE: THE HYPOTHESIS

In the test of the difference between two means, there were two treatment conditions, and comparison was made of the difference between their means. In one-way analysis of variance there are k treatment conditions, where k may be 2 *or some larger number.* At the conclusion of the analysis, comparison may be made among the means of the several treatment conditions. In the development to follow, we shall use the term *subgroup* to identify those individuals subject to a particular treatment condition. These individuals may constitute a sample or perhaps a population, depending on what we wish to talk about. Thus we may speak of k subgroups, k subgroup sample means, or k subgroup population means.

One-way analysis of variance is very closely related to the t test of the difference between two *independent* means. In fact, the outcome of analysis of variance applied to the special case of two subgroups is identical with that of the t test. The *t* test, therefore, may be thought of as a special case of one-way analysis of variance, or, conversely, one-way analysis of variance may be considered as an extension of the *t* test between independent groups to problems involving more than two groups. Like the *t* test, the analysis of variance is suited to samples of any size.

In one-way analysis of variance, subjects are assigned *independently* and *at random* to the *k* treatment conditions. The several treatment conditions may be identified by letters such as *D, E, F, . . .* and the subgroup population means as μ_D, μ_E, μ_F, . . . If the different treatment applied to the subgroups has no differential effect on the variable under observation, then we may expect these subgroup population means to be equal. To inquire as to whether variation in treatment made a difference, we therefore test the null hypothesis:

$$H_0: \mu_D = \mu_E = \mu_F = \cdots$$

against the alternative that they are unequal in some way. In testing the hypothesis of no difference between *two* means, a distinction was made between directional and nondirectional alternative hypotheses. Such a distinction no longer makes sense when the number of subgroups exceeds two. In the multigroup analysis of variance, H_0 may be false in any one of a number of ways. For example, two or more subgroup means may be alike while the remainder differ, all may be different, etc.

22.3 THE EFFECT OF DIFFERENTIAL TREATMENT ON SUBGROUP MEANS

Suppose three subgroups of ten cases each have been selected independently and at random and that differential treatment has been applied. If the difference in treatment has no effect, the distribution of scores in the three subgroups might appear as shown on the next page in Figure 22.1. Note that:

1 μ_D, μ_E, and μ_F all have the same value.
2 The subgroup sample means vary to some extent about the subgroup population means.
3 Scores vary about their subgroup sample means, and to a similar extent in each subgroup.

The second and third points are in accord with what we have learned about the influence of random sampling variation.

Now suppose that the three treatments *did* have a differential effect. In this case, the distribution of scores in the three subgroups might appear as shown in Figure 22.2. By inspection, we note the following:

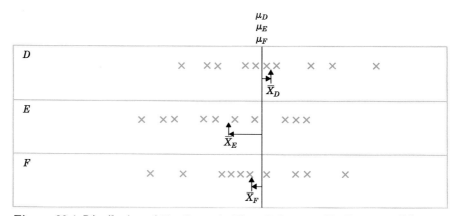

Figure 22.1 *Distribution of Ten Scores in Three Subgroups: No Treatment Effect.*

1 μ_D, μ_E, and μ_F have different values.

2 The subgroup sample means vary about their subgroup population means and to an extent similar to that above. However,

3 *Variation among subgroup sample means is substantially greater than when there was no difference among subgroup population means.*

4 Scores vary about their subgroup sample means and to an extent similar to that above.

A key to inquiry about the possible differential effect of the three treatments lies in the amount of variation shown among the several subgroup sample means. Of course, we would not expect $\bar{X}_D$, $\bar{X}_E$, and $\bar{X}_F$ all to have the same value even when $\mu_D = \mu_E = \mu_F$. These means are subject to random sampling variation. But how

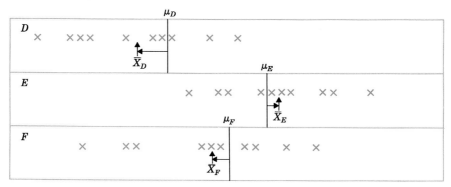

Figure 22.2 *Distribution of Ten Scores in Three Subgroups: Treatment Effect Present.*

much variation is expected when the subgroup population means are equal? Fortunately, we have ways of finding out.

If there is no treatment effect, $\mu_D = \mu_E = \mu_F$, and we may treat the three samples as though they came from the same population. Remember that the standard error of the mean measures the amount of variation expected among means of random samples drawn from the same population. If $\mu_D = \mu_E = \mu_F$, we should find the actual variation of our three sample means to be similar, within limits of random sampling fluctuation, to that predicted by the standard error of the mean. On the other hand, if the three subgroup population means are unequal, we should find greater variation among the three sample means. If variation among the subgroup means is so great as to be unlikely to occur when the null hypothesis is true, we will want to reject that hypothesis.

22.4 MEASURES OF VARIATION: THREE SOURCES

The comparison we are after could be conducted quite satisfactorily along the lines developed in the previous section. However, the traditional procedures of analysis have followed a slightly different viewpoint, although one wholly consonant with the reasoning of the previous section. We shall follow this viewpoint because of its universality and because it is more adaptable when one considers advanced forms of the analysis of variance.

Study of the examples of the last section reveals three situations in which an index of variability might be obtained. They are:

1 Variability of the scores about the mean of all scores. This will be reflected by the deviation: $(X - \bar{\bar{X}})$ where $\bar{\bar{X}}$ is the grand mean of all scores.

2 Variability of scores about their subgroup sample means. This will be reflected by the deviation: $(X - \bar{X})$, where $\bar{X}$ is the mean of the subgroup that contains X.

3 Variability of subgroup sample means about the grand mean of all scores. This will be reflected by the deviation: $(\bar{X} - \bar{\bar{X}})$.

The last two are of particular importance in analysis of variance. *Variability of scores within each subgroup is of interest because it is a measure of inherent variation, free from the influence of differential treatment which may affect the several groups.*† Within a given subgroup, all subjects receive the *same* treatment, so differences among scores cannot be attributed to differential treatment.

---

† In analysis of variance, variance of this kind is sometimes called *error variance.*

Variability of subgroup sample means, an *among*-groups contrast, is also of interest, because it reflects *two* sources of variation:

1 *Inherent variation,* free from the influence of treatment effect.

2 Variation attributable to differences between subgroup population means, if any, and therefore *variation attributable to treatment effect, if any.*

We need to develop (1) a measure of variation that reflects only inherent variation, and (2) a measure that reflects inherent variation plus treatment effect, if present, and (3) a means of comparing the two measures. If the subgroup population means are equal, we will expect the two sources of variability to yield measures of the same order, but if not, the measure reflecting treatment effect should be larger. In the next section we develop the two measures of variability and in Section 22.9 the method for comparing them.

22.5 WITHIN-GROUPS AND AMONG-GROUPS VARIANCE ESTIMATES

True to its name, analysis of variance is concerned with the *variance* as a measure of variability. You will remember (Section 6.5) that the variance of a set of scores is the square of the standard deviation. Thus, σ^2 is the variance of a population of scores, and $\sigma_{\bar{X}}^2$ is the variance of the sampling distribution of means. It is also important to know that an unbiased estimate of a population variance is made by calculating the sum of the squares of the deviations of each score from the sample mean, and *dividing by the number of degrees of freedom associated with that sum of squares* (see Section 19.8). This general relationship can be summarized by the equation

$$s^2 = \frac{SS}{df}$$

where the letters SS stand for "sum of squares (of deviation scores)."

We will use the symbol σ^2 to mean the variance inherent in the population of scores, *free from the influence of treatment effect*. In the example of Section 22.3, an estimate of σ^2 could be made from any one of the three subgroups by taking the sum of the squares of the deviations of scores in that group from the subgroup mean and dividing by the appropriate number of degrees of freedom. However, on the assumption that the subgroup population variances are the same for all subgroups (the *assumption of homogeneity of variance*), a better estimate may be made by combining information from these several subgroups. Following the line of thought first described in Section 19.8, such an estimate may be made by pooling the sums of squares of deviation scores from the several subgroups and dividing by the sum of the degrees of freedom characterizing each of the subgroups. This estimate is called the *within-groups variance estimate;* we shall symbolize it by s_W^2. Formula 22.1 shows this variance estimate in deviation score form:

Within-Groups Variance Estimate $s_W^2 = \dfrac{SS_W}{df_W} = \dfrac{\sum(X_D - \bar{X}_D)^2 + \sum(X_E - \bar{X}_E)^2 + \cdots}{(n_D - 1) + (n_E - 1) + \cdots}$ (22.1)

where: X_D is a score in subgroup D, etc.
$\quad\quad\;\; \bar{X}_D$ is the mean of subgroup D, etc.
$\quad\quad\;\; n_D$ is the number of elements in subgroup D, etc.

The numerator of this expression is called the *within-groups sum of squares* (SS_W) and the denominator the *within-groups degrees of freedom* (df_W).

Another estimate of σ^2 is required, one that will reflect influence of the treatment effect (if any) as well as inherent variation. A variance estimate that reflects both of these influences can be formed by finding the deviation of each of the k subgroup means from the grand mean of the combined distribution, squaring each deviation, summing the squares, and dividing that sum by $k - 1$, the number of degrees of freedom associated with that sum of squares:†

$$\frac{\sum\limits^{k}(\bar{X} - \bar{\bar{X}})^2}{k - 1}$$

But this formula estimates *variance of means,* whereas s_W^2 estimates *variance of scores.* The two measures can be directly compared *only* if they are in the same terms, so we need a way of converting the measure of means to a measure of scores.

Such a conversion can be developed from the (estimated) standard error of the mean, $s_{\bar{X}} = s_X/\sqrt{n}$. Squaring both sides of this equation we have: $s_{\bar{X}}^2 = s_X^2/n$. Solving this equation for s_X^2, it reads:

$$s_X^2 = ns_{\bar{X}}^2$$

If we substitute our measure of variance of subgroup means for $s_{\bar{X}}^2$ in the equation immediately above, we obtain the desired estimate of variability of scores. This estimate is called the *among-groups variance estimate* and is symbolized by s_A^2.‡ When the subgroups are of equal size, the formula for this estimate, in deviation score form, is:

Among-Groups Variance Estimate: Subgroups of Equal Size $s_A^2 = \dfrac{SS_A}{df_A} = n\dfrac{\sum\limits^{k}(\bar{X} - \bar{\bar{X}})^2}{k - 1}$ (22.2)

---

†The mean of the combined distribution of scores is also the mean of the subgroup means.
‡It is also common to refer to s_W^2 and s_A^2 as *mean squares* and to symbolize them MS_W and MS_A. We shall continue to use the former designations in this chapter.

where: $\bar{X}$ is the mean of a subgroup

$\bar{\bar{X}}$ is the mean of the combined distribution of scores (grand mean)

k is the number of subgroups

n is the number of scores in each subgroup

The numerator of this formula is called the *among-groups sum of squares* (SS_A).

If there is no treatment effect, the subgroup sample means will tend to cluster about $\bar{\bar{X}}$ as predicted by the standard error of the mean, and s_A^2 will be an unbiased estimate of inherent variation, σ^2. It will, therefore, estimate the same quantity as that estimated by s_W^2. On the other hand, if there is a treatment effect, the sum of squares of the deviations of the $\bar{X}$'s about $\bar{\bar{X}}$ will tend to be larger, and s_A^2 will tend to be larger than s_W^2.

The formula above is appropriate when n, the number of scores in a subgroup, is the same for all subgroups. When sample size differs among subgroups, the appropriate formula is:

Among-Groups Variance Estimate:
Subgroups of Unequal Size
$$s_A^2 = \frac{\sum\limits_{}^{k} n_i(\bar{X}_i - \bar{\bar{X}})^2 \dagger}{k - 1} \qquad (22.3)$$

where: n_i is the number of scores in the ith subgroup and $\bar{X}_i$ is the mean of the ith subgroup.

To calculate the numerator of Formula 22.3, find the deviation of the subgroup mean from $\bar{\bar{X}}$, square it, and multiply by the number of cases in the subgroup. When this is done for each subgroup, sum the k products so obtained.

22.6 PARTITION OF SUMS OF SQUARES AND DEGREES OF FREEDOM

To complete the analysis of variance, we require a means of comparing s_W^2 and s_A^2. But first, it will be instructive to work a simple example, showing the procedure for finding these two variance estimates. The example will not only help to make the procedure more concrete but will demonstrate two rather surprising and useful facts.

Suppose there are three treatment groups, D, E, and F, and that the first consists of three scores while the others are comprised of two scores each.‡ The scores in each group are shown in the table at the top of the next page.

---

†$\Sigma n_i(\bar{X}_i - \bar{\bar{X}})^2$ means: $n_D(\bar{X}_D - \bar{\bar{X}})^2 + n_E(\bar{X}_E - \bar{\bar{X}})^2 + \cdots$
‡The number of scores will serve for explanatory purposes but is too small for practical work.

$$\bar{X} = 6 \quad \begin{array}{l} \bar{X}_D = 6 \\ \bar{X}_E = 7 \\ \bar{X}_F = 5 \\ \end{array} \quad \begin{array}{ccc} D & E & F \\ 3 & 4 & 2 \\ 5 & 10 & 8 \\ 10 & & \end{array}$$

First, calculate the mean of each subgroup and the mean of all scores combined. These values are shown at the left of the table. Next, calculate

$$SS_W = \Sigma(X_D - \bar{X}_D)^2 + \Sigma(X_E - \bar{X}_E)^2 + \cdots$$
$$= [(3 - 6)^2 + (5 - 6)^2 + (10 - 6)^2]$$
$$+ [(4 - 7)^2 + (10 - 7)^2] + [(2 - 5)^2 + (8 - 5)^2] = 62$$

Then calculate:

$$df_W = (n_D - 1) + (n_E - 1) + \cdots$$
$$= (3 - 1) + (2 - 1) + (2 - 1) = 4$$

Finally, calculate:

$$s_W{}^2 = \frac{SS_W}{df_W} = \frac{62}{4} = 15.5$$

Similarly, calculate

$$SS_A = \sum^{k=3} n_i(\bar{X}_i - \bar{\bar{X}})^2$$
$$= 3(6 - 6)^2 + 2(7 - 6)^2 + 2(5 - 6)^2 = 4.0$$

Then calculate

$$df_A = (k - 1) = (3 - 1) = 2$$

And finally:

$$s_A{}^2 = \frac{SS_A}{df_A} = \frac{4.0}{2} = 2.0$$

These two estimates are all that is needed to conduct the analysis of variance. But we remember from Sec. 22.4 that a third estimate is possible, one made from the deviation of each score from the mean of all scores. Such an estimate could be formed by dividing the *total sum of squares:*

Total Sum of Squares
$$SS_T = \sum^{\substack{\text{all} \\ \text{scores}}} (X - \bar{\bar{X}})^2 \qquad (22.4)$$

by the number of degrees of freedom associated with it:

$$df_T = \sum^{k} n_i - 1$$

Now this variance estimate is of no use in analysis of variance, for reasons we shall learn in Sec. 22.9. But it will prove to be instructive to calculate the total sum of squares:

$$SS_T = \sum^{\substack{\text{all} \\ \text{scores}}}(X - \bar{\bar{X}})^2$$
$$= (3 - 6)^2 + (5 - 6)^2 + (10 - 6)^2 + (4 - 6)^2 + (10 - 6)^2$$
$$+ (2 - 6)^2 + (8 - 6)^2 = 66$$

and

$$df_T = \sum^{k} n_i - 1$$
$$= (3 + 2 + 2) - 1$$
$$= 6$$

In our example, $SS_W = 62$, $SS_A = 4$, and $SS_T = 66$, the sum of the first two values. This relationship holds in *any* analysis of variance: *the within-groups sum of squares plus the among-groups sum of squares equals the total sum of squares:*

$$SS_T = SS_W + SS_A$$

In our example, $df_W = 4$, $df_A = 2$, and $df_T = 6$, the sum of the first two values. This relationship also holds in *any* analysis of variance: *the number of degrees of freedom associated with SS_W plus the number of degrees of freedom associated with SS_A equals the number of degrees of freedom associated with SS_T:*

$$df_T = df_W + df_A$$

These are the characteristics that give rise to the name, analysis of variance. The sum of squares that contributes to total variance, and the number of degrees of freedom, may be analyzed, or partitioned, into component parts, each attributable to different sources. Proof of these two equalities is given in the Note at the end of the chapter.

In analysis of variance, it is convenient to present a summary table indicating source, and the corresponding sum of squares, degrees of freedom, and variance estimate. Such a table is shown in Table 22.1. One advantage of such a table is that it shows the basic result of the analysis very clearly. Another is that it makes clear that the several sums of squares add to equal the total sum of squares and that the several degrees of freedom add to equal the total number of degrees of freedom. Note that the table does not show the useless s_T^2.

22.7 RAW SCORE FORMULAS FOR ANALYSIS OF VARIANCE

So far, we have discussed analysis of variance in terms of sums of squares of deviation scores. This approach helps to see what is happening. When the goal is

Table 22.1 *Table of Analysis of Variance, Showing the Partition of Sums of Squares and Degrees of Freedom*

Source	df	SS	(MS) s^2
Among Groups	2	4.00	2.00
Within Groups	4	62.00	15.50
Total	6	66.00	

ease of computation rather than understanding, raw score formulas are more practical than those expressed in deviation scores. The raw score formulas for SS_W, SS_A, and SS_T appear below:

Within-Groups Sum of Squares: Raw Score Formula

$$SS_W = \sum^{\substack{\text{all}\\\text{scores}}} X^2 - \left[\frac{\left(\sum X_D\right)^2}{n_D} + \frac{\left(\sum X_E\right)^2}{n_E} + \cdots \right] \tag{22.5}$$

Among-Groups Sum of Squares: Raw Score Formula

$$SS_A = \left[\frac{\left(\sum X_D\right)^2}{n_D} + \frac{\left(\sum X_E\right)^2}{n_E} + \cdots \right] - \frac{\left(\sum^{\substack{\text{all}\\\text{scores}}} X\right)^2}{\sum n_i} \tag{22.6}$$

Total Sum of Squares: Raw Score Formula

$$SS_T = \sum^{\substack{\text{all}\\\text{scores}}} X^2 - \frac{\left(\sum^{\substack{\text{all}\\\text{scores}}} X\right)^2}{\sum n_i} \tag{22.7}$$

SS_W and SS_A yield the desired variance estimates when divided by the appropriate number of degrees of freedom:

Within-Groups Variance Estimate
$$s_W^2 = \frac{SS_W}{\sum (n_i - 1)} \tag{22.8}$$

Among-Groups Variance Estimate
$$s_A^2 = \frac{SS_A}{k - 1} \tag{22.9}$$

where: n_i is the number of cases in the ith subgroup and k is the number of subgroups.

According to Formulas 22.5 and 22.6, the basic quantities which require computational labor are (1) the sum of the squares of all the scores, (2) the sum of all the scores, and (3) the sum of the scores in each subgroup. It is easy to arrange computational routine to find the third quantity as part of the procedure of finding the second.

We may apply these formulas to the problem of the previous section, by way of illustration. Once again, the distribution of scores:

D	E	F
3	4	2
5	10	8
10		

$$SS_W = 3^2 + 5^2 + 10^2 + 4^2 + 10^2 + 8^2$$
$$- \left[\frac{(3 + 5 + 10)^2}{3} + \frac{(4 + 10)^2}{2} + \frac{(2 + 8)^2}{2} \right]$$

$$= 318 - 256 = 62$$

$$SS_A = \frac{(3 + 5 + 10)^2}{3} + \frac{(4 + 10)^2}{2} + \frac{(2 + 8)^2}{2}$$
$$- \frac{(3 + 5 + 10 + 4 + 10 + 2 + 8)^2}{3 + 2 + 2}$$

$$= 256 - 252 = 4$$

Note that the values obtained for SS_W and SS_A are exactly the same as those obtained by the deviation score formulas in the previous section.

It is easier to see what number of degrees of freedom corresponds to each sum of squares when working with deviation scores than when working with raw scores. For reference, let us summarize:

$$df_W = \sum (n_i - 1)$$
$$df_A = k - 1$$
$$df_T = \sum n_i - 1$$

where: n_i is the number of cases in the ith subgroup and k is the number of subgroups.

In the problem illustrated above, these values are: $df_W = 4$, $df_A = 2$, and $df_T = 6$.

22.8 **THE *F* DISTRIBUTION**

To compare the two estimates, s_W^2 and s_A^2, we must consider the probability distribution of the *F* ratio, a statistic named in honor of R. A. Fisher. *F* is formed by the ratio of two unbiased estimates of σ^2, the population variance.

F Ratio $$F = s_1^2/s_2^2 \qquad\qquad (22.10)$$

The tabled values of *F* describe the distribution of *F* when:

1 The population of scores is normally distributed.

2 Two sample estimates, s_1^2 and s_2^2 have been made of the same population variance, σ^2.

3 The scores comprising each estimate have been selected at random from the population.

4 The two estimates are independent.

If these conditions have been met, *F* will have the distribution characteristics given in Table H, in Appendix F. To use this table, we enter it with the number of degrees of freedom associated with the estimate appearing in the numerator of *F*, and the number of degrees of freedom associated with the estimate appearing in the denominator. Like the *t* distribution, the *F* distribution is actually a family of curves, depending on the number of degrees of freedom associated with the variance estimates. The distribution of *F* is shown in Figure 22.3 for 4 degrees of freedom in the numerator and 20 degrees of freedom in the denominator.

Note that this distribution is skewed positively. This is intuitively reasonable. If two estimates are made of the same value (σ^2), the estimate placed in the numerator

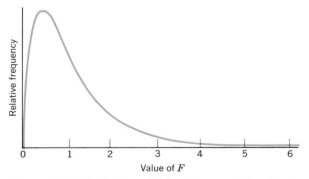

Figure 22.3 *Distribution of F for 4 Degrees of Freedom in the Numerator and 20 Degrees of Freedom in the Denominator. From* Statistical Inference *by Helen M. Walker and Joseph Lev. Copyright 1953 by Holt, Rinehart and Winston, Inc. Reprinted by permission of Holt, Rinehart and Winston, Inc.*

may be smaller than that in the denominator, in which case F will be less than 1.00, but not less than zero. But if the estimate placed in the numerator is larger than that in the denominator, the F ratio may be much larger than 1.00.

22.9 COMPARING s_W^2 AND s_A^2 ACCORDING TO THE F TEST

From the analysis of variance of the data of our sample (Section 22.6), we have two estimates of σ^2: s_W^2 and s_A^2. We form them into an F ratio:

$$F_{calc} = \frac{s_A^2}{s_W^2} = \frac{2}{15.5} = .13$$

Now s_A^2 estimates variance inherent in the scores plus variance attributable to treatment differences (if any), whereas s_W^2 estimates only variance inherent in the scores. If the assumptions have been satisfied *and there is no treatment effect*, both s_A^2 and s_W^2 estimate the same quantity, σ^2, and F_{calc} will be distributed as F_{tabled}. If, on the contrary, there is a treatment effect, this will tend to inflate s_A^2, and F_{calc} will be larger than otherwise.

To test the hypothesis that $\mu_D = \mu_E = \mu_F$, we must compare the calculated value of F with the values of F which would occur through random sampling if the hypothesis were true. Now *if s_A^2 is always placed in the numerator of F, as is customary, the hypothesis of equality of subgroup population means will be rejected only if the calculated value of F is* larger *than expected.* Consequently, the region of rejection is placed entirely in the *upper* tail of the F distribution. In our example, there were 2 degrees of freedom associated with s_A^2 and 4 degrees of freedom associated with s_W^2. Turn to Table H, and locate the entries corresponding to $df = 2$ in the numerator and $df = 4$ in the denominator.† Assuming that we wish to adopt the 5% significance level, the critical value of F is 6.94. This is the value of such magnitude that it would be equalled or exceeded but 5% of the time in random sampling when the hypothesis is true. Beyond this value, therefore, lies the region of rejection, as shown in Figure 22.4. It is clear that the obtained value of $F = .13$ lies much below that critical value, and the null hypothesis will be accepted.

We are now in a position to appreciate why F is calculated from s_A^2 and s_W^2 rather than involving s_T^2 in some way. Recall from Section 22.8 that the numerator and denominator of F must consist of *independent* estimates. The two estimates that we use *are* independent if samples have been selected at random from a normally distributed population, but neither of these estimates is independent of s_T^2.

The calculations for one-way analysis of variance are summarized in Table 22.2.

---

† Be sure to keep straight which df characterizes the numerator and which the denominator. Note that tabled entries are not the same for 4 and 2 df as they are for 2 and 4 df.

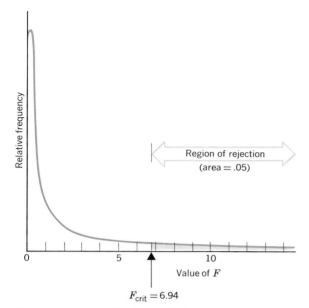

Figure 22.4 *Distribution of F for 2 and 4 Degrees of Freedom.*

This table duplicates the information of Table 22.1, except that the calculated and critical values of F are now shown. The critical value of F is obtained from Table H, in Appendix F, according to the degrees of freedom characterizing the numerator and denominator of F_{calc} and level of significance (α) chosen. Since F_{calc} is smaller than F_{crit}, the hypothesis that $\mu_D = \mu_E = \mu_F$ cannot be rejected.

   The rather low value of F brings up a point of interest. To what are we to attribute a very *low* value of F? If the assumptions are correct, a low F simply means that the subgroup means are closer together than might ordinarily be expected. Other possibilities include error in the calculations or selection of the wrong model of analysis of variance.

Table 22.2 *Outcome of the One-Way Analysis of Variance*

Source	df	SS	s^2	Calc'd value of F	Crit. value of F ($\alpha = .05$)
Among Groups	2	4.00	2.00	$F = s_A^2/s_W^2 = .13$	6.94
Within Groups	4	62.00	15.50		
Total	6	66.00			

22.10 REVIEW OF ASSUMPTIONS

Several assumptions have been mentioned as necessary for the analytic model presented to be entirely correct. We collect them here for purposes of review:

1 The subgroup populations are normally distributed.

2 Samples are drawn at random.

3 Selection of elements comprising any subgroup is independent of selection of elements of any other subgroup.

4 The variances of the several subgroup populations are the same for all subgroups (homogeneity of variance).

As with the *t* test for independent means, moderate departure from conditions specified in the first and fourth requirements will not unduly disturb the outcome of the test. Resistance to such disturbance is enhanced when sample size rises. In any event, tiny samples are hardly worth while because of the substantial risk of committing a Type II error. If there is a choice, it is desirable to select samples of equal size for the subgroups. This will make computation a little simpler, minimize the effect of failing to satisfy the condition of homogeneity of variance, and, for a given Σn_i, minimize the probability of committing a Type II error.

The most troublesome problem is probably that of obtaining random samples. Attention is called to an earlier discussion of this problem in Section 15.11.

The third assumption (independent samples) reminds us that the analysis described in this chapter is not appropriate for repeated measures on the same subjects nor when matched subjects have been assigned to treatment groups. Other techniques of analysis of variance are designed to handle problems of this sort.

When samples are quite small and there is serious question about the assumption of normality, one possible alternative is the Kruskal-Wallis nonparametric one-way analysis of variance. See chapter 24 (Section 24.5).

22.11 TWO-WAY ANALYSIS OF VARIANCE

One analysis of variance design, a step up in complexity, permits the simultaneous study of the effect of two types of treatment conditions. For example, we may wish to study the relative legibility of type using different styles of type and different amounts of illumination. Suppose we decide to use three styles of type and two degrees of illumination. In analysis of variance, an independent variable (such as style of type) is known as a *treatment*, and the varied conditions of an independent variable are known as *levels* of that treatment. Thus in the example above, there are two treatments—style of type and amount of illumination; the first treatment has three levels, and the second has two. It is common to refer to a study of this kind as

Table 22.3 *Two-Way Analysis of Variance: Sample Subgroup Means*

Level of illumination	Style of type		
	A	*B*	*C*
High	$\bar{X} = 33$	$\bar{X} = 40$	$\bar{X} = 33$
Low	$\bar{X} = 23$	$\bar{X} = 35$	$\bar{X} = 8$

a "3 × 2" (read 3 *by* 2) design. Each of the two treatments represents a separate question, and a possible interaction between the two can be assessed as a third question.

With our 3 × 2 design, there are six combinations of type style and illumination level. To begin, we assign *at random,* say, 15 subjects to each of the six possible treatment combinations. Table 22.3 illustrates the six means that might result. We now consider the three questions that this design permits us to study. First, it is possible to inquire whether style of type made a difference in the legibility score. There is greater generality to the outcome of this test than if it were conducted in the form of a "basic" experiment. In a basic experiment, illumination would be fixed at some arbitrarily chosen level, and the conclusions would apply only to situations characterized by *that* level of illumination. In this experiment, conclusions are not so restricted.

Second, it is possible to inquire whether level of illumination made a difference in the subjects' legibility score. Once again, the conclusions are broader than if a study of the effect of illumination had been conducted using only a single type style. Another benefit of this design now appears: we have been able to answer *two* questions for the price of *one.* If the two questions had been conceived separately, and a one-way analysis of variance conducted (each based on the same number of observations), *twice* the number of observations would have been required.

Third, we are able to examine a new and important question, one that can not be answered by the simple *t* test or by the one-way analysis of variance: *whatever the difference among the several styles of type, is it the same for both levels of illumination?* In analysis of variance, this question is referred to as one of *interaction* effect, and an *F* can be calculated to test for interaction. If the test for interaction is significant, it means that differences attributable to styles of type are *not* the same for both levels of illumination. This can be illustrated more clearly by graphic representation of the several subgroup means, as shown in Figure 22.5. In this figure, straight lines connect those subgroup means characterized by a particular level of illumination. According to Figure 22.5, it appears that legibility is somewhat improved by greater illumination irrespective of style of type. However, if the effect of level of illumination were the *same* for all type styles, we would expect the two lines to be parallel (within limits of random sampling fluctuation). This does not seem to

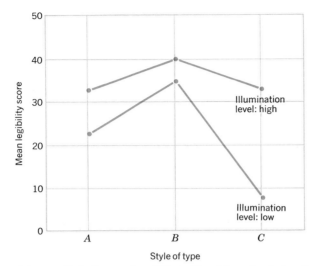

Figure 22.5 *Interaction Effect: Two-Way Analysis of Variance.*

be the case.† Specifically, type style C appears especially to suffer under the condition of low illumination.

In general, the question of interaction between two treatments may be phrased this way: *Whatever the difference among the several levels of one treatment, is it the same for each of the levels of the other treatment?* Earlier, we phrased the question of interaction, "Whatever the difference among the several styles of type, is it the same for both levels of illumination?" But the question could, with equal validity, be stated: "Whatever the difference between the two levels of illumination, is it the same for each of the three styles of type?" In some studies it will appear better to look at the question one way rather than the other; try both ways to decide.

This question of interaction of factors is easy to overlook when the approach is through the design of the basic experiment, but it is obviously very important. As a further example, suppose that teaching method A has been shown superior to teaching method B among fast learners. Will the same superiority of method hold for slow learners? The question is one of interaction of method and learning ability.

22.12 THE PROBLEM OF UNEQUAL NUMBER OF SCORES

In one-way analysis of variance, it is quite possible to assign a different number of subjects to the several levels of the treatment, although certain advantages follow

---

†In effect, the *F* test for interaction examines the question of whether the two lines depart significantly from a parallel relationship.

when the number of subjects is the same for each level. These advantages were described in Section 22.10.

The question of keeping the number of cases equal is more critical in two-way analysis of variance. In most cases, if the number of cases per cell is unequal, adjustments will have to be made to the data before proceeding. These adjustments may reduce the power of the test or may require some new assumptions that cannot easily be verified. They will all require more work, although that factor can be counteracted by using commonly available computer packages that have adjustment routines. *The best advice, then, is to be sure to assign an equal number of cases* when more than one treatment is involved in analysis of variance. The procedures described in the sections that follow are based on the assumption that there are an equal number of cases per cell.

Despite one's best effort in this regard, it occasionally happens that one or more subjects will be lost from the study. Perhaps an animal died from unknown causes or a human subject fell out of the study as a result of measles or the flu. *If you feel sure that the reason for the loss is unrelated to the treatment condition,* then one of the adjustment procedures will be in order. A good elementary discussion of these procedures is given by Linton and Gallo, and more advanced discussion appears in books by Kirk and by Winer.†

Unfortunately, it sometimes appears that there is differential loss from the several combinations of treatment levels that can be attributed to the particular conditions of the study. For example, if some conditions are more burdensome on the subject (perhaps some conditions require the subject to return several times), we may find that there is greater loss of subjects under these particular conditions. If so, it is reasonable to think that perhaps the subjects who *did* participate are, as a group, more highly motivated and more cooperative than those who participated in other treatment conditions. There is, of course, no statistical adjustment that can rectify this problem.

22.13 A PROBLEM IN TWO-WAY ANALYSIS OF VARIANCE

Analysis of variance (of whatever type) is often referred to by a contraction of its name: *ANOVA*. We shall use this term from time to time. Now let us begin the step-by-step development of two-way analysis of variance. Remember that we always assign *an equal number of cases to each combination of treatment conditions.*

---

†M. Linton and P. S. Gallo, Jr. *The Practical Statistician: Simplified Handbook of Statistics,* Brooks/Cole Publishing Company, Monterey, Cal., 1975.
R. E. Kirk, *Experimental Design: Procedures for The Behavioral Sciences,* Brooks/Cole Publishing Company, Monterey, Cal., 1968.
B. J. Winer, *Statistical Principles in Experimental Design,* 2nd ed., McGraw-Hill Book Company, Inc., New York, 1971.

In a learning experiment, we may want to know whether there is a difference in performance among three kinds of motivation and also whether there is a difference between two conditions of practice. The table below shows the 12 scores that might be obtained in such a study, if two subjects were assigned at random to each of the six possible combinations of kind of motivation and condition of practice.† We shall designate the three conditions of motivation as C_1, C_2, and C_3, (column effect), and the two conditions of practice as R_1 and R_2 (row effect).

Kind of Motivation

		C_1	C_2	C_3
Condition	R_1	4,4	2,3	8,6
of Practice	R_2	6,8	5,4	10,13

In what is to follow, we shall use the following symbolism:

X: scores in general

X_{C_i}: scores in the ith column

X_{R_i}: scores in the ith row

$\bar{X}_{C_i}$: mean of the ith column

$\bar{X}_{R_i}$: mean of the ith row

$\bar{\bar{X}}$: mean of all scores

We will develop four variance estimates:

s_{WC}^2 (*within-cells estimate*), derived from the discrepancy between scores within each cell. This measure is of interest because it is free from the influence of possible differences between columns (column effect), possible differences between rows (row effect), and also any interaction effect, if present. It therefore measures only inherent variation, and is analogous to s_W^2 in one-way ANOVA.

s_C^2 (*column estimate*), derived from the differences between column means. If the difference in kind of motivation has no effect, then $\mu_{C_1} = \mu_{C_2} = \mu_{C_3}$, and variation among column means ($\bar{X}_{C_1}$, $\bar{X}_{C_2}$, and $\bar{X}_{C_3}$) will be affected only by inherent variation. Under these circumstances, s_C^2 will estimate the same quantity estimated by s_{WC}^2. If there is a difference among kinds of motivation, s_C^2 will tend to be larger than otherwise. It is therefore analogous to s_A^2 in one-way ANOVA.

† The number of cases is too small for a practical study but will serve to illustrate the calculations involved.

$s_R{}^2$ (*row estimate*), derived from the differences between row means. If the difference in condition of practice has no effect, then $\mu_{R_1} = \mu_{R_2}$, and variation among row means ($\bar{X}_{R_1}$ and $\bar{X}_{R_2}$) will be affected only by inherent variation. It is therefore just like $s_C{}^2$, except that it is sensitive to row effect rather than to column effect.

$s_{R \times C}{}^2$ (*interaction estimate*), derived from the discrepancy between the means of the several cells and the values predicted for each on the assumption of no interaction at the population level.† If there is no interaction, $s_{R \times C}{}^2$ will be responsive only to inherent variation and will estimate the same quantity estimated by $s_{WC}{}^2$. If interaction is present, $s_{R \times C}$ will respond to it and will therefore tend to be larger.

Each of three variance estimates, $s_C{}^2$, $s_R{}^2$, and $s_{R \times C}{}^2$, is responsive (1) to the presence of the effect for which it is named (column effect, row effect, and interaction effect), and (2) to inherent variation. $s_{WC}{}^2$, *on the other hand, is responsive only to inherent variation.* When the three estimates are at hand, F's may be formed by placing each in turn in the numerator and $s_{WC}{}^2$ in the denominator. A significantly large F will then serve as an indicator of the presence of the effect specially associated with the kind of estimate placed in the numerator.

22.14 PARTITION OF THE SUM OF SQUARES FOR TWO-WAY ANOVA

In two-way analysis of variance, we divide the total sum of squares (SS_T) into four components:

$$SS_T = SS_C + SS_R + SS_{R \times C} + SS_{WC}$$

where: SS_T is the total sum of squares, generated from the deviation of each score from the mean of all scores, $(X - \bar{\bar{X}})$

SS_C is the sum of squares for columns, generated from the deviation of each column mean from the mean of all scores, $(\bar{X}_{C_i} - \bar{\bar{X}})$

SS_R is the sum of squares for rows, generated from the deviation of each row mean from the mean of all scores, $(\bar{X}_{R_i} - \bar{\bar{X}})$

$SS_{R \times C}$ is the sum of squares for interaction, generated from the deviation of each cell mean from the value predicted for that cell on the assumption of no interaction

SS_{WC} is the sum of squares within cells, generated from the deviation of each score from its cell mean, $(X - \bar{X}_{\text{cell}})$

---

† It is customary to read $R \times C$ as R *by* C; thus we speak of the "row by column interaction."

This time, we will bypass the deviation score formulas, since the raw score formulas are more practical for computation.

SS_T is calculated in the same way as for one-way ANOVA:

Total Sum of Squares

$$SS_T = \sum_{\substack{\text{all} \\ \text{scores}}} X^2 - \frac{\left(\displaystyle\sum_{\substack{\text{all} \\ \text{scores}}} X \right)^2}{n_{\substack{\text{all} \\ \text{scores}}}} \tag{22.7}$$

SS_C is calculated from the column totals and the grand total:

Column Sum of Squares

$$SS_C = \frac{\left(\sum X_{C_1} \right)^2}{n_{C_1}} + \frac{\left(\sum X_{C_2} \right)^2}{n_{C_2}} + \cdots - \frac{\left(\displaystyle\sum_{\substack{\text{all} \\ \text{scores}}} X \right)^2}{n_{\substack{\text{all} \\ \text{scores}}}} \tag{22.11}$$

Similarly, SS_R is calculated from the row totals and the grand total:

Row Sum of Squares

$$SS_R = \frac{\left(\sum X_{R_1} \right)^2}{n_{R_1}} + \frac{\left(\sum X_{R_2} \right)^2}{n_{R_2}} + \cdots - \frac{\left(\displaystyle\sum_{\substack{\text{all} \\ \text{scores}}} X \right)^2}{n_{\substack{\text{all} \\ \text{scores}}}} \tag{22.12}$$

SS_{WC} is calculated from the individual scores and from the cell totals:

Within Cells Sum of Squares

$$SS_{WC} = \sum_{\substack{\text{all} \\ \text{scores}}} X^2 - \sum_{\substack{\text{all} \\ \text{cells}}} \left[\frac{\left(\displaystyle\sum_{}^{\text{cell}} X \right)^2}{n_{\text{cell}}} \right] \tag{22.13}$$

The second half of the last expression means that we are to find the total of the scores in a given cell, square it, and divide by the number of cases in the cell. Repeating this operation for each cell, the resultant quantities are summed and that sum is subtracted from ΣX^2. It is really rather easier than it sounds. Let us illustrate with the data of the table in the previous section:

$$SS_T = 4^2 + 4^2 + 6^2 + 8^2 + \cdots + 13^2$$

$$- \frac{(4 + 4 + 6 + 8 + \cdots + 13)^2}{12} = 110.92$$

$$SS_C = \frac{(4 + 4 + 6 + 8)^2}{4} + \frac{(2 + 3 + 5 + 4)^2}{4} + \cdots$$

$$- \frac{(4 + 4 + 6 + 8 + \cdots + 13)^2}{12} = 68.17$$

$$SS_R = \frac{(4 + 4 + 2 + 3 + 8 + 6)^2}{6} + \frac{(6 + 8 + 5 + 4 + 10 + 13)^2}{6}$$
$$- \frac{(4 + 4 + 6 + 8 + \cdots + 13)^2}{12} = 30.09$$

$$SS_{WC} = 4^2 + 4^2 + 6^2 + 8^2 + \cdots + 13^2$$
$$- \left[\frac{(4 + 4)^2}{2} + \frac{(6 + 8)^2}{2} + \frac{(2 + 3)^2}{2} + \cdots \right] = 9.50$$

Since the several components (SS_C, SS_R, $SS_{R \times C}$, and SS_{WC}) sum to equal SS_T, we may most easily find $SS_{R \times C}$ by subtraction:

$$SS_{R \times C} = SS_T - (SS_C + SS_R + SS_{WC})$$
$$= 110.92 - (68.17 + 30.09 + 9.50)$$
$$= 3.16$$

Be sure to check your calculations; an error anywhere along the line will also cause an error in $SS_{R \times C}$. And remember that a negative sum of squares (!) is impossible; it results from an error in calculation.

22.15 DEGREES OF FREEDOM IN TWO-WAY ANALYSIS OF VARIANCE

The total number of degrees of freedom also may be divided into components associated with each sum of squares:

$$df_T = df_C + df_R + df_{R \times C} + df_{WC}$$

In counting degrees of freedom, we shall let C equal the number of columns, R equal the number of rows, and n_{WC} equal the number of scores within each cell. Since there are C deviations involved in the computation of SS_C, $df = C - 1$; similarly, $df_R = R - 1$. In computing SS_{WC}, we consider the deviation of each score in the cell from the cell mean. Consequently, each cell contributes $n_{WC} - 1$ degrees of freedom, and

$$df_{WC} = \overset{\substack{\text{all} \\ \text{cells}}}{\sum} (n_{WC} - 1)$$

Computation of SS_T involves as many deviations as there are scores, or $(R)(C)(n_{WC})$ of them; consequently, df_T is one less than this number. Finally, $df_{R \times C} = (R - 1)(C - 1)$. Applying this information to the present problem, we have:

$$df_C = (C - 1) = 2$$
$$df_R = (R - 1) = 1$$
$$df_{R \times C} = (R - 1)(C - 1) = 2$$

$$df_{WC} = \sum (n_{WC} - 1) = 6$$

$$df_T = (R)(C)(n_{WC}) - 1 = 11$$

Note that the degrees of freedom for the first four components sum to 11, the number of degrees of freedom accorded to SS_T.

22.16 COMPLETING THE ANALYSIS

To complete the analysis, each variance estimate (s^2) is calculated by dividing each component sum of squares by the number of degrees of freedom associated with it, as in one-way ANOVA. Then, the three F's are calculated by dividing s_C^2, s_R^2, and $s_{C \times R}^2$, by s_{WC}^2. The resultant values are shown in Table 22.4.

We now turn to the tabled values of F (Table H, in Appendix F) to learn what magnitude must be reached or exceeded to declare significance. We shall assume that $\alpha = .05$ has been selected for all tests. Since the F for column effect and the F for interaction have 2 df associated with the numerator and 6 df associated with the denominator, the critical value of F is 5.14. The F for row effect has 1 and 6 df associated with it, and the critical value is 5.99. These values are shown at the far right in Table 22.4. The obtained F's for column effect and row effect both exceed their critical values; consequently, the hypotheses that $\mu_{C_1} = \mu_{C_2} = \mu_{C_3}$ and that $\mu_{R_1} = \mu_{R_2}$ are rejected. The obtained F for interaction, on the other hand, is not significant.

To return to the substantive problem, the analysis gives reason to believe that the differences in motivation (column effect) made a difference in performance and that the difference in condition of practice also made a difference in performance. The nonsignificant outcome of the test for interaction means that there are no grounds for believing that the relative effect of the three kinds of motivation differed between the two practice conditions, or, if we wish to put it the other way around, that there are no grounds for believing that the relative effect of the two conditions of practice differed among the three motivational conditions.

Table 22.4 *Outcome of the Two-Way Analysis of Variance*

Source	df	SS	s^2	Calcd. value of F	Crit. value of F ($\alpha = .05$)
Columns	2	68.17	34.09	$F = s_C^2/s_{WC}^2 = 21.58$	5.14
Rows	1	30.09	30.09	$F = s_R^2/s_{WC}^2 = 19.04$	5.99
Columns × rows	2	3.16	1.58	$F = s_{R \times C}^2/s_{WC}^2 = 1.00$	5.14
Within cells	6	9.50	1.58		
Total	11	110.92			

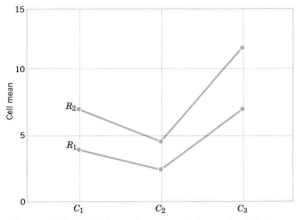

Figure 22.6 *Cell Means for a 2 × 2 Analysis of Variance: Data from Section 22.13.*

22.17 STUDYING THE OUTCOME OF TWO-WAY ANOVA

If the outcome of any of the three F tests is significant, it will generally be useful to calculate the several cell means and study them. To see what is going on, these may be cast in a table, as in the earlier example shown in Table 22.3, or, even better, in graphic form, as in Figure 22.5. For the present problem, Figure 22.6 shows the six cell means. The line labeled R_1 shows the means for the R_1 condition of practice under the several kinds of motivation (C_1, C_2, and C_3). The line labeled R_2 shows the means for the R_2 condition of practice under the same circumstances. This figure shows that one condition of practice was consistently superior to the other. Similarly, we see that there were differences in performance according to the several levels of motivation employed. The nonsignificant interaction component is reflected by the fact that the two lines are reasonably parallel.

In any event, look carefully at the means and their relationship to one another to see if the results make sense. If they don't, the first step is to hunt for possible computational error.

22.18 INTERACTION AND THE INTERPRETATION OF MAIN EFFECTS

The column effect and the row effect are called *main effects*. In our example, the tests for both main effects were significant. Interpretation of such an outcome is

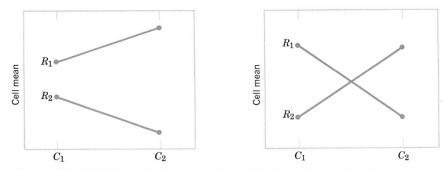

Figure 22.7 *Cell Means for 2 × 2 Analysis of Variance: Interaction Present.*

clear when there is no interaction. However, when interaction is present, the meaning of tests for main effects may be clouded. Consider Figure 22.7, which shows two possible outcomes in which significant interaction is present in a 2 × 2 analysis of variance. In the first part of this picture (at the left), it is apparent that one row condition (R_1) results in rather higher scores than the other. At the same time, it appears that the difference between R_1 and R_2 is greater under the condition C_2 than under C_1.

The second part of Figure 22.7 shows an interesting possibility. The average effect of R_1 (under condition C_1 and C_2) is not different from the average effect of R_2, a fact that would be reflected by a nonsignificant F in the test for row effect. Similarly, the average effect of C_1 (under conditions R_1 and R_2) is not different from the average effect of C_2. At the same time, the nonparallel lines show the strong interaction effect that is present. According to the data, high performance may be expected when R_1 occurs in combination with C_1 *or* when R_2 occurs in combination with C_2.

A hypothetical situation may help in understanding the meaning of such a finding. Suppose we wish to compare the effectiveness of two teachers and of two teaching methods. It might be that one teacher is quite effective when using one method and not so effective when using the other, whereas just the reverse is true for the other teacher.

It should be clear that it is particularly important to study the several values of the cell means when the test for interaction is significant. As Figure 22.7 shows, the meaning of the outcome of the tests for main effects is highly dependent on the particular nature of the interaction effect.

22.19 ALTERNATIVES TO THE GENERAL *F* TEST FOR A TREATMENT EFFECT

In analysis of variance, the overall F test for a treatment examines the hypothesis of no difference among population means of all subgroups of the treatment. Often it is more interesting to inquire about the difference between certain subgroup means than to ask the one overall question. For example, suppose we want to compare the effectiveness of these three methods of instruction: lecture, lecture + movie, and lecture + audio tape. It would make sense to construct two comparisons: (1) lecture v. the average of the two methods that use supplementary material, and (2) lecture + movie v. lecture + audio tape.

The logic of the study will suggest the particular comparisons to be made, as it does in the example above. If so, we will know in advance what comparisons would interest us. Comparisons chosen this way are called *planned comparisons*. In some studies, comparisons come to our attention only on inspection of the outcome of the data or perhaps simply "because they were there." Either way, they are selected without a planned rationale. Such comparisons are known as *post hoc comparisons*.

Perhaps our study was a "fishing expedition": we wanted to learn what different conditions affect performance, but had no particular advance reason for looking at the (*post hoc*) comparison that now intrigues us. That comparison came to our attention because it appeared that it might yield a difference large enough to mean something. Now when the null hypothesis is true, just by chance some sample differences will be large. Consequently, when a difference is chosen from among the several that might be examined *because* it appears large, there is a better-than-usual chance of claiming a significant difference, when in fact the difference was only due to chance. Even when a comparison is made simply because "no stone should be left unturned," the same problem faces us: the greater the number of comparisons made, the greater the likelihood of claiming a significant difference, when in fact there is no difference. Recall that using the 5% significance level means that in every 20 independent tests when the null hypothesis is true, we expect 1 out of 20 to prove (falsely) to be significant; if 40 tests, 2 significant; and so on. See Section 16.9 for a more extended treatment of this problem of multiple comparisons.

Consequently, a different strategy is desirable for examining *post hoc* comparisons than for evaluating planned comparisons. There are numerous methods of making comparisons of both types, and some of them are quite specialized. We will develop just one method for each, but these methods have the advantage of applicability to a wide variety of experimental circumstances. As we shall see, the way the comparison is constructed will be the same for both planned and *post hoc* comparisons; the difference is in the way the comparison is evaluated.

22.20 CONSTRUCTING A COMPARISON

Suppose a treatment in analysis of variance consists of a control condition (*A*) and three experimental conditions (*B*, *C*, and *D*). If we wish to compare the control condition with the average of the experimental conditions, the desired comparison can be expressed as:

$$\bar{X}_A \text{ v.} \frac{\bar{X}_B + \bar{X}_C + \bar{X}_D}{3}, \text{ or}$$

$$1\,\bar{X}_A \text{ v. } (\tfrac{1}{3}\bar{X}_B + \tfrac{1}{3}\bar{X}_C + \tfrac{1}{3}\bar{X}_D)$$

The hypothesis we propose to test is, of course, about the difference at the population level:

$$H_0: 1\,\mu_A - \tfrac{1}{3}\mu_B - \tfrac{1}{3}\mu_C - \tfrac{1}{3}\mu_D = 0$$

Note that:

1 In a comparison, two quantities are contrasted with each other. In the example above it is the mean of A with the average of the means of the remaining conditions: B, C, and D.

2 Each term in the comparison is multiplied by a coefficient. In the example, $+1$ is the coefficient for μ_A and $-\tfrac{1}{3}$ is the coefficient for μ_B, μ_C, and μ_D.

3 The total of the positive coefficients equals the total of the negative coefficients.

Other contrasts are of course possible. If we had wished to compare the average of A and B with the average of C and D, the contrast would be:

$$\frac{\bar{X}_A + \bar{X}_B}{2} \text{ v.} \frac{\bar{X}_C + \bar{X}_D}{2}, \text{ or more formally:}$$

$$\tfrac{1}{2}\bar{X}_A + \tfrac{1}{2}\bar{X}_B - \tfrac{1}{2}\bar{X}_C - \tfrac{1}{2}\bar{X}_D$$

Similarly, for $\bar{X}_A$ v. $\bar{X}_B$, we have:

$$1\,\bar{X}_A - 1\,\bar{X}_B$$

and for a comparison of the average of A and B with D:

$$\tfrac{1}{2}\bar{X}_A + \tfrac{1}{2}\bar{X}_B - 1\,\bar{X}_D$$

In general, a comparison, K, may be expressed as

A Comparison $K = a_A\bar{X}_A + a_B\bar{X}_B + \cdots + a_k\bar{X}_k$ (22.14)

where: a_A, a_B, etc. are the coefficients for the several levels of the treatment, and k is the number of levels of the particular treatment.

If some levels are not included in the comparison, the coefficients of the means of these subgroups are assigned the value zero.

To sum up, a comparison is constructed as follows:

1 Decide what conditions (levels of a treatment) are to be compared.

2 Select coefficients for the means of the treatment levels to be used in the comparison, assigning coefficients of zero to means not involved in the

comparison, and making certain that the algebraic sum of all coefficients is zero. Calculation of a comparison is illustrated in Section 22.22; see Table 22.5.

22.21 STANDARD ERROR OF A COMPARISON

In order to evaluate a comparison, we need to calculate its standard error. The standard error of a comparison is:

Standard Error of a Comparison

$$s_K = \sqrt{ s_{\text{error}}^2 \left(\frac{a_A{}^2}{n_A} + \frac{a_B{}^2}{n_B} + \cdots + \frac{a_k{}^2}{n_k} \right) } \qquad (22.15)$$

where: s_{error}^2 is the variance estimate that would constitute the denominator of the overall F test ($s_W{}^2$ in one-way ANOVA; $s_{WC}{}^2$ in two-way ANOVA)

a_A is the coefficient of the mean of the subgroup A, etc.

n_A is the number of cases in subgroup A, etc.

The number of degrees of freedom associated with this standard error is the number associated with s_{error}^2: $\overset{k}{\sum}(n_i - 1)$ for one-way ANOVA; $\overset{\text{cells}}{\sum}(n_{WC} - 1)$ for two-way ANOVA. Use of Formula 22.15 is demonstrated in the next section.

22.22 EVALUATING A PLANNED COMPARISON

The procedure described in this section is best applied to those comparisons that have been specified in advance of collecting the data. If used for a *post hoc* comparison, the probability of rejecting a true null hypothesis may be substantially higher than α, its nominal value. For the same reason, we should make no more comparisons than are necessary.

A comparison, planned or otherwise, may be evaluated by hypothesis testing or by interval estimation. We shall illustrate the latter. The limits of the confidence interval are given by the rule:

Rule for Constructing an Interval Estimate of a Planned Comparison

$$K \pm t_p s_K \qquad (22.16)$$

where: K is the comparison

s_K is the standard error of the comparison

t_p is the magnitude of Student's t for which p is the probability of obtaining a value so deviant or more so (in either direction)

p is $1 - C$

C is the confidence coefficient

The number of degrees of freedom associated with t_p is the number associated with s_K. The procedure for constructing a confidence interval on κ (kappa), the population value of a comparison, is illustrated in Table 22.5.

Table 22.5 *Constructing a Confidence Interval for a Planned Comparison*

Given:

	Treatment condition				
	A	B	C	D	
$\bar{X}$	38	41	46	44	
n	20	30	20	30	$s_W^2 = 30$

Problem: Construct the 95% confidence interval for κ, the population value of the comparison μ_B v. $\frac{1}{2}(\mu_C + \mu_D)$.

Solution:

Step 1: Select the appropriate coefficients:

$$a_A = 0,\ a_B = +1,\ a_C = -\tfrac{1}{2},\ a_D = -\tfrac{1}{2}$$

Step 2: Calculate the standard error of the comparison:

$$s_K = \sqrt{s_{error}^2 \left(\frac{a_A^2}{n_A} + \frac{a_B^2}{n_B} + \frac{a_C^2}{n_C} + \frac{a_D^2}{n_D} \right)}$$

$$= \sqrt{30 \left(\frac{0^2}{20} + \frac{(+1)^2}{30} + \frac{(-\frac{1}{2})^2}{20} + \frac{(-\frac{1}{2})^2}{30} \right)} = 1.27$$

Step 3: Calculate K, the sample value of the comparison:

$$K = a_A \bar{X}_A + a_B \bar{X}_B + a_C \bar{X}_C + a_D \bar{X}_D$$
$$= (0)(38) + (+1)(41) + (-\tfrac{1}{2})(46) + (-\tfrac{1}{2})(44) = -4$$

Step 4: Select the appropriate tabled value of t:

Since $C = .95$ and

$$df_W = \Sigma(n_i - 1) = (20 - 1) + (30 - 1) + (20 - 1) + (30 - 1) = 96,$$
$$t_p = 1.984 \text{ (using } df = 100)$$

Step 5: Calculate the interval limits:

LL $= K - t_p s_K$	UL $= K + t_p s_K$
$= -4 - (1.984)(1.27)$	$= -4 + (1.984)(1.27)$
$= -6.52$	$= -1.48$

Step 6: Express the outcome formally:

$$C(-6.52 \leq \kappa \leq -1.48) = .95$$

In this illustration we find that the average of μ_C and μ_D must be greater than μ_B by a matter of 1.48 to 6.52 points.

If we prefer to think of this problem as one of testing the hypothesis of no difference between μ_B and the average of μ_C and μ_D, note that the interval does not include the value zero. This tells us that a nondirectional test at the .05 level of significance would have resulted in rejection of that null hypothesis.

Once again, make no more comparisons than are supported by the reasons behind the study. If a comparison is to be made "because it is there" or because the outcome of the data suggested it, it is better to evaluate it as a *post hoc* comparison.

22.23 CONSTRUCTING INDEPENDENT COMPARISONS

If possible, it is highly desirable to construct comparisons that are independent of each other.† From among the k means of the levels of a treatment one may construct a set of $k - 1$ comparisons that are nearly mutually independent. When subgroup sample size is equal, it can be done as follows:

1 Construct the first comparison using all levels of the treatment. For example, if there are four subgroups, the first comparison might be: 1A v. $(\frac{1}{3}B + \frac{1}{3}C + \frac{1}{3}D)$.

2 The second comparison must be constructed wholly from subgroups that fall on *one* side of the first comparison. In the example, only a comparison involving B, C, and D will meet this criterion. Again, use *all* available subgroups. We might, for example, choose: 1 C v. $(\frac{1}{2}B + \frac{1}{2}D)$.

3 Construct the third comparison by applying the procedure of step 2 to the comparison just obtained. In our example only one comparison is now possible: 1 B v. 1 D. Note that we now have a set of $k - 1 = 3$ comparisons constructed from the $k = 4$ treatment means, and that this is in accord with the rule stated in the second sentence of this section.

Alternative sets of comparisons constructed in this way are possible. In the example, one possibility is: $(\frac{1}{2}A + \frac{1}{2}B)$ v. $(\frac{1}{2}C + \frac{1}{2}D)$, 1 A v. 1 B, and 1 C v. 1 D.

Although comparisons within a particular set approach mutual independence, this cannot be said for comparisons selected from more than one set. Consequently, in consideration of the reasons for doing the study, we decide in advance which set would be most appropriate and choose comparisons from that set only.

Comparisons constructed this way are called *orthogonal comparisons*. Adequacy

---

†Independent comparisons provide nonoverlapping information, whereas dependent comparisons do not. Further, if comparisons are independent, it is possible to calculate the probability of committing at least one Type I error, whereas for dependent comparisons this calculation usually is not possible.

of the procedure rests on reasonable approximation to the assumptions that sub-group populations are normally distributed with equal variance and that sub-group n's are equal. Moderate departure from these conditions will not be crucial.

22.24 EVALUATING A POST HOC COMPARISON

A procedure widely useful for making *post hoc* comparisons is that devised by Scheffé.† It permits evaluation of any and all comparisons, independent or not, including those suggested by the outcome of the study. There is, as we shall shortly discover, a price to be paid for this privilege.

A Scheffé comparison is calculated exactly as described in Sec. 22.20. However, to evaluate it we must calculate:

$$F' = (k - 1)F_{\text{crit}}$$

where: k is the total number of subgroup means for the given treatment (whether or not included in the comparison)

F_{crit} is the tabled value of F for the given level of significance, with $df = k - 1$ for the numerator, and, for the denominator, the df associated with s_K.‡

The confidence interval for a Scheffé comparison is constructed by the rule:

Rule for Constructing an Interval Estimate of a Post Hoc Comparison
$$K \pm (\sqrt{F'} \times s_K) \qquad (22.17)$$

where: K is the comparison

     s_K is the standard error of a comparison

     F' is the critical value of F for a Scheffé comparison

For the example appearing in Table 22.5, F' is calculated from the critical value of F corresponding to the .05 significance level and with $df = 3$ for the numerator and $df = 96$ for the denominator:

$$F' = (k - 1)F_{\text{crit}}$$
$$= (4 - 1)(2.70) = 8.10$$

The limits of the 95% confidence interval are:

$$\text{LL} = K - (\sqrt{F'} \times s_K) \qquad\qquad \text{UL} = K + (\sqrt{F'} \times s_K)$$
$$= -4 - (\sqrt{8.10} \times 1.27) \qquad\qquad = -4 + (\sqrt{8.10} \times 1.27)$$
$$= -7.61 \qquad\qquad\qquad\qquad = -.39$$

---

†H. Scheffé, *The Analysis of Variance*, John Wiley & Sons, Inc., New York, 1959.

‡If a confidence coefficient of .95 is desired, F_{crit} is that value corresponding to the .05 significance level; similarly $C = .99$ corresponds to $\alpha = .01$.

Expressed formally:
$$C(-7.61 \leqq \kappa \leqq -.39) = .95$$

Strictly speaking, the Scheffé procedure is applicable only in a situation where a preliminary overall F test for the treatment has shown significance. If such a test has shown significance, then there exists at least one comparison for which the null hypothesis will be rejected at the same level of significance. The advantage of the Scheffé method is that if the test of applicability has been met, 95% of all intervals so constructed will (over the long run) include the true values. As many comparisons as are desired may be made, whether independent or not. The price for such flexibility is that each comparison yields wider limits than if it had been planned. Compare the limits obtained above with those for the same comparison obtained in step 6, Table 22.5 (Section 22.22): $C(-6.52 \leqq \kappa \leqq -1.48) = .95$.

NOTE

Partition of the Sum of Squares and of Degrees of Freedom in One-way Analysis of Variance (*Ref:* Section 22.6)
$$(X - \bar{\bar{X}}) = (X - \bar{X}) + (\bar{X} - \bar{\bar{X}})$$
and squaring both sides,
$$(X - \bar{\bar{X}})^2 = (X - \bar{X})^2 + 2(X - \bar{X})(\bar{X} - \bar{\bar{X}}) + (\bar{X} - \bar{\bar{X}})^2$$
Summing *within* each subgroup,

$$\sum^{n_i}(X - \bar{\bar{X}})^2 = \sum^{n_i}(X - \bar{X})^2 + 2(\bar{X} - \bar{\bar{X}}) \sum^{n_i}(X - \bar{X}) + n_i(\bar{X} - \bar{\bar{X}})^2$$

Since $\Sigma(X - \bar{X}) = 0$ (See Note 5.2), the middle term drops out.
Then summing over the k subgroups,

$$\sum^{k}\left[\sum^{n_i}(X - \bar{\bar{X}})^2\right] = \sum^{k}\left[\sum^{n_i}(X - \bar{X})^2\right] + \sum^{k} n_i(\bar{X} - \bar{\bar{X}})^2, \text{ or}$$
$$SS_T \qquad = \qquad SS_W \qquad + \qquad SS_A$$
Counting degrees of freedom for each term,

$$\sum^{k} n_i - 1 = \sum^{k}[n_i - 1] + [k - 1]$$
$$df_T \qquad = \qquad df_W \quad + \quad df_A$$
Proof of the proposition follows from

$$\sum^{k} n_i - 1 = \sum^{k} n_i - k + k - 1$$

$$\sum^{k} n_i - 1 = \sum^{k} n_i - 1$$

PROBLEMS AND EXERCISES

Identify:

one-way analysis of variance

within-groups variance estimate

among-groups variance estimate

SS

n_i

k

$\bar{\bar{X}}$

s_W^2

s_A^2

Σn_i

MS

sum of squares

mean square

F ratio

F distribution

two-way analysis of variance

ANOVA

treatment

levels of a treatment

s_{WC}^2

$s_{R \times C}^2$

interaction effect

main effect

planned comparison

post hoc comparison

K

κ

s_K

orthogonal comparison

Scheffé comparison

F'

1 With reference to Table H, what tabled value of F is so great that it would be exceeded in random sampling only 5% of the time when there are: (*a*) 5 degrees of freedom in the numerator and 20 in the denominator? (*b*) 20 degrees of freedom in the numerator and 5 in the denominator? (*c*) 3 degrees of freedom in the numerator and 40 in the denominator? (*d*) 6 degrees of freedom in the numerator and 100 in the denominator?

Data 22A

There are three subjects in each of three treatment groups. Scores are as follows:

Group L:	2,	7,	3
Group M:	7,	9,	5
Group N:	9,	12,	9

2 Approach the following problems through the deviation score formulas. For Data 22A: (*a*) Find SS_W, SS_A, and SS_T. Does $SS_W + SS_A = SS_T$? (*b*) What are the values of df_W, df_A, and df_T? Does $df_W + df_A = df_T$? (*c*) Find s_W^2 and s_A^2. (*d*) Present the outcome developed so far in an analysis of variance table. (*e*) Test the hypothesis that $\mu_L = \mu_M = \mu_N$ at $\alpha = .05$ and state your conclusions.

3 Repeat Problem 2 using the raw score formulas.

4 In the analysis of variance F test, why is it that only the area in the upper tail of the F distribution is of interest?

Data 22B

Group O:	2,	5,	6
Group P:	4,	7,	11,	8
Group Q:	8,	8,	12,	15,	15

5 Approach the following problem through the deviation score formulas. For Data 22B: (a) Find SS_W, SS_A, and SS_T. (b) What are the values of df_W, df_A, and df_T? (c) Find s_W^2 and s_A^2. (d) Present the outcome so far developed in an analysis of variance table. (e) Test the hypothesis that $\mu_O = \mu_P = \mu_Q$ at $\alpha = .05$ and $\alpha = .01$, and state your conclusions.

6 Repeat Problem 5 using the raw score formulas.

7 Which approach do you recommend for Data 22B: the raw score approach or the deviation score approach? Explain.

8 In a one-way analysis of variance, an equal number of subjects were distributed among the several subgroups. (a) If $df_A = 3$ and $df_W = 84$, how many subgroups were there? How many subjects were assigned to each subgroup? What is the numerical value of df_T? (b) If $s_A^2 = 170$ and $s_W^2 = 50$, was there a significant treatment effect if $\alpha = .05$? If $\alpha = .01$? Justify. (Use nearest table values to answer this question.)

9 A one-way analysis of variance resulted in finding a significant treatment effect. The subgroup means were: $\bar{X}_A = 63.7$, $\bar{X}_B = 68.9$, $\bar{X}_C = 61.8$, $\bar{X}_D = 62.2$. What interpretation seems plausible?

10 An experimenter wishes to evaluate the effectiveness of four teaching methods among three kinds of students. The study is conducted as a two-way analysis of variance, and each combination of method and type of student is represented by five subjects. (a) What df characterizes each of the SS's that will be calculated? (b) If the tests are conducted at the 5% level of significance, what is the critical value of F for testing difference among methods? For difference among types of students? For interaction?

Data 22C

	Col 1	Col 2
Row 1	2, 4	1, 5
Row 2	3, 6	3, 4

11 Suppose the eight numbers shown in the body of the table entitled Data 22C represent scores obtained in a two-way analysis of variance. (a) Find df_T, df_C, df_R, df_{WC}, and $df_{R \times C}$. (b) Find SS_T, SS_C, SS_R, SS_{WC}, and $SS_{R \times C}$. (c) Calculate the several variance estimates appropriate to two-way ANOVA, and present the results so far developed in a table. (d) Calculate the F's required to test the main effects and the interaction effect. Draw the statistical conclusions appropriate when $\alpha = .05$.

12 "A good way to begin computation of two-way ANOVA is to find, for each cell, the number of raw scores, the sum of them, and the sum of their squares." Would you agree? Explain.

Data 22D

	Teaching machine	Conventional method
Bright students	5, 7, 9	10, 11, 15
Ordinary students	5, 10, 9	4, 8, 6

13 An experiment is designed to test the relative effectiveness of the teaching machine method of instruction as compared with the conventional method. Two samples of three subjects each were selected from among students of good aptitude and assigned to the two methods of instruction, as shown in Data 22D. Two samples of the same size were selected from among students of ordinary ability and assigned to the same methods of instruction (also shown in Data 22D). In the test trial, the 12 students earned the scores shown in Data 22D. (a) Find df_T, df_C, df_R, df_{WC}, and $df_{R \times C}$. (b) Find SS_T, SS_C, SS_R, SS_{WC}, and $SS_{R \times C}$. (c) Calculate the several variance estimates appropriate to two-way ANOVA, and present the results so far developed in an analysis of variance table. (d) Calculate the F's required to test the main effects and the interaction effect. Draw the statistical conclusions appropriate when $\alpha = .05$ and $\alpha = .01$. (e) Construct a graph of the cell means in the manner of Figure 22.7. (f) In the light of the statistical outcome (d) and the graph (e), what appears to be the essential sense of the study?

Data 22E

Source	df	s^2
Columns	4	18.0
Rows	3	36.0
Columns × rows		30.0
Within cells		12.0
Total		

14 Relative to Data 22E, suppose that 5 subjects had been assigned to each cell. (a) State the values of: $df_{R \times C}$, df_{WC}, df_T. (b) Make the possible F tests, using $\alpha = .05$. (c) What can we say about the meaning of the outcome of the test for row effect?

Data 22F

Source	df	s^2		
Among	4	250	$\bar{X}_A = 26.0$	$\bar{X}_D = 33.0$
Within	120	100	$\bar{X}_B = 25.0$	$\bar{X}_E = 29.0$
Total	124		$\bar{X}_C = 27.0$	
			$n = 25$ per subgroup	

15 Relative to Data 22F, (a) construct K, the sample value of the comparison, for evaluating the difference between the mean of A and the average of the remaining subgroups, and the difference between the average of B and C v. the average of D and E. (b) Calculate the standard error of these two comparisons. (c) Determine the 95% confidence interval for the two comparisons, and express the outcome formally. (d) State in words what each of these expressions means. (e) If the null hypothesis had been used in these two comparisons, what conclusions would have been reached?

16 (a) How many comparisons would there be in a complete set of "independent" comparisons for Data 22F? (b) Identify one such set. (c) Identify a different set.

17 (a) Redo part (c) of Problem 15 using $\alpha = .05$, but treating the two comparisons as post hoc. (b) If the null hypothesis had been used in each comparison, what conclusions would have been reached?

CHAPTER 23

23.1 INTRODUCTION

In previous chapters, problems in hypothesis testing have been concerned with hypotheses about summary characteristics of a distribution (or distributions), such as the mean, or the correlation coefficient. In this chapter, we introduce the *chi-square statistic,* which may be used to test hypotheses about entire frequency distributions. The central question is how to make an inference about a population distribution from the evidence contained in a sample distribution. To approach this question, one compares the obtained (sample) frequencies characterizing the several categories (or class intervals) of the distribution with those frequencies expected according to the researcher's hypothesis. The methods of this chapter, then, are used for inference about frequencies, *and, since proportions may be converted to frequencies, about proportions.*

As originally developed, this approach was intended for distributions of a

Inference about Frequencies

categorical nature, i.e. those in which the several classes consist of unordered, qualitative categories, such as eye color, sex, or political affiliation. However, it may also be used with continuous, quantitative variables by treating the several class intervals as "categories."

23.2 A PROBLEM IN DISCREPANCY BETWEEN EXPECTED AND OBTAINED FREQUENCIES

Is there a difference, among four brands of cola drink, in the proportion of consumers who prefer the taste of each? This question might be answered by allowing subjects to taste each of the four brands and then declare their preference. Of course, suitable experimental conditions must be provided to control for

Table 23.1 *Expected and Obtained Frequency of Preference for Four Brands of Cola* (*100 Subjects*)

	Brand A	Brand B	Brand C	Brand D	
Obtained frequency	$f_o = 20$	$f_o = 31$	$f_o = 28$	$f_o = 21$	$\Sigma f_o = 100$
Expected frequency	$f_e = 25$	$f_e = 25$	$f_e = 25$	$f_e = 25$	$\Sigma f_e = 100$

possible extraneous influences, such as knowledge of brand name or order of presentation. Suppose an appropriately designed experiment is conducted among 100 subjects selected at random, and the *obtained frequencies* of preference (f_o's) are as indicated in Table 23.1. To answer the question, we shall hypothesize that the cola drinks do not differ in regard to the proportion of people who prefer each. According to this null hypothesis, the expected proportionate preference for each cola is $1/4$, and the *expected frequency* of preference (f_e) for each is $(1/4)(100) = 25$.

The expected frequencies are those that would, *on the average,* occur in indefinite repetitions of such an experiment when no differential preference exists. In any one experiment, we anticipate that the obtained frequency of choices will vary from the expected frequencies in accord with random sampling variation. But how much variation is reasonable to expect? Some measure of discrepancy is needed as well as a means of testing whether the obtained discrepancy is within the bounds of random sampling variation.

23.3 CHI-SQUARE (χ^2) AS A MEASURE OF DISCREPANCY BETWEEN EXPECTED AND OBTAINED FREQUENCIES

The *chi-square* statistic, χ^2, provides a measure of the discrepancy between expected and obtained frequencies. Its basic formula, suited to this task, is:

Chi-Square
$$\chi^2 = \sum \left[\frac{(f_o - f_e)^2}{f_e} \right] \tag{23.1}$$

where: f_e is the expected frequency and f_o is the obtained frequency and summation is over the number of discrepancies characterizing a given problem.

For the data of Table 23.1 there are four discrepancies, and chi-square is calculated as follows:

$$\chi^2_{calc} = \frac{(20-25)^2}{25} + \frac{(31-25)^2}{25} + \frac{(28-25)^2}{25} + \frac{(21-25)^2}{25}$$

$$= \frac{(-5)^2 + 6^2 + 3^2 + (-4)^2}{25} = 3.44$$

Examination of the formula and the illustrated calculation reveals several points of interest about χ^2:

1 χ^2 cannot be negative since all discrepancies are squared; both positive and negative discrepancies make a positive contribution to the value of χ^2.

2 χ^2 will be zero only in the unusual event that each obtained frequency exactly equals the expected frequency.

3 Other things being equal, the larger the discrepancy between the f_e's and their corresponding f_o's, the larger χ^2 will be.

4 *But,* it is not the size of the discrepancy alone that accounts for a contribution to the value of χ^2; it is the size of the discrepancy *relative to the magnitude of the expected frequency.*

This is intuitively reasonable. For example, if we toss a number of coins and inquire as to the number of "heads," f_e is 6 when 12 coins are tossed and 500 when 1000 coins are tossed. If 11 heads are obtained in 12 tosses, the discrepancy is 5—most unusual. However, if 505 heads are obtained in 1000 tosses, the discrepancy is also 5—hardly a rarity.

5 The value of χ^2 depends on the *number* of discrepancies involved in its calculation. For example, if the experiment described above had been limited to three brands of cola instead of four, there would be one less discrepancy to contribute to the total of χ^2. The method of evaluating χ^2 must therefore take this factor into account. This is done by considering the number of *degrees of freedom* (*df*) associated with the particular χ^2, as explained in Section 23.5.

23.4 THE LOGIC OF THE CHI-SQUARE TEST

Although the chi-square test is conducted in terms of frequencies, *it is best viewed conceptually as a test about proportions.* For example, in the cola experiment, we explore the possibility that in the population of consumers, the *proportion* of individuals preferring each brand is $1/4$. The hypothesized proportions are derived from a substantive question of interest to the researcher, and, as usual, *the hypothesis concerns the population proportions,* not sample proportions. Our concern with the sample is simply to see whether it is in reasonable accord with what is hypothesized to be true of the population.

To conduct the test, we must generate expected frequencies, and these are obtained for each category by multiplying the proportion hypothesized to characterize that category in the population by sample size. Thus, the expected frequency of preference for Brand A is $(1/4)(100) = 25$. An expected frequency is the mean of the obtained frequencies that would occur on indefinite repetitions of such an experiment when the hypothesis is true and sampling is random.

When the hypothesis is true, the several obtained frequencies will vary from their corresponding expected frequencies according to the influence of random sampling fluctuation. The calculated value of χ^2 will be smaller when agreement between f_o's and f_e's is good and larger when it is not.

When the hypothesized f_e's are *not* the true ones, the set of discrepancies between f_o and f_e will tend to be larger than otherwise, and, consequently, so will the calculated value of χ^2. To test the hypothesis, we must learn what calculated values of χ^2 would occur under random sampling when the hypothesis is true. Then we will compare the χ^2 calculated from our particular sample with this distribution of values. If it is so large that such a value would rarely occur when the hypothesis is true, the hypothesis will be rejected. For example, if the 5% significance level is adopted, the hypothesis will be rejected for values of χ^2 so large that their prior probability of occurrence is .05 or less.

23.5 CHI-SQUARE AND DEGREES OF FREEDOM

To evaluate a given χ^2, the number of degrees of freedom (df) associated with it must be taken into account. The concept of degrees of freedom has been encountered earlier (chapter 19). In that setting, df proved to be a function of sample size. However, *in χ^2 problems with frequency data, the number of degrees of freedom is determined by the number of $(f_o - f_e)$ discrepancies that are independent of each other,* and are therefore "free to vary."

In considering what this means, it may be easier to think of the number of obtained frequencies which may be written independently. The key to understanding is that the *total* number of observations must be considered as fixed. In the cola problem, for example, there are 100 responses. In the four cells corresponding to the four brands of cola, any three of the f_o's are free to vary. But, once three are determined, the fourth is fixed since the total of all four must be 100. There are, therefore, 3 degrees of freedom for the cola problem. If the experiment had been conducted with three colas rather than four, there would be 2 degrees of freedom. In general, the number of degrees of freedom for problems of this type will be $C - 1$, where C is the number of categories involved.

The cola problem is an example of one general class of problems that may be approached through the chi-square test. Other classes of problems exist, as we shall see. For these, determination of the number of degrees of freedom proceeds somewhat differently, although according to the same general principle. This question will be considered as it arises.

23.6 THE RANDOM SAMPLING DISTRIBUTION OF CHI-SQUARE

When the hypothesis to be tested is true *and certain conditions hold,* the sampling distribution formed by the values of χ^2 calculated from repeated random samples closely follows a known theoretical distribution. These conditions will be discussed in Section 23.7. Actually, there is a *family* of sampling distributions of χ^2, each member corresponding to a given number of degrees of freedom. Figure 23.1 shows several of the theoretical models of the sampling distribution for differing values of *df*.

Table G in Appendix F may be used to determine the probability of obtaining a sample χ^2 greater than a specified amount. To use this table, it must be entered with the appropriate *df*. For example, the table shows that when $df = 1$, the probability is .05 of obtaining a χ^2 equal to or greater than 3.84.

We may return to the cola problem to illustrate the table's use in conducting a

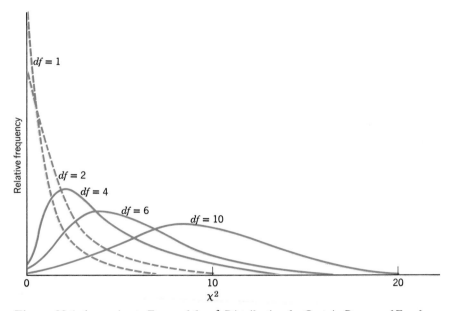

Figure 23.1 *Approximate Forms of the χ^2 Distribution for Certain Degrees of Freedom. Reproduced with permission from: E. F. Lindquist,* Design and Analysis of Experiments in Psychology and Education, *Houghton Mifflin Co., Boston, 1953.*

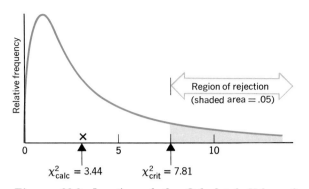

Figure 23.2 *Location of the Calculated Value of χ^2 Relative to the Expected Distribution of χ^2 when $df = 3$.*

test. If the test is conducted at the 5% significance level, we must identify the value of χ^2 so large that it will be equaled or exceeded but 5% of the time in random sampling when the null hypothesis is true. In the cola problem, $df = 3$, and entering Table G with this value, we find that the critical value is 7.81. The test situation is illustrated in Figure 23.2. The value of χ^2 calculated from the experimental data is 3.44 and falls short of the critical point. The $(f_o - f_e)$ discrepancies are therefore of a magnitude small enough to be reasonably expected when the null hypothesis is true, and the hypothesis will not be rejected.

It is useful to know that the mean of any member of the family of (tabled) chi-square distributions is always the same as the number of degrees of freedom associated with that particular distribution. In the illustration just concluded, $\mu_{\chi^2} = df = 3$. If our obtained value of χ^2 had been less than 3, we would know without having to look in the table that this value must lead to acceptance of the null hypothesis.

23.7 ASSUMPTIONS IN THE USE OF THE THEORETICAL DISTRIBUTION OF CHI-SQUARE

The percentage points of the distribution of χ^2, as recorded in Table G, follow from certain theoretical considerations. The distribution of χ^2 is therefore a theoretical model, and obtained values of χ^2 may be expected to follow this distribution exactly only when the assumptions appropriate to this model are satisfied. What are these assumptions?

1 It is assumed that the sample drawn is a random sample from the population about which inference is to be made. In practice, this requirement is seldom fully met: the discussion in Section 15.11 is quite as relevant here as there.

2 It is assumed that observations are independent. For example, in the cola experiment, utilizing 100 randomly selected subjects, the preference of one individual is not predictable from that of any other. But suppose each subject had been given three trials. There would then be 300 responses from the 100 subjects. In all likelihood the three responses of each subject are not independent of each other. If so, the chi-square model is not appropriate. In general, *the set of observations will not be completely independent when their number exceeds the number of subjects.*

3 It is assumed that, in repeated experiments, observed frequencies will be normally distributed about expected frequencies. With random sampling, this *tends* to be true. There are two important ways in which this assumption may be violated:

   (a) When f_e is small, the distribution of f_o's about f_e tends to be positively skewed. For instance, when $f_e = 3, f_o$ can be no more than three points lower, but it may range to a greater distance above. In subsequent discussion of the χ^2 model, suitable cautionary rules of thumb will be offered according to the particular circumstances.

   (b) Pearson's theoretical distribution of chi-square is smooth and continuous. In other words, the theoretical distribution makes allowance for the possibility that a particular χ^2 may have *any* fractional value, such as 3.645, 3.646, etc. On the other hand, the obtained values of χ^2 actually form a discrete distribution.† The reason is that adjacent values of f_o can differ *only* in terms of full units. For example, in the cola problem, the first discrepancy is: $f_o - f_e = 20 - 25$. The *least* amount by which this discrepancy can be greater is: $f_o - f_e = 19 - 25$, a full unit larger. Comparing the obtained values of χ^2, which form a discrete series, with the continuous distribution of theoretical values may result in a degree of error. The importance of this discrepancy is, fortunately, minimal unless both n and df are small. A correction exists when $df = 1$ and will be explained as the circumstance arises.

23.8 THE ALTERNATIVE HYPOTHESIS

In the chi-square test, the null hypothesis is that in the population distribution the proportional frequency in each subcategory equals a specified value. In the cola

---

† See Section 2.5 for discussion of discrete and continuous measures.

experiment, these values were predicated upon equal preference among the four brands. In this experiment, if the hypothesis is false, it could be that a preference exists for the first of the colas but that the remainder are equally, if less, attractive. It could also be false in that the first two are preferred above the second two, or that a difference in preference exists in numerous other ways. As we have found, when the true expected frequencies differ from the hypothesized expected frequencies *in any way,* the obtained value of χ^2 tends to be enlarged. It is for this reason that *the region of rejection always appears in the* upper tail *of the sampling distribution of χ^2.*

According to the procedure described earlier, the critical value of χ^2 is determined by setting the area in the upper tail of the χ^2 distribution equal to α, the level of significance, and rejecting the null hypothesis if $\chi^2_{calc} \geq \chi^2_{tabled}$. We now see that this constitutes a nondirectional test, since *whatever the direction of the discrepancies between observed and expected frequencies,* larger discrepancies result in a numerically higher value of χ^2_{calc}. In the cola experiment and in others like it, H_A, the alternative hypothesis, is simply that the null hypothesis is untrue in some (any) way. Note that the distinction between a directional test and a nondirectional one, encountered earlier, is not pertinent here.

In the special case when chi-square has one degree of freedom, it is possible to perform a one-tailed test if the logic of the study calls for it. When $df = 1$ (only), $\chi^2 = z^2$. We may therefore calculate $z = \sqrt{\chi^2_{calc}}$ and compare that value with the critical one-tailed value of normally distributed $z(z_{crit} = 1.645$ for $\alpha = .05$; $z_{crit} = 2.33$ for $\alpha = .01$). The null hypothesis should be rejected *only* for differences in the direction specified in the alternative hypothesis. The one-tailed test will be illustrated in Section 23.10.

What of the other tail of the chi-square distribution? A very low obtained value of χ^2 means that, *if the assumptions have been met and the calculation is correct,* the obtained frequencies are rather closer to the expected frequencies than chance would ordinarily allow. A very small value of χ^2 has no significance other than to remind us to check on the adequacy of our procedure.

23.9 CHI-SQUARE AND THE 1 × C TABLE

The development of the cola problem has taken place over several sections; it is now time to consider the general problem that that application exemplifies and to summarize the procedure. That problem illustrates one of the several classes of problems for which χ^2 may be useful in testing the discrepancy between expected and obtained frequencies. The class of problems to which the cola problem belongs may be termed the "*one-variable case,*" because it always involves the categories of a single variable. Problems of this class are sometimes said to be characterized by a 1 × C table, where C is the number of categories or class intervals.

In the $1 \times C$ table, χ^2 may be used to test whether the relative frequencies characterizing the several categories (or class intervals) of a sample frequency distribution are in accord with the set of such values hypothesized to be characteristic of the population distribution. In any such problem, the hypothesized relative frequency of occurrence in each class interval is dictated by the substantive hypothesis of interest. In the cola problem, the hypothesized proportions derive from interest in the possibility that the four brands are equally attractive.

The hypothesized proportions need not be equal. For example, one of Mendel's findings regarding heredity holds that plants bred in a particular way will show one of four characteristics and that the relative frequency of those characteristics will occur according to the ratio $9:3:3:1$. In an experiment designed to test this hypothesis, the ratios will be converted into relative frequencies such that their sum equals 1.00. Thus, the relative frequencies, or proportions, are: $p_1 = 9/16$, $p_2 = 3/16$, $p_3 = 3/16$, and $p_4 = 1/16$. Suppose plants are bred in the specified manner and a sample of 256 seedlings is obtained. Upon examining the characteristics of these seedlings, some exhibit one characteristic and some another, as indicated in Table 23.2. The expected frequencies, obtained by multiplying each of the above-hypothesized relative frequencies by 256, are also shown in the table. Calculating χ^2 according to Formula 23.1, we have:

$$\chi^2 = \frac{(130 - 144)^2}{144} + \frac{(55 - 48)^2}{48} + \frac{(50 - 48)^2}{48} + \frac{(21 - 16)^2}{16} = 4.03$$

For problems of this general class, the number of degrees of freedom is one less than the number of categories, and here, therefore, $df = 3$. Is the discrepancy between expected and obtained frequencies so great as to be beyond the realm of chance? We turn to the χ^2 function (Table G), and find that when $df = 3$, a χ^2 of 7.81 or greater would occur by chance 5% of the time when the hypothesis is true. Our χ^2 is not so rare an event (the table shows that its probability of occurrence is between .20 and .30). If the test is conducted at the 5% significance level, we have therefore no reason to reject the statistical hypothesis. The sample outcome is in reasonable agreement with Mendel's hypothesis.

It should be mentioned that the chi-square test is not satisfactory when the expected frequencies are very small. Discussion of the issues involved and recommendations for practice will be found in Section 23.11.

Table 23.2 *Expected and Obtained Frequency of Occurrence of Four Inherited Plant Characteristics*

Type 1	Type 2	Type 3	Type 4	
$f_o = 130$	$f_o = 55$	$f_o = 50$	$f_o = 21$	$\Sigma f_o = 256$
$f_e = 144$	$f_e = 48$	$f_e = 48$	$f_e = 16$	$\Sigma f_e = 256$

23.10 THE 1 × 2 TABLE AND THE CORRECTION FOR DISCONTINUITY

Suppose we want to know if light or dark enters into a preference of rats when given two alternative routes at a choice point in a maze. A study may be designed that incorporates controls designed to guard against extraneous factors such as a tendency for the animal always to choose alternatives that are on a particular side. If, then, 50 rats are afforded the opportunity of choosing between two routes, one light and the other dark, the obtained frequencies may appear as follows:

$$\text{light: } f_o = 15 \qquad \text{dark: } f_o = 35$$

If illumination makes no difference, the proportionate preference should be $1/2$ for each side, and the two f_e's are each $(1/2)(50) = 25$. By Formula 23.1:

$$\chi^2 = \frac{(15 - 25)^2}{25} + \frac{(35 - 25)^2}{25} = \frac{(-10)^2}{25} + \frac{10^2}{25} = 8.00$$

In this problem, the number of degrees of freedom is equal to one. In the special circumstance that $df = 1$, a correction may be applied to compensate for the error involved in comparing calculated values of χ^2, which form a discontinuous distribution, with the theoretical tabled values of χ^2, which form a continuous distribution. This correction is known as *Yates' correction*, or the *correction for discontinuity*, and consists in reducing the discrepancies between f_o and f_e by .5 before squaring. Thus, the corrected value of χ^2 is:

$$\chi^2 = \frac{(\,|15 - 25| - .5)^2}{25} + \frac{(\,|35 - 25| - .5)^2}{25}$$

$$= \frac{(9.5)^2}{25} + \frac{(9.5)^2}{25} = 7.22$$

The vertical bars in the formula indicate that $1/2$ unit is to be subtracted from the *absolute* discrepancy (discrepancy taken without regard to sign) before squaring.

We have 1 degree of freedom, and if the usual nondirectional test is conducted at the 5% significance level, $\chi^2_{\text{crit}} = 3.84$. Since χ^2_{calc} exceeds that value, the hypothesis will be rejected. Apparently, light or dark is a factor in the rat's choice. In Section 23.8 we learned that a one-tailed test was possible when $df = 1$. In the present problem, suppose the logic of the study called for rejection of the null hypothesis only if the evidence points toward a significant preference for the dark route. First, note that the evidence from the sample shows a greater proportion of choices of the dark route (if it did not, there would be no point in pursuing the matter further). Next, calculate $z = \sqrt{\chi^2_{\text{calc}}} = \sqrt{7.22} = 2.69$. For the one-tailed test at $\alpha = .05$, $z_{\text{crit}} = 1.645$, so the null hypothesis is rejected.

Yates' correction is always applicable to chi-square tests of hypotheses about frequencies when $df = 1$. It makes less difference when the number of observations is large, but because it is easy to apply and improves the accuracy of the test, it ought always to be used. It is *not* a satisfactory correction when $df > 1$; there is no simple alternative. Fortunately, the need for a correction is slight when $df > 1$, so we need not be concerned.

Earlier (Section 23.7), we learned that the chi-square test is not satisfactory when expected frequencies are very small. When $df = 1$, both f_e's ought to equal or exceed 5. Further discussion appears in the next section.

Finally, note that this test may be conceived as a test about a single proportion. We may identify P as the proportion of choices of dark routes in the population of possible choices, and $(1 - P)$ as the proportion of choices of light routes.† For the problem illustrated above, we could write:

$$H_0: P = .50$$
$$H_A: P \neq .50$$

where P is the population value of the proportion. In the same example, the sample value is $p = 35/50$. The test of a single proportion is therefore conceptually analogous to the test of a single mean. The difference is simply in the test statistic involved; i.e. $\bar{X}$ or p.

Just as with single means, it is possible to construct an interval estimate of P. This is explained in Section 23.18.

23.11 SMALL EXPECTED FREQUENCIES AND THE CHI-SQUARE TEST

In Section 23.7, we learned that the χ^2 test is dependent on the assumption that the f_o's will be normally distributed about their f_e's. When f_e is quite small, the distribution of f_o's tends to be skewed, and the theoretical chi-square model will not be adequate. The matter is of greater consequence when df is small than when it is large.

Knowledgeable statisticians vary in their recommendations, but none argues that the test is satisfactory when $df = 1$ *and* when any f_e is less than 5 (some propose 10). We shall support the more liberal criterion: *all f_e's should equal or exceed 5 when $df = 1$.* Please note that the requirement concerns *expected* frequencies and not obtained frequencies.

There is even less agreement when $df > 1$. One suggestion frequently offered for contingency tables (see Section 23.12) is that if no more than 1/5 of the expected frequencies are less than 5, then an expected frequency as low as 1 is allowable.‡

---

†P may be arbitrarily identified with either of the two categories (but not with both). Thus the outcome of the test would be the same if P were defined as the proportion of choices of *light* routes.

‡W. G. Cochran, "Some methods for strengthening the common χ^2 tests," *Biometrics* **10**(1954):417–51.

For problems involving one degree of freedom, procedures alternative to chi-square are available when expected frequencies fall below permissible levels. These procedures are described in other volumes. Several appropriate references are listed in Section 23.19.

23.12 CONTINGENCY TABLES AND THE HYPOTHESIS OF INDEPENDENCE

So far, we have considered the application of chi-square to the one-variable case. It also has important application to the analysis of bivariate frequency distributions. For example, suppose we poll 400 students on a college campus and ask what role they feel students should have in determining the college curriculum. We may wish to analyze the nature of their response in relation to college major of the respondents. Do students with different majors see their role in the same way?

To study this question, the data are classified in a bivariate distribution, as indicated in Table 23.3. As an example of the information conveyed by the table, note that of the 400 students, 200 were majors in Humanities and Arts, and of the 200 Humanities and Arts majors, 72 thought that students should be voting members of the college curriculum committee.

In many ways, this table is similar to the bivariate frequency distributions encountered in the study of correlation (see chapter 9). Indeed, the major difference is that the two variables (student's major and student's role) are both qualitative

Table 23.3 Classification of Responses of 400 College Students to the Question: *"How Should Students Participate in Determining the Curriculum?"*

		Desired Role of Students			
		Recommendation through student association	Nonvoting membership on college curriculum committee	Voting membership on college curriculum committee	f_{row}
College Major of Respondents	Humanities and Arts	46	82	72	200
	Science	42	38	20	100
	Business	52	40	8	100
	f_{col}	140	160	100	$n = 400$

variables rather than quantitative variables.† As with a correlation table, we may ask whether there is a relationship between the two variables in the population sampled. That is, is classification of response independent of classification of the respondent's major, or is one contingent upon the other in some way?

Bivariate frequency distributions of the type illustrated in Table 23.3 are known as *contingency tables*. From such a table we may inquire what cell frequencies would be expected if the two variables are independent of each other in the population. Then, chi-square may be used to compare the obtained cell frequencies with those expected under the hypothesis of independence. If the $f_o - f_e$ discrepancies are small, χ^2 will be small, suggesting that the two variables of classification could be independent. Conversely, a large χ^2 will point toward a contingent relationship.

23.13 THE HYPOTHESIS OF INDEPENDENCE AS A HYPOTHESIS ABOUT PROPORTIONS

In general, the hypothesis of independence in a contingency table is equivalent to hypothesizing that *the proportionate distribution of frequencies in the population for any row is the same for all rows*, or that *in the population the proportionate distribution of frequencies for any column is the same for all columns*. So again the hypothesis to be tested by χ^2 may be thought of as one concerning proportions. For the data of Table 23.3, if the role students assign to themselves is unrelated to their major, then *on a proportional basis* the role assigned should be the same for students from each of the three majors. To calculate χ^2, we begin by calculating the proportion of cases appearing in each column (i.e. proportion of cases when the three student majors are combined). This is done by dividing each column total by the grand total. For the data of Table 23.3, these proportions are calculated as follows:

Recommendation through student association	Nonvoting membership on college curriculum committee	Voting membership on college curriculum committee
$p = 140/400 = .35$	$p = 160/400 = .40$	$p = 100/400 = .25$

In the absence of a dependent relationship, we should expect the distribution of proportions *in each row* to approximate these figures. The *expected* cell proportions are therefore the same as those calculated.above: they are shown in Table 23.4.

---

†For ordinary Pearson r, both variables are continuous and quantitative. For the chi-square test, either or both *may* be unordered, qualitative variables.

Table 23.4 *Expected Cell Proportions for Each Row in a Contingency Table (Data from Table 23.3)*

		Student Role		
		Advisory	Nonvoting member	Voting member
Student Major	Humanities and Arts	$p_e = .35$	$p_e = .40$	$p_e = .25$
	Science	$p_e = .35$	$p_e = .40$	$p_e = .25$
	Business	$p_e = .35$	$p_e = .40$	$p_e = .25$
	Total	$p = \dfrac{140}{400} = .35$	$p = \dfrac{160}{400} = .40$	$p = \dfrac{100}{400} = .25$

23.14 FINDING EXPECTED FREQUENCIES IN A CONTINGENCY TABLE

Under the hypothesis of independence of classification of the two variables in the population, the expected cell frequencies are easily generated from the expected cell proportions: in each row, simply *multiply the row total by the expected proportion for each cell in that row.* In the present example, the result is as shown in Table 23.5. Obtained frequencies (from Table 23.3) are also shown in this table.

To sum up, frequencies expected under the hypothesis of independence in a contingency table may be calculated as follows:

1 Find the column proportions by dividing each column total (f_{col}) by the grand total (n). In the illustration they are .35, .40, and .25, respectively. The sum of these proportions should always be unity.

2 Multiply each row total by these column proportions; the result in each instance is the expected cell frequency (f_e) for cells in that row. This is shown in the cells of Table 23.5. Keep the result to one decimal place.

3 Check to see that the total of the expected frequencies in any row or in any column equals that of the observed frequencies. If not, there is an error in calculation.

In the illustration above, cell values of f_e were obtained by multiplying column proportions by row totals. The same result could be obtained by finding the row proportions and multiplying by column totals.

Table 23.5 *Expected and Obtained Frequency of Response to a Question Asked of College Students (Data from Table 23.3)*

		Student Role			
		Advisory	Nonvoting member	Voting member	f_{row}
Student Major	Humanities and Arts	$f_e = .35 \times 200 = 70$ $f_o = 46$	$f_e = .40 \times 200 = 80$ $f_o = 82$	$f_e = .25 \times 200 = 50$ $f_o = 72$	200
	Science	$f_e = .35 \times 100 = 35$ $f_o = 42$	$f_e = .40 \times 100 = 40$ $f_o = 38$	$f_e = .25 \times 100 = 25$ $f_o = 20$	100
	Business	$f_e = .35 \times 100 = 35$ $f_o = 52$	$f_e = .40 \times 100 = 40$ $f_o = 40$	$f_e = .25 \times 100 = 25$ $f_o = 8$	100
		$f_{\text{col}} = 140$	$f_{\text{col}} = 160$	$f_{\text{col}} = 100$	$n = 400$
		$p_{\text{col}} = \dfrac{140}{400} = .35$	$p_{\text{col}} = \dfrac{160}{400} = .40$	$p_{\text{col}} = \dfrac{100}{400} = .25$	

23.15 CALCULATION OF χ^2 AND DETERMINATION OF SIGNIFICANCE IN A CONTINGENCY TABLE

Now that the expected and obtained frequencies are at hand for each cell (Table 23.5), χ^2 may be calculated according to Formula 23.1.† As usual, each $(f_o - f_e)$ discrepancy is squared and divided by f_e. The sum of these nine components is the calculated value of χ^2.

$$\chi^2 = \frac{(46 - 70)^2}{70} + \frac{(42 - 35)^2}{35} + \frac{(52 - 35)^2}{35} + \frac{(82 - 80)^2}{80} + \frac{(38 - 40)^2}{40}$$
$$+ \frac{(40 - 40)^2}{40} + \frac{(72 - 50)^2}{50} + \frac{(20 - 25)^2}{25} + \frac{(8 - 25)^2}{25} = 40.28$$

How many degrees of freedom are associated with this χ^2? To figure degrees of freedom in a contingency table, we consider that the column totals and the row totals are fixed and ask how many cell frequencies are free to vary. In general, for

---

†With as many component cells (9) as there are in this problem, an alternative (and equivalent) formula may save a little computational work: $\chi^2 = \sum^{\text{cells}} (f_o^2/f_e) - \sum^{\text{cells}} f_o$. For the present problem, this formula yields: $\chi^2 = 46^2/70 + 42^2/35 + \cdots + 8^2/25 - 400 = 40.28$.

an $R \times C$ contingency table, their number (and therefore the number of degrees of freedom) is $(C - 1)(R - 1)$, where C is the number of columns and R is the number of rows. For the problem currently under consideration, $df = (3 - 1)(3 - 1) = 4$.

If the hypothesis of independence of classification is true at the population level, we should expect that random sampling will produce obtained values of χ^2 that are in accord with the tabled distribution of that statistic. If the hypothesis is false in any way, the calculated value of χ^2 will tend to be larger than otherwise. As before, then, the region of rejection is placed in the upper tail of the tabled distribution. For $df = 4$, Table G shows that when the test is conducted at $\alpha = .05$, $\chi^2_{\text{crit}} = 9.49$, and when $\alpha = .01$, $\chi^2_{\text{crit}} = 13.28$. The calculated χ^2 is 40.28, a value exceeding both critical points. Accordingly, the hypothesis of independence is rejected.

The same cautions voiced earlier concerning small expected frequencies apply to χ^2 as calculated from contingency tables. See Section 23.11 for advice on this matter.

Since the contingency table is analogous to the correlation table, it might be thought that χ^2, like r, provides a measure of strength of association. Although χ^2 may be converted into such a measure, it does not, by itself, serve this function. The purpose of the chi-square test as applied to a contingency table is to examine the hypothesis of independence between the two variables. Consequently, it is more nearly analogous to the test of the hypothesis, in a correlation table, that the true correlation is zero.

23.16 INTERPRETATION OF THE OUTCOME OF A CHI-SQUARE TEST

Finding that χ^2 is significant only opens the door to explanatory analysis. The simplest way to study what is happening is to convert the observed cell frequencies to proportions and to compare these proportions (p_o's) with the expected cell proportions (p_e's). To calculate the observed proportions, we divide each obtained cell frequency by the total number of cases in the row in which that cell falls: $p_o = f_o / f_{\text{row}}$. These calculations are illustrated in Table 23.6.

Now let us inspect this table. We take each column in turn and *within the column* compare each proportion with the others and with the expected proportion as shown at the bottom of the table. Although figures in the center column show little variation from row to row, the story is different in the two outer columns. Tentatively, it appears that Humanities and Arts majors differ from Business majors in more strongly favoring the fullest student participation and that Science majors fall somewhere in between.

Table 23.6 *Obtained Frequencies Expressed as Proportions of the Row Totals*
(*Data from Table 23.3*)

		Student Role			
		Advisory	Nonvoting member	Voting member	f_{row}
Student Major	Humanities and Arts	$p_o = \dfrac{46}{200} = .23$	$p_o = \dfrac{82}{200} = .41$	$p_o = \dfrac{72}{200} = .36$	200
	Science	$p_o = \dfrac{42}{100} = .42$	$p_o = \dfrac{38}{100} = .38$	$p_o = \dfrac{20}{100} = .20$	100
	Business	$p_o = \dfrac{52}{100} = .52$	$p_o = \dfrac{40}{100} = .40$	$p_o = \dfrac{8}{100} = .08$	100
		$p_{col} = .35$	$p_{col} = .40$	$p_{col} = .25$	$n = 400$

This conclusion should be taken as a tentative hypothesis rather than as a confirmed fact. Remember that a significant outcome of the chi-square test is directly applicable *only to the data taken as a whole*. The χ^2 which we obtained is inseparably a function of the nine contributions (one from each cell) composing it. We can not say for sure whether one group is responsible for the finding of significance or whether all are involved.

We should also remember that when large samples are involved, *proportionately* small differences may be responsible for statistically significant differences. This does not appear to be a vital factor in the present example, but it could be if n were substantially larger. Paying attention to proportions rather than frequencies will help curb undue excitement upon obtaining a significant outcome in a large sample.

In the problem used to illustrate the contingency table, we proceeded by determining the proportionate distribution of scores in the several rows. From the explanation of the hypothesis to be tested as developed in Section 23.13, it is apparent that the problem could with equal validity have been explored by studying the proportionate distribution of scores in the several columns. In this case we would be asking if the proportionate distribution for a column might be the same for all columns. To proceed along this line, we would convert each f_o in a column to a proportion of the column total and would compare these proportions with those obtained by converting each of the row totals to a proportion of the grand total. According to the logic of the problem, one may sometimes make more sense than the other, so some thought should be given to this matter before beginning the analysis. Of course, if you are used to one procedure, this problem could be handled by deciding in advance which variable to place on the vertical axis and which on the horizontal.

23.17 THE 2 × 2 CONTINGENCY TABLE

Although the 2 × 2 contingency table is one kind of $R \times C$ table, it deserves special consideration. The 2 × 2 table affords one degree of freedom. Consequently, Yates' correction is applicable (see Section 23.10). We may, if we wish, proceed to treat this table in exactly the same way as afforded an $R \times C$ table, except that each $(f_o - f_e)$ discrepancy would be reduced by .5 before squaring. However, the formula for calculating χ^2 given below will produce a result exactly equivalent, and with less work. Because the test is improved by Yates' correction, the formula incorporates that feature:

Chi-Square for a 2 × 2 Table

$$\chi^2 = \frac{n[\,|AD - BC| - (n/2)]^2}{(A + B)(C + D)(A + C)(B + D)} \tag{23.2}$$

where: A, B, C, and D are the obtained frequencies in the four cells of the contingency table:

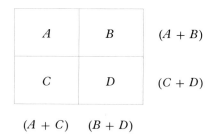

Note that the four quantities in parentheses in the denominator are the marginal totals of the table. In the numerator of Formula 23.2, the vertical bars indicate that $n/2$ (Yates' correction) is to be subtracted from the *absolute* difference between AD and BC before squaring.

We illustrate the procedure with analysis of answers of undergraduate psychology majors who contemplate graduate study to a question about their degree objective. Responses are cross-classified according to sex of the respondent, as indicated in Table 23.7. Following the procedure just described, χ^2 is calculated as follows:

$$\chi^2 = \frac{190[\,|(42)(32) - (58)(58)| - (190/2)]^2}{(42 + 58)(58 + 32)(42 + 58)(58 + 32)}$$

$$= \frac{190[\,|1344 - 3364| - 95]^2}{(100)(90)(100)(90)}$$

$$= \frac{190(1925)^2}{(9000)^2} = 8.69$$

Table 23.7 *Educational Objective of 190 Undergraduate Psychology Students Who Contemplate Graduate Study*

	Master's Degree	Doctorate	
Male	A 42	B 58	$(A + B) = 100$
Female	C 58	D 32	$(C + D) = 90$

$(A + C) = 100$ $(B + D) = 90$ $n = 190$

When $\alpha = .01$ and $df = 1$, the critical value of χ^2 is 6.64. The obtained value of χ^2 exceeds this value, and the hypothesis must therefore be rejected. The obtained frequencies could be converted to proportions in the manner described in the previous section, but in this case the conclusion seems reasonably clear without doing so: in the population that we sampled, male students differ from female students in that they more frequently aspire to the doctorate.

Remember the cautions applicable when *expected* frequencies are small; see Section 23.11.

Just as the 1×2 chi-square table is related to testing a hypothesis about a single proportion, so is the 2×2 table related to the test of the difference between two proportions from independent samples. For the data of Table 23.7, we could write:

$$H_0: P_M - P_F = 0$$
$$H_A: P_M - P_F \neq 0$$

where P_M is the population value of the proportion of males who aspire to the master's degree and P_F is the same figure for females. Again, it is possible to construct an interval estimate on the difference between two proportions. The next section describes how.

23.18 INTERVAL ESTIMATES ABOUT PROPORTIONS

In Section 23.10 we saw that the chi-square test applied to a 1×2 table corresponded to a test of the hypothesis that the population value of a proportion was some particular quantity. In the section immediately above, we also noted that the application of chi-square to a 2×2 table corresponded to a test of the difference between two proportions. Often we may prefer to apply the technique of interval estimation rather than hypothesis testing to these two situations (see Section 18.8). Finding a satisfactory approach to the construction of confidence intervals here is not an easy task because of two problems. First, the standard error of the sampling distribution requires the population value of proportions for which we have only sample estimates. Second, for samples of limited size, the shape of the sampling distribution is not always symmetrical. Specifically, it will be symmetrical about a true proportion of .5, but it tends more and more to be skewed as the true proportion departs from this value. This effect, small at first, develops with increasing rapidity as the true proportion value approaches more closely .0 or 1.0. For a rough idea of what is happening, you might turn to Figure 20.1 (chapter 20). Although that concerned sample values of the correlation coefficient, the idea is much the same. The procedures for constructing confidence intervals that follow are subject to the two sources of error. In general, they will produce acceptable results *if* we remember to use them with reasonably large samples and in situations where the proportions do not too closely approach .0 or 1.0. As a rule of thumb, use these procedures for a single proportion only when the smaller of np or $n(1 - p)$ equals or exceeds 5. For the difference between two proportions, *each* of the two proportions should meet this requirement.

For P, the single population proportion, we may use the rule:

Approximate Rule for Constructing a 95% Confidence Interval for P
$$p + \left(\frac{1}{2n} \pm 1.96 \sqrt{\frac{p(1 - p)}{n}} \right) \qquad (23.3)$$

where: P is the population value of the proportion
p is the sample value of the proportion
n is the number of cases in the sample

For the preferences of 50 rats for light or dark described in Section 23.10, $p_L = 15/50 = .30$ and $n = 50$. Therefore the limits of the interval are:

$$\text{UL} = .30 + \left(\frac{1}{2(50)} + 1.96 \sqrt{\frac{(.30)(.70)}{50}} \right) = .30 + .14 = .44$$

$$\text{LL} = .30 - \left(\frac{1}{2(50)} + 1.96 \sqrt{\frac{(.30)(.70)}{50}} \right) = .30 - .14 = .16$$

and the outcome may be written: $C(.16 \leq P \leq .44) = .95$. If $C = .99$ is preferred, substitute 2.58 for 1.96. To avoid excessive error, when p is approximately .5 it would be desirable that n be perhaps 30 or more. Should p be as low as .10, something in excess of 100 cases will be in order.

For $P_X - P_Y$, the difference between two population proportions, we may use:

Approximate Rule for Constructing a
95% Confidence Interval for $P_X - P_Y$

$$(p_X - p_Y) \pm \left(\frac{n_X + n_Y}{2n_X n_Y} + 1.96 \sqrt{\frac{p_X(1 - p_X)}{n_X} + \frac{p_Y(1 - p_Y)}{n_Y}} \right) \qquad (23.4)$$

For the data of Table 23.7, the proportion of males aspiring to the doctorate is $p_M = 58/100 = .58$ and that of females is $p_F = 32/90 = .36$. The interval limits for the difference in proportions at the population level are:

$$\text{UL} = (.58 - .36) + \left(\frac{100 + 90}{2(100)(90)} + 1.96 \sqrt{\frac{(.58)(.42)}{100} + \frac{(.36)(.64)}{90}} \right)$$

$$= .22 + .15 = .37$$

$$\text{LL} = (.58 - .36) - \left(\frac{100 + 90}{2(100)(90)} + 1.96 \sqrt{\frac{(.58)(.42)}{100} + \frac{(.36)(.64)}{90}} \right)$$

$$= .22 - .15 = .07$$

and the outcome may be written:

$$C(.07 \leqq (P_M - P_F) \leqq .37) = .95$$

23.19 OTHER APPLICATIONS OF CHI-SQUARE

If you pursue advanced studies in statistics, you will find that the chi-square function is a useful mathematical model for a surprising variety of statistical questions, some having to do with frequencies and some not. We have considered its application only to problems involving discrepancies between obtained and expected frequencies. Even in this realm, two major classes of problems were selected for consideration from among a larger group. Some indication of the richness of application of this technique is owed before closing.

As a special application of the one-variable case, chi-square may be used to test goodness-of-fit. Is it possible that scores in a given distribution may be considered as a random sample from a normally distributed population? The degrees of freedom must be calculated in a special way for this test.

We have used chi-square to test hypotheses about proportions among independent samples. It may also be used to test hypotheses about proportions obtained from dependent samples.

In Section 23.15, it was mentioned that chi-square is not in itself a measure of association when applied to a contingency table but that it is possible to derive measures of association from it. The *contingency coefficient* is such a measure; it applies to contingency tables in which the dimensions are greater than 2×2. In 2×2 tables, the *phi coefficient* (derived also from chi-square) serves the same function. See Section 9.10 (chapter 9) for further comment.

Finally, the chi-square distribution may be used in a test that has nothing to do with the discrepancy between expected and obtained frequency. Specifically, it may be used to test the hypothesis that the population variance equals some specified quantity. Alternatively, it may be used to provide an interval estimate of the population variance, based on the obtained sample value.

Description of the application of chi-square to such problems may be found in other books. Among them are volumes by Hays, McNemar, and Siegel.†

PROBLEMS AND EXERCISES

Identify:

categorical data	contingency table
obtained frequency	hypothesis of independence
expected frequency	f_o
chi-square statistic	f_e
chi-square distribution	p_o
$1 \times C$ table	p_e
$R \times C$ table	p
correction for discontinuity	

1 One hundred students take a multiple-choice test. There are 80 questions, and each has five alternatives. To Question 36, the frequency of responses was as follows:

Alternative:	A	B	C	D	E
Frequency of response:	15	40	5	12	28

(*a*) Test the hypothesis, at $\alpha = .05$ and $.01$, that the students were just guessing on this item. (*b*) Suppose Alternative B is the correct answer: (1) What is the obtained frequency of correct and incorrect answers? (2) What is the expected frequency of correct and incorrect answers if the students are just guessing? (3) Test the hypothesis, at $\alpha = .05$ and $.01$, that the frequency of correct and incorrect answers is in accord with chance.

†W. L. Hays, *Statistics for the Social Sciences*, 2nd ed., Holt, Rinehart and Winston, New York, 1973.

Q. McNemar, *Psychological Statistics*, 4th ed., John Wiley & Sons, Inc., New York, 1969.

S. Siegel, *Nonparametric Methods for the Behavioral Sciences*, McGraw-Hill Book Co., New York, 1956.

2 A student took the test described in Problem 1 and answered all the questions. Twenty-five of his answers were correct. (a) If he were just guessing, and if his answers to the questions were independent of each other, how many questions would we expect he would answer correctly? (b) Test the hypothesis, at $\alpha = .05$ and $.01$, that his frequency of correct and incorrect answers is in accord with chance.

3 In a grocery store, customers who pass by are asked to sample three cheese spreads and to declare their preference for one. Frequency of choice is as follows:

Spread:	A	B	C
Frequency of choice:	20	39	25

(a) Test the hypothesis of equal preference, using $\alpha = .05$ and $.01$. (b) Test the hypothesis that spread B is as popular as the other two combined, using $\alpha = .05$ and $.01$. (c) It is argued that it is proper to examine the question raised in part (b) of this problem if it were hypothesized in advance of collecting the data, but that if the hypothesis were generated by the finding that spread B was more popular than the rest, it would be improper. Explain.

4 In the χ^2 test, why is it that only the area in the upper tail of the χ^2 distribution is of interest?

5 A standard of physical strength is set for men, and it is claimed that 50% of men will meet it. In a sample of eight men, one surpasses the standard, and seven fall short. It is proposed to use χ^2 to test whether these results are significantly discrepant from those claimed. Any objection?

6 To a question of attitude, the responses of men and women are categorized as follows:

	disagree	undecided	agree
males	40	25	70
females	25	20	30

Test the hypothesis that attitude is independent of the sex of the respondent. Use $\alpha = .05$ and $.01$.

7 The mechanical aptitude scores of different types of workers were as follows:

	30–49	50–69	70 and above
unskilled	20	30	10
semiskilled	10	40	30
skilled	5	10	20

(a) Test the hypothesis that test score is independent of job classification. Use $\alpha = .05$ and $.01$.
(b) Translate each obtained frequency into proportion relative to its row frequency. Do the same for the expected frequencies. Comparing the two, and in view of your answer to (a), what interpretation appears likely?

8 Senior psychology majors were asked about their plans for a job. Those who said they

wanted to teach the subject are represented below:

	teach in a junior college	teach in a college or university
male	32	28
female	24	4

(a) Test the hypothesis that teaching aspiration is independent of sex of the respondent, using Formula 23.2. Use $\alpha = .05$. (b) What are the expected proportions of teaching preference for each sex under the hypothesis of independence? (c) What are the obtained proportions? (d) The lower right cell frequency is small. Is it really legitimate to use the χ^2 test of independence with these data? Explain.

9 In one large factory, 100 employees were judged to be highly successful and another 100 marginally successful. All workers were asked, "Which do you find most important to you personally, the money you are able to take home or the satisfaction you feel from doing the job?" In the first group 45% found the money more important, but in the second group 65% responded that way. Test the hypothesis of no difference in response using χ^2. Use $\alpha = .05$.

10 χ^2 as described in this chapter would be appropriate for testing equality of accident liability among four divisions of an industry but not for testing equality of accident liability of the industry's workers among the months of January, February, March, and April. Why not?

11 The example in Section 23.10 concerned the preference for light or dark of 50 rats. Suppose the question had concerned the preference of one particular rat. We might give it 50 trials and use the χ^2 test in the same way. Would that be permissible? Explain.

12 A simple random sample of residences is drawn from a large city. It is found that 35 percent of these contain one or more color television sets. Establish the 95% confidence interval for the population proportion if sample size were (a) 300, and (b) 1200.

13 Treat problem 9 as a problem in proportions: construct the 95% confidence interval for the difference between the proportion of workers in the successful group and the proportion in the less successful group who feel that the money is more important.

CHAPTER 24

24.1 INTRODUCTION

The statistical techniques considered from the beginning through chapter 22 are very efficient statistics and are for the most part the techniques of choice for data analysis in the behavioral sciences. Many of them are accompanied by assumptions that sound rather risky but that usually prove not to be troublesome. For example, normality of subgroup populations and homogeneity of variance are assumed for the t test of the difference between means of independent samples and also for one-way analysis of variance. Nevertheless, we have learned that these tests are quite "robust" in the face of violation of these assumptions; that is, rather substantial departure from these conditions may not seriously invalidate the tests when sample size is moderate to large. However, a problem can arise when the distributional assumptions are materially violated *and sample size is small*.

Some Order Statistics (Mostly)

This chapter is largely concerned with alternative procedures that require less restrictive conditions. Since there is a price for everything, we shall not be surprised to learn that these procedures are somewhat less efficient than the standard techniques when the assumptions necessary for the latter are fully met. In this chapter we present a few of these alternative techniques. Except for the Sign Test (Section 24.6), these procedures lose relatively little in efficiency—but look carefully to see what their limitations might be.

Most of the tests described here are based on order.† "Order" measures, among other things, circumvent assumptions about the shape of the distribution, although the measures described here require that the underlying variable be continuous. In addition to advantages already cited, these measures are typically quite easy to use, requiring substantially less computation than their counterparts described else-

---

† It would be good background to study Section 2.7, with particular reference to the ordinal scale of measurement, and 2.8, which discusses some of the "scale problems" that can confront the investigator.

where in this text. That is, they are easier to use when sample size is small, although sometimes that advantage diminishes as sample size increases.

Hypothesis testing and interval estimation procedures described through chapter 22 focus on the mean of a distribution or the difference between means of two (or more) distributions. The parallel techniques described here are less specific. The usual hypothesis is simply that the distributions are not different, rather than that there is no difference among the distributions with respect to some particular measure of central tendency. This is mildly annoying, because it suggests (correctly) that "significance" could result from some unknown combination of differences in central tendency, variability, and symmetry. However, if distributions are not of greatly differing shape, most are indeed good tests of location, even though they do not specifically refer to a particular measure of central tendency.

The measures described in this chapter might be given special consideration when:

1 The data as gathered are already in the form of ranks.

2 There is substantial reason to believe that the distributional assumptions required for the more efficient techniques may be violated *and* when sample size is small.

3 Rapidity of analysis and ease of computation are special considerations.

24.2 TIES IN RANK

A problem that arises quite frequently in translating scores to ranks is that of identical scores that therefore cause ties in rank. Most rank order procedures are based on the assumption that the underlying measure is continuous and that therefore theoretically there are no ties.

There are various ways to deal with ties in rank.† A simple and reasonably satisfactory scheme is to assign each of the consecutive scores in a tie the mean of the ranks that would be available to them. According to this principle, the following 9 scores

4	5	5	8	11	11	11	15	19

would be assigned these ranks:

1	2.5	2.5	4	6	6	6	8	9

This procedure usually has little or no effect on the mean but tends to reduce the variance. Fortunately, the disturbance created in the statistic being calculated is usually slight unless perhaps as many as a third of all scores are involved in ties.

When scores are fairly numerous, and especially when there are ties in rank, it

---

† J. V. Bradley, *Distribution-free Statistical Tests,* Prentice-Hall, Inc., Englewood Cliffs, N. J., 1968.

is easy to make a mistake in assigning ranks. A useful check follows from the fact that the sum of ranks equals $n(n + 1)/2$, where n is the number of scores being ranked. This holds whether or not there are ties in rank.

24.3 SPEARMAN'S RANK ORDER CORRELATION COEFFICIENT

Spearman's correlation coefficient, r_S, is closely related to the Pearson correlation coefficient.† In fact, if the paired scores are both in the form of ranks (and there are no ties in rank), calculation of r_S and Pearson r will yield identical outcomes. When would one want to use the rank order coefficient? Suppose 10 aspects of a job are listed, such as hours of work, working conditions, quality of supervision, wages, etc. Suppose we ask workers to place these job aspects in rank order according to their importance and suppose we also ask their supervisors to rank the same aspects according to the importance that they believe workers would assign. We may now ask about the extent to which one worker agrees with another and the extent to which supervisors understand workers' feelings. The degree of agreement between any two persons can be studied by calculating the coefficient of correlation between the ranks they assign to the 10 job aspects. Since the data are in the form of ranks, r and r_S will yield the same coefficient, and r_S will be preferred because it is simpler to calculate.

In another situation, photographic portraits of 12 persons are shown to a subject who is requested to place the portraits in rank order with respect to estimated IQ. The extent to which subjects can make such judgments will then be studied by determining the correlation between the rank order assigned and measured IQ. In this case, one set of measures is in rank form and one is not. It might be convenient to convert measured IQ to rank order and use the Spearman coefficient.

r_S is also used on occasion when both sets of measures are in score form. In this case, each set of measures is translated into rank form, assigning 1 to the lowest score, 2 to the next lowest, etc. Then the calculation proceeds as shown below. When would one do this? Sometimes the scale properties of the measures appear doubtful (see Sections 2.7 and 2.8). If it can be concluded that what matters is that one score is higher than another and that *how much higher* is not really important, translating scores to ranks will be suitable. At other times the scale properties are not in question, but the pairs of scores are few in number. In this case, working r_S by hand will be less demanding than calculating r by desk or pocket calculator (unless the calculator has capacity for single-key calculation of r). In any event, the typical circumstance for use of r_S is one in which n is rather small. When n is large,

---

†The Spearman rank order correlation coefficient is sometimes called Spearman Rho, and symbolized ρ. You will remember that in this book, ρ is reserved for the population value of Pearson r.

the proportion of tied ranks is apt to increase, and the work of translating scores to ranks becomes progressively more burdensome and error-prone.

The formula for the Spearman rank correlation coefficient is:

Spearman Rank Order Correlation Coefficient
$$r_s = 1 - \frac{6 \sum D^2}{n(n^2 - 1)} \qquad (24.1)$$

where: D is the difference between a pair of ranks

n is the number of pairs of ranks

Suppose an instructor was curious about the relation between the time the 15 members of his class took to complete an examination and the number of points earned on it. After the test, the examination booklets form a pile on his desk; the bottom booklet is the first one turned in and the remainder are in the order in which they were submitted. With regard to time required to complete, he assigns a rank of 1 to the first paper turned in and succeeding ranks according to the order of completion. After he has scored the tests, he records order of completion and score obtained as shown in Table 24.1. He then converts the test scores to ranks,

Table 24.1 *Calculation of r_s*

Subject	Order of turn-in X	Test Score Y	Rank of X R_X	Rank of Y R_Y	D = $R_X - R_Y$	D^2
A	1	28	1	6.5	−5.5	30.25
B	2	21	2	2	0.	0.
C	3	22	3	3.5	−.5	.25
D	4	22	4	3.5	.5	.25
E	5	32	5	10	−5.	25.
F	6	36	6	13	−7.	49.
G	7	33	7	11	−4.	16.
H	8	39	8	15	−7.	49.
I	9	25	9	5	4.	16.
J	10	30	10	8	2.	4.
K	11	20	11	1	10.	100.
L	12	28	12	6.5	5.5	30.25
M	13	31	13	9	4.	16.
N	14	38	14	14	0.	0.
O	15	34	15	12	3.	9.
n = 15						$\sum D^2 =$ 345.00

$$r_s = 1 - \frac{6 \sum D^2}{n(n^2 - 1)} = 1 - \frac{6(345)}{15(15^2 - 1)} = .38$$

assigning a rank of 1 to the lowest score. Since two scores are tied, the average of the ranks available for them is assigned to each, according to the procedure explained in Section 24.2. The set of paired ranks appears in the columns headed R_X and R_Y. Next, the differences between the pairs of ranks are recorded in the column headed D. If the algebraic signs are retained, a useful check may be had from the fact that ΣD must be zero. Values of D are then squared and summed, and the calculation of r_S is completed as shown in the table.† The value of r_S is $+.38$, suggesting that there may be some tendency for those who turn their papers in early to be those earning poorer scores.

Exact procedures have been developed for testing the hypothesis of no correlation for very small samples, but good results may be had for $n \geq 10$ by finding the critical values required for significance for $df = n - 2$ in Table E in Appendix F. This is the same table used to determine significance of Pearson r. For the present problem, Table E shows that for $df = n - 2 = 13$, a coefficient of $\pm.514$ or larger would be needed to reject the hypothesis of no correlation for a two-tailed test at $\alpha = .05$. The obtained coefficient of .38 therefore fails to meet this test and the null hypothesis of no correlation in the population is retained.

24.4 TEST OF LOCATION FOR TWO INDEPENDENT GROUPS: THE MANN-WHITNEY TEST

This test is an alternative to the t test of the difference between means of two independent samples. It might be considered when samples are small and the distributional assumptions necessary for the t test come seriously into question (see Section 19.14). The null hypothesis concerns the identity of the two population distributions rather than the identity of the two means, medians, or whatever. Nevertheless, if the two population distributions are of even moderately similar shape and variability, it is an excellent test of central tendency. Since the test is on ranks, the most closely corresponding measure of central tendency is the median. Consequently, when evaluating the outcome of the test described here, a comparison of the two medians comes first to mind (see Section 5.8 for properties of the median).

The test itself is sometimes known as the Wilcoxon rank-sum test, in honor of the man who first thought of the basic idea in modern times.‡ Mann and Whitney offered a variant particularly directed toward the problem described here; we will refer to the test under their names to avoid the confusion that might be generated

---

†In squaring tied ranks, it is useful to remember that $(n + .5)^2 = n(n + 1) + .25$.
‡F. Wilcoxon, "Individual Comparisons by Ranking Methods", *Biometrics* **1**, (1945): 80–83.

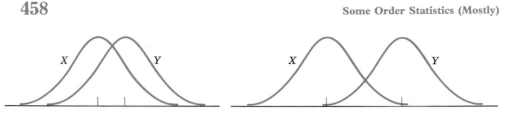

Figure 24.1 *Distributions that Overlap by Different Amounts.*

by the fact that another test described in this chapter is usually known by Wilcoxon's name.†

The nature of the test is easy to understand at an intuitive level. Suppose there are two groups whose distributions are as shown at the left in Figure 24.1; we see that they overlap to a substantial extent. Suppose that the two distributions were combined and all scores were ranked from 1 (the lowest score) to $n_X + n_Y$ (the highest score). The ranks of the scores in the X group will tend to be somewhat lower than those of the scores in the Y group; consequently the sum of the ranks of the X group (ΣR_X) will tend to be lower than the sum of the ranks of the Y group (ΣR_Y). If the two groups were more widely separated, as shown at the right in Figure 24.1, the discrepancy between ΣR_X and ΣR_Y would be even greater. The Mann-Whitney test is based on exactly this discrepancy. It derives from the probability of obtaining a sum of ranks for one distribution that differs from the expected sum of ranks (under the hypothesis of equality of the two distributions) by more than a given amount.

The procedure for conducting the test is as follows:

1 Label the two groups X and Y; *if one group contains fewer cases than the other, it must be labeled* X.

2 Combine all scores into one distribution of $n_X + n_Y$ cases. Then assign the rank of 1 to the lowest score, 2 to the next lowest, etc., until all scores are ranked.

3 Find ΣR_X, the sum of the ranks of all scores in the X distribution.

Table J in Appendix F gives critical values of ΣR_X corresponding to one-tailed probabilities of .005, .01, .025, and .05 for n_X values from 3 to 15, and n_Y values from 3 to 15.

4 Locate the row of entries in Table J that corresponds to n_X and n_Y. Then follow procedure a), b), or c) below, depending on the nature of the alternative hypothesis:

   a) H_A: $X \neq Y$. Find the pair of numbers corresponding to the column heading equal to $\alpha/2$ (if $\alpha = .05$, use heading designated .025). Reject

---

†H. B. Mann and D. R. Whitney, "On a Test of Whether One of Two Random Variables is Stochastically Larger Than the Other", *Annals of Mathematical Statistics* **18,** (1947): 50-60.

H_o if ΣR_{Xcalc} equals or falls below the lower number *or* if it equals or exceeds the higher number.

b) $H_A: X < Y$. Find the pair of numbers corresponding to the column heading equal to α (if $\alpha = .05$, use heading designated .05). Reject if ΣR_{Xcalc} equals or falls below the lower number.

c) $H_A: X > Y$. Find the pair of numbers corresponding to the column heading equal to α (if $\alpha = .05$, use heading designated .05). Reject if ΣR_{Xcalc} equals or exceeds the higher number.

When sample sizes are too large to use Table J, the statistic

$$z = \frac{\Sigma R_X - .5\,[n_X(n_X + n_Y + 1)]}{\sqrt{\dfrac{n_X n_Y(n_X + n_Y + 1)}{12}}}$$

is approximately normally distributed.† Negative values of z imply $X < Y$ and positive values imply $X > Y$.

The following example illustrates the conduct of the test: Nine children are given an arithmetic achievement test and their scores are noted. They then receive daily practice on arithmetic problems. At the end of each practice session their papers are marked by a teacher's aide, who praises them for the number they got right and states that she thinks they might do even better in the next few days. Eight other children are treated the same except for the statements of the teacher's aide. She points out the problems they missed and tells them that they should be able to do better than that. At the end of two weeks, all children are retested on a parallel form of the arithmetic achievement test, and their "gain scores" over the two-week period are noted. Examination of these scores reveals that they are skewed positively, so it is decided to evaluate the outcome with the Mann-Whitney test rather than with the t test for independent means. A two-tailed test will be conducted at the 5% level of significance. Gain scores are as follows:

Criticism (X):	-3	-2	0	0	2	5	7	9	
Praise (Y):	0	2	3	4	10	12	14	19	21

Note that some scores will be tied in rank. Ranks for these scores are assigned according to the procedure explained in Section 24.2, and the X ranks are then summed:

Criticism (X):	1	2	4	4	6.5	10	11	12	
Praise (Y):	4	6.5	8	9	13	14	15	16	17

$$\Sigma R_X = 50.5$$

We enter Table J with $n_X = 8$, $n_Y = 9$, and $\alpha = .05$ (for a two-tailed test we look in the column headed .025) and find that the critical values of ΣR_X are 51 and 93.

---

† The normal curve model will be an even better fit if the magnitude of the numerator is reduced by .5. This is a correction for discontinuity, like that used for chi-square with $df = 1$.

Since $\Sigma R_X = 50.5$ falls below the lower critical value, the null hypothesis is rejected. The low value of $\Sigma R_{X\text{calc}}$ indicates that the gains of the criticized group generally fell below those of the praised group. This is confirmed when we note the median of the gains of the criticized group is 1 whereas that of the praised group is 10.

If, for purposes of demonstration, we figure the outcome from the formula, we have:

$$z = \frac{50.5 - .5\,[8(8 + 9 + 1)]}{\sqrt{\dfrac{(8)(9)(8 + 9 + 1)}{12}}} = -2.07$$

or, if the numerator is reduced by .5 to correct for discontinuity, $z = -2.02$. These values fall just below $z = -1.96$, the critical value of normally distributed z corresponding to $\alpha = .05$ with a two-tailed test.

The fundamental assumptions for this test are random sampling with replacement and no ties in rank. As in the example illustrated, a moderate number of tied ranks do not substantially disturb the sense of the outcome.

24.5 TEST OF LOCATION AMONG SEVERAL INDEPENDENT GROUPS: THE KRUSKAL-WALLIS TEST

This test is an alternative to the one-way analysis of variance (completely randomized design). It may be thought of as an extension of the Mann-Whitney test to more than two groups. Like the Mann-Whitney test (and like one-way analysis of variance), it is for independent groups. The null hypothesis concerns the identity of the several population distributions rather than the identity of some particular measure of central tendency for the several populations. Under ordinary circumstances, however, it is a good test for location. When examining a significant outcome, the median is probably the best statistic to use, although the mean might be considered if distributional properties are not peculiar. See the first paragraph of Section 24.4 for an earlier discussion.

Suppose the scores from k subgroups were combined and all scores ranked from 1 (the lowest score) to $n_1 + n_2 + \cdots + n_k$ (the highest score). Separating the subgroups again, we might determine the mean of the ranks of scores in each subgroup and also the mean of the ranks for all scores combined. If the samples all came from identical populations, we would expect the subgroup rank means to vary to some extent (consonant with the influence of random variation) about the overall rank mean. If, however, the samples come from different populations, we would expect the subgroup means to vary more widely. The trick is to find out how much variation is so great that it would be unlikely to result as a consequence of random sampling variation when the null hypothesis is true. The Kruskal-Wallis test proceeds on exactly this basis, examining the magnitude of the k discrepancies between mean subgroup rank and overall mean rank, and finally comparing the total magnitude of the discrepancies with what might be expected by chance.† Those who have studied one-way analysis of variance will recognize the similarity of rationale there and here. In any event, Figures 22.1 and 22.2 (in chapter 22) are worth studying, because they present pictorially the essence of the argument developed above.

The test statistic for the Kruskal-Wallis procedure is:

The Kruskal-Wallis
Test Statistic: H

$$H = -3(\Sigma n_i + 1) + \frac{12}{\sum n_i \left(\sum n_i + 1 \right)} \left[\frac{\left(\sum R_1 \right)^2}{n_1} + \frac{\left(\sum R_2 \right)^2}{n_2} + \cdots \right] \quad (24.2)$$

where: ΣR_1 is the sum of the ranks in subgroup 1, etc.

n_1 is the number of cases in subgroup 1, etc.

Σn_i is the number of cases in all subgroups combined

Exact probabilities have been tabled for various values of H, but only for tiny samples. With three groups and 4 or more cases per group, the chi-square distribution may be used to evaluate H and will give good approximate results. (With more than three groups, some groups can have as few as 2 or 3 cases.) Compare H_{calc} with tabled values of χ^2 (Table G in Appendix F) for $df = k - 1$, where k is the number of groups. Since H reflects the magnitude of the discrepancies and is not sensitive to their direction, the region of rejection lies in the upper tail of the χ^2 distribution. Consulting the column of Table G headed by .05, for example, leads to the critical value of χ^2 (or H) for a nondirectional test at $\alpha = .05$. Reject the null hypothesis for H_{calc} that equals or exceeds the tabled value.

Suppose three styles of type, A, B, and C, were studied for their legibility and the legibility scores were as shown in Table 24.2. Differences are to be studied according to $\alpha = .01$. If the Kruskal-Wallis test is chosen to examine possible differences, the first step will be to combine the $6 + 6 + 5 = 17$ scores into a single distribution and to assign the scores ranks beginning with 1 for the lowest score and ending with 17 for the highest. Note that the score of 26 appears three

---

† The Kruskal-Wallis test statistic (H) developed in this section does not, on inspection, immediately reveal that it is responding as described. Some formulas for H show it clearly, but the one presented here has been modified to minimize calculation effort.

Table 24.2 *Test for the Difference in Legibility of Three Type Styles According to the Kruskal-Wallis Procedure*

	Type Style				
A		B		C	
score	rank	score	rank	score	rank
22	3	26	8	23	4
24	5	36	16	30	12
21	2	27	10	29	11
17	1	37	17	26	8
26	8	33	15	31	13
25	6	32	14		
n_i　6		6		5	
$\sum R_i$　25		80		48	

$\sum R = 25 + 80 + 48 = 153$

$\sum R = \sum n_i \left(\sum n_i + 1 \right) / 2 = 17(17 + 1)/2 = 153$, check.

$$H = -3\left(\sum n_i + 1 \right) + \frac{12}{\sum n_i \left(\sum n_i + 1 \right)} \left[\frac{\sum R_1^2}{n_1} + \frac{\sum R_2^2}{n_2} + \cdots \right]$$

$$= -3(17 + 1) + \frac{12}{17(17 + 1)} \left[\frac{(25)^2}{6} + \frac{(80)^2}{6} + \frac{(48)^2}{5} \right]$$

$$= -54 + .0392[1631.63]$$

$$= 9.96$$

$df = k - 1 = 3 - 1 = 2$; $\chi^2_{\text{crit}} = 9.21$ for $\alpha = .01$,

so H_0 is rejected at $\alpha = .01$.

times, and so the average of the three ranks available for these scores (8) is assigned to each. This follows the procedure described in Section 24.2 for ties in rank. ΣR_i, the sum of the ranks for each subgroup, is determined and recorded below the body of the table. A check on the assignment of ranks may be had from the fact that

$$\overset{\text{all}}{\sum} R = \Sigma n_i (\Sigma n_i + 1)/2$$

which is shown immediately below the sum of the ranks in the subgroups (ΣR_i). Next follows the calculation of H, yielding a value of 9.96. Using the chi-square distribution to evaluate H, $df = k - 1 = 3 - 1 = 2$. For $\alpha = .01$ and $df = 2$,

Table G in Appendix F gives $\chi^2_{crit} = 9.21$. Since $H = \chi^2_{calc} = 9.96$ falls beyond that value, the null hypothesis is rejected.

As with the Mann-Whitney test for two independent groups, the effect of ties in rank is not great unless there are many of them. See Section 24.2 for procedure in dealing with ties and for problems involved when many ranks are tied.

The measure that first comes to mind for exploring a significant difference is the median. For the present example, median scores for groups A, B, and C are 23, 14.5, and 29. One is not limited to the overall test of significance; as for analysis of variance, it is possible to make multiple comparisons. Bradley and Gibbons, among others, show how this may be done.†

Assumptions for the Kruskal-Wallis test are the same as for the Mann-Whitney test: random sampling with replacement and no ties in rank.

24.6 TEST OF LOCATION FOR TWO DEPENDENT GROUPS: THE SIGN TEST

The Sign Test and Wilcoxon's Signed Ranks Test are commonly used to test for a difference in location for two dependent groups. Each has an important advantage that the other does not. We present the Sign Test in this section and the Wilcoxon test in the next. Let us suppose that an investigator wishes to study the effect of the physical arrangements in a sorting task. Each of 20 subjects is given a shuffled deck of 52 playing cards and asked to sort them according to suit, putting them into four labeled boxes placed in front of him. The time required for the subject to complete the sort is recorded. We shall suppose that speed of performance improves with practice but not generally beyond the 15th trial. Our investigator gives his subjects 20 trials, rearranges the order in which the sorting boxes are placed before the subject, and conducts another trial. Let us suppose that the sorting times for trial 20 and 21 are those indicated in Table 24.3.

To inquire as to whether rearrangement of the sorting boxes made a difference in performance, one might elect to test the significance of the difference of mean sorting time for trial 20 and trial 21. If so, the appropriate procedure is that for dependent samples, since both trials involve the same subjects.

A different approach is possible. Let us assign the symbol "+" to a pair of observations when the sorting time on trial 21 is higher than for trial 20, and "−" when the opposite occurs. Such a classification is indicated in Table 24.3.

Now if the conditions under which the two trials were conducted make no difference, we would expect that there would be as many "pluses" as "minuses,"

† J. V. Bradley, *Distribution-free Statistical Tests,* Prentice-Hall, Inc., Englewood Cliffs, N. J., 1968. J. D. Gibbons, *Nonparametric Methods for Quantitative Analysis,* Holt, Rinehart and Winston, New York, 1976.

Table 24.3 *Time (in Seconds) for Two Trials in a Card Sorting Task for 20 Subjects*

	Time				Time		
Subject	Trial 20	Trial 21	Difference	Subject	Trial 20	Trial 21	Difference
1	51	53	+	11	39	45	+
2	40	47	+	12	48	50	+
3	42	40	−	13	50	55	+
4	54	63	+	14	47	52	+
5	48	55	+	15	51	50	−
6	42	48	+	16	42	46	+
7	39	40	+	17	47	50	+
8	50	54	+	18	54	58	+
9	47	46	−	19	58	60	+
10	57	61	+	20	51	54	+

within limits of sampling fluctuation. This question is open to interpretation in terms of chi-square. The expected and obtained frequencies of "plus" and "minus" are shown below.

$$
\begin{array}{ccc}
 & (-) & (+) \\
f_o: & 3 & 17 \\
f_e: & 10 & 10
\end{array}
$$

Chi-square is calculated as described in Section 23.10:

$$\chi^2 = \frac{(|f_{o+} - f_{e+}| - .5)^2}{f_{e+}} + \frac{(|f_{o-} - f_{e-}| - .5)^2}{f_{e-}}$$

$$\chi^2 = \frac{(|17 - 10| - .5)^2}{10} + \frac{(|3 - 10| - .5)^2}{10} = \frac{(6.5)^2}{10} + \frac{(6.5)^2}{10} = 8.45$$

With 1 degree of freedom, χ^2 must reach or exceed 3.84 to be significant at the 5% level, and 6.64 to be significant at the 1% level (these values are determined from Table G in Appendix F and are for a nondirectional test). Our χ^2 surpasses both of these critical values. It is clear that reordering the position of the sorting boxes made a difference in performance.

In conducting a test according to these principles, it will occasionally occur that some of the differences will be zero and cannot, therefore, be categorized as + or −. This dilemma may be solved in one of several ways. Probably the simplest is to ignore such cases, reduce *n* accordingly, and proceed with the test on the remaining values.

Evaluating the Sign Test by χ^2 will give reasonable accuracy for 10 or more pairs of scores. Below that number it is better to use a small sample approach (the binomial test). Siegel, among many authors, shows how this test may be made.[†]

[†] S. Siegel, *Nonparametric Methods for the Behavioral Sciences,* McGraw-Hill Book Company, New York, 1956.

The assumptions required for this test are that the $X - Y$ differences have been randomly drawn from the population of difference scores and that sampling is with replacement. A third assumption is that no difference is exactly zero. With regard to the last assumption, using the method described above will be reasonably satisfactory provided the number of zeros is small.

The special advantages of the sign test are its ease of application and assumptions that are less restrictive than those for the Wilcoxon Signed Ranks Test. Its disadvantage is that it is rather less sensitive, since it disregards some information that the other takes into account. Specifically, each "plus" simply indicates that the sorting time on trial 21 is higher than that for the same subject on trial 20, but no account is taken of how much higher.

When the dependent sample case was introduced in earlier chapters, we learned that there can be some special problems when the situation involves the same rather than different but matched subjects or when assignment of treatment condition to members of a pair is not random. See Sections 17.12 and 21.14 for further information.

24.7 TEST OF LOCATION FOR TWO DEPENDENT GROUPS: WILCOXON'S SIGNED RANKS TEST

The Wilcoxon test is an alternative to the Sign Test (and also to the t test of the difference between two dependent means). It is more sensitive than the Sign Test, but it demands an assumption that we may not be willing to make. More about this later.

Suppose we are studying the effect of a drug on the performance of mental operation—for example, on the speed and accuracy of addition and subtraction of figures. Ten pairs of subjects are formed, matched according to their performance on a pretest score earned on similar arithmetic problems. Members of each pair are randomly assigned to two treatments: the drug and a placebo. At an appropriate time after ingesting the substance (active or inert), they take the test. Their scores are recorded in the columns headed X and Y in Table 24.4. We wish to know whether the drug made a difference in performance; we decide to conduct a two-tailed test at $\alpha = .05$ and to use the Wilcoxon Signed Ranks Test. The procedure is described below, and the calculations are shown in Table 24.4.

1 Record the paired scores in two columns. In the table these appear under the headings X and Y.

2 Obtain the difference between members of each pair.

3 If any difference be zero, disregard it in subsequent calculations and reduce n, the number of pairs of scores, accordingly.

Table 24.4 *Testing the Difference Between Two Dependent Samples: The Wilcoxon Signed Ranks Test*

Pair	(placebo) X	(drug) Y	$\lvert X - Y\rvert$	Rank of $\lvert X - Y\rvert$	Signed Rank of $X - Y$	$\Sigma R_+ =$ W_+	$\Sigma R_- =$ W_-
1	24	28	4	2	-2		2
2	39	29	10	6.5	$+6.5$	6.5	
3	29	34	5	3.5	-3.5		3.5
4	28	21	7	5	$+5$	5	
5	25	28	3	1	-1		1
6	32	15	17	10	$+10$	10	
7	31	17	14	8	$+8$	8	
8	33	28	5	3.5	$+3.5$	3.5	
9	31	16	15	9	$+9$	9	
10	22	12	10	6.5	$+6.5$	6.5	
				$\Sigma\lvert X - Y\rvert =$ $55 =$ $n(n+1)/2$		$W_+ =$ 48.5	$W_- =$ 6.5

Since W_- is smaller than W_+, it is the test statistic. Consulting Table K (in Appendix F), the critical value for a two-tailed test at $\alpha = .05$ and with 10 pairs of scores is 8. Since the absolute value of W_- is smaller, the null hypothesis is rejected; it appears that the drug resulted in reduced performance.

4 *Disregard the sign of the differences obtained,* and then supply ranks to the absolute magnitude of the differences, assigning a rank of 1 to the smallest of the differences, 2 to the next smallest, etc. Ties in rank are handled as described in Section 24.2; assign each of the consecutive scores in a tie the mean of the ranks available for those scores. The outcome is shown in the column headed: Rank of $\lvert X - Y\rvert$.†

5 Next, resupply the appropriate sign of the differences to the rank of the differences. This is shown in the column headed: Signed Rank of $X - Y$.

6 The test statistic will be the sum of the ranks with a negative sign or the sum of the ranks with a positive sign, *whichever is smaller.* We will call the former W_- and the latter W_+. Often it will be obvious which to calculate; for purposes of completeness, both are shown in Table 24.4.

7 Table K in Appendix F presents critical values for one- and two-tailed tests at the usual levels of significance. Compare the smaller of the obtained values of W_- and W_+ (*disregarding the sign*) with the entry in the

---

†A check on the accuracy of assignment of ranks may be obtained by calculating the sum of these unsigned ranks: it should equal $n(n+1)/2$, where n is the number of pairs of scores ranked.

table corresponding to n, α, and the nature of your alternative hypothesis. For a two-tailed test, reject the null hypothesis if the calculated value *equals or is less than the tabled value.* For a one-tailed test, the sign of the test statistic must also be taken into account. A positive sign means that X is greater than Y, and a negative sign means the opposite. However, since your test statistic is the *smaller* of the two sums, rejecting the null hypothesis for a very small sum of negative ranks means that positive ranks predominate and that therefore $X > Y$. Similarly, if the test statistic is positive, it indicates that $X < Y$.

When the sample size is too large to use Table K, the statistic

$$z = \frac{W_+ - .25n(n + 1)}{\sqrt{\dfrac{n(n + 1)(2n + 1)}{24}}}$$

is approximately normally distributed.† If it is more convenient, substitute W_- (again, disregard its sign) for W_+ in the formula.

We can see immediately why this test is more sensitive than the Sign Test. That test responded only to the direction of the difference between a pair of scores, whereas the Wilcoxon test uses additional information about the size of the difference. For useful interpretation of the outcome of the Wilcoxon test, we must assume that differences between pairs of scores can be placed in rank order. In behavioral science that may often be a hazardous assumption. Is it true that the difference between a score of 20 and 25 is the same as between 40 and 45? That depends on (often unknown) scale properties of the measure. See Section 2.8 for further comment on this matter.

For the test itself, the assumptions are random assignment of treatment condition to members of a pair (and independent assignment among different pairs), no differences of zero, and no ties in rank. See the last paragraph of Section 24.6 for comment on the hazards of the dependent-samples design.

PROBLEMS AND EXERCISES

Identify:

Spearman coefficient	Kruskal-Wallis test
r_S	Sign test
rank-order correlation	Wilcoxon Signed Ranks test
Mann-Whitney test	

---

† The normal curve model will be an even better fit if the magnitude of the numerator is reduced by .5 to give a correction for discontinuity.

1 Two judges at an art show are asked to place the six pictures that reached the "finals" in order of merit. Their rankings are:

Pictures:	A	B	C	D	E	F
Judge A:	3	2	6	4	1	5
Judge B:	2	1	5	3	4	6

(a) Calculate r_S, the Spearman rank-order coefficient of correlation, as an index of agreement between the two judges. (b) Is r_S significantly different from zero according to a two-tailed test at the 5% significance level? Show the basis for your answer. (c) Do you have any qualification for your answer to (b)? Explain.

2 For the data of Problem 1, if you calculated Pearsonian r as the index of agreement between the two judges, would you expect r to be identical with r_S as obtained above? Explain.

3 Consider the data in Problem 1, chapter 9. Translate these scores to ranks and compute r_S, the Spearman coefficient.

4 Pearsonian r, calculated for the data of Problem 3 above, is $+.59$. Does this agree with the r_S you calculated in Problem 3? Explain.

5 Consider the data in Problem 2, chapter 9. Translate these scores to ranks and compute r_S.

6 What value of r_S would be needed to reject the hypothesis of no correlation at the 5% significance level if there were 15 pairs of scores? 25 pairs of scores?

7 In a large class, 14 students required a make-up examination. The instructor gave the same test to everyone but because of the circumstances could find a quiet environment for only 6 of the students. The other 8 had to take their test in a noisy location. If assignment to testing environment can be considered random, and if their scores were

Noisy environment:	55,	38,	46,	63,	35,	61,	56,	47
Quiet environment:	62,	56,	47,	65,	59,			

is the difference in performance significant according to a two-tailed test using $\alpha = .05$? Use the appropriate order statistic to develop your answer. Interpret the outcome using appropriate descriptive statistics.

8 Rework Problem 7 using the large sample (z) approach and making the correction for discontinuity.

9 Conduct a two-tailed test at the 5% level of significance of the difference between the X and Y scores in the data of Problem 5, chapter 17. Use the Mann-Whitney test.

10 (a) Apply the Mann-Whitney test to the data of Problem 6, chapter 17. Conduct a nondirectional test using $\alpha = .05$. (b) Do you have any reservation about applying the test to these data? Explain.

11 Apply the Kruskal-Wallis test to the scores given in Data 22A (chapter 22), using $\alpha = .05$. Do you have any reservation about applying this test to these data? Explain.

12 Apply the Kruskal-Wallis test to the scores given in Data 22B (chapter 22). Use $\alpha = .05$.

13 In a given problem situation, 12 children are praised on one occasion, and blamed on another. Their reactions, subsequent to the problem situation, are judged for aggressive reactions toward others. Ratings of aggressive behavior are as follows:

Children:	A	B	C	D	E	F	G	H	I	J	K	L
Praise:	6	8	2	1	4	5	6	9	8	7	7	3
Blame:	7	11	4	5	3	7	9	8	9	11	9	6

Examine, by the sign test, the hypothesis of no difference between the two treatments. Use $\alpha = .05$ and $.01$.

14 Eleven pipe smokers were blindfolded and given a pipe of tobacco to smoke. At a later session the same subjects were blindfolded again and given a pipe to smoke. This time the pipe contained a heated coil rather than tobacco, so the subjects drew in nothing but warm air. At both sessions blood pressure was measured before and after puffing the pipe. Below is a record of change in blood pressure during each session (a positive number represents an increase; a negative number a decrease):

Subject:	A	B	C	D	E	F	G	H	I	J	K
1st session (tobacco):	12	4	6	17	14	4	20	7	0	10	7
2nd session (warm air):	14	4	6	14	6	5	11	2	−4	3	7

(*a*) Test for a difference between scores at the first session and those at the second. Use the sign test to make a two-tailed test at the 5% significance level. (*b*) What appears to be interesting about the data aside from the result of the comparison you made in (*a*)? (*c*) What comments do you have about the way the study was conducted?

15 Eleven male subjects responded to an attitude questionnaire designed to evaluate tendency to view females in stereotype roles. A month later they were shown a film that illustrated the ways in which women have often been placed unfairly at a disadvantage relative to men. Four months later the subjects again responded to the attitude questionnaire. Scores from both time periods are shown below (the higher the score the greater the bias):

Subject:	A	B	C	D	E	F	G	H	I	J	K
Before:	21	25	31	26	21	31	28	24	27	24	22
After:	13	26	35	24	17	24	22	27	17	19	18

(*a*) Conduct a nondirectional test for a difference in response between the two time periods. Use the Wilcoxon Signed Ranks test and the 5% significance level. (*b*) Do you feel that the way the study was conducted is adequate? Explain.

16 Rework Problem 15(*a*) using the large sample (z) Wilcoxon approach and making the correction for discontinuity.

17 Repeat Problem 14(*a*), but evaluate the outcome with the Wilcoxon Signed Ranks test.

APPENDIX A
REVIEW OF BASIC MATHEMATICS

CONTENTS

A.1 INTRODUCTION

This appendix offers information about basic skills which are useful in an introductory course in statistics. It is not intended to be a comprehensive compendium, nor should it be considered as an initial unit of instruction for those who have no knowledge of the subject. It is intended primarily as a reminder of principles formerly learned, but possibly covered with mental cobwebs.

A pretest appears below, covering many (*but not all*) of the principles stated in the remaining sections. If you can answer all of these questions correctly, you would do well to skim the subsequent sections, looking for principles which seem unfamiliar. Questions are keyed to particular sections in this appendix, so if you miss a question you will know where to look to review the principles involved. Answers to the pretest questions will be found at the end of this appendix.

Listed below are three books which may be helpful for those who desire further review. They are listed in order of increasing comprehensiveness. All are designed for self-instruction.

1. A. R. Baggaley, *Mathematics for Introductory Statistics,* John Wiley & Sons, Inc., New York, 1969 (paperback).
2. V. A. Clark, and M. E. Tarter, *Preparation for Basic Statistics,* McGraw-Hill Book Co., New York, 1968 (paperback).
3. H. M. Walker, *Mathematics Essential for Elementary Statistics,* rev. ed., Holt, Rinehart and Winston, Inc., New York, 1951.

A.2 PRETEST OF MATHEMATICAL SKILLS

Reference for questions 1–4: Section A.3.

1 What symbol, inserted between 3 and 2, indicates that 3 is greater than 2?   _____

2 The reciprocal of 2/3 is   _____

3 $|-8| = ?$ _____

4 Write $(ab)^2$ another way   _____

Reference for questions 5–11: Section A.4.

5 $2 - (-4) = ?$ _____

6 $(3)(-4) = ?$ _____

7 $(-3)(-4) = ?$ _____

8 $(2)(-3)(-2)(-2) = ?$ _____

9 $(2)(-3)(0)(-1) = ?$ _____

10 $2 - 4(3/4) = ?$ _____

11 $-4/-2 = ?$ _____

Reference for questions 12–18: Section A.5.

12 Does $(abc)^2 = abc^2$?   _____

13 Does $a^2 + b^2 = (a + b)^2$?   _____

14 Does $\dfrac{a^2}{b^2} = \left(\dfrac{a}{b}\right)^2$?   _____

15 Does $\sqrt{4b} = 2\sqrt{b}$?   _____

16 Does $\sqrt{a^2 + b^2} = a + b$?   _____

17 Does $\sqrt{\dfrac{a^2}{b^2}} = \dfrac{a}{b}$?   _____

18 The square of $\sqrt{a} = ?$ _____

Reference for questions 19–23: Section A.6.

19 $3/12 =$ what percent?   _____

20 Simplify: $\dfrac{2ab^2}{a}$ _____

21 Simplify: $\dfrac{a}{\dfrac{ab}{c}}$ _____

22 Does $\dfrac{a - b}{c} = \dfrac{a}{c} - \dfrac{b}{c}$?   _____

23 Does $12/15 = 4/5$?   _____

Reference for questions 24–29: Section A.7.

24 $a - (b - a) = ?$ _____

25 $a(X + Y) = ?$ _____

26 $2ab^2 - 2b$ may be expressed as the product of what two quantities?   _____

27 $(X + 4)(Y - 2) = ?$ _____

28 $(X - Y)^2 = ?$ _____

29 $\left\{20 - 3\left[3 + \left(\dfrac{12}{4}\right)\right]\right\}^2 = ?$ _____

Reference for questions 30–36: Section A.8.

30 $Y - 3 = 2$ $Y =$ _____

31 $2Y = -6$ $Y =$ _____

32 $(3/4)Y = 12$ $Y =$ _____

33 $\dfrac{2}{Y} = 3$ $Y =$ _____

34 $2(Y - 2) = 4$ $Y =$ _____

35 $3Y - 3 = 2Y + 5$ $Y =$ _____

36 $\sqrt{Y^2 - 9} = k$ $Y =$ _____

Reference for questions 37–44: Section A.9.

37 The graph of a linear function is what kind of line?   _____

38 Among the following, which are linear equations? Write the *letters* corresponding to those equations which are linear functions on the line provided at the end of this question.

(*a*) $Y = 3X - 4$

(*b*) $3Y = 4X + 2$

(*c*) $Y - 3 = (7 + 2X)/3$

(*d*) $Y/2 = 20 - 4(X - 1)$

(*e*) $Y^2 = 3X + 2$

(*f*) $\sqrt{Y} = X - 3$

(*g*) $Y = X^2 - 2X + 1$

(*h*) $Y = -4$ _____

(score **38** correct only if all parts are correct)

If $Y = bX + a$, what are the values of b and a for:

39 $Y = -X + 20$ $b =$ _____; $a =$ _____

40 $Y = 3X - 14$ $b =$ _____; $a =$ _____

41 $Y = -7X$ $b =$ _____; $a =$ _____

42 $Y = -3$ $b =$ _____; $a =$ _____

(score **39–42** correct only if both parts of each question are correct)

If $Y = 2X - 30$, then

43 When $X = 20$, $Y = ?$ _____

44 When $X = 10$, $Y = ?$ _____

Reference for questions 45 and 46: Section A.10.

$100^2 = 10{,}000$ and $102^2 = 10{,}404$. If we assumed that change in the square proceeded at the same rate as change in the number to be squared, we would estimate that:

45 $101^2 = ?$ _____

46 $(100.5)^2 = ?$ _____

Questions 47–50 are to be answered without the aid of tables.

Reference for questions 47 and 48: Section A.11.

47 $800^2 = ?$ _____

48 $.8^2 = ?$ _____

Reference for questions 49 and 50: Section A.12.

49 $\sqrt{90,000} = ?$ _____

50 $\sqrt{1.44} = ?$ _____

A.3 SYMBOLS AND THEIR MEANING

Symbol	*Meaning*
$X \neq Y$	X is not equal to Y.
$X \sim Y$ or $X \approx Y$	X is approximately equal to Y.
$X > Y$	X is greater than Y.
$X < Y$	X is less than Y.
$X \geqq Y$	X is equal to, or greater than Y.
$X < W < Y$	W is greater than X, but less than Y.
$X \leqq W \leqq Y$	W is not less than X, nor greater than Y.
$X \pm Y$	As used in this book, it always identifies two limits: $X + Y$ and $X - Y$.
$|X|$	The *magnitude* of X without regard to its sign; e.g., $|+3| = 3$ and $|-3| = 3$.
XY or $(X)(Y)$	The product of X and Y; X times Y.
$\dfrac{X}{Y}$ or X/Y	Alternative ways of indicating X divided by Y.
$\dfrac{Y}{X}$	The *reciprocal* of $\dfrac{X}{Y}$.
$\dfrac{1}{Y}$	The *reciprocal* of Y $\left(\text{reciprocal of } \dfrac{Y}{1}\right)$.
$(X)\left(\dfrac{1}{Y}\right)$	The product of X and the reciprocal of Y; an alternative way of writing X/Y.
$(XY)^2$	The square of the product of X and Y.
$X^2 Y^2$	The product of X^2 and Y^2; it is the same as $(XY)^2$.

XY^2	The product of X and Y^2; the "*square*" *sign modifies* Y *but not* X.
∞	Infinity; a number indefinitely large.
4 or $+4$	When a *specific* number is written without a sign in front of it, a positive number is intended. Negative numbers are so indicated, e.g., -4.

A.4 ARITHMETIC OPERATIONS INVOLVING POSITIVE AND NEGATIVE NUMBERS

Problem	*Comment*
$3 - 12 = -9$	To subtract a larger number from a smaller one, subtract the smaller from the larger and reverse the sign.
$3 + (-12) = -9$	Adding a negative number is the same as subtracting that number.†
$3 - (-12) = 15$	Subtracting a negative number is the same as adding it.†
$-3 - 12 = -15$	The sum of two negative numbers is the negative sum of the two numbers.
$(3)(-12) = -36$	The product of two numbers is negative when *one* of the two is negative.
$(-3)(-12) = 36$	The product of two numbers is positive when *both* are negative.
$(-2)^2 = 4$	The square of a negative number is positive, since to square is to multiply a number by itself.
$(-2)(3)(-4) = 24$	The product of more than two numbers is obtained by finding the product of any two of them, multiplying that product by one of the remaining numbers, and continuing this process as needed. Thus: $(-2)(3) = -6$, and $(-6)(-4) = 24$.
$(2)(0)(4) = 0$	The product of several terms is zero if any one of them is zero.

† An equivalent instruction is: "When a positive sign precedes parentheses, the parentheses may be removed without changing the sign of the terms within, but when a negative sign precedes, reverse the signs of these terms." (See Section A.7.)

$2 + 3(-4) = 2 - 12 = -10$

In an additive sequence, reduce each term before summing. In the example, obtain the product *first*, then add it to the other term.

$\dfrac{-4}{2} = -2$

When *one* of the numbers in a fraction is negative, the quotient is negative.

$\dfrac{-4}{-2} = 2$

When *both* numbers in a fraction are negative, the quotient is positive.

A.5 SQUARES AND SQUARE ROOTS

Problem

Comment

$[(2)(3)(4)]^2 = (2^2)(3^2)(4^2)$
$\quad 24^2 \quad\;\; = \;(4)(9)(16)$
$\quad 576 \quad\;\; = \quad\; 576$

The square of a product equals the product of the squares.

$(2 + 3 + 4)^2 \neq 2^2 + 3^2 + 4^2$
$\quad\quad 9^2 \quad \neq \; 4 + 9 + 16$
$\quad\quad 81 \quad\; \neq \quad\quad 29$

The square of a sum does *not* equal the sum of the squares.

$\left(\dfrac{4}{16}\right)^2 = \dfrac{4^2}{16^2}$

$\left(\dfrac{1}{4}\right)^2 = \dfrac{16}{256}$

$\dfrac{1}{16} = \dfrac{1}{16}$

The square of a fraction equals the fraction of the squares.

$\sqrt{(4)(9)(16)} = \sqrt{4}\,\sqrt{9}\,\sqrt{16}$
$\quad\; \sqrt{576} \quad = \quad (2)(3)(4)$
$\quad\quad 24 \quad\;\; = \quad\quad 24$

The square root of a product equals the product of the square roots.

$\sqrt{9 + 16} \neq \sqrt{9} + \sqrt{16}$
$\quad \sqrt{25} \quad \neq \quad 3 + 4$
$\quad\; 5 \quad\; \neq \quad\;\; 7$

The square root of a sum does *not* equal the sum of the square roots.

$\sqrt{\dfrac{4}{16}} = \dfrac{\sqrt{4}}{\sqrt{16}}$

$\sqrt{\dfrac{1}{4}} = \dfrac{2}{4}$

$\dfrac{1}{2} = \dfrac{1}{2}$

The square root of a fraction equals the fraction of the square roots.

$(\sqrt{4})^2 = 4$
$\quad 2^2 \;\; = 4$
$\quad 4 \;\; = 4$

The square of a square root is the same quantity found under the square root sign. Another example: $(\sqrt{x^2 - c})^2 = x^2 - c$.

A.6 FRACTIONS

Problem	Comment
$\dfrac{1}{4} = .25$	To convert the ratio of two numbers to a decimal fraction, divide the numerator by the denominator.
$\begin{aligned}.25 &= (100)(.25)\% \\ &= 25\%\end{aligned}$	To convert a decimal fraction to percent, multiply by 100.
$\begin{aligned}\left(\dfrac{3}{5}\right)(16) &= \dfrac{(3)(16)}{5} \\ &= \dfrac{48}{5} \\ &= 9.6\end{aligned}$	To multiply a quantity by a fraction, multiply the quantity by the numerator of the fraction, and divide that product by the denominator of the fraction.
$\dfrac{16}{4} = \left(\dfrac{1}{4}\right)(16) = 4$	To divide by a number is the same as multiplying by its reciprocal.
$\dfrac{16}{\frac{4}{5}} = \left(\dfrac{5}{4}\right)(16) = 20$	To divide by a fraction, multiply by its reciprocal.
$\begin{aligned}\dfrac{3+4-2}{8} &= \dfrac{3}{8} + \dfrac{4}{8} - \dfrac{2}{8} \\ &= \dfrac{5}{8}\end{aligned}$	When the numerator of a fraction is a sum, the numerator may be separated into component additive parts, each divided by the denominator.
$\begin{aligned}\dfrac{3}{8} + \dfrac{4}{8} - \dfrac{2}{8} &= \dfrac{3+4-2}{8} \\ &= \dfrac{5}{8}\end{aligned}$	When the several terms of a sum are fractions having a common denominator, the sum may be expressed as the sum of the numerators, divided by the common denominator.
$\begin{aligned}\dfrac{(3)(15)}{5} &= \dfrac{(3)(3)(\cancel{5})}{\cancel{5}} \\ &= 9\end{aligned}$	When the numerator and/or denominator of a fraction is the product of two or more terms, identical terms appearing in the numerator and denominator may be cancelled.
$\begin{aligned}\left(\dfrac{1}{5}\right)\left(\dfrac{2}{7}\right)\left(\dfrac{3}{11}\right) &= \dfrac{(1)(2)(3)}{(5)(7)(11)} \\ &= \dfrac{6}{385}\end{aligned}$	The product of several fractions equals the product of the numerators divided by the product of the denominators.

A.7 OPERATIONS INVOLVING PARENTHESES

Problem	*Comment*
$2 + (4 - 3 + 2)$ $= 2 + 4 - 3 + 2$ $= 5$	When a positive sign precedes parentheses, the parentheses may be removed without changing the signs of the terms within.
$2 - (4 - 3 + 2)$ $= 2 - 4 + 3 - 2$ $= -1$	When a negative sign precedes parentheses, they may be removed if signs of the terms within are reversed.
$a(b + c) = ab + ac$ A numerical example: $2(3 + 4) = 2(3) + 2(4)$ $2(7) = 6 + 8$ $14 = 14$	When a quantity within parentheses is to be multiplied by a number, *each* term within the parentheses must be so multiplied.
$2a + 4ab^2 = (2a)(1) + (2a)(2b^2)$ $= 2a(1 + 2b^2)$ A numerical example: $(6 + 8) = (2)(3) + (2)(4)$ $14 = 2(3 + 4)$ $14 = (2)(7) = 14$	When all terms of a sum contain a common multiplier, that multiplier may be factored out as a multiplier of the remaining sum.
$3 + (1 + 2)^2 = 3 + 3^2$ $= 3 + 9 = 12$	When parentheses are modified by squaring or some other function, take account of the modifier before combining with other terms.
$\left[100 - 40\left(\dfrac{20}{10}\right)\right] + \left[\dfrac{20}{10} + (40 - 30)\right]$ $= [100 - 40(2)] + [2 + 10]$ $= [100 - 80] + 12$ $= \quad 20 \quad + \quad 12$ $= 32$	When an expression contains nesting parentheses, *perform those operations required to remove the most interior parentheses first.* Simplify the expression by working outward.
$(a + b)(c - d) = ac - ad + bc - bd$ A numerical example: $(2 + 3)(5 - 4)$ $= (2)(5) + (2)(-4) + (3)(5) + (3)(-4)$ $= \quad 10 \quad - \quad 8 \quad + \quad 15 \quad - \quad 12$ $= 5$	The product of two sums may be obtained by multiplying each element of one term by each element of the other term.
$(a - b)^2 = a^2 - 2ab + b^2$ A numerical example: $(2 - 4)^2 = 2^2 + 2(2)(-4) + (-4)^2$ $(-2)^2 = 4 - \quad 16 \quad + \quad 16$ $4 \quad = 4$	The square of a binomial equals the square of the first term, plus two times the product of the two terms, plus the square of the second term.

A.8 EQUATIONS IN ONE UNKNOWN

To solve an equation in an unknown, we must work to isolate the unknown, unmodified and by itself, on one side of the equation, and everything else on the other side of the equation. In working toward this goal, one side of the equation may be altered if the other side is altered in the *same* way. Alteration by adding, subtracting, multiplying, dividing, squaring, taking the square root, or taking the reciprocal may each be useful, depending on circumstances. *In each of the problems illustrated below, we shall suppose that it is required to solve for Y.*

Problem	*Comment*
$Y + 3 = 4$ *Operation:* subtract 3 from both sides $Y = 1$	Subtracting 3 isolates Y on one side of the equation.
$3Y = 12$ *Operation:* divide both sides by 3 $Y = 4$	Dividing by 3 isolates Y.
$\dfrac{Y}{3} = 4$ *Operation:* multiply both sides by 3 $Y = 12$	Multiplying by 3 isolates Y.

    Many problems require two or more successive operations to isolate the unknown. Several examples are given below. The order of operations is generally important, although sometimes there is more than one economical solution. Steps in a solution should be thought out in advance, as if it were a miniature chess game.

Problem	*Comment*
$\dfrac{3}{Y} = 4$ *1st Operation:* take the reciprocal of both sides $\dfrac{Y}{3} = \dfrac{1}{4}$ *2nd Operation:* multiply both sides by 3 $Y = \dfrac{3}{4}$	Y must be dug out of the denominator, and taking the reciprocal is one way to do it. Can you think of another way?
$2Y - 4 = 8$ *1st Operation:* add 4 to both sides $2Y = 12$ *2nd Operation:* divide both sides by 2 $Y = 6$	In this problem, the two operations could be performed in reverse order with no loss of efficiency.

$2(4 - Y) = 12$
1st Operation: perform the indicated multiplication
$8 - 2Y = 12$
2nd Operation: subtract 8 from both sides
$-2Y = 4$
3rd Operation: divide both sides by -2
$Y = -2$

There is another way to isolate Y; can you think of it?

$5Y - 3 = Y + 5$
1st Operation: subtract Y from both sides
$4Y - 3 = 5$
2nd Operation: add 3 to both sides
$4Y = 8$

3rd Operation: divide both sides by 4
$Y = 2$

Like terms must be collected in solving an equation.

Sometimes it is required to solve an equation for an unknown when the constants are expressed by letters, rather than numbers (e.g., A, B, C, etc.). The same principles hold. Here are two examples (we are to solve for Y):

$\dfrac{C}{Y + K} = A$
1st Operation: take the reciprocal of both sides
$\dfrac{Y + K}{C} = \dfrac{1}{A}$
2nd Operation: multiply both sides by C
$Y + K = \dfrac{C}{A}$
3rd Operation: subtract K from both sides
$Y = \dfrac{C}{A} - K$

A different solution is possible.

$\sqrt{Y^2 - C^2} = A$
1st Operation: square both sides
$Y^2 - C^2 = A^2$
2nd Operation: add C^2 to both sides
$Y^2 = A^2 + C^2$
3rd Operation: take the square root of both sides
$Y = \sqrt{A^2 + C^2}$

This problem becomes a nightmare unless the first operation is to square both sides.

A.9 THE LINEAR FUNCTION: AN EQUATION IN TWO VARIABLES

The equation, $Y = 2X + 20$, is really a sentence expressing the functional relation between two variables. It states: "If X is . . . , then Y is . . ." Table A.1 shows several ways in which that sentence may be completed, each of which is in agreement with the above equation.

When the graph of an equation is a straight line, the equation is said to express a *linear function*. $Y = 2X + 20$ is an equation of a straight line, so we may say that Y is a linear function of X. It is easy to tell when an equation describes a straight line; the variables in such an equation are always expressed as an additive (but not multiplicative) function of "just plain X and Y". Thus the equations below at the left are linear functions, whereas those at the right are not:

Linear Functions	Nonlinear Functions
$Y - 3X = 12$	$Y - 3X^2 = 12$
$\dfrac{2Y + 3}{4} = 16X$	$\dfrac{2Y + 3}{4} = 16\sqrt{X}$
$2Y + 1 = \dfrac{2X - 3}{7}$	$\dfrac{4}{5(2Y - 3)} = \dfrac{2 \log X - 3}{7}$
$Y = 4$	$2XY = 3$

The equation at the bottom on the left is of special importance. Although it does not contain the variable X, it is still the equation of a straight line. If we think of it as a sentence relating X and Y, it says: "Y has the value $+4$ for any and all values of X." Its graph would be a horizontal line lying 4 units above the intersection of the two axes.

A linear function expressing the relation between two variables can always be reduced to the form: $Y = bX + a$, where a and b are *constants*, and X and Y are *variables*. In the

Table A.1 *Values of Y Corresponding to Particular Values of X when* $Y = 2X + 20$

If X is	Then Y is
$+20$	$+60$
$+15$	$+50$
$+10$	$+40$
$+5$	$+30$
0	$+20$
-5	$+10$
-10	0
-15	-10
-20	-20

equation $Y = 2X + 20$, $b = +2$, and $a = +20$. Here are several other linear functions, together with the values of a and b:

Equation	Values of a and b
$Y = -3X - 20$	$b = -3$, $a = -20$
$Y = -X + 2$	$b = -1$, $a = +2$
$Y = 4$	$b = 0$, $a = +4$
$Y = 3X$	$b = +3$, $a = 0$

In elementary statistics, we encounter linear functions which are not initially expressed in this simplest form. In statistical computation, it is often required to simplify the expression, and put it in this form. For example (see Section 8.4):

$$X_n = \left(\frac{S_n}{S_o}\right)X_o + \bar{X}_n - \left(\frac{S_n}{S_o}\right)\bar{X}_o$$

where: X_n and X_o are variables and the other symbols stand for constants. If the values of the constants are:

$$\bar{X}_o = 70 \qquad S_o = 10$$
$$\bar{X}_n = 100 \qquad S_n = 20$$

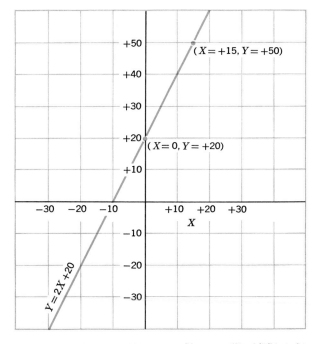

Figure A.1 *Graph of the Linear Function:* $Y = 2X + 20$.

the equation becomes:

$$X_n = \left(\frac{20}{10}\right)X_o + 100 - \left(\frac{20}{10}\right)(70)$$
$$X_n = 2X_o + 100 - 140$$
$$X_n = 2X_o - 40$$

It is now apparent that the equation is in the form: $Y = bX + a$, where $b = +2$ and $a = -40$. The constants b and a have particular meanings which help to interpret a given linear function. This aspect is explored in Section 12.3.

Since two points determine a straight line, the graph of a linear function is easy to construct. Let X be any convenient numerical value, substitute that value in the equation, and determine the corresponding numerical value of Y. The pair of numerical values of X and Y identify one point on the line. Repeat this operation, using another convenient value for X. These values identify a second point on the line. Find the location of each point on the graph, and draw a straight line through them.

This process may be illustrated with the equation $Y = 2X + 20$, described at the beginning of this section. Referring to Table A.1, we find that when $X = 0$, $Y = +20$. The point thus identified is shown in Figure A.1. When $X = +15$, $Y = +50$; this point is also shown in Figure A.1. In practical work, it is a good idea to find a third point as a check on computational accuracy. If the third point does not lie on the line drawn through the other two, a mistake has been made. Compare other pairs of values appearing in Table A.1 with the graph. For example, Table A.1 states that when $X = -15$, $Y = -10$. Does this point fall on the line?

A.10 LINEAR INTERPOLATION

Suppose Johnny is 64 inches tall on his sixteenth birthday, and 68 inches tall on his seventeenth birthday. If we wish to estimate how tall he was at sixteen and a half, we might assume that growth proceeded at a constant rate during the year, and conclude that he was probably 66 inches tall at that time. If we wished to estimate his height at age sixteen and three-quarters, we would proceed on the assumption that three-quarters of the growth had taken place when three-quarters of the time interval had passed. His height at that time is therefore estimated to be 64 in. + (3/4)(4 in.) = 67 in.

The means of estimating Johnny's height described above is called *linear interpolation*. The term "interpolation" implies that values exterior to the one desired are known, and that this knowledge is used to help estimate it. The adjective "linear" tells us that the rate of change is assumed to be constant. If it is, the equation relating the variable used to assist in prediction to the variable being predicted is one which describes a straight line. In the example above, it is assumed that age and stature are linearly related.

In evaluating this procedure, we must focus on the assumption that the relationship is really linear. Indeed, as with the height–age relationship, it is often known that it is not. *This will not matter much if the relation is close to a linear one, or if the two values between which interpolation takes place are close together.*

A.11 HOW TO USE A TABLE OF SQUARES OF NUMBERS

Finding the squares of numbers is a problem occurring frequently in statistical calculation. Most statistics books, including this one, include a table of squares in the appendix. The table in this book gives squares of numbers from 1.00 to 10.00, in intervals of .01. If the number is one of these, the square may be read directly from the table. However, the table is useful even when the number is not one of those tabulated.

The rule is: Consider the number to be squared. Move the decimal point whatever number of places, and in whatever direction is required to produce a number which may be found in the table. Read the square of this number from the table. With regard to this answer, *shift the decimal point two places for every one place it was moved in the original number, and in the opposite direction.*

Example: Find 670^2.

Step 1: Shift the decimal *two places to the left,* and find the square from the table:
$$6\,70.^2 = 6.70^2 = 44.8900$$

Step 2: Shift the decimal *four places to the right:*
$$670^2 = 44.8900 = 448900$$

Example: Find $.21^2$.

Step 1: Shift the decimal *one place to the right,* and find the square from the table:
$$.2\,1^2 = 2.10^2 = 4.4100$$

Step 2: Shift the decimal *two places to the left:*
$$.21^2 = 04.4100 = .0441$$

A.12 HOW TO USE A TABLE OF SQUARE ROOTS

Finding square root is also a problem frequent in statistical calculation. The table in this book gives the square root of numbers from 1.00 to 10.00, in intervals of .01. If the number is one of these, the root may be read directly from the table in the column headed $\sqrt{N}$. The table also gives the square root of numbers from 10.0 to 100.0, in intervals of .1. These values may be found by using the column headed $\sqrt{10N}$. For example, to find $\sqrt{25}$ we observe that $\sqrt{25} = \sqrt{(10)(2.5)}$; it may be found in the column headed $\sqrt{10N}$ opposite the entry $N = 2.50$. However, the table is also useful when the number is not one of those tabulated in the $\sqrt{N}$ or $\sqrt{10N}$ columns.

The rule is: Consider the number for which the square root is desired. Move the decimal point *two places at a time* in whatever direction is required to produce a number which may be found in the table. Read the square root of this number from the table. With regard to this answer, *shift the decimal point one place in the opposite direction for every two places it was moved in the original number.*

Example: Find $\sqrt{670}$.

Step 1: Shift the decimal *two places to the left,* and find the square root from the table:

$$\sqrt{6\underset{\smile}{\ 70.}} = \sqrt{6.70} = 2.58844$$

Step 2: Shift the decimal *one place to the right:*

$$\sqrt{670} = 2.\underset{\smallsmile}{5\ 8}844 = 25.8844$$

Example: Find $\sqrt{6700}$.

Step 1: Shift the decimal *two places to the left,* and find the square root from the $\sqrt{10N}$ column in the table:

$$\sqrt{67\underset{\smile}{\ 00.}} = \sqrt{67.00} = 8.18535$$

Step 2: Shift the decimal *one place to the right:*

$$\sqrt{6700} = 8.\underset{\smallsmile}{1\ 8}535 = 81.8535$$

Example: Find $\sqrt{.00067}$.

Step 1: Shift the decimal *four places to the right,* and find the square root from the table:

$$\sqrt{.0006\underset{\smallsmile}{\ 7}} = \sqrt{6.70} = 2.58844$$

Step 2: Shift the decimal *two places to the left:*

$$\sqrt{.00067} = \underset{\smile}{\ 02.}58844 = .0258844$$

These rules are based on the principle stated in Section A.5 that $\sqrt{ab} = \sqrt{a}\ \sqrt{b}$. For example, $\sqrt{.00067} = \sqrt{(.0001)(6.70)} = \sqrt{.0001}\ \sqrt{6.70} = .01\ \sqrt{6.70} = .01(2.58844) = .0258844$. Similarly, $\sqrt{670} = \sqrt{(100)(6.70)} = \sqrt{100}\ \sqrt{6.70} = 10(2.58844) = 25.8844$.

Sometimes a number contains more significant digits than can be used in finding square root by the table. If the loss in accuracy is tolerable, the solution is to round the number to three significant digits before entering the table. For example:

$$\sqrt{6275.41}\ \text{may be rounded to}\ \sqrt{6280}$$
$$\sqrt{.03214}\ \ \text{may be rounded to}\ \sqrt{.0321}$$

When a greater degree of accuracy is desired, methods such as those described by Walker may be used.†

One point in finding square roots is worth special attention; inadequate recognition of it often leads to error. We expect the square root of a number to be a smaller number. This is so only when the number of which the root is required is greater than one. *When the number is between zero and one, its square root is larger (but less than one).* For example, $\sqrt{25} = 5$, but $\sqrt{.25} = .5$.

A.13 FINDING SQUARE ROOT WITH AN ELECTRONIC CALCULATOR

Finding square root on a pocket calculator is an easy calculation, and even easier if the instrument has a memory. Be sure the calculator is set to operate with a floating decimal.

---

†H. M. Walker, *Mathematics Essential for Elementary Statistics,* rev. ed., Holt, Rinehart and Winston, Inc., New York, 1951, Chapter 15.

The method shown below is one of successive approximation. First, select a number that approximates the square root of the number. We will call it *1st approx.* Then we obtain a second (and better) approximation by the following formula:

$$\sqrt{n} = \text{approximately } \frac{1}{2}\left(\frac{n}{\textit{1st approx.}} + \textit{1st approx.}\right) = \textit{2nd approx.}$$

Substituting the second approximation in place of the first approximation, repeat the calculation, obtaining a third (and still better) approximation. The procedure converges quickly on the correct answer, so very frequently this third approximation will be accurate enough. Check to see by squaring it and comparing the result with n. If necessary, repeat the procedure one more time.

Example: Find $\sqrt{40}$.

Guessed approximation: 6.

Calculate: *2nd approx.* $= \frac{1}{2}\left(\frac{40}{6} + 6\right) = 6.3333333$

The square of this approximation is 40.11.

$$\textit{3d approx.} = \frac{1}{2}\left(\frac{40}{6.3333333} + 6.3333333\right)$$
$$= 6.3245614$$

and the square of this approximation is 40.000077.

A.14 ANSWERS TO PRETEST QUESTIONS

1. $>$	**18.** a	**35.** 8
2. $3/2$	**19.** 25	**36.** $\sqrt{k^2 + 9}$
3. 8	**20.** $2b^2$	**37.** straight line
4. a^2b^2	**21.** c/b	**38.** a, b, c, d, and h
5. 6	**22.** yes	**39.** $b = -1$, $a = 20$
6. -12	**23.** yes	**40.** $b = 3$, $a = -14$
7. 12	**24.** $2a - b$	**41.** $b = -7$, $a = 0$
8. -24	**25.** $aX + aY$	**42.** $b = 0$, $a = -3$
9. zero	**26.** $2b$ and $(ab - 1)$	**43.** 10
10. -1	**27.** $XY + 4Y - 2X - 8$	**44.** -10
11. 2	**28.** $X^2 - 2XY + Y^2$	**45.** 10,202
12. no	**29.** 4	**46.** 10,101
13. no	**30.** 5	**47.** 640,000
14. yes	**31.** -3	**48.** .64
15. yes	**32.** 16	**49.** 300
16. no	**33.** $2/3$	**50.** 1.2
17. yes	**34.** 4	

APPENDIX B

SUMMATION RULES

In the algebraic transformation of statistical equations, there are three basic rules of summation which come into frequent play. The first is:

Rule 1: *When a quantity which is itself a sum or difference is to be summed, the summation sign may be distributed among the separate terms of the sum.* That is:

$$\sum (X + Y) = \sum X + \sum Y \tag{B.1}$$

Proof of this proposition is:

$$\sum (X + Y) = (X_1 + Y_1) + (X_2 + Y_2) + \cdots + (X_n + Y_n)$$
$$= (X_1 + X_2 + \cdots + X_n) + (Y_1 + Y_2 + \cdots + Y_n)$$
$$= \sum X + \sum Y$$

By extension of the proof, it follows that:

$$\sum (X + Y + W) = \sum X + \sum Y + \sum W, \text{ etc.}$$

The second rule is:

Rule 2: *The sum of a constant equals the product of the constant and the number of times the constant appears.* That is:

$$\sum a = na \tag{B.2}$$

Proof of this proposition is apparent from the consequences of proposition B.1:

$$\sum (X + a) = (X_1 + a) + (X_2 + a) + \cdots + (X_n + a)$$
$$= (X_1 + X_2 + \cdots + X_n) + (a + a + \cdots + a)$$
$$= \sum X + \sum a$$

which follows from proposition B.1. Since the number of a's to be summed is the same as the number of scores to be summed, it is clear that there are n of them, and that $\sum a = na$.

The third rule is:

Rule 3: *The sum of the product of a constant and a variable is equivalent to the product of the constant and the sum of the variable.* That is:

$$\sum aX = a \sum X \qquad\qquad \text{(B.3)}$$

Proof of this proposition is:

$$\begin{aligned}
\sum aX &= aX_1 + aX_2 + \cdots + aX_n \\
&= a(X_1 + X_2 + \cdots + X_n) \\
&= a \sum X
\end{aligned}$$

These three rules can be combined, and extended. Several illustrations are given below, and the rules involved are listed at the right. In the illustrations, a and b represent constants, and X and Y are variables.

1. $\Sigma(X + 2) = \Sigma X + 2n$ B.1, B.2

2. $\Sigma(X^2 - 1) = \Sigma X^2 - n$ B.1, B.2

   Note: If X is a variable, so is X^2.

3. $\Sigma 2a = 2an$ B.2

4. $\Sigma ab^2 XY^2 = ab^2 \Sigma XY^2$ B.3

5. $\Sigma a(Y + 3)^2 = a\Sigma(Y + 3)^2$ B.3

   Note: If Y is a variable, so is $(Y + 3)^2$.

6. $\Sigma(2X - 3) = 2\Sigma X - 3n$ B.1, B.2, B.3

7. $\Sigma(Y - a)^2 = \Sigma(Y^2 - 2aY + a^2)$

              $= \Sigma Y^2 - 2a\Sigma Y + na^2$ B.1, B.2, B.3

APPENDIX C

LIST OF SYMBOLS

Symbols used in this book are identified below. Numbers in parentheses indicate the page on which each symbol is introduced and defined, and where pronunciation is given for Greek letters.

GREEK LETTER SYMBOLS

α	level of significance, probability of a Type I error (253)
β	probability of a Type II error (276)
$1 - \beta$	power of a test (364)
η	correlation ratio (156)
κ	population value of a comparison (418)
μ, μ_X	mean of a population (65)
$\mu_{\bar{X}}$	mean of the sampling distribution of means (223)
ρ_{XY}	population Pearsonian correlation coefficient (143)
Σ	the sum of (64)
σ, σ_X	standard deviation of a population (86)
σ^2, σ_X^2	variance of a population (85)
σ_r	standard error of r (351)
$\sigma_{\bar{X}}$	standard error of the mean (223)
$\sigma_{\bar{X}-\bar{Y}}$	standard error of the difference between two means (291, 298)
ϕ	phi coefficient (156)
χ^2	chi-square (428)

ENGLISH LETTER SYMBOLS

a	Y intercept of a line (201)
b	slope of a line (202)

490

C	a constant (64)
C	confidence coefficient (313)
C_j	jth centile (36)
D	differences between paired scores (299)
$\bar{D}$	mean difference between paired scores (299)
d	discrepancy between an hypothesized value and the true value (374)
$\boldsymbol{d_1, d_2}$	discrepancy between sample and population characteristic expressed in standard score units (316, 317)
df	degrees of freedom (329, 331)
F	variance ratio (401)
f	frequency (32)
f_e	expected frequency (428)
f_o	obtained frequency (428)
H	test statistic for the Kruskal-Wallis test (461)
H_A	alternative hypothesis (253)
H_0	null hypothesis (253)
i	class interval width (32)
K	a constant (64)
K	sample value of a comparison (416)
k	coefficient of alienation (207)
k	number of subgroups in analysis of variance (390)
Mdn	median (64)
Mo	mode (64)
MS	mean square, or variance estimate (395n)
N	number of cases in a population (32)
n	number of cases in a sample (32)
n_i	number of cases in the ith subgroup (396)
P	population value of a proportion (446)
p	sample value of a proportion (446)
Pr	probability (235)
Q	semiinterquartile range (83)
r, r_{XY}	sample Pearsonian correlation coefficient (143, 146)
r^2	coefficient of determination (209)
r_s	Spearman's rank order correlation coefficient (455)
S, S_X	standard deviation of a sample (86)
$S^2, S_X{}^2$	variance of a sample (85)
$S_{Y'}{}^2$	variance of predicted scores (210)
S_{YX}	standard error of estimate (185)
$S_{YX}{}^2$	variance of obtained scores about their predicted scores (209)
s, s_X	estimate of a population standard deviation (252)
$s^2, s_X{}^2$	unbiased estimate of a population variance (278)
$s_A{}^2$	among-groups variance estimate (395, 396)
$s_C{}^2$	column variance estimate (408)
$s_{\bar{D}}$	estimate of the standard error of the mean of difference scores (301)
s_K	standard error of a comparison (417)
$s_p{}^2$	pooled estimate of the population variance (336–337)

$s_R{}^2$	row variance estimate (409)
$s_{R \times C}{}^2$	row by column interaction variance estimate (409)
$s_W{}^2$	within-groups variance estimate (395)
$s_{WC}{}^2$	within-cells variance estimate (408)
$s_{\bar{X}}$	estimate of the standard error of the mean (252)
$s_{\bar{X}-\bar{Y}}$	estimate of the standard error of the difference between two means (291, 298, 337)
SS	sum of squares (394)
T	T score (135)
t	Student's t statistic (328–329)
t_p	t beyond which a given proportion of values fall (341)
W_+, W_-	test statistic for the Wilcoxon Signed Ranks test (466)
w	maximum desired discrepancy between sample and population characteristic in an interval estimate (318)
X	raw scores (63)
$\bar{X}$	mean of a sample (65)
$\bar{X}_c$	mean of a combined distribution (73)
$\bar{\bar{X}}$	mean of all scores, or grand mean (393)
x	deviation score (84)
Y	raw scores (64)
$\bar{Y}$	mean of a sample (65)
Y'	predicted raw score (182)
y	deviation score (84)
z	z score, or standard score (113)
"z"	approximate z score (256)
z_p	z score beyond which a given proportion of values fall (312)
z'_Y	predicted z score (181)
$\mathbf{Z'}$	Fisher's logarithmic transformation of ρ (354–355)
$\mathbf{z'}$	Fisher's logarithmic transformation of r (354–355)

APPENDIX D
USEFUL FORMULAS

These are most of the computing formulas appearing in the book. The reference is to the section number where each formula is introduced and defined.

Sample Mean	$\bar{X} = \dfrac{\sum X}{n}$	Sec. 5.5
Sum of Squares of Deviation Scores (Raw Score Formula)	$\sum x^2 = \sum X^2 - \dfrac{\left(\sum X\right)^2}{n}$	Sec. 6.7
Sample Standard Deviation	$S = \sqrt{\dfrac{\sum x^2}{n}}$	Sec. 6.6
Estimate of the Population Standard Deviation	$s = \sqrt{\dfrac{\sum x^2}{n-1}}$	Sec. 15.4
General Formula for a z Score	$z = \dfrac{\text{score} - \text{mean}}{\text{standard deviation}}$	Sec. 13.10
z Score from a Raw Score	$z = \dfrac{X - \bar{X}}{S}$	Sec. 7.2
Raw Score from a z Score	$X = \bar{X} + zS$	Sec. 7.8

Sum of Products of Deviation Scores (Raw Score Formula)	$$\sum xy = \dfrac{\left(\sum X\right)\left(\sum Y\right)}{n}$$	Sec. 9.5
Pearson Correlation Coefficient	$$r = \dfrac{\sum xy}{\sqrt{\left(\sum x^2\right)\left(\sum y^2\right)}}$$	Sec. 9.5
Predicted z_Y from the Straight Line of Best Fit	$$z'_Y = rz_X$$	Sec. 11.3
Predicted Y from the Straight Line of Best Fit	$$Y' = r\left(\dfrac{S_Y}{S_X}\right)X - r\left(\dfrac{S_Y}{S_X}\right)\bar{X} + \bar{Y}$$	Sec. 11.4
Standard Error of Estimate (Y)	$$S_{YX} = S_Y\sqrt{1 - r^2}$$	Sec. 11.6
Standard Error of the Mean	$$\sigma_{\bar{X}} = \dfrac{\sigma}{\sqrt{n}}$$	Sec. 13.7
Estimate of the Standard Error of the Mean	$$s_{\bar{X}} = \dfrac{s}{\sqrt{n}} = \dfrac{S}{\sqrt{n-1}}$$	Sec. 15.4
Addition Theorem of Probability: Outcomes Mutually Exclusive	$$\mathrm{Pr}(A \text{ or } B) = \mathrm{Pr}(A) + \mathrm{Pr}(B)$$	Sec. 14.3
Multiplication Theorem of Probability: Independent Events	$$\mathrm{Pr}(A \text{ and } B) = \mathrm{Pr}(A) \times \mathrm{Pr}(B)$$	Sec. 14.3
Test Statistic: Hypothesis about a Single Mean	$$\text{``}z\text{''} = t = \dfrac{\bar{X} - \mu_{\text{hyp}}}{s_{\bar{X}}}$$	Sec. 15.6 Sec. 19.2
Estimate of the Standard Error of the Difference between Two *Independent* Means	$$s_{\bar{X}-\bar{Y}} = \sqrt{s_{\bar{X}}^2 + s_{\bar{Y}}^2}$$	Sec. 17.4
(Same as above; Alternative Computing Formulas)	$$s_{\bar{X}-\bar{Y}} = \sqrt{\dfrac{s_X^2}{n_X} + \dfrac{s_Y^2}{n_Y}} = \sqrt{\dfrac{S_X^2}{n_X - 1} + \dfrac{S_Y^2}{n_X - 1}}$$	Sec. 17.4

Estimate of the Standard Error of the Difference between Two Independent Means (Assuming Homogeneity of Variance)

$$s_{\bar{X}-\bar{Y}} = \sqrt{\frac{\sum x^2 + \sum y^2}{(n_X - 1) + (n_Y - 1)}\left(\frac{1}{n_X} + \frac{1}{n_Y}\right)}$$

Sec. 19.8

(Same as above when $n_X = n_Y$)

$$s_{\bar{X}-\bar{Y}} = \sqrt{\frac{\sum x^2 + \sum y^2}{n(n - 1)}}$$

Sec. 19.8

Estimate of the Standard Error of the Difference between Two *Dependent* Sample Means

$$s_{\bar{X}-\bar{Y}} = \sqrt{s_{\bar{X}}^2 + s_{\bar{Y}}^2 - 2rs_{\bar{X}}s_{\bar{Y}}}$$

Sec. 17.9

Test Statistic: Hypothesis about the Difference between Two *Independent* Means, Normal Distribution Model

$$\text{``}z\text{''} = \frac{(\bar{X} - \bar{Y}) - (\mu_X - \mu_Y)_{\text{hyp}}}{\sqrt{s_{\bar{X}}^2 + s_{\bar{Y}}^2}}$$

Sec. 17.5

Test Statistic: Hypothesis about the Difference between Two *Independent* Means, t Distribution Model

$$t = \frac{(\bar{X} - \bar{Y}) - (\mu_X - \mu_Y)_{\text{hyp}}}{\sqrt{\frac{\sum x^2 + \sum y^2}{(n_X - 1) + (n_Y - 1)}\left[\frac{1}{n_X} + \frac{1}{n_Y}\right]}}$$

Sec. 19.8

Test Statistic: Hypothesis about the Difference between Two *Dependent* Means

$$\text{``}z\text{''} = t = \frac{(\bar{X} - \bar{Y}) - (\mu_X - \mu_Y)_{\text{hyp}}}{\sqrt{s_{\bar{X}}^2 + s_{\bar{Y}}^2 - 2rs_{\bar{X}}s_{\bar{Y}}}}$$

Sec. 17.9
Sec. 19.10

Approximate Rule for Interval Estimate of μ

$$\bar{X} \pm z_p s_{\bar{X}}$$

Sec. 18.3

Interval Estimate of μ

$$\bar{X} \pm t_p s_{\bar{X}}$$

Sec. 19.11

Sample Size for Interval Estimate of μ of Given Width

$$n = \left(\frac{\sigma z_p}{w}\right)^2$$

Sec. 18.6

Approximate Rule for Interval Estimate of $\mu_X - \mu_Y$	$(\bar{X} - \bar{Y}) \pm z_p s_{\bar{X}-\bar{Y}}$	Sec. 18.4
Rule for Interval Estimate of $\mu_X - \mu_Y$	$(\bar{X} - \bar{Y}) \pm t_p s_{\bar{X}-\bar{Y}}$	Sec. 19.12
Sample Size for Interval Estimate of $\mu_X - \mu_Y$, *Independent* Samples	$n = 2\left(\dfrac{\sigma z_p}{w}\right)^2$	Sec. 18.6

Within-Groups Sum of Squares, Raw Score Formula

$$SS_W = \sum^{\substack{\text{all} \\ \text{scores}}} X^2 - \left[\frac{\left(\sum X_A\right)^2}{n_A} + \frac{\left(\sum X_B\right)^2}{n_B} + \cdots\right]$$

Sec. 22.7

Among-Groups Sum of Squares, Raw Score Formula

$$SS_A = \left[\frac{\left(\sum X_A\right)^2}{n_A} + \frac{\left(\sum X_B\right)^2}{n_B} + \cdots\right] - \frac{\left(\sum^{\substack{\text{all} \\ \text{scores}}} X\right)^2}{\sum n_i}$$

Sec. 22.7

Total Sum of Squares, Raw Score Formula

$$SS_T = \sum^{\substack{\text{all} \\ \text{scores}}} X^2 - \frac{\left(\sum^{\substack{\text{all} \\ \text{scores}}} X\right)^2}{\sum n_i}$$

Sec. 22.7

Within-Groups Degrees of Freedom	$df_W = \sum(n_i - 1)$	Sec. 22.5
Among-Groups Degrees of Freedom	$df_A = k - 1$	Sec. 22.5
Within-Groups Variance Estimate	$s_W^2 = \dfrac{SS_W}{df_W}$	Sec. 22.5
Among-Groups Variance Estimate	$s_A^2 = \dfrac{SS_A}{df_A}$	Sec. 22.5
F Ratio	$F_{\text{calc}} = \dfrac{s_A^2}{s_W^2}$	Sec. 22.9

Column Sum of Squares	$$SS_C = \left[\frac{\left(\sum X_{C_1} \right)^2}{n_{C_1}} + \frac{\left(\sum X_{C_2} \right)^2}{n_{C_2}} + \cdots \right] - \frac{\left(\sum\limits_{\substack{\text{all} \\ \text{scores}}} X \right)^2}{n_{\substack{\text{all} \\ \text{scores}}}}$$	Sec. 22.14
Row Sum of Squares	$$SS_R = \left[\frac{\left(\sum X_{R_1} \right)^2}{n_{R_1}} + \frac{\left(\sum X_{R_2} \right)^2}{n_{R_2}} + \cdots \right] - \frac{\left(\sum\limits_{\substack{\text{all} \\ \text{scores}}} X \right)^2}{n_{\substack{\text{all} \\ \text{scores}}}}$$	Sec. 22.14
Within-Cells Sum of Squares	$$SS_{WC} = \sum\limits_{\substack{\text{all} \\ \text{scores}}} X^2 - \sum\limits_{\substack{\text{all} \\ \text{cells}}} \left[\frac{\left(\sum\limits^{\text{cell}} X \right)^2}{n_{\text{cell}}} \right]$$	Sec. 22.14
$R \times C$ Interaction Sum of Squares	$$SS_{R \times C} = SS_T - (SS_C + SS_R + SS_{WC})$$	Sec. 22.14
Degrees of Freedom for Columns	$$df_C = C - 1$$	Sec. 22.15
Degrees of Freedom for Rows	$$df_R = R - 1$$	Sec. 22.15
Degrees of Freedom for $R \times C$ Interaction	$$df_{R \times C} = (R - 1)(C - 1)$$	Sec. 22.15
Within-Cells Degrees of Freedom	$$df_{WC} = \sum\limits^{\substack{\text{all} \\ \text{cells}}} (n_{WC} - 1)$$	Sec. 22.15
A Comparison (ANOVA)	$$K = a_A \bar{X}_A + a_B \bar{X}_B + \cdots + a_k \bar{X}_k$$	Sec. 22.20
Standard Error of a Comparison	$$s_K = \sqrt{s_{\text{error}}^2 \left(\frac{a_A^2}{n_A} + \frac{a_B^2}{n_B} + \cdots + \frac{a_k^2}{n_k} \right)}$$	Sec. 22.21
Rule for Interval Estimate of a Planned Comparison	$$K \pm t_p s_K$$	Sec. 22.22

F' for a Scheffé Comparison	$F' = (k - 1)F_{\text{crit}}$	Sec. 22.24
Rule for Interval Estimate of a Scheffé Comparison	$K \pm (F' \times s_K)$	Sec. 22.24
Chi-Square: General Formula	$\chi^2 = \sum \left[\dfrac{(f_o - f_e)^2}{f_e} \right]$	Sec. 23.3
Chi-Square: Alternative Formula	$\chi^2 = \sum \left(\dfrac{f_o^2}{f_e} \right) - \sum f_o$	Sec. 23.15
Chi-Square: 2×2 Table (Includes Yates' Correction)	$\chi^2 = \dfrac{n \left[\,\lvert AD - BC \rvert - \left(\frac{n}{2} \right) \right]^2}{(A + B)(C + D)(A + C)(B + D)}$	Sec. 23.17
Rule for 95% Confidence Interval for P	$p \pm \left(\dfrac{1}{2n} + 1.96 \sqrt{\dfrac{p(1 - p)}{n}} \right)$	Sec. 23.18
Rule for 95% Confidence Interval for $P_X - P_Y$	$(p_X - p_Y) \pm \left(\dfrac{n_X + n_Y}{2n_X n_Y} \right.$ $\left. + 1.96 \sqrt{\dfrac{p_X(1 - p_X)}{n_X} + \dfrac{p_Y(1 - p_Y)}{n_Y}} \right)$	Sec. 23.18
Sum of a Set of Ranks	$\dfrac{n(n + 1)}{2}$	Sec. 24.2
Spearman Rank Order Correlation Coefficient	$r_S = 1 - \dfrac{6 \sum D^2}{n(n^2 - 1)}$	Sec. 24.3

APPENDIX E
ANSWERS TO PROBLEMS AND EXERCISES

CHAPTER 1

1 (*a*) first (*b*) both (*c*) second (*d*) first (*e*) first.

2 Information about behavior of persons in general gives one some idea how he or she might behave. Since the results of a group are generalized, the individual's behavior may or may not be typical of the group.

3 The three percentages are answers to three *different* questions. Contributing factors to the different percentages include: some instructors are full-time and some are part-time; not all courses carry the same number of units; not all instructors teach the same number of courses.

4 Yes; it is the question that is important, not the tool used to study it.

CHAPTER 2

1 It is better not to do so. In the best statistical sense, the population is the set of test scores in the first instance and the set of heights in the second.

2 (*a*) number of chairs in a room (*b*) number of chairs in a particular room (*c*) the set of numbers representing chair counts for each room.

3 (*a*) presence or absence of a TV in a residence (*b*) presence or absence of a TV in a particular residence (*c*) the set of such records for each residence.

4 Weigh at the same time of day, use the same scale, wear the same clothing (or lack of it!).

5 Type and difficulty of material to be studied, physical study conditions (light, noise, etc.), length of study period.

6 (*a*) continuous (*b*) continuous (*c*) discrete (*d*) discrete (*e*) discrete (*f*) continuous (the underlying variable is continuous) (*g*) continuous (*h*) continuous.

7 Discrete: one cannot have a fractional number of accidents. Continuous: if number of accidents is viewed as an indicator of the proclivity toward safety of an individual, the underlying variable is presumably continuous.

8 It could be considered either way. Exact: fractional errors may not be possible. Approximate: underlying variable being measured (amount learned) is best viewed as continuous.

9 (*a*) too detailed for practical concern (*b*) weight fluctuates; perhaps better rounded to the nearest pound (*c*) too coarse for most purposes.

10 Yes; nominal.

11 Ordinal.

12 Ordinal; intervals are not equal.

13 Interval.

14 Interval; although a given rise in temperature represents the same increase in heat at different points on the scale, the zero point is arbitrary.

15 Yes; since a given numerical interval has the same meaning at any point along the scale, an interval of 20 points is twice that of 10 points no matter where the two intervals are located.

16 (*a*) yes (*b*) yes   In each case, a given interval represents the same difference no matter where it is located along the scale.

17 (*a*) no; the true zero is no longer called zero (*b*) yes; zero remains zero, and although any interval is magnified by 10, all similar intervals are also so magnified, and so remain equal.

CHAPTER 3

1 (*a*) 51.5–52.5   (*b*) 17–18 yrs.   (*c*) 750–850 yds.   (*d*) 455–465 lb.   (*e*) .55–.65 in.   (*f*) .465–.475 sec.

2 Using 10–20 class intervals reaches a balance between convenience and accuracy. The limits are arbitrary in that no critical change takes place as one crosses them.

3 (*a*) not all intervals are of the same width (*b*) intervals are not continuous; scores of 32–37 are omitted (*c*) top interval is open-ended (*d*) between 10 and 20 intervals would be better.

4 (Answers to parts (*b*) to (*d*), inclusive, may differ from those given, depending on the width of class interval selected.)

   1) (*a*) 39   (*b*) 3   (*c*) 36–38; 35.5–38.5   (*d*) 37.

   2) (*a*) 63   (*b*) 5   (*c*) 50–54; 49.5–54.5   (*d*) 52.

   3) (*a*) 144   (*b*) 10   (*c*) 20–29; 19.5–29.5   (*d*) 24.5.

   4) (*a*) 43   (*b*) 3   (*c*) -22 to -20; -22.5 to -19.5 (*d*) -21.

   5) (*a*) 2.34   (*b*) .20   (*c*) 1.10–1.29; 1.095–1.295   (*d*) 1.195.

   6) (*a*) 534   (*b*) 50   (*c*) 250 to 299; 249.5–299.5   (*d*) 274.5.

5 9.5–19.5; 14.5; 0–9.5; 4.5; yes, as $-.5$ to 9.5 because negative scores are possible.

6 46.5–47.5, 47.5–48.5, 48.5–49.5; 47, 48, 49.

7 (*a*)

score limits	f
56–58	2
53–55	0
50–52	4
47–49	10
44–46	4
41–43	11
38–40	14
35–37	9
32–34	8
29–31	8
26–28	5
23–25	3
20–22	2

(*b*)

score limits	f
54–56	2
51–53	2
48–50	8
45–47	4
42–44	7
39–41	10
36–38	16
33–35	9
30–32	6
27–29	6
24–26	7
21–23	1
18–20	2

(*b*) No, the 6 scores are all scores of 29.

(*c*) Yes; in the first distribution, the scores of the interval containing the most (47–49) are part of two different intervals (45–47, 48–50) in the second distribution.

8

score limits	f
55–59	2
50–54	4
45–49	10
40–44	16
35–39	22
30–34	10
25–29	11
20–24	5

In this distribution, the irregularities are smoothed out and one can see the characteristic shape of the distribution better; apparently the scores tend to pile up more toward the center than in the extremes.

9

score limits	f	%f
56–58	2	2
53–55	0	0
50–52	4	5
47–49	10	12
44–46	4	5
41–43	11	14
38–40	14	18
35–37	9	11
32–34	8	10
29–31	8	10
26–28	5	6
23–25	3	4
20–22	2	2

10

score limits	f	%f
54–56	2	2
51–53	2	2
48–50	8	10
45–47	4	5
42–44	7	9
39–41	10	12
36–38	16	20
33–35	9	11
30–32	6	8
27–29	6	8
24–26	7	9
21–23	1	1
18–20	2	2

11 (*a*) Group 1 (*b*) Group 2 (*c*) Group 2.

12 (*a*) 87.5–90.5 (*b*) 81.5–84.5 (*c*) 78.5–81.5 (*d*) 69.5–72.5.

13 *N.B.* There are other ways than that given below to construct a frequency distribution with acceptable characteristics. Answers to Questions 14,15, and 16 are given relative to the distribution shown here.

(*a*) score limits	f	(*b*) cum f	(*c*) cum %f
80–81	2	50	100
78–79	2	48	96
76–77	5	46	92
74–75	7	41	82
72–73	9	34	68
70–71	6	25	50
68–69	8	19	38
66–67	4	11	22
64–65	4	7	14
62–63	2	3	6
60–61	1	1	2

14 (*a*) 64.5 (*b*) 67.9 (*c*) 72.6 (*d*) 79.0.

15 _____

16 (*a*) C_{96} (*b*) C_{10} (*c*) C_{41} (*d*) C_{78}.

17 Yes, a centile may have any value that scores have; it is the *score* point below which a certain percent of scores fall.

18

Score	(*a*) %f A	B	(*b*) Cum. f A	B	(*c*) Cum. %f A	B
155–159	0	2		50		100
150–154	1	4	150	49	100	98
145–149	3	14	148	47	99	94
140–144	5	24	144	40	96	80
135–139	8	20	137	28	91	56
130–134	9	14	125	18	83	36

Score	(a) %f		(b) Cum. f.		(c) Cum. %f	
	A	B	A	B	A	B
125–129	17	8	111	11	74	22
120–124	15	6	86	7	57	14
115–119	12	0	63	4	42	8
110–114	13	4	45	4	30	8
105–109	8	2	25	2	17	4
100–104	5	0	13	1	9	2
95– 99	2	2	5	1	3	2
90– 94	1	0	2	0	1	0

% frequency distribution is more meaningful when comparing two distributions of unequal n's.

19 (a) 110.8 (b) 125.3 (c) 130.0 (d) 143.4.

20 ———

21 (a) C_{91} (b) C_{62} (c) C_4 (d) C_2.

22 (a) 117.0 (b) 129.5.

23 $c = \ell + \left(\dfrac{cf_c - cf_\ell}{f}\right)i.$

where: C: centile
  ℓ: lower limit of class interval containing the centile
  cf_c: number of scores lying below centile
  cf_ℓ: number of scores lying below ℓ
  i: width of the class interval
  f: frequency of scores in the interval

24 Rounding error; yes, if rounding error tends to be consistently in one direction.

CHAPTER 4

1 Graphs of widely differing appearance may be constructed from the same distribution; under some circumstances, the graphic representation may be misleading. But salient features of the data may be more visible in graphic representation.

2 A large graph is better if values are to be read from it; it is easier to construct with accuracy and easier to read; a small graph would be acceptable if used only to show pertinent features, not to read values.

3 ———

4 ———

5 ———

6 ———

7 Bar diagram should be constructed in terms of *percentage* frequency; %f (males): 6, 16, 28, 27, 24, and %f (females): 21, 17, 28, 15, 19. Males are proportionally fewer at the freshman level and proportionally more numerous at the senior and graduate level.

8 (a) 63 or 64 (b) 68 (c) 72 or 73 (d) 81.

9 (a) C_7 (b) C_{53} (c) C_7 (d) C_{96}.

10 ———; although the spread of r.t. under the two conditions is similar, a greater proportion of subjects react more quickly to the simple stimulus.

11 ——

12 (*a*) —— (*b*) The cumulative function appears smoother; faster r.t. with the simple stimulus is shown by the fact that this distribution lies mainly to the left of the other.

13 ——

14 (*a*) —— (*b*) Comment is similar to that of Problem 12; performance is consistently better with Method B.

15 (*a*) —— (*b*) distribution A falls to the right of distribution B (*c*) horizontal space occupied by distribution B is greater (*d*) cumulative curves (*e*) the noncumulated distribution shows the frequency of a particular score or range of scores; the cumulative distribution shows the frequency of scores below a particular score point and is better for identifying the position of a score relative to the group.

16 No, the relationship between frequencies and percents is a directly proportional one.

17 (*a*) rises quickly at first, then less rapidly (*b*) rises more slowly at first, then quickly (*c*) rises at uniform rate (*d*) center shows less rapid rise than portions immediately preceding or following.

CHAPTER 5

1 $\bar{X} = 16.4$; Mdn $= 13.0$.

2 $\bar{X} = 19.5$; Mdn $= 20.5$.

3 $\bar{X} = 32.25$; Mdn $= 31.0$.

4 (*a*) 57.0 (*b*) 55.2 (*c*) 55.0.

5 (*a*) 56.5 (*b*) 55.5 (*c*) 55.6.

6 The assumption that the midpoint represents the scores in the interval is approximated differently in the two distributions.

7 (*a*) $Mo = 86.0$ (*b*) $Mdn = 81.0$ (*c*) $\bar{X} = 79.76$.

8 (*a*) $Mo = 87.0$ (*b*) $Mdn = 81.0$ (*c*) $\bar{X} = 79.80$.

No, the Mo differs and the $\bar{X}$ differs in the second decimal although the Mdn is the same; we expect these differences because of loss of accuracy in grouping scores, and that loss takes place differently depending on how the scores are grouped.

9 $Mdn = 122.1$ $Mo = 127.0$.

10 $Mdn = 138.0$ $Mo = 142.0$.

11 (*a*) 41 (*b*) 16 (*c*) 42 (*d*) 7 (*e*) 62.

12 The mean is the measure that best reflects the total of the scores.

13 The median; it is a reasonably stable measure but not so responsive as the mean to the few deviant scores.

14 The median; it is the only relatively stable measure that can be found for open-ended distributions.

15 negatively skewed.

16 negatively skewed.

17 Fig. 4.11 D, E, or F.

18 56.4.

19 (*a*) to give the appropriate weight to each $\bar{X}$ according to the number of cases upon which $\bar{X}$ is based (*b*) when all subgroups are based on the same number of cases.

20 Yes, if "average" refers to $\bar{X}$, in a positively skewed distribution the Mdn will be less than $\bar{X}$, and thus more than half earn less than the mean income.

21 The mean; more amenable to arithmetic and algebraic manipulation, appropriate for other important statistical formulas and procedures, and least sensitive to sampling fluctuation.

22 Yes, in popular use the term *average* is often used indiscriminately for any measure; if one organization uses one index and the other another, their statements could be "consistent," assuming the distribution of wages is skewed.

23 (a) $\overline{X - C} = \dfrac{\sum (X - C)}{n} = \dfrac{\sum X}{n} - \dfrac{nC}{n} = \bar{X} - C$

(b) $\overline{(X/C)} = \dfrac{\sum (X/C)}{n} = \dfrac{(1/C)\sum X}{n} = \bar{X}/C$

CHAPTER 6

1 (a) 109   (b) 13.7.

2 Simple stimulus: range $= 199$ Q $= 25.4$.

Complex stimulus: range $= 199$ Q $= 25.4$.

Variability of the two in terms of range and Q is equal.

3 (a) 5; 5   (b) 1.7   (c) 1.7   (d) 1.7   (e) the raw score method is easier.

4 1.9; 1.9; 1.9

5 (a) 20.0   (b) 4.0   (c) 10.0.

6 2.2

7 11.1, 6.6; 47.4, 7.2; 143.8, 6.8

8 29.00, 3.03

9 58.50, 5.02

10 40.25, 9.97

11 Simple stimulus: $\bar{X} = 193.1$, $S_X = 40.7$

Complex stimulus: $\bar{Y} = 215.0$, $S_Y = 37.6$

The mean reaction time to simple stimuli is rather less than to complex stimuli; variability is similar.

12 For simple stimulus, the range (200) is 4.9S, and the expected range of scores (given a normal distribution) in a sample of size 50 is approximately 4 to 5S; for complex stimulus, the range (200) is 5.3S, and the expected range of scores in a sample of size 150 is approximately 5–6S. The obtained standard deviations therefore appear reasonable.

13 The mean, range, and S would be affected; $\bar{X}$ and S respond to the exact position of every score in the distribution, and the range is a function of the distance between the lowest and highest score. The median is unaffected since it only reflects *how many* scores are above and below it, not what their values are. Similarly, Q will be unaffected since C_{75} will be unchanged.

14 Most resistant to sampling fluctuation, important in advanced statistical procedures.

15 $\bar{X}$ and S_X give no information regarding the shape of the distribution.

16 Q is the only relatively stable measure of variability appropriate for an open-ended distribution.

17 His students not only have more knowledge of science but are more homogeneous in their knowledge; they may therefore be ready for a more advanced curriculum than generally offered and are more alike than expected in their readiness for science study.

18 Data 6D: diff. = .15 st. dev., a small difference (distributions overlap more than 90%). Data 6E: diff. = .71 st. dev., a substantial difference (distributions overlap less than 80%).

CHAPTER 7

(Answers to some problems in this chapter may differ from those given below depending on when rounding has been introduced into the calculations.)

1 (*a*) .16 (*b*) .02 (*c*) .001 (*d*) .02 (*e*) .001.

2 (*a*) .84 (*b*) .50 (*c*) .98.

3 (*a*) .30 (*b*) .14 (*c*) .68 (*d*) .95 (*e*) .997.

4 (*a*) 120 (*b*) 56 (*c*) 272 (*d*) 380 (*e*) 399.

5 (*a*) .20 (*b*) .37 (*c*) .92 (*d*) .18.

6 (*a*) .31 (*b*) .16 (*c*) .21 (*d*) .93 (*e*) .30 (*f*) .87 (*g*) .09 (*h*) .31.

7 (*a*) 20 (*b*) 990 (*c*) 890 (*d*) 40 (*e*) 90 (*f*) 490 or if carried to another decimal:

   (*a*) 23 (*b*) 994 (*c*) 894 (*d*) 40 (*e*) 92 (*f*) 493.

8 (*a*) +1.64 (*b*) +1.96 (*c*) +2.33 (*d*) +2.58.

9 (*a*) ±2.58 (*b*) ±1.96 (*c*) ±.67.

10 (*a*) +.84 (*b*) +.39 (*c*) −.52 (*d*) −1.55 (*e*) ±.92.

11 (*a*) +1.28 (*b*) +.31 (*c*) −.77 (*d*) −1.55 (*e*) ±.67.

12 (*a*) 33.2 (*b*) 25.3 (*c*) 19.1 (*d*) 18.6 (*e*) 23.1, 26.9.

13 (*a*) 130.8 (*b*) 94.2 (*c*) 91.7 (*d*) 77.3 (*e*) 80.8, 119.2.

CHAPTER 8

1 Nothing, a score is uninterpretable without a frame of reference.

2 (*a*) 110 (*b*) 125 (*c*) 85 (*d*) 55.

3 (*a*) 540 (*b*) 473 (*c*) 440 (*d*) 490.

4 (*a*) $X_n = 1.67 X_o + 5.0$.

   (*b*) 110; 125; 85; 55.

5 (*a*) $X_n = 3.33 X_o + 140.0$.

   (*b*) 540; 473; 440; 490.

6 (*a*) C_{31} (*b*) C_{98} (*c*) C_{69} (*d*) C_{89}.

7 *Mdn;* the mean of centile ranks may be different from the centile rank of the mean of the raw scores or other standard scores, depending upon the shape of the distribution, but the *Mdn* of a set of centile ranks will be the same as the centile rank of the median score.

8 Since the shapes of the two distributions are different (aptitude scores positively skewed, achievement scores negatively skewed), comparison of standard scores will not be appropriate; may use centile ranks or convert scores to derived score distributions that have identical shapes as well as identical means and standard deviations (e.g. T scores).

9 Greatest gain is made by Student B, least by Student A.

10 (a) $\bar{X}_{\text{Mary}} = 74$; $\bar{X}_{\text{Beth}} = 56$.

(b)

	Mary's z	Beth's z
Test X:	-1.5	$+1.5$
Test Y:	$+1.5$	-1.5
	$\bar{z}_{\text{Mary}} = 0$	$\bar{z}_{\text{Beth}} = 0$

(c) When scores from different distributions are averaged, the scores are weighted according to the standard deviation of the distribution from which each came; in this case, Mary has a higher raw score mean than Beth because she performed better on the test with greater variability, whereas Beth performed better on the test with the lesser variability.

11 Just take the mean of the raw scores, since the ratio of the two standard deviations (which is responsible for weighting) is already in the desired ratio of 2 to 1.

12 Principle of comparative measurement is not used; for example, a score of 90% might be either high or low compared with other persons.

13 Only when the mean and median are the same. This would not be true if the distribution were skewed.

14 Only for those rare scores more than 5 standard deviations below the mean.

CHAPTER 9

1 (a) $+.59$ (b) $+.59$ (c) Rounding error may result in slightly different answers. (d) Raw score method; it uses one-digit whole numbers rather than two-digit fractional numbers.

2 (a) $-.76$ (b) $\bar{X} = 5.2$, $\bar{Y} = 6.2$, $S_X = 2.04$, $S_Y = 1.84$.

3 (a) $-.46$ (b) $\bar{X} = 6.5$, $\bar{Y} = 6.25$, $S_X = 1.1$, $S_Y = 2.2$.

4 (a) $.95$ (b) $\bar{X} = 4.0$, $\bar{Y} = 6.7$, $S_X = 2.2$, $S_Y = 3.1$.

5 (a) $r = -.60$ (b) to (f) unchanged (g) $r < .60$

6 (a) ⎯⎯⎯ (b) $\bar{X} = 38.1$ $\bar{Y} = 77.5$ $S_X = 4.28$ $S_Y = 4.67$.

7 (a) $.60$ (b) $\bar{X} = 18.4$, $\bar{Y} = 39.4$, $S_X = 6.9$, $S_Y = 7.8$.

8 (a) $.52$ (b) $\bar{X} = 21.0$, $\bar{Y} = 41.1$, $S_X = 8.5$, $S_Y = 10.8$.

9 ⎯⎯⎯

10 ⎯⎯⎯

CHAPTER 10

1 The age of drivers may not be the determining factor in driving safety; perhaps older drivers are more experienced or because of seniority are assigned easier, less traveled routes and/or day shifts.

2 Both strength of grip and arithmetic achievement score are dependent on maturational level. Maturational level is a variable in the elementary school sample but essentially a constant in the college sample.

3 (*a*) _____ (*b*) The bivariate distribution is both discontinuous and nonlinear; yes, the discontinuity tends to result in a higher value of *r*, and Pearson *r* tends to underestimate the relationship when data are nonlinear, since scores do not "hug" the straight line of best fit as well as they would the curved line of best fit.

4 (*a*) _____ (*b*) The distribution lacks homoscedasticity, and both distributions are positively skewed; homoscedasticity: *r* is a measure of the *average* strength of relationship and will underestimate that strength among low scores and overestimate it among high scores.

5 Both coefficients are subject to substantial sampling variation because of small sample size ($n = 15$), so it could be that the present difference is due simply to sampling variation.

6 Although both industries employ "assembly workers," the job duties may be quite different. If so, what predicts well for one type of job may not do so for another.

7 Production method may not involve manual dexterity in one company; the kind of unit produced by the two companies may be quite different; the two tests used may measure different aspects of manual dexterity.

CHAPTER 11

1 When regression is linear; when the bivariate distribution is a sample rather than a population bivariate distribution.

2 (1) The resulting regression equation is more readily interpretable. (2) The regression line location and the correlation coefficient are more stably determined than otherwise.

3 (*a*) $Y' = .00233X + 1.35$ (*b*) 2.48; 3.00 (*c*) linearity of regression (*d*) .303 (*e*) .29; .06; 1.89–3.07 (*f*) .95; .50; 2.79–3.21 (*g*) linearity; homoscedasticity; that the distribution of obtained *Y* scores (for a particular *X*) is normal.

4 $z'_Y = +.50z_X$.

5 $Y' = .933X + 53.3$ (*b*) 109.3; 81.3 (*c*) .91; .26; 72.4–146.2 (*d*) .27; .46; 64.9–97.7.

6 $z'_Y = +.70z_X$.

7 (*a*) $+1.20$ (*b*) 62 (*c*) 56 (*d*) 44 (*e*) 38 (*f*) 50.

8 The sum of the squares of errors of prediction will be minimized.

9 (*a*) No, the term "$+40$" characterizes a *raw* score regression equation (*b*) no, the term "*X*" will disappear from the right side of the raw score regression equation when $r = 0$ (*c*) only if S_X and S_Y are equal.

CHAPTER 12

1 _____

2 The range of talent for IQ will be less among retarded children, so the correlation will be lower.

3 Since all persons in the group are highly creative, the range of talent is small. The two variables would probably correlate much more substantially in a random sample taken from the general population.

4 Restriction of range; there is probably less variation in ability among experienced pilots, so the correlation will be lower.

5 There is likely to be less variability in ability among currently employed workers than among job applicants; we therefore expect a lower correlation coefficient for the employed.

6 No; lower when combined since spelling score means for each group differ but IQ means are about the same; the regression line fitted to the pooled data lies among the two distributions so that the ratio of S_{YX}^2 to S_Y^2 is larger than in either sample alone.

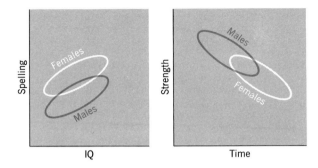

7 No; it is likely that women's mean grip strength is lower and 100 yd. dash time is higher than for men, so that in the pooled distribution the ratio of S_{YX}^2 to S_Y^2 is smaller and the correlation coefficient is of greater magnitude for the pooled data.

8 (a) No (b) Y increases by 2 units for each unit increase in X.

9 (a) It is negative (b) Y decreases 5 units for each unit increase in X.

10 Yes, when the regression line passes through the point where $Y' = 0$ when $X = 0$.

11 $\bar{Y} = 12$, $r = 0$.

12 (a) $z = +.25$ (b) $Y = 105$ (c) $Y = 86$.

13 Yes, since the parents are selected because of their low IQ, the facts of regression suggest that the mean IQ of their offspring will be substantially higher than their own. The proposal will be less effective than supposed.

14 Regression on the mean is expected; their retest mean should be somewhat closer to the mean (100) of the general population.

15 The safety course may have been beneficial, but because of regression on the mean, one would expect improvement even if the course were of no value.

16 (a) The proportion of the maximum possible predictive error (when $r = 0$) remaining is .99, .95, .80, and .44, respectively. (b) The proportion of variance in one variable that is accounted for by changes in the other variable is .01, .09, .36, and .81, respectively. (c) The proportion of correct placements in excess of chance is .03, .10, .20, and .35, respectively.

17 (a) The existing proportion of the maximum possible predictive error is reduced from .97 to .87. (b) The proportion of the total Y variance associated with changes in X is increased from .06 to .25. (c) The proportion of correct placements in excess of chance increased from .08 to .17. (d) no.

18 $S_{YX} = 0$ because all points are on the regression line and thus there is no predictive error.

19 When $r = 0$, $Y' = \bar{Y}$. Therefore $\Sigma(Y - Y')^2/n = \Sigma(Y - \bar{Y})^2/n = S_Y^2$.

20 $S_Y^2 = S_{YX}^2 + S_{Y'}^2$; if $S_{YX} = 0$, $S_Y = S_{Y'}$; this condition occurs when $r = \pm1.00$.

21 When $r = 0$; see answer to 19.

CHAPTER 13

1 Random sampling differences in the constituency of the class might account for the drop.

2 (a) .25 (b) 25.

3 (a) 1/6   (b) 1/3   (c) 2/3.

4 .95.

5 (a) .16   (b) .13.

6 (a) .19   (b) .32.

7 (a) .008   (b) .005.

8 (a) 159.3   (b) 139.7–160.3.

9 (a) 115.9   (b) 116.1–123.9.

10 (a) 153.2   (b) 145.9–154.1.

CHAPTER 14

1 Empirical—they are derived from experience in similar circumstances.

2 (a) *Die #1:* 1 1 1 1 1 1 2 2 2 2 2 2 3 3 3 3 3 3 4 4 4 4 4 4 5 5 5 5 5 5 6 6 6 6 6 6
      Die #2: 1 2 3 4 5 6 1 2 3 4 5 6 1 2 3 4 5 6 1 2 3 4 5 6 1 2 3 4 5 6 1 2 3 4 5 6

  (b) *Sum of points:*   2   3   4   5   6   7   8   9   10   11   12
      relative f: 1/36 2/36 3/36 4/36 5/36 6/36 5/36 4/36 3/36 2/36 1/36

  (c) 1/36   (d) 3/36 or 1/12   (e) 6/36 or 1/6   (f) 15/36 or 5/12; 30/36   (g) 1/36; 1/1296.

3 (a) 3/16   (b) 10/16   (c) 6/16.

4 (a) 1/2704   (b) 1/169   (c) 1/16   (d) 1/169   (e) 2/169.

5 _____

6 (a) 2.5%   (b) 5.1%   (c) 29.2%.

7 (a) $\mu = 5.0$; $\sigma = 3.63$

(b) Samples	(c) $\bar{X}$	(d) $\bar{X}$	f
1,1	1.0	1.0	1
1,2	1.5	1.5	2
1,4	2.5	2.0	1
1,7	4.0	2.5	2
1,11	6.0	3.0	2
2,1	1.5	4.0	3
2,2	2.0	4.5	2
2,4	3.0	5.5	2
2,7	4.5	6.0	2
2,11	6.5	6.5	2
4,1	2.5	7.0	1
4,2	3.0	7.5	2
4,4	4.0	9.0	2
4,7	5.5	11.0	1
4,11	7.5		
7,1	4.0		
7,2	4.5		
7,4	5.5		
7,7	7.0		
7,11	9.0		
11,1	6.0		
11,2	6.5		
11,4	7.5		
11,7	9.0		
11,11	11.0		

(e) $\mu_{\bar{X}} = 5.0$, $\sigma_{\bar{X}} = 2.57$ (f) $\sigma_{\bar{X}} = 2.57$ (g) yes, 5   (h) yes, 2.57   (i) No; however it is more like the normal curve than is the population of 5 scores. This is in accord with the Central Limit Theorem.

8 _____

9 (a) 0   (b) 12/2652, or 1/221   (c) 156/2652, or 1/17   (d) 16/2652, or 4/663.

10 (a) 100/190   (b) 90/190   (c) 58/100   (d) 58/190;   (58/100)(100/190) = 58/190   or (58/90)(90/190) = 58/190.   (e) 90/361   (f) (42 + 58 + 32)/190 = 132/190;   (100/190) + (90/190) − (58/190) = 132/190.

CHAPTER 15

1 Dividing Σx^2 by 99 rather than 100 makes little difference, but dividing by 2 rather than 3 would make a substantial difference; S and s will be similar unless n is small.

2 ± 1.64.

3 (a) $\Sigma x^2 = 11.0$ (b) $s_X = 1.92$ (c) $s_{\bar{X}} = .96$ (d) $S_X = 1.66$ (e) $s_{\bar{X}} = .96$ (f) (should be).

4 (a) $z_{obt} = +2.50$, $z_{crit} = \pm 1.96$; reject H_0 (b) $z_{obt} = +2.50$, $z_{crit} = \pm 2.58$; accept H_0 (c) .0062; .0124.

5 (a) $z_{obt} = +2.50$, $z_{crit} = +1.64$; reject H_0;   (b) $z_{obt} = +2.50$, $z_{crit} = +2.33$; reject H_0.

6 $z_{obt} = +2.50$, $z_{crit} = -1.64$; accept H_0.

7 $H_0: \mu = 123$, $H_A: \mu \neq 123$;   (a) $z_{obt} = -1.50$, $z_{crit} = \pm 1.96$ accept H_0 (b) $z_{obt} = -1.50$, $z_{crit} = \pm 2.58$; accept H_0 (c) .1336.

8 $H_0: \mu = 123$; $H_A: \mu \neq 123$;   (a) $z_{obt} = -2.75$, $z_{crit} = \pm 1.96$; reject H_0 (b) $z_{obt} = -2.75$, $z_{crit} = \pm 2.58$; reject H_0 (c) .006.

9 (a) $z_{obt} = -2.45$, $z_{crit} = \pm 1.96$ (reject H_0 at $\alpha = .05$), $z_{crit} = \pm 2.58$ (accept H_0 at $\alpha = .01$)   (b) accept H_0 at both levels; reject H_0 at both levels (c) because σ is estimated and n is very small.

10 (a) $z_{obt} = +2.27$, reject H_0 at $\alpha = .05$, accept H_0 at $\alpha = .01$ (b) reject H_0 at $\alpha = .05$, accept H_0 at $\alpha = .01$; accept H_0 at both levels.

11 Yes; the sample mean is so deviant that its probability of occurrence in random sampling (when H_0 is true) is .05 or less; it seems unlikely that this sample mean came from the population defined by H_0.

12 No; we can say only that H_0 *could* be true; given our sample statistics, there are many other hypotheses that if tested would be accepted and therefore could also be true.

13 $H_0: \mu = 100$, $H_A: \mu < 100$ (a) $z_{obt} = -2.00$, $z_{crit} = -1.64$; reject H_0 (b) $z_{obt} = -2.00$, $z_{crit} = -2.33$; accept H_0 (c) .0228.

14 (a) Heavy usage of the library may be expected just prior to midterms; thus, this sample would not represent general library usage.   (b) This sample is likely to be biased in favor of "library users," as opposed to those who seldom frequent the library.   (c) It may be that freshman English students use the library more or less than students in general, so the sample may not be satisfactory.   (d) Humanities and Arts majors may use the library more or less than Science majors, Business majors, etc., and thus not be representative of the population desired (all students at S.U.).   (e) These early risers may not be representative of all students; perhaps the more ambitious sign up for 8:00 AM classes and use the library more often.

CHAPTER 16

1 Accept the null hypothesis; the evidence does not point toward the validity of the alternative hypothesis.

2 The choice stems from the logic of the inquiry, not the nature of the sample outcome.

3 If interest is *only* in a difference in a particular direction, a one-tailed test is appropriate; one may expect the outcome to be in a specific direction but yet be interested in discovering a discrepancy if it appeared in the other direction.

4 Rejecting H_0 means that we have found a statistic so deviant that its probability of occurrence when H_0 is true is rare enough for us to conclude that it is not reasonable to believe H_0 is true; accepting H_0 means that we do not have sufficient evidence to reject H_0; it does not mean H_0 is probably true but only that it *could* be true.

5 (a) Using small samples avoids the problem of finding a statistical difference with a very large n when the actual discrepancy is so small as to be practically unimportant. (b) If n is very small, it is difficult to discover a difference unless the true discrepancy is very large.

6 (a) .75 (b) 102.25 (c) no, it is only a small fraction of a standard deviation above the hypothesized value (d) .15.

7 No, .95 is the probability of accepting H_0 *when* it is true, not the probability that it *is* true.

8 No, .95 does not refer to the likelihood that H_0 is false, but to the likelihood of accepting H_0 when it is true.

9 Using $\alpha = .05$, we would expect 1 out of 20 tests to show "significance" when the null hypothesis was true. 1 out of 18 is quite in line with this expectation; the test may well prove worthless.

10 (a) $\alpha = 1.00$ (b) $\beta = 0$.

11 (a) $\alpha = 2/3$ (b) $\beta = 1/3$.

12 (a) $\alpha = 0$ (b) $\beta = 2/3$.

13 (a) $\alpha = 0$ (b) $\beta = 1/3$.

14 _____

CHAPTER 17

1 (a) $H_0: \mu_X - \mu_Y = 0$; $H_A: \mu_X - \mu_Y \neq 0$ (b) $s_{\bar{X}-\bar{Y}} = 5.0$ (c) $z = -2.00$ (d) at $\alpha = .05$, reject H_0; at $\alpha = .01$, accept H_0.

2 At $\alpha = .05$, reject H_0; at $\alpha = .01$ accept H_0.

3 Accept H_0 at both levels.

4 (a) $H_0: \mu_X - \mu_Y = 0$; $H_A: \mu_X - \mu_Y \neq 0$ (b) $s_{\bar{X}-\bar{Y}} = 2.83$ (c) $z = +2.47$ (d) at $\alpha = .05$ reject H_0; at $\alpha = .01$ accept H_0.

5 (a) $H_0: \mu_X - \mu_Y = 0$; $H_A: \mu_X - \mu_Y \neq 0$ (b) $s_X = 1.87$; $s_Y = 1.87$ (c) $(s_{\bar{X}-\bar{Y}} = 1.18$; $z = +2.54)$ at $\alpha = .05$ reject H_0; at $\alpha = .01$ accept H_0.

6 (a) $H_0: \mu_X - \mu_Y = 0$; $H_A: \mu_X - \mu_Y \neq 0$ (b) $s_X = 1.87$; $s_Y = 1.73$ (c) $(s_{\bar{X}-\bar{Y}} = 1.14$; $z = -4.38)$ at $\alpha = .05$ reject H_0; at $\alpha = .01$ reject H_0.

7 Independent: matching involves a variable. In this case grade in school is a constant for both groups, not a variable.

8 (a) $H_0: \mu_X - \mu_Y = 0$; $H_A: \mu_X - \mu_Y \neq 0$ (b) $s_{\bar{X}-\bar{Y}} = 1.80$ (c) $z = +1.67$: accept H_0 at both levels.

9 (a) $H_0: \mu_X - \mu_Y = 0$; $H_A: \mu_X - \mu_Y \neq 0$ (b) $\bar{X} = 5.6$ $\bar{Y} = 3.4$ $S_X = 1.85$ $S_Y = 1.85$ (c) $r = +.57$
(d) $s_{\bar{X}-\bar{Y}} = .86$ (e) $z = +2.56$: at $\alpha = .05$ reject H_0; at $\alpha = .01$ accept H_0.

10 (a) $\bar{D} = 2.2$; $s_{\bar{D}} = .86$ (b) $z = +2.56$; same (c) at $\alpha = .05$, reject H_0; at $\alpha = .01$ accept H_0.

11 _____

12 (a) 2.58 (b) 2.98 (c) Total n is the same (60), but $s_{\bar{X}-\bar{Y}}$ is smaller when $n_X = n_Y$.

CHAPTER 18

1 (a) 60.65–65.35 (b) 59.90–66.10 (c) 61.03–64.97.

2 (a) 61.82–64.18 (b) 61.45–64.55
2.36 vs 4.70 3.10 vs 6.20
4 times the number of cases halve the width of the interval

3 (a) $C[109.16 \leq \mu \leq 124.84] = .95$
(b) $C[106.68 \leq \mu \leq 127.32] = .99$
(c) $C[114.32 \leq \mu \leq 119.68] = .50$

4 (a) $C[-19.8 \leq (\mu_X - \mu_Y) \leq -.2] = .95$
(b) $C[-22.9 \leq (\mu_X - \mu_Y) \leq +2.90] = .99$
(c) $C[-13.35 \leq (\mu_X - \mu_Y) \leq -6.65] = .50$

5 (a) $C[1.45 \leq (\mu_X - \mu_Y) \leq 12.55] = .95$
(b) $C[-.30 \leq (\mu_X - \mu_Y) \leq 14.30] = .99$
(c) $C[5.10 \leq (\mu_X - \mu_Y) \leq 8.90] = .50$

6 (a) $C[-.53 \leq (\mu_X - \mu_Y) \leq 6.53] = .95$
(b) $C[-1.64 \leq (\mu_X - \mu_Y) \leq 7.64] = .99$

7 $d_1 = .20$; rather precise: μ should be within $.20\sigma$ of $\bar{X}$.

8 $d_1 = .39$; only moderately precise: μ should be with $.39\sigma$ of $\bar{X}$.

9 (a) $C(2.75 \leq \mu \leq 3.05) = .95$ (b) _____ (c) $d_1 = .49$ (d) not too precise: μ should be with $.49\sigma$ of $\bar{X}$ (e) n is too small for accurate evaluation

10 $d_2 = .45$ (or .44), which suggests only moderate precision: $\mu_X - \mu_Y$ should be within $.44\sigma$ of $\bar{X} - \bar{Y}$.

11 $C[-.88 \leq (\mu_X - \mu_Y) \leq -.01] = .95$.

12 $d_2 = .33$; $\mu_X - \mu_Y$ should be within 33σ of $\bar{X} - \bar{Y}$, moderately precise.

13 96.

14 166.

15 (a) 69 (b) 42.

16 (a) 120 (b) 72.

17 (a) accept H_0 (b) reject H_0 (c) a confidence interval contains all those values that if hypothesized would be accepted.

18 (a) -5 (b) reject H_0.

19 (a) $+5$ (b) accept H_0.

20 (a) $z = +5.0$ (b) it is very unlikely that a difference this large could have arisen by chance when H_0 is true (c) $C(81.8 \leq \mu \leq 84.2) = .95$ (d) chances are high that μ falls within 81.8–84.2 (e) the former suggests that 80 is an unlikely value for μ and that 83 is far from 80; the latter suggests that the limits of sampling variation are very narrow (because of the large n), and that therefore 80 is an unlikely value for μ

CHAPTER 19

1 Because the mean of the 3 scores, $\bar{X}$, is fixed, only 2 of the 3 scores in $\sum\limits^{3}(X - \bar{X})^2$ are free to vary; in $\sum\limits^{3}(X - \mu)^2$, μ does not result in such a restriction, so all 3 scores are free to vary.

2 (a) $+2.602$ (b) -1.341.

3 (a) $\pm.706$ (b) ±1.860 (c) ±2.306 (d) ±3.355.

4 (a) .10 (b) .90 (c) .95 (d) .925.

5 (a) $p < .01$ (b) $p < .05$ (c) $p < .05$ (d) $p < .20$ (e) $p < .05$.

6 (a) accept H_0: $t_{\text{crit}} = \pm2.262$ (b) reject H_0: $t_{\text{crit}} = \pm2.093$ (c) reject H_0: $t_{\text{crit}} = +1.833$.

7 (a) $t_{\text{calc}} = +2.0$, $t_{\text{crit}} = \pm2.132$, accept H_0. (b) $t_{\text{calc}} = -1.67$, $t_{\text{crit}} = -1.753$, accept H_0.

8 (a) $s_X = 2.45$ ($s_{\bar{X}} = 1.09$) (b) $t_{\text{calc}} = -2.75$ (c) $t_{\text{crit .05}}$ for $df = 4$: ±2.776, accept H_0 (d) $t_{\text{crit .01}}$ for $df = 4$: ±4.604, accept H_0.

9 (a) $t_{\text{obt}} = +2.27$; $t_{\text{crit .05}}$ for $df = 4$: ±2.776, accept H_0; $t_{\text{crit .01}} = \pm4.604$, accept H_0 (b) $t_{\text{crit .05}}$ for $df = 4$: $+2.132$, reject H_0; $t_{\text{crit .01}} = +3.747$, accept H_0 (c) accept H_0 at both levels.

10 (a) $s_{\bar{X} - \bar{Y}} = 1.25$ (b) $t_{\text{calc}} = -4.80$, t_{crit} for $df = 30$: ±2.042, reject H_0.

11 (a) H_0: $\mu_X - \mu_Y = 0$; H_A: $\mu_X - \mu_Y \neq 0$ (b) $s_{\bar{X} - \bar{Y}}$ (pooled) $= 1.18$ (c) $t_{\text{calc}} = +2.54$, $t_{\text{crit .05}}$ for 8 $df = \pm2.306$, reject H_0; $t_{\text{crit .01}}$ for 8 $df = \pm3.355$, accept H_0.

12 (a) H_0: $\mu_X - \mu_Y = 0$; H_A: $\mu_X - \mu_Y \neq 0$ (b) $s_X = 1.87$, $s_Y = 1.73$ (c) $s_{\bar{X} - \bar{Y}} = 1.14$, $t_{\text{crit .05}}$ for 8 $df = \pm2.306$, reject H_0; $t_{\text{crit .01}}$ for 8 $df = \pm3.355$, reject H_0.

13 (a) H_0: $\mu_X - \mu_Y = 0$; H_A: $\mu_X - \mu_Y \neq 0$ (b) $s_{\bar{X} - \bar{Y}} = 2.41$ (c) $t_{\text{calc}} = 1.66$, $t_{\text{crit .05}}$ for $df = 15$: ±2.131, accept H_0; $t_{\text{crit .01}}$ for $df = 15$: ±2.947, accept H_0.

14 (a) $C[43.60 \leq \mu_X \leq 56.40] = .95$
   (b) $C[41.16 \leq \mu_X \leq 58.84] = .99$
   (c) $C[47.93 \leq \mu_X \leq 52.07] = .50$

15 (a) $C[1.97 \leq \mu_X \leq 8.03] = .95$
   (b) $C[-.02 \leq \mu_X \leq 10.02] = .99$
   (c) $C[4.19 \leq \mu_X \leq 5.81] = .50$

16 (a) $C[-8.55 \leq (\mu_X - \mu_Y) \leq -3.45] = .95$
   (b) $C[-9.44 \leq (\mu_X - \mu_Y) \leq -2.56] = .99$

17 (a) $C[.28 \leq (\mu_X - \mu_Y) \leq 5.72] = .95$
   (b) $C[-.96 \leq (\mu_X - \mu_Y) \leq 6.96] = .99$

18 (a) $C[-1.14 \leq (\mu_X - \mu_Y) \leq 9.14] = .95$
   (b) $C[-3.10 \leq (\mu_X - \mu_Y) \leq 11.10] = .99$

CHAPTER 20

1 At $\alpha = .10$, $r_{\text{crit}} = \pm.344$, reject H_0; at $\alpha = .05$, $r_{\text{crit}} = \pm.404$, accept H_0; at $\alpha = .01$, $r_{\text{crit}} = \pm.515$, accept H_0.

2 (a) $r_{\text{crit}} = \pm.374$, reject H_0 (b) $r_{\text{crit}} = \pm.590$, accept H_0 (c) $r_{\text{crit}} = -.360$ reject H_0 (d) $r_{\text{crit}} = -.337$, accept H_0.

3 Yes, for a two-tailed test $r_{\text{crit .01}} = .081$.

4 (a) H_0: $\rho_{males} - \rho_{females} = 0$, H_A: $\rho_{males} - \rho_{females} \neq 0$ (b) $z_{calc} = +1.26$, $\alpha = .05$, $z_{crit} = \pm 1.96$, accept H_0; at $\alpha = .01$, $z_{crit} = \pm 2.58$, accept H_0.

5 (a) $C[.52 \leq \rho \leq .75] = .95$ (b) $C[.48 \leq \rho \leq .78] = .99$ (c) $C[.54 \leq \rho \leq .73] = .90$.

6 (a) $C[-.01 \leq \rho \leq .75] = .95$ (b) $C[-.16 \leq \rho \leq .81] = .99$ (c) $C[.08 \leq \rho \leq .71] = .90$.

7 $r = .75$ suggests a strong relationship, but with the small sample we find it is not great enough to reject the hypothesis that $\rho = 0$ at $\alpha = .05$.

8 Yes, $r_{crit} = \pm .088$. Although significantly different from zero, the relationship is so low that it is of little importance.

CHAPTER 21

1 _____

2 (a) .92 (b) .83.

3 (a) .68 (b) .86.

4 (a) .83 (b) .48.

5 (a) .48 (b) .36.

6 (a) H_0: $\mu = 80$; H_A: $\mu \neq 80$ (b) 43.

7 (a) 55 (b) 168 (c) 36.

8 (a) Let X represent warned students and Y represent unwarned students; then H_0: $\mu_X - \mu_Y = 0$; H_A: $\mu_X - \mu_Y > 0$ (b) 346.

9 (a) 321 (b) 90 (c) 416.

10 (a) Type of disorder, severity of disorder, personal factors such as sex, membership in cultural subgroup, and age (b) effect of suggestion (that "therapy will help"), strength of motivation for recovery (as evidenced by coming regularly for treatment during the 10 weeks), effect of someone paying attention to the person (in contrast to therapy).

11 Both reduce the standard error of the difference, thus tending to reduce β.

12 A little less than one standard deviation.

CHAPTER 22

1 (a) 2.71 (b) 4.56 (c) 2.84 (d) 2.19.

2 (a) $SS_W = 28$, $SS_A = 54$, $SS_T = 82$; yes (b) $df_W = 6$, $df_A = 2$, $df_T = 8$; yes (c) $s_W^2 = 4.67$, $s_A^2 = 27.00$

(d)

source	df	SS	s^2
within groups	6	28	4.67
among groups	2	54	27.00
total	8	82	

(e) $F = 27.00/4.67 = 5.78$; $F_{.05} = 5.14$; reject H_0.

3 (see problem no. 2)

4 Only a large F is evidence for rejecting H_0.

5 (a) $SS_W = 82.87, SS_A = 104.05, SS_T = 186.92$ (b) $df_W = 9, df_A = 2, df_T = 11$ (c) $s_W^2 = 9.21$, $s_A^2 = 52.03$

(d)

source	df	SS	s^2
within groups	9	82.87	9.21
among groups	2	104.05	52.03
total	11	186.92	

(e) $F = 52.03/9.21 = 5.65$; $F_{.05} = 4.26$ (reject H_0), $F_{.01} = 8.02$ (accept H_0).

6 (see problem no. 5)

7 The raw score approach is simpler computationally.

8 (a) 4, 22, 87 (b) $F_{crit\ .05} = 2.72$, $F_{crit\ .01} = 4.04$ $F_{obt} = 3.4$, difference is significant at .05 level, not at .01.

9 Means of groups A, C, and D appear quite similar, but that of B is substantially higher. The significant difference may be owed to B.

10 (a) $df_{methods} = 3$, $df_{students} = 2$, $df_{within\ cells} = 48$, $df_{methods \times students} = 6$, $df_{total} = 59$

(b) methods: $F_{crit} = 2.80$; students: $F_{crit} = 3.19$; interaction: $F_{crit} = 2.30$.

11

source	df	SS	s^2	F	F_{crit}
C	1	.50	.50	$.50/3.75 = .13$	7.71, n.s.
R	1	2.00	2.00	$2.00/3.75 = .53$	7.71, n.s.
$C \times R$	1	.50	.50	$.50/3.75 = .13$	7.71, n.s.
within cells	4	15.00	3.75		
total	7	18.00			

12 Yes, these values are the raw materials from which (in proper combination) all SS's are calculated.

13 (a), (b), (c), (d):

source	df	SS	s^2	F	
C	1	6.75	6.75	$6.75/5.50 = 1.23$, n.s.	$F_{crit\ .05} = 5.32$;
R	1	18.75	18.75	$18.75/5.50 = 3.41$, n.s.	$F_{crit\ .01} = 11.26$
$C \times R$	1	36.75	36.75	$36.75/5.50 = 6.68$, sig. at	
w.c.	8	44.00	5.50	.05, not at .01	
total	11	106.25			

(e)

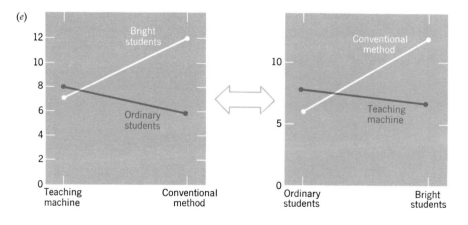

(f) The relative effectiveness of the methods depends on the kind of student with which they are used. The results suggest that under the conventional method bright students learn rapidly, but under the teaching machine method, progress is similar for both types of students.

14 (a) 12, 80, 99   (b) $F_{Col} = 1.50$, $F_{crit} = 2.48$, accept H_0; $F_{Row} = 3.00$, $F_{crit} = 2.72$, reject H_0; $F_{C \times R} = 2.50$, $F_{crit} = 1.88$, reject H_0 (c) The significant row effect should be studied in the light of the significant interaction before its meaning will be clear.

15 (a) $\kappa_1 = -2.5$, $\kappa_2 = -5.0$ (b) $s_{\kappa_1} = 2.24$, $s_{\kappa_2} = 2.00$ (c) $C_1(-6.94 \leq \kappa \leq +1.94) = .95$, $C_2(-8.96 \leq \kappa \leq -1.04) = .95$ (d) We can be 95% confident that the difference between the population mean of A and the average of the population means of the other subgroups falls somewhere between -6.94 points (μ_A being lower) and $+1.94$ points (μ_A being higher); we can be 95% confident that the difference between the average of μ_B and μ_C is less than the average of μ_D and μ_E by somewhere between 1.04 and 8.96 points   (e) accepted in the first comparison, rejected in the second.

16 (a) 4   (b) ———

17 (a) $C_1(-9.50 \leq \kappa \leq +4.50) = .95$, $C_2(-11.25 \leq \kappa \leq +1.25) = .95$ (b) accepted in both comparisons

CHAPTER 23

1 (a) $\chi^2_{calc} = 38.9$, for $df = 4$, $\chi^2_{.05} = 9.49$, reject H_0; $\chi^2_{.01} = 13.28$, reject H_0
(b) obtained frequencies: 40 correct, 60 incorrect; expected frequencies: 20 correct, 80 incorrect
(c) $\chi^2_{calc} = 23.76$, for $df = 1$, $\chi^2_{.05} = 3.84$, reject H_0; $\chi^2_{.01} = 6.63$, reject H_0

2 (a) 16   (b) $\chi^2_{calc} = 5.65$, for $df = 1$, $\chi^2_{.05} = 3.84$, reject H_0; $\chi^2_{.01} = 6.63$, accept H_0.

3 (a) $\chi^2_{calc} = 6.93$, for $df = 2$, $\chi^2_{.05} = 5.99$, reject H_0; $\chi^2_{.01} = 9.21$, accept H_0
(b) $\chi^2_{calc} = .30$, for $df = 1$, $\chi^2_{.05} = 3.84$, accept H_0; $\chi^2_{.01} = 6.63$, accept H_0
(c) α states the probability of obtaining given deviancy when selecting at random. When an event is chosen for study of its demonstrated deviancy, the probability of finding significance when none exists is greater than α.

4 Since all discrepancies are squared, both positive and negative discrepancies make a positive contribution to the value of χ^2. Only large, positive values are possibly indicative of nonchance discrepancies.

5 The f_e values are (each) 4, less than adequate for the χ^2 model.

6 $\chi^2_{calc} = 3.10$, for $df = 2$, $\chi^2_{.05} = 5.99$, accept H_0; $\chi^2_{.01} = 9.21$, accept H_0.

7 (a) $\chi^2_{calc} = 21.94$, for $df = 4$, $\chi^2_{.05} = 9.49$, reject H_0; $\chi^2_{.01} = 13.28$, reject H_0

(b)		30–49	50–69	70–up
obtained	unskilled	.33	.50	.17
cell	semiskilled	.12	.50	.38
proportions	skilled	.14	.29	.57
expected	unskilled	.20	.46	.34
cell	semiskilled	.20	.46	.34
proportions	skilled	.20	.46	.34

The three classes of workers are dissimilar with regard to mechanical aptitude. It appears that aptitude level is higher with higher skill classification of workers, though this conclusion goes beyond the overall χ^2 test.

8 (a) $\chi^2_{\text{calc}} = 7.30$, for $df = 1$, $\chi^2_{.05} = 3.84$, reject H_0

(b)

	Junior College	College-University
male	.64	.36
female	.64	.36

(c)

	Junior College	College-University
male	.53	.47
female	.86	.14

(d) Yes; although $f_o < 5$, $f_e > 5$

9 $\chi^2_{\text{calc}} = 7.29$, for $df = 1$, $\chi^2_{.05} = 3.84$, reject H_0.

10 In part the same workers would be involved in the comparison by months, and thus the samples will not be independent.

11 It would be necessary to assume each of the 50 trials is independent of the others, which is almost certainly wrong.

12 (a) $C(.294 \leq P \leq .406) = .95$ (b) $C(.323 \leq P \leq .377) = .95$.

13 $C[-.345 \leq (P_s - P_{us}) \leq -.055] = .95$.

CHAPTER 24

1 (a) $+.60$ (b) $df = 4$, $r_{\text{crit}} = .811$, accept H_0 (c) n is too small for proper evaluation by Table E.

2 Yes, the scores are in the form of ranks and there are no ties.

3 $+.47$.

4 No, because differences between adjacent scores are not proportional to differences between adjacent ranks, and because of ties in rank.

5 $-.75$.

6 $+.514$, $\pm.396$.

7 No, $\Sigma R_X = 45$, within the critical values 21–49 for the Mann-Whitney test. $Mdn_{\text{quiet}} = 59$, $Mdn_{\text{noisy}} = 51$; in the sample those in the quiet environment performed better, but the difference was not significant.

8 $z = +1.39$, not significant.

9 Not significant at $\alpha = .05$: $\Sigma R_X = 37$, critical values are 17–38.

10 (a) Significant at .05 level: $\Sigma R_X = 15$, critical values are 17–38   (b) More than 2/3 of the scores are involved in ties in rank

11 $\chi^2_{\text{crit}} = 5.99$ for $df = 2$, $H = 5.36$, n.s. A minimum of 4 cases for each of the 3 groups is recommended for satisfactory application of the χ^2 distribution.

12 $\chi^2_{\text{crit}} = 5.99$ for $df = 2$, $H = 6.80$, significant.

13 $\chi^2_{\text{calc}} = 4.08$, $df = 1$; $\chi^2_{.05} = 3.84$, reject H_0, $\chi^2_{.01} = 6.63$, accept H_0.

14 (a) $\chi^2_{\text{calc}} = 1.13$, $\chi^2_{\text{crit}} = 3.84$, n.s.
(b) blood pressure rose for *both* groups
(c) There is no control for an order effect (see Section 21.14), since tobacco was always used on the first trial and warm air on the second; it would be useful to run a third series of trials in which

subjects drew in warm air *and were aware of it;* when ties are dropped, only 8 cases remain: too few for χ^2 to be wholly adequate.

15 (*a*) $W_- = 9$, $W_{crit} = 10$, reject H_0 (*b*) factors other than the film may have been operative; it is not clear that the film is responsible for the difference.

16 $z = -2.09$, reject H_0.

17 $W_- = 3$, $W_{crit} = 3$, reject H_0.

APPENDIX F

STATISTICAL TABLES

CONTENTS

Table A Squares and Square Roots.[a] (*Use of this table is described in Appendix A. See Sections A.11 and A.12.*)

N	N^2	$\sqrt{N}$	$\sqrt{10N}$	N	N^2	$\sqrt{N}$	$\sqrt{10N}$
1.00	1.0000	1.00000	3.16228	1.50	2.2500	1.22474	3.87298
1.01	1.0201	1.00499	3.17805	1.51	2.2801	1.22882	3.88587
1.02	1.0404	1.00995	3.19374	1.52	2.3104	1.23288	3.89872
1.03	1.0609	1.01489	3.20936	1.53	2.3409	1.23693	3.91152
1.04	1.0816	1.01980	3.22490	1.54	2.3716	1.24097	3.92428
1.05	1.1025	1.02470	3.24037	1.55	2.4025	1.24499	3.93700
1.06	1.1236	1.02956	3.25576	1.56	2.4336	1.24900	3.94968
1.07	1.1449	1.03441	3.27109	1.57	2.4649	1.25300	3.96232
1.08	1.1664	1.03923	3.28634	1.58	2.4964	1.25698	3.97492
1.09	1.1881	1.04403	3.30151	1.59	2.5281	1.26095	3.98748
1.10	1.2100	1.04881	3.31662	1.60	2.5600	1.26491	4.00000
1.11	1.2321	1.05357	3.33167	1.61	2.5921	1.26886	4.01248
1.12	1.2544	1.05830	3.34664	1.62	2.6244	1.27279	4.02492
1.13	1.2769	1.06301	3.36155	1.63	2.6569	1.27671	4.03733
1.14	1.2996	1.06771	3.37639	1.64	2.6896	1.28062	4.04969
1.15	1.3225	1.07238	3.39116	1.65	2.7225	1.28452	4.06202
1.16	1.3456	1.07703	3.40588	1.66	2.7556	1.28841	4.07431
1.17	1.3689	1.08167	3.42053	1.67	2.7889	1.29228	4.08656
1.18	1.3924	1.08628	3.43511	1.68	2.8224	1.29615	4.09878
1.19	1.4161	1.09087	3.44964	1.69	2.8561	1.30000	4.11096
1.20	1.4400	1.09545	3.46410	1.70	2.8900	1.30384	4.12311
1.21	1.4641	1.10000	3.47851	1.71	2.9241	1.30767	4.13521
1.22	1.4884	1.10454	3.49285	1.72	2.9584	1.31149	4.14729
1.23	1.5129	1.10905	3.50714	1.73	2.9929	1.31529	4.15933
1.24	1.5376	1.11355	3.52136	1.74	3.0276	1.31909	4.17133
1.25	1.5625	1.11803	3.53553	1.75	3.0625	1.32288	4.18330
1.26	1.5876	1.12250	3.54965	1.76	3.0976	1.32665	4.19524
1.27	1.6129	1.12694	3.56371	1.77	3.1329	1.33041	4.20714
1.28	1.6384	1.13137	3.57771	1.78	3.1684	1.33417	4.21900
1.29	1.6641	1.13578	3.59166	1.79	3.2041	1.33791	4.23084
1.30	1.6900	1.14018	3.60555	1.80	3.2400	1.34164	4.24264
1.31	1.7161	1.14455	3.61939	1.81	3.2761	1.34536	4.25441
1.32	1.7424	1.14891	3.63318	1.82	3.3124	1.34907	4.26615
1.33	1.7689	1.15326	3.64692	1.83	3.3489	1.35277	4.27785
1.34	1.7956	1.15758	3.66060	1.84	3.3856	1.35647	4.28952
1.35	1.8225	1.16190	3.67423	1.85	3.4225	1.36015	4.30116
1.36	1.8496	1.16619	3.68782	1.86	3.4596	1.36382	4.31277
1.37	1.8769	1.17047	3.70135	1.87	3.4969	1.36748	4.32435
1.38	1.9044	1.17473	3.71484	1.88	3.5344	1.37113	4.33590
1.39	1.9321	1.17898	3.72827	1.89	3.5721	1.37477	4.34741
1.40	1.9600	1.18322	3.74166	1.90	3.6100	1.37840	4.35890
1.41	1.9881	1.18743	3.75500	1.91	3.6481	1.38203	4.37035
1.42	2.0164	1.19164	3.76829	1.92	3.6864	1.38564	4.38178
1.43	2.0449	1.19583	3.78153	1.93	3.7249	1.38924	4.39318
1.44	2.0736	1.20000	3.79473	1.94	3.7636	1.39284	4.40454
1.45	2.1025	1.20416	3.80789	1.95	3.8025	1.39642	4.41588
1.46	2.1316	1.20830	3.82099	1.96	3.8416	1.40000	4.42719
1.47	2.1609	1.21244	3.83406	1.97	3.8809	1.40357	4.43847
1.48	2.1904	1.21655	3.84708	1.98	3.9204	1.40712	4.44972
1.49	2.2201	1.22066	3.86005	1.99	3.9601	1.41067	4.46094
1.50	2.2500	1.22474	3.87298	2.00	4.0000	1.41421	4.47214
N	N^2	$\sqrt{N}$	$\sqrt{10N}$	N	N^2	$\sqrt{N}$	$\sqrt{10N}$

[a] From Table I of P. Hoel. *Elementary Statistics,* 2nd ed., John Wiley & Sons, Inc., New York, 1966, with permission of the publisher.

N	N²	√N	√10N	N	N²	√N	√10N
2.00	4.0000	1.41421	4.47214	2.50	6.2500	1.58114	5.00000
2.01	4.0401	1.41774	4.48330	2.51	6.3001	1.58430	5.00999
2.02	4.0804	1.42127	4.49444	2.52	6.3504	1.58745	5.01996
2.03	4.1209	1.42478	4.50555	2.53	6.4009	1.59060	5.02991
2.04	4.1616	1.42829	4.51664	2.54	6.4516	1.59374	5.03984
2.05	4.2025	1.43178	4.52769	2.55	6.5025	1.59687	5.04975
2.06	4.2436	1.43527	4.53872	2.56	6.5536	1.60000	5.05964
2.07	4.2849	1.43875	4.54973	2.57	6.6049	1.60312	5.06952
2.08	4.3264	1.44222	4.56070	2.58	6.6564	1.60624	5.07937
2.09	4.3681	1.44568	4.57165	2.59	6.7081	1.60935	5.08920
2.10	4.4100	1.44914	4.58258	2.60	6.7600	1.61245	5.09902
2.11	4.4521	1.45258	4.59347	2.61	6.8121	1.61555	5.10882
2.12	4.4944	1.45602	4.60435	2.62	6.8644	1.61864	5.11859
2.13	4.5369	1.45945	4.61519	2.63	6.9169	1.62173	5.12835
2.14	4.5796	1.46287	4.62601	2.64	6.9696	1.62481	5.13809
2.15	4.6225	1.46629	4.63681	2.65	7.0225	1.62788	5.14782
2.16	4.6656	1.46969	4.64758	2.66	7.0756	1.63095	5.15752
2.17	4.7089	1.47309	4.65833	2.67	7.1289	1.63401	5.16720
2.18	4.7524	1.47648	4.66905	2.68	7.1824	1.63707	5.17687
2.19	4.7961	1.47986	4.67974	2.69	7.2361	1.64012	5.18652
2.20	4.8400	1.48324	4.69042	2.70	7.2900	1.64317	5.19615
2.21	4.8841	1.48661	4.70106	2.71	7.3441	1.64621	5.20577
2.22	4.9284	1.48997	4.71169	2.72	7.3984	1.64924	5.21536
2.23	4.9729	1.49332	4.72229	2.73	7.4529	1.65227	5.22494
2.24	5.0176	1.49666	4.73286	2.74	7.5076	1.65529	5.23450
2.25	5.0625	1.50000	4.74342	2.75	7.5625	1.65831	5.24404
2.26	5.1076	1.50333	4.75395	2.76	7.6176	1.66132	5.25357
2.27	5.1529	1.50665	4.76445	2.77	7.6729	1.66433	5.26308
2.28	5.1984	1.50997	4.77493	2.78	7.7284	1.66733	5.27257
2.29	5.2441	1.51327	4.78539	2.79	7.7841	1.67033	5.28205
2.30	5.2900	1.51658	4.79583	2.80	7.8400	1.67332	5.29150
2.31	5.3361	1.51987	4.80625	2.81	7.8961	1.67631	5.30094
2.32	5.3824	1.52315	4.81664	2.82	7.9524	1.67929	5.31037
2.33	5.4289	1.52643	4.82701	2.83	8.0089	1.68226	5.31977
2.34	5.4756	1.52971	4.83735	2.84	8.0656	1.68523	5.32917
2.35	5.5225	1.53297	4.84768	2.85	8.1225	1.68819	5.33854
2.36	5.5696	1.53623	4.85798	2.86	8.1796	1.69115	5.34790
2.37	5.6169	1.53948	4.86826	2.87	8.2369	1.69411	5.35724
2.38	5.6644	1.54272	4.87852	2.88	8.2944	1.69706	5.36656
2.39	5.7121	1.54596	4.88876	2.89	8.3521	1.70000	5.37587
2.40	5.7600	1.54919	4.89898	2.90	8.4100	1.70294	5.38516
2.41	5.8081	1.55242	4.90918	2.91	8.4681	1.70587	5.39444
2.42	5.8564	1.55563	4.91935	2.92	8.5264	1.70880	5.40370
2.43	5.9049	1.55885	4.92950	2.93	8.5849	1.71172	5.41295
2.44	5.9536	1.56205	4.93964	2.94	8.6436	1.71464	5.42218
2.45	6.0025	1.56525	4.94975	2.95	8.7025	1.71756	5.43139
2.46	6.0516	1.56844	4.95984	2.96	8.7616	1.72047	5.44059
2.47	6.1009	1.57162	4.96991	2.97	8.8209	1.72337	5.44977
2.48	6.1504	1.57480	4.97996	2.98	8.8804	1.72627	5.45894
2.49	6.2001	1.57797	4.98999	2.99	8.9401	1.72916	5.46809
2.50	6.2500	1.58114	5.00000	3.00	9.0000	1.73205	5.47723
N	N²	√N	√10N	N	N²	√N	√10N

Table A (*Continued*)

N	N²	$\sqrt{N}$	$\sqrt{10N}$	N	N²	$\sqrt{N}$	$\sqrt{10N}$
3.00	9.0000	1.73205	5.47723	3.50	12.2500	1.87083	5.91608
3.01	9.0601	1.73494	5.48635	3.51	12.3201	1.87350	5.92453
3.02	9.1204	1.73781	5.49545	3.52	12.3904	1.87617	5.93296
3.03	9.1809	1.74069	5.50454	3.53	12.4609	1.87883	5.94138
3.04	9.2416	1.74356	5.51362	3.54	12.5316	1.88149	5.94979
3.05	9.3025	1.74642	5.52268	3.55	12.6025	1.88414	5.95819
3.06	9.3636	1.74929	5.53173	3.56	12.6736	1.88680	5.96657
3.07	9.4249	1.75214	5.54076	3.57	12.7449	1.88944	5.97495
3.08	9.4864	1.75499	5.54977	3.58	12.8164	1.89209	5.98331
3.09	9.5481	1.75784	5.55878	3.59	12.8881	1.89473	5.99166
3.10	9.6100	1.76068	5.56776	3.60	12.9600	1.89737	6.00000
3.11	9.6721	1.76352	5.57674	3.61	13.0321	1.90000	6.00833
3.12	9.7344	1.76635	5.58570	3.62	13.1044	1.90263	6.01664
3.13	9.7969	1.76918	5.59464	3.63	13.1769	1.90526	6.02495
3.14	9.8596	1.77200	5.60357	3.64	13.2496	1.90788	6.03324
3.15	9.9225	1.77482	5.61249	3.65	13.3225	1.91050	6.04152
3.16	9.9856	1.77764	5.62139	3.66	13.3956	1.91311	6.04979
3.17	10.0489	1.78045	5.63028	3.67	13.4689	1.91572	6.05805
3.18	10.1124	1.78326	5.63915	3.68	13.5424	1.91833	6.06630
3.19	10.1761	1.78606	5.64801	3.69	13.6161	1.92094	6.07454
3.20	10.2400	1.78885	5.65685	3.70	13.6900	1.92354	6.08276
3.21	10.3041	1.79165	5.66569	3.71	13.7641	1.92614	6.09098
3.22	10.3684	1.79444	5.67450	3.72	13.8384	1.92873	6.09918
3.23	10.4329	1.79722	5.68331	3.73	13.9129	1.93132	6.10737
3.24	10.4976	1.80000	5.69210	3.74	13.9876	1.93391	6.11555
3.25	10.5625	1.80278	5.70088	3.75	14.0625	1.93649	6.12372
3.26	10.6276	1.80555	5.70964	3.76	14.1376	1.93907	6.13188
3.27	10.6929	1.80831	5.71839	3.77	14.2129	1.94165	6.14003
3.28	10.7584	1.81108	5.72713	3.78	14.2884	1.94422	6.14817
3.29	10.8241	1.81384	5.73585	3.79	14.3641	1.94679	6.15630
3.30	10.8900	1.81659	5.74456	3.80	14.4400	1.94936	6.16441
3.31	10.9561	1.81934	5.75326	3.81	14.5161	1.95192	6.17252
3.32	11.0224	1.82209	5.76194	3.82	14.5924	1.95448	6.18061
3.33	11.0889	1.82483	5.77062	3.83	14.6689	1.95704	6.18870
3.34	11.1556	1.82757	5.77927	3.84	14.7456	1.95959	6.19677
3.35	11.2225	1.83030	5.78792	3.85	14.8225	1.96214	6.20484
3.36	11.2896	1.83303	5.79655	3.86	14.8996	1.96469	6.21289
3.37	11.3569	1.83576	5.80517	3.87	14.9769	1.96723	6.22093
3.38	11.4244	1.83848	5.81378	3.88	15.0544	1.96977	6.22896
3.39	11.4921	1.84120	5.82237	3.89	15.1321	1.97231	6.23699
3.40	11.5600	1.84391	5.83095	3.90	15.2100	1.97484	6.24500
3.41	11.6281	1.84662	5.83952	3.91	15.2881	1.97737	6.25300
3.42	11.6964	1.84932	5.84808	3.92	15.3664	1.97990	6.26099
3.43	11.7649	1.85203	5.85662	3.93	15.4449	1.98242	6.26897
3.44	11.8336	1.85472	5.86515	3.94	15.5236	1.98494	6.27694
3.45	11.9025	1.85742	5.87367	3.95	15.6025	1.98746	6.28490
3.46	11.9716	1.86011	5.88218	3.96	15.6816	1.98997	6.29285
3.47	12.0409	1.86279	5.89067	3.97	15.7609	1.99249	6.30079
3.48	12.1104	1.86548	5.89915	3.98	15.8404	1.99499	6.30872
3.49	12.1801	1.86815	5.90762	3.99	15.9201	1.99750	6.31664
3.50	12.2500	1.87083	5.91608	4.00	16.0000	2.00000	6.32456
N	N²	$\sqrt{N}$	$\sqrt{10N}$	N	N²	$\sqrt{N}$	$\sqrt{10N}$

N	N²	√N̄	√10N̄	N	N²	√N̄	√10N̄
4.00	16.0000	2.00000	6.32456	4.50	20.2500	2.12132	6.70820
4.01	16.0801	2.00250	6.33246	4.51	20.3401	2.12368	6.71565
4.02	16.1604	2.00499	6.34035	4.52	20.4304	2.12603	6.72309
4.03	16.2409	2.00749	6.34823	4.53	20.5209	2.12838	6.73053
4.04	16.3216	2.00998	6.35610	4.54	20.6116	2.13073	6.73795
4.05	16.4025	2.01246	6.36396	4.55	20.7025	2.13307	6.74537
4.06	16.4836	2.01494	6.37181	4.56	20.7936	2.13542	6.75278
4.07	16.5649	2.01742	6.37966	4.57	20.8849	2.13776	6.76018
4.08	16.6464	2.01990	6.38749	4.58	20.9764	2.14009	6.76757
4.09	16.7281	2.02237	6.39531	4.59	21.0681	2.14243	6.77495
4.10	16.8100	2.02485	6.40312	4.60	21.1600	2.14476	6.78233
4.11	16.8921	2.02731	6.41093	4.61	21.2521	2.14709	6.78970
4.12	16.9744	2.02978	6.41872	4.62	21.3444	2.14942	6.79706
4.13	17.0569	2.03224	6.42651	4.63	21.4369	2.15174	6.80441
4.14	17.1396	2.03470	6.43428	4.64	21.5296	2.15407	6.81175
4.15	17.2225	2.03715	6.44205	4.65	21.6225	2.15639	6.81909
4.16	17.3056	2.03961	6.44981	4.66	21.7156	2.15870	6.82642
4.17	17.3889	2.04206	6.45755	4.67	21.8089	2.16102	6.83374
4.18	17.4724	2.04450	6.46529	4.68	21.9024	2.16333	6.84105
4.19	17.5561	2.04695	6.47302	4.69	21.9961	2.16564	6.84836
4.20	17.6400	2.04939	6.48074	4.70	22.0900	2.16795	6.85565
4.21	17.7241	2.05183	6.48845	4.71	22.1841	2.17025	6.86294
4.22	17.8084	2.05426	6.49615	4.72	22.2784	2.17256	6.87023
4.23	17.8929	2.05670	6.50384	4.73	22.3729	2.17486	6.87750
4.24	17.9776	2.05913	6.51153	4.74	22.4676	2.17715	6.88477
4.25	18.0625	2.06155	6.51920	4.75	22.5625	2.17945	6.89202
4.26	18.1476	2.06398	6.52687	4.76	22.6576	2.18174	6.89928
4.27	18.2329	2.06640	6.53452	4.77	22.7529	2.18403	6.90652
4.28	18.3184	2.06882	6.54217	4.78	22.8484	2.18632	6.91375
4.29	18.4041	2.07123	6.54981	4.79	22.9441	2.18861	6.92098
4.30	18.4900	2.07364	6.55744	4.80	23.0400	2.19089	6.92820
4.31	18.5761	2.07605	6.56506	4.81	23.1361	2.19317	6.93542
4.32	18.6624	2.07846	6.57267	4.82	23.2324	2.19545	6.94262
4.33	18.7489	2.08087	6.58027	4.83	23.3289	2.19773	6.94982
4.34	18.8356	2.08327	6.58787	4.84	23.4256	2.20000	6.95701
4.35	18.9225	2.08567	6.59545	4.85	23.5225	2.20227	6.96419
4.36	19.0096	2.08806	6.60303	4.86	23.6196	2.20454	6.97137
4.37	19.0969	2.09045	6.61060	4.87	23.7169	2.20681	6.97854
4.38	19.1844	2.09284	6.61816	4.88	23.8144	2.20907	6.98570
4.39	19.2721	2.09523	6.62571	4.89	23.9121	2.21133	6.99285
4.40	19.3600	2.09762	6.63325	4.90	24.0100	2.21359	7.00000
4.41	19.4481	2.10000	6.64078	4.91	24.1081	2.21585	7.00714
4.42	19.5364	2.10238	6.64831	4.92	24.2064	2.21811	7.01427
4.43	19.6249	2.10476	6.65582	4.93	24.3049	2.22036	7.02140
4.44	19.7136	2.10713	6.66333	4.94	24.4036	2.22261	7.02851
4.45	19.8025	2.10950	6.67083	4.95	24.5025	2.22486	7.03562
4.46	19.8916	2.11187	6.67832	4.96	24.6016	2.22711	7.04273
4.47	19.9809	2.11424	6.68581	4.97	24.7009	2.22935	7.04982
4.48	20.0704	2.11660	6.69328	4.98	24.8004	2.23159	7.05691
4.49	20.1601	2.11896	6.70075	4.99	24.9001	2.23383	7.06399
4.50	20.2500	2.12132	6.70820	5.00	25.0000	2.23607	7.07107
N	N²	√N̄	√10N̄	N	N²	√N̄	√10N̄

N	N²	√N̄	√10N̄	N	N²	√N̄	√10N̄
5.00	25.0000	2.23607	7.07107	5.50	30.2500	2.34521	7.41620
5.01	25.1001	2.23830	7.07814	5.51	30.3601	2.34734	7.42294
5.02	25.2004	2.24054	7.08520	5.52	30.4704	2.34947	7.42967
5.03	25.3009	2.24277	7.09225	5.53	30.5809	2.35160	7.43640
5.04	25.4016	2.24499	7.09930	5.54	30.6916	2.35372	7.44312
5.05	25.5025	2.24722	7.10634	5.55	30.8025	2.35584	7.44983
5.06	25.6036	2.24944	7.11337	5.56	30.9136	2.35797	7.45654
5.07	25.7049	2.25167	7.12039	5.57	31.0249	2.36008	7.46324
5.08	25.8064	2.25389	7.12741	5.58	31.1364	2.36220	7.46994
5.09	25.9081	2.25610	7.13442	5.59	31.2481	2.36432	7.47663
5.10	26.0100	2.25832	7.14143	5.60	31.3600	2.36643	7.48331
5.11	26.1121	2.26053	7.14843	5.61	31.4721	2.36854	7.48999
5.12	26.2144	2.26274	7.15542	5.62	31.5844	2.37065	7.49667
5.13	26.3169	2.26495	7.16240	5.63	31.6969	2.37276	7.50333
5.14	26.4196	2.26716	7.16938	5.64	31.8096	2.37487	7.50999
5.15	26.5225	2.26936	7.17635	5.65	31.9225	2.37697	7.51665
5.16	26.6256	2.27156	7.18331	5.66	32.0356	2.37908	7.52330
5.17	26.7289	2.27376	7.19027	5.67	32.1489	2.38118	7.52994
5.18	26.8324	2.27596	7.19722	5.68	32.2624	2.38328	7.53658
5.19	26.9361	2.27816	7.20417	5.69	32.3761	2.38537	7.54321
5.20	27.0400	2.28035	7.21110	5.70	32.4900	2.38747	7.54983
5.21	27.1441	2.28254	7.21803	5.71	32.6041	2.38956	7.55645
5.22	27.2484	2.28473	7.22496	5.72	32.7184	2.39165	7.56307
5.23	27.3529	2.28692	7.23187	5.73	32.8329	2.39374	7.56968
5.24	27.4576	2.28910	7.23878	5.74	32.9476	2.39583	7.57628
5.25	27.5625	2.29129	7.24569	5.75	33.0625	2.39792	7.58288
5.26	27.6676	2.29347	7.25259	5.76	33.1776	2.40000	7.58947
5.27	27.7729	2.29565	7.25948	5.77	33.2929	2.40208	7.59605
5.28	27.8784	2.29783	7.26636	5.78	33.4084	2.40416	7.60263
5.29	27.9841	2.30000	7.27324	5.79	33.5241	2.40624	7.60920
5.30	28.0900	2.30217	7.28011	5.80	33.6400	2.40832	7.61577
5.31	28.1961	2.30434	7.28697	5.81	33.7561	2.41039	7.62234
5.32	28.3024	2.30651	7.29383	5.82	33.8724	2.41247	7.62889
5.33	28.4089	2.30868	7.30068	5.83	33.9889	2.41454	7.63544
5.34	28.5156	2.31084	7.30753	5.84	34.1056	2.41661	7.64199
5.35	28.6225	2.31301	7.31437	5.85	34.2225	2.41868	7.64853
5.36	28.7296	2.31517	7.32120	5.86	34.3396	2.42074	7.65506
5.37	28.8369	2.31733	7.32803	5.87	34.4569	2.42281	7.66159
5.38	28.9444	2.31948	7.33485	5.88	34.5744	2.42487	7.66812
5.39	29.0521	2.32164	7.34166	5.89	34.6921	2.42693	7.67463
5.40	29.1600	2.32379	7.34847	5.90	34.8100	2.42899	7.68115
5.41	29.2681	2.32594	7.35527	5.91	34.9281	2.43105	7.68765
5.42	29.3764	2.32809	7.36206	5.92	35.0464	2.43311	7.69415
5.43	29.4849	2.33024	7.36885	5.93	35.1649	2.43516	7.70065
5.44	29.5936	2.33238	7.37564	5.94	35.2836	2.43721	7.70714
5.45	29.7025	2.33452	7.38241	5.95	35.4025	2.43926	7.71362
5.46	29.8116	2.33666	7.38918	5.96	35.5216	2.44131	7.72010
5.47	29.9209	2.33880	7.39594	5.97	35.6409	2.44336	7.72658
5.48	30.0304	2.34094	7.40270	5.98	35.7604	2.44540	7.73305
5.49	30.1401	2.34307	7.40945	5.99	35.8801	2.44745	7.73951
5.50	30.2500	2.34521	7.41620	6.00	36.0000	2.44949	7.74597
N	N²	√N̄	√10N̄	N	N²	√N̄	√10N̄

N	N²	√N	√10N	N	N²	√N	√10N
6.00	36.0000	2.44949	7.74597	6.50	42.2500	2.54951	8.06226
6.01	36.1201	2.45153	7.75242	6.51	42.3801	2.55147	8.06846
6.02	36.2404	2.45357	7.75887	6.52	42.5104	2.55343	8.07465
6.03	36.3609	2.45561	7.76531	6.53	42.6409	2.55539	8.08084
6.04	36.4816	2.45764	7.77174	6.54	42.7716	2.55734	8.08703
6.05	36.6025	2.45967	7.77817	6.55	42.9025	2.55930	8.09321
6.06	36.7236	2.46171	7.78460	6.56	43.0336	2.56125	8.09938
6.07	36.8449	2.46374	7.79102	6.57	43.1649	2.56320	8.10555
6.08	36.9664	2.46577	7.79744	6.58	43.2964	2.56515	8.11172
6.09	37.0881	2.46779	7.80385	6.59	43.4281	2.56710	8.11788
6.10	37.2100	2.46982	7.81025	6.60	43.5600	2.56905	8.12404
6.11	37.3321	2.47184	7.81665	6.61	43.6921	2.57099	8.13019
6.12	37.4544	2.47386	7.82304	6.62	43.8244	2.57294	8.13634
6.13	37.5769	2.47588	7.82943	6.63	43.9569	2.57488	8.14248
6.14	37.6996	2.47790	7.83582	6.64	44.0896	2.57682	8.14862
6.15	37.8225	2.47992	7.84219	6.65	44.2225	2.57876	8.15475
6.16	37.9456	2.48193	7.84857	6.66	44.3556	2.58070	8.16088
6.17	38.0689	2.48395	7.85493	6.67	44.4889	2.58263	8.16701
6.18	38.1924	2.48596	7.86130	6.68	44.6224	2.58457	8.17313
6.19	38.3161	2.48797	7.86766	6.69	44.7561	2.58650	8.17924
6.20	38.4400	2.48998	7.87401	6.70	44.8900	2.58844	8.18535
6.21	38.5641	2.49199	7.88036	6.71	45.0241	2.59037	8.19146
6.22	38.6884	2.49399	7.88670	6.72	45.1584	2.59230	8.19756
6.23	38.8129	2.49600	7.89303	6.73	45.2929	2.59422	8.20366
6.24	38.9376	2.49800	7.89937	6.74	45.4276	2.59615	8.20975
6.25	39.0625	2.50000	7.90569	6.75	45.5625	2.59808	8.21584
6.26	39.1876	2.50200	7.91202	6.76	45.6976	2.60000	8.22192
6.27	39.3129	2.50400	7.91833	6.77	45.8329	2.60192	8.22800
6.28	39.4384	2.50599	7.92465	6.78	45.9684	2.60384	8.23408
6.29	39.5641	2.50799	7.93095	6.79	46.1041	2.60576	8.24015
6.30	39.6900	2.50998	7.93725	6.80	46.2400	2.60768	8.24621
6.31	39.8161	2.51197	7.94355	6.81	46.3761	2.60960	8.25227
6.32	39.9424	2.51396	7.94984	6.82	46.5124	2.61151	8.25833
6.33	40.0689	2.51595	7.95613	6.83	46.6489	2.61343	8.26438
6.34	40.1956	2.51794	7.96241	6.84	46.7856	2.61534	8.27043
6.35	40.3225	2.51992	7.96869	6.85	46.9225	2.61725	8.27647
6.36	40.4496	2.52190	7.97496	6.86	47.0596	2.61916	8.28251
6.37	40.5769	2.52389	7.98123	6.87	47.1969	2.62107	8.28855
6.38	40.7044	2.52587	7.98749	6.88	47.3344	2.62298	8.29458
6.39	40.8321	2.52784	7.99375	6.89	47.4721	2.62488	8.30060
6.40	40.9600	2.52982	8.00000	6.90	47.6100	2.62679	8.30662
6.41	41.0881	2.53180	8.00625	6.91	47.7481	2.62869	8.31264
6.42	41.2164	2.53377	8.01249	6.92	47.8864	2.63059	8.31865
6.43	41.3449	2.53574	8.01873	6.93	48.0249	2.63249	8.32466
6.44	41.4736	2.53772	8.02496	6.94	48.1636	2.63439	8.33067
6.45	41.6025	2.53969	8.03119	6.95	48.3025	2.63629	8.33667
6.46	41.7316	2.54165	8.03741	6.96	48.4416	2.63818	8.34266
6.47	41.8609	2.54362	8.04363	6.97	48.5809	2.64008	8.34865
6.48	41.9904	2.54558	8.04984	6.98	48.7204	2.64197	8.35464
6.49	42.1201	2.54755	8.05605	6.99	48.8601	2.64386	8.36062
6.50	42.2500	2.54951	8.06226	7.00	49.0000	2.64575	8.36660
N	N²	√N	√10N	N	N²	√N	√10N

N	N²	√N	√10N	N	N²	√N	√10N
7.00	49.0000	2.64575	8.36660	7.50	56.2500	2.73861	8.66025
7.01	49.1401	2.64764	8.37257	7.51	56.4001	2.74044	8.66603
7.02	49.2804	2.64953	8.37854	7.52	56.5504	2.74226	8.67179
7.03	49.4209	2.65141	8.38451	7.53	56.7009	2.74408	8.67756
7.04	49.5616	2.65330	8.39047	7.54	56.8516	2.74591	8.68332
7.05	49.7025	2.65518	8.39643	7.55	57.0025	2.74773	8.68907
7.06	49.8436	2.65707	8.40238	7.56	57.1536	2.74955	8.69483
7.07	49.9849	2.65895	8.40833	7.57	57.3049	2.75136	8.70057
7.08	50.1264	2.66083	8.41427	7.58	57.4564	2.75318	8.70632
7.09	50.2681	2.66271	8.42021	7.59	57.6081	2.75500	8.71206
7.10	50.4100	2.66458	8.42615	7.60	57.7600	2.75681	8.71780
7.11	50.5521	2.66646	8.43208	7.61	57.9121	2.75862	8.72353
7.12	50.6944	2.66833	8.43801	7.62	58.0644	2.76043	8.72926
7.13	50.8369	2.67021	8.44393	7.63	58.2169	2.76225	8.73499
7.14	50.9796	2.67208	8.44985	7.64	58.3696	2.76405	8.74071
7.15	51.1225	2.67395	8.45577	7.65	58.5225	2.76586	8.74643
7.16	51.2656	2.67582	8.46168	7.66	58.6756	2.76767	8.75214
7.17	51.4089	2.67769	8.46759	7.67	58.8289	2.76948	8.75785
7.18	51.5524	2.67955	8.47349	7.68	58.9824	2.77128	8.76356
7.19	51.6961	2.68142	8.47939	7.69	59.1361	2.77308	8.76926
7.20	51.8400	2.68328	8.48528	7.70	59.2900	2.77489	8.77496
7.21	51.9841	2.68514	8.49117	7.71	59.4441	2.77669	8.78066
7.22	52.1284	2.68701	8.49706	7.72	59.5984	2.77849	8.78635
7.23	52.2729	2.68887	8.50294	7.73	59.7529	2.78029	8.79204
7.24	52.4176	2.69072	8.50882	7.74	59.9076	2.78209	8.79773
7.25	52.5625	2.69258	8.51469	7.75	60.0625	2.78388	8.80341
7.26	52.7076	2.69444	8.52056	7.76	60.2176	2.78568	8.80909
7.27	52.8529	2.69629	8.52643	7.77	60.3729	2.78747	8.81476
7.28	52.9984	2.69815	8.53229	7.78	60.5284	2.78927	8.82043
7.29	53.1441	2.70000	8.53815	7.79	60.6841	2.79106	8.82610
7.30	53.2900	2.70185	8.54400	7.80	60.8400	2.79285	8.83176
7.31	53.4361	2.70370	8.54985	7.81	60.9961	2.79464	8.83742
7.32	53.5824	2.70555	8.55570	7.82	61.1524	2.79643	8.84308
7.33	53.7289	2.70740	8.56154	7.83	61.3089	2.79821	8.84873
7.34	53.8756	2.70924	8.56738	7.84	61.4656	2.80000	8.85438
7.35	54.0225	2.71109	8.57321	7.85	61.6225	2.80179	8.86002
7.36	54.1696	2.71293	8.57904	7.86	61.7796	2.80357	8.86566
7.37	54.3169	2.71477	8.58487	7.87	61.9369	2.80535	8.87130
7.38	54.4644	2.71662	8.59069	7.88	62.0944	2.80713	8.87694
7.39	54.6121	2.71846	8.59651	7.89	62.2521	2.80891	8.88257
7.40	54.7600	2.72029	8.60233	7.90	62.4100	2.81069	8.88819
7.41	54.9081	2.72213	8.60814	7.91	62.5681	2.81247	8.89382
7.42	55.0564	2.72397	8.61394	7.92	62.7264	2.81425	8.89944
7.43	55.2049	2.72580	8.61974	7.93	62.8849	2.81603	8.90505
7.44	55.3536	2.72764	8.62554	7.94	63.0436	2.81780	8.91067
7.45	55.5025	2.72947	8.63134	7.95	63.2025	2.81957	8.91628
7.46	55.6516	2.73130	8.63713	7.96	63.3616	2.82135	8.92188
7.47	55.8009	2.73313	8.64292	7.97	63.5209	2.82312	8.92749
7.48	55.9504	2.73496	8.64870	7.98	63.6804	2.82489	8.93308
7.49	56.1001	2.73679	8.65448	7.99	63.8401	2.82666	8.93868
7.50	56.2500	2.73861	8.66025	8.00	64.0000	2.82843	8.94427
N	N²	√N	√10N	N	N²	√N	√10N

N	N²	√N	√10N	N	N²	√N	√10N
8.00	64.0000	2.82843	8.94427	8.50	72.2500	2.91548	9.21954
8.01	64.1601	2.83019	8.94986	8.51	72.4201	2.91719	9.22497
8.02	64.3204	2.83196	8.95545	8.52	72.5904	2.91890	9.23038
8.03	64.4809	2.83373	8.96103	8.53	72.7609	2.92062	9.23580
8.04	64.6416	2.83549	8.96660	8.54	72.9316	2.92233	9.24121
8.05	64.8025	2.83725	8.97218	8.55	73.1025	2.92404	9.24662
8.06	64.9636	2.83901	8.97775	8.56	73.2736	2.92575	9.25203
8.07	65.1249	2.84077	8.98332	8.57	73.4449	2.92746	9.25743
8.08	65.2864	2.84253	8.98888	8.58	73.6164	2.92916	9.26283
8.09	65.4481	2.84429	8.99444	8.59	73.7881	2.93087	9.26823
8.10	65.6100	2.84605	9.00000	8.60	73.9600	2.93258	9.27362
8.11	65.7721	2.84781	9.00555	8.61	74.1321	2.93428	9.27901
8.12	65.9344	2.84956	9.01110	8.62	74.3044	2.93598	9.28440
8.13	66.0969	2.85132	9.01665	8.63	74.4769	2.93769	9.28978
8.14	66.2596	2.85307	9.02219	8.64	74.6496	2.93939	9.29516
8.15	66.4225	2.85482	9.02774	8.65	74.8225	2.94109	9.30054
8.16	66.5856	2.85657	9.03327	8.66	74.9956	2.94279	9.30591
8.17	66.7489	2.85832	9.03881	8.67	75.1689	2.94449	9.31128
8.18	66.9124	2.86007	9.04434	8.68	75.3424	2.94618	9.31665
8.19	67.0761	2.86182	9.04986	8.69	75.5161	2.94788	9.32202
8.20	67.2400	2.86356	9.05539	8.70	75.6900	2.94958	9.32738
8.21	67.4041	2.86531	9.06091	8.71	75.8641	2.95127	9.33274
8.22	67.5684	2.86705	9.06642	8.72	76.0384	2.95296	9.33809
8.23	67.7329	2.86880	9.07193	8.73	76.2129	2.95466	9.34345
8.24	67.8976	2.87054	9.07744	8.74	76.3876	2.95635	9.34880
8.25	68.0625	2.87228	9.08295	8.75	76.5625	2.95804	9.35414
8.26	68.2276	2.87402	9.08845	8.76	76.7376	2.95973	9.35949
8.27	68.3929	2.87576	9.09395	8.77	76.9129	2.96142	9.36483
8.28	68.5584	2.87750	9.09945	8.78	77.0884	2.96311	9.37017
8.29	68.7241	2.87924	9.10494	8.79	77.2641	2.96479	9.37550
8.30	68.8900	2.88097	9.11043	8.80	77.4400	2.96648	9.38083
8.31	69.0561	2.88271	9.11592	8.81	77.6161	2.96816	9.38616
8.32	69.2224	2.88444	9.12140	8.82	77.7924	2.96985	9.39149
8.33	69.3889	2.88617	9.12688	8.83	77.9689	2.97153	9.39681
8.34	69.5556	2.88791	9.13236	8.84	78.1456	2.97321	9.40213
8.35	69.7225	2.88964	9.13783	8.85	78.3225	2.97489	9.40744
8.36	69.8896	2.89137	9.14330	8.86	78.4996	2.97658	9.41276
8.37	70.0569	2.89310	9.14877	8.87	78.6769	2.97825	9.41807
8.38	70.2244	2.89482	9.15423	8.88	78.8544	2.97993	9.42338
8.39	70.3921	2.89655	9.15969	8.89	79.0321	2.98161	9.42868
8.40	70.5600	2.89828	9.16515	8.90	79.2100	2.98329	9.43398
8.41	70.7281	2.90000	9.17061	8.91	79.3881	2.98496	9.43928
8.42	70.8964	2.90172	9.17606	8.92	79.5664	2.98664	9.44458
8.43	71.0649	2.90345	9.18150	8.93	79.7449	2.98831	9.44987
8.44	71.2336	2.90517	9.18695	8.94	79.9236	2.98998	9.45516
8.45	71.4025	2.90689	9.19239	8.95	80.1025	2.99166	9.46044
8.46	71.5716	2.90861	9.19783	8.96	80.2816	2.99333	9.46573
8.47	71.7409	2.91033	9.20326	8.97	80.4609	2.99500	9.47101
8.48	71.9104	2.91204	9.20869	8.98	80.6404	2.99666	9.47629
8.49	72.0801	2.91376	9.21412	8.99	80.8201	2.99833	9.48156
8.50	72.2500	2.91548	9.21954	9.00	81.0000	3.00000	9.48683
N	N²	√N	√10N	N	N²	√N	√10N

Table A (*Continued*)

N	N²	√N	√10N	N	N²	√N	√10N
9.00	81.0000	3.00000	9.48683	9.50	90.2500	3.08221	9.74679
9.01	81.1801	3.00167	9.49210	9.51	90.4401	3.08383	9.75192
9.02	81.3604	3.00333	9.49737	9.52	90.6304	3.08545	9.75705
9.03	81.5409	3.00500	9.50263	9.53	90.8209	3.08707	9.76217
9.04	81.7216	3.00666	9.50789	9.54	91.0116	3.08869	9.76729
9.05	81.9025	3.00832	9.51315	9.55	91.2025	3.09031	9.77241
9.06	82.0836	3.00998	9.51840	9.56	91.3936	3.09192	9.77753
9.07	82.2649	3.01164	9.52365	9.57	91.5849	3.09354	9.78264
9.08	82.4464	3.01330	9.52890	9.58	91.7764	3.09516	9.78775
9.09	82.6281	3.01496	9.53415	9.59	91.9681	3.09677	9.79285
9.10	82.8100	3.01662	9.53939	9.60	92.1600	3.09839	9.79796
9.11	82.9921	3.01828	9.54463	9.61	92.3521	3.10000	9.80306
9.12	83.1744	3.01993	9.54987	9.62	92.5444	3.10161	9.80816
9.13	83.3569	3.02159	9.55510	9.63	92.7369	3.10322	9.81326
9.14	83.5396	3.02324	9.56033	9.64	92.9296	3.10483	9.81835
9.15	83.7225	3.02490	9.56556	9.65	93.1225	3.10644	9.82344
9.16	83.9056	3.02655	9.57079	9.66	93.3156	3.10805	9.82853
9.17	84.0889	3.02820	9.57601	9.67	93.5089	3.10966	9.83362
9.18	84.2724	3.02985	9.58123	9.68	93.7024	3.11127	9.83870
9.19	84.4561	3.03150	9.58645	9.69	93.8961	3.11288	9.84378
9.20	84.6400	3.03315	9.59166	9.70	94.0900	3.11448	9.84886
9.21	84.8241	3.03480	9.59687	9.71	94.2841	3.11609	9.85393
9.22	85.0084	3.03645	9.60208	9.72	94.4784	3.11769	9.85901
9.23	85.1929	3.03809	9.60729	9.73	94.6729	3.11929	9.86408
9.24	85.3776	3.03974	9.61249	9.74	94.8676	3.12090	9.86914
9.25	85.5625	3.04138	9.61769	9.75	95.0625	3.12250	9.87421
9.26	85.7476	3.04302	9.62289	9.76	95.2576	3.12410	9.87927
9.27	85.9329	3.04467	9.62808	9.77	95.4529	3.12570	9.88433
9.28	86.1184	3.04631	9.63328	9.78	95.6484	3.12730	9.88939
9.29	86.3041	3.04795	9.63846	9.79	95.8441	3.12890	9.89444
9.30	86.4900	3.04959	9.64365	9.80	96.0400	3.13050	9.89949
9.31	86.6761	3.05123	9.64883	9.81	96.2361	3.13209	9.90454
9.32	86.8624	3.05287	9.65401	9.82	96.4324	3.13369	9.90959
9.33	87.0489	3.05450	9.65919	9.83	96.6289	3.13528	9.91464
9.34	87.2356	3.05614	9.66437	9.84	96.8256	3.13688	9.91968
9.35	87.4225	3.05778	9.66954	9.85	97.0225	3.13847	9.92472
9.36	87.6096	3.05941	9.67471	9.86	97.2196	3.14006	9.92975
9.37	87.7969	3.06105	9.67988	9.87	97.4169	3.14166	9.93479
9.38	87.9844	3.06268	9.68504	9.88	97.6144	3.14325	9.93982
9.39	88.1721	3.06431	9.69020	9.89	97.8121	3.14484	9.94485
9.40	88.3600	3.06594	9.69536	9.90	98.0100	3.14643	9.94987
9.41	88.5481	3.06757	9.70052	9.91	98.2081	3.14802	9.95490
9.42	88.7364	3.06920	9.70567	9.92	98.4064	3.14960	9.95992
9.43	88.9249	3.07083	9.71082	9.93	98.6049	3.15119	9.96494
9.44	89.1136	3.07246	9.71597	9.94	98.8036	3.15278	9.96995
9.45	89.3025	3.07409	9.72111	9.95	99.0025	3.15436	9.97497
9.46	89.4916	3.07571	9.72625	9.96	99.2016	3.15595	9.97998
9.47	89.6809	3.07734	9.73139	9.97	99.4009	3.15753	9.98499
9.48	89.8704	3.07896	9.73653	9.98	99.6004	3.15911	9.98999
9.49	90.0601	3.08058	9.74166	9.99	99.8001	3.16070	9.99500
9.50	90.2500	3.08221	9.74679	10.00	100.0000	3.16228	10.00000
N	N²	√N	√10N	N	N²	√N	√10N

Table B Areas under the Normal Curve Corresponding to Given Values of z[a]

Column 2 gives the proportion of the area under the entire curve which is between the mean ($z = 0$) and the positive value of z. Areas for negative values of z are the same as for positive values, since the curve is symmetrical.

Column 3 gives the proportion of the area under the entire curve which falls beyond the stated positive value of z. Areas for negative values of z are the same, since the curve is symmetrical.

z	Area between mean and z	Area beyond z	z	Area between mean and z	Area beyond z
1	*2*	*3*	*1*	*2*	*3*
0.00	.0000	.5000	0.15	.0596	.4404
0.01	.0040	.4960	0.16	.0636	.4364
0.02	.0080	.4920	0.17	.0675	.4325
0.03	.0120	.4880	0.18	.0714	.4286
0.04	.0160	.4840	0.19	.0753	.4247
0.05	.0199	.4801	0.20	.0793	.4207
0.06	.0239	.4761	0.21	.0832	.4168
0.07	.0279	.4721	0.22	.0871	.4129
0.08	.0319	.4681	0.23	.0910	.4090
0.09	.0359	.4641	0.24	.0948	.4052
0.10	.0398	.4602	0.25	.0987	.4013
0.11	.0438	.4562	0.26	.1026	.3974
0.12	.0478	.4522	0.27	.1064	.3936
0.13	.0517	.4483	0.28	.1103	.3897
0.14	.0557	.4443	0.29	.1141	.3859

[a]From Appendix 2 of R. Clarke, A. Coladarci, and J. Caffrey, *Statistical Reasoning and Procedures,* Charles E. Merrill Books, Inc., Columbus, Ohio, 1965, with permission of the publisher.

Table B (Continued)

z	Area between mean and z	Area beyond z	z	Area between mean and z	Area beyond z
1	2	3	1	2	3
0.30	.1179	.3821	0.65	.2422	.2578
0.31	.1217	.3783	0.66	.2454	.2546
0.32	.1255	.3745	0.67	.2486	.2514
0.33	.1293	.3707	0.68	.2517	.2483
0.34	.1331	.3669	0.69	.2549	.2451
0.35	.1368	.3632	0.70	.2580	.2420
0.36	.1406	.3594	0.71	.2611	.2389
0.37	.1443	.3557	0.72	.2642	.2358
0.38	.1480	.3520	0.73	.2673	.2327
0.39	.1517	.3483	0.74	.2704	.2296
0.40	.1554	.3446	0.75	.2734	.2266
0.41	.1591	.3409	0.76	.2764	.2236
0.42	.1628	.3372	0.77	.2794	.2206
0.43	.1664	.3336	0.78	.2823	.2177
0.44	.1700	.3300	0.79	.2852	.2148
0.45	.1736	.3264	0.80	.2881	.2119
0.46	.1772	.3228	0.81	.2910	.2090
0.47	.1808	.3192	0.82	.2939	.2061
0.48	.1844	.3156	0.83	.2967	.2033
0.49	.1879	.3121	0.84	.2995	.2005
0.50	.1915	.3085	0.85	.3023	.1977
0.51	.1950	.3050	0.86	.3051	.1949
0.52	.1985	.3015	0.87	.3078	.1922
0.53	.2019	.2981	0.88	.3106	.1894
0.54	.2054	.2946	0.89	.3133	.1867
0.55	.2088	.2912	0.90	.3159	.1841
0.56	.2123	.2877	0.91	.3186	.1814
0.57	.2157	.2843	0.92	.3212	.1788
0.58	.2190	.2810	0.93	.3238	.1762
0.59	.2224	.2776	0.94	.3264	.1736
0.60	.2257	.2743	0.95	.3289	.1711
0.61	.2291	.2709	0.96	.3315	.1685
0.62	.2324	.2676	0.97	.3340	.1660
0.63	.2357	.2643	0.98	.3365	.1635
0.64	.2389	.2611	0.99	.3389	.1611

Table B (*Continued*)

z	Area between mean and z	Area beyond z	z	Area between mean and z	Area beyond z
1	*2*	*3*	*1*	*2*	*3*
1.00	.3413	.1587	1.35	.4115	.0885
1.01	.3438	.1562	1.36	.4131	.0869
1.02	.3461	.1539	1.37	.4147	.0853
1.03	.3485	.1515	1.38	.4162	.0838
1.04	.3508	.1492	1.39	.4177	.0823
1.05	.3531	.1469	1.40	.4192	.0808
1.06	.3554	.1446	1.41	.4207	.0793
1.07	.3577	.1423	1.42	.4222	.0778
1.08	.3599	.1401	1.43	.4236	.0764
1.09	.3621	.1379	1.44	.4251	.0749
1.10	.3643	.1357	1.45	.4265	.0735
1.11	.3665	.1335	1.46	.4279	.0721
1.12	.3686	.1314	1.47	.4292	.0708
1.13	.3708	.1292	1.48	.4306	.0694
1.14	.3729	.1271	1.49	.4319	.0681
1.15	.3749	.1251	1.50	.4332	.0668
1.16	.3770	.1230	1.51	.4345	.0655
1.17	.3790	.1210	1.52	.4357	.0643
1.18	.3810	.1190	1.53	.4370	.0630
1.19	.3830	.1170	1.54	.4382	.0618
1.20	.3849	.1151	1.55	.4394	.0606
1.21	.3869	.1131	1.56	.4406	.0594
1.22	.3888	.1112	1.57	.4418	.0582
1.23	.3907	.1093	1.58	.4429	.0571
1.24	.3925	.1075	1.59	.4441	.0559
1.25	.3944	.1056	1.60	.4452	.0548
1.26	.3962	.1038	1.61	.4463	.0537
1.27	.3980	.1020	1.62	.4474	.0526
1.28	.3997	.1003	1.63	.4484	.0516
1.29	.4015	.0985	1.64	.4495	.0505
1.30	.4032	.0968	1.65	.4505	.0495
1.31	.4049	.0951	1.66	.4515	.0485
1.32	.4066	.0934	1.67	.4525	.0475
1.33	.4082	.0918	1.68	.4535	.0465
1.34	.4099	.0901	1.69	.4545	.0455

Table B (*Continued*)

z	Area between mean and z	Area beyond z	z	Area between mean and z	Area beyond z
1	*2*	*3*	*1*	*2*	*3*
1.70	.4554	.0446	2.05	.4798	.0202
1.71	.4564	.0436	2.06	.4803	.0197
1.72	.4573	.0427	2.07	.4808	.0192
1.73	.4582	.0418	2.08	.4812	.0188
1.74	.4591	.0409	2.09	.4817	.0183
1.75	.4599	.0401	2.10	.4821	.0179
1.76	.4608	.0392	2.11	.4826	.0174
1.77	.4616	.0384	2.12	.4830	.0170
1.78	.4625	.0375	2.13	.4834	.0166
1.79	.4633	.0367	2.14	.4838	.0162
1.80	.4641	.0359	2.15	.4842	.0158
1.81	.4649	.0351	2.16	.4846	.0154
1.82	.4656	.0344	2.17	.4850	.0150
1.83	.4664	.0336	2.18	.4854	.0146
1.84	.4671	.0329	2.19	.4857	.0143
1.85	.4678	.0322	2.20	.4861	.0139
1.86	.4686	.0314	2.21	.4864	.0136
1.87	.4693	.0307	2.22	.4868	.0132
1.88	.4699	.0301	2.23	.4871	.0129
1.89	.4706	.0294	2.24	.4875	.0125
1.90	.4713	.0287	2.25	.4878	.0122
1.91	.4719	.0281	2.26	.4881	.0119
1.92	.4726	.0274	2.27	.4884	.0116
1.93	.4732	.0268	2.28	.4887	.0113
1.94	.4738	.0262	2.29	.4890	.0110
1.95	.4744	.0256	2.30	.4893	.0107
1.96	.4750	.0250	2.31	.4896	.0104
1.97	.4756	.0244	2.32	.4898	.0102
1.98	.4761	.0239	2.33	.4901	.0099
1.99	.4767	.0233	2.34	.4904	.0096
2.00	.4772	.0228	2.35	.4906	.0094
2.01	.4778	.0222	2.36	.4909	.0091
2.02	.4783	.0217	2.37	.4911	.0089
2.03	.4788	.0212	2.38	.4913	.0087
2.04	.4793	.0207	2.39	.4916	.0084

Table B (*Continued*)

z	Area between mean and z	Area beyond z	z	Area between mean and z	Area beyond z
1	2	3	1	2	3
2.40	.4918	.0082	2.75	.4970	.0030
2.41	.4920	.0080	2.76	.4971	.0029
2.42	.4922	.0078	2.77	.4972	.0028
2.43	.4925	.0075	2.78	.4973	.0027
2.44	.4927	.0073	2.79	.4974	.0026
2.45	.4929	.0071	2.80	.4974	.0026
2.46	.4931	.0069	2.81	.4975	.0025
2.47	.4932	.0068	2.82	.4976	.0024
2.48	.4934	.0066	2.83	.4977	.0023
2.49	.4936	.0064	2.84	.4977	.0023
2.50	.4938	.0062	2.85	.4978	.0022
2.51	.4940	.0060	2.86	.4979	.0021
2.52	.4941	.0059	2.87	.4979	.0021
2.53	.4943	.0057	2.88	.4980	.0020
2.54	.4945	.0055	2.89	.4981	.0019
2.55	.4946	.0054	2.90	.4981	.0019
2.56	.4948	.0052	2.91	.4982	.0018
2.57	.4949	.0051	2.92	.4982	.0018
2.58	.4951	.0049	2.93	.4983	.0017
2.59	.4952	.0048	2.94	.4984	.0016
2.60	.4953	.0047	2.95	.4984	.0016
2.61	.4955	.0045	2.96	.4985	.0015
2.62	.4956	.0044	2.97	.4985	.0015
2.63	.4957	.0043	2.98	.4986	.0014
2.64	.4959	.0041	2.99	.4986	.0014
2.65	.4960	.0040	3.00	.4987	.0013
2.66	.4961	.0039	3.01	.4987	.0013
2.67	.4962	.0038	3.02	.4987	.0013
2.68	.4963	.0037	3.03	.4988	.0012
2.69	.4964	.0036	3.04	.4988	.0012
2.70	.4965	.0035	3.05	.4989	.0011
2.71	.4966	.0034	3.06	.4989	.0011
2.72	.4967	.0033	3.07	.4989	.0011
2.73	.4968	.0032	3.08	.4990	.0010
2.74	.4969	.0031	3.09	.4990	.0010

Table B (*Continued*)

z	Area between mean and z	Area beyond z		z	Area between mean and z	Area beyond z
1	*2*	*3*		*1*	*2*	*3*
3.10	.4990	.0010		3.20	.4993	.0007
3.11	.4991	.0009		3.21	.4993	.0007
3.12	.4991	.0009		3.22	.4994	.0006
3.13	.4991	.0009		3.23	.4994	.0006
3.14	.4992	.0008		3.24	.4994	.0006
3.15	.4992	.0008		3.30	.4995	.0005
3.16	.4992	.0008		3.40	.4997	.0003
3.17	.4992	.0008		3.50	.4998	.0002
3.18	.4993	.0007		3.60	.4998	.0002
3.19	.4993	.0007		3.70	.4999	.0001

Table C *Values of* z *Corresponding to Divisions of the Area under the Normal Curve into a Larger Proportion and a Smaller Proportion*[a]

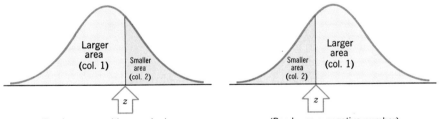

The larger area	z	The smaller area		The larger area	z	The smaller area
1	*2*	*3*		*1*	*2*	*3*
.500	.0000	.500		.525	.0627	.475
.505	.0125	.495		.530	.0753	.470
.510	.0251	.490		.535	.0878	.465
.515	.0376	.485		.540	.1004	.460
.520	.0502	.480		.545	.1130	.455

[a] Modified from: *Fundamental Statistics in Psychology and Education* by J. P. Guilford. Copyright © 1965, McGraw-Hill Book Co., Inc. Used by permission of McGraw-Hill Book Co., Inc.

Table Continued on Following Page

Table C (*Continued*)

| The larger area | z | The smaller area | | The larger area | z | The smaller area |
1	2	3		1	2	3
.550	.1257	.450		.730	.6128	.270
.555	.1383	.445		.735	.6280	.265
.560	.1510	.440		.740	.6433	.260
.565	.1637	.435		.745	.6588	.255
.570	.1764	.430				
				.750	.6745	.250
.575	.1891	.425		.755	.6903	.245
.580	.2019	.420		.760	.7063	.240
.585	.2147	.415		.765	.7225	.235
.590	.2275	.410		.770	.7388	.230
.595	.2404	.405				
				.775	.7554	.225
.600	.2533	.400		.780	.7722	.220
.605	.2663	.395		.785	.7892	.215
.610	.2793	.390		.790	.8064	.210
.615	.2924	.385		.795	.8239	.205
.620	.3055	.380				
				.800	.8416	.200
.625	.3186	.375		.805	.8596	.195
.630	.3319	.370		.810	.8779	.190
.635	.3451	.365		.815	.8965	.185
.640	.3585	.360		.820	.9154	.180
.645	.3719	.355				
				.825	.9346	.175
.650	.3853	.350		.830	.9542	.170
.655	.3989	.345		.835	.9741	.165
.660	.4125	.340		.840	.9945	.160
.665	.4261	.335		.845	1.0152	.155
.670	.4399	.330				
				.850	1.0364	.150
.675	.4538	.325		.855	1.0581	.145
.680	.4677	.320		.860	1.0803	.140
.685	.4817	.315		.865	1.1031	.135
.690	.4959	.310		.870	1.1264	.130
.695	.5101	.305				
				.875	1.1503	.125
.700	.5244	.300		.880	1.1750	.120
.705	.5388	.295		.885	1.2004	.115
.710	.5534	.290		.890	1.2265	.110
.715	.5681	.285		.895	1.2536	.105
.720	.5828	.280				
				.900	1.2816	.100
.725	.5978	.275		.905	1.3106	.095

Table C (*Continued*)

The larger area	z	The smaller area	The larger area	z	The smaller area
1	*2*	*3*	*1*	*2*	*3*
.910	1.3408	.090	.970	1.8808	.030
.915	1.3722	.085	.975	1.9600	.025
.920	1.4051	.080	.980	2.0537	.020
.925	1.4395	.075	.985	2.1701	.015
.930	1.4757	.070	.990	2.3263	.010
.935	1.5141	.065	.995	2.5758	.005
.940	1.5548	.060	.996	2.6521	.004
.945	1.5982	.055	.997	2.7478	.003
.950	1.6449	.050	.998	2.8782	.002
.955	1.6954	.045	.999	3.0902	.001
.960	1.7507	.040	.9995	3.2905	.0005
.965	1.8119	.035			

Table D Student's t Distribution[a]

The first column identifies the specific t distribution according to its number of degrees of freedom. Other columns give the proportion of the area under the entire curve which falls beyond the tabled positive value of t. Areas for negative values of t are the same, since the curve is symmetrical.

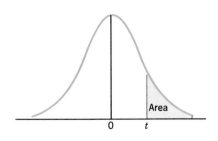

			Area in one tail			
df	.25	.10	.05	**.025**	.01	**.005**
1	1.000	3.078	6.314	12.706	31.821	63.657
2	0.816	1.886	2.920	4.303	6.965	9.925
3	0.765	1.638	2.353	3.182	4.541	5.841
4	0.741	1.533	2.132	2.776	3.747	4.604
5	0.727	1.476	2.015	2.571	3.365	4.032
6	0.718	1.440	1.943	2.447	3.143	3.707
7	0.711	1.415	1.895	2.365	2.998	3.500
8	0.706	1.397	1.860	2.306	2.896	3.355
9	0.703	1.383	1.833	2.262	2.821	3.250

[a] Modified from Section 2.1, *Handbook of Statistical Tables* by Donald B. Owen. Copyright © 1962, Addison-Wesley, Reading, Mass. Courtesy of the U.S. Energy Research and Development Adm.

Table Continued on Following Page

Table D (Continued)

Area in one tail

df	.25	.10	.05	.025	.01	.005
10	0.700	1.372	1.812	2.228	2.764	3.169
11	0.697	1.363	1.796	2.201	2.718	3.106
12	0.696	1.356	1.782	2.179	2.681	3.054
13	0.694	1.350	1.771	2.160	2.650	3.012
14	0.692	1.345	1.761	2.145	2.624	2.977
15	0.691	1.341	1.753	2.132	2.602	2.947
16	0.690	1.337	1.746	2.120	2.584	2.921
17	0.689	1.333	1.740	2.110	2.567	2.898
18	0.688	1.330	1.734	2.101	2.552	2.878
19	0.688	1.328	1.729	2.093	2.540	2.861
20	0.687	1.325	1.725	2.086	2.528	2.845
21	0.686	1.323	1.721	2.080	2.518	2.831
22	0.686	1.321	1.717	2.074	2.508	2.819
23	0.685	1.320	1.714	2.069	2.500	2.807
24	0.685	1.318	1.711	2.064	2.492	2.797
25	0.684	1.316	1.708	2.060	2.485	2.787
26	0.684	1.315	1.706	2.056	2.479	2.779
27	0.684	1.314	1.703	2.052	2.473	2.771
28	0.683	1.312	1.701	2.048	2.467	2.763
29	0.683	1.311	1.699	2.045	2.462	2.756
30	0.683	1.310	1.697	2.042	2.457	2.750
31	0.682	1.310	1.696	2.040	2.453	2.744
32	0.682	1.309	1.694	2.037	2.449	2.738
33	0.682	1.308	1.692	2.034	2.445	2.733
34	0.682	1.307	1.691	2.032	2.441	2.728
35	0.682	1.306	1.690	2.030	2.438	2.724
36	0.681	1.306	1.688	2.028	2.434	2.720
37	0.681	1.305	1.687	2.026	2.431	2.715
38	0.681	1.304	1.686	2.024	2.429	2.712
39	0.681	1.304	1.685	2.023	2.426	2.708
40	0.681	1.303	1.684	2.021	2.423	2.704
45	0.680	1.301	1.679	2.014	2.412	2.690
50	0.679	1.299	1.676	2.009	2.403	2.678
55	0.679	1.297	1.673	2.004	2.396	2.668
60	0.679	1.296	1.671	2.000	2.390	2.660
70	0.678	1.294	1.667	1.994	2.381	2.648
80	0.678	1.292	1.664	1.990	2.374	2.639
90	0.677	1.291	1.662	1.987	2.368	2.632
100	0.677	1.290	1.660	1.984	2.364	2.626
120	0.676	1.289	1.658	1.980	2.358	2.617
150	0.676	1.287	1.655	1.976	2.352	2.609

Table D (*Continued*)

df	Area in one tail					
	.25	.10	.05	*.025*	.01	*.005*
200	0.676	1.286	1.652	1.972	2.345	2.601
300	0.675	1.284	1.650	1.968	2.339	2.592
400	0.675	1.284	1.649	1.966	2.336	2.588
500	0.675	1.283	1.648	1.965	2.334	2.586
1000	0.675	1.282	1.646	1.962	2.330	2.581
∞	0.674	1.282	1.645	1.960	2.326	2.576

Table E *Values of the Correlation Coefficient Required for Different Levels of Significance when* $H_0: \rho = 0$ [a]

df	Levels of significance for a one-tailed test			
	.05	.025	.01	.005
	Levels of significance for a two-tailed test			
	.10	*.05*	.02	*.01*
1	.988	.997	.9995	.9999
2	.900	.950	.980	.990
3	.805	.878	.934	.959
4	.729	.811	.882	.917
5	.669	.754	.833	.874
6	.622	.707	.789	.834
7	.582	.666	.750	.798
8	.549	.632	.716	.765
9	.521	.602	.685	.735
10	.497	.576	.658	.708
11	.476	.553	.634	.684
12	.458	.532	.612	.661
13	.441	.514	.592	.641
14	.426	.497	.574	.623
15	.412	.482	.558	.606
16	.400	.468	.542	.590
17	.389	.456	.528	.575
18	.378	.444	.516	.561
19	.369	.433	.503	.549
20	.360	.423	.492	.537

[a] Table E is taken from Table V.A of Fisher: *Statistical Methods for Research Workers,* published by Oliver & Boyd Limited, Edinburgh, and by permission of the author and publishers. Supplementary values were calculated at San Jose State University by K. Fernandes.

Table Continued on Following Page

Table E (*Continued*)

df	Levels of significance for a one-tailed test			
	.05	.025	.01	.005
	Levels of significance for a two-tailed test			
	.10	.05	.02	.01
21	.352	.413	.482	.526
22	.344	.404	.472	.515
23	.337	.396	.462	.505
24	.330	.388	.453	.496
25	.323	.381	.445	.487
26	.317	.374	.437	.479
27	.311	.367	.430	.471
28	.306	.361	.423	.463
29	.301	.355	.416	.456
30	.296	.349	.409	.449
32	.287	.339	.397	.436
34	.279	.329	.386	.424
36	.271	.320	.376	.413
38	.264	.312	.367	.403
40	.257	.304	.358	.393
42	.251	.297	.350	.384
44	.246	.291	.342	.376
46	.240	.285	.335	.368
48	.235	.279	.328	.361
50	.231	.273	.322	.354
55	.220	.261	.307	.339
60	.211	.250	.295	.325
65	.203	.240	.284	.313
70	.195	.232	.274	.302
75	.189	.224	.265	.292
80	.183	.217	.256	.283
85	.178	.211	.249	.275
90	.173	.205	.242	.267
95	.168	.200	.236	.260
100	.164	.195	.230	.254
120	.150	.178	.210	.232
150	.134	.159	.189	.208
200	.116	.138	.164	.181
300	.095	.113	.134	.148
400	.082	.098	.116	.128
500	.073	.088	.104	.115
1000	.052	.062	.073	.081

Table F *Values of Fisher's* z' *for Values of* r[a]

r	z'	r	z'	r	z'	r	z'	r	z'
.000	.000	.200	.203	.400	.424	.600	.693	.800	1.099
.005	.005	.205	.208	.405	.430	.605	.701	.805	1.113
.010	.010	.210	.213	.410	.436	.610	.709	.810	1.127
.015	.015	.215	.218	.415	.442	.615	.717	.815	1.142
.020	.020	.220	.224	.420	.448	.620	.725	.820	1.157
.025	.025	.225	.229	.425	.454	.625	.733	.825	1.172
.030	.030	.230	.234	.430	.460	.630	.741	.830	1.188
.035	.035	.235	.239	.435	.466	.635	.750	.835	1.204
.040	.040	.240	.245	.440	.472	.640	.758	.840	1.221
.045	.045	.245	.250	.445	.478	.645	.767	.845	1.238
.050	.050	.250	.255	.450	.485	.650	.775	.850	1.256
.055	.055	.255	.261	.455	.491	.655	.784	.855	1.274
.060	.060	.260	.266	.460	.497	.660	.793	.860	1.293
.065	.065	.265	.271	.465	.504	.665	.802	.865	1.313
.070	.070	.270	.277	.470	.510	.670	.811	.870	1.333
.075	.075	.275	.282	.475	.517	.675	.820	.875	1.354
.080	.080	.280	.288	.480	.523	.680	.829	.880	1.376
.085	.085	.285	.293	.485	.530	.685	.838	.885	1.398
.090	.090	.290	.299	.490	.536	.690	.848	.890	1.422
.095	.095	.295	.304	.495	.543	.695	.858	.895	1.447
.100	.100	.300	.310	.500	.549	.700	.867	.900	1.472
.105	.105	.305	.315	.505	.556	.705	.877	.905	1.499
.110	.110	.310	.321	.510	.563	.710	.887	.910	1.528
.115	.116	.315	.326	.515	.570	.715	.897	.915	1.557
.120	.121	.320	.332	.520	.576	.720	.908	.920	1.589
.125	.126	.325	.337	.525	.583	.725	.918	.925	1.623
.130	.131	.330	.343	.530	.590	.730	.929	.930	1.658
.135	.136	.335	.348	.535	.597	.735	.940	.935	1.697
.140	.141	.340	.354	.540	.604	.740	.950	.940	1.738
.145	.146	.345	.360	.545	.611	.745	.962	.945	1.783
.150	.151	.350	.365	.550	.618	.750	.973	.950	1.832
.155	.156	.355	.371	.555	.626	.755	.984	.955	1.886
.160	.161	.360	.377	.560	.633	.760	.996	.960	1.946
.165	.167	.365	.383	.565	.640	.765	1.008	.965	2.014
.170	.172	.370	.388	.570	.648	.770	1.020	.970	2.092
.175	.177	.375	.394	.575	.655	.775	1.033	.975	2.185
.180	.182	.380	.400	.580	.662	.780	1.045	.980	2.298
.185	.187	.385	.406	.585	.670	.785	1.058	.985	2.443
.190	.192	.390	.412	.590	.678	.790	1.071	.990	2.647
.195	.198	.395	.418	.595	.685	.795	1.085	.995	2.994

[a] From *Statistical Methods*, 2nd ed., by Allen L. Edwards. Copyright © 1954, 1967 by Allen L. Edwards. Reprinted by permission of Holt, Rinehart and Winston, Inc.

Table G   The χ^2 Distribution[a]

The first column identifies the specific χ^2 distribution according to its number of degrees of freedom. Other columns give the proportion of the area under the entire curve which falls above the tabled value of χ^2.

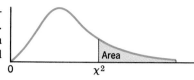

Area

0 χ^2

				Area in the upper tail					
df	.995	.99	.975	.95	.90	.10	**.05**	.025	**.01**	.005
1	.000039	.00016	.00098	.0039	.016	2.71	3.84	5.02	6.63	7.88
2	.010	.020	.051	.10	.21	4.61	5.99	7.38	9.21	10.60
3	.072	.11	.22	.35	.58	6.25	7.81	9.35	11.34	12.84
4	.21	.30	.48	.71	1.06	7.78	9.49	11.14	13.28	14.86
5	.41	.55	.83	1.15	1.61	9.24	11.07	12.83	15.09	16.75
6	.68	.87	1.24	1.64	2.20	10.64	12.59	14.45	16.81	18.55
7	.99	1.24	1.69	2.17	2.83	12.02	14.07	16.01	18.48	20.28
8	1.34	1.65	2.18	2.73	3.49	13.36	15.51	17.53	20.09	21.96
9	1.73	2.09	2.70	3.33	4.17	14.68	16.92	19.02	21.67	23.59
10	2.16	2.56	3.25	3.94	4.87	15.99	18.31	20.48	23.21	25.19
11	2.60	3.05	3.82	4.57	5.58	17.28	19.68	21.92	24.72	26.76
12	3.07	3.57	4.40	5.23	6.30	18.55	21.03	23.34	26.22	28.30
13	3.57	4.11	5.01	5.89	7.04	19.81	22.36	24.74	27.69	29.82
14	4.07	4.66	5.63	6.57	7.79	21.06	23.68	26.12	29.14	31.32
15	4.60	5.23	6.26	7.26	8.55	22.31	25.00	27.49	30.58	32.80
16	5.14	5.81	6.91	7.96	9.31	23.54	26.30	28.85	32.00	34.27
17	5.70	6.41	7.56	8.67	10.09	24.77	27.59	30.19	33.41	35.72
18	6.26	7.01	8.23	9.39	10.86	25.99	28.87	31.53	34.81	37.16
19	6.84	7.63	8.91	10.12	11.65	27.20	30.14	32.85	36.19	38.58
20	7.43	8.26	9.59	10.85	12.44	28.41	31.41	34.17	37.57	40.00
21	8.03	8.90	10.28	11.59	13.24	29.62	32.67	35.48	38.93	41.40
22	8.64	9.54	10.98	12.34	14.04	30.81	33.92	36.78	40.29	42.80
23	9.26	10.20	11.69	13.09	14.85	32.01	35.17	38.08	41.64	44.18
24	9.89	10.86	12.40	13.85	15.66	33.20	36.42	39.36	42.98	45.56
25	10.52	11.52	13.12	14.61	16.47	34.38	37.65	40.65	44.31	46.93
26	11.16	12.20	13.84	15.38	17.29	35.56	38.89	41.92	45.64	48.29
27	11.81	12.88	14.57	16.15	18.11	36.74	40.11	43.19	46.96	49.64
28	12.46	13.56	15.31	16.93	18.94	37.92	41.34	44.46	48.28	50.99
29	13.12	14.26	16.05	17.71	19.77	39.09	42.56	45.72	49.59	52.34
30	13.79	14.95	16.79	18.49	20.60	40.26	43.77	46.98	50.89	53.67
40	20.71	22.16	24.43	26.51	29.05	51.81	55.76	59.34	63.69	66.77
50	27.99	29.71	32.36	34.76	37.69	63.17	67.50	71.42	76.15	79.49
60	35.53	37.48	40.48	43.19	46.46	74.40	79.08	83.30	88.38	91.95
70	43.28	45.44	48.76	51.74	55.33	85.53	90.53	95.02	100.42	104.22
80	51.17	53.54	57.15	60.39	64.28	96.58	101.88	106.63	112.33	116.32
90	59.20	61.75	65.65	69.13	73.29	107.56	113.14	118.14	124.12	128.30
100	67.33	70.06	74.22	77.93	82.36	118.50	124.34	129.56	135.81	140.17
120	83.85	86.92	91.58	95.70	100.62	140.23	146.57	152.21	158.95	163.64

[a] Modified from Table 8: E. Pearson, and H. Hartley, *Biometrika Tables for Statisticians,* Vol. 1, 3rd ed., University Press, Cambridge, 1966, with permission of the Biometrika Trustees.

Note: When $df > 30$, the critical value of χ^2 may be found by the following approximate formula: $\chi^2 = df[1 - (2/9df) + z\sqrt{2/9df}]^3$, where z is the normal deviate above which lies the same proportionate area in the normal curve. For example, to find the value of χ^2 which divides the upper 1% of the distribution from the remainder when $df = 30$, we calculate: $\chi^2 = 30(1 - .00741 + 2.3263\sqrt{.0074074})^3 = 50.91$ which compares closely with the tabled value of 50.89.

Table H The F Distribution.[a] *Values of F Corresponding to 5% (Roman Type) and 1% (**Boldface Type**) of the Area in the Upper Tail*

The specific F distribution must be identified by the number of degrees of freedom characterizing the numerator and the denominator of F.

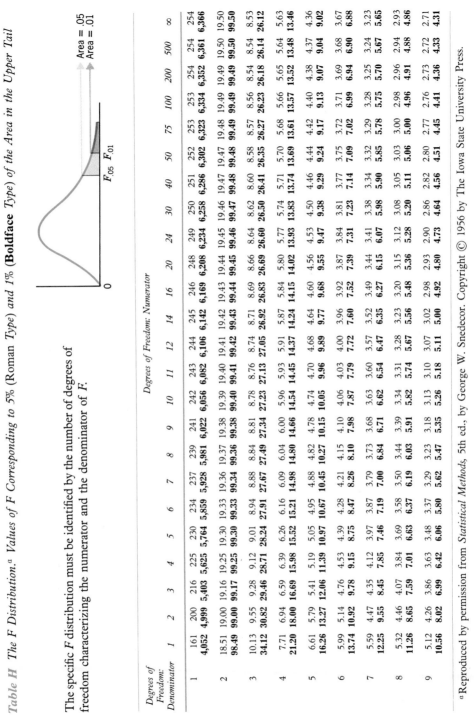

Degrees of Freedom: Denominator	Degrees of Freedom: Numerator																							
	1	2	3	4	5	6	7	8	9	10	11	12	14	16	20	24	30	40	50	75	100	200	500	∞
1	161 **4,052**	200 **4,999**	216 **5,403**	225 **5,625**	230 **5,764**	234 **5,859**	237 **5,928**	239 **5,981**	241 **6,022**	242 **6,056**	243 **6,082**	244 **6,106**	245 **6,142**	246 **6,169**	248 **6,208**	249 **6,234**	250 **6,258**	251 **6,286**	252 **6,302**	253 **6,323**	253 **6,334**	254 **6,352**	254 **6,361**	254 **6,366**
2	18.51 **98.49**	19.00 **99.00**	19.16 **99.17**	19.25 **99.25**	19.30 **99.30**	19.33 **99.33**	19.36 **99.34**	19.37 **99.36**	19.38 **99.38**	19.39 **99.40**	19.40 **99.41**	19.41 **99.42**	19.42 **99.43**	19.43 **99.44**	19.44 **99.45**	19.45 **99.46**	19.46 **99.47**	19.47 **99.48**	19.47 **99.48**	19.48 **99.49**	19.49 **99.49**	19.49 **99.49**	19.50 **99.50**	19.50 **99.50**
3	10.13 **34.12**	9.55 **30.82**	9.28 **29.46**	9.12 **28.71**	9.01 **28.24**	8.94 **27.91**	8.88 **27.67**	8.84 **27.49**	8.81 **27.34**	8.78 **27.23**	8.76 **27.13**	8.74 **27.05**	8.71 **26.92**	8.69 **26.83**	8.66 **26.69**	8.64 **26.60**	8.62 **26.50**	8.60 **26.41**	8.58 **26.35**	8.57 **26.27**	8.56 **26.23**	8.54 **26.18**	8.54 **26.14**	8.53 **26.12**
4	7.71 **21.20**	6.94 **18.00**	6.59 **16.69**	6.39 **15.98**	6.26 **15.52**	6.16 **15.21**	6.09 **14.98**	6.04 **14.80**	6.00 **14.66**	5.96 **14.54**	5.93 **14.45**	5.91 **14.37**	5.87 **14.24**	5.84 **14.15**	5.80 **14.02**	5.77 **13.93**	5.74 **13.83**	5.71 **13.74**	5.70 **13.69**	5.68 **13.61**	5.66 **13.57**	5.65 **13.52**	5.64 **13.48**	5.63 **13.46**
5	6.61 **16.26**	5.79 **13.27**	5.41 **12.06**	5.19 **11.39**	5.05 **10.97**	4.95 **10.67**	4.88 **10.45**	4.82 **10.27**	4.78 **10.15**	4.74 **10.05**	4.70 **9.96**	4.68 **9.89**	4.64 **9.77**	4.60 **9.68**	4.56 **9.55**	4.53 **9.47**	4.50 **9.38**	4.46 **9.29**	4.44 **9.24**	4.42 **9.17**	4.40 **9.13**	4.38 **9.07**	4.37 **9.04**	4.36 **9.02**
6	5.99 **13.74**	5.14 **10.92**	4.76 **9.78**	4.53 **9.15**	4.39 **8.75**	4.28 **8.47**	4.21 **8.26**	4.15 **8.10**	4.10 **7.98**	4.06 **7.87**	4.03 **7.79**	4.00 **7.72**	3.96 **7.60**	3.92 **7.52**	3.87 **7.39**	3.84 **7.31**	3.81 **7.23**	3.77 **7.14**	3.75 **7.09**	3.72 **7.02**	3.71 **6.99**	3.69 **6.94**	3.68 **6.90**	3.67 **6.88**
7	5.59 **12.25**	4.74 **9.55**	4.35 **8.45**	4.12 **7.85**	3.97 **7.46**	3.87 **7.19**	3.79 **7.00**	3.73 **6.84**	3.68 **6.71**	3.63 **6.62**	3.60 **6.54**	3.57 **6.47**	3.52 **6.35**	3.49 **6.27**	3.44 **6.15**	3.41 **6.07**	3.38 **5.98**	3.34 **5.90**	3.32 **5.85**	3.29 **5.78**	3.28 **5.75**	3.25 **5.70**	3.24 **5.67**	3.23 **5.65**
8	5.32 **11.26**	4.46 **8.65**	4.07 **7.59**	3.84 **7.01**	3.69 **6.63**	3.58 **6.37**	3.50 **6.19**	3.44 **6.03**	3.39 **5.91**	3.34 **5.82**	3.31 **5.74**	3.28 **5.67**	3.23 **5.56**	3.20 **5.48**	3.15 **5.36**	3.12 **5.28**	3.08 **5.20**	3.05 **5.11**	3.03 **5.06**	3.00 **5.00**	2.98 **4.96**	2.96 **4.91**	2.94 **4.88**	2.93 **4.86**
9	5.12 **10.56**	4.26 **8.02**	3.86 **6.99**	3.63 **6.42**	3.48 **6.06**	3.37 **5.80**	3.29 **5.62**	3.23 **5.47**	3.18 **5.35**	3.13 **5.26**	3.10 **5.18**	3.07 **5.11**	3.02 **5.00**	2.98 **4.92**	2.93 **4.80**	2.90 **4.73**	2.86 **4.64**	2.82 **4.56**	2.80 **4.51**	2.77 **4.45**	2.76 **4.41**	2.73 **4.36**	2.72 **4.33**	2.71 **4.31**

[a]Reproduced by permission from *Statistical Methods*, 5th ed., by George W. Snedecor. Copyright © 1956 by The Iowa State University Press.

Table Continued on Following Page

Degrees of Freedom: Numerator

Degrees of Freedom: Denominator	1	2	3	4	5	6	7	8	9	10	11	12	14	16	20	24	30	40	50	75	100	200	500	∞
10	4.96 **10.04**	4.10 **7.56**	3.71 **6.55**	3.48 **5.99**	3.33 **5.64**	3.22 **5.39**	3.14 **5.21**	3.07 **5.06**	3.02 **4.95**	2.97 **4.85**	2.94 **4.78**	2.91 **4.71**	2.86 **4.60**	2.82 **4.52**	2.77 **4.41**	2.74 **4.33**	2.70 **4.25**	2.67 **4.17**	2.64 **4.12**	2.61 **4.05**	2.59 **4.01**	2.56 **3.96**	2.55 **3.93**	2.54 **3.91**
11	4.84 **9.65**	3.98 **7.20**	3.59 **6.22**	3.36 **5.67**	3.20 **5.32**	3.09 **5.07**	3.01 **4.88**	2.95 **4.74**	2.90 **4.63**	2.86 **4.54**	2.82 **4.46**	2.79 **4.40**	2.74 **4.29**	2.70 **4.21**	2.65 **4.10**	2.61 **4.02**	2.57 **3.94**	2.53 **3.86**	2.50 **3.80**	2.47 **3.74**	2.45 **3.70**	2.42 **3.66**	2.41 **3.62**	2.40 **3.60**
12	4.75 **9.33**	3.88 **6.93**	3.49 **5.95**	3.26 **5.41**	3.11 **5.06**	3.00 **4.82**	2.92 **4.65**	2.85 **4.50**	2.80 **4.39**	2.76 **4.30**	2.72 **4.22**	2.69 **4.16**	2.64 **4.05**	2.60 **3.98**	2.54 **3.86**	2.50 **3.78**	2.46 **3.70**	2.42 **3.61**	2.40 **3.56**	2.36 **3.49**	2.35 **3.46**	2.32 **3.41**	2.31 **3.38**	2.30 **3.36**
13	4.67 **9.07**	3.80 **6.70**	3.41 **5.74**	3.18 **5.20**	3.02 **4.86**	2.92 **4.62**	2.84 **4.44**	2.77 **4.30**	2.72 **4.19**	2.67 **4.10**	2.63 **4.02**	2.60 **3.96**	2.55 **3.85**	2.51 **3.78**	2.46 **3.67**	2.42 **3.59**	2.38 **3.51**	2.34 **3.42**	2.32 **3.37**	2.28 **3.30**	2.26 **3.27**	2.24 **3.21**	2.22 **3.18**	2.21 **3.16**
14	4.60 **8.86**	3.74 **6.51**	3.34 **5.56**	3.11 **5.03**	2.96 **4.69**	2.85 **4.46**	2.77 **4.28**	2.70 **4.14**	2.65 **4.03**	2.60 **3.94**	2.56 **3.86**	2.53 **3.80**	2.48 **3.70**	2.44 **3.62**	2.39 **3.51**	2.35 **3.43**	2.31 **3.34**	2.27 **3.26**	2.24 **3.21**	2.21 **3.14**	2.19 **3.11**	2.16 **3.06**	2.14 **3.02**	2.13 **3.00**
15	4.54 **8.68**	3.68 **6.36**	3.29 **5.42**	3.06 **4.89**	2.90 **4.56**	2.79 **4.32**	2.70 **4.14**	2.64 **4.00**	2.59 **3.89**	2.55 **3.80**	2.51 **3.73**	2.48 **3.67**	2.43 **3.56**	2.39 **3.48**	2.33 **3.36**	2.29 **3.29**	2.25 **3.20**	2.21 **3.12**	2.18 **3.07**	2.15 **3.00**	2.12 **2.97**	2.10 **2.92**	2.08 **2.89**	2.07 **2.87**
16	4.49 **8.53**	3.63 **6.23**	3.24 **5.29**	3.01 **4.77**	2.85 **4.44**	2.74 **4.20**	2.66 **4.03**	2.59 **3.89**	2.54 **3.78**	2.49 **3.69**	2.45 **3.61**	2.42 **3.55**	2.37 **3.45**	2.33 **3.37**	2.28 **3.25**	2.24 **3.18**	2.20 **3.10**	2.16 **3.01**	2.13 **2.96**	2.09 **2.89**	2.07 **2.86**	2.04 **2.80**	2.02 **2.77**	2.01 **2.75**
17	4.45 **8.40**	3.59 **6.11**	3.20 **5.18**	2.96 **4.67**	2.81 **4.34**	2.70 **4.10**	2.62 **3.93**	2.55 **3.79**	2.50 **3.68**	2.45 **3.59**	2.41 **3.52**	2.38 **3.45**	2.33 **3.35**	2.29 **3.27**	2.23 **3.16**	2.19 **3.08**	2.15 **3.00**	2.11 **2.92**	2.08 **2.86**	2.04 **2.79**	2.02 **2.76**	1.99 **2.70**	1.97 **2.67**	1.96 **2.65**
18	4.41 **8.28**	3.55 **6.01**	3.16 **5.09**	2.93 **4.58**	2.77 **4.25**	2.66 **4.01**	2.58 **3.85**	2.51 **3.71**	2.46 **3.60**	2.41 **3.51**	2.37 **3.44**	2.34 **3.37**	2.29 **3.27**	2.25 **3.19**	2.19 **3.07**	2.15 **3.00**	2.11 **2.91**	2.07 **2.83**	2.04 **2.78**	2.00 **2.71**	1.98 **2.68**	1.95 **2.62**	1.93 **2.59**	1.92 **2.57**
19	4.38 **8.18**	3.52 **5.93**	3.13 **5.01**	2.90 **4.50**	2.74 **4.17**	2.63 **3.94**	2.55 **3.77**	2.48 **3.63**	2.43 **3.52**	2.38 **3.43**	2.34 **3.36**	2.31 **3.30**	2.26 **3.19**	2.21 **3.12**	2.15 **3.00**	2.11 **2.92**	2.07 **2.84**	2.02 **2.76**	2.00 **2.70**	1.96 **2.63**	1.94 **2.60**	1.91 **2.54**	1.90 **2.51**	1.88 **2.49**
20	4.35 **8.10**	3.49 **5.85**	3.10 **4.94**	2.87 **4.43**	2.71 **4.10**	2.60 **3.87**	2.52 **3.71**	2.45 **3.56**	2.40 **3.45**	2.35 **3.37**	2.31 **3.30**	2.28 **3.23**	2.23 **3.13**	2.18 **3.05**	2.12 **2.94**	2.08 **2.86**	2.04 **2.77**	1.99 **2.69**	1.96 **2.63**	1.92 **2.56**	1.90 **2.53**	1.87 **2.47**	1.85 **2.44**	1.84 **2.42**
21	4.32 **8.02**	3.47 **5.78**	3.07 **4.87**	2.84 **4.37**	2.68 **4.04**	2.57 **3.81**	2.49 **3.65**	2.42 **3.51**	2.37 **3.40**	2.32 **3.31**	2.28 **3.24**	2.25 **3.17**	2.20 **3.07**	2.15 **2.99**	2.09 **2.88**	2.05 **2.80**	2.00 **2.72**	1.96 **2.63**	1.93 **2.58**	1.89 **2.51**	1.87 **2.47**	1.84 **2.42**	1.82 **2.38**	1.81 **2.36**
22	4.30 **7.94**	3.44 **5.72**	3.05 **4.82**	2.82 **4.31**	2.66 **3.99**	2.55 **3.76**	2.47 **3.59**	2.40 **3.45**	2.35 **3.35**	2.30 **3.26**	2.26 **3.18**	2.23 **3.12**	2.18 **3.02**	2.13 **2.94**	2.07 **2.83**	2.03 **2.75**	1.98 **2.67**	1.93 **2.58**	1.91 **2.53**	1.87 **2.46**	1.84 **2.42**	1.81 **2.37**	1.80 **2.33**	1.78 **2.31**
23	4.28 **7.88**	3.42 **5.66**	3.03 **4.76**	2.80 **4.26**	2.64 **3.94**	2.53 **3.71**	2.45 **3.54**	2.38 **3.41**	2.32 **3.30**	2.28 **3.21**	2.24 **3.14**	2.20 **3.07**	2.14 **2.97**	2.10 **2.89**	2.04 **2.78**	2.00 **2.70**	1.96 **2.62**	1.91 **2.53**	1.88 **2.48**	1.84 **2.41**	1.82 **2.37**	1.79 **2.32**	1.77 **2.28**	1.76 **2.26**

24	4.26 / 7.82	3.40 / 5.61	3.01 / 4.72	2.78 / 4.22	2.62 / 3.90	2.51 / 3.67	2.43 / 3.50	2.36 / 3.36	2.30 / 3.25	2.26 / 3.17	2.22 / 3.09	2.18 / 3.03	2.13 / 2.93	2.09 / 2.85	2.02 / 2.74	1.98 / 2.66	1.94 / 2.58	1.89 / 2.49	1.86 / 2.44	1.82 / 2.36	1.80 / 2.33	1.76 / 2.27	1.74 / 2.23	1.73 / 2.21
25	4.24 / 7.77	3.38 / 5.57	2.99 / 4.68	2.76 / 4.18	2.60 / 3.86	2.49 / 3.63	2.41 / 3.46	2.34 / 3.32	2.28 / 3.21	2.24 / 3.13	2.20 / 3.05	2.16 / 2.99	2.11 / 2.89	2.06 / 2.81	2.00 / 2.70	1.96 / 2.62	1.92 / 2.54	1.87 / 2.45	1.84 / 2.40	1.80 / 2.32	1.77 / 2.29	1.74 / 2.23	1.72 / 2.19	1.71 / 2.17
26	4.22 / 7.72	3.37 / 5.53	2.98 / 4.64	2.74 / 4.14	2.59 / 3.82	2.47 / 3.59	2.39 / 3.42	2.32 / 3.29	2.27 / 3.17	2.22 / 3.09	2.18 / 3.02	2.15 / 2.96	2.10 / 2.86	2.05 / 2.77	1.99 / 2.66	1.95 / 2.58	1.90 / 2.50	1.85 / 2.41	1.82 / 2.36	1.78 / 2.28	1.76 / 2.25	1.72 / 2.19	1.70 / 2.15	1.69 / 2.13
27	4.21 / 7.68	3.35 / 5.49	2.96 / 4.60	2.73 / 4.11	2.57 / 3.79	2.46 / 3.56	2.37 / 3.39	2.30 / 3.26	2.25 / 3.14	2.20 / 3.06	2.16 / 2.98	2.13 / 2.93	2.08 / 2.83	2.03 / 2.74	1.97 / 2.63	1.93 / 2.55	1.88 / 2.47	1.84 / 2.38	1.80 / 2.33	1.76 / 2.25	1.74 / 2.21	1.71 / 2.16	1.68 / 2.12	1.67 / 2.10
28	4.20 / 7.64	3.34 / 5.45	2.95 / 4.57	2.71 / 4.07	2.56 / 3.76	2.44 / 3.53	2.36 / 3.36	2.29 / 3.23	2.24 / 3.11	2.19 / 3.03	2.15 / 2.95	2.12 / 2.90	2.06 / 2.80	2.02 / 2.71	1.96 / 2.60	1.91 / 2.52	1.87 / 2.44	1.81 / 2.35	1.78 / 2.30	1.75 / 2.22	1.72 / 2.18	1.69 / 2.13	1.67 / 2.09	1.65 / 2.06
29	4.18 / 7.60	3.33 / 5.42	2.93 / 4.54	2.70 / 4.04	2.54 / 3.73	2.43 / 3.50	2.35 / 3.33	2.28 / 3.20	2.22 / 3.08	2.18 / 3.00	2.14 / 2.92	2.10 / 2.87	2.05 / 2.77	2.00 / 2.68	1.94 / 2.57	1.90 / 2.49	1.85 / 2.41	1.80 / 2.32	1.77 / 2.27	1.73 / 2.19	1.71 / 2.15	1.68 / 2.10	1.65 / 2.06	1.64 / 2.03
30	4.17 / 7.56	3.32 / 5.39	2.92 / 4.51	2.69 / 4.02	2.53 / 3.70	2.42 / 3.47	2.34 / 3.30	2.27 / 3.17	2.21 / 3.06	2.16 / 2.98	2.12 / 2.90	2.09 / 2.84	2.04 / 2.74	1.99 / 2.66	1.93 / 2.55	1.89 / 2.47	1.84 / 2.38	1.79 / 2.29	1.76 / 2.24	1.72 / 2.16	1.69 / 2.13	1.66 / 2.07	1.64 / 2.03	1.62 / 2.01
32	4.15 / 7.50	3.30 / 5.34	2.90 / 4.46	2.67 / 3.97	2.51 / 3.66	2.40 / 3.42	2.32 / 3.25	2.25 / 3.12	2.19 / 3.01	2.14 / 2.94	2.10 / 2.86	2.07 / 2.80	2.02 / 2.70	1.97 / 2.62	1.91 / 2.51	1.86 / 2.42	1.82 / 2.34	1.76 / 2.25	1.74 / 2.20	1.69 / 2.12	1.67 / 2.08	1.64 / 2.02	1.61 / 1.98	1.59 / 1.96
34	4.13 / 7.44	3.28 / 5.29	2.88 / 4.42	2.65 / 3.93	2.49 / 3.61	2.38 / 3.38	2.30 / 3.21	2.23 / 3.08	2.17 / 2.97	2.12 / 2.89	2.08 / 2.82	2.05 / 2.76	2.00 / 2.66	1.95 / 2.58	1.89 / 2.47	1.84 / 2.38	1.80 / 2.30	1.74 / 2.21	1.71 / 2.15	1.67 / 2.08	1.64 / 2.04	1.61 / 1.98	1.59 / 1.94	1.57 / 1.91
36	4.11 / 7.39	3.26 / 5.25	2.86 / 4.38	2.63 / 3.89	2.48 / 3.58	2.36 / 3.35	2.28 / 3.18	2.21 / 3.04	2.15 / 2.94	2.10 / 2.86	2.06 / 2.78	2.03 / 2.72	1.98 / 2.62	1.93 / 2.54	1.87 / 2.43	1.82 / 2.35	1.78 / 2.26	1.72 / 2.17	1.69 / 2.12	1.65 / 2.04	1.62 / 2.00	1.59 / 1.94	1.56 / 1.90	1.55 / 1.87
38	4.10 / 7.35	3.25 / 5.21	2.85 / 4.34	2.62 / 3.86	2.46 / 3.54	2.35 / 3.32	2.26 / 3.15	2.19 / 3.02	2.14 / 2.91	2.09 / 2.82	2.05 / 2.75	2.02 / 2.69	1.96 / 2.59	1.92 / 2.51	1.85 / 2.40	1.80 / 2.32	1.76 / 2.22	1.71 / 2.14	1.67 / 2.08	1.63 / 2.00	1.60 / 1.97	1.57 / 1.90	1.54 / 1.86	1.53 / 1.84
40	4.08 / 7.31	3.23 / 5.18	2.84 / 4.31	2.61 / 3.83	2.45 / 3.51	2.34 / 3.29	2.25 / 3.12	2.18 / 2.99	2.12 / 2.88	2.07 / 2.80	2.04 / 2.73	2.00 / 2.66	1.95 / 2.56	1.90 / 2.49	1.84 / 2.37	1.79 / 2.29	1.74 / 2.20	1.69 / 2.11	1.66 / 2.05	1.61 / 1.97	1.59 / 1.94	1.55 / 1.88	1.53 / 1.84	1.51 / 1.81
42	4.07 / 7.27	3.22 / 5.15	2.83 / 4.29	2.59 / 3.80	2.44 / 3.49	2.32 / 3.26	2.24 / 3.10	2.17 / 2.96	2.11 / 2.86	2.06 / 2.77	2.02 / 2.70	1.99 / 2.64	1.94 / 2.54	1.89 / 2.46	1.82 / 2.35	1.78 / 2.26	1.73 / 2.17	1.68 / 2.08	1.64 / 2.02	1.60 / 1.94	1.57 / 1.91	1.54 / 1.85	1.51 / 1.80	1.49 / 1.78
44	4.06 / 7.24	3.21 / 5.12	2.82 / 4.26	2.58 / 3.78	2.43 / 3.46	2.31 / 3.24	2.23 / 3.07	2.16 / 2.94	2.10 / 2.84	2.05 / 2.75	2.01 / 2.68	1.98 / 2.62	1.92 / 2.52	1.88 / 2.44	1.81 / 2.32	1.76 / 2.24	1.72 / 2.15	1.66 / 2.06	1.63 / 2.00	1.58 / 1.92	1.56 / 1.88	1.52 / 1.82	1.50 / 1.78	1.48 / 1.75
46	4.05 / 7.21	3.20 / 5.10	2.81 / 4.24	2.57 / 3.76	2.42 / 3.44	2.30 / 3.22	2.22 / 3.05	2.14 / 2.92	2.09 / 2.82	2.04 / 2.73	2.00 / 2.66	1.97 / 2.60	1.91 / 2.50	1.87 / 2.42	1.80 / 2.30	1.75 / 2.22	1.71 / 2.13	1.65 / 2.04	1.62 / 1.98	1.57 / 1.90	1.54 / 1.86	1.51 / 1.80	1.48 / 1.76	1.46 / 1.72
48	4.04 / 7.19	3.19 / 5.08	2.80 / 4.22	2.56 / 3.74	2.41 / 3.42	2.30 / 3.20	2.21 / 3.04	2.14 / 2.90	2.08 / 2.80	2.03 / 2.71	1.99 / 2.64	1.96 / 2.58	1.90 / 2.48	1.86 / 2.40	1.79 / 2.28	1.74 / 2.20	1.70 / 2.11	1.64 / 2.02	1.61 / 1.96	1.56 / 1.88	1.53 / 1.84	1.50 / 1.78	1.47 / 1.73	1.45 / 1.70

Table Continued on Following Page

Table H (Continued)

Degrees of Freedom: Numerator

Degrees of Freedom: Denominator	1	2	3	4	5	6	7	8	9	10	11	12	14	16	20	24	30	40	50	75	100	200	500	∞
50	4.03 **7.17**	3.18 **5.06**	2.79 **4.20**	2.56 **3.72**	2.40 **3.41**	2.29 **3.18**	2.20 **3.02**	2.13 **2.88**	2.07 **2.78**	2.02 **2.70**	1.98 **2.62**	1.95 **2.56**	1.90 **2.46**	1.85 **2.39**	1.78 **2.26**	1.74 **2.18**	1.69 **2.10**	1.63 **2.00**	1.60 **1.94**	1.55 **1.86**	1.52 **1.82**	1.48 **1.76**	1.46 **1.71**	1.44 **1.68**
55	4.02 **7.12**	3.17 **5.01**	2.78 **4.16**	2.54 **3.68**	2.38 **3.37**	2.27 **3.15**	2.18 **2.98**	2.11 **2.85**	2.05 **2.75**	2.00 **2.66**	1.97 **2.59**	1.93 **2.53**	1.88 **2.43**	1.83 **2.35**	1.76 **2.23**	1.72 **2.15**	1.67 **2.06**	1.61 **1.96**	1.58 **1.90**	1.52 **1.82**	1.50 **1.78**	1.46 **1.71**	1.43 **1.66**	1.41 **1.64**
60	4.00 **7.08**	3.15 **4.98**	2.76 **4.13**	2.52 **3.65**	2.37 **3.34**	2.25 **3.12**	2.17 **2.95**	2.10 **2.82**	2.04 **2.72**	1.99 **2.63**	1.95 **2.56**	1.92 **2.50**	1.86 **2.40**	1.81 **2.32**	1.75 **2.20**	1.70 **2.12**	1.65 **2.03**	1.59 **1.93**	1.56 **1.87**	1.50 **1.79**	1.48 **1.74**	1.44 **1.68**	1.41 **1.63**	1.39 **1.60**
65	3.99 **7.04**	3.14 **4.95**	2.75 **4.10**	2.51 **3.62**	2.36 **3.31**	2.24 **3.09**	2.15 **2.93**	2.08 **2.79**	2.02 **2.70**	1.98 **2.61**	1.94 **2.54**	1.90 **2.47**	1.85 **2.37**	1.80 **2.30**	1.73 **2.18**	1.68 **2.09**	1.63 **2.00**	1.57 **1.90**	1.54 **1.84**	1.49 **1.76**	1.46 **1.71**	1.42 **1.64**	1.39 **1.60**	1.37 **1.56**
70	3.98 **7.01**	3.13 **4.92**	2.74 **4.08**	2.50 **3.60**	2.35 **3.29**	2.23 **3.07**	2.14 **2.91**	2.07 **2.77**	2.01 **2.67**	1.97 **2.59**	1.93 **2.51**	1.89 **2.45**	1.84 **2.35**	1.79 **2.28**	1.72 **2.15**	1.67 **2.07**	1.62 **1.98**	1.56 **1.88**	1.53 **1.82**	1.47 **1.74**	1.45 **1.69**	1.40 **1.62**	1.37 **1.56**	1.35 **1.53**
80	3.96 **6.96**	3.11 **4.88**	2.72 **4.04**	2.48 **3.56**	2.33 **3.25**	2.21 **3.04**	2.12 **2.87**	2.05 **2.74**	1.99 **2.64**	1.95 **2.55**	1.91 **2.48**	1.88 **2.41**	1.82 **2.32**	1.77 **2.24**	1.70 **2.11**	1.65 **2.03**	1.60 **1.94**	1.54 **1.84**	1.51 **1.78**	1.45 **1.70**	1.42 **1.65**	1.38 **1.57**	1.35 **1.52**	1.32 **1.49**
100	3.94 **6.90**	3.09 **4.82**	2.70 **3.98**	2.46 **3.51**	2.30 **3.20**	2.19 **2.99**	2.10 **2.82**	2.03 **2.69**	1.97 **2.59**	1.92 **2.51**	1.88 **2.43**	1.85 **2.36**	1.79 **2.26**	1.75 **2.19**	1.68 **2.06**	1.63 **1.98**	1.57 **1.89**	1.51 **1.79**	1.48 **1.73**	1.42 **1.64**	1.39 **1.59**	1.34 **1.51**	1.30 **1.46**	1.28 **1.43**
125	3.92 **6.84**	3.07 **4.78**	2.68 **3.94**	2.44 **3.47**	2.29 **3.17**	2.17 **2.95**	2.08 **2.79**	2.01 **2.65**	1.95 **2.56**	1.90 **2.47**	1.86 **2.40**	1.83 **2.33**	1.77 **2.23**	1.72 **2.15**	1.65 **2.03**	1.60 **1.94**	1.55 **1.85**	1.49 **1.75**	1.45 **1.68**	1.39 **1.59**	1.36 **1.54**	1.31 **1.46**	1.27 **1.40**	1.25 **1.37**
150	3.91 **6.81**	3.06 **4.75**	2.67 **3.91**	2.43 **3.44**	2.27 **3.14**	2.16 **2.92**	2.07 **2.76**	2.00 **2.62**	1.94 **2.53**	1.89 **2.44**	1.85 **2.37**	1.82 **2.30**	1.76 **2.20**	1.71 **2.12**	1.64 **2.00**	1.59 **1.91**	1.54 **1.83**	1.47 **1.72**	1.44 **1.66**	1.37 **1.56**	1.34 **1.51**	1.29 **1.43**	1.25 **1.37**	1.22 **1.33**
200	3.89 **6.76**	3.04 **4.71**	2.65 **3.88**	2.41 **3.41**	2.26 **3.11**	2.14 **2.90**	2.05 **2.73**	1.98 **2.60**	1.92 **2.50**	1.87 **2.41**	1.83 **2.34**	1.80 **2.28**	1.74 **2.17**	1.69 **2.09**	1.62 **1.97**	1.57 **1.88**	1.52 **1.79**	1.45 **1.69**	1.42 **1.62**	1.35 **1.53**	1.32 **1.48**	1.26 **1.39**	1.22 **1.33**	1.19 **1.28**
400	3.86 **6.70**	3.02 **4.66**	2.62 **3.83**	2.39 **3.36**	2.23 **3.06**	2.12 **2.85**	2.03 **2.69**	1.96 **2.55**	1.90 **2.46**	1.85 **2.37**	1.81 **2.29**	1.78 **2.23**	1.72 **2.12**	1.67 **2.04**	1.60 **1.92**	1.54 **1.84**	1.49 **1.74**	1.42 **1.64**	1.38 **1.57**	1.32 **1.47**	1.28 **1.42**	1.22 **1.32**	1.16 **1.24**	1.13 **1.19**
1000	3.85 **6.66**	3.00 **4.62**	2.61 **3.80**	2.38 **3.34**	2.22 **3.04**	2.10 **2.82**	2.02 **2.66**	1.95 **2.53**	1.89 **2.43**	1.84 **2.34**	1.80 **2.26**	1.76 **2.20**	1.70 **2.09**	1.65 **2.01**	1.58 **1.89**	1.53 **1.81**	1.47 **1.71**	1.41 **1.61**	1.36 **1.54**	1.30 **1.44**	1.26 **1.38**	1.19 **1.28**	1.13 **1.19**	1.08 **1.11**
∞	3.84 **6.64**	2.99 **4.60**	2.60 **3.78**	2.37 **3.32**	2.21 **3.02**	2.09 **2.80**	2.01 **2.64**	1.94 **2.51**	1.88 **2.41**	1.83 **2.32**	1.79 **2.24**	1.75 **2.18**	1.69 **2.07**	1.64 **1.99**	1.57 **1.87**	1.52 **1.79**	1.46 **1.69**	1.40 **1.59**	1.35 **1.52**	1.28 **1.41**	1.24 **1.36**	1.17 **1.25**	1.11 **1.15**	1.00 **1.00**

Table I Random Digits[a]

11339	19233	50911	14209	39594	68368	97742	36252	27671	55091
96971	19968	31709	40197	16313	80020	01588	21654	50328	04577
07779	47712	33846	84716	49870	59670	46946	71716	50623	38681
71675	95993	08790	13241	71260	16558	83316	68482	10294	45137
32804	72742	16237	72550	10570	31470	92612	94917	48822	79794
14835	56263	53062	71543	67632	30337	28739	17582	40924	32434
15544	14327	07580	48813	30161	10746	96470	60680	63507	14435
92230	41243	90765	08867	08038	05038	10908	00633	21740	55450
33564	93563	10770	10595	71323	84243	09402	62877	49762	56151
84461	55618	40570	72906	30794	49144	65239	21788	38288	29180
91645	42451	83776	99246	45548	02457	74804	49536	89815	74285
78305	63797	26995	23146	56071	97081	22376	09819	56855	97424
97888	55122	65545	02904	40042	70653	24483	31258	96475	77668
67286	09001	09718	67231	54033	24185	52097	78713	95910	84400
53610	59459	89945	72102	66595	02198	26968	88467	46939	52318
52965	76189	68892	64541	02225	09603	59304	38179	75920	80486
25336	39735	25594	50557	96257	59700	27715	42432	27652	88151
73078	44371	77616	49296	55882	71507	30168	31876	28283	53424
31797	52244	38354	47800	48454	43304	14256	74281	82279	28882
47772	22798	36910	39986	34033	39868	24009	97123	59151	27583
54153	70832	37575	31898	39212	63993	05419	77565	73150	98537
93745	99871	37129	55032	94444	17884	27082	23502	06136	89476
81676	51330	58828	74199	87214	13727	80539	95037	73536	16862
79788	02193	33250	05865	53018	62394	56997	41534	01953	13763
92112	61235	68760	61201	02189	09424	24156	10368	26527	89107
87542	28171	45150	75523	66790	63963	13903	68498	02981	25219
37535	48342	48943	07719	20407	33748	93650	39356	01011	22099
95957	96668	69380	49091	90182	13205	71802	35482	27973	46814
34642	85350	53361	63940	79546	89956	96836	81313	80712	73572
50413	31008	09231	46516	61672	79954	01291	72278	55658	84893
53312	73768	59931	55182	43761	59424	79775	17772	41552	45236
16302	64092	76045	28958	21182	30050	96256	85737	86962	27067
96357	98654	01909	58799	87374	53184	87233	55275	59572	56476
38529	89095	89538	15600	33687	86353	61917	63876	52367	79032
45939	05014	06099	76041	57638	55342	41269	96173	94872	35605
02300	23739	68485	98567	77035	91533	62500	31548	09511	80252
59750	14131	24973	05962	83215	25950	43867	75213	21500	17758
21285	53607	82657	22053	29996	04729	48917	72091	57336	18476
93703	60164	19090	63030	88931	84439	94747	77982	61932	21928
15576	76654	19775	77518	43259	82790	08193	63007	68824	75315
12752	33321	69796	03625	37328	75200	77262	99004	96705	15540
89038	53455	93322	25069	88186	45026	31020	52540	10838	72490
62411	56968	08379	40159	27419	12024	99694	68668	73039	87682
45853	68103	38927	77105	65241	70387	01634	59665	30512	66161
84558	24272	84355	00116	68344	92805	52618	51584	75964	53021
45272	58388	69131	61075	80192	45959	76992	19210	27126	45525
68015	99001	11832	39832	80462	70468	89929	55695	77524	20675
13263	92240	89559	66545	06433	38634	36645	22350	81169	97417
66309	31466	97705	46996	69059	33771	95004	89037	38054	80853
56348	05291	38713	82303	26293	61319	45285	75784	50043	44438

[a] From pp. 99 and 100 of The Rand Corporation, *A Million Random Digits with 100,000 Normal Deviates,* The Free Press, Glencoe, Ill., 1955, with permission of the Rand Corporation.

Table Continued on Following Page

Table I (*Continued*)

93108	77033	68325	10160	38667	62441	87023	94372	06164	30700
28271	08589	83279	48838	60935	70541	53814	95588	05832	80235
21841	35545	11148	34775	17308	88034	97765	35959	52843	44895
22025	79554	19698	25255	50283	94037	57463	92925	12042	91414
09210	20779	02994	02258	86978	85092	54052	18354	20914	28460
90552	71129	03621	20517	16908	06668	29916	51537	93658	29525
01130	06995	20258	10351	99248	51660	38861	49668	74742	47181
22604	56719	21784	68788	38358	59827	19270	99287	81193	43366
06690	01800	34272	65497	94891	14537	91358	21587	95765	72605
59809	69982	71809	64984	48709	43991	24987	69246	86400	29559
56475	02726	58511	95405	70293	84971	06676	44075	32338	31980
02730	34870	83209	03138	07715	31557	55242	61308	26507	06186
74482	33990	13509	92588	10462	76546	46097	01825	20153	36271
19793	22487	94238	81054	95488	23617	15539	94335	73822	93481
19020	27856	60526	24144	98021	60564	46373	86928	52135	74919
69565	60635	65709	77887	42766	86698	14004	94577	27936	47220
69274	23208	61035	84263	15034	28717	76146	22021	23779	98562
83658	14204	09445	41081	49630	34215	89806	40930	97194	21747
78612	51102	66826	40430	54072	62164	68977	95583	11765	81072
14980	74158	78216	38985	60838	82836	42777	85321	90463	11813
63172	28010	29405	91554	75195	51183	65805	87525	35952	83204
71167	37984	52737	06869	38122	95322	41356	19391	96787	64410
78530	56410	19195	34434	83712	50397	80920	15464	81350	18673
98324	03774	07573	67864	06497	20758	83454	22756	83959	96347
55793	30055	08373	32652	02654	75980	02095	87545	88815	80086
05674	34471	61967	91266	38814	44728	32455	17057	08339	93997
15643	22245	07592	22078	73628	60902	41561	54608	41023	98345
66750	19609	70358	03622	64898	82220	69304	46235	97332	64539
42320	74314	50222	82339	51564	42885	50482	98501	02245	88990
73752	73818	15470	04914	24936	65514	56633	72030	30856	85183
97546	02188	46373	21486	28221	08155	23486	66134	88799	49496
32569	52162	38444	42004	78011	16909	94194	79732	47114	23919
36048	93973	82596	28739	86985	58144	65007	08786	14826	04896
40455	36702	38965	56042	80023	28169	04174	65533	52718	55255
33597	47071	55618	51796	71027	46690	08002	45066	02870	60012
22828	96380	35883	15910	17211	42358	14056	55438	98148	35384
00631	95925	19324	31497	88118	06283	84596	72091	53987	01477
75722	36478	07634	63114	27164	15467	03983	09141	60562	65725
80577	01771	61510	17099	28731	41426	18853	41523	14914	76661
10524	20900	65463	83680	05005	11611	64426	59065	06758	02892
93815	69446	75253	51915	97839	75427	90685	60352	96288	34248
81867	97119	93446	20862	46591	97677	42704	13718	44975	67145
64649	07689	16711	12169	15238	74106	60655	56289	74166	78561
55768	09210	52439	33355	57884	36791	00853	49969	74814	09270
38080	49460	48137	61589	42742	92035	21766	19435	92579	27683
22360	16332	05343	34613	24013	98831	17157	44089	07366	66196
40521	09057	00239	51284	71556	22605	41293	54854	39736	05113
19292	69862	59951	49644	53486	28244	20714	56030	39292	45166
79504	40078	06838	05509	68581	39400	85615	52314	83202	40313
64138	27983	84048	42631	58658	62243	82572	45211	37060	15017

Table J *Critical Values of* ΣR_X *for the Mann-Whitney (Wilcoxon) Rank-Sum Test*[a]

		$n_X = 3$						$n_X = 4$		
n_Y	**.005**	.01	**.025**	.05		n_Y	**.005**	.01	**.025**	.05
3				6–15		4			10–26	11–25
4				6–18		5		10–30	11–29	12–28
5			6–21	7–20		6	10–34	11–33	12–32	13–31
6			7–23	8–22		7	10–38	11–37	13–35	14–34
7		6–27	7–26	8–25		8	11–41	12–40	14–38	15–37
8		6–30	8–28	9–27		9	11–45	13–43	14–42	16–40
9	6–33	7–32	8–31	10–29		10	12–48	13–47	15–45	17–43
10	6–36	7–35	9–33	10–32		11	12–52	14–50	16–48	18–46
11	6–39	7–38	9–36	11–34		12	13–55	15–53	17–51	19–49
12	7–41	8–40	10–38	11–37		13	13–59	15–57	18–54	20–52
13	7–44	8–43	10–41	12–39		14	14–62	16–60	19–57	21–55
14	7–47	8–46	11–43	13–41		15	15–65	17–63	20–60	22–58
15	8–49	9–48	11–46	13–44						

		$n_X = 5$						$n_X = 6$		
n_Y	**.005**	.01	**.025**	.05		n_Y	**.005**	.01	**.025**	.05
5	15–40	16–39	17–38	19–36		6	23–55	24–54	26–52	28–50
6	16–44	17–43	18–42	20–40		7	24–60	25–59	27–57	29–55
7	16–49	18–47	20–45	21–44		8	25–65	27–63	29–61	31–59
8	17–53	19–51	21–49	23–47		9	26–70	28–68	31–65	33–63
9	18–57	20–55	22–53	24–51		10	27–75	29–73	32–70	35–67
10	19–61	21–59	23–57	26–54		11	28–80	30–78	34–74	37–71
11	20–65	22–63	24–61	27–58		12	30–84	32–82	35–79	38–76
12	21–69	23–67	26–64	28–62		13	31–89	33–87	37–83	40–80
13	22–73	24–71	27–68	30–65		14	32–94	34–92	38–88	42–84
14	22–78	25–75	28–72	31–69		15	33–99	36–96	40–92	44–88
15	23–82	26–79	29–76	33–72						

		$n_X = 7$						$n_X = 8$		
n_Y	**.005**	.01	**.025**	.05		n_Y	**.005**	.01	**.025**	.05
7	32–73	34–71	36–69	39–66		8	43–93	45–91	49–87	51–85
8	34–78	35–77	38–74	41–71		9	45–99	47–97	51–93	54–90
9	35–84	37–82	40–79	43–76		10	47–105	49–103	53–99	56–96
10	37–89	39–87	42–84	45–81		11	49–111	51–109	55–105	59–101
11	38–95	40–93	44–89	47–86		12	51–117	53–115	58–110	62–106
12	40–100	42–98	46–94	49–91		13	53–123	56–120	60–116	64–112
13	41–106	44–103	48–99	52–95		14	54–130	58–126	62–122	67–117
14	43–111	45–109	50–104	54–100		15	56–136	60–132	65–127	69–123
15	44–117	47–114	52–109	56–105						

[a]Adaptation of Table 1 in L. R. Verdooren, "Extended Tables of Critical Values for Wilcoxon's Test Statistic," *Biometrika*, **50**, 177–186 (1963), with permission of the author and the Biometrika Trustees.

Table Continued on Following Page

Table J (*Continued*)

	$n_X = 9$					$n_X = 10$			
n_Y	**.005**	.01	**.025**	.05	n_Y	**.005**	.01	**.025**	.05
9	56–115	59–112	62–109	66–105	10	71–139	74–136	78–132	82–128
10	58–122	61–119	65–115	69–111	11	73–147	77–143	81–139	86–134
11	61–128	63–126	68–121	72–117	12	76–154	79–151	84–146	89–141
12	63–135	66–132	71–127	75–123	13	79–161	82–158	88–152	92–148
13	65–142	68–139	73–134	78–129	14	81–169	85–165	91–159	96–154
14	67–149	71–145	76–140	81–135	15	84–176	88–172	94–166	99–161
15	69–156	73–152	79–146	84–141					

	$n_X = 11$					$n_X = 12$			
n_Y	**.005**	.01	**.025**	.05	n_Y	**.005**	.01	**.025**	.05
11	87–166	91–162	96–157	100–153	12	105–195	109–191	115–185	120–180
12	90–174	94–170	99–165	104–160	13	109–203	113–199	119–193	125–187
13	93–182	97–178	103–172	108–167	14	112–212	116–208	123–201	129–195
14	96–190	100–186	106–180	112–174	15	115–221	120–216	127–209	133–203
15	99–198	103–194	110–187	116–181					

	$n_X = 13$					$n_X = 14$			
n_Y	**.005**	.01	**.025**	.05	n_Y	**.005**	.01	**.025**	.05
13	125–226	130–221	136–215	142–209	14	147–259	152–254	160–246	166–240
14	129–235	134–230	141–223	147–217	15	151–269	156–264	164–256	171–249
15	133–244	138–239	145–232	152–225					

	$n_X = 15$			
n_Y	**.005**	.01	**.025**	.05
15	171–294	176–289	184–281	192–273

Table K *Critical Values for the Smaller of* W_+ *or* W_- *for the Wilcoxon Signed Ranks Test*[a]

	Levels of significance for a one-tailed test			
	.05	.025	.01	.005
	Levels of significance for a two-tailed test			
number of pairs	.10	.05	.02	.01
4	—			
5	0	—		
6	2	0	—	
7	3	2	0	—
8	5	3	1	0
9	8	5	3	1
10	10	8	5	3
11	13	10	7	5
12	17	13	10	7
13	21	17	12	10
14	25	21	16	13
15	30	25	19	16

[a] Adaptation of Table C of C. H. Craft and C. Van Eeden, *A Nonparametric Introduction to Statistics,* © Copyright, The MacMillan Company, 1968, New York.

INDEX